HISTORY OF EDUCATION IN GREAT BRITAIN

S. J. CURTIS, M.A., Ph.D.

FORMERLY READER IN EDUCATION IN THE UNIVERSITY OF LEEDS

With a Foreword by W. R. NIBLETT, B.A., B.LITT.
Professor of Education, University of London Institute of Education

UNIVERSITY TUTORIAL PRESS LTD

9-10 GREAT SUTTON STREET, LONDON, E.C.1

Published 1948
Second Edition 1950
Third Edition 1953
Fourth Edition 1957
Reprinted 1961
Fifth Edition 1963
Sixth Edition 1965
Seventh Edition 1967

PRINTED IN GREAT BRITAIN BY UNIVERSITY TUTORIAL PRESS LTD, FOXTON
NEAR CAMBRIDGE

FOREWORD

By W. R. Niblett, B.A., B.Litt.

Professor of Education, University of London Institute of Education

Why should we spend time in studying the long history of the educational provision made in this island? Facts about the history of education are notoriously difficult to remember and not least when an examination paper is waiting, in front of one's eyes, to be answered. The complex sequences of events, the tortuous negotiations which have preceded the carrying through of so many reforms, the changing currents of public opinion, studied in detachment, have a way of seeming unreal, boring, irrelevant. And, of course, studied in detachment (with one's eye on an examination ahead), so they are.

But the true history of education can hardly be studied in detachment. For it is a record of the provision made by our fathers for us, and by their fathers for them, back through many generations. Those apparently tortuous negotiations conceal battles of principle — battles which have their contemporary counterparts recorded in *The Times Educational Supplement*, *Hansard*, and the local Press. The history of education is the history of a gradually widening conception of what education itself is, a history still nearer its beginning than its end. Wherever we may live there are within reach of us visible embodiments of the Victorian ideas of the purpose of schools in the very architecture of the schools themselves. Our teaching to-day is guided, guarded, informed, and influenced, by the history of education within these shores.

In this concentrated book, filled with knowledge and hard facts— but with many things in it of direct and personal human interest —Dr. Curtis has given us plenty of clues for tracking modern issues and controversies back through the centuries to mediaeval times. The examples he draws upon in text and footnote are often northern examples and none the worse for that, whether the reader be from

iii

the south or the north. His chapters on Education in Scotland give valuable material for work in comparative education. As he says, he has tried to show "some of the main ways in which it has both influenced, and been influenced by, events in England." There is still room for more of such two-way traffic.

As we read any history of education it is well to remember for our comfort that however defective the actual educational provision in any period, even to-day, may be, education in the broad sense was and is always taking place—through home and family life, in the contacts of field and factory, in church and market and street, as well as in schools and universities. It is well to remember, too, that what goes on in schools, and how it goes on, depends not only on the great statesmen, the strong headmasters, and the ardent administrators, with whose work and contribution this book is necessarily chiefly concerned, but on the creative ideas of those men and women of many nations to whose thinking about education we owe so much—the Platos and the Lockes, the Rousseaus and the Froebels, the McMillans and the Montessoris, the Bubers and the Deweys, down the ages.

W. R. NIBLETT. ·

PREFACE TO THE FIRST EDITION

THIS book has been written to meet the needs of students in University Education Departments and Training Colleges. It will appeal also to the general reader interested in the development of education and in current problems concerning educational progress.

The origin and growth has been considered not only of schools, primary and secondary, but also of universities and other educational institutions and agencies. The important differences between the English and Scottish systems and the influence of each on the other has been considered.

The bibliography has been carefully planned to guide readers wishing to study in greater detail individual topics in which they are particularly interested.

The author would like to express his gratitude to his colleagues and friends who have assisted him in so many ways. In particular, he wishes to acknowledge the debt he owes to Professor W. R. Niblett for his kindness in contributing the Foreword and for his helpful advice and criticism when the book was in proof; to his colleague, Mrs. A. Whitehead, for permission to use the letters and prospectus on pp. 226-7 [pp. 548-9 in the Sixth Edition], and to Miss W. F. Robson, who so kindly assisted in reading the proofs. Finally, he would like to thank his wife, not only for her help in the arduous task of checking the proofs and index but also for the lively encouragement she gave him when he was writing this book.

S. J. C.

PREFACE TO THE SIXTH EDITION

SINCE 1963 the developments in education have accelerated. The Newsom and Robbins Reports have been published and some of their recommendations have been accepted. This has necessitated an enlarged Chapter XVII. The history is brought up to the beginning of November 1964. Additions have been made to the Bibliography and Date Chart.

S. J. C.

NOTE TO THE SEVENTH EDITION

THE developments in education have continued to accelerate and the history is brought up to the middle of 1967. Additions have been made to the Bibliography, Date Chart, and Index.

S. J. C.

CONTENTS

HISTORY OF EDUCATION IN GREAT BRITAIN

CHAPTER I

ENGLISH SCHOOLS BEFORE THE REFORMATION

"An institution older than the House of Commons, older than the Universities, older than the Lord Mayor, older even than the throne or nation itself." In these words, A. F. Leach emphasised the antiquity of the school of York Minster, of which St. Peter's, York, is the lineal descendant. In these days, when men are apt to associate education predominantly with the State, it is useful to remind ourselves and others that our English schools were the creation of the Church and took their rise almost at the same time as the introduction of Christianity into this island. No doubt schools existed in Roman Britain both before and after Christianity was accepted as the religion of the Empire, but all traces of them were swept away by the Anglo-Saxon invasions of the 5th and 6th centuries.

England received its Christianity through two streams, the Continental in the south-east and the Celtic in the north. As the Continental was the first, it is logical to suppose that the earliest schools were established in Kent, and in the controversy as to which is the oldest school, Canterbury or York, the evidence seems to point in favour of the former. It should, however, be noted that even at the present day, the word "school" is ambiguous. It may either refer to the building in which instruction is given to pupils, *i.e.* the schoolhouse, or it may indicate the assembly of pupils and teachers met together for the respective purposes of learning and teaching. There is a close parallel in the use of the word "church" which can be used to indicate either a body of people united by the bond of common belief and worship, or the actual building in which the worship is carried out. In modern usage, school, often, but not exclusively, emphasises the building, but in mediaeval times the essential idea was that of a number of scholars who gathered together to listen to a master. The pupils might be adults or they might be children. The teaching might be conducted in the open air, within a monastery or a church, or even in the dwelling-place of the master. The practice of setting aside a special building for the purposes of education only arose at a comparatively late period. Thus, when we refer to a school at Canterbury or York existing during the Saxon period, it must not be assumed that a particular building was earmarked to house the master and his pupils. A relic of the mediaeval usage is to be found in the term, the Honours School of a University, or the Schools of Oxford.

Augustine landed in England in 597 and after the conversion of Ethelbert, King of Kent, he was permitted to establish his episcopal see in the royal city of Canterbury. Augustine's mission was a difficult one. He was attempting to Christianise a people who, unlike the barbarian invaders of the Continent, had only the slightest acquaintance with the Roman tongue, Roman customs, and the Roman religion. Hence it was necessary for his missionaries to teach the Latin language to the native priests who were to perform the services in that tongue, and to those nobles who were to understand the new doctrines. Thus the teaching of Latin went hand in hand with the teaching of Christianity.

When the first cathedral church of Christ at Canterbury was established, it is practically certain that a school connected with it started at about the same time. The lineal descendant of this school is the King's School, Canterbury, its title referring not to the original patron, Ethelbert, but to Henry VIII who refounded it. As other sees were founded at Rochester, London, and the town of Dunwich, now swept away by the sea, similar schools on the model of Canterbury were started.

The evidence for this is afforded by the Ecclesiastical History of Bede who tells us, "At that time (631) the king of East Anglia was Sigebert, a good and religious man, who sometime before had received baptism while in exile in Gaul. On his return home, as soon as he had recovered his kingdom, wishing to imitate what he had seen well arranged among the Gauls, he instituted a school in which boys might be taught grammar (*litterae*). In this enterprise he was assisted by Bishop Felix, who came to him from Kent and brought with him ushers and teachers after the fashion of the Canterbury folk." [1] The school founded by Sigebert was Dunwich, and Bede expressly states that Canterbury served as its model. The controversy as to which is the oldest school in England is quite simply settled, for as Leach tells us, "The first churches

[1] III, 18.

were Bishops' churches or cathedrals invariably planted as the Bishop's see in the chief cities of the kingdom in which the Bishop himself was established. The schools were annexed to, or rather were part of, the foundation of the churches. We have only, therefore, to look for the first endowed cathedral, and there we shall find the first endowed grammar or Public School, and for the second to find the second, and so on."[1]

The first preaching of Christianity to the north was due to Paulinus, who was sent from Kent to convert Edwin of Northumbria and his people. The work of Paulinus was shortlived. Penda, the heathen king of Mercia, with the assistance of his Welsh allies, defeated and slew Edwin at Heathfield in 633. Paulinus fled from Northumbria leaving behind James the deacon to look after the remnant of Christians. When the Christian King Oswald returned to Northumbria, Bede tells us, "when the number of the faithful increased, James acted as master to many in church, chanting after the Roman or Canterbury fashion [*i.e.* teaching the use of the Gregorian chant]." Oswald had learnt his Christianity in the monastery of Iona, and it was natural that he should turn to the Abbot of Iona to send a missionary to convert his subjects. The mission was undertaken by Aidan, and although Oswald was later defeated and slain by Penda, the work accomplished by the Celtic mission was of a permanent character. The reference of Bede to the work of James the deacon indicates that what in later ages was known as a song-school had been established at York.

Thus we find that from the earliest days of the Church in this country the forerunners of at least two different types of school were established. Other types came into existence at a later date, but wherever a cathedral or minster was built, there developed the twin schools of grammar and song. The same is true of Scotland. The important fact, so often forgotten in modern times when the State plays such a predominant part in education, is that the English schools were the offspring of the Church, which regarded them as one of its chief instruments in Christianising and civilising the people. Hence the Church, since it provided the only organised education that existed, exercised complete control over the schools which were under the jurisdiction of the ecclesiastical authorities. Until the Reformation, all schoolmasters, with very few exceptions, were clergy, and scholars were in orders, though not necessarily

[1] In a letter to *The Times Educational Supplement*, 3rd January 1911.

major orders.   It is essential to grasp this point to understand the
controversies of the early 19th century.   When the Church of
England claimed continuity with the mediaeval Church, she also
claimed to be the one body responsible for education in the country.
This claim had the support of history and tradition, but those who
advanced it failed to realise the changed circumstances of the time
in which they lived.

The early Fathers were vehemently opposed to the training given
in the grammar-schools of the Empire.   Their main object was to
further the spread of the Christian faith and it seemed to them that
the literary curriculum of the grammar-schools was so bound up
with pagan myth and legend as to be inimical to the new religion.
They found themselves confronted with a very real practical
problem.   Tertullian and Origen, who had received a classical
education themselves, sought to solve the difficulty by suggesting
that much of the best in Greek and Roman literature had been
borrowed from the sacred writings, and Augustine of Hippo openly
proclaimed the legitimacy of "spoiling the Egyptians," *i.e.* making
use of all those elements of pagan learning which were not opposed
to the faith.   This, however, did not represent the general outlook,
especially in the West, and for a considerable period the Church
was hostile to pagan learning.   Even such a liberal-minded man
as Gregory the Great scolded one of his French bishops, saying in
a letter, "it has come to our knowledge that your brotherhood
teaches grammar to certain persons; which we take all the worse
as it converts what we formerly said to lamentation and mourning,
since the praise of Christ cannot lie in one mouth with the praise
of Jupiter."

The needs of the new kingdoms which arose out of the ruins
of the Empire eventually forced the Church to reconsider the aim
of education.   On the one hand it was necessary to produce loyal
sons of the Church whose aim in this life was to procure the
salvation of their souls in the next, but there was also the need
to train the clergy to act as intelligent leaders.   As the organisation
of the new kingdoms grew more complex, there developed the
necessity for keeping up the supply of officials.   "The clerks supplied
not only the chaplains, but the civil servants, secretaries, attorneys,
and land stewards of the age.   Domesday Book and the vast
number of accounts, title-deeds, charters and the like legal
documents, which still survive, were their work.   Some of the
feudal establishments, therefore, included a number of learned

persons, or furnished the nucleus of an educated society, in the narrow sense of the phrase as used to-day." [1]

For such people, as for the clergy, a knowledge of the Latin language was essential. Thus we find that the study of Latin, which sometimes included a small amount of literature, was one of the main subjects in the mediaeval grammar-schools. According to Leach, the early schools took as their model the only possible one, the grammar-school of the later Roman Empire. This has been denied by some writers who trace these schools back to the early Christian schools, e.g. schools for catechumens, catechetical, and episcopal schools.[2] The probability is that both influences were at work in shaping the schools, and the effect of Christian tradition is seen in the importance attached to instruction in religion and morals.

The history of the English pre-Reformation schools falls roughly into three periods, each of which is characterised by certain important features. The first, which may be called the Formative period, starts with the introduction of Christianity and ends with the completion of the Norman Conquest. The next period, which is one of Development, is brought to a close by the Black Death, 1349, and the last, an age of Consolidation, is terminated by the Renaissance and Reformation. Although it is not the purpose of this chapter to attempt a detailed account of English schools and scholars of the Middle Ages, yet it is important to consider the educational developments of each of the above periods and to draw attention to factors which affected schools of later days.

The records of the early period provide somewhat scanty information. Thus, although Leach's claim that Canterbury was the seat of our oldest school may be accepted, its truth is rather a matter of inference from what Bede has to say than of direct evidence. We do know, however, that the school of Canterbury was flourishing shortly after the arrival of Archbishop Theodore of Tarsus in 669. It was known as the "School of the Archbishop and the City," but for nearly three centuries after the death of Theodore, there is a complete blank. Absence of records, however, is not evidence that the school for a time ceased to exist.

In the same way, evidence is lacking for the continuity of the school at York. We do not know for how long James the deacon

[1] J. W. Adamson. *A Short History of Education*, p. 13, C.U.P., 1922.
[2] A. W. Parry. *Education in England in the Middle Ages*, pp. 22-3, U.T.P., 1920.

carried on the school after the triumph of Penda, but shortly after the Synod of Whitby in 664 the school appears in history once more. It seems that, from the beginning of the 8th century, the right of appointing the master of the school was assumed by the Archbishop of York. The first master was Egbert (about 705). He was followed by Albert (about 750), whose pupil, and successor in 766, was the famous Alcuin of York. After Alcuin, with the exception of a brief reference in 849, no further record exists until 1094. The reason for the silence was the destruction of the well-known library by the Normans in 1069. After the Harrying of the North, the Archbishop seems to have re-established the school.

Similar schools were established in connection with other cathedrals, *e.g.* Winchester, 648, Worcester, 685, together with Lichfield and Hereford at approximately the same time. The school of York is always associated with the name of Alcuin, who, together with Albert, founded the famous cathedral library, the catalogue of which is still extant. This shows that it contained a complete collection of the Church Fathers, the Latin grammarians, and a representative assembly of Latin classical writers.

Alcuin gives an illuminating description of the curriculum of the school in those early days. "There he (Albert) moistened thirsty hearts with divers streams of teaching and varied dews of study ; busily giving to some the arts of the science of grammar (*grammaticae rationis artes*), pouring into others the streams of the tongues of orators ; these he polished on the whet-stone of law, those he taught to sing in Aeonian chant, making others play on the flute of Castaly, and run with the lyre over the hills of Parnassus. But others, the said master made to know the harmony of heaven and the sun, the labours of the moon, the five belts of the sky, the seven planets, the laws of the fixed stars, their rising and setting, the movements of the air and the sun, the earth's quake, the nature of men, cattle, birds, and beasts, the different kinds of number and various (geometrical) figures ; and he gave sure return to the festival of Easter ; above all, revealing the mysteries of holy writ, for he opened the abysses of the old and rude law." [1]

This account of the studies of the school of York suggests that they were encyclopaedic in range, and the reader will discover that they consisted mainly in the Seven Liberal Arts, a term which is explained later in this chapter. He should note that the one

[1] Quoted by A. F. Leach. *The Schools of Medieval England*, pp. 58-9, Methuen, 1915.

institution undertook the teaching of all subjects from what we should now call the school to the university stage. Differentiation in function found little place in the early schools of England, and even in the later Middle Ages there was much overlapping between one institution and another. It seems, however, that on the Continent, differentiation of function in the schools was beginning to appear. The evidence for this development is afforded by the letters of Alcuin. Archbishop Eanbald I was contemplating retirement from his office in 795. At this time, Alcuin was in France, engaged in founding schools in the dominions of Charles the Great. Letters were sent asking Alcuin to return to England so that his knowledge and experience might be available in the choice of a new archbishop. Alcuin could not be spared, and in his absence Eanbald II was elected archbishop.

When Alcuin heard of the appointment, he wrote a letter to Eanbald to congratulate him on his accession, and offered him the following advice. "With holy solicitude, make provision for masters to teach the pupils. According to the customs of the Gauls, arrange for the clerks to be separated into those who read books, those who serve the chanting of the services, and those who are assigned to the study of writing. Let each of these divisions have its own masters, lest having nothing to do, they wander from place to place and busy themselves with idle frivolities or become slaves to other foolish pursuits. My dearest son, consider all these things most carefully, so that in the chief city of our people, there may be found a fount of goodness and learning from which the thirsty wayfarer or the lover of ecclesiastical lore, may be able to draw what his soul desires.

"You, who are most diligent in the practice of apostolic piety, turn over with care in your mind where you can establish guest houses or hospitals in which a daily welcome may be offered to the poor and to travellers, and they may have sustenance at your expense." [1]

This letter is of first-rate importance. Although there is no evidence to show that Alcuin's counsel was acted upon immediately, it anticipates the development that was to take place in the future, when the grammar and song schools were organised as separate establishments, and the writing-school, having been

---

[1] There appear to be two errors in the original manuscript; *clero* should obviously be *clerici*, and *illorum* (since the letter was written from Gaul) should be read as *Gallorum*. These corrections do not affect the meaning of the advice, and Alcuin's intentions are perfectly clear.

relegated to an inferior position, carried out the functions of a primary school.

In the early days of the Church in this country, the bishop not only supervised his diocese, but he also undertook the office of a teacher. Thus Wilfrid of Ripon personally instructed the sons of noblemen. As the business of the diocese grew more burdensome, the bishop found it necessary to delegate part of the teaching. St. John of Beverley, who occupied the see of York from 705 to 718, is described by Bede as teaching a school which included both clerics and laymen and seems to have been both a grammar and a song school.[1] John was an elderly man (he had previously been Bishop of Hexham) and for several years before he retired he had found the business of the diocese pressing heavily upon him. To ease his burden, he appointed Wilfrid II as his deputy in the city of York. In a similar way, so Alcuin informs us in his poem on the Archbishops of York (*De Pontificibus et Sanctis Ecclesiae Eboracensis Carmen*), Archbishop Egbert appointed Albert as master in York (*et simul Euborica praefertur in urbe magister*). This shows that the bishop had delegated the office of teaching to a person who ranked next to him in authority. When Albert in his turn was raised to the archbishopric, his love of learning was so great that Alcuin records with some surprise that he still continued to teach and expound the Scriptures.

During this formative period, the process of delegation seems to have taken place in stages. In the first stage, the bishop delegated the teaching of the grammar and song schools whilst retaining what afterwards became the theological school. The next step was when the bishop's duties became so onerous that he was forced to abandon teaching altogether. His deputy took charge of all the schools. The final stage belongs to the period of development when the bishop's deputy became head of the theological school but the grammar and song schools had separate officers. Thus the bishop's deputy eventually became known as the chancellor (*cancellarius*) and the schoolmaster and precentor were in charge of the grammar and song schools respectively. It will be necessary to describe this process of delegation in some detail when we consider the period of development, since we find a certain amount of confusion amongst writers on the history of education in regard to the status of the chancellor, his duties, and his relation to the schoolmasters of the diocese. It will be sufficient at this point to

[1] *Ecclesiastical History*, Bk. V, Ch. vi.

emphasise that in the pre-Conquest schools, the process of devolution was well on its way.

In the 8th and 9th centuries English schools and scholars enjoyed an international reputation. This was the result of the labours of men like Wilfrid of Ripon, Albert, and Alcuin. The latter was so outstanding a personality in the history of early education that it is worth while summarising his accomplishments in England and on the Continent. Evidently the prestige of the school of York had travelled far and wide, for we find that pupils from other lands were sent to Alcuin to obtain a training which was not available to them in their own countries. Thus, some time between 760 and 770, Liudgar and Sigibold came from Utrecht to study under Alcuin at York. After spending a year in the school, Liudgar returned to his own home, but he had been so impressed with the teaching of Alcuin that he obtained permission to come back and stay another four years at York.

After the death of Archbishop Albert, Northumbria passed through a period of unrest. One king after another succeeded to the throne in the space of a very few years. Possibly the ensuing disorder had much to do with Alcuin's decision to leave the school of York. He also deeply felt the loss of his bishop and friend to whom he was genuinely attached. During Albert's lifetime, Alcuin had accompanied the archbishop to the Continent when the two scholars went in search of books for the library. In the course of these visits Alcuin made many friends, and in 781 he became acquainted with Charles the Great. Charles soon discovered that Alcuin was the kind of man he required to organise the schools of his empire. Permission was obtained from the king of Northumbria and Archbishop Eanbald for Alcuin to stay on the Continent and undertake the organisation of the palace school, which was intended for the sons of the noblemen at the court of Charles. The Englishman collected round him a band of accomplished scholars and as head of the palace school acted as a kind of Minister of Education for Charles. Alcuin returned once more to England in 790 but he soon went back to France where he spent the rest of his days. The school of York was always in his thoughts, as evidenced by the letter of advice he sent to Eanbald about the reorganisation of the school. In his old age, Alcuin retired to become Abbot of Tours, where he died on Whit-Sunday, 804.

Many of Alcuin's letters are still extant and show him to have been a most lovable character who possessed a strong sense of

humour.   One letter to his old companions at York reminds them
how they trained him in his early years and with paternal floggings
brought him to man's estate.   On another occasion he playfully
warned the canons against falling in love or getting tipsy.   On his
last visit to York he seems to have found the cold very trying after
his long stay in France, for he wrote to his servant, asking him to
send some warm clothing and a supply of wine "because the acidity
of the beer in these parts plays havoc with my stomach."

The mention of the palace school of Charlemagne for the sons
of courtiers, raises the question whether a like development occurred
in England.   According to his biographer, Asser, Alfred the Great
seems to have contemplated some such thing, but Asser's testimony
cannot by any means be taken as accurate.   If Alfred did establish
a palace school, it was not continued after his death.   Alfred's
fame as a patron of education rests upon his earnest attempt to
repair the ravages wrought by the Viking invasions.   He tells us that
as the result of the raids, "So great was the decay of learning among
Englishmen that there were very few on this side Humber, and I
ween not many north of it, who could understand the Mass or
translate a letter from Latin into English.   No, I cannot remember
one such, south of the Thames, when I came to the throne."
Alfred's work of restoration consisted in his translations and in his
invitations to famous scholars to visit England and assist him in
his task.   It was in this way that both Asser and Grimbald came
to dwell at Alfred's court.   One of Alcuin's successors in the palace
school was the famous philosopher, Scotus Erigena.   William of
Malmesbury asserts that some time after 872, Erigena was invited
to England by Alfred, where he became head of the school connected with the monastery of Malmesbury and met his end by being
stabbed to death with the pens of his infuriated pupils.   A good
deal of controversy has raged over the trustworthiness of William's
statement.[1]

Dunstan has always been reputed an important patron of
schools and learning, but such a crop of legends has developed
around his activities that it is difficult to dissociate the truth from
error.   Aelfric was a pupil of Dunstan and his authorship of an
Anglo-Saxon grammar, a *Glossary*, and the well-known *Colloquy*,
testify that education had made considerable progress.   Aelfric

---

[1] The evidence for Erigena's residence at Malmesbury is discussed at length
by R. L. Poole, *Illustrations of the History of Medieval Thought and Learning*,
pp. 273-85, S.P.C.K., 1920.

became Abbot of Eynsham about 1005 and his *Colloquy* gives us an insight into the teaching methods of these early schools. Latin was taught as a spoken language, and for this purpose vocabulary books and readers were necessary. The former were known as Colloquies and took the form of dialogues into which words and phrases useful in everyday life were introduced.

Speaking of Aelfric's *Colloquy*, Dr. Coulton says: "It gives us a very vivid picture of school at that time. To begin with, we find the rough material. The teacher asks: 'Who are you here before me?' and one pupil answers for 'us boys' (*nos pueri*). The list of pupils includes a professed monk, ploughmen, shepherds, cowherds, fishermen, fowlers, merchants, shoemakers, hunters, and bakers. We must not, of course, take this catalogue too literally; the writer's business was to bring in as many occupations as possible in order to increase the vocabulary of his scholars. . . . Next, the book throws light upon discipline. The teacher asks: 'Are you ready to be flogged while you learn?' (*Vultis flagellari in discendo?*). The pupils answer: 'We would rather be flogged for learning's sake than be ignorant,' but they add ingratiatingly: 'We know that thou art a humane man, and wilt not beat us unless our conduct compels thee.'"[1]

The second period of mediaeval education extends from the third quarter of the 11th century to about the time of the Black Death, when the universities had become securely established and organised. The 12th century itself was an age of considerable intellectual activity, only exceeded in the vigour of its efforts and achievements by the Scholastic Renaissance of the following century and the Humanistic Renaissance which ushered out the Middle Ages. This intellectual ferment was largely the product of two causes: the increased attention given to the study of law, especially canon law and Roman law as expressed in the Digest of Justinian, and the infiltration into Western Europe of the *Organon* or logical works of Aristotle. On the authority of John of Salisbury, we know that by 1162 the whole of the *Organon* was in the possession of the West. It was also the 12th-century Renaissance which brought about the foundation of the mediaeval universities, and as soon as they were established we begin to obtain a clearer picture of the organisation of education in this country. Records become more plentiful and they show that not only the founding of schools went on with renewed vigour as soon as the confusion which was

[1] G. G. Coulton. *Medieval Panorama*, p. 403, C.U.P., 1938.

created by the Conquest had disappeared, but they enable us to obtain more certain knowledge about the different types of school which existed.

The first two important changes were direct effects of the Conquest. To a considerable extent, Saxon schoolmasters were replaced by Normans, and thus began the practice of translating Latin into Norman-French instead of English. Another innovation was due to the policy of Archbishop Lanfranc, who was determined to reform the English Church by replacing, wherever possible, the secular establishments of the cathedrals by regulars. He naturally began with his own cathedral church of Canterbury, which had been severely damaged by fire in 1067. The actual establishment of Canterbury in pre-Norman times is unknown, but the frequent use of the phrase "the Archbishop and his clerks," suggests a large element of seculars. Lanfranc replaced them by members of regular monastic orders, as was also the case at Rochester, Winchester, and Worcester. The school at Canterbury was maintained, but instead of remaining as an integral part of the cathedral establishment supervised by a permanent member of the Chapter, it was put under the jurisdiction of the archbishop, who had so many cares that we may assume he had little time to spare for the interests of the school. That the school of Canterbury continued is attested by the fact that when the first Franciscans came to England about 1220, certain of them were lodged in the schoolhouse of Canterbury. This also shows that by this time it had become the custom to set aside a special building for the use of the school.

The records of the 12th century indicate that the educational organisation of the Church was taking on a definite pattern, and the tendency towards differentiation of function, already developing in the pre-Norman schools, now resulted in a clearer line of demarcation between different types of school. Some writers have distinguished between Latin and vernacular schools, and have considered the former as providing a secondary and the latter an elementary type of education. This distinction is by no means an absolute one since in many so-called Latin schools a part of the teaching was in the vernacular, which in the early part of the period was often Norman-French, and in some schools which have been claimed as elementary, the pupils were taught to sing the Latin of the Church services. In any case, we must remember that the elementary school, in the meaning of the term in later ages, did not exist.

The most important distinction was that between the grammar-school and other types.   The actual term "grammar-school" was not in common use much before the 14th century.   Its first appearance in English seems to have been in 1387 when John of Trevisa used the phrase "gramer scole" in his translation of Ralph Higden's *Polychronicon*.   There is, however, no doubt that the cathedral establishments of the early period included a school which was to all intents and purposes a grammar-school.

Other schools were attached to monasteries and at first prepared novices who wished to become monks, but after a time they admitted lay youths as well.   Leach[1] contends that the number of schools of monastic origin has been greatly exaggerated. He points out that the word minster can only be translated into Latin by the word monastery, which in the early English period meant any large church, just as monasteriolum, or little minster, referred to any small church, even an ordinary parish church.   In later times, the word minster was applied exclusively to cathedrals or collegiate churches of secular clergy, like York, Ripon, Beverley, and Southwell Minsters in the north, Lincoln and Lichfield in eastern England or the midlands, and Wimborne Minster in the south.

Indeed, it should not be assumed that because a school was attached to a monastery or placed under the care of the Abbot, it was a monastic school.   Thus St. Alban's School, usually attributed to Abbot Ulsinus, 948, was certainly in existence in 1097.   In the abbacy of Richard Daubney (1097-1119), the secular Geoffrey de Gorham was sent from the Continent to become the master of the school at St. Albans.   Later, the mastership was held by Alexander Nequam, the author of many punning verses, also a secular.   He was master from 1185 to 1195, when he was appointed Bishop of Cirencester.   This is an example of a grammar-school under the jurisdiction of an abbey, staffed by seculars, and differing in no respects from other grammar-schools of the time except that it received distinction from the fact that it educated Nicholas Breakspear, afterwards Adrian IV, the only Englishman ever to occupy the Papal Chair.   It is a matter of dispute to what extent the internal schools of the monasteries were open to pupils from outside.   The practice seems to have varied from age to age, but at no time were the pupils very numerous.

Whatever its origin, the grammar-school provided what may be called the secondary education of the Middle Ages.   Another type

[1] A. F. Leach. *The Schools of Medieval England*, p. 57, Methuen, 1915.

of school, the song-school, was in existence. We have already met with the instance of the song-school at York, which probably existed side by side with the grammar-school from the earliest times. As a rule the song-schools were quite distinct from the grammar-schools, though in small foundations they were frequently housed under one roof. In such cases, the grammar master was always senior to the song master, as their stipends indicate. At Northallerton in 1426, the school included what may be called the three departments of grammar, song, and reading. Jesus College, Rotherham, employed a grammar master whose salary was £10, a song master who received £6 13s. 4d., and a writing master at £5 6s. 8d. The aim of the song-school was to train youths who were engaged in the singing of the Church services. Chaucer, in the *Prioresses Tale*, describes a "litel scole" where, the Prioress tells us, the pupils learned

> ". . . to singen and to rede
> As smale children doon in hir childhede."

A small choir-boy, "a widwes sone, a litel clergeon seven yeer of age," attended this school and sat "in the scole at his prymer." He heard the older children singing the Alma Redemptoris Mater and he committed the words to memory, but he could not understand them. One of the older boys tried to explain its meaning but he could not go far because,

> "I can no more expounde in this matere;
> I lerne song, I can but smal grammere."

The little boy made up his mind to learn the hymn for himself.

> "Though that I for my prymer shal be shent
> And shal be beten thryes in an houre."

He learnt it so thoroughly that he was able to sing it "wel and boldely," and when going to school in the morning, and again when coming home at night, he sang the hymn to himself.

> "Twyes a day it passed thurgh his throte,
> To scoleward and homward whan he wente."

Besides the song-schools there were reading-and-writing schools, and, in the passage above, Chaucer is giving us a picture of a tiny boy learning his primer in a reading-and-writing school which was attached to a song-school for older choristers.

It was during this middle period that the cathedral establishments became stabilised and the offices and duties of the precentor and chancellor were clearly differentiated. The clearest picture of what occurred is presented by the history of the cathedral of York. In 1069 the whole of the north was in rebellion against William I and the Norman garrison at York was massacred.   During the fighting, the cathedral was destroyed by fire and with it perished the great library which had been created through the labours of Albert and Alcuin.   William's vengeance on the rebels and the desolation he wrought in Northumbria are well known.   He found York a city of ruins, and one of his first acts was to set about the restoration of the cathedral.   Thomas of Bayeux was appointed archbishop. The work of restoration carried out by this Norman ecclesiastic is described by Hugh the Chanter, *i.e.* the precentor.   Thomas re-established the school of York and appointed a schoolmaster. Hugh tells us that only three of the seven canons remained and the cathedral had been completely gutted.   The original number of canons was restored, the church received a new roof, and a refectory and dormitory were built.   According to the continental custom, a provost was appointed to preside over the canons and the diocese was divided among the archdeacons.

About twenty years later, Archbishop Thomas, acting upon advice which had been tendered to him, entirely reorganised the establishment and appointed four principal dignitaries.   The dean took the place of the provost and next in rank came the precentor, who was in charge of the music of the cathedral, and the treasurer, who was responsible for the ornaments of the church.   The schoolmaster (*magister scolarum*), who had previously been appointed, was the fourth dignitary or *maior persona*.   The same kind of change had been taking place in other cathedral establishments, *e.g.* at Salisbury and Lincoln.

In 1120 Thurstan was elected archbishop, and we are told in the history of Hugh the Chanter, that the newly elected archbishop visited the Pope at Blois to seek consecration without having to swear obedience to Canterbury.   Thurstan was accompanied by two archdeacons and the schoolmaster, who in this connection was described as *scolasticus*.[1]   It is probable that the latter was Hugh,

---

[1] The term *scolasticus* was not in common use in England, though it is frequently met with in accounts of schools on the Continent.   During the early mediaeval period in Scotland, there was a person who was known as the *scolasticus* or *scoloc*, but he was a scholar who had passed beyond the stage of being merely a pupil and was employed as a kind of assistant teacher.   The Scottish equivalent to the English chancellor in those days was the Ferleyne.

Thus Adamson seems to be at fault when he writes: "At first the actual conduct of the scholastic work of the cathedral was a duty of the chancellor, who in this capacity was termed *scolasticus*."   (*Op. cit.*, p. 5.)

who may have held this office before he became precentor. At this time the title of chancellor and schoolmaster seems to have been interchangeable. The same was true of St. Paul's, where the schoolmaster regularly used the title *magister scolarum*. Richard of Stortford, who became master of St. Paul's in 1181, signed his documents as *magister scolarum Londoniensium*. The bishop of London considered that the stipend of the schoolmaster was insufficient and he assigned to the office certain tithes from lands at Fulham and Barnes. A later addition to the document which awarded the extra emoluments reads, "Note of tithes granted to the schoolmaster, now the chancellor." John of Kent, who succeeded Richard, used the title of chancellor in a deed of 1205.

This development can be illustrated from the records of York Minster. A dispute had arisen about the order of precedence of the cathedral dignitaries. Archdeacon Ralph asserted that the third dignitary in order of rank was the Archdeacon of York. An appeal was made to the Pope, who ordered the Abbot of Welbeck and the Priors of Newburgh and Pontefract to investigate the claim. The papal commissioners took the evidence of those clergy who had been longest at York, and concluded that the chancellor was the third dignitary of the cathedral (*invenimus quod cancellaria est tertia dignitas in ecclesia Eboracensi*). They gave judgment that the chancellor, Simon of Apulia, had precedence in all things of Ralph, Archdeacon of York. The date of the decision is 1191 and it suggests that the separation between the duties of the chancellor and the schoolmaster had only recently been made.

The statutes of the cathedral of York were not put into writing until 1307, but they claimed to represent the customs of that church for at least a century before this date. The section headed: "Of the chancellor and his office" is so significant in the light it throws upon the duties performed by that dignitary, that a full translation is appended.

"The chancellor, who in ancient time was called the schoolmaster, should be a master in theology and should actually teach close to the church. It is his duty to make the appointments to the grammar-schools (*scholas grammaticales*). He must appoint a master in arts to the grammar-school at York, who should be an individual who gives promise of being efficient. According to the ancient custom of this church, he should hold office for not more than three years, though in special circumstances his tenure may be extended for a further year.

"The chancellor must preach a sermon to the people on the first Sundays of Advent and Lent, and at the synod he is to preach to the clergy. He is also to assign the dates on which others are to preach. He is to be in charge of the seal for citations (*i.e.* for legal business). It is his duty, and that of the sub-chancellor, to make a roll of the readers, to grant the licence authorising them to read, and to hear them before the vestry office.

"He must also keep the records of important events in the history of the cathedral. On double feasts he is to assign the lessons to the readers, but when the dean or any other of the four dignitaries are appointed to read, the sub-chancellor is to see that they are notified and also the canons, so that they may choose their own reader.

"The sub-chancellor also has the duty of seeing that there is no deficiency in the reading in the choir and chapter-house, nor amongst the incense bearers and deacons.

"For these duties, the sub-chancellor is to be paid the sum of twenty shillings a year from the grammar-school endowment."

These statutes demonstrate quite clearly that the chancellor was expected to teach the theological school, and the fact that a master of arts was required for the grammar-school shows that the latter was of some standing. It should be noted that the chancellor appointed the masters to the grammar-schools of the diocese and that in his work in the cathedral he was assisted by the sub-chancellor. The statutes also detail the duties of the precentor and indicate that by this time the song-school and the grammar-school had become distinct establishments. The duties of the latter dignitary were parallel to those of the chancellor. The statutes laid down that he was to appoint the master of the song-school, supervise all matters pertaining to that school, and settle all disputes. The precentor was responsible for the singing in the choir, and the vicars' sub-chanter assisted him in the latter work The actual choir arrangements were in the hands of the vicars' sub-chanter, who kept a roll of the choir-boys, made sure that they knew their parts, and punished them when necessary (*cum necesse fuerit, castigare*). Like the sub-chancellor, the sub-chanter received twenty shillings a year from the song-school endowment.[1]

[1] The results of recent research into the cathedral establishments are given in the following study. K. Edwards, *The English Secular Cathedrals in the Middle Ages*, University of Manchester Press, 1949. The office and duties of the chancellor are discussed on pp. 180-7.

Throughout the greater part of the Middle Ages the Church exercised a close supervision over the schools. This did not mean that the schoolmaster was necessarily in holy orders, and there is evidence that in some of the schools, especially towards the end of the period, he might be a layman. Thus, in 1432, John Sevenoaks, the founder of Sevenoaks Grammar School, definitely ordered that the master should not be a clergyman. The Church controlled education by conferring the right to teach through the chancellor's licence, a rule which also applied to the universities. The system of licensing schoolmasters was widespread, and the Third Lateran Council of 1179 laid down that no charge was to be made for the issue of the licence (*Pro licentia docendi nihil exigi debet vel promitti*). Thus began the system of licensing schoolmasters which was not finally abolished until 1869.[1]

There were, however, some masters who defied the regulations and opened unlicensed or "adulterine" schools. One of the best-known examples is the series of disputes which distracted the district of Beverley in the early 14th century. Beverley Grammar School was a very ancient foundation dating from pre-Conquest days when the Minster was established. Nothing is known of the early history of Beverley Grammar School. The first mention of it is in the history of the miracles of St. John of Beverley, written by Ketell who informs us that in the year 1100 a new schoolmaster was appointed. He was an excellent man in every way until he cast his eyes upon a pretty girl with whom he fell hopelessly in love. He kept his passion a secret, but the effect upon him was disastrous. He neglected his studies and his discipline fell to pieces. His passion so preyed upon him that he became pale and emaciated. One morning he remained in church after matins to seek the aid of St. John of Beverley. The saint responded to his tears and prayers and the schoolmaster arose from his knees completely healed and once more became the perfect schoolmaster.

A certain Thomas of Brompton, Rector of Beverley Grammar School, on 27th October 1304, cited one "Robert Dalton, clerk, unmindful of his [soul's] health" as an unlicensed schoolmaster, who kept school in a district which fell within the jurisdiction of the Minster. Walter Kelsay, clerk to the Minster chapter, warned Dalton

[1] Endowed Schools Act, 1869, Clause 21. "In every scheme, the Commissioners shall provide for the abolition of all jurisdiction of the Ordinary relating to the licensing of masters in any endowed school, or of any jurisdiction arising from such licensing."

to relinquish his school within nine days under pain of excommunication, and forbade him to teach in Beverley in the future. Evidently
Dalton obeyed the decision of the chapter for the time being, but
he was not the only unlicensed schoolmaster to trouble the
authorities. A few months later, Stephen of Garton was warned
against keeping an adulterine, *i.e.* an unlicensed school, at Kelk
in the liberty of Beverley. No sooner was this case disposed of
when a third clerk, Geoffrey of Sancton, summoned before the
chapter for practising as a schoolmaster, turned the tables upon
Thomas of Brompton by instituting an action against him. The
issue of the action is not recorded in the chapter roll, but later in
1305, Geoffrey of Sancton was warned about his behaviour. He
refused to give up his school, was excommunicated and then boy-
cotted, "to avoid him and cause others to avoid him, until, excluded
from common intercourse, suffused with shame he may be inclined
to the grace of humility and the issue of reconciliation." Geoffrey
was unable to stand against the clerical boycott and made his
submission in January 1306. A few months later, Robert Dalton's
name cropped up again. He was warned once more and finally
had to desist from teaching.[1]

Another example of the claim to the monopoly of teaching is
afforded by Gloucester Grammar School. In this case, an action
was brought in the Court of Common Pleas and was heard by the
Lord Chief Justice and two judges. The school at Gloucester
was originally attached by Henry I, about the year 1100, to St.
Oswald's collegiate church. In 1137 it was transferred to
Llanthony Abbey, a house of the Augustinian canons, a short
distance out of the town. The right of patronage of the priory
of Llanthony seems to have been resented by the people of
Gloucester and resulted in an inquiry of 1286-7 by the bishop, who
upheld the claim of the prior of Llanthony and directed other
schools established in the city to be suspended. In order to
confirm the right, the priory obtained a royal charter. The lawsuit of 1410 was instituted by John Hamlyn, master of the school,
who sought to restrain Thomas More from teaching an unlicensed
school in the city. Normally the appeal would have been made to
the ecclesiastical authorities, but, influenced no doubt by the fact
that the charter had been obtained from the Crown, Hamlyn
brought an action of trespass against More in the civil court. He

[1] A. F. Leach. *The Schools of Medieval England*, pp. 182-3, Methuen,
1915.

pleaded that owing to the competition of the rival school his emoluments had fallen off considerably, and he claimed damages. The full text of the proceedings is given by Montmorency in Appendix I to his *State Intervention in English Education.* The Lord Chief Justice ruled that the act of keeping a school did not constitute an offence against the Common Law of England.[1] The law did not recognise a monopoly except in the case of the universities and the ancient schools. If an offence had been committed, it was a question for the ecclesiastical courts, and the plaintiff must seek his remedy there. Once again a principle was enunciated which was not observed in practice, for we shall see that a few years later Henry VI granted a monopoly to his royal foundation at Eton.

Perhaps the most amusing case is that of the grammar-school at Canterbury in the early 14th century. In the Middle Ages, Canterbury was not a free school and tuition fees were paid until its refoundation by Henry VIII. The Rector of the school in 1321 was Ralph of Waltham. During his tenure of office, Robert de Henneye, Rector of St. Martin's outside the city walls, taught a school in his parish. This school appears to have been a reading-and-writing school and he was allowed to take as many pupils for elementary education as he could obtain. In addition, he was permitted to teach grammar to a number of pupils, who were not to exceed thirteen in number. Probably the grammar pupils paid higher fees and Robert was anxious to increase the number. Ralph contended that this infringed his monopoly and he sent his usher to pay surprise visits to the rival school to count the grammar boys and report if they exceeded the permitted number. Robert seems to have got wind of the visits, for it was alleged that whenever the usher appeared the excess pupils were concealed, and produced when the visit had terminated. Ralph appealed to the archbishop, who, after holding an inquiry, confirmed that Robert was only entitled to thirteen grammar boys and threatened him with excommunication if he should take more than this number.[2]

---

[1] The Lord Chief Justice, in giving his decision, ruled that the education of children is a spiritual matter (*le doctrine et enformation des enfants est chose espiritual*) and therefore came under the jurisdiction of the Church courts, not the civil courts. This judgment was used by the Church party in the 19th century to support the claim of the Church to exclusive control of education, but both those who employed it and those who opposed it failed to understand the real significance of the decision.

[2] See Woodruff and Cape, *History of the King's School, Canterbury,* pp. 28-30, Mitchell Hughes and Clarke, 1908.

A frequent cause of dispute was concerning the respective rights of the grammar-school master on the one hand and the masters of the song and reading-and-writing schools on the other. We have already emphasised that these schools, although they gave what we should now term an elementary instruction, must not be regarded in the light of the elementary schools of the 19th century. In a great many cases they were in the nature of preparatory schools, teaching reading and writing to pupils who would afterwards enter the grammar-school. At Warwick, a dispute between the respective rights of the grammar and song masters was settled by the statutes of the school. Unfortunately, the statutes are not dated and we are unable to tell if they were drawn up in 1215 or 1315. The statutes record: "For an everlasting remembrance of the matter, we, Robert of Leicester, Dean of the Collegiate church of the Blessed Mary of Warwick, with the counsel of our brethren, decree and order that the Master of the Grammar School for the time being shall devote himself diligently to the information and instruction of his scholars in grammar. . . . That all material for strife and disagreement, which we learn has hitherto arisen between the Master and Music School-master over the Donatists and little ones learning their first letters and the psalter may be put a stop to for ever, after due inquiry in the matter and with the advice of our brethren, and so that the Masters and each of them may receive their due, and that undue encroachment of scholars on one side and the other may cease for the future; we decree and direct to be inviolably observed that the present Grammar Master and his successors shall have the Donatists, and thenceforward have, keep, and teach scholars in grammar and the art of dialectic if he shall be expert in that art, while the Music Master shall keep and teach those learning their first letters, the psalter, music and song." [1] The Donatists were those pupils who were studying the *Ars Minor* of Donatus, the elementary textbook on the parts of speech. In this case the Donatists were given to the grammar master, and the song master was given those who had not begun their Donat. In other cases it was decided that some of the Donatists might be taught by other masters, as in the example previously quoted of the thirteen boys at Canterbury School.

The rise of the universities resulted in a further development. The schools for higher studies connected with the cathedral establishments tended to disappear and become absorbed in the

[1] A. F. Leach. *History of Warwick School*, pp. 65-6, Constable, 1906.

Theological Faculties of the universities, except in places where the cathedral was remote from a university. At the same time, the function of the grammar-school became more sharply defined. It was now a feeder for the universities and provided that training in Latin, elementary logic, and rhetoric, which was necessary for a would-be entrant to university studies. Thus began that close connection between the grammar-schools and the universities which has remained so marked a feature even in modern times. The universal demand thus created resulted in the foundation of new schools, and their number rapidly increased after the commencement of the 13th century.

Since the grammar-schools of this period began to be thought of as feeders for the universities, their curriculum was now designed as an introduction to university studies and we no longer find that encyclopaedic range of subjects which characterised the school at York in the time of Alcuin. A much-quoted passage of William Fitzstephen, taken from the preface of his biography of Thomas a' Becket and preserved for posterity by John Stow in his *Survey of London*, 1596, indicates the nature of grammar-school studies in the middle of the 12th century. "In London, the three principal churches have famous schools privileged and of ancient dignity, though sometimes through personal favour to some one noted as a philosopher more schools are allowed. [The schools were St. Paul's, the school of the Arches, or St. Mary-le-Bow, and that of St. Martin's-le-Grand. Stow unfortunately creates confusion in his account by identifying the two latter with Westminster and Bermondsey, which at that time were outside London.] On feast days the Masters celebrate assemblies at the churches, arrayed in festive garb. The scholars hold disputations, some argumentatively, others by way of question and answer. These roll out enthymemes, those use the forms of perfect syllogisms. Some dispute merely for show, as they do at collections; others for the truth which is the grace of perfection. The sophists and those training in sophistry are pronounced happy because of the mass and volume of their words; others play upon words. Those learning rhetoric with rhetorical speeches speak to the point with a view to persuasion, being careful to observe the precepts of their art, and to leave out nothing that belongs to it."

Apart from this being a description of what we may almost call a 12th-century Speech Day in which the scholars, and not some person imported from outside, provided the entertainment, the reference throws a most valuable light upon the grammar-school studies of the period. In the technical language of the time, the schools were concerned with the first three of the Seven Liberal Arts. In the Middle Ages, theology was considered the queen of studies, to which philosophy served as an introduction. The studies which led to the supreme study of theology were known generally as the Seven Liberal Arts. The Arts (or sciences) were termed liberal from *liber*, free, and constituted the course of study suitable for the freeman as contrasted with the Practical and Mechanical Arts which were learned and practised by slaves in the classical period.[1] The conception of the Liberal Arts takes us back to Greece, at least as far as Plato, and passed over to Rome with other aspects of Greek thought. The idea was given more definite form by the late Latin writers, Augustine and Martianus Capella in the 5th century, and Boethius and Cassiodorus in the 6th. The two latter were responsible for fixing the number of the arts as seven, no doubt due to Proverbs ix. 1, "Wisdom hath builded her house, she hath hewn out her seven pillars."

The arts were divided into the Trivium and Quadrivium. This division was first indicated by Boethius (475-525), who, in his treatise on arithmetic, showed the relation of that study to the other sciences of geometry, astronomy, and music. Speaking of the four, he wrote: "This, then, is that Quadrivium in which those must travel whose mind being raised above the senses, is brought to the heights of intelligence." The distinction between the Trivium and the Quadrivium was completed by Isidore of Seville (570-636), who, in his *Etymologiae,* produced an encyclopaedia of all the knowledge as was available to his day. The conception of the Seven Liberal Arts exercised a profound influence on after ages. We have already met with the practical application of the idea in the curriculum of the school at York under Albert and Alcuin. Even as late as the 18th century, many school books contained allegorical illustrations depicting the Arts.[2]

[1] This contrast was maintained in the Middle Ages, as witness the references to the Seven Mechanical Arts in the works of Hugh of St. Victor in the 12th century and St. Bonaventure in the 13th. The latter, in his *De reductione Artium ad Theologiam,* classifies the Mechanical Arts as the manufacture of clothes (*lanificium*), the making of weapons (*armatura*), agriculture and hunting (which also include the trades of bakers, cooks, and butchers), navigation, the theatrical art, and medicine. In the universities, the latter became an additional art added to the Quadrivium.

[2] A useful sketch of the meaning and development of the Liberal Arts is given in the *Spens Report on Secondary Education,* Appendix II, H.M.S.O., 1938.

The subjects of the Trivium consisted of Grammar, Rhetoric, and Dialectic (logic); and of the Quadrivium, Arithmetic, Geometry, Astronomy, and Music. In many of the cathedral schools before the foundation of the universities, the subjects of the Trivium were taught to younger pupils and those of the Quadrivium to older pupils. John of Salisbury, in his *Metalogicus,* described in great detail the curriculum of the School of Chartres as it was under Bernard of Chartres in the 12th century. From his account, we find that grammar was employed merely as an introduction to the reading of classical literature, for which study Chartres was famous, but he is careful to add: "Since then less time and less care have been bestowed on grammar, and persons who profess all arts, liberal and mechanical, are ignorant of the primary art, without which a man proceeds in vain to the rest." As the universities developed, the grammar-schools confined their teaching to the Trivium, the remaining studies being considered as those proper to the university.

As already stated, grammar, *i.e.* the study of Latin grammar, was for practical reasons the most important of the school subjects. It is not usually realised that training in the Latin tongue was as vocational in the Middle Ages as is, say, training in engineering at the present day. Most of the teaching was oral. Manuscripts were scarce, so that the usual method of teaching consisted in the master reading from his own manuscript and dictating notes. The text-book used in the early period was the *Ars Minor* of Donatus, the teacher of St. Jerome who flourished at Rome in the middle of the 4th century. Donatus produced two works on grammar, the *Ars Minor* and the *Ars Maior.* The latter work was studied for the bachelor's degree in Arts at Oxford in the 13th century. The grammar of Donatus was so widely used that the term "Donat" was employed to describe an elementary work on any subject whatever. In some schools the *Institutio de Arte Grammatica* of Priscian (6th century) was used. This book contained a large number of quotations by way of illustration from classical authors, and was divided into eighteen parts, sixteen concerned with accidence and two with syntax. Later, in the 12th century, another competitor appeared, Alexander of Villa Dei. His book was written in crude verse and its quotations were taken from Scripture or colloquial Latin. The use of colloquies has already been mentioned.

Logic received some attention and was at first encouraged by the Church authorities as a means of detecting heresies. After the Renaissance, when the opposition to Scholasticism was in full swing, the study of logic in schools tended to be discouraged, since it was considered to be closely allied to the doctrines and methods of the Schoolmen. Rhetoric in the schools was really a training in the art of writing letters and official documents. Some little time was given to what may be called ecclesiastical arithmetic, *i.e.* the rules for fixing the date of Easter and other feasts, and perhaps the elements of computation through the use of the abacus or ball frame.[1]

The period of consolidation presents a number of important and interesting features. Following the development of the collegiate system at the universities, a revival of it began amongst the secular clergy. In many parts of the country new collegiate churches, each with its grammar and song school, arose. Leach considers that Howden, in 1266, was one of the earliest. Others quickly followed and "from this time to the dissolution of colleges in 1548, scarcely a year passed without witnessing the foundation of a college at the university, or a collegiate church with its grammar school attached, generally in the native place of its founder. The only difference between the university college, with its church attached, and the collegiate church with its schools of grammar and song attached, was that the latter were primarily for religious services and secondarily for education, and the former were primarily for education and secondarily for religious services. The collegiate church was *ad orandum et studendum,* the house of scholars at the university *ad studendum et orandum.* Both were indifferently spoken of as colleges." [2]

In a similar way, grammar-schools were founded as adjuncts to the colleges of Oxford and Cambridge. Thus, in the Statutes of the House of the Scholars of Merton, 1270, Walter de Merton enjoined that "some single individual, being a member of the collegiate body, is to be a grammarian, and must entirely devote himself to the study of grammar ; and he is to be furnished, at the expense of the house, with a proper supply of books and other requisites: he is to have the care of the students in grammar, and to him too the more advanced in years may have recourse without a blush." [3]

---

[1] Foster Watson seems to over-emphasise the place of logic in the schools. See *The Old Grammar Schools,* p. 7, C.U.P., 1916.

[2] A. F. Leach. *The Schools of Medieval England,* p. 167, Methuen, 1915.

[3] *The Foundation Statutes of Merton College, Oxford,* ed. E. F. Percival, p. 16, William Pickering, 1847.

A further provision of the statutes attached a grammar-school to Merton's foundation. "I will and enact that if any young children of my kin need support in consequence of the death or poverty of their parents, while they are under early instruction in the rudiments of knowledge, in such case the Warden shall cause them, to the number of thirteen, to be educated in the house until they can make their way in the schools (of the university), if they turn out to be of ability for that purpose." [1]

The proof that Merton's will was carried out is shown by the accounts of the college grammar-school. In 1277 there were eleven boys, four living in the college and the remainder in the town under the care of Thomas of Wallingford. The Master of Grammar is described as the Master of Glomery. The latter was a corruption of the word "grammar," and was not only in use at Cambridge, as Rashdall states, but, as we have seen, at Oxford and also at other places in England and on the Continent. The accounts also state that the sum of 4d. a quarter for each boy is to be paid as tuition fee to the Master of Glomery. When Archbishop Peckham visited Merton in 1284, he found grave abuses existing both in the college and the school, and in his ordinances he says: "Furthermore, the founders of your college, perceiving that the clergy of England, for the most part, expressed themselves very inaccurately in the learned languages, decreed that you should educate scholars under a grammatical tutor, and that the works of grammatical authors should be kept in the library to perfect you in the learned languages. But as this has hitherto been neglected, we prescribe, under the penalty imposed on disobedience, that so far as possible the transgression be corrected according to rule. And we will that the works of Papia and Hughico, together with the summary of Brico, be procured and fastened on a public table, so that all who frequent the library may have facility of consulting them." [2] Other grammar-schools in connection with the colleges followed in imitation of the example of Merton, e.g. William Waynflete's foundation of Magdalen College School.

One of the outstanding characteristics of this period was that the customs according to which the schools were governed now began to appear in written form as statutes. No doubt the examples of the statutes of Merton and Peterhouse assisted in the growth of this procedure. Thus we have instances of early statutes at Lincoln

[1] *The Foundation Statutes of Merton College, Oxford*, ed. E. F. Percival, p. 65, William Pickering, 1847.　　　　　　　　　　　　[2] *Ibid.*, p. 56.

in 1236, St. Paul's about 1250, and at York in 1307. The latter claimed to be a codification of the ancient customs which for centuries had been observed in the cathedral and the school of York. As distinguished ecclesiastics and lay noblemen began to found new schools, it was only natural that they should put into legal form the regulations for the government of these institutions. This development reached its maturity in the statutes of Winchester and Eton.

The Black Death of 1349, followed by other outbreaks in 1361 and 1367, seriously affected every aspect of national life, but nowhere were its results more apparent than amongst the clergy and in the schools and universities. It put an end, for many years, to the creation of new colleges and schools. At Cambridge, when Corpus Christi[1] and Clare Colleges were founded to repair the ravages caused by the Black Death, no other foundation is recorded for over a century, and the development of the Oxford colleges was hindered for nearly forty years. The mortality amongst the educated sections of the population was enormous, so that there was an insufficiency of clerics to fill posts in the Church and the State.

It has often been stated that one of the earliest consequences of the Black Death was the almost complete disappearance of the French language in schools. The Black Death was probably a contributory cause, but it must be remembered that for some time Normans and Saxons had been drawn together in an English nation and that for more than ten years before the coming of the plague, England and France had been at war. French had been discarded in 1362 as the language of the law-courts and of Parliament. John of Trevisa (1326-1412) informs us that John of Cornwall, the master of Merton College School, "changed the learning in grammar schools and construction of French into English . . . so that now [1385] . . . in all the grammar schools of England children leave French and construe and learn in English, and have thereby advantage on one side and disadvantage on the other. Their advantage is that they learn their grammar in less time than children were wont to do. The disadvantage is that now children of the grammar school know no more French than does their left heel, and that is harmful if they should pass the sea and travel in strange lands."

[1] Corpus Christi College originated from the gild of the same name, whose headquarters were situated south of St. Bene't's Church. Although it was officially named the "College of Corpus Christi and the Blessed Virgin Mary," for nearly 500 years it was called Bene't College. When the old entrance to the churchyard was closed in 1827, the college reverted to its official title.

The Black Death, by seriously reducing the number of scholars fit to teach in grammar-schools, was instrumental in bringing about the foundation of the first English institution for the training of schoolmasters.[1]   In 1439 William Byngham petitioned the King for authority to erect a mansion called God's House in Cambridge for the training of grammar-school masters.   The House was to accommodate "twenty-four scholars for to commence in grammar, and a priest to govern them."   In his petition, Byngham declared : "your poor beseecher hath found in western land, over the east party of the way leading from Hampton to Coventry and so forth no farther north than Ripon, 70 schools void or more that were occupied all at once within 50 years past, because that there is so great scarcity of masters of grammar, whereof as now be almost none, nor none may be had in your Universities over those that needs must be occupied still there."[2]   Evidently Byngham's venture was not a permanent one, for the house was permitted to fall into decay and was later refounded as Christ's College by the Lady Margaret, mother of Henry VII.

The lack of priests resulted in a great increase in pluralism. William of Wykeham, after the plague of 1361, is reported to have obtained sixteen preferments in the space of eighteen months.   His rapid rise to wealth and fame was such that he may be considered as the millionaire of the 14th century.   After certain minor advancements, Wykeham was elected to the see of Winchester in 1366 and was made Chancellor in the following year.   When, in 1371, Parliament attacked the King's ministers, he lost the office of Chancellor, and later, at the instrumentality of John of Gaunt, Wykeham was impeached for fraudulent misuse of public funds, and his episcopal estates were sequestrated.   They were, however, soon returned to him and, on the accession of Richard II, Wykeham received a full pardon.

Wykeham had long been a patron of education, and as early as 1369 he was buying land at Oxford with a view to a new foundation.   In 1379 he executed a charter for the foundation of "Saint Marie College of Winchester in Oxford," which should have a warden and seventy scholars.   The actual building of the college proceeded apace and it was formally opened in 1386.   The college

---

[1] As early as 1200, the Council of Westminster, after ordering that priests should teach freely any children brought to them, also required that all priests should have a school for schoolmasters in their houses.   We have no means of discovering how far this injunction was obeyed.

[2] G. G. Coulton.   *Medieval Panorama*, p. 391, C.U.P., 1938.

was known as New College to distinguish it from Oriel, the older St Mary College in Oxford. The statutes of New College show quite clearly Wykeham's reasons for his foundation. "Further, compassionating the general disease of the clerical army, which through the want of clergy caused by pestilence, wars, and other miseries of the world, we have seen grievously wounded, in order that one may be able partly to relieve it, since in truth we cannot wholly cure it, for this truly in our small way we willingly spend our labours." A further reason was the growing strength of the Lollard movement. Wykeham saw that educated clergy were a necessity if the new doctrines were to be successfully checked.

At the time that Wykeham was busy with the preparations for the erection of New College, he was also making arrangements for the second part of his project. In 1373 he entered into an agreement with Richard of Herton to take charge for ten years in Winchester of "the poor scholars whom the said Lord Bishop maintains and will continue to maintain at his own expense." A house in the parish of St. John's, outside the East Gate, was purchased as a dwelling-place for the "poor scholars." In the meantime, Wykeham was maturing his plans for building a permanent home for them. In 1378 he obtained a Bull from Urban VI for the founding of "Saint Marie College of Winchester," and when the royal licence was granted a site was chosen and, after some delay, building operations commenced in 1387. They were not completed until 28th March 1394, when, with much ceremony, the formal opening of the college took place.[1]

Wykeham's College at Winchester represents the beginning of a new era in the foundation of schools. As we have seen, collegiate schools had existed long before his time, but Winchester was on a larger and grander scale than the earlier colleges, and became a model for subsequent foundations. From Winchester, his scholars were to go to the sister foundation at Oxford to study arts, philosophy, and theology. The Winchester statutes show a marked development in clarity and comprehension over the statutes of earlier schools. The innovation of Wykeham, however, has been admirably described by Leach in his well-known history of the college.

[1] There seems to be some confusion in regard to the date of the formal opening of Winchester. The problem is discussed by A. F. Leach (*A History of Winchester College*, Chap xi, "Our Opening Day").

"The really important new departure was taken, a real step in advance made, when Wykeham made his School a separate and distinct foundation, independent of the Oxford College.   Others had erected Collegiate Churches for university students.   He erected one for school-boys.   The old Collegiate Churches had kept Grammar Schools, and flourishing Grammar Schools, but they were, though inseparable accidents, still accidents.   The new Collegiate Churches at the University, called Colleges, substituted grown scholars for priests, and study for services, as the essence of the institution, but the school-boys remained an accident, and a rather unimportant accident.   In Winchester College the accident became the essence.   The corporate name of 'Warden and scholars, clerks,' stamped the School and the school-boys as the aim and object of the foundation.   The Collegiate Church form was preserved, the Fellows occupying the place of Canons, but instead of the boys being subordinate to the Canons the Canons were subsidiary to the boys.   For the first time a school was established as a sovereign and independent corporation existing by and for itself, self-centred, self-controlled." [1]

In his foundation deed of 1382, Wykeham, after a reference to the founding of New College, states quite clearly the purpose of Winchester.   "As experience, the mistress of life, already teaches, grammar is the foundation, gate, and source of all other liberal arts, without which they cannot be known, nor can any one arrive at their pursuit. . . . There are, too, and will be hereafter, one may believe, many poor scholars, busied in school studies, suffering from want of money and poverty, whose means barely suffice, or will suffice, in the future, to enable them to continue and become proficient in the art of grammar.   For such poor and needy scholars, clerks, now and hereafter, in order that they may stay and be busy at school, and more freely and liberally profit in the faculty and science of grammar, and become as is desirable, more fit for the sciences or liberal arts . . . we propose, by the help of God, out of the means and goods given us by God, to hold out helping hands, and give the assistance of charity in the form underwritten."   The deed appointed as Warden, Thomas of Canle and directed that the Warden and scholars "shall in the same college, live together as collegial and collegiate persons."

The earlier statutes of Winchester are not extant, and we only possess the revised statutes of the year 1400.   From these we find

[1] A. F. Leach.   *A History of Winchester College*, pp. 89-90, Duckworth, 1899.

that the original establishment consisted of the Warden, the Head Master, ten Fellows, three Chaplains, an Usher, seventy scholars, three chapel clerks, sixteen choristers, making a total of 105. In addition, there was a considerable domestic staff. The statutes show that, although Winchester was on a larger scale than previous schools, it was essentially a grammar-school. In spite of the fact that at present it is frequently described as our oldest public school, it is important to remember that the term "public school" did not acquire the sense it often has now until the 18th century. The public schools were no different in their origin from other grammar-schools. In its mediaeval usage, the word "public" simply meant open to scholars from all parts of the country, with no restrictions as to place of residence, as was the case in many schools. In this sense, St. Albans can claim, with a good deal of justice, to be one of the oldest public schools. The reference to the "poor and needy scholars" (*pauperes et indigentes*), will be discussed later in this chapter.

Winchester was intended to be an independent college, though closely connected with New College. Thus, the latter elected the Warden, who was a past or present Fellow of New College. The Fellows of Winchester were to have been, or were to be in the future, Fellows of New College. Also, each year the Warden and two Fellows from New College held a visitation at Winchester. It was on the occasion of their visit that scholars of Winchester were elected to proceed to New College and new scholars for the school were chosen. The statutes contain the regulations for conducting the election. First priority was to be given to the founder's kin. The remainder were to be "poor and needy scholars, of good character and well conditioned, of gentlemanly habits, able for school, completely learned in reading, plain song and old Donatus." They were to be between the ages of eight and twelve, but in exceptional cases boys up to sixteen could be admitted if they showed sufficient promise. Preference was to be afforded to those who came from the estates of the two foundations. Next in order came natives of the diocese of Winchester, and then those from Oxford, Berks, Wilts, Somerset, Essex, Middlesex, Dorset, Kent, Sussex, and Cambridge, and finally those born in other parts of England. Scholars could stay at school until the age of eighteen.

In addition to the scholars, the statutes directed that not more than ten sons of noble persons might be admitted, provided "that by occasion thereof prejudice, loss or scandal in no wise arise to the Warden, priests, scholars, clerks or any of the servants of the same." These were called Commoners or Gentleman Commoners because they paid to have their commons, *i.e.* common meals and residence, with the Fellows. According to the records, the first commoners appeared in 1395. By the second term they were eleven in number, though one of them was termed *puer officialis*. We may suspect that he was what in later ages was termed a pupil-teacher. The amount paid for commons seems to have varied from 9d. to 16d. per week, according to the individual's station in life. By 1412 we find that there were from eighty to one hundred commoners, and the complaint of overcrowding was made. Only ten of the commoners were living in college. The rest were "street commoners" or Oppidans, who lodged near the college. Some of them are supposed to have lived in St. Elizabeth's College, which was on the site of the Warden's Garden. At a later period special quarters were provided for them by the Head Master. It is important to note that here we have the beginnings of the present public-school system in which the majority of the pupils are fee-payers and not free scholars.

At first the Warden was the most important officer and the Head Master (*Magister Informator*)[1] was merely the teacher, but as time went on he became very much more important. The stipend of the Warden was £20 a year ; that of the Informator £10, whilst the Fellows received £5. The Head Master was allowed an Usher (*Hostiario*) as an assistant, and the latter was paid at the rate of £3 6s. 8d. a year. At times there were other assistants, known as *co-adiutores*. The Head Master was not permitted by statute to receive money or presents from the scholars, but there was no such restriction in regard to the commoners. One suspects that they contributed liberally to the Head's expenses.

The college records provide us with a clear picture of schoolboy life in the Middle Ages at such an institution as Eton or Winchester. There was no general holiday until 1518 when, for the first time in its history, school was closed. There were plenty of holy days on which boys did not attend lessons, and certain boys were allowed to go home between Whitsun and August (*Exeats*). Any scholar who was absent for more than a month relinquished his place. Christmas was a season of great festivity. Not only did the college receive visits from minstrels and players, but on Holy Innocents' Day the curious ceremony of the feast of the Boy

---

[1] The headmaster of Winchester still signs his prizes as "Informator."

Bishop took place. One of the most handsome boys was chosen to be a bishop and the remainder took the parts of the prebends, canons, and other clergy. In reality, positions were reversed, and whilst the boys sang the services the clergy took subordinate parts. One can imagine with what glee the boys occupying the stalls of the Master and the Fellows sang, "He hath put down the mighty from their seats." The ceremony of the Boy Bishop was not by any means peculiar to Winchester. We find it at Eton and St. Paul's and in many of the other collegiate schools such as Jesus College, Rotherham. At Bristol, the mayor and corporation attended the Boy Bishop's sermon and received his blessing. The ceremony was proscribed by Henry VIII in 1541.

It is difficult with the scanty materials available to give anything like a complete picture of the daily routine at Winchester. The time of rising was fixed by mattins, which varied according to summer or winter from four to six o'clock a.m. After mattins came school-work. Breakfast was at nine and only the younger scholars were allowed to partake. The older ones were thought to be sturdy enough to wait until dinner at noon. The other main meal was supper at about six. All fast days were kept with the usual abstinence from flesh meat, but there is no evidence that the boys were insufficiently fed. Beer for the table was brewed in the college itself.

All scholars were obliged to receive the tonsure, the first step towards holy orders, before the end of their first year at school. Their head was shaved by the porter, and the inventory of the Porter's Lodge for 1413 contains amongst its items three basins, six shaving cloths, and four razors. All scholars were ordered to wear long gowns. Their colour is unknown except that black gowns were forbidden. The choristers, or Quiristers, did not live in college for the first half-year, but after this they were eligible for election and received their education free in return for waiting in Hall and making the beds of the Fellows.

Wykeham has been credited with the institution of Prefects or Praepostors. The boys were divided into Prefects and Inferiors, and the statutes certainly ordered that in the scholars' chambers there should be at least three scholars of good repute and older than the rest to superintend their studies and report on them to the Warden or Master when required to do so. This idea, however, was not original, for it seems to have been borrowed from the statutes of Merton, which prescribed, "There is to be one person in every chamber, where scholars are resident, of more mature age than the others, who is also to have a superintendence over the other fellows, and who is to make his report of their morals and advancement in learning to the Warden." [1]

Wykeham does not seem to have drawn up any regulations concerning sports and games. In his desire to protect the fabric, his statutes forbid "uproarious and inordinate sports" in the college precincts. He says: "Inasmuch as below the said Hall is the school-room wherein scholars should study, who by wrestlings, dancings, leapings, singings, clamours, tumults and inordinate noises, and the spilling of water, beer and other liquids, in the said Hall, may be sore hindered from their studies and may sustain grave damage to their books and clothes: now we forbid all such doings, and each offender shall pay for the damage done by himself in such matters." The main exercise seems to have been that of walking in procession to Hills (*ad montem*). The hill in question was St. Catherine's Hill, about a mile from the college. No satisfactory explanation of the custom has been forthcoming. It may be that scholars could there indulge in ball games and archery without interference. The practice was developed at Eton in 1452, and there Montem was held each year at about the time of the Feast of the Conversion of St. Paul. The custom led eventually to rowdyism, and was abolished at Eton in 1847.

The schoolroom below Hall which is mentioned in the above extract from the statutes was the original schoolroom, and is the only ancient school building of the 14th century which now remains. A 16th-century description gives us a picture of it as it existed before modern restoration altered some of its original features. The room was at first forty-five feet six inches in length and twenty-eight feet ten inches in breadth. With such dimensions, one can well understand the complaint about overcrowding made in 1412. The Hall above was supported by four posts, of which one remains. There are raised steps in each window, on which sat the eighteen Prefects to supervise the work of the Inferiors. On the walls hung a map of the world, Quintilian's Code of School Laws, and the famous device, "*Aut disce aut discede, manet sors tertia, caedi*," which has been translated by "Learn, leave, or be licked." Under the *Aut disce* originally stood the rostrum from which boys declaimed their exercises in rhetoric.

[1] *The Foundation Statutes of Merton College, Oxford*, ed. E. F. Percival, pp. 18-19, William Pickering, 1847.

Wykeham's foundation was sure to have its imitators. One of these was Archbishop Chicheley of Canterbury, who founded the college school at Higham Ferrers in Northamptonshire, and the College of All Souls, Oxford, in 1422 and 1438 respectively. The most important college which took Winchester for a model was that of Eton, founded by Henry VI in 1440. Its scholars were intended to pass on to King's College, Cambridge. Henry paid several visits to Winchester to study the organisation of the school, and when he had decided the lines on which Eton should be run, he persuaded the headmaster of Winchester, William Wayneflete, to be Eton's first Provost. Wayneflete brought with him from Winchester five scholars, an ex-scholar, and a commoner, to form the nucleus of the new college. The statutes of Eton, with certain modifications, were modelled on those of Winchester. Henry seems to have been more mindful of recreation than Wykeham, for he set aside sufficient ground for archery, and there is every reason to believe that some kind of football was played at Eton in quite early times.

Henry issued in 1446 a warrant in which he granted a monopoly to the Provost of Eton and his successors. This is one of the earliest occasions on which the term "public" was applied to a grammar-school, and it is again another sign that in the beginning the public schools of to-day were not different from, but had a common origin in, the mediaeval grammar-schools. The terms "public" and "general" emphasised the non-local character of Eton, which drew its scholars from all parts of the kingdom. This necessitated boarding in the houses of the Fellows. The boarders were known, as at Winchester, by the name oppidans, in distinction from the scholars who were borne on the foundation. There were two classes of oppidans at Eton: the higher class was composed of sons of noblemen and were not to exceed twenty in number. They dined with the chaplain and usher. The lower class dined with the scholars and choristers, and paid less for their board. Both classes received their tuition free.

Eton passed through troublous times during the Wars of the Roses. Because Eton was a foundation of the House of Lancaster, Edward IV, when he became King, obtained a Bull abolishing the college, and annexed the buildings to St. George's, Windsor. Wayneflete, now Bishop of Winchester, and Westbury, the Provost, were able to restore the college in 1467 and to obtain the revocation of the Bull. Edward seems later to have taken Eton into his favour again and paid several visits to the college. In 1489, as a

consequence of a petition presented by Eton and King's College
to Henry VII, a commission of inquiry was appointed and the two
colleges received back much of the property taken from them by
the Yorkist kings.

The third of our ancient public schools, Westminster, is from
one point of view the oldest. The actual date of its commencement
is unknown, but it is probable that when, in 1179, Pope Alexander
III ordered all cathedrals and monasteries to maintain a school, the
great Benedictine monastery of Westminster was unlikely to have
disobeyed. The rules for the behaviour of 13th-century schoolboys
preserved in the chapter library at Westminster are thought to have
applied to the scholars of that school. The boys, on rising in the
morning, were to make their beds, say their prayers, and wash
themselves before proceeding to church. "They were not to carry
in their hands bows, sticks or stones, and were not to run, jump,
chatter or play any trick on a townsman . . . on the way. In church
they were to endeavour to fix their eyes on the altar and to copy the
good customs of their elders, and they were neither to laugh nor
to giggle if anyone should happen to read or sing indifferently. . . .
On holidays the boys were to keep to a definite place assigned
beforehand for playing in moderation . . . but should any boy be
found with dice in his possession, he must taste a stroke of the rod
for each pip of the dice." [1]

It is beyond doubt that from 1363 there was a permanent school
in the Almonry of the Abbey, though it was never a large one,
probably containing not more than twenty-eight boys. Leach
arrives at this number in an interesting manner. "The payments
for cloth enable us to determine with tolerable certainty the status
of the almonry schoolmaster and the size of his school. The five
yards of cloth allowed him was the same as the allowance to the
usher at Winchester College, three yards less than the head master's,
and his fur coat cost 16d. or 18d., while the head master's at Winchester cost 3s. 4d. He was sometimes a married man, and therefore not in holy orders. The number of boys can be deduced from
the amount of cloth. Three or four pieces were bought, of twenty-
four yards in the piece, which, at four yards a boy, would give
eighteen to twenty-four boys." [2] The payment of cloth to the master
and the boys remind us that at that time the clothing trade was
the staple trade of England.

[1] L. E. Tanner. *Westminster School*, pp. 1-2, Country Life Ltd., 1934.
[2] A. F. Leach. *The Schools of Medieval England*, p. 220, Methuen, 1915.

Westminster was one of many instances which arose in the 13th century of a grammar-school under the supervision of the monastic almoner. At first, the grammar and song schools seem to have been combined, but in 1479 the records show that the two establishments were separate. The monastery was dissolved in 1540, but the King issued a charter for the refoundation of the school, and Alexander Nowell was appointed as Head Master in 1543. The development of Westminster into a large public school belongs, therefore, to the post-Reformation period.

One of the striking characteristics of the later Middle Ages was the very large number of schools which originated in association with a chantry. Some of these were primary schools, but most of them were either grammar-schools originally or became grammar-schools at a later date. The custom developed for wealthy individuals, who in earlier years might have endowed a church or a monastery, to found a chantry, which maintained one or more priests to say Masses for the repose of the founder and the souls of other specified persons. In most cases, the duties of a chantry priest involved the teaching of a school. Foster Watson claimed that the earliest recognised case of the foundation of a school in a chantry was that of Lady Berkeley in 1348, who was the founder of what was known later as Wotton-under-Edge Grammar School of Lady Margaret.[1] This claim does not seem to be substantiated, for Adamson states that the earliest chantries were founded in the 12th century, and Leach gives numerous instances of chantries and schools founded much earlier than Lady Berkeley's, *e.g.* the Free School of Crewkerne, Somerset, connected with the Trinity chantry, 1310 ; Ashburton Grammar School, Devon, and the chantry of St. Lawrence, 1314 ; and the chantry school of St. Petronilla at Harlow, Essex, 1324.

One of the earliest instances of a grammar-school springing from a chantry is that of Appleby Grammar School. As a matter of fact, Appleby originated from two chantry bequests, both much earlier than the date assigned by Foster Watson to Wotton-under-Edge. The first was the chantry of De Goldington, at the altar of St. Mary in the Church of St. Lawrence. He assigned five and a half marks yearly for the chantry priest. The deed is dated 1286. The mayor and corporation of Appleby claimed the right of

[1] Foster Watson. *The Old Grammar Schools*, p. 3, C.U.P., 1916. This school, however, can lay claim to another record. It was the first English school to possess a playground, and Lady Berkeley prescribed that whilst the pupils were at play they should be supervised by the master and the usher.

appointing the chantry priest, who was the schoolmaster. An interesting relic of this claim is that until 1886 the headmaster of the grammar-school had the right to occupy the corporation pew in the Church of St. Lawrence. The second chantry, dedicated to St. Nicholas, the patron saint of schoolboys, was founded by Robert de Threkeld in 1331. It seems that the same priest served both chantries. This was not unusual in cases where the chantry bequest was not sufficient by itself to maintain a priest. In 1388 the town was sacked by the Scots, but the chantry school was left standing. The rest of the days of the chantry school were occupied in a contest between the mayor and corporation and the vicar of St. Lawrence over the right of appointing the schoolmaster. In 1518 the dispute seems to have gone in favour of the corporation. When we come to consider the mediaeval Scottish schools, we shall find that the civic authorities claimed similar rights over them, and the proximity of Appleby to the Border may have influenced the corporation in this particular case. The chantry was dissolved in 1548, but the school was allowed to remain. In 1569 the dispute about the appointment of the master was raised once more, and to settle it the corporation applied to the Queen for a charter. This was granted in 1574, but the present title of the foundation as the Queen Elizabeth's Grammar School should not delude us into thinking that it originated at that date.

Another example of a grammar-school which sprang from a chantry is that of Leeds Grammar School.

Thomas Clarell, who was Vicar of Leeds from 1430 to 1469, was buried in his own chantry in Leeds parish church. The object of the Clarell Chantry was "to pray for the soule of Kynge Edwarde the iiijth and Quene Elizabeth, the founder's soule and all Cristen soules, and to do dyvyne service." Freehold lands worth £4 13d. 4d. per annum were acquired for the support of the chantry. The original endowment was doubled by further gifts of land and it is highly probable that some kind of school, most likely a grammar-school, was taught by the chantry priest. We certainly find a reference in the will of 1496 to the "prestes, clarkes, and scolers" of Leeds. When the chantry was dissolved, the chantry priest was a certain William Sheafield who was granted a small pension. At his death in 1552, Sheafield left a will bequeathing the rent of certain properties "to the use and for findinge sustentation and livinge of one honest substantial learned man to be a schoole maister to teach and instruct freely for ever all such younge schollars youthes and children as shall come and resort to him from time to time to be taught instructed and informed in such a school house as shall be founded erected and buylded by the paryshioners of the sayde towne and parishe of Leedes." He also named twelve executors to see his wishes carried out.

Another founder of the school was William Ermystead, priest, who refounded Skipton Grammar School in 1548 and Birstall Grammar School in 1556. In 1555 he set aside certain property the rent of which should go "to the finding of one prieste sufficientlie learned to teache a free gramer schole within the towne of Leeds in the Countie of Yorke for ever for all such as shall repaire thereunto without takinge of any money more or lesse for teaching of the said children or schollers saveing of one pennie of everie scholler to enter his name in the Mayster's booke yf the Scholler have a pennie and yf not to enter and continue freelie withoute any paieing, whiche said prieste and his successors by the Grace of God and by my will and mynde saie Masse three daies in everie weeke in the parish church of Leeds aforesaid."

Wakefield Grammar School developed from a chantry school. The commission of inquiry appointed by the Chantries Act of 1547 noted, with regard to Wakefield Parish, "the Chauntry called Thurstone Chauntry in the seid paryshe churche—Edward Wood, Incombent, lii yeres of age, well learned and teacheth youth there, hath no other lyving than the profits of the said Chauntrie." In a similar manner, Skipton Grammar School originated in the chantry of St. Nicholas, established some time before 1492 by Peter Toller, whose object is expressed as, "to pray for his sowl and all Christian sowles, and to help to do and manteyn dyvyne service in the said quere, and also to keep a grammer skole to the children of the same towne." The altar of St. Nicholas was established in Skipton Parish Church in 1475, when Toller became Dean of Craven, so that the school may have originated at that date. The frequent dedication of chantries to St. Nicholas, the patron of schoolboys, in itself emphasises the close connection between the chantries and the schools.

The craft and merchant gilds of the Middle Ages, which through their apprenticeship system trained artisans and skilled craftsmen, were closely associated with the Church and paid priests to officiate for them. In addition, there were numerous religious gilds and brotherhoods, all of which maintained a priest. Frequently one of the duties of the priest was to teach Latin grammar, and some of the gilds maintained schools such as Ludlow Grammar School, founded by the Palmers' Gild, and the school connected with the Gild of St. Nicholas at Worcester. The foundation of the Grammar School of Stratford-on-Avon, which was attended by Shakespeare, was closely connected with the gilds of that town. Sometimes the gild priest was also a chantry priest; at others, he might be a "morrow mass priest,"[1] who celebrated an early Mass attended by folk on their way to work. It should not be thought that the gild schools were merely vocational. They were similar to the grammar-schools which sprang from cathedrals and collegiate churches. In the same way, hospitals and almshouses frequently maintained schools.

Ripon Grammar School was probably a pre-Conquest foundation, but it does not appear in written history until 1348, when the Sheriff of Yorkshire was ordered to arrest the master on a charge of felony. His crime was that he had become mixed up in some kind of rebellion, but, fortunately for him, he could not be found. The school became associated with the gilds of the town, and the events which followed form a most important commentary on the economic conditions of the later Middle Ages and their effect upon schoolmasters. Although the all-round wealth of the country had been growing during the 15th century, money was declining in value. We know from the chantry certificate of the commissioners of Henry VIII that the stipend of the schoolmaster at Ripon was £2 per annum. For many years this had been insufficient to maintain him, and in order to provide him with a living wage he had been given a chantry in the minster. The gilds also came to his rescue and he was allowed the use of the rents from certain lands which were known as the School or Rood lands. The master was

---

[1] An interesting example of the "morrow mass priest" is afforded by the chantry certificate for the chantry connected with the school of Pontefract. "The Chauntrie of Corpus Christi in the sayde Churche. Richard Ridgall, incumbent. Havynge no foundacion but put in by the Mayre and his bretherne, To th' entente to say the morrowe masse in the said church and to survey the amendynge of the high wayes about the said towne, which masse is done by 5 o'clock in the mornynge." Richard, when he had concluded his mass, evidently had time on his hands, and was able to undertake the duties of a highway surveyor and to teach in the school. At the dissolution, the school-master of Pontefract had to make do on a stipend of £2 19s. 2d. a year. A complaint was made that he "doth not his endeavour and diligence in the due education and bringing up of children." The appointment of the master was given to the corporation, and in 1583 Elizabeth ordered the stipends of several small schools in the neighbourhood to be compounded and given to the master of Pontefract. His new salary was £25 7s. 2d. The school fell into decay and was refounded by George III in 1782 under the title of the King's School. (See *Charity Commissioners' Reports, Yorkshire West Riding*, 1819-37, pp. 734-7.)

not permitted to augment his income by charging fees to his pupils, since Ripon was a free school. The lands mentioned above belonged to the Rood or Gild of the Holy Cross in Ripon. It seems to have been quite a common practice for a gild to devote part of its income to help out the 15th-century schoolmaster and so to preserve the grammar-schools as free schools. In the example of Ripon, there was a curious sequel.

The Chantries Act dissolved gilds as well as chantries. The total income from the gild lands at Ripon was £8 7s. 2d. When the Chantry Commissioners visited Ripon, the townsfolk endeavoured to conceal the fact that the property consisted in gild lands. Probably they thought they would be able to preserve their school by this means. In any case, once the lands had been surrendered, if they wished to continue the school it would have been necessary to buy back the lands from the Crown. All might have gone well had they not attempted to dismiss the master, Edmund Browne, on the grounds that he was a Papist; "he was commonly reputed and taken for a misliker of Christ's religion now established." Browne evidently informed the authorities of the real facts about the lands, and a number of involved lawsuits followed. The school was reconstituted in 1555 as the Free Grammar School of Queen Mary.

After this brief account of the development of the pre-Reformation schools of this country, one is in a position to consider certain problems that arise in connection with mediaeval education. In the first place, was any provision made for primary education in the mediaeval scheme?

Adamson quotes a number of instances where grammar-schools of the later Middle Ages extended their teaching to younger children who were taught to read and write. Some of these small schools survived the Reformation and thus secured the continuity of primary education in this country.

The Church, through decrees of councils and episcopal charges, frequently reminded parish priests of their duty to maintain schools and teach freely all children of the parish who came to them. It is important to realise that girls as well as boys attended such "parish schools." We have no means of estimating the value of this teaching or how consistently it was carried out. One suspects that it varied greatly with individual parish priests and was often of the nature of the teaching given in a Sunday School, though probably there were some priests who taught children of their parishioners to read and write.

Some writers (*e.g.* S. C. Parker, *A Textbook in the History of Modern Elementary Education*, Ginn, 1912) have stressed the tardy development of vernacular schools. As we said previously, it must not be supposed that facilities for elementary education existed in England comparable to the elementary schools of the 19th century, but there is evidence that the type of school we have been considering was more widespread than has usually been acknowledged. Leach quotes a number of instances of primary schools existing at the beginning of the reign of Edward VI. Three examples will illustrate this point.

1. The Guylde of the Trinitie in Barnard Castell.

"The said Guylde was founded and endowed with certen landes, by Gifte of the brethern and other benefactors of the same, of auncyent tyme, to fynde a preste to be namyd the Guylde preste, to say masse dayly at the 6th houre of the clocke in the mornyng, and to kepe a free Grammar scoole and a Songe scoole for all the children of the towne." [1]

2. Parish of Kingsley, Staffordshire.

The chantry priest was directed "to kepe scole, and to teche pore mens children of the seid parishe grammer, and to rede and sing." [2]

3. Parish of Bromyard, Worcestershire.

"Sir John Bastenall, Incombente and scole master ther, of the age of [blank] yeres, a man of good conversacion and well lerned, which teachith chylderne, and doth brynge upe vertuously in redying, wryttynge, and in gramer." [3]

In northern Italy and Germany, the situation was entirely different. The development of banking and the growth of commerce and industry demanded that a comparatively large proportion of the population should be able to read, write, and keep accounts. Thus we have the rise of the German reading-and-writing schools in which the teaching was in the vernacular and which can be considered as elementary schools in some respect similar to the English schools of the 18th century. In Germany, also, the town councils took a prominent part in the founding and maintenance of these schools.

[1] A. F. Leach. *English Schools at the Reformation*, p. 61, Pt. II, "Extracts from Chantry Certificates and Warrants," Constable, 1896.
[2] *Ibid.*, p. 200.   [3] *Ibid.*, p. 98.

Childrey, in Berkshire, is an interesting example of a school with an upper division for those who required grammar teaching. The priest was to teach the alphabet, the Paternoster, the Ave, the Creed, and all that was necessary for serving at Mass. The boys also received doctrinal instruction in the articles of faith, the ten commandments, and the method of making a confession. They were also taught good manners and to honour their parents. Those who proceeded to the upper division were to be instructed in grammar, but the priest was to give his services gratis, though he could accept presents freely offered.

The scarcity of references to primary schools in the Middle Ages is responsible for the belief, held until recently, that little or no provision was made for elementary teaching. The lack of documentary evidence is partly due to the fact that many primary schools were ephemeral, and partly because vernacular schools were considered as much less important than the Latin schools. Nevertheless, unless considerable numbers of them existed, it is difficult to explain how boys who entered the grammar-schools were able to read and write. Many of these schools had no schoolhouse, but the scholars were taught in the parish church by the priest or the clerk.

One interesting example is that of Threlkeld School, near Keswick in Cumberland. The school may have existed as early as 1220, but there is good reason to believe that it was flourishing in the 15th century. When the Lancastrians were defeated at Towton, in 1461, Henry, the young Lord Clifford, and his mother proceeded in disguise to Threlkeld village. His father, "the black Clifford," had been slain at Towton and the Yorkists were seeking the young boy's life. He is said to have lived for fourteen years in a shepherd's home at Threlkeld and to have received his education in the village school, which seems to have been held in the parish church. It was given a permanent schoolhouse through the will of Anthony Gilbanke, in 1659, and was endowed as a free school. The present building was erected in 1849, and the school is now known as Threlkeld Church of England School.

Many of the grammar-schools are distinctly described as "Free Grammar Schools," and the title became almost universal in Tudor times. Some controversy has arisen in regard to the meaning of the term "free." One theory, advanced by Dr. Kennedy, headmaster of Shrewsbury School, and submitted in 1862 to the Public

Schools Commission, was that the freedom of the school simply implied that it was free from external control whether of a cathedral or monastic chapter or of a college. This view has generally been abandoned. Another interpretation is that a "free school" was a school in which a liberal, *i.e.* a freeman's education, was provided. Parry puts forward the view that the freedom of the school consisted in its not being restricted to any particular class of pupils, but opening its doors to all comers. In other words, a free school was a public school.[1] He argues that some monastery and cathedral schools only admitted certain classes of pupils. Also, in certain towns and parishes the schools were only open to inhabitants of the district; and those who came from outside the neighbourhood, foreigners, as they were called, were not admitted. He quotes as an example the entry in the York Episcopal Registers of June 1289, concerning the schools of Kinoulton, which were open to parishioners only: "all other clerks and strangers whatsoever being kept out and by no means admitted to the school."

According to his view, the term "public" gradually became a substitute for "free" school. He concludes: "We may consequently regard the institution of 'free' grammar schools as marking a stage in the policy of breaking down the barriers which separated parish from parish, and township from township." This theory has much to commend it. Undoubtedly, in later times, the terms "free grammar-school" and "public grammar-school" were often interchangeable. Thus the charter of Giggleswick emphasises that the master is "to teach indifferently [*i.e.* impartially] the poor as well as the rich, the parishioners as well as the stranger." Some schools, however, resembled Sedburgh, founded by Roger Lupton and described in the foundation deed of 1527 as the "Free Grammar School of Mayster Roger Lupton." Although there were no restrictions to the entry of foreigners, preference was to be given to the founder's kin and boys of the district. The master was enjoined to "teche frely gramer after the maner, forme, and use of some laudable, notable, and famous scole of England, and especiall my kinsmen and theym of Sedber, Dent, and Garstall, and then all others without any exaction or chalenge of their stipend or wages beside my allowance." There is no doubt that when he founded Sedbergh, Lupton had Eton in mind.

[1] A. W. Parry. *Education in England in the Middle Ages*, pp. 67-71, U.T.P., 1920.

Leach's theory is generally accepted at the present time. It does justice to the points put forward by Parry, but it interprets "free" in the literal meaning of the word. Leach held that a "free" school meant undoubtedly a school in which, because of its endowment, all or some of the scholars, the poor, or the inhabitants of the place, or a certain number, were freed from fees for teaching. This view is well supported by numerous foundation deeds, if it is realised that entrance fees, money paid for extras,[1] and fees contributed by pupils who were not eligible for the freedom of the school, were not incompatible with the idea of a free school. Some grammar-schools were not free in the sense that fees were paid by all their pupils, and many schools which were free were not grammar-schools, but provided a more elementary type of education.

Frequently parents made a voluntary offering to the schoolmaster for his care of their children. Needless to say, such gratuities, where not expressly forbidden in the foundation deeds, were encouraged, and set a precedent. One interesting contribution in the late Middle Ages and Tudor times was the "cockpenny." Cockfighting was a widespread form of sport for boys and masters, especially in northern England. The cockpenny was a levy to provide the cocks and pay incidental expenses. The foundation deed of Manchester Grammar School forbade the masters to take any money such as "cockpenny, victor penny, potation penny." At Sedbergh, the cockpenny was transformed in the 18th and 19th centuries into an offering of £1 1s. to the Headmaster and 10s. 6d. to the Usher paid on Shrove Tuesday. Pocklington Grammar School still preserves its ancient cock-fighting bell.

Leach's theory receives support from the example of Sedbergh mentioned above. We have also seen the predicament in which the master of Ripon found himself through not being able to charge

---

[1] There is very little information to be obtained about extras paid for in mediaeval schools. In the 16th century we find many instances of payments which probably had the support of long-standing custom. Thus nearly all free grammar-schools charged entrance fees which usually ranged from a penny to a shilling. Sometimes boys of the neighbourhood or kinsmen of the founder were exempt from entrance fees. Occasionally, the amount of the entrance fee was graded according to the social status of the pupil, varying from 10s. for the son of a lord to 4d. for the son of an ordinary citizen. In some schools fees were charged for light, heat, and cleaning. At Guildford, 8d. a year was charged and was allotted as follows: 1d. per quarter for brooms and rods, 4d. at Michaelmas for providing wax candles to light the school in the dark winter mornings and evenings. Instances were not uncommon where the pupils brought their own wax candles (tallow candles were usually not accepted) and their contribution to the school fire.

fees to supplement his inadequate stipend.[1] Roger Sutton, who was
described as Rector of Beverley Grammar School, argued in 1312
that no more than seven choristers could be admitted to the school
as free scholars (*liberi*). The chapter inquired into the ancient
traditions and customs of the church and school, and ruled that
there was no restriction to the number who could be admitted
without paying fees. At Jesus College, Rotherham, founded by
Archbishop Rotherham in 1483, the grammar, song, and writing
masters were to "diligently teach without exaction of money or
anything else" (*absque pecunie vel alterius rei cuiscunque exac-
cione*). That this rule was observed is attested by the Chantry
Certificate of 1548, which states: "The sayd Colledge was founded
for a preacher to preach 12 sermons every yere, three scholemasters
of free scholes, viz. grammer, song, and wryting, 6 pore children,
a butler, and a coke." The Chantry Certificate for Newland,
Gloucestershire, tells us that amongst the duties of the chantry priest
was "to kepe a Gramer scoole halfFree; that is to seye, taking of
scolers lerning gramer 8d. the quarter, and of others lerning to
rede 4d. the quarter."[2]

There is also another possible interpretation of the term "free"
which, strangely enough, seems to have been overlooked. During
the 13th century, the estates of the Church were increasing at an
alarming rate, and this was having a serious effect upon the revenue
of the King. A feudal king was almost completely dependent on his
feudal dues, *e.g.* scutage, escheat in the case of lack of heirs,
wardships, and fines for treasonable conduct. With the income he
obtained from such sources, he had to carry on the business of government. Landowners tried to avoid the demands made upon them.
As in modern times people have escaped the high rate of income-tax
by residing in the Channel Islands, so in the Middle Ages one
method of evasion consisted in granting lands to an ecclesiastical
corporation such as an abbey or a cathedral chapter and afterwards

[1] The idea of the free grammar-school spread extensively during the Tudor
period, and we find the charters of these schools commencing with the phrase,
"the Free Grammar School of King Edward VI" or "of Queen Elizabeth."
The following extracts from Tudor foundations are typical: Keighley: "The
master shall instruct in the English, Latin, and Greek languages free and without
any reward or stipend whatever." Archbishop Holgate's Schools: "The
master shall teach grammar—without taking any stipend, wages or other exaction
of the scholars." Heath Grammar School, Halifax: "For the admission and
teaching of every scholar of the town and parish of Halifax, of what condition
soever, nothing shall be demanded."

[2] Quoted by J. W. Adamson, *The Illiterate Anglo-Saxon*, p. 52, C.U.P.,
1946.

receiving them back as a tenant. Any marked growth of this practice resulted in an appreciable diminution in the royal income, and as a counter Edward I persuaded Parliament to enact the Statute of Mortmain in 1279. This law prohibited the grant of land to the Church under pain of forfeiting it to the Crown. The statute contained a good many loop-holes and it was necessary to close them by further legislation in 1391.

It was, however, possible for a founder to obtain a dispensation from the King exempting him from the Statute of Mortmain. This was granted even in cases where property was left to a monastery. If it could be proved that the bequest was a charitable one, the claim to be freed from the operation of the statute was so much the stronger. Thus a founder who left land and property to endow a college or a school could plead that his bequest was a charitable one, if he provided that a portion of the entrants should be educated without paying fees. Many founders wished to benefit their own district and were quite willing to make such a stipulation. In order to be freed from the operation of the statute, such a person would apply for a licence in Mortmain. Thus Archbishop Rotherham obtained a licence in Mortmain in 1482 as a prelude to founding Jesus College. The same was true of Renaissance and post-Reformation schools. The letters patent of Edward VI, authorising the refoundation of Giggleswick in 1553, provided the governors with a licence in Mortmain giving them power to acquire additional land (*licenciam specialem liberam*). In a similar way, he issued, in the warrant for letters patent for refounding Sedbergh School, a licence in Mortmain. "With a lycense also that the said Gouernours may receyve by way of gifte or purchas other landes and heredytamentes hereafter to the value of xx^{li}, with such other convenyent clauses to be contegned in the said graunte as in other Free Scoles erected by the Kinges Maiestie."

To sum up: the meaning of the term "free" grammar-school is not altogether clear. We meet with similar difficulty in saying what was intended by speaking of a "free" town. There seem to have been two conditions for a free school which to a certain extent were interdependent. The founder was granted a licence freeing his gift from the operation of Mortmain, but the condition of the licence may have been that the school should receive a proportion of pupils who did not pay fees. In addition, many schools were free to receive scholars from any part of the kingdom, though certain preferences could be operative. The licence in Mortmain also freed the school from external interference whether by a monastery, a cathedral, or even the Crown itself.

The phrase, "poor scholars," *pauperes et indigentes scolares,* as we find it expressed in the statutes of Winchester College, is frequently used to describe the type of pupil who attended the free grammar-schools. Much controversy has raged over the meaning for the term "poor." Leach maintains that the schools were not for the very poor—the destitute—, but for the relatively poor, *i.e.* sons of tradesmen, skilled artisans, country gentry, and yeoman farmers.

Parry takes an opposite point of view and considers that even such outstanding schools as Eton and Winchester were originally intended for "boys whose parents were poor and needy." [1] He adds, "The only condition of admission, practically, was that these boys would subsequently proceed to the universities, in order that their course of preparation for the priesthood might be completed."

Leach, dealing with the early 16th century, admits, "That occasionally bright boys were snatched up out of the ranks of the real poor and turned into clerics, to become lawyers, civil servants, bishops, is not to be doubted. But it was the middle classes, whether country or town, the younger sons of the nobility, or farmers, the lesser land-holders, the prosperous tradesmen, who created a demand for education, and furnished the occupants of Grammar Schools." [2]

One fact does stand out quite clearly—namely, that very few of the nobility sent their sons to be educated at the grammar-schools.

As Trevelyan writes, "The sons of the nobility and gentry were educated in various ways, differing according to the rank or the personal views of their parents. Some stayed in the manor house and were taught letters by the chaplain, field sports by the forester, and the use of arms by an old retainer or a neighbour knight. More usually they were sent away from home, an English practice that seemed heartless to foreigners, but was perhaps more good than bad in its results. Some sat in the grammar schools, conning Latin cheek by jowl with the ablest sons of burghers and yeomen. Others went to smaller private schools, even then sometimes kept by a married master. Others again were boarded in monasteries under the special care of the abbot." [3]

[1] A. W. Parry. *Education in England in the Middle Ages,* p. 201, U.T.P., 1920.
[2] A. F. Leach. *English Schools at the Reformation,* p. 109, Constable, 1896.
[3] G. M. Trevelyan. *English Social History,* p. 76, Longmans, 1946.

Leach quotes the foundation statutes of William of Wykeham's College of Winchester, to the effect that every boy on entering took an oath, "I have nothing whereby I know I can spend beyond five marks a year," *i.e.* an income of £3 6s. 8d. He points out that these "poor" boys were permitted to have an income greater than that enjoyed by sixty-seven incumbents in the diocese of Winchester.

Coulton supports the view of Leach. He writes: "The constant use of the word 'poor' in foundation statutes has led modern readers very naturally to imagine that benefactors' endowments were originally intended for a class very much worse off than those who enjoy them at present. This, however, rests upon a misunderstanding of medieval common-form. By Canon Law it was strictly forbidden to transfer to secular purposes any endowment which had been given to the Church. But nearly all the endowments conferred on our colleges were of that kind. Peterhouse and Corpus Christi at Cambridge, for instance, were both founded mainly on the income of a parish church, which was served by the Fellows. It was therefore necessary for the foundation deed to emphasise the fact that the new institution was itself one of pious charity. Leach and Rashdall have both shown conclusively that foundation statutes anticipated, not a proletarian standard of scholastic life, but that of the middle, and not even of the lower middle class." [1]

Montmorency states that before 1406, the year the Statute of Artificers was passed by Parliament, "the first Statute of Education," as he calls it, "the class that chiefly attended the grammar schools, whether in town or country, were the children of free, non-gentle persons." [2]

So far, this statement agrees with the assertion of Leach that these pupils were the sons of the relatively poor. His further argument does not seem conclusive. He agrees that in the 14th century there was no large class of destitute persons. The non-gentle population of England consisted of the free and the non-free. The latter consisted of villeins, cottagers, and the lowest social class of all, the villeins in gross, who were not only tied to the manor but could be even sold at the will of their lord. We know that the Peasants' Revolt of 1381 was a great uprising of the non-free classes and after its failure, although the restrictions of the Statute

---

[1] G. G. Coulton. *Medieval Panorama*, p. 403, C.U.P., 1938.
[2] J. E. G. de Montmorency. *State Intervention in English Education*, p. 26, C.U.P., 1902.

of Labourers were enforced outwardly in a stricter way than ever, yet throughout the 15th century the distinction between the free and the non-free classes tended to become less and less.

One result was that even as early as 1391, children of the non-free began to make their way into the grammar-schools so that they could rise in the social scale.   This fact is indicated by the petition presented by the Commons to Richard II in this year, asking the King to forbid villeins sending their children to school to "learn clergie."   This phrase is significant.   All persons who could read Latin were deemed to be in orders (though not necessarily major orders) and could claim benefit of clergy.   All clerics were freemen. The King rejected the petition and a few years later the statute of 1406, mentioned above, proclaimed that "every man or woman of what state or condition that he be, shall be free to set their son or daughter to take learning at any school that pleaseth them within the realm."

In the 13th and 14th centuries there are numerous examples of villeins being fined for sending their sons to school without permission of their lords, and Leach quotes several instances by way of illustration.   Villeins willingly paid fines to send their children to school, not so much because of a desire to see them educated as to secure their freedom from bondage.   An educated man was deemed a clerk and enjoyed the status of a freeman.   There were several reasons which moved the Commons to make their petition, amongst them being the fear that any great spread of education amongst the masses would entirely upset the existing system of land tenure by depriving them of the labour of the villeins.   One thing, however, Montmorency forgets because of his legal training.   The Statute of Artificers stated a principle, but that is one thing; to get the principle acted upon is quite another, especially in the Middle Ages. The statute had removed the legal restriction under which the villeins suffered and it became possible for a labourer's son to make his way up the social ladder, provided always that he was a boy of outstanding ability.

Thus the 14th-century schools even in the towns, but more especially in the country, would contain a sprinkling of boys of this type, but it does not affect the contention of Leach that the majority of the pupils of the grammar-schools were from what we should now call the middle classes.   The limit of five marks a year which applied to the foundation scholars of Winchester was an upper limit.   We have already seen that the statutes provided for a limited number of commoners. One may trace some kind of parallel in the position as regards free places in secondary schools in the decade before the Second World War. Pupils awarded free places, or rather those who accepted the free places which were awarded, were rarely the destitute. The very poor found themselves unable to accept the offer of an award because they had need of the child's earnings, and his keep and other incidental expenses were more than the parents could afford. But sons of parents whose income was above a fixed amount could not benefit by the scholarship. Leach appears to be justified when he writes: "The poor whom Wykeham wished to help were, as he says, those who had means enough to send their sons to grammar schools but not enough to send them on to the universities; the younger sons of lords and squires, the landed gentry in the county, the burgesses and traders in the towns. The notion that the endowments of Winchester or any other school before Christ's Hospital, which was for foundlings and the gutter pauper, have been perverted from the patrimony of the poor into an appanage of the rich, will not bear investigation." [1] As the Fleming Report warns us, "If we wish to suggest changes in the method of entry of the Public Schools, and in particular to make this entry available to a less restricted range of society than is now the case, we must base our reasons for doing so on the present needs of the country, whose children they were founded to educate, rather than on the inevitably uncertain interpretation of phrases in use five or six hundred years ago." [2]

So far we have been discussing the education of boys during the mediaeval period. Was there any equivalent form of education for girls? The evidence for the existence of schools for girls is still very scanty, though here and there fresh instances are coming to light. One can say quite definitely that there was nothing resembling the grammar-school for the education of girls. Most girls received their training at home from their mothers. Amongst the upper and middle classes it seems to have consisted in what we should now call domestic duties. Girls were trained in all that pertained to the management of the household, in first-aid, sick-nursing and the use of simple herbs for healing, and in various kinds of needlework, as the beautiful tapestry and embroidery of the Middle Ages testify.

[1] A. F. Leach. *The Schools of Medieval England*, pp. 207-8, Methuen, 1915.
[2] *The Public Schools*, Board of Education Report, p. 9, H.M.S.O., 1944.

When young, girls of the upper classes took part in the games and field sports, such as hawking, with their brothers. We know that quite a number of women of these classes were able to read and write, and that some, like Chaucer's Prioress, were able to speak French, but the evidence that these accomplishments were learnt at school is very slight. Adamson writes: "In the roll of the Corpus Christi Guild of Boston, under the year 1404, occurs the name of Maria Mareflete, '*magistra scolarum*,' a phrase which by analogy may be rendered 'school mistress,' or, where more than one teacher is in question, 'head mistress.' Was this lady the head of an independent girls' school, or a teacher of girls, or of 'petties' in the grammar school itself? The material for an answer is not forthcoming." [1]

Montmorency, in a note, says: "To what extent girls' schools existed must be sought for in local records. That there were many such schools there is no reason to doubt. Alfred appears to have attempted something in the way of schools for girls. The term 'schoolmistress' was in use quite early. In Dan Michel's *Ayenbite of Inwyt*, written in the Kentish dialect in A.D. 1340, Avarice is referred to as 'The maystresse thet heth zuo greate scole thet alle guoth thrin nor to lyerni.' . . . Probably schools for girls were conducted by nuns and were thus under the control of the Church." [2]

Daughters of the nobility were sometimes educated by private tutors. Thus Elizabeth of York, daughter of Edward IV, was taught to read and write English by a scrivener from London, and later in life she claimed to be able to write in French and Spanish. Girls and even little boys from wealthy families were occasionally sent to nunneries for their education. The ecclesiastical authorities did not favour the maintenance of convent schools, since they considered that the intrusion of persons from the outside world was upsetting to convent discipline.[3] Convent schools do not seem to have appeared until the latter half of the 14th century, a period when church discipline was becoming somewhat lax.

Abbot Gasquet quotes the instance of Thomas Hunte, who sent his two daughters to a convent, presumably to be educated.

---

[1] J. W. Adamson. *A Short History of Education*, p. 74, C.U.P., 1922.

[2] J. E. G. de Montmorency. *State Intervention in English Education*, p. 12, C.U.P., 1902.

[3] Aelred, Abbot of Rievaulx, Yorkshire, advises the anchoress to whom he is writing, "Do not allow boys and girls to come to you. There are some anchoresses who turn their anchorage into a school." Migne, *Patrol. Lat.*, Vol. XXXII, col. 1453.

He paid 17s. 4d. each for food, but no mention is made of the kind of training they received. Lady Beaumont sent her daughter to a convent and was charged £2 13s. 4d. a year. She paid only £2 and the convent authorities did not press for payment of the remainder, probably because they did not wish to offend Lord Beaumont. The latter paid a visit to his daughter and he was charged $1\frac{1}{2}$d. for "1 shoulder le molton" and 8d. for two lambs. Robert Aske, the leader of the Pilgrimage of Grace, asserted as one reason for opposing the suppression of the religious foundations that "in nunneries their daughters were brought up in virtue." [1]

In the 13th century forty-two schoolmasters and twenty-one schoolmistresses are mentioned in the returns made to the Chancellor at Paris, but it is possible that some of the schoolmistresses may have taught small boys. In 1484 authority was given to Perette la Couppenoire "to conduct the school of St. Germain l'Auxerrois and to teach and instruct girls (*puellas*) in good manners, in grammatical letters (*litteris grammaticalibus*) and in other things lawful and honourable" for the space of one year. [2] The convent of Farwell, in 1367, was allowed a nun to educate one child, provided it was not of the male sex over seven years of age. At the Dissolution there were between thirty and forty "gentylmens childern" at Polesworth, Warwickshire, but these may have been all small boys.

J. E. G. de Montmorency states that the convent of St. Mary's, Winchester, had twenty-six daughters of the nobility entrusted to it in 1537. He reproduces the register of the pupils. [3]

Bryget Plantaganet, dowghter unto the Lord Vyounte Lysley.
Mary Pole, dowghter unto Sr Gefferey Pole, knyght.
Brygget Coppeley, dowghter unto Sir Roger Coppeley, knyght.
Elizabeth Phyllpot, dowghter unto Sr Peter Phyllpot, knyght.

Margery Tyrrell	Emme Bartue
Adryan Tyrrell	Myldrid Clerke
Johanne Barbabe	Anne Lacy
Amy Dyngley	Isold Apulgate
Elizabeth Dyngley	Elizabeth Legh
Jane Dyngley	Mary Legh
Ffrances Dyngley	Alienor Merth
Susan Tycheborne	Johanne Sturgys
Elizabeth Tycheborne	Johanne Ffyldes
Mary Justyce	Johanne Ffrances
Agnes Aylmer	Jane Raynysford. xxvi.

---

[1] Abbot Gasquet. *English Monastic Life*, p. 162, Methuen, 1904.
[2] J. W. Adamson. *A Short History of Education*, p. 74, C.U.P., 1922.
[3] Article entitled "The Medieval Education of Women in England," *The Journal of Education*, June 1909.

He also quotes from Fuller's 1655 edition of his *Church History*. "Nunneries also were good Shee-schools, wherein the girles and maids of the neighbourhood were taught to read and work; and sometimes a little Latine was taught them therein. Yea, give me leave to say, if such Feminine Foundations has still continued . . . haply the weaker sex . . . might be heightened to a higher perfection than hitherto hath been obtained."

Miss Rickert quotes an instance of a mediaeval boarding-school for boys which, about 1380, was run by a layman. The evidence is contained in a charming letter written to Sir Edmund de Stonor by his chaplain. The latter was on a visit to Sir Edmund's son, who had been ill, and no doubt the chaplain had been sent to obtain news of his health. The boy was now recovering and the chaplain reported: "He is beginning to learn Donatus slowly, as is right enough so far. He has that copy of Donatus which I was afraid was lost. Indeed, I have never seen a boy get such care as he has had during his illness. The master and his wife prefer that some of his clothes should be left at home, because he has far too many, and fewer would be enough; and his clothes, through no fault of theirs, might easily be torn and spoiled."[1] How far this was but an isolated example is impossible to say.

It is certain that girls often attended the parish schools. Thus Elizabeth, daughter of William Garrard, a draper of London, was taught in a primary school by Sir William Barbour, priest, and we are told that there were thirty children in the school and the master taught them the Paternoster, the Ave, and the Creed, and "ferther learnyng." Certain anchoresses accepted girls as pupils, but the practice was frowned upon by the authorities. The well-known mystic and anchoress, Dame Juliana of Norwich, is supposed to have been educated by the nuns of Carrow, and we are told that "This nunnery had for many years been a school or place of education for the young ladies of the chief families of the diocese who boarded with and were educated by the nuns."[2]

Authorities differ widely as to the distribution of schools in the Middle Ages. Leach estimates the population of England, basing it on the Poll Tax returns, as about 2¼ millions in 1377. He regards this as an over- rather than an under-estimate. He calculates that this would give 400 schools in forty counties, or one

[1] *Chaucer's World.* Edith Rickert, ed. Clair Olson and Martin Crow pp. 115-16, O.U.P., 1948.
[2] Gertrude Robinson. *In a Mediaeval Library*, p. 76, Sands and Co., 1918

grammar-school for every 5,625 people, and contrasts this proportion with that revealed by the Schools Inquiry Report of 1864, of one school to every 23,750 people.[1]

G. G. Coulton calculates 26,000 pupils for a population of about five millions at the Dissolution. He concludes that if the provision of schools in 1931 was at the mediaeval rate, "we should have only 182,000 pupils, spaced among nearly 4,000 schools, whose average standard inclined rather to the elementary than to the grammar class. Yet we have in fact, according to *Whitaker's Almanack* for 1931, 1,300 secondary schools with an aggregate of 200,000 boys and 180,000 girls, to which must be added 20,000 elementary schools with an attendance of 5,000,000, that is, nearly thirty times more scholars in proportion to population."[2]

[1] A. F. Leach. *The Schools of Medieval England*, pp. 329-31, Methuen, 1915.
[2] G. G. Coulton. *Medieval Panorama*, p. 388, C.U.P., 1938.

CHAPTER II

THE MEDIAEVAL UNIVERSITIES

It is no exaggeration to say that the university was the greatest invention of the Middle Ages, and the most important legacy bequeathed by them to the modern world. As stated in the previous chapter, the universities were a product of the great intellectual revival of the 12th century. Before the foundation of universities, there were schools attached to certain cathedrals and monasteries in which advanced learning flourished, but many of these schools lacked organisation and continuity. Their existence entirely depended upon the ability of the teachers connected with them. For example, the School of Chartres in the 11th and 12th centuries enjoyed a considerable reputation on account of a series of illustrious scholars who taught there.[1]

The earliest university was that of Salerno, but as this remained predominantly a medical school, it had little influence upon the growth of universities in this country. During the first half of the 12th century, Irnerius, the famous teacher of Roman Law, and Gratian, the equally distinguished exponent of Canon Law, drew numerous students to the law schools of Bologna. Gradually, towards the second half of the 12th century, the University of Bologna came into existence. Since, in the early days, Bologna was essentially a law university, the most important development taking place, from our point of view, was in Paris.

The schools of Paris were unknown to history before the close of the 9th century, and for over two hundred years they were overshadowed by the fame of other places such as Chartres. The cathedral school of Paris, which was really the origin of the later university, became known through the teaching of its master, William of Champeaux. To this school came Peter Abelard, first as the pupil and then as the opponent of William. When Abelard began to teach, he attracted scholars from all parts of Europe, but it would be an exaggeration to claim him as the founder of the University of Paris. Except for his own personal qualities there was nothing to distinguish his school from others which were

---

[1] Bernard of Chartres, died 1130; Theoderic of Chartres, died about 1155, whose disciple was John of Salisbury; and William of Conches (1080-1154), who was tutor to Henry II of England.

beginning to flourish in the same city. There were three great churches which became famous for their schools: the cathedral school taught by William of Champeaux, the school of the Collegiate Church of Ste Geneviève, and the school of the Canons of S. Victor, known to posterity because of the renowned theologians and mystics, Hugh and Richard of S. Victor. Abelard himself taught on the "Mount" of Ste Geneviève. Although during his lifetime the school of Ste Geneviève was thronged with students, by the middle of the century it had, with S. Victor, materially declined in importance. This left the cathedral school in a position of pre-eminence.

Nevertheless, it must be admitted that it was due to Abelard that two of the indispensible conditions for the formation of a university were to be found at Paris in the middle years of the 12th century, namely the existence of a large number of students and a multiplicity of masters. The actual date at which this collection of students and masters became organised into the University of Paris is unknown, but it is certain that it came into being some time between 1170 and 1175. The University of Paris received a charter from Philip Augustus in 1200 and was fully recognised by the Pope in 1231, but it was an acknowledged institution many years before its official recognition. Its importance for us lies in the fact that it was the mother of our own ancient universities.

In the 12th century the word "university" had quite a different meaning from that which it bears to-day. *Universitas* simply meant a gild or corporation and there were universities of merchants and tailors as well as of scholars. For their own mutual benefit and protection, scholars and teachers formed themselves into associations, and we come across the terms *universitas scholarium* and *universitas magistrorum*. At Bologna, the wealthy students of law formed a university of scholars which was far more important than the teachers who were employed and ruled by them. The University of Paris was an association of masters and served as the model for Oxford. Thus in mediaeval times the word *universitas* signified an association of scholars or masters and it was a later development to apply the term to the collection of buildings in which the teaching took place.

The usual mediaeval term for a university was *studium generale*. Any "school" or place of learning was a *studium*, but a *studium generale* was open to scholars from all lands and instruction was given in at least one "faculty" other than arts. In the 13th century, it became the custom for a *studium generale* to secure recognition through a Papal Bull which granted to the masters of the university the *ius ubique docendi*, the right to teach in any similar institution. Oxford received official confirmation of its rights and privileges by the Bull of Innocent IV in 1254. Dr. Coulton reminds us: "The universities rose and attained their great influence by the same natural growth which created trade unions in modern Britain and has made them, in their present power and organisation, almost a fourth estate of the realm. It is true that, by about 1300, lawyers had worked out the theory that papal or imperial licence was necessary for the founding of a university, but even these lawyers had to admit that long custom might count also, and that we might have a university ' by custom ' (*ex consuetudine*), as genuine as if it had been a papal or imperial foundation." [1]

The origin of Oxford University has been a matter of controversy. We can dismiss at once the ancient legend that Oxford was founded by Alfred the Great. The view which received support from Leach, that the university was a natural growth from the priory of St. Frideswide, is also open to objection. Dr. Rashdall's theory, expounded in his *Universities of Europe in the Middle Ages*, [2] is not now generally accepted. He believed that Oxford owed its commencement as a *studium generale* to the quarrel between Henry II and Beckett, when in 1167 all English clergy abroad were ordered by the King to return home. The scholars who migrated from Paris eventually set up a new *studium generale* at Oxford. However this may be, two facts stand out quite clearly. In the first place there were schools at Oxford in the earlier part of the 12th century. Thus, in 1133, Robert Pullus, a prominent theologian, was teaching at Oxford. There is also evidence that Vacarius, the famous Lombard jurist, lectured at Oxford, but there is some doubt whether he taught before or after 1167. Secondly, there is clear evidence that a *studium generale* existed at Oxford about 1185. Giraldus Cambrensis, the Welsh traveller and man of letters,

---

[1] G. G. Coulton. *Medieval Panorama*, p. 395, C.U.P., 1938.

[2] O.U.P., new edition 1936, reprinted 1942. The new edition is edited by Sir F. M. Powicke and A. B. Emden, and contains many valuable notes and criticisms. The English universities are dealt with in Vol. III. The attention of the reader is drawn to Chapter xii, in which Rashdall expounds his theory, and to Appendix I which contains Leach's criticism and Rashdall's reply. Rashdall's theory of the migration from Paris in 1167 would place the origin of the latter university much earlier than generally supposed. The state of learning, and of the schools, in England during the 11th and 12th centuries requires a much more thorough investigation than has so far been attempted.

visited Oxford at that time and read his newly written *Topographia Hibernica* before an assembly of the masters and scholars.

The origin of Cambridge is generally attributed to a quarrel between the scholars and townsfolk of Oxford in 1209, which resulted in the migration of a large body of Oxford scholars to Cambridge.[1] The legend ascribing the foundation of Cambridge to the Spanish prince, Cantaber, 531, was merely an attempt to find an origin which should be earlier than the alleged foundation of Oxford by Alfred. It is not certain whether there were schools at Cambridge before 1209, but by 1231 there is documentary evidence of an organised university there.

Whether Rashdall's theory of the origin of Oxford is accepted or not, there is no doubt that both Oxford and Cambridge were, in their early days, strongly influenced by the customs and traditions of Paris. Certain features of the organisation of Paris were reproduced, but the English universities possessed some important characteristics of their own. At Paris, the scholars were organised into four Nations: the French, the Normans, the Picards, and the English. At the outbreak of the Hundred Years' War, the English withdrew and their place was taken by the Germans. In the same way, at Oxford and Cambridge, scholars were divided into Nations. At Oxford, those who came from north of the Trent formed the Northern, and the remainder the Southern, Nation. Scotsmen were in the former Nation, and Welshmen and Irishmen in the latter. The Nations were represented by their Proctors, who, although retaining the names of Northern and Southern, became representatives elected by the whole Faculty of Arts when the Nations were amalgamated in 1274. Sometimes quarrels broke out between Northerners and Southerners. At Cambridge, in 1261, a riot between the Nations, in which the townsfolk joined, led to the plundering of houses and the burning of records.

One of the main differences between the English universities and the University of Paris consisted in the position held by the

---

[1] In 1334 a similar quarrel caused a migration of Oxford scholars to Stamford and produced such an impression that, up to 1827, no man was allowed to take his master's degree at Oxford without swearing an oath that he would never lecture at Stamford. It was on this occasion that the famous knocker of Brasenose was left at Stamford and remained there until it was purchased by the college in 1890. There were other migrations to Northampton in 1261 and Salisbury in 1238. Neither of these attempts to found new universities persisted for any length of time. There was, however, always the chance that the *studium generale* might be transferred to another town, a fact that caused Walter de Merton to hesitate before he finally decided to place his college at Oxford.

Chancellor. In the previous chapter, attention was drawn to the functions of the episcopal chancellor. The Chancellor of Notre Dame, as the representative of the bishop, issued to masters, whether of schools or in the university, the licence or the right to teach. He was not a member of the university and it was not long before he came into conflict with the Rector, the head of the Nations. As the result of a long dispute, the Chancellor lost power and became merely the official who issued the licence on conditions prescribed by the *universitas* of masters. The latter were much assisted in their struggle by the Papacy. At the English universities, matters turned out very differently. Oxford and Cambridge were not cathedral cities and no chancellor is mentioned until the legatine ordinance of 1214. It is possible either that the licence to teach was issued by the archdeacon or that the masters chose an official of their own to grant the licence. What actually occurred in this early period is a matter for conjecture, and when Robert Grosseteste of Lincoln was appointed to the office of Chancellor of Oxford, we have, as Rashdall describes, the "almost unique combination of the functions of a continental Chancellor with those of a continental Rector." [1] The Chancellor was not only the bishop's representative, but he was also the head of the magisterial gild. Hence there could be no contest between Chancellor and masters as occurred at Paris. The Chancellor became less dependent on the bishop and more representative of the university. This independence on the part of the university was almost entirely due to the fact that Oxford was not the seat of a bishopric. The same process took place at Cambridge, although somewhat later. Thus, unlike Paris, the Chancellor of the English universities was not only the head of the university body, but also a member of it.

Another distinction lies in the growth of the collegiate system which was once supposed to be peculiar to England. In the early days of the universities, scholars lived in what lodgings they could find and the masters taught in hired rooms. The custom grew up at Paris, and was followed at Oxford and Cambridge, of students living together in houses which they hired for themselves. This practice was more satisfactory than living in lodgings. It was usual to elect one member who would be responsible to the rest. He was known as the *magister*, but at first it was not necessary that he should be a Master of Arts. Gradually these *hospitia*, or hostels,

[1] H. Rashdall. *The Universities of Europe in the Middle Ages*, Vol. III, p. 42, O.U.P., 1942.

came under the control of the university. Frequently the hostel was due to the public spirit of some benefactor who endowed it as a house for poor scholars. One of the best known of these "houses of scholars" was that founded at Paris by Robert de Sorbon, but he was by no means the earliest benefactor. In the middle of the 13th century, William of Durham endowed a house at Oxford known as Great University Hall, which became, about 1280, University College.[1] Sir John Balliol, in penance for the injuries he had inflicted upon his neighbours across the border, agreed to support a number of poor scholars at Oxford. In 1282 his widow, Devorguilla, the Lady of Galloway, added extra endowments towards the "House of Balliol."

Some of the houses or halls received further endowments, and when later they became recognised as legal corporations, they developed into colleges. The transition from a hostel to a college is illustrated by the foundation of Walter de Merton, Chancellor of England and Bishop of Rochester, which was described in the previous chapter. Through his statutes, which aimed at regulating the corporate life of the Fellows, Merton College developed from an endowed hostel into a self-governing college, subject to a Warden, with Deans to watch over the morals of the Fellows, and three Bursars to manage the property. Complaints against the Warden could be made to the Patron or Visitor, who had the authority to deprive the Warden of his office if necessary.

Colleges developed in a similar manner at Paris, but whilst at the latter university the authorities quickly took over the control

[1] It is important to remember that the early colleges at Oxford were founded to enable their members to lead a common life. The idea that the senior members or Fellows should be responsible for the studies of the younger was introduced by Wykeham. Very little is known of William of Durham in his younger days. He was one of the five English masters who left Paris when the university dispersed in 1229. After some years at Rouen, he was appointed Rector of Wearmouth, one of the richest livings in the diocese of Durham, in 1237. In 1248, he contested the property rights of the living with Bishop Nicholas of Farnham, and his appeal to Rome necessitated a visit to the Continent. William died at Rouen on his journey back to England and he left in his will 310 marks to the University of Oxford for the maintenance of 10, 11, or 12 masters. The exact terms of the will are unknown, so that it is impossible to know whether William merely intended the university to use the money for certain individual scholars, or whether he wished to establish a college similar to those which were springing up in Paris. It is clear, however, that by 1280, statutes had been devised to regulate the life of the small community, which at that time consisted of only four masters. The statutes were revised and elaborated in 1292 and again in 1311, and the connection of the Hall with Durham was emphasised. The title of the Scholars of William of Durham (*Scholares Willelmi de Dunelmia*) was given to the community. It retained this name until 1573 when it was officially known as "the Master and Fellows of the College of the Great Hall of the University of Oxford."

of the colleges, at Oxford and at Cambridge, where in 1284 Peterhouse adopted statutes similar to those of Merton, the colleges began to develop in independence of the universities. This process was accelerated by the policy of Wykeham and of Henry VI. Wykeham arranged that the head of New College was not only to manage the house but was also to supervise the education of the scholars. This was carried out by the Fellows who became tutors and drew an additional allowance for their tutorial work from the college funds. So far the tutorial work was supplementary to the lectures of the public schools of the university. The same policy was carried a stage further by Henry VI in his foundation of King's College, Cambridge. The King obtained a Papal Bull excluding the college from the jurisdiction of the Chancellor of the University. This was not accepted without protest and modification, but it represented one more step in the development of colleges as independent of university control. At Paris the university exercised full control over the colleges until they were swept away by the French Revolution.

It is a mistake to regard the mediaeval colleges as being designed for undergraduates. They were for scholars, that is bachelors and masters who were studying for higher degrees in law, theology, and medicine. The ordinary undergraduate was not a member of the college and, if he was permitted to live in it, was a kind of paying guest. "One foundation (All Souls) remains to-day as a reminder that a college can survive without undergraduates; in the 14th century such a college was the rule rather than the exception. Thus the number of those in residence at the earliest Oxford colleges was small, and it has been estimated that in the middle of the 14th century the six colleges did not contain more than seventy-three members."[1] The undergraduates lived in the hostels or halls and often in private lodgings. It was not until the 15th century that the number of undergraduates living in the colleges began to grow and Commoners were admitted, i.e. students not on the foundation who paid fees for tuition and maintenance.[2]

Much has been written about the size of the student population of the mediaeval universities. People of the Middle Ages were much given to exaggeration, so that we should not be astonished at some of the amazing claims which were made. Thirty thousand seems to have been a favourite number both for Paris and Oxford,

[1] S. C. Roberts. *British Universities*, p. 13, Collins, 1947.
[2] Pensioner is the Cambridge equivalent to the Oxford Commoner.

but such claims are fantastic, as both Rashdall and Coulton demonstrate. It is difficult to find reliable evidence about numbers in the early days of the universities, but from the 15th century the roll of those who graduated and the lists of halls afford some data. It is probable that even in the early days when Paris was the only university in north-western Europe, the numbers never exceeded 5,000, and that by the beginning of the 15th century they had fallen to about 3,000. In the same way Oxford may have approached the 3,000 mark, but by the beginning of the 15th century the total was somewhere in the neighbourhood of 1,500, and by 1450 it fell to below a thousand.

There were frequent quarrels between the students and the townsfolk. The latter regarded the students as lawless young men who were always creating disturbances. The students were always complaining of the extortionate prices demanded by the townsfolk for food and lodgings. Some of the fights between town and gown reached serious dimensions. The most famous was on St. Scholastica's Day, 10th February 1354. It began in a tavern quarrel. Some Oxford clerks complained of the wine served to them in an inn near Carfax. "The vintner giving them stubborn and saucy language, they threw the wine and vessel at his head." The innkeeper, on the advice of his friends, rang the bell of St. Martin's Church. The townsfolk assembled, and armed with bows and arrows, began to attack the students who, in turn, summoned reinforcements by ringing the bell of St. Mary's. In spite of statutes forbidding the carrying of weapons, the scholars appeared armed and the battle went on until night without a fatal casualty on either side. Unfortunately, the townsmen opened battle again on the next day and invaded the scholars' houses. This time, considerable numbers were killed and wounded. When the trouble was investigated, the King supported the university and gave it jurisdiction over the city and control of the market. The town was placed under an interdict which was only lifted when the mayor, the bailiffs, and the chief citizens agreed to perform an annual penance. A similar riot took place at Cambridge in 1381.

The system of academic degrees began towards the close of the 12th century. We have seen that the *universitas* was an association either of masters or students, and that in the north-western universities it consisted of the members of the masters' gild. There is a very close connection between the craft-gilds and the gilds of learning. The undergraduate was an apprentice to learning, and when he first came to the university his name was placed upon the *matricula,* or list of students, kept by each master. Hence the modern term, matriculation. Just as the apprentice to the tailor, saddler, or goldsmith became a journeyman after a number of years, so too, the award of the title of Bachelor showed that the apprentice to learning had passed through the first half of his course satisfactorily, and now, although still a pupil, he could undertake a certain amount of teaching under the direction of a master. After further time spent in teaching and study, which varied in length according to the Faculty and the period of history, the bachelor might become a master.[1] Some masters continued to teach at the university and were known as Regent Masters (*magistri actu regentes*), whilst others taught in schools and were called Non-Regent Masters (*magistri non regentes*).

The candidate for the degree of bachelor had to take a preliminary test (Responsions) which involved a disputation in logic and grammar with a master. If he passed this successfully, he presented himself before a board of examiners consisting of three (later four) masters of his faculty who satisfied themselves that he had fulfilled the conditions of residence and attended the necessary lectures. They then proceeded to ask him questions about the contents of the books he had studied. Having passed this test with credit, he was allowed to *determine.* The Determination took the form of a disputation in which the candidate eventually determined, or summed up and gave a definite solution of, the problem he had chosen. At Paris the disputation took place in the Vicus Stramineus (Straw Street), so called because, for the sake of warmth, the floors of the examination halls were strewn with straw. The audience before whom the exercise took place consisted of the masters and fellow students of the candidate, but the disputation was also open to the general public. Cases were known in which the determiner's friends rushed into the street and collected an audience from the passers-by. A successful determination was frequently followed by some kind of banquet.

[1] It originally took three years to become a Bachelor, another four for the Mastership, and five or more years, according to the Faculty, for the Doctorate. As time went on, the period of residence demanded grew shorter, and at the English universities, residence became unnecessary after the bachelor's degree. On the Continent, the baccalaureate tended either to disappear or to become the equivalent of matriculation. Originally the term "degree" (*gradus*) was confined to the baccalaureate which was looked upon as a step to the mastership. The term Faculty at first denoted the capacity to teach a subject or group of subjects, but later it came to stand for the whole collection of masters and students of those subjects.

It is important to realise that the master's degree originally possessed a double aspect. From one point of view, it was essentially a licence to teach, and the authority conferring the licence was the Chancellor. From another, it consisted in the formal recognition of the candidate by the masters' gild as one of their number. This ceremony was known as Inception, and in the course of it the newly appointed master was presented with the insignia of his office, the black *cappa* of the master, the magisterial biretta, and the book. The significance of the handing over the tools of the trade (*traditio*) is admirably illustrated by the inception of a Master of Grammar at Cambridge in the 15th century.

This mastership has been specially instituted for those who wished to teach in grammar-schools and is another instance of the close connection between the grammar-schools and the universities. The candidate attended early mass at St. Mary's Church. "When mass is done, fyrst shall begynne the acte in Gramer. The Father shall have hys sete . . . the Proctor shall say, Incipiatis. When the Father hath argyude as shall plese the Proctor, the Bedeyll[1] in Arte shall bring the Master of Gramer to the Vyce-chancelar, delyveryng hym a Palmer[2] wyth a Rodde, whych the Vyce-chancelar shall gyve to the seyde Master in Gramer, and so create hym Master. Then shall the Bedell purvay for every master in Gramer a shrewde[3] Boy, whom the master in Gramer shall bete openlye in the Scolys, and the master in Gramer shall give the Boy a Grote for Hys Labour, and another Grote to hym that provydeth the Rode and the Palmer." It was in this way that the newly fledged master approved his ability to teach in a grammar-school.

The two events which produced a profound change in the development of the European universities were the introduction of the Aristotelian corpus into the West and the activities of the great mendicant orders of Franciscans and Dominicans. We have already noted that by 1162 western Europe possessed the whole of the *Organon,* or Logical works of Aristotle. The remainder of the Aristotelian writings had an interesting history. Syrian scholars translated them into their own tongue, and when the Arab conquerors established the Caliphate of Bagdad, they founded a school of translators who rendered these Syriac versions into Arabic.

---

[1] *Bedel* or *beadle* = the Vice-Chancellor's mace-bearer and attendant.
[2] *Palmer* = a flat piece of wood used to inflict punishment by smiting the palm of the hand.   [3] *Shrewde* = mischievous.

Naturally the text suffered greatly in the double process of trans-lation, but errors grew more numerous when Latin translations of Arabic versions of Syriac translations of the Greek originals trickled into western Europe via Spain.

This, however, is only part of the story. Quite a number of neo-Platonic writings, which often possessed a strongly pantheistic flavour, were ascribed to Aristotle and the doctrines taught in them became associated with his name. The Arabs were no mean scholars and they began to produce commentaries on the works of Aristotle. The greatest of the Arabian commentators were Avicenna (980-1037) and Averroes (1125-98). The latter was responsible for the doctrine of the unity of the intellect, a view which asserted that there is a single intellectual principle operating throughout the whole human race. Christian thinkers strongly opposed this doctrine, since it seemed to them to contradict the belief in the immortality of the individual human soul.

When the Aristotelian writings and the Arab commentaries began to be studied in the University of Paris, the ecclesiastical authorities became thoroughly alarmed. Thus the Council of Sens, held at Paris in 1210, prohibited the reading of Aristotle under pain of excommunication, and in 1215 the Papal Legate, Robert Curzon, renewed the prohibition. In 1229 the Pope intervened and appointed three Parisian masters to examine the new works and to make a faithful translation of them. Owing to the difficulty of reconciling Aristotle with dogma, this was not done; but in spite of the prohibitions, the works of Aristotle were read and studied in the Faculty of Arts. It was not, however, until 1263 that Urban IV officially recognised the Aristotelian philosophy and permitted it to be studied in the schools.

Before this time, Augustinian philosophy and theology had been predominant in the schools. Although Augustine still remained the most important authority in theology, a large number of the masters at Paris and Oxford adopted the Aristotelian philosophy. This change had been largely brought about by the work of two great thinkers: Albert of Cologne (1193-1280) and his famous pupil, St. Thomas Aquinas (1226-74). The former succeeded in popularising Aristotle in the West. The latter, through his friend William of Moerbeke, Archbishop of Corinth, a distinguished Greek scholar, was able to obtain accurate translations of Aristotle, and produced the scholastic synthesis of faith and reason with which his name will always be associated.

By the close of the 13th century, even those who were most inimical to the Aristotelian philosophy had adopted its terminology and many of its methods. This did not come about without a struggle, and the critical year was 1270 when Siger de Brabant, the leader of the Picard Nation at Paris, boldly proclaimed that Averroes had interpreted Aristotle correctly. His conclusions were strenuously attacked by Aquinas, who was not so much concerned with what Aristotle did or did not say, but was bent upon synthesising what was true in Aristotle with the Christian faith. Averroism was condemned at Paris in 1270 and again in 1277. In the latter year, a similar condemnation was promulgated at Oxford.

Scholastic philosophy reached its culmination in the universities of the 13th century. It was both a philosophy and a teaching method, and it is the latter aspect which is of chief interest to the student of education. As we shall see, its method of presentation was strongly influenced by the form taken by the lectures and disputations of the mediaeval universities. Nineteenth-century writers on philosophy and education had many scathing remarks to make about the trivial matters discussed and the barren results of scholasticism. The present century has witnessed a revival of interest in mediaeval studies, and it is now realised that the greatest of the mediaeval thinkers had something to say which concerned not only their own time but future ages also. To the eager throngs of 13th-century students who crowded the lecture-halls of Paris or Oxford, the problems debated seemed anything but trivial. The standards of any age must eventually be judged by the works of its more advanced thinkers, and if we are to condemn mediaeval learning and culture by the mediocre scholarship and barbarous Latinity of its lesser exponents, then the present day would not appear so illustrious if university education was measured solely by the accomplishments of undistinguished pass-graduates. Leach was one of the first to point out that the standards of mediaeval learning were considerably higher than had previously been supposed.

During the life of its founder, the order of St. Francis was more interested in the winning of souls than in education, and was even inclined to view secular learning with strong suspicion. There was, however, amongst the Dominicans, even in their early days, a marked intellectual interest. The acceptance of the Aristotelian corpus and the works of other non-Christian writers raised the problem of assimilating these new influences with Christian belief

and tradition. Such a course appeared, especially to the Dominicans, as an absolute necessity if Christian civilisation was to be
preserved. Though this was not always explicitly recognised, in
particular amongst the Franciscans, the decision ultimately taken
was fraught with results of the utmost importance. We have only
to call to mind that it was two Dominicans, Albert and Aquinas,
who secured for Aristotle a permanent place in the curriculum of
the universities. The coming of the mendicants to the universities
was destined to provoke some serious disturbances.

At Paris, the Dominicans were the first to appear, and from the
start they received a somewhat uncertain welcome. The universities owed their foundation to the seculars, who, with the regular
monastic orders, viewed the newcomers with suspicion which
deepened later to actual hostility. The Dominicans came to Paris
in 1217 and were followed a few years later by the Franciscans.
A tavern riot, in which the civic authorities rather unwisely intervened, caused the Great Dispersion of 1229. The secular masters
refused to teach and many of them retired to the smaller cathedral
schools at Angers, Toulouse, and Rheims. Henry III of England
invited to this country those who wished to emigrate and his offer
was accepted by a considerable number of foreign scholars who
settled at Oxford and Cambridge. As the professors had departed
from Paris, the Dominicans were able to obtain two Chairs in
theology in 1229 and 1231 respectively. The Franciscans also
obtained two Chairs in the university.

When the seculars returned, their opposition to the mendicants
grew intense and was still active even at the close of the century.
The mendicants, however, had come to stay, since their cause was
supported by the Papacy and their struggle directed by two such
able leaders as St. Bonaventure and St. Thomas Aquinas. It was
the opposition to the mendicants which was largely responsible for
the development of the secular colleges of the University of Paris.

The Dominicans appeared at Oxford in 1220 and the Franciscans five years later. At first they received a kindly welcome and
for a time lived harmoniously with the seculars. Eventually, the
aggressive policy of the Dominicans brought about a quarrel with
the secular members of the university. The root cause of the dispute
was the policy of the Dominicans of extending their influence in the
university without submitting to its regulations. For example, the
friars claimed a dispensation from the obligation of graduating in
arts before proceeding to the master's degree in theology. Events

reached such a pitch in 1313 that a lawsuit commenced which ended in an appeal to Rome. Although a compromise agreement was reached in 1320, the costs of litigation put the university badly in debt and it was saved from bankruptcy only by a levy made by the Convocations of Canterbury and York. At Cambridge the Dominicans were more successful in gaining their ends. The Franciscans profited by the unpopularity of the Dominicans, and, through the outstanding ability of Robert Grosseteste, Roger Bacon, and especially Duns Scotus, gained an ascendancy at Oxford. The first of these teachers, although he never entered the order, was for many years reader at the Franciscan priory.

The Franciscan influence at Oxford was an important factor in developing the interests of the university along lines different from those of Paris. The policy of the early 13th-century popes had been to foster the growth of Paris so that it would become not only the university of France, but also the centre of theological studies for the whole of western Europe. Indeed, in the 13th century, Paris was the leading university in Europe, but its influence declined in the following century, and eventually it succumbed to the growing power of the French monarchy and was finally handed over to the jurisdiction of Parliament. As Paris declined, so Oxford began to take its place as the leader in European thought, but the attraction of theological studies was never as strong as at the former university. The important interests at Oxford were in the realm of mathematics, languages, and natural science. Roger Bacon once claimed that Oxford was the only European university at which the mathematical sciences were completely taught.

Although he has tended to be obscured by the fame of his pupil Roger Bacon, the real originator of this bias at Oxford was Robert Grosseteste, its first chancellor. Grosseteste was a remarkable personality. He was a distinguished linguist, and in the days when a knowledge of Greek was exceptional, he translated several of the works of Aristotle and the writings of the Pseudo-Dionysius the Areopagite from the original Greek. His theory of light as the essence of the spatial universe came very near to the modern conceptions of ether and energy, whilst his studies in optics led him to apply mathematical methods to natural science. In all this he had an apt follower in Roger Bacon. The scientific tradition was carried on into the 14th century by William of Ockham and his followers, who manifested that practical outlook and empirical approach which for so long characterised English thought.

During the 13th and 14th centuries, Cambridge was quite a small university in comparison with Oxford, but in the 15th century the reputation of Cambridge was much enhanced. Oxford had become infected by the teaching of Wycliffe and for this reason both Church and Crown favoured Cambridge. Attention was paid to the discipline of undergraduates at both universities. Statutes were promulgated prohibiting students from carrying arms and the disciplinary regulations were extended to those living in halls. Fines were imposed for breaches of the regulations. Gambling and practice with arms incurred a fine of fourpence. A farthing was exacted from students who shouted and sang when others were studying or wished to sleep. Those who came into the college after 8 p.m. in winter or 9 p.m. in summer, or spoke English in place of Latin, were fined a farthing. The penalty for sleeping out, or bringing in a friend for the night without permission from the principal, was one penny. Regulations forbade the wearing of extravagant and unbecoming dress, and behaviour at table was controlled by rigid rules. Certain offences were punished by flogging, which is surprising at a period when the average age of students was rising rapidly.

The teaching method of the mediaeval universities took two forms, that of the *lectio* and that of the *quaestio*. The *lectio* consisted in the reading and explanation of a textbook in the classroom. The lecturer read the text paragraph by paragraph, and at the end of each one commented on its content. Some lecturers read very rapidly whilst others were so slow and deliberate in their delivery that students could take down verbatim both text and commentary. This seems to have had a considerable effect on the sales of the booksellers, and several regulations of the early days of the universities require the lecturer to read at a normal conversational pace.

The *quaestio* was extremely important in the theological faculties. It can be regarded as an exercise in disputation between the professor and his pupils. There were two kinds of disputation. The ordinary disputations were closely connected with topics arising out of the lectures and were held several times a year. The problems debated were often of considerable complexity and it was possible for the disputation to range over several university sessions. The ordinary disputations of celebrated masters were committed to writing under the title of *quaestiones disputatae*. All the details concerning the procedure are not yet known, but much has been

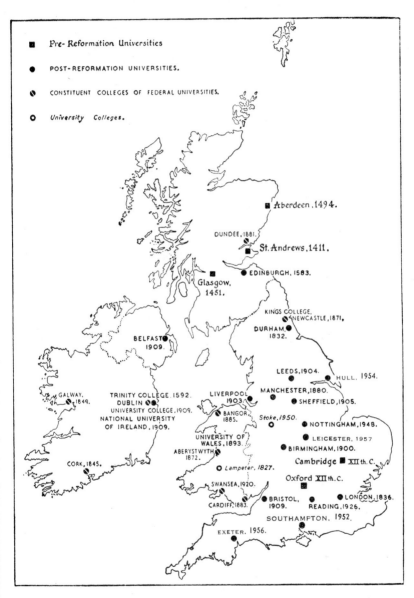

Pre-Reformation Universities

POST-REFORMATION UNIVERSITIES.

CONSTITUENT COLLEGES OF FEDERAL UNIVERSITIES.

University Colleges.

Aberdeen, 1494.

DUNDEE, 1881.

St. Andrews, 1411.

EDINBURGH, 1583.

Glasgow, 1451.

KINGS COLLEGE, NEWCASTLE, 1871.

DURHAM, 1832.

BELFAST 1909.

LEEDS, 1904.

HULL, 1954.

GALWAY, 1849.

TRINITY COLLEGE, 1592. DUBLIN UNIVERSITY COLLEGE, 1909. NATIONAL UNIVERSITY OF IRELAND, 1909.

LIVERPOOL 1903.

MANCHESTER, 1880.

SHEFFIELD, 1905.

BANGOR, 1885.

Stoke, 1950.

NOTTINGHAM, 1948.

UNIVERSITY OF WALES, 1893.

LEICESTER, 1957

BIRMINGHAM, 1900.

ABERYSTWYTH, 1872.

Cambridge XIIth.C.

CORK, 1845.

Lampeter, 1827.

Oxford XIIth.C.

SWANSEA, 1920.

BRISTOL, 1909.

LONDON, 1836.

CARDIFF, 1883.

READING, 1926.

SOUTHAMPTON, 1952.

EXETER, 1956.

UNIVERSITIES AND UNIVERSITY COLLEGES OF GREAT BRITAIN AND IRELAND, 1957.
(For the new Universities see p. 646.)

done by such writers as Mandonnet and Grabmann to enable us to construct a picture of what occurred.

The example of a disputation concerned with a simple topic and lasting two days will give a picture of the procedure. On the first day, with the master presiding, his bachelor answered difficulties (*obiectiones*) raised by other masters, bachelors, and scholars. On the following day, the master grouped the arguments and objections proposed on the previous day, and then in the *sed contra,* announced his own solution, quoting some authoritative text in support of it. He then established his own solution by means of a series of arguments. This was known as the master's determination (*determinatio magistralis*). The final step was to dispose of each objection in turn. The reader can easily verify this procedure by reference to the plan on which any "article" in the *Summa Theologica* of St. Thomas Aquinas is organised.

In addition to the ordinary disputations, special disputations were held twice a year, usually in Advent and Lent. These were known as *disputationes quodlibetales,* since any student was at liberty to raise whatsoever problem he pleased. Obviously the problems were unrelated, but in the written report of the disputations, known as the *Quodlibeta,* some attempt was made to group them under their respective headings. Most of the *Quodlibeta* of the famous masters such as Aquinas, Duns Scotus, and William of Ockham, are still extant.

CHAPTER III

ENGLISH SCHOOLS AND UNIVERSITIES IN THE TUDOR PERIOD

In the 16th century, the course of English education was profoundly influenced by the twin movements of the Renaissance and the Reformation. The influence of the Renaissance was the earlier and its effects were already being felt in English schools in the 15th century.

Leach corrects the common error that the Renaissance was due to the introduction of Greek. "Through an unfortunate misrepresentation by the self-lauding reformers of the sixteenth century, the Renaissance has in the educational sphere come to be considered as synonymous with the introduction of Greek into the curriculum of schools, and particularly with Colet's statutes for the 'newe Scole of Powles' in 1510, in which for the first time Greek was suggested as a desideratum, though not demanded as a *sine qua non*, the High Master being required to be one who knew Greek, 'Yf swyche could be gotten.' . . . The revival of Greek was an effect, not the cause of the Renaissance. . . . It was not the introduction of Greek at Winchester and Eton, New College and Magdalen, and its appearance in the statutes of St. Paul's School, which made them the great schools and colleges of the day and their scholars the leading Humanists of their age. On the contrary, Greek was introduced in those colleges and schools because they were the advanced institutions of the day. Because they were scholarly and literary they took to Greek. It was not Greek which made them scholarly and literary." [1]

He quite correctly insists that the very term "Renaissance" is misleading. There was no rebirth of learning because learning had never died out. The old jibe of the 19th century that the Middle Ages were the Dark Ages has been answered by the work of modern scholars. The difference between the Middle Ages and the period which followed them was a difference of attitude and it may be summed up in the one word, Humanism. As he writes, "The true virtue of what is known as the Renaissance is much better

[1] A. F. Leach. *The Schools of Medieval England*, pp. 246-8, Methuen, 1915.

73

expressed in the term Humanism. It is not the introduction of Greek or the imitation of Cicero, the preference for the study of grammar over dialectic, or for the details of philology instead of the niceties of logic, which constitute the Renaissance. It was the substitution of humanism for divinity, of this world for the next, as the object of living, and therefore of education, that differentiated the humanists from their predecessors. For a thousand years the attention of educated mankind had been concentrated on its latter end, or on what was feared to follow it. Not life, but death, had been the subject of culture. Not how to prepare for life but how to prepare for death was the sole object of education. The humanist's progress consisted in the adoption of the dogma, 'The noblest study of mankind is man.' " [1]

It is necessary to realise that the Renaissance was a very slow and gradual movement, and we must not expect that its far-reaching effects on the English schools were developed in the course of a few years. We can trace its beginning long before the close of the mediaeval period and its practical results in the foundation of the great collegiate schools of Winchester and Eton. The ordinary grammar-schools showed little outward change in their curriculum. They remained essentially Latin schools, but gradually the aim of Latin studies became not so much an end in itself as a means towards the study of the literature of ancient Rome. Greek was introduced, but in most of the schools it took second place to Latin. One of the practical difficulties in introducing Greek was the scarcity of good Greek scholars and teachers. In a few schools, Hebrew was taught. The first appearance of Hebrew seems to have been at Archbishop Holgate's school at York in 1547, where the master was to have "understandinge in the Hebrew, Greek, and Latin tongues." The first English teacher of Greek at Oxford was William Grocyn, who taught at Magdalen in 1491. It was introduced to Eton by William Horman, who was headmaster from 1485 to 1494, and then became headmaster of Winchester from 1494 to 1502. There is, however, sufficient evidence to show that it was not until Greek scholars became more numerous after the middle of the 16th century that Greek studies became more widespread in the schools. Even at Eton in 1560, the teaching of Greek seems to have been left to the discretion of the master.

Dean Colet's foundation of St. Paul's School in 1509 is an example of a typical Renaissance grammar-school. Leach considers

[1] A. F. Leach. *The Schools of Medieval England*, pp. 248-9, Methuen, 1915.

that it was a refoundation and enlargement of the school which for many centuries had been attached to the Cathedral of St. Paul's. On the other hand, J. H. Lupton asserts that the old school continued its independent existence to the beginning of the 17th century as a choristers' school.[1] However this may be, Colet's statutes, which were planned with reference to even the smallest details, represent a distinct advance in the conception of what a grammar-school should be.

Colet was a wealthy man, and although not a Greek scholar himself, his friendship with Erasmus and the leaders of the Humanist movement showed that he was thoroughly in sympathy with the new trends of thought. He made over the whole of his London estate, which in modern money exceeded £60,000, to the Mercers' Company in trust for his foundation. "The Honourable Company of Mercers of London, that is to saye, The Maister and all the Wardens, and all the Assistence of The Felowshyppe, shall have all the care and charge, rule, and governaunce of the Scole, and they shall every yere chose of their Companye Eleven, honeste and substantiall men, called The Surveyors of the Schole, whiche in the name of the hoole Felowship shall take all the charge and besinesse about the Schole, for that one year." [2]

The school was to be in charge of a High Master who should be appointed by the Wardens of the Mercers' Company. He was to be "a man hoole in body, honest and vertuous, and lerned in good and cleane Latin literature, and also in Greke, yf such may be gotten ; a Wedded man, a Single man, or a Preste that hath no benefice with cure, nor service that may lett the due besinesse in the Scole." The High Master's stipend was £35 with a house and livery gown. Under him was a Surmaster with a salary of £18 and a house, and a Chaplain to sing Mass in the school chapel and "pray for the Children to prosper in good life and in good literature, to the Honour of God and Our Lord Christ Jesu." The chaplain should assist in the school and teach the children "the Catechyzom and Instruction of the Articles of the Faythe, and the Ten Commandments in Inglishe." For this he was to receive £8 a year ; he lodged in the master's house and was given a livery gown of the value of 26s. 8d.

[1] Life of Dean Colet, p. 160, 2nd ed., 1909.
[2] The statutes are printed in full in N. Carlisle, The Endowed Grammar Schools of England and Wales, 1818.

Colet was fortunate in obtaining William Lily, whom he had known at Magdalen, as the High Master. The appointment of a layman as headmaster of a large school was uncommon, but it was by no means the first of its kind. Lily was succeeded in 1522 by John Rightwyse, a Cambridge scholar. There seems to have been a difficulty in finding a suitable successor to Lily, for one of the Cambridge scholars declared, "Who would put up with the life of a schoolmaster who could get a living in any other way?"

St. Paul's was designed as a day-school for the sons of upper-middle-class people. The number of pupils was fixed at 153, and they were to be "children of all Nations and Contres indifferently." The number 153 was an allusion to the Miraculous Draught of Fishes (John xxi. 11) and the holidays and half-holidays amounted to seven score and thirteen, which again added up to 153. Before a child was admitted, the master ascertained whether he could say the Catechism and was able to read and write. Each pupil paid 4d. to have his name placed on the register, and the admission pence were given to the poor scholar who swept the school and cleaned the seats. In every form, the head pupil was seated in a chair as the form president.

The school hours were from seven to eleven o'clock in the mornings, and from one to five in the afternoons. Prayers were said in the morning, at noon, and in the evening. Boys were to come provided with wax candles at the expense of their friends. These cost about a shilling a pound, eight times as much as tallow candles. This is another proof that the school was for the sons of the well-to-do. Cock-fighting was prohibited. Every 28th December, Holy Innocents' Day, the whole school proceeded to the cathedral to hear the sermon of the Boy Bishop, and after the High Mass each scholar made an offering of "a penny to the Childe Byshop, and with them the maisters and surveyors of the Scole."

Colet left instructions about the curriculum. Speaking of the general principles underlying school studies, he ordained, "As touching in this Scole what shall be taught of the Maisters, and learned of the Scolers, it passeth my witte to devyse, and determine in particular, but in general to speake and sume what to saye my mynde, I wolde they were taught always in good literature bothe Laten and Greke and good autors such as have the verrye Romayne eloquence joyned with wisdome with clean and chaste Laten, other in verse or in prose." This ordinance clearly exhibits the Renaissance spirit.

In a letter of Erasmus written to his friend Justas Jonas, an interesting description of the school in its early days is given. "He divided the School into four apartments. The first viz., the Porch and Entrance, is for Catechumens, or the Children to be instructed in the principles of Religion ; where no Child is to be admitted, but what can read or write. The second apartment is for the lower Boys, to be taught by the Second Master or Usher. The third, for the Upper forms, under the Head Master ; which two parts of the School are divided by a curtain, to be drawn at pleasure. Over the Master's chair is an image of the Child Jesus of admirable work, in the gesture of teaching ; whom all the boys, going and coming, salute with a short hymn ; and there is a representation of God the Father, saying, 'Hear ye him' ; these words being written at my suggestion. The Fourth, or last apartment, is a little Chapel for Divine Service. The School has no corners, or hiding places ; nothing like a cell or closet. The boys have their distinct forms, or benches, one above another. Every form holds sixteen ; and he that is head, or captain of each form, has a little kind of desk by way of pre-eminence." [1]

One of the immediate changes of the Renaissance was that produced in methods of teaching owing to the invention of printing. Books became more plentiful, and the oral instruction of mediaeval days was superseded by written methods with greater reliance on the textbook.

The Humanist renaissance produced two outstanding treatises on education. The first was the *The Boke named the Governor* written by Sir Thomas Elyot in 1531. It was described by Professor Laurie as "the first full exposition of the Humanistic point of view, not only in English but also in England." [2] Elyot was born in Wiltshire about 1490 and chose the law as his profession. He rose to some eminence as a lawyer and was appointed, by Cardinal Wolsey, Clerk to the Privy Council. When a young man, Elyot was a member of the distinguished circle of Humanist scholars who gathered at Sir Thomas More's house at Chelsea. Although he had not studied at the university, he received instruction at the hands of Linacre, one of the most accomplished Greek scholars of the age. He had first-hand knowledge of the classical authors and was

[1] Erasmus evidently made an error in his calculations, for 8 forms of 16 boys each gives a total of 128. We know that the five upper classes had 18 boys each, and the three lower 21 each, a total of 153.

[2] S. S. Laurie. *Studies in the History of Educational Opinion from the Renaissance*, Chapter v, C.U.P., 1903

strongly influenced by the Italian writers on education of the previous century.

The Governor was dedicated to the King, and its main theme was the education of "a gentleman which is to have authority in the public weal." Elyot emphasises the Humanist ideals which afford a discipline for the growing mind, and advocates, in addition to physical pursuits and training in skill at arms, the acquisition of such courtly accomplishments as music and dancing. Although Elyot was not averse to men of ability making their way into high offices of State, he was chiefly concerned with the sons of gentry who were destined for a life of public service. Like most Humanists, he began his scheme of instruction with the infant and he pointed out the importance of imitation from the earliest stages. He was in agreement with the principles of Erasmus, whose writings he had studied, and he drew attention to the three essential factors in the training of young children—the importance of developing the habit of clear and refined speech, the utilisation of play in the early stages of instruction, and the "direct method" of learning a foreign language, which in this case was Latin.

After the age of seven, Elyot would have the child taken from the company of women and given into the charge of a tutor which should be "an ancient and worshipful man" and one of such temperament and character that "the child by imitation following may grow to be excellent." As in the Middle Ages, very few of the sons of the nobility were sent to school and even those who did attend usually took their tutors with them. In addition to Latin, the tutor should give instruction in Greek, and special attention should be devoted to the reading of classical writers in both prose and poetry. In fact, Elyot regards the latter as more important than prose. "Poetry was the first philosophy that ever was known, and through it children have always gained their first lessons in right conduct."

At the age of fourteen the boy should begin his study of the writers on rhetoric, not only classical authors, but such works as those of Erasmus. The voyages of discovery had awakened interest in the newly found lands, and Elyot recommends a study of geometry and astronomy coupled with training in the use of maps. The Greek and Roman historians should also be studied, because from them the young man will gain his first experiences of military, political, and moral wisdom.

By this time the young man will have reached the age of seventeen and the time is ripe for him to begin the study of philosophy.

He should begin by reading the first two books of Aristotle's *Ethics* and then continue with the *De Officiis* of Cicero, the prophetical and historical writings of the Old Testament, and finally *The Institution of a Christian Prince* "the little book of the most excellent Doctor Erasmus." Elyot thinks that the common mistake of schoolmasters is to introduce their pupils to studies before they have arrived at the age when they can appreciate them. "Lord God, how many good and clean wits of children be now-a-days perished by ignorant schoolmasters!"

On coming of age, the young "governor" should study the laws of his country, not with a view to becoming a professional lawyer, but as a part of the liberal education suited to one whose life is to be spent in the public service. Side by side with academic studies, the young man should receive a training in outdoor pursuits such as wrestling, running, swimming, hunting, hawking, and, above all, archery. He recommends chess as an indoor recreation, but the youth should be warned against the perils of dice.

The second important Renaissance book on education is *The Scolemaster* of Roger Ascham. The author was a Yorkshireman by birth who came under the Renaissance influence at Cambridge where he took his bachelor's degree in 1534. Ascham distinguished himself in his Greek studies, and after some experience in teaching private pupils, he was appointed university lecturer in Greek. His Latin style was so excellent that he was also given the post of Public Orator and was in charge of the Latin correspondence of the university. In 1548 he came to court to supervise the studies of the young Princess Elizabeth. It is a tribute to his skill as a tutor that his pupil became one of the best-read monarchs of the age. *The Scolemaster* was not published until after his death in 1568.

Ascham was concerned with the education of the child, who at the age of seven entered a grammar-school. He considered the question of the pupil's reading a very important one, and he would have him go direct to the Latin authors instead of reading about them. He thought that the greatest mistake in current practice consisted in giving the child a few lessons in grammar and then plunging him into the writing of Latin composition. This resulted in the formation of bad linguistic habits which were difficult to eradicate. Ascham's own method of teaching Latin was as follows. He advocated the selection made by Sturmius of the *Epistles* of Cicero as a basis for the instruction. First of all the child ought to be taught the content of the passage. He should then make an

English translation and parse every word of the original. After this, he should make a final English version which he should show to his master. The latter would take his book from him and set him to turn the English translation back into Latin. When this has been completed, the child is to receive back his textbook and compare his Latin version with the original. Whenever he has done well, the master should praise him and say, "Here do ye well." ". . . For I assure you, there is no such whetstone to sharpen a good wit, and encourage a will to learning, as is praise."

Ascham believed in the child being taught on the translation method and he would not allow him to speak Latin since this would ruin his style. When the grammatical stage of learning the language has been completed, the master should turn his attention to improving the pupil's Latin style, and Ascham gives details of the different kinds of exercises which he thinks efficacious for this purpose. He has no patience with those who are content with the knowledge of one language, but thinks that where possible the pupil should also learn Greek.

Ascham has much to say on the subject of school discipline. In fact, in his preface he informs us that it was his strong feelings about discipline which prompted him to write the book. Some boys had run away from the severe discipline of Eton, and Ascham soundly condemned the barbarous floggings which were all too common in his day and even much later. His opinion was "that young children should rather be allured to learning by gentleness and love, than compelled to learning by beating and fear." He disagrees with the common view that children have a natural distaste for learning. Where this is so, the blame is to be attached to the schoolmaster. No boy should ever be punished because he is slow in learning, but he would not withold corporal punishment in cases of moral delinquency. Ascham knew no psychology, but he was a shrewd practical schoolmaster with a kindly nature and a strong vein of common sense. His book was read by Mulcaster and Brinsley, and its influence can be traced in both their writing and their practice.

The effects of the Reformation were in some ways a disaster to English education. The Reformers as a whole were supporters of learning and encouraged the study of Greek as a means to the reading of the New Testament. It was the policy of the Tudor monarchs which caused the mischief. Henry VIII's breach with Rome led to the closing of the monastic schools, but the damage done was comparatively small as these schools did not represent the main stream of English education. Moreover, Henry himself was an extremely well-educated man and had a proper regard for learning. The dissolution of the chantries was far more damaging. We have already mentioned that the majority of the chantries supported a grammar-school from their endowments. Henry VIII commenced the work of dissolution by the Act of 1545, but it is doubtful if more than two or three were actually dissolved by this law.

The real blow fell in 1547 when a similar Act of Edward VI completely abolished the chantries. It is quite true that in the preamble to the Act it was suggested that the endowments would be better used for education and for assisting the poor. It also stipulated that schools were only to be continued when the maintenance of a school was mentioned in the "first foundation and ordinance thereof." This meant the closure of a large number of schools, both grammar and other types. Even those which were permitted to remain were very badly hit. In most cases the lands of the chantry were confiscated and the school given a fixed annual sum which, owing to the rapid fall in the value of money in Tudor times, reduced many to severe financial straits. Elementary schools maintained by chantries were unable to continue. The Government threw the responsibility for elementary education upon the clergy. Gradually, elementary education fell into the hands of private individuals who were often, in character and attainments, unfit for the job. It was not until the 18th century, when the efforts of individuals and the philanthropic societies were turned to the education of the masses, that elementary education revived. Nevertheless, we shall see that there were a few survivors of the primary schools which ensured the continuity of elementary education.

The Tudors have often been lauded as patrons of education and the founders of our grammar-schools. To believe this is to ignore all the work which was carried out by the mediaeval schools. The more modern view, based on ample evidence, is rather that they were the destroyers of schools. "Never was a great reputation more easily gained and less deserved than that of King Edward VI as a founder of schools. If the ordinary educated person were asked to whom our system of secondary education was mainly due, and who was the founder of most of the grammar schools on which it chiefly rests, he would answer, without hesitation, Edward VI. The magnificent foundations of Christ's Hospital and Birmingham

Grammar School, and the numerous Edward VI Grammar Schools which stud the country, would rise up before his mind, and he would give the credit of them to their reputed founder. Even to those people who credit Wykeham with the foundation of our public school system in founding Winchester, and credit Henry VIII with the cathedral schools, such as the King's School, Canterbury, Edward VI still stands out as *par excellence* the founder of schools and patron saint of industrious schoolboys." [1]

There is plenty of contemporary evidence to support the modern view. Thomas Lever, Master of St. John's College, Cambridge, complains about conditions in the middle years of the 16th century. Lever refers to the avowed intentions of the Acts dissolving the chantries as "the alteration, change, or amendment of the same, and converting to good and godly uses, as in erecting grammar schools, to the education of youth in virtue and godliness, the further augmenting of the universities, and better provisions for the poor and needy." This plain speaking, delivered in a sermon preached to the King and the nobles in 1550, was the means of saving the chantry school of Sedbergh. The second witness is Thomas Williams, Speaker of the House of Commons, who in 1562 drew the Queen's attention to the fact, "I daresay a hundred schools want in England, which before this time had been: and if in every school there had been but an hundred scholars, yet that had been ten thousand; so that now I doubt whether there be so many learned men in England, as the number wants of these Scholars."

It is because of the number of schools bearing the name of the reigning monarch that the Tudors have been considered patrons of learning. The King's Schools (Henry VIII), and Edward VI and Queen Elizabeth's grammar-schools, are practically all refoundations of schools which had previously existed. Moreover, it is very doubtful if the Tudor sovereigns were even the prime movers in the work of refoundation. As a rule they complied with the request of the town or district for the re-establishment of old grammar-schools. In addition, quite a number of schools were refounded by wealthy merchants or noblemen who, from loyalty to the sovereign, when they had obtained a charter, applied the royal title to the revived school.

For example, the Wakefield Grammar School was granted a royal charter by Elizabeth, 19th November 1591, as a result of a petition of the inhabitants of the town.. This school was probably

---

[1] A. F. Leach. *English Schools at the Reformation*, p. 1, Constable, 1896.

a revival of an older school which is mentioned as existing in 1547 in connection with the chantry at the parish church. The initial paragraph of the charter runs as follows, "Elizabeth, By the grace of God, Quene of England, Fraunce and Irelande, defender of the faithe, etc., to all men to whom thies present letters shall comme sendith greting. Bee it knowen unto you that wee at the humble sute made unto us by the Inhabitants of the Towne and parisshe of Wakefilde in our countie of Yorke for a free Grammar Scoole there to be erected and establisshed for ever for the contynuall teachinge instructinge and bringing up of children and youthe in good lernynge, namlie those belonginge to the said parisshe of Wakefilde, Of our special grace certen knowledge and meere motion Wee doe will graunte and ordayne for us our heires and successors that hereafter there be and shalbe one Grammer Scoole in the saide Towne of Wakefilde which shalbe called the free Grammer Scoole of Quene Elizabeth att Wakefilde for the teachinge instructinge and bringinge up of children and youthe in Grammer and other good learnynge to contynue to that use forever." [1]

The Free Grammar School of Queen Elizabeth at Horncastle, Lincolnshire, was granted letters patent by the Queen at the request of Lord Clinton (afterwards Earl of Lincoln) in 1599. The text of the Queen's letter makes it clear that the foundation was at the request of Lord Clinton. "The Queen to all whom it may concern etc. Health. Whereas our well beloved and faithful Counsellor and Subject Edward Fynes knight of the most noble Order of the Garter Lord Clynton and Saye and our great Admiral of England, hath humbly prayed us that we would condescend that a Grammar School be erected founded and established in the Town of Horncastle in our County of Lincoln for the good Education and Instruction of Boys and Youth there . . . we will grant and ordain that henceforth there may and shall be a Grammar School in the Town of Horncastle aforesaid which shall be called the Free Grammar School of Queen Elizabeth."

There is an amusing incident connected with the charter of Otley Grammar School, Yorks. The school was founded in 1608 as the result of the will of Thomas Cave, a chapman or travelling merchant of Wakefield, who bequeathed the sum of £250 for the purpose of founding a grammar-school in the town from which his

[1] The old schoolhouse near the market is now the Cathedral School and is used as a secondary modern school. The building has recently been scheduled as an ancient monument.

family had sprung. The charter was granted by James I in response
to "the petition of certain substantial inhabitants of the Parish of
Otley." In 1606 the Rev. W. Harrison, Vicar of Otley, was sent
to London by the governors to ask for a foundation charter. The
form of the charter had been agreed beforehand, but Harrison
inserted the last phrase of the following paragraph. ". . . We do
name, constitute and appoint our well beloved William Harrison,
Batchelor of Arts, being a learned, honest, religious, and discreet
man, to be the first and present Schoolmaster of the said Free
Grammar School of Prince Henry at Otley, to *continue in the said
office and place for and during his natural life.*" Evidently his
honesty did not prevent him from inserting the phrase in italics
himself. The governors resented this action and reported that "itt
was of his own contentment, but high offence to the Parishioners."
At first they thought of seeking redress in the law-courts, but
wiser counsels prevailed and in 1622 they persuaded Harrison to
vacate his office, "for and in consideration of a certaine some of
money to me in hand payde."

The foundation or refoundation of schools by wealthy individuals was a common tendency of the latter part of Elizabeth's reign
and was also noticeable during the early Stuart period. In an
earlier age, these benefactors would have shown their piety and
public spirit by building a church or endowing a chantry. In a
changed age, they exhibited the same virtues in providing for the
education of future generations. In districts where a grammar-
school was already in existence, such benefactors found a means
of displaying their charity by enlarging the foundations in their
neighbourhood.

Thus Thoresby, the well-known historian of Leeds, tells us that
the wealthy cloth merchant of that town, John Harrison, not only
built the beautiful Jacobean Church of St. John in 1634, but
provided a new schoolhouse for the grammar-school in 1624.
Speaking of the school, Thoresby says, "The famous Mr. Harrison
removed it . . . to a pleasant Field of his own which he surrounded
with a substantial Wall and then in the midst of the Quadrangle
built the present Fabrick of the School."

The 16th-century grammar-schools, like their mediaeval counterparts, stressed the study of Latin grammar, but now the grammar
was beginning to be regarded as the first stage in the acquisition of
a sound knowledge of Latin. The first Latin Grammar printed in
English was written by John Stanbridge, who was usher at Magdalen

College School. It was a distinct improvement on the doggerel verse of Alexander of Villa Dei, and the declensions and conjugations were set out in a much clearer form than in the earlier Grammars, e.g. *Amo/as/at, Amamus/atis/ant.* Several of the larger schools adopted his Grammar. It is worthy of note that William Lily, the first High Master of St. Paul's School and the author of the celebrated Grammar which bears his name, came from Magdalen College School. The variety of Grammars published in the early 16th century caused considerable confusion in the schools, and resulted in the first definite act of State intervention in the affairs of the schools. Henry VIII, by royal proclamation, ordered Lily's Grammar to be used exclusively in all grammar-schools in the realm. "We will and command and straitly charge all you schoolmasters and teachers of grammar within this realm and other our dominions, as ye intend to avoid our displeasure and have our favour, to teach and learn your scholars this English introduction here insuing, and the Latin grammar annexed to the same and none other."

The Grammar was a composite work in which Erasmus, and Robertson the headmaster of Magdalen College School, shared. The early part of the Grammar for use with younger pupils explained the accidence in English, and later, William Haine, of Merchant Taylors' School, translated the remainder under the title of *Lily's Rules Construed.* The Grammar first appeared in 1515 and after various alterations and additions reached its final form in 1574, when it was entitled *A Short Introduction of Grammar, generally to be used: compiled and set forth for the bringing up of all those that intend to attain the knowledge of the Latin tongue.*

Colet wrote the preface to the Grammar and in the following words the attitude of this great scholar and schoolmaster towards schoolboys is distinctly shown. "Judging that nothing may be too soft nor too familiar for little children, specially learning a tongue with them at all strange; in which little book I have left many things out on purpose, considering the tenderness and capacity of small minds. . . . Wherefore I pray you all, little babes, all little children, learn gladly this little treatise, and commend it diligently unto your memories, trusting of this beginning ye shall proceed and grow to perfect literature, and come at the last to be great clerks. And lift up your little white hands for me, which prayeth for you to God, to whom be all honour and imperial majesty and glory." In spite of these kindly words, Lily's Grammar caused multitudes of schoolboys tears during the next two and a half centuries.[1] The Grammar treats exceptions at great length and deals with the declension of Greek forms, all of which must have made it a difficult book for beginners. Nevertheless, Lily had come to stay. In the Canons of the Church of England, in 1604, its use was prescribed and one of the questions to be asked at the bishop's visitation was concerning the use of the Grammar. Archbishop Parker, in his second visitation to the cathedral church of Canterbury, inquired of the dean and chapter, "Whether your schoolmasters teach any other grammar than such as is approved by the Queen's Majesty's Injunctions." Lily's Grammar was used throughout the 17th century. It was slightly revised in 1758 under the title of the *Eton Latin Grammar,* and held its own until superseded in 1867 by the *Public Schools Latin Primer.*

The Grammar, however, did show certain improvements on earlier Grammars in arrangement and clarity.   The declensions were better spaced and set out in clearer form than in Stanbridge's Grammar, *e.g.* "The seconde is when the Genitive case singular endith in i, the Dative in o, the Accusative in um, the Vocative for the most part like the Nominative, the Ablative in o. The Nominative plural in i, the Genitive in orum, the Dative in is, the Accusative in os, the Vocative lyke the Nominative, the Ablative in is: as in example.

		Singulariter				Pluraliter	
Hic	Vir		Nominat.	hic magister		Nomin.	hi magistri
His	Liber		Genit.	huius magistri		Ge.	horū magistrorū
Haec	Colus		Dativo	huic magistro		Dati.	his magistris
His	Logos		Accus.	hunc magistrū		Accu.	hos magistros
			Vocativo	ô magister		Vocat.	ô magistri
			Abla.	ab hoc magistro		Ab.	ab his magistris

Present   Singular   Amo, amas, amat
          Plural   Amamus, amatis, amant

Brinsley's *Ludus Literarius or the Grammar Schoole,* published in 1612, is a mine of information about the work done in the 16th and 17th century grammar-schools. Brinsley enjoyed a brilliant career as the master of the grammar-school at Ashby-de-la-Zouch in Leicestershire, but was suspended from teaching, about 1619, on account of his Puritan views. His book is in the form of a dialogue between two schoolmasters and was "intended for the helping of the younger sort of Teachers, and of all Schollers." When Philoponus is asked how he would ensure that boys knew their grammar,

---

[1] The author's copy of Lily's Grammar is a leather-covered book, 5½ in. by 3½ in., and was in use at St. Bees' Grammar School. On the fly-leaf, in a copperplate schoolboy hand, under the date 1751, is written, "This work is strongly recommended for bothering a fellow's brains."

he replies, "The continuall use of the bookes of construing of Lillies Rules, by causing them to learne to construe, and to keepe their Grammar rules, onely by the helpe of those translations." A large part of the book is taken up by showing the best way of teaching the rules of Lily's Grammar, but Brinsley tells us a good deal about the other Latin work of the grammar-school.

The study of grammar was closely bound up with the making of vocabularies. Each day, the master dictated a list of words which the pupils learnt by heart. These were tested and revised frequently so that the pupils quickly acquired a store of Latin words and phrases. The *Colloquia* of Erasmus, 1516, was widely used and later the *Exercitatio Linguae Latinae* of Vives, 1539, found favour in many English schools. The latter was translated by Foster Watson in 1908 under the title of *Tudor Schoolboy Life*.

All this work was preparatory to the reading of Latin authors. Cicero was the most highly esteemed, and Vergil, Terence, and Ovid followed next. Caesar and Livy were read, but were not considered elementary texts as nowadays. Certain mediaeval Christian writers, and even contemporary works, were often included. Almost as important as construing a Latin author was the writing of a composition. This took the form of writing short, simple sentences in the junior classes, but with the older pupils Ascham's method was much used. Brinsley gives examples of the way in which letter-writing was taught. Finally, the pupils encountered the most difficult exercise of all, Latin verse composition. A large number of these verse exercises are still extant (including the youthful efforts of Edward VI), and some show the straits to which the young authors were put. When their Latin gave out, they often intercalated English words.

Latin was taught as a living language and, in many schools, in order to gain fluency, pupils spoke Latin all the time in class and at meals. Severe penalties threatened those who lapsed into English. Brinsley suggests the appointment of two prefects in each form to prevent the speaking of English. He admits that speaking Latin on all occasions is "exceeding hard," and "one will wink at another if they be out of the master's hearing."

Greek, as was previously said, was second in importance to Latin, and the methods of teaching the language were similar to those employed in Latin, though less intensive. When the teaching of Greek became more common in the latter half of the 16th century,

TIME-TABLE OF A TYPICAL ELIZABETHAN GRAMMAR-SCHOOL, 1598

(*Schools Inquiry Commission*, Vol. VII, pp. 262-3.)

Classes III, IV, and V were taught by the master; Classes I and II by the usher. In winter the school closed at 4 p.m.

	MONDAY	TUESDAY	WEDNESDAY	THURSDAY	FRIDAY	SATURDAY
Class V 7-11 a.m.	Prose theme. Lecture in Cicero or Sallust or Caesar's *Commentaries*.	Verse theme. Lecture same as Monday.	Prose theme. Lecture in Vergil or Ovid's *Metamorphosis*, or Lucan.	Lecture in Vergil, etc., same as Wednesday.	Verse theme. Repetition of the week's lectures.	Examination in lecture of previous afternoon.
1-5 p.m.	Latin Syntax or Greek Grammar or Figures of Sysenbrote.[1] Home lessons and exercises given out and prepared.	Latin Syntax, etc., same as Monday.	Latin Syntax, etc., same as Monday.	Half-holiday.	Repetition continued. Lecture on Horace, or Lucan, or Seneca's *Tragedies*.	Declamation on a given subject by several senior scholars. Catechism and New Testament.
Class IV 7-11 a.m.	Lecture on Cicero's *de Senectue* or *de Amicitia*, or on Justin.[2]	Lecture on Cicero, etc., as on Monday.	Lecture on Ovid's *Tristia*, or *de Ponto*, or on Seneca's *Tragedies*.	Lecture, etc., as on Wednesday.	Verse theme, and repetition of the week's lectures.	Examination in lecture of previous afternoon.
1-5 p.m.	Prose theme. Latin Syntax or Greek Grammar or Figures of Sysenbrote. Home lessons and exercises given out and prepared.	Verse theme. Latin Syntax, etc., as on Monday.	Prose theme. Latin Syntax, etc., as on Monday.	Half-holiday.	Repetition continued. Lecture on Ovid's *Fasti*.	Catechism and New Testament.

Class III **7-11 a.m.**	Lecture on the letters of Ascham, or Sturm's Cicero's *Letters*,³ or Terence. Paraphrase of a sentence.	Lecture on As-cham, etc., as on Monday. *Vulgaria* in Prose.	Lectures on Palen-genius, or the Psalms of Hess. Paraphrase of a sentence.	Lecture on Palen-genius or the Psalms of Hess.	*Vulgaria* in Prose, and repetition of the week's lectures.	Examination in lecture of previous afternoon.
1-5 p.m.	Latin Syntax or Greek Grammar or Figures of Sysenbrote.¹ Home lessons and exercises given out and prepared.	Latin Syntax, etc., as on Monday.	Latin Syntax, etc., as on Monday.	Half-holiday.	Repetition con-tinued. Lecture on Eras-mus' *Apophthegms*.	Catechism and New Testament.
Class II **7-11 a.m.**	Lecture on *Colloquies* of Erasmus or on *Dia-logues* of Corderius.	Lecture, etc., same as on Monday.	Lecture on the Cato senior, or Cato junior.	Lecture, etc., same as on Wednesday.	Repetition of the week's lectures.	Examination in lecture of previous afternoon.
1-5 p.m.	Translations from English into Latin. Home lessons and exercises given out and prepared.	Translations as on Mondays.	Translations as on Mondays.	Half-holiday.	Repetition con-tinued. Lecture on *Æsop's Fables*.	Writing out the Catechism in English. Arithmetic.
Class I **7-11 a.m.**	The Royal Grammar.	The Royal Gram-mar.	The Royal Gram-mar.	The Royal Gram-mar.	Repetition of the work of the week.	Examination in lecture of previous afternoon.
1-5 p.m.	The English Testa-ment, or the Psalms of David, in English.	As on Monday.	As on Monday.	Half-holiday.	Repetition con-tinued. Lecture on *Æsop's Fables*.	Writing out the Catechism in English. Arithmetic.

¹ J. Susenbrotus, a German, who died in 1543. Wrote an epitome of Rhetoric in 1540.
² Justinian's *Institutes*.
³ Sturm published a selection of Cicero's *Epistles*. He was Rector of the school at Strasbourg.

pupils read the Gospel of St. John and Nowell's *Greek Catechism*, construing both books into Latin. Few schools proceeded to the reading of Greek classical authors. We hear that Westminster was famous for its Hebrew and even experimented in introducing Arabic.

History and geography were taught incidentally in connection with the authors read. The only other subjects were writing and arithmetic and a little geometry and astronomy to the higher forms. The grammar-schools were inclined to shy at the teaching of reading and writing. These were considered subjects for the "petties," *i.e.* the little ones in the primary or the preparatory school. Every boy was supposed to be able to read and write[1] when he entered the grammar-school, though in practice it was often necessary to teach these arts to pupils. Brinsley believed in giving an hour's practice each day in writing, preferably at one o'clock, "when their hands are warmest and nimblest." Some grammar-schools sent their pupils, after morning or afternoon school, to a writing-master. As this was not usually possible for country schools, writing was often taught by a travelling teacher, who spent several weeks at each school. Arithmetic was of much less importance, and since the teaching was either at the end of the day or on a half-holiday, it was not popular with the pupils nor with the usher who had to teach it. Brinsley, in his *Grammar Schoole,* shows us the shortcomings of the average grammar-school pupil with regard to arithmetic. He writes: "You shall have schollers, almost readie to go to the Universitie, who yet can hardly tell you the number of Pages, Sections, Chapters, or other divisions in their books, to finde what they should. And it is, as you say, a great & foule want; because, without the perfect knowledge of these numbers, schollers cannot helpe themselves by the Indices, or Tables of such bookes, as they should use, for turning to anything of a sodaine." [2]

We have to remember that, when Brinsley wrote, most pages and chapters were numbered with the roman numerals. The arabic notation, although gaining popularity on the Continent in the 15th century, did not come into use in England until the following century. The first authentic use of the arabic notation

---

[1] Cf. Wakefield Grammar School. "None shall be admitted to be taught as scholars in this school, upon what pretext soever, unless he be able in tolerable sort to read English and be promoted to the accidence . . . and because this school is not ordained for petties but for grammarians, we will that all the scholars under the master's teaching shall be tied to the speaking of Latin."

[2] *The Grammar Schoole,* by John Brinsley, ed. by E. T. Campagnac, p. 25, University of Liverpool Press, 1917.

is said to be at St. Andrews at the close of the 15th century. Brinsley considers that it is quite easy to teach the roman notation and he suggests a method of doing it. He also refers to the arabic notation, calling it "the numbers by Figures" in contrast to "the numbers by letters," and he explains the principles of the decimal system. He thinks the understanding of these two notations is sufficient for the average pupil. "In a word, to tell what any of these numbers stand for, or how to set downe any of them; will performe fully so much as is needfull for your ordinarie Grammar scholler. If you do require more for any, you must seeke Record's Arithmetique, or other like Author's and set them to the Cyphering school." [1]

Dr. Robert Recorde, to whom Brinsley refers, was a Tenby physician who had graduated at Cambridge. He is said to have been physician to Edward VI and Mary. He wrote four books on arithmetic, algebra, geometry, and astronomy, called, respectively, *The Ground of Artes, The Whetstone of Witte, The Pathway to Knowledge,* and *The Castle of Knowledge.* Recorde was the first English writer to introduce the common symbols for equality, addition, subtraction, and multiplication, and he explains the sign of equality as "a pair of paralleles or gemowe (twin) lines of one length, thus, =, because noe 2 thynges can be more equalle." He deals with two kinds of arithmetic: pen-arithmetic and arithmetic carried out with counters. The former is the type of arithmetic with which we are familiar, but counter-arithmetic was a means of reckoning numbers which could be learnt by those who could neither read nor write. [2] It was by means of counters that the ordinary tradesman kept his accounts. Pen-arithmetic was usually known as ciphering. It was generally taught to scholars proceeding to the university, but the art of casting accounts was useful to boys who would later be apprenticed. This distinction explains the references to arithmetic in the following Elizabethan schools:—

Tideswell, Derby, 1560. The master to teach grammar and, for the petties, the figures and characteristics of letters.

St. Olave's Grammar School, Southwark, 1561. The master to teach children to write and read and cast accounts.

[1] *The Grammar Schoole,* by John Brinsley, ed. by E. T. Campagnac, p. 26, University of Liverpool Press, 1917.
[2] Foster Watson gives an interesting account of arithmetic with counters in his *The Beginnings of the Teaching of Modern Subjects in England,* pp. 301-3, Pitman, 1909.

Bungay, Suffolk, 1592.   The schoolmaster and scholars to keep
school every Saturday and every half-holiday until 3 p.m.,
"for writing and casting accounts with the pen and counters
according to their capacities."

Stainmore, Westmorland, 1594.   Instruction of children in reading,
writing, and accounts.

Wellingborough, Northampton, 1596.   Master and usher to teach
Latin, and also reading, writing, and accounts.

Aldenham, Herts, 1599.   The usher to teach English, writing,
ciphering, and accounts.

As an example of Recorde's pen-arithmetic, his method of
multiplication throws light upon the practice of his time, and also
upon the origin of our present symbol for multiplication. Suppose
we have to multiply eight by seven. The reader should realise that
the multiplication table was unknown at that date, so that the only
way of multiplying, say, four by three, was to set down four three
times and find the total by addition. Recorde tells us that the first
step in his method is to set down the seven under the eight, and
opposite them the differences between these two numbers and ten,
e.g. ${}^8_7 \times {}^2_3$. By addition, we find that twice three is six, so that
six is our units digit. We then either subtract three from eight, or
two from seven, which gives us five as the tens digit.

The same method applies to numbers over ten e.g. 12×13,
${}^{12}_{13} \times {}^2_3$, except that instead of taking three from twelve, we add
and thus obtain 156 as the answer. Larger numbers still can
be multiplied together by using the method in stages, but this must
be left to the reader's ingenuity. The method admits of a simple
algebraic proof.

The subject ranking next in importance to grammar was the
instruction given in religion and morals, and the value attached to
religious education was enhanced by the Reformation. At Wakefield, the master swore, "The youth of this scole I shall diligentlie
instruct in religion learning and good manners."

The statutes of Harrow insisted, "The schoolmaster shall have
regard to the manners of his scholars and see that they come not
uncombed unwashed ragged or slovenly; but above all things he
shall punish severely lying, picking and stealing, fighting, filthiness
or wantonness of speech and such like." The statutes of Newcastle
Grammar School, 1600, directed that "youth should be well founded
from their tenderest years in the rudiments of true religion and

instructed in learning and good manners." After the Reformation the religious teaching was based upon the Bible and the Catechism. The latter had been compiled by Dean Nowell and was practically identical with that contained in the Book of Common Prayer. Older scholars used Latin or Greek versions of the Catechism.

The Injunctions of Queen Elizabeth, 1559, laid down the lines on which the religious instruction should proceed.

XLI. "That all teachers of children shall stir and move them to live and do reverence to God's true religion now truly set forth by public authority."

XLII. "They shall accustom their scholars reverently to learn such sentences or scriptures as shall be most expedient to induce them to all godliness."

XLIII. "Every parson, vicar, or curate shall upon every holy-day and every second Sunday in the year, hear and instruct the youth of the parish for half an hour at the least before evening prayer in the Ten Commandments, the Articles of Belief, and the Lord's Prayer; and diligently examine them, and teach the Catechism set forth in the Book of Public Prayer."

In all the grammar-schools, the school session began and ended with religious exercises which varied from a few set prayers prescribed by the founder to an elaborate service.[1]

All pupils were obliged to attend divine service on Sundays and holy days. Thus the statutes of Dronfield, Derbyshire, enjoin, "I ordain that the scholars do upon every Sunday and Holyday in the morning resort orderly to the school, and that they go thence into the church, two and two in rank, that they carry their service book with them, and answer the versicles in the Psalms as the clerk of the parish doth, that they kneel at such times of the celebration of Divine Service according as it is in that behalf prescribed in the Book of Common Prayer, and that they stand up at the reading of the Creed, and bow at the sacred name of Jesus, and that as many as be of capacity do take in writing the notes of the preacher's sermons, and give account of them on Monday morning to the master."

Great attention was paid to the inculcation of good manners both in school and at the table. A. F. Leach tells us that the boys at Wells were given minute directions about their manners and behaviour. They were to cut their bread at dinner, not gnaw it

[1] Examples of school prayers and services are given in J. H. Brown, *Elizabethan Schooldays*, pp. 55-61, Blackwell, 1933.

with their teeth nor tear it with their nails.   When drinking, their mouths were to be empty, not full, and they were not to pick their teeth with their knives.[1]

Games and sport took a prominent place in school life. Most of the games were of the type that would keep the pupils' bodies fit and healthy, such as running, wrestling, leap-frog, and above all archery. In some districts a crude type of football was played which was condemned by Elyot, but thought by Mulcaster to be useful. Hand-ball and stool-ball, which were in a way ancestors of fives and cricket, were very popular.

When Harrow School was founded by John Lyon, parents were expected to provide their boys with "bowshafts, bowstrings, and a bracer." Bowls was usually forbidden, lest in the bowling-alleys the youth got into bad company. Mulcaster discusses the value of different sports and exercises, and we have seen that cock-fighting was one of the most popular pastimes. Nevertheless, it was strictly prohibited at some schools such as St. Paul's, Merchant Taylors', and Manchester.

Some of the smaller schools were taught by one master, but usually there was also an usher, or assistant master. Very large schools had more than one usher. For example, St. Paul's and Merchant Taylors' had three, and Shrewsbury four, assistants. The master was in charge of the upper and the usher of the lower classes.   The appointment of the master was sometimes in the hands of the founder and his heirs, or the governing body of the school, or the bishop, or a college at one of the universities.   Upon appointment, he usually took a formal oath declaring that he would carry out his duties in a satisfactory manner.   The statutes of Wakefield Grammar School enumerate the duties of the school-master in great detail.   First and foremost comes the duty of instructing his pupils in religion, and he is directed to teach and examine his scholars in the principles of the Christian religion between one and two o'clock every Saturday. He is also charged to see that the pupils attend church on Sunday, "where his carefull eye shall overview their carriage and behaviour, their attention, also and diligence in noting the heads of instruction delivered by the preacher." On Monday morning he is to examine his scholars in the sermon and to deal with offenders who have been absent or negligent, "either by word, or by the rod, as the quality of the offence deserveth."

[1] A. F. Leach. *English Schools at the Reformation*, p. 105, Constable, 1896.

He is instructed to teach Lily's Latin Grammar and the Greek Grammar generally used in the colleges of Cambridge. There also follows a list of the Latin and Greek texts which are to be studied. "These duties by the master thus performed, yet lies there upon him a last duty of informing his youth in good nurture and manners which are themselves an ornament to religion and good learning."

The duties of the usher are similar to those of the master, but, "It shall further appertain to the office and duty of the usher to instruct the younger sort of scholars in the rudiments of the Latin tongue, and in the Latin grammar. . . . The usher shall at his best leisure, set them copies or get them copies set by some of the scholars, and appoint them one hour for writing every teaching day afternoon in which their writing he shall oversee and instruct them."

When the pupils are proficient they are to be transferred from the usher's to the master's class. On appointment, the master and the usher swore an oath to carry out their duties diligently. The master's stipend was to be £26 13s. 4d., paid quarterly, and the usher's £10. This was rather more than the average stipend which worked out at £16 10s. and £9 respectively. In small country schools the stipend was a mere pittance, but the master's salary at a large school like Shrewsbury was £40. When these amounts are stated in modern terms (at present they would have to be multiplied by something over twenty), they compare favourably with the pre-war scales for teachers, especially as in most cases the master had a house and received capitation fees and other payments. As a rule the usher was appointed and dismissed by the master with or without the consent of the governors.

The qualifications required for the master varied with different schools. Sometimes these are described in vague and indefinite terms, such as, "a learned and painful schoolmaster," "a pious, learned, and sober man," "a true member of the Church of England as by law established, a good grammar scholar, and an expert writer, and arithmetician." Some statutes state specifically that the master must be a graduate of Oxford or Cambridge. At Wakefield, the master must be an M.A. of Oxford or Cambridge; at Bradford, "a discreet and fit person, who should have taken the degree of M.A."; at Otley, "One mete man for knowledge religion and life, being well reported of and having taken the degree of Master of Arts or Batchelor of Arts." He must also be "perfect in ye Latin and Greek tongue; and a temperate man, fearinge God and of True Religion and Godly conversation, not contentious, not usinge or bent to any outward Faculty or given to Drunk'ness, swearinge, dyseing, cardinge or other unlawfull game." Some schools insisted that the master should be in priest's orders, *e.g.* Leeds, Skipton; and others that he should be single, *e.g.* Almondbury. In all cases he must be loyal to the Established Church and of good moral character. At Oundle, the Table of Orders states, "Neither the master or usher shall be common gamesters, haunters of taverns, neither to exceed in apparell, nor in any other ways to be an infamy to the School, or give evil example to the scholars, to whom in all points they ought to be themselves of honest continent and Godly behaviour."

One master and an usher were frequently not sufficient to staff the school and we find a kind of monitorial system in certain schools. Thus, at Manchester in 1525, the statutes state, "The High Master shall alway appoint one of his scollers, as he thinketh best, to instruct and teach in the one end of the scole all infants that come there to learn their A.B.C. primer and forthe till they begin gramyer, and in every month to choose another new scoller so as to teach infants." At Winchester, it was long the custom for senior boys to teach younger ones. This was all the more necessary, since boys were sent to the grammar-school at an early age. Brinsley thought seven or eight years was the best age, so that a boy would be ready to enter the university at about fifteen.

The masters maintained order in the schools by severe measures. In most pictures of 16th and 17th century schoolmasters and their schools, the master is depicted with a birch or rod. Brinsley was a very humane man and deprecated whipping for incapacity. "Now this extreme whipping, all men know what a dislike it breedeth in the children, both of the schoole, and of all learning, as that they will think themselves very happy, if the parents will set them to any servile or toiling business, so that they may keep from schoole. And it also workes in them a secret hatred of their Masters." [1] He would, however, use the rod for moral offences and he speaks of it as "God's instrument to cure the evils of their conditions, to drive out that folly which is bound up in their hearts, so to save their soules from hell, and to give them wisdome." [2] Brinsley recommends reproof, loss of place in the form, or the giving of a black mark which he terms the "blacke Bill" as punishments for minor offences. The master or usher may also keep the boys at their

[1] John Brinsley. *The Grammar Schoole*, Chap. xxvii.
[2] *Op. cit.*, Chap. xxix.

tasks while the rest play, but, knowing boys, he advises, "But herein there must be a speciall care, when they are thus restrained from play, that either Master or Usher, if it can be conveniently, have an eye to them, that they do their taskes." [1] As a last resort, appeal may be had to corporal punishment, but the master should know how to administer it properly. Care must be taken not to inflict injury upon the scholar by smiting him across the back or upon the head. "When you are to correct any stubborne or unbroken boy, you make sure with him to hold him fast ; as they are inforced to do, who are to shoo or to tame an unbroken colt. To this end to appoint three or four of your Schollers, whom you know to be honest, and strong inough, or moe if neede be, to lay hands upon him together, to hold him fast, over some fourme, so that he cannot stirre hand nor foot ; or else if no other remedy will serve, to hold him to some post (which is farre the safest and free from inconvenience) so as he cannot in any way hurt himselfe or others, be he never so peevish." [2]

Many masters were not as kindly as Brinsley would have them be. Thus, at Otley in 1652, the master, Mr. Brown, was dismissed by the governors. The charges against him were that there was no proof that he was a graduate as he pretended to be and that "he strapt ffrancis Tomlinson for takinge pears out of his grandmother's orchard and beat him unmercifully; and that he did beat, Henry, the son of Jonas Flesher, pulled off the hair of his head, and punished him."

School hours were very long in the 16th and 17th centuries. At Eton, in 1528, the boys rose at 5 a.m., school started at 6 a.m., breakfast was at 9 a.m., and school was resumed at 9.45 a.m. Dinner was at 11 a.m. and, in the afternoon, school lasted from 1 p.m. to 5 p.m. At Wakefield, in 1607, school was from 6 (sunrise in winter) to 11 a.m., and then from 1 p.m. to 6 p.m. At Winchester, in 1550, school was for $7\frac{1}{2}$ hours each day with two periods of prep, making in all ten hours. Unpunctuality was punished by whipping.

Holidays were shorter than in modern schools. Saints' Days were kept as holidays (Holy Days), and on the Rogation Days the whole school followed their elders round the boundaries of the parish. The pupils' memories of the boundaries were refreshed by whipping, bumping against trees, or being thrown into the stream where the boundaries crossed it.

[1] John Brinsley. *The Grammar Schoole*, Chap. xxix.   [2] *Ibid.*, Chap. xxix.

The school year was divided into four quarters, but the usual number of vacations was three: Christmas, Easter, and Whitsuntide. Their length varied, but averaged about three weeks at Christmas, and a fortnight at Easter and Whitsun. In addition, two half-holidays a week were common, though, as we have seen, many pupils had to spend this time in learning to write and compute. Altogether, the boy spent about twice the time in school that his modern counterpart does.

In the previous chapter we emphasised that the English schools were developed in close connection with the Church which exercised a very close supervision of education. By means of the licensing power, the Church, at the Reformation, had the practical control of education throughout the country. In 1553 Queen Mary ordered Bonner, Bishop of London, to "examine all schoolmasters and teachers of children and, finding them suspect in any ways, to remove them and place Catholic men in their rooms." [1]

Elizabeth had a specially difficult problem to solve. On the one hand, she was faced by the "Recusants" who favoured the old order and did not accept the Elizabethan settlement. On the other, she was obliged to deal with the returned exiles of the previous reign whose desire was to see the Reformation carried further on Continental lines. Many of these became the Puritans of the later years of the 16th century.

In 1559 the Queen's Injunctions contained the order, "that no man shall take upon him to teach but such as shall be allowed by the Ordinary, and found meet as well for his learning and dexterity in teaching, as for sober and honest conversation, and also for right understanding of God's true religion."

The latter phrase implied acceptance of the Elizabethan settlement. In 1580 the Separatist movement had grown and the Privy Council ordered an examination of all schoolmasters and tutors by the bishop or his representatives. If they were found corrupt or unworthy, they were to be deprived of their posts and replaced by sound and fit men. The Archbishop of Canterbury issued the following two items of inquiry:

"IV. Item. What schoolmasters are within your parish, and what their names are, that teach publicly or privately within any man's house within your parish, of what state, calling, or condition

---

[1] Quoted by N. Wood. *The Reformation and English Education*, p. 54, Routledge, 1931.

soever he or they be, in whose house or houses any such school-master or teacher is?

"V. Item. Whether any such schoolmaster, or schoolmasters, is reported known or suspected to be backward in the religion now established by the laws of this realm, that, are thought any way to be secret hinderers thereof?" [1]

The reference to teaching in private houses was due to the activities of priests who were suspected of giving instruction in religion to the households of Roman Catholic gentlemen in which they served as tutors. The carrying out of these instructions was left largely to the local justices of the peace, who were in many cases unwilling to take action unless their attention was expressly drawn to the facts. Many Roman Catholics had availed themselves of occasional conformity to secure their safety, but after the Papal excommunication of Elizabeth they had to make a definite choice. In spite of the persecution, we do hear of cases where schools were opened and continued for some time until an informer forced the local magistrates to take action.

Canon LXXVII of the Church of England, 1604, ordained that "No man shall teach either in public school or private house, but such as shall be allowed by the Bishop of the Diocese, or Ordinary of the place, under his hand and seal, being found meet as well for his learning and dexterity in teaching, as for sober and honest conversation, and also for right understanding of God's true religion; and also except he shall first subscribe to the first and third Articles afore-mentioned simply and to the two first clauses of the said Article." In other words, the intending schoolmaster must first accept the royal supremacy and declare his belief in the apostolic character of the Established Church. The same attitude was prevalent throughout the Stuart period. The Act of Uniformity, 1662, required every schoolmaster to declare his conformity to the liturgy of the Church of England. A further Act of 1665 forbade Protestant Dissenters from teaching publicly or privately, under a penalty of £40. In fact, at the end of the 17th century, the Church exercised as great a control over schoolmasters as at any period of the Middle Ages. It was not until 1779 that Dissenters gained full freedom to teach in schools. The same right was not accorded to Roman Catholics until 1790. Even then,

[1] Quoted by J. E. G. de Montmorency. *State Intervention in English Education*, p. 94, C.U.P., 1902. On page 96, Montmorency gives the text of the licence issued by Archbishop Whitgift to William Swetnam to teach a school within the City of London.

both Protestant Dissenters and Roman Catholics attending the universities suffered under certain disabilities.

In the latter part of Elizabeth's reign, Roman Catholics found it impossible to have their sons educated in England. If they were sent to the ordinary grammar-schools and their religion was discovered they were usually expelled. The only solution of the problem was to send their children abroad to be educated. Allen had set up a school at Douai in the Low Countries for the education of priests. He had intended to include a grammar-school in his foundation, but circumstances would not admit of it for some years. Douai started its life in 1568, but after a short space of ten years the students were expelled by the townsfolk, and it was some years before they were able to return. Allen had expected this and had made arrangements for the college to be transferred to Rheims. By 1580 there were 200 students at the college or at the preparatory schools at Eu in Normandy, Pont-a-Musson, and Verdun. There was no place in the original college for younger pupils, and when Rheims was given up after the assassination of the Duke of Guise in 1588, the younger boys were sent to the Jesuits at Douai. The English Government was quite aware of what was happening and an Act of 1585 threatened with very heavy penalties any parent sending his child overseas to be educated. He was liable to a fine of £100, and his son forfeited the right of inheritance. Moreover, it was a serious offence to send money overseas to these children. In 1592 the college at Eu was moved to St. Omer, where it continued until the expulsion of the Jesuits from France in 1762.

Burnley Grammar School is a curious example of a school which outwardly conformed to the Elizabethan settlement but remained to all intents and purposes a Catholic school. The earliest mention of the school was in 1532, and from this we learn that it was a chantry school taught by Stephen Smith who is decribed as chantry priest and schoolmaster. When the chantries were dissolved, Gilbert Fairbank held this office, and, at the opening of the re-endowed school in 1559, he was appointed as headmaster. There is no indication that he changed his faith and his will suggests that he was still a Catholic. His successor, Lawrence Yeates (1566-80), was also an adherent of the old faith. "An enquiry into the condition of the Reformed Faith in Lancashire in 1591 revealed the facts that 'no house was worse than Mr. Yeates, the Schoolmaster of Blackburn,' that 'his wife, daughter, and maid were recusants,' the maid had 'done much hurt among the scholars,' and that the Schoolmaster himself had harboured a papist recusant priest. Five of the pupils of Mr. Yeates at Blackburn fled overseas because of their zeal for Catholicism." [1] If this was his record after he was appointed headmaster of Blackburn Grammar School, there seems no reason to doubt that he held the same beliefs when he was at Burnley. Contemporary records show that the majority of the governors were Catholics and that the school trained a number of boys who afterwards became priests, some of whom were executed under the penal laws. This Catholic bias, which was a reflection of the strength of Catholicism in Lancashire during Elizabeth's reign, continued through the first half of the Stuart period. In 1646 the Puritans obtained a majority on the governing body, and for the rest of the century the Puritan influence was predominant.

It is very difficult to assess the provision of primary education during the 16th century. The records are scanty and widely dispersed, and mostly contained in parish church registers. No systematic study of these from the point of view of education has yet been made, and such a research would be a stupendous task. However, there are clear indications that primary education was more widespread than was formerly believed. Apart from the numerous instances where the grammar-school provided instruction in elementary subjects either by means of the usher or by senior pupils, there are cases where separate schools were built for elementary scholars. Sometimes they served the function of preparatory schools for the grammar-school. This was increasingly necessary, since in the latter part of the 16th century the grammar-schools had become more efficient, and the demand that pupils should be able to read and write before entering upon the grammar course began to be more widely made. At other times, the elementary school was an end in itself, being content to teach reading, writing, and accounts, and sending very few pupils on to the grammar-school.

Leach mentions forty-five schools which provided an elementary education, and this does not by any means exhaust the list. In addition to primary schools which survived the Reformation, there were certain schools, originally founded as grammar-schools, whose fortunes declined and which became in fact elementary schools. Further evidence is afforded by the inquiries into endowed schools

[1] W. Bennett. *A History of the Burnley Grammar School*, p. 13, published at the Burnley Grammar School, 1940.

undertaken in 1842 and listed in the Digest of Schools and Charities for Education. Amongst the non-classical endowed schools, the names of 168 schools of unknown date are given. These may be presumed to be the schools of an elementary character which survived the Reformation. Moreover, evidence is forthcoming which indicates that the number of people in the 16th century who were able to read and write English was far greater than has hitherto been thought. Professor Adamson points out "that the Paston letters (written during the 15th century) were written in English and this demonstrates that the reading and writing of English was not confined to those who had been pupils at grammar schools." [1] This was truer still of the next century. The Privy Council took severe measures against people who distributed handbills or fixed them to the doors of townsfolk's houses. This action is difficult to explain unless we assume that the knowledge of reading and writing was fairly common. All the English reformers laid great emphasis upon opportunities for reading the Bible in English, and they themselves wrote a large number of religious works in the vernacular. The supposition is that these were addressed to a sufficiently wide reading public as to make them worth while. The conclusion which seems best in answer to this problem is that in every town and in many large villages there existed one or more persons who gave instruction in reading and writing. In what cases this instruction was given privately and in what cases it was provided in a school are questions we have no means of answering accurately. Leach quotes the example of Falmouth in 1547 where the children of the poor were taught by the bellringer,[2] and Launceston where similar instruction was given by an aged man chosen by the mayor.[3] Certain vestry records show that on occasions this instruction received rate aid. Thus, in 1561, the overseers' accounts of the City of Westminster contain the following entry, "To Bull for teaching a childe —viii d." [4] These instances appear to be cases of instruction given by private individuals. Others, however, suggest the existence of some kind of primary school.

Montmorency instances the example of the vestry of Hackney who, in 1613, appointed a schoolmaster who was allowed to charge up to 4d. a week for teaching grammar to the children of the parish, and up to 2d. a week for teaching English reading

---

[1] *Short History of Education*, pp. 82-3.
[2] *English Schools at the Reformation*, p. 31.   [3] *Ibid.*, p. 34.
[4] J. E. G. de Montmorency, *op. cit.*, p. 191.

only.[1] Foster Watson quotes the example of St. Olave's, South-wark. The churchwardens, speaking of their Free School, in 1561, say: "We have great number of poor people in our parish who are not able to keep their children at grammar. But we are desirous to have them taught the principles of Christian religion and to write, read and cast accounts and so to put them forth to prentice." [2]

He also mentions the churchwardens' accounts of 1653 at Darlington, "Edward Holmes a poor scholar at the Petit School for half-yr's teaching 3s. 3d.," and "Dame Seamer for her wages for teaching a boy one year 4/-." [3] Is the latter an early instance of a dame-school?

A. F. Leach gives several examples. From the Beverley accounts: "They agreed the same day [i.e. 1572] that the Governors shall appoint one Maister for to teach pettyes in this Borow; and to have 53s. 4d. allowed; and the Grammar Maister to be no more charged with teaching pettyes." [4] This looks as though the master of the grammar-school had objected strenuously to the task of teaching small children to read and write. From the Rotherham accounts, 1635: "Item glasse for the Petty Schoole. 8d." [5]

The Clerk's School at Skipton is an interesting example of a pre-Elizabethan primary school which survived until 1814 when it was superseded by the National School. The school was founded by Ermysted in 1555, seven years after he had refounded Skipton Grammar School. That it was his intention to endow the Clerk's School for elementary instruction is clear from the foundation deed. The endowment was left for "the finding and maintaining of one Clerk sufficiently learned to teach Children the Spell and Read the A.B.C. called the ABsc, the Primer and Psalter in Latin and not in English, and teach them to sing plain Song perfectly, and to teach them daily and diligently upon every Week Day without taking of any Money . . . except one Penny of every Scholar at the Entry to put his name in the School Master's Book, and if the Scholar have not a Peny, to let him enter for nothing." The school seems to have been taught by the parish clerk. During the 18th century it received financial assistance from Lady Hastings and Lord Thanet, though later it was compelled through circumstances to admit some fee-paying scholars. The Clerk's School at Skipton

---

[1] J. E. G. de Montmorency, op. cit., p. 192.
[2] The English Grammar Schools to 1660, p. 158.   [3] Ibid.
[4] Early Yorkshire Schools, Vol. I, p. 118.   [5] Op. cit., Vol. II, p. 210.

is one of the rare cases in which the same founder was responsible for the establishment of both a grammar and a petty school.[1]

We know that the Church included the instruction of the young as one of the duties of the incumbent of the parish and that the "school" was frequently held in the church porch or in a room above the porch. How far this instruction went beyond the teaching of religion and morals depended upon the individual clergyman.

One of the most interesting writers on education in the Elizabethan period was Richard Mulcaster. When, in 1561, the Merchant Taylors' Guild established the grammar-school of that name, Mulcaster was appointed Master at a salary of £10, a dwelling, and a small addition by way of fees. Amongst his pupils were Edmund Spenser the poet, and Andrews, Bishop of Winchester. In 1576 Mulcaster was appointed Master of St. Paul's School at a salary of £36 and residence. In his two books, the *Positions,* and the *First Part of the Elementarie,* he develops views considerably in advance of his age. He writes in English because "though I appeal to the learned who understand Latin, I wish to reach also the unlearned, who understand only English, and whose interests are to be the more considered that they have fewer chances of information." He also declares that "My purpose is to help the whole business of teaching even from the very first foundation, that is to say, not only what is given in the Grammar School, and what follows afterwards, but also the elementary training which is given to infants from their first entrance, until they are thought fit to pass on to the Grammar School."[2]

He thinks that education should start with reading and should then pass on to the arts of writing, drawing, and music, and he has much to say how these should be taught. If there had been little opportunity for elementary education, Mulcaster's suggestions would have been useless. He would not limit education to boys, but he would not advocate higher education for girls. "I do not advocate sending young maidens to public Grammar Schools, or to the Universities as this has never been the custom in this country."[3] In addition to the elementary skills of reading, writing, and music, Mulcaster suggests needlework and housewifery. We know of a

---

[1] A full account of the school is given in A. M. Gibbon's excellent *History of the Ancient Free Grammar School of Skipton-in-Craven*, Appendix C, University Press of Liverpool, 1947.

[2] J. Oliphant. *The Educational Writings of Richard Mulcaster*, p. 4, James Maclehose, 1903.   [3] *Ibid.*, p. 51.

few references to schools for girls in the Middle Ages and there are occasional mentions of schoolmistresses after the Reformation, but the education of girls, such as it was, took place mainly in the home. Amongst the wealthier people a girl was taught by a private tutor or governess, but in middle-class homes, and amongst the poor, the girl's mother was usually the only teacher.

What may be termed the technical education of the Tudor period was provided by the apprenticeship system. In the first chapter, the work of the gilds in founding chantries and endowing grammar-schools was mentioned. The merchant and craft gilds grew up during the 12th and 13th centuries. After the Black Death, the merchant gilds declined in importance whilst the craft gilds took their place. The latter tended to become exclusive by restricting the right of entry, so that the craft was a preserve for members and their relatives. In the Middle Ages, the apprentice who had completed his training could look forward to becoming first a journeyman, then, after a certain number of years, a master craftsman. From the 15th century onwards, the tendency grew for the journeyman to remain as a journeyman, and the masterships to be restricted to those born in the gild. At the same time, within the gilds themselves, a sharp social distinction between the poorer and richer masters began to manifest itself.

In London the more wealthy gild members could afford to wear the special livery of the gild, and gradually the whole control of the association began to fall into the hands of the "liverymen." The result was that the respective status of the apprentice and journeyman became more rigorously defined. A cleavage began to take place between the actual craftsman and the merchant who sold his produce. The merchants formed themselves into powerful associations, and in this way the important merchant companies such as the Grocers, the Drapers, and the Mercers developed. As we saw earlier in this chapter, the government of St. Paul's School was given to the rich Mercers' Company.

In 1563 the Elizabethan Parliament passed the Statute of Apprentices, which fixed seven years as the period of apprenticeship in all trades and industries, and restricted it to parents who held freehold of the annual value of forty shillings. The enrolling of an apprentice was a solemn ceremony. The would-be apprentice promised to serve his master faithfully and to keep secret the craft mysteries entrusted to him. He bound himself to good behaviour and to remain single during the period of his apprenticeship. The master swore that he would receive the youth into his own house, feed and clothe him, and teach him the craft. The usual age for apprenticeship was twelve.

A written agreement between the parent and the master was drawn up, and when this was signed and sealed, the document was torn into two parts, one being kept by the parent and the other by the master. If any dispute about the terms arose, the two halves of the agreement were produced and, if their jagged or indented edges fitted together, that was proof that the document was genuine. Hence the name "indentures." The parent paid a fee at the signing of the indentures, and during the last years of the apprenticeship the master usually gave the youth a small amount of pocket money. At the end of the apprenticeship, the young man had to decide whether he would work for a master as a journeyman or whether he could afford to open an establishment of his own and become "free of his craft." Before he could do this, it was necessary for him to submit a piece of work of his own for inspection by the master and wardens of his craft.

Some of the members of the livery companies were men of great wealth and became public benefactors by endowing schools and colleges or providing scholarships from the grammar-schools to the universities. Thus Sir Thomas White of Reading instituted a number of scholarships at Oxford to be held by pupils of Reading Grammar School, and later in life (1555), he founded St. John's College, Oxford. Laurence Sheriff, of the Grocers' Company, bequeathed his estates to found Rugby School in 1567. Another member of the same Company, Sir William Laxton, left certain tenements in the City of London to endow a free grammar-school at Oundle in 1556. Another of London's famous merchants was Sir Andrew Judd who was born at Tonbridge. The school formerly attached to the Priory of St. Mary Magdalene had been dispersed at the Dissolution, and Judd determined to restore the educational facilities of the town by endowing a grammar-school. In 1553 he obtained a royal charter and left property in the City and in St. Pancras for his foundation, which was to be administered by the Skinners' Company. In the 19th century, part of this land was sold to the Midland Railway Company at an enhanced value, a transaction which ensured the financial stability of Tonbridge School at a time when rebuilding became necessary. Merchant Taylors' School was founded in 1561 by the Worshipful Company of Merchant Taylors. The moving spirits in the foundation were

Richard Hilles and Sir Thomas White, who were both liverymen of the company.

One effect of the Renaissance upon the universities was the foundation of new colleges. Corpus Christi was founded at Oxford by Bishop Fox of Winchester. His first intention was to found a monastery, but he was dissuaded from this by his friend Bishop Oldham, the founder of Manchester Grammar School, who prophesied, "What, my lord, shall we build houses and provide livelihoods for a company of bussing monks whose end and fall we ourselves may live to see." Corpus Christi was founded in 1516 and its statutes reflect the influence of the Renaissance. The studies of the students were to be mainly classical, and two readers in Greek and Humanity (Latin literature) were appointed. This was the first lectureship in Greek to be established at Oxford. It was ordered that the commentaries of the ancient fathers were to be used instead of those of the mediaeval doctors which "are far inferior in learning as in date." Before their admission, students were able to "write off a Latin letter, to compose fair verses, to have been initiated into logic, and to have some little training in plain song." At Cambridge, Fisher was the first Professor of Divinity, and it was his influence which encouraged Lady Margaret, mother of Henry VII, to found St. John's College.

The outstanding Renaissance foundation was Christ Church, Oxford. Wolsey had contemplated building Cardinal College which should be the most magnificent home of learning in Europe, and, in order to endow it, embarked on the dangerous precedent of suppressing a number of smaller monasteries and using their revenues for his foundation. When Wolsey fell from royal favour, his foundation narrowly escaped suppression. Henry VIII stopped the work for a time, but in 1546 he allowed it to be continued and united the college, under the name of Christ Church, with the new bishopric of Oxford, transferred from Osney. This explains why the dean of Christ Church became the head of a college and of a cathedral chapter.

The Reformation affected the universities by reducing the number of their students and the endowments of the colleges. There was for a time a danger that the universities might suffer the same fate as the monasteries, but Henry VIII was himself no mean scholar and replied to his courtiers whose appetite had not been sated by the spoils of the religious houses, "Sirs, I judge no land in

England better bestowed than that which is given to our Universities." The convents and halls of the religious orders which had formed an important part of mediaeval Oxford and Cambridge were suppressed. At first, Oxford showed considerable opposition to the religious changes, but Cambridge eagerly embraced Protestantism. For some time the attention of students and masters was focused on theological controversy rather than on sound learning.

With the accession of Elizabeth, the fortunes of the universities began to improve, but the Reformation had completely changed their mediaeval character. Oxford had hitherto been the leading university, but now Cambridge took this place, partly because it was a more staunch supporter of the Elizabethan settlement, and partly because Cecil Lord Burleigh, Elizabeth's trusted Minister, was its Chancellor throughout the greater part of the reign. The number of undergraduates preparing for secular careers greatly increased. The college system finally supplanted the halls and lodgings of mediaeval days. Students and masters were compelled to assent to the Thirty-Nine Articles and the royal supremacy.

A change took place in the type of student who entered the universities   The poor scholar of mediaeval times was fast disappearing, and as early as 1549 Latimer declared, in a sermon preached before Edward VI, "There be none now but great men's sons in colleges and their fathers look not to have them preachers." The system by which Fellows of the college acted as private tutors to groups of about half a dozen students was developing. This new departure was on the whole good since the universities had grossly neglected the teaching of students, but it also had its weaknesses in the tendency for the tutor to neglect the poorer scholar in favour of the richer William Harrison wrote in 1587, "The manner to live in these universities is not as in some other of foreign countries we see daily to happen, where the students are enforced for want of such houses to dwell in common inns and taverns, without all order or discipline. But in these our colleges we live in such exact order, and under so precise rules of government, as that ... Erasmus ... did not let to compare the trades in living of students in these two places even with the very rules and orders of the ancient monks. . . . In most of our colleges there are also great numbers of students, of which many are found by the revenues of the houses and other by the purveyances and help of their rich friends. . . . They were erected by their founders at the first only for poor men's sons, whose parents were not able to bring them up unto learning; but now they have the least benefit of them, by reason the rich do so encroach upon them. . . . In some grammar schools likewise which send scholars to these universities, it is lamentable to see what bribery is used; for, ere the scholar can be preferred, such bribage is made that poor men's children are commonly shut out, and the richer sort received. . . . Besides this, being for the most part either gentlemen or rich men's sons, they oft bring the universities into much slander. For, standing upon their reputation and liberty, they ruffle and roist it out, exceeding in apparel and haunting riotous company (which draweth them from their books unto another trade); and for excuse, when they are charged with breach of all good order, think it sufficient to say that they be gentlemen, which grieveth many not a little." [1]

[1] From *Life in Shakespeare's England.*   J. Dover Wilson, pp. 64-5, C.U.P., 1911.

CHAPTER IV

ENGLISH SECONDARY AND UNIVERSITY EDUCATION IN THE 17TH AND 18TH CENTURIES

The spirit of Humanism which had entered the ancient grammar-schools at the Renaissance like a breath of life had almost spent itself at the end of the 16th century. In their curriculum and methods of instruction the schools had settled down to a narrow, formal, and academic outlook which was out of contact with the growing demands of the age. The discovery and settlement of new lands resulting in a great expansion of commerce, the new outlook which was developing as a consequence of the growth of mathematical and scientific knowledge, the freshly awakened spirit of philosophy, and the rich contributions to life and thought made by perhaps the greatest period in the history of our literature, had little impact upon the schools, which concentrated upon the learning of Latin grammar and the rather pedantic study of a few classical authors. More and more, the grammar-schools occupied themselves with the task of preparing their pupils for entrance to the universities, from which they would emerge to become clergymen, lawyers, doctors, or even schoolmasters, and thus help to perpetuate the system. The moribund state of the universities was reflected in the schools.

Even before the end of Elizabeth's reign, dissatisfaction was being expressed with the "gerund-grinding" of the grammar-schools. As the schools and universities were increasingly felt to be out of touch with the growing interests of the outside world, new suggestions were put forward, in the shape of Academies which would supply a type of education lacking in the grammar-schools. As early as 1570, Sir Humphrey Gilbert proposed a "Queen Elizabeth's Academy" which should teach "matters of action meet for present practice, both of peace and war." Besides the classics, Gilbert advocated the study of logic and rhetoric, moral and natural philosophy, law, heraldry, dancing, music, and riding. These subjects were to be taught in English, since the vernacular was the tongue in use in all the operations of everyday life. Gilbert's proposals came to nothing, but they showed the way people were thinking. There were also several interesting attempts either to found new schools or to readapt existing schools so that they would be in closer contact with the changing demands of the times.

One well-known example was the addition to the curriculum of Christ's Hospital. The foundation of this institution was the consequence of a sermon preached before Edward VI by Bishop Ridley. The King was deeply moved and ordered him "to take out of the streets all the fatherless children and other poor men's children that were not able to keep them, and to bring them up to the late dissolved house of the Greyfriars, which they devised to be a Hospital for them, where they should have meat, drink, and clothes, lodging and learning and officers to attend upon them." The work of reconstructing the Franciscan convent was taken in hand, and by November 1552 nearly 400 children were brought into residence. One of the last acts of Edward VI was the signing of a charter, 26th June 1553, which incorporated the five Royal Hospitals. The other four were those of St. Bartholomew, Bethlehem, the Bridewell, and St. Thomas, which were intended as refuges for the sick, maimed, and destitute.

Small as well as older children were admitted to Christ's Hospital, girls as well as boys, and teachers were provided to teach the alphabet, reading, and writing to the younger pupils. If any pupils showed little inclination to learning, as soon as their elementary studies were completed they were to be apprenticed. Many of the boys looked forward to leaving school and entering upon a career of adventure in the Indies or America. It was found necessary to curb this youthful enthusiasm, and a statute was promulgated forbidding children to be sent overseas without the consent of their parents. Those who made good progress in their lessons were to be retained in the school "in the hope of preferrment to the Universitie." In later days these were known as the "Grecians."

In 1673 the Mathematical School of Christ's Hospital was opened to provide for the instruction of forty boys, generally known as "King's Boys," in grammar, arithmetic, and the art of navigation. Charles II promised to pay £1,000 annually for seven years and, after that, £370 10s. each year for apprenticing, to captains of the Indian Navy, those who had completed their course. Books, maps, globes, and mathematical instruments were provided, but in spite of the King's support and the active encouragement of Pepys, Halley, Sir Isaac Newton, and Samuel Travers, the school did not make much headway. The lack of success of this experiment was largely the result of incompetent management.

Christ's Hospital originated as a charity school, and the familiar blue coat, yellow stockings, leather belt, and white neck-band were a badge of servitude, and not, as now, a mark of the antiquity of the foundation. Even at the close of the 18th century the school was still regarded as a high-class charity school. The original building was unable to accommodate all the children, and a daughter house was opened for the younger ones at Hertford. The regulations were gradually changed so that all classes of children, even those not connected with the City of London, could be admitted.

In the 17th century a number of private schools to teach navigation were opened, and some of the grammar-schools near the sea coast included mathematics and navigation in the time-table. Thus, in 1679, Dartmouth Grammar School appointed a master to teach English, navigation, and mathematics. Unfortunately, this broadening of the curriculum only affected a very limited number of schools.

The courtly academy for the education of the sons of the nobility, which flourished on the Continent, never really developed in this country. In 1640 a proposal was made in the House of Lords for founding an academy to train young noblemen and gentlemen, but once more nothing came of it. The English aristocracy preferred to have their sons educated by private tutors. It was towards the end of the 17th century that the differentiation between the great public schools and the remainder of the grammar-schools became more marked. Winchester, because of the scale of its foundation, and Eton, because of its royal patron, had always been pre-eminent amongst the English schools. Other schools, on account of their size or antiquity, or because of the social status of many of their pupils, began to occupy a more prominent position. They were frequently referred to as "the great schools," but the term "public school" had not yet attained its modern significance. One important development should be noted, namely the increase of non-foundation scholars admitted on payment of fees as compared with those on the foundation who received their tuition gratis. The same change was taking place in the smaller grammar-schools. Although compelled by their statutes to admit foundation scholars without payment, many of the schools, owing to depreciation in the value of money, found their endowments insufficient to meet the expenses of the school. The only solution was to admit more fee-payers, and if the statutes forbade this, the school tended to sink into insignificance.   Some schools were fortunate in possessing endowments in real property situated on the outskirts of London and the large towns.   As the cities expanded, the property grew in value and offset, or more than offset, the declining value of money. Others, however, whose endowment consisted of a few fields in the heart of the country, or on the slopes of the Pennines, were very badly hit.   This process was to continue for the next two hundred years, so that, in the mid-19th century, the Taunton Commission considered the term "free grammar-school" a complete misnomer.

Criticisms of the grammar-schools became more frequent in the 17th century, but they had little effect upon the existing institutions. They bore fruit in an entirely new type of school which will be discussed later.   One of the most influential critics was Sir Francis Bacon.   "The position of Bacon in the history of education, as in the history of human thought, is usually either much exaggerated or under-valued.   On the one hand he was not the discoverer of a new method of thought, for he had predecessors as well as co-labourers. . . . Nor on the other hand was he a man who simply repeated what was a time-worn familiarity with all great thinkers." [1]

Bacon's contention was that the universities and schools occupied themselves with words rather than things, and were dominated by the authorities of the past.   He thought that the schools produced too many scholars who proceeded to the universities, and that while the professions tended to be overcrowded there was a lack in the country and towns, of both servants for husbandry and apprentices for trade.   This view was expressed in a letter he wrote to Thomas Sutton, who proposed founding a hospital and school in the Charterhouse of Smithfield.   Bacon's influence on Wolfgang Ratke and Comenius is well known.   The latter was invited to England by the Long Parliament as a member of a commission for the reform of education.   The Civil War made the sitting of the commission impossible, so that after waiting some months, until he saw the hopelessness of the situation, Comenius left for Sweden in 1642.

Milton's *Tractate of Education*, 1644, was still more trenchant in its criticisms of the traditional system.   He considered that the error of the schools was threefold.   They concentrated on formal grammar and exercises in composition, they paid no attention to

---

[1] Paul Monroe. *A Text-Book in the History of Education*, p. 477, Macmillan, 1907.

the literary side of language, and they confined themselves entirely to the language and literature of Greece and Rome. The *Tractate* was dedicated to Master Samuel Hartlib, who was the most enthusiastic advocate in England of the views of Comenius. In a letter to Hartlib, Milton denounced "the many mistakes which have made learning generally so unpleasing and so unsuccessful." Milton's cure as expressed in the *Tractate* was almost as bad as the evil it was intended to mend. He says, quite soundly, "We do amiss to spend seven or eight years merely in scraping together so much miserable Latin and Greek, as might be learnt otherwise easily and delightfully in one year." When, however, he describes the curriculum for a boy from the age of twelve to twenty-one, he gives a most impracticable programme. If carried out in practice, the result would have been mental indigestion, so many and unrelated are the studies advocated. Moreover, the whole of the complicated information was to be gathered from books mainly in Latin and in Greek. The most important contribution of the *Tractate* is Milton's well-known definition of the end of education: "I call therefore a complete and generous education that which fits a man to perform justly, skillfully, and magnanimously all the offices both private and public of Peace and War."

The third critic was John Locke, whose views were expressed both in his philosophical works and in his *Thoughts concerning Education,* 1692. Locke, although himself a product of Westminster School (Hebrew and Arabic were taught to the upper forms in addition to Latin and Greek), thought so badly of the public schools of his age that he preferred to rely on the services of a private tutor. ". . . You think it worth while to hazard your son's innocence and virtue for a little Greek and Latin. How any one's being put into a mixed herd of unruly boys, and there learning to wrangle at Trap or rook at Span Farthing fits him for civil conversation or business, I do not see. And what qualities are ordinarily to be got from such a troop of Play-fellows as Schools usually assemble together from parents of all kinds, that a father should so much covet, is hard to divine." Locke thoroughly disapproved of the studies and methods of teaching in the schools. "When I consider what ado is made about a little Latin and Greek, how many years are spent in it, and what a noise and business it makes to no purpose, I can hardly forbear thinking that the parents of children still live in fear of the Schoolmaster's Rod." The constant repetition needed in order to learn by heart extracts from classical authors, calls forth his scorn. "Languages are to be learned only by reading and talking, and not by scraps of authors got by heart; which when a man's head is stuffed with, he has got the just furniture of a pedant, than which there is nothing less becoming a gentleman." When, however, Locke leaves criticism and comes to the constructive side of his programme, his suggestions are quite as impracticable as those of Milton.   Like the latter, he took an encyclopaedic view and believed in education covering the whole of human knowledge and accomplishments.   It is noteworthy that amongst the subjects he would have taught are French, arithmetic, chronology, history, and geometry.   As the pupil grows older he should learn astronomy, ethics, the civil and common law, and natural philosophy.   In addition, he should be taught certain accomplishments such as riding, fencing, wrestling, and dancing; and should be familiar with at least one trade.

The English grammar-schools were largely unaffected by the criticisms of the period and by the new ideas developing on the Continent.   In justice to them, it is difficult to see how they could have made any major alterations in the traditional curriculum, bound as they were by their foundation-statutes and tied to the Church by the requirements of the licence to teach.   After the Restoration, a new type of school arose which was able to exercise the freedom denied to the older institutions.   The Act of Uniformity and the Five Mile Act were aimed at Protestant Dissenters who carried on the profession of schoolmaster.   At the same time Nonconformist tutors at the universities were expelled.   Many of these tutors opened academies for training candidates for the ministry, but other pupils were accepted as well.   During the 17th century, the academies were carried on more or less under conditions of secrecy.

Thus the academy at Rathmell, near Settle, Yorks, founded by Richard Frankland, the earliest institution of its kind in the north of England, had to move several times during its short existence, 1669-98.   It seems that two distinct colleges were founded in the Newington Green district of London.   The earlier one owes its origin to Theophilus Gale, who was ejected from his Fellowship at Oxford in 1660.   One of his pupils was Isaac Watts, the famous hymnologist.   This college was dissolved in 1705 at the death of Thomas Rowe, Gale's successor.   The second college was due to Charles Morton, who was a distinguished mathematician. It was opened about 1675 and has sometimes been confused with the earlier one. It numbered among its pupils Samuel Wesley, the father of the evangelist, and Daniel Defoe, the author. From these two men we learn a good deal about the curriculum followed. Wesley wrote: "This Academy were indeed the most considerable, having annext a fine Garden, Bowling Green, Fish Pond, and within a laboratory and some not inconsiderable rarities with air-pump, thermometer and all sorts of mathematical instruments." From Defoe we learn that, in addition to the classical languages, the pupils studied French, Italian, Spanish, mathematics, natural science, history, geography, logic, and politics.

The academy at Sheriffhales in Shropshire, where Harley Earl of Oxford and St. John Lord Bolingbroke received their education, is well known. One academy, Gloucester, could boast of two famous pupils who occupied high offices in the Established Church. One was Secker, who became Archbishop of Canterbury, the other Joseph Butler, later Bishop of Durham, the most distinguished English moral philosopher of the 18th century. The Gloucester Academy was originally opened in that city in 1708, but was forced to seek more favourable accommodation at Tewkesbury in 1712. Its principal, Samuel Jones, developed oriental languages as a special study, for, in addition to the classics and mathematics, instruction was given in Hebrew, Chaldee, and Syriac. One of the later academies was Warrington, 1757-86. A very detailed description of the curriculum has been furnished. The course of studies covered three years. In the first year the pupils studied arithmetic, algebra, geometry, and French. The second year's course emphasised mathematics (trigonometry; instruction in navigation was given when desired) and natural science, together with "the easier parts of Astronomy applied to the use of Globes and the general system of the Universe." The concluding year was divided between natural science (chemistry), and morality and Christian evidences. The Academy also provided instruction in writing, drawing and design, bookkeeping, and geography. Joseph Priestley, the discoverer of oxygen and later minister of Mill Hill Chapel, Leeds, was for a time one of the lecturers. In his *Essay on a Course of Liberal Education for Civil and Active Life,* 1765, he describes a curriculum somewhat similar to that adopted at Warrington. He emphasised that the range of studies should include not only those aiming at a university career or one of the learned professions, but also those subjects which would be useful for any department of life.

The reader will have noticed the very wide range of studies proposed in the academies. A later writer criticised their curriculum on the basis that "the grand error in almost every dissenting academy has been the attempt to teach and to learn too much." The encyclopaedic range of studies may have been due to the views of Milton, but it is more likely that the deciding factor was the variety of professions the students had in view, including that of teaching in similar establishments.

When the restrictions upon Dissenters keeping school were removed in 1779, the need for the older academies disappeared. Their place was taken by a large number of private schools opened in London and the large industrial centres, and modelled upon the older academies.   These institutions had a free hand in experiment-ing with new subjects and fresh ideas and provided a pattern for the reform of secondary education in later years.

During the 17th century, the Jesuits attempted to open schools in England.   Stanley Grange was started in 1633.   One of the boys became a Protestant and informed the authorities, who could no longer turn a blind eye to the existence of the school.   It was broken up, but re-formed on a smaller scale in 1638.   There is also evidence that similar schools were opened in other parts of the country.   On the accession of James II, the Jesuits were given permission to establish a school in the Savoy which contained "at least two hundred Catholick Scollers and about as many Protestants," but the Revolution of 1688 brought such ventures to an end.

Locke's denunciation of the grammar and public schools, although it had little effect in improving them, was of considerable assistance in emptying them of some of their most promising pupils. His advice to provide private tutors was followed by large numbers of the upper classes, who sent their sons, after a period of private tuition, to tour the Continent rather than to study at Oxford and at Cambridge.   Private schools sprang up to cater for the needs of the middle classes.   The effect of this is seen in the declining number of pupils at the grammar-schools and of students at the universities.   Another effect was the widening of the distinction between the local and non-local grammar-schools, the latter becoming, in the 18th century, institutions for the education of the wealthier classes.

A very detailed account of the life and studies of an English grammar-school in the middle of the 17th century is presented by

Charles Hoole in his book, *A New Discovery of the Old Art of Teaching Schoole*, published in 1660.[1]   The author was born at Wakefield in 1610, and after being a pupil at Wakefield Grammar School, he studied at Lincoln College, Oxford.   He returned from the university to occupy the post as master of the Free Grammar School at Rotherham, an appointment which he held until 1642. A few years later we find him in London as a very successful teacher of a private school in Aldersgate Street.   In 1660 he became Prebendary of Lincoln, and ended his life as Rector of Stock in Essex.   Thus his treatise contained the fruits of his experience as a practical schoolmaster and incorporated much that he had learned in his school-days from his master at Wakefield, Mr. Robert Doughty.   In addition to his principal work, Hoole published a number of school books, including a version of Comenius's *Orbis Pictus*.   He was also well acquainted with the pedagogical literature of his period, especially Brinsley's *Grammar School*.

The book is divided into four parts with titles as follows: —

I The Petty School.   Shewing a way to teach little children to read English with delight and profit.

II The Usher's Duty, or a Platforme of Teaching Lillies Grammar.

III The Master's Method, or the Exercising of Scholars in Grammars, Authors, and Exercises; Greek, Latine, and Hebrew.

IV Scholastick Discipline, or the Way of ordering a Grammar Schoole, Directing the not-experienced how he may profit every particular Scholar, and avoid confusion amongst a multitude.

Hoole's idea of a petty school, although he thought of it mainly as a means of preparation for the grammar-school, is interesting because it also gave attention to the education of those pupils who would not proceed to study the classics.   These should remain in school and spend their time in reading more English, and in writing and arithmetic.   He declares, in a spirit reminiscent of Mulcaster, that the aim of this additional training is to ensure that the children "will gain such a habit and delight in reading as to make it their chief recreation when liberty is afforded them" (Chap. v).   For this purpose he recommends such works as *The Practice of Piety, The*

---

[1] A modern reprint of Hoole's treatise has been edited by E. T. Campagnac, Liverpool, 1913.

Practice of Quietness, The Whole Duty of Man, to be followed by the reading of *The History of Queen Elizabeth,* or poetry, as Herbert's *Poems* and Quarl's *Emblems.*

Like Mulcaster, Hoole would like to see a petty school in every town and large village, where "all such poor boys as can conveniently frequent it may be taught gratis, but the more able sort of neighbors may pay for their children's teaching as if the school was not free, for they will find it no small advantage to have such a school amongst them" (Chap. vi). He suggests a salary of £20 per annum for the master, with permission to take boarders if he wishes. Hoole had examples of the kind of school he wished to see, for he continues, "And I am rather induced to propound such a thing because that late eminent, Dr. Bathurst, lately deceased, Mr. Gouge, and some others yet living did, out of their own good affection to learning, endeavor at their own charge to promote the like." The petty school should be divided into four forms, and the children of the upper form should take it in turn to be monitors. "Let them every evening, after all the lessons are said, give a bill to the master of their names that are absent, and theirs that have committed any disorder, and let him be very moderate in correcting, and be sure to make a difference betwixt those faults that are viciously enormous and those that are but childish transgressions. Where admonitions readily take place, it is needless trouble to use a rod, and as for a ferule I wish it were utterly banished out of all schools" (Chap. vii). There should be a master to every form and no class should exceed forty in number.

The usher's work is to teach the three lowest forms of the grammar-school.[1] It mainly consists in the teaching of Lily's *Latin Grammar.* Hoole knew how distasteful this study was to schoolboys, and he recommends the use of the *Orbis Pictus,* the pictorial Latin primer produced by Comenius. We can hear the experienced schoolmaster speaking when he says, "There is a great disproportion betwixt a child's capacity and the accidence itself. Children are led most by sense, and the grammar rules, consisting in general doctrines, are too subtile for them. Children's wits are weak, active, and lively, whereas grammar notions are abstractive, dull, and lifeless; boys find no sap nor sweetness in them, because they know not what they mean, and tell them the meaning of the same rule never so often over, their memories are so waterish that the

[1] The work of the different forms is set out in tabular form by Foster Watson in *The Old Grammar Schools,* pp. 101-10, C.U.P., 1916.

impression (if any were made in the brain) is quickly gone out again" (Chap. ii).

The upper three forms are taught by the master. In the fourth form, pupils, after reading the Latin Testament, should be introduced to Greek, and learn to read from the Greek Testament. They should study rhetoric and write Latin verses. Hoole prefers Camden's *Greek Grammar*, "though perhaps it be not so facile or complete as some later printed, especially those that are set out by my worthy friends, Mr. Busbie of Westminster, and Mr. Dugard of Merchant Tailor's School" (Chap. i). Hoole would also make use of the delight that boys find in acting. "When you meet with an act that is full of affection and action, you may cause some of your scholars, after they have learned it, to act it, first in private amongst themselves, and afterwards in the open school before their fellows; and herein you must have a main care of the pronunciation, and acting every gesture to the very life." In the next form they should write Greek verses, and in the sixth they should begin the study of Hebrew. The school should possess a library of about 250 to 300 books, including Latin and Greek authors, grammars, dictionaries, works on rhetoric and on theology, medicine, and law. The type of library Hoole had in mind may still be seen at such schools as the Wakefield and Richmond (Yorks) Grammar Schools.

The last division of the book on discipline gives much information about the daily routine of the school. Hoole distinguishes between the "great" or collegiate schools, "classical" or grammar-schools, and "mixed" schools which taught both petties and grammarians. Many of the latter were unsatisfactory, partly because "the master is overburdened with too many petty scholars" and partly because many of the parents "will not spare their children to learn if they can but find them any employment about their domestic affairs, whereby they may save a penny." Another source of weakness is the constant change of ushers, who leave their schools "as soon as they can fit themselves for a more easy profession, or obtain a more profitable place."

We learn that these schools occasionally sent a bright pupil to the university, though this was more commonly the function of the grammar-school. The latter suffered from the competition of the "great schools" and had but few scholarships to offer. Hoole's remarks about the condition of English education anticipate the conclusions of the royal commissions in the middle of the 19th century: "Comparing all the schools which we have in England with some that I read of in other countries . . . we evidently see how many places of education beyond the seas do quite outstrip us."

Many boys came to the grammar-school without having passed through a petty school. Hoole recommends that they should be sent to a writing-and-arithmetic master in the nearest town. Sometimes an itinerant teacher of writing would visit a country grammar-school, and, after giving the younger boys a grounding, would leave the master to give them further practice. "The best season for such a man's coming is about May Day, partly because the days are then pretty long, and partly because it will be requisite for such as are then getting their grammar rudiments, to learn to write before they come to translations."

School holidays generally consisted of a fortnight at Christmas, Easter, and Whitsuntide, respectively. School hours were as long as in Tudor times. Lessons commenced at six or seven o'clock in the morning and lasted until eleven. The afternoon sessions finished at three on Thursdays, four on Tuesdays, and five on Mondays, Wednesdays, and Fridays. Saturday was a holiday.

Hoole was evidently a good practical schoolmaster who put into operation ideas he had obtained from Mulcaster and Brinsley, but we look in vain for any conceptions of a wider and more liberal character, for example those advocated by Milton or the Continental reformers such as Comenius or Hartlib. If the curriculum of so outstanding a schoolmaster was as restricted as Hoole's treatise shows, we wonder what the condition of schools run by lesser men must have been.

If the 17th century witnessed the decline of the grammar-schools, the 18th century displayed secondary education at its very lowest level. Two causes were contributory. One was the steady decline in the standards of both social and official life during the reigns of the first two Georges. There is no need to stress the wholesale corruption of public life under the long dominance of Walpole, the cold formality of the religion of the Established Church, and the deterioration in morals and manners of all classes of the community. All this occurred when the thin veneer of culture, which was shown so prominently in early 18th-century literature, concealed the real disintegration which was taking place in English life and manners. The 18th century was a most astounding period in history. At the top was a culture which has had few equals in its polish and refinement. The middle classes were self-satisfied and sensual. The one quality which received universal condemnation was enthusiasm. Throughout the century the governing classes were acutely aware of the danger of revolution coming from below. The manners, morals, and life, of the submerged classes cause the modern student conflicting feelings of pity and disgust.

The other cause was the slow transition during which England, from being almost an entirely agricultural country, became the leading industrial nation of the world.

The governments of the time did not understand what was happening, and failed to control or direct the course of the Industrial Revolution. Hence it was allowed to take its own course, until the evils which it engendered grew to such magnitude that at length government intervention became a necessity.

Yet, at the same time, this astounding century represented a most glorious epoch in the history of our country. It was an age when the Empire grew at a most rapid rate, and even the check to its growth occasioned by the American revolt was compensated by the acquisition of new territories in Australia and India. The restrained classical style in literature gave way to the warmth and emotional fervour of the Romantic revival of the early 19th century. Great things were accomplished in art, music, natural science, philosophy, discovery, and invention. Finally, the philanthropic and humanitarian movements prepared the way and were in turn fostered by a new outburst of religious fervour both inside and outside the Established Church, and laid the foundations of the social reforms and educational progress of the next century.

It was not, however, until the close of the century that these developments affected secondary education. The grammar-schools, bound by their foundation statutes, were unable to change their narrow classical curriculum even if they wished to. Some schools with meagre endowments became institutions which provided only an elementary education.

Carlisle, in his *Endowed Grammar Schools of England and Wales,* lists 475 schools. In addition to those schools which returned no answer to his questionnaire, eighty-two had either ceased to exist or had become primary schools by 1818. In his preface, he writes: "It is painful, however, to relate, that many of our numerous and ample Endowments have fallen to decay, by the negligence or cupidity of ignorant or unprincipled Trustees; who have silently, or by connivance, suffered the furtive alienation of the very Lands which they were called upon so solemnly to defend, and which were in great measure ordained for the Education of their own Children." The following are typical of the comments made by Carlisle: —

Childrey, near Wantage: "It is at present 'a mere Day-school,' in which the children of the Parish are taught to write and read, by a Master who barely possesses these attainments himself."

(Vol. I, p. 33.)

Buckingham: "It is of little note in any respect,—none but the children of the Lower classes having been educated here, for time immemorial. There are six boys only in the School." (*Ibid.*, p. 47.)

Saffron Walden: "The School-room has lately been repaired by The Corporation, and One Hundred and Forty boys are daily taught therein on The National System of Education."

(*Ibid.*, p. 442.)

Bishop's Stortford: "The Grammar School of Bishop's Stortford no longer exists. The whole Establishment, together with the School-house, is in ruins. The Library, which is considered a scarce and valuable collection of books, is deposited at The Vicarage, but they are also going to decay." (*Ibid.*, p. 554.)

Banbury (the school of John Standbridge): "for many years past it has totally ceased—and the building in which it was kept, is now let to a Plush Manufacturer by The Corporation."

(Vol. II, p. 294.)

Monk's Kirby, Warwickshire (endowment £300): "The Master is most illiterate and unfit for the office. He attends occasionally at the School, where he has nothing to do, and there is no Usher appointed." (*Ibid.*, p. 600.)

Pocklington, Yorks (endowment £1,000-£1,200): "The Lower School-room is made use of as a Saw-pit and Barn,—that the Master has not attended for the last Twelve months—and that the Usher, being deaf, the Children have necessarily been sent to other Schools." (*Ibid.*, p. 864.)

A few schools, showing more courage and initiative than the rest, added such modern subjects as elementary mathematics, modern languages, bookkeeping, and dancing. As these were extras and involved the engagement of additional staff, special fees were charged to pupils taking these subjects. The attempt of the grammar-schools to improve their condition received a severe shock at the hands of the Lord Chancellor, Lord Eldon, in the decision which he gave in the well-known Leeds Grammar School case. As in most schools, the number of pupils at Leeds had steadily declined, and during the years 1791-6 reached its low-water mark of forty-four. The Committee of Charitable Uses, which acted as the governing body of the school, suggested bad teaching and a deterioration in discipline as partial causes, but attributed the main cause to the inadequacy of the curriculum. The only subjects taught were Latin, Greek, and divinity, although the fact that John Smeaton, the famous engineer and builder of the Eddystone lighthouse, was a pupil of the school, suggests that some mathematics was taught to selected pupils. Leeds at this time was an example of one of the growing industrial and commercial communities springing up over a large part of northern England. The curriculum of the grammar-school was unlikely to attract the wealthy manufacturers and merchants of the town. Accordingly, as early as 1777, the Committee resolved "as soon as convenient with respect to Rents and Profits of School to appoint a Master for the purpose of teaching to Write and Account such Boys as shall attend at the Free School to learn Latin and Greek, and also that another Master shall be appointed to teach the French tongue and other Foreign languages, and that sufficient salaries shall be appointed for such masters."

Nothing, however, was done about the matter until the appointment of Mr. Whiteley as headmaster in 1789. A sub-committee, called to consider the introduction of the new subjects, reported that Mr. Whiteley did not agree and that he was supported by the Usher. The only way out of the difficulty was an appeal to the law-courts. In 1797 a Master in Chancery held an inquiry whether it would be "proper and for the benefit of the Charity to have any other Master or masters to teach writing, arithmetic, and other languages besides the Greek and the Latin." He quoted the testimony of the Committee that Leeds had "a very extensive Foreign Trade" and that the introduction of new studies would be useful to the townsfolk and increase the number of pupils. He added that there was nothing in the endowment which excluded the teaching of any useful kind of learning and he suggested adding a German and a French master, and one to teach mathematics. As for writing and arithmetic, there was a variety of schools catering for these subjects, and to teach them free at the grammar-school would harm these institutions rather than benefit the townsfolk.

The report did not satisfy the Committee and drew forth the protest from the masters that the "School was intended for a Grammar School only, and not for algebra, the mathematics or the modern languages." In view of this disagreement, the case was heard by Lord Eldon as Lord Chancellor. In his judgment, delivered in July 1805, he emphasised that the argument must stand or fall by the facts and not by expediency. The intention of the founder was to establish a grammar-school, and, according to Dr. Johnson, a grammar-school was defined as an institution "for teaching grammatically the learned languages." The court could not sanction "the conversion of that Institution by filling a school intended for that mode of Education with scholars learning the German and French languages, Mathematics, and anything save Greek and Latin." The policy of the Committee would turn the school into a commercial academy. "This is a scheme to promote the benefits of the Merchants of Leeds. It is not that the poor Inhabitants are to be taught reading and writing English, but the Clerks and Riders of the Merchants are to be taught French and German to carry on a Trade. I fear the effect would be to turn out the poor Latin and Greek scholars altogether."

Leach comments on the case as follows: "This decision carried dismay to all interested in the advancement of education and nearly killed half the schools in the country." In justice to Lord Eldon, it may be said that he had before him numerous examples of grammar-schools which were no longer grammar-schools, but which had in fact become primary schools. He also showed respect to the declared intentions of the founder and brushed aside the plea that had the founder lived in modern times his bequest would have been worded differently. Lord Eldon's attitude presents a striking contrast to many education authorities, central and local, who seem to ride roughshod over the intentions of founders as expressed in the foundation-deeds of schools.

Leach's comment is not fully justified, for even at Leeds we find that Mr. Whiteley himself appointed additional masters and volunteered to teach mathematics to the higher forms, and in 1806 the Committee resolved (a) "that the teaching under proper restrictions of branches of the Mathematics as are usually taught to young men proceeding to their admission to the University would induce Persons to send their Boys to the School to learn Greek and Latin and would thereby tend to promote the object of the Founder"; (b) no boy should learn any other science unless at the same time "he pursued also Classical learning"; (c) "that no boy should start the learning of other sciences until he could construe the Latin Testament."

Subsequent decisions by Lord Eldon supported the judgment delivered in the Leeds Grammar School case, and he has been frequently charged with delaying the cause of reform for two generations. The truth is that he was determined to uphold the essential features of the grammar-schools as enunciated by their founders, but he was not averse to the introduction of other subjects provided the studies specified in the foundation were taught. The introduction of modern subjects in the very school in which the dispute had arisen makes his point of view sufficiently clear. Several large grammar-schools which possessed enough funds for the purpose obtained private Acts of Parliament authorising the introduction of subjects not mentioned in the foundation. An example is Macclesfield, which obtained a private Act in 1838, enabling the governors to establish a Modern Free School in addition to the grammar-school. Modern subjects (exclusive of the classics) could be taught subject to the consent of the governors. After an unsuccessful attempt in Parliament to reverse Lord Eldon's decision, the Grammar Schools Act of 1840 gave freedom to grammar-school governors to introduce subjects other than those provided for in the foundation.

The condition of the public schools was almost as deplorable as the grammar-schools, and their curriculum was just as restricted. Dr. Thomas James, who was headmaster of Rugby from 1778 to 1794 and who was a really able schoolmaster, has left us minute details of the 18th-century public-school curriculum. When Dr. Butler, who had been an assistant at Rugby, was appointed to Shrewsbury, he sought advice from his old Head. James replied willingly and in great detail. Not only did he give advice about the methods of running a large boarding-school, but he also furnished detailed information about the work of the different forms at Rugby. Dr. Butler's famous grandson, the author of *Erewhon,* included this account in the life of his grandfather. From this we learn that the bulk of the work of the lower forms to the VIth was entirely classical. In the lowest form the boys learnt nothing but Latin grammar. In the second and third forms certain authors were studied and the pupils worked exercises in Latin prose and verse composition. Greek was begun in the third form, and through-out the school the unending grind at grammar, translation, Latin and Greek prose, and verse exercises went on.   Any other subjects were taught on what were supposedly holidays.   On holidays the boys attended school from ten to eleven in the morning and two to three in the afternoon.   On half-holidays they attended from two to three o'clock.   In these periods the lower forms learnt writing and arithmetic, and the fifth form geography and algebra. It is probable that the latter subject was taught by Dr. James himself.   At any rate, he afterwards confessed that this weekly mathematical period "wearied his body to excess and made it hot, or, at any rate, perspire too much."   Some years earlier, in 1766, James had prepared an account of the work done at Eton, and we find it followed lines similar to those at Rugby.

The moral state of the schools came in for some sharp criticism. It was asserted that the life of the pupils was rough and brutal, and many parents from the wealthier sections of the community so dreaded sending their sons to the larger boarding-schools that they either utilised the services of private tutors or sent them on the Grand Tour.   It was in this way that many of the polished gentle-men scholars of the 18th century were produced, a type well exemplified by Ashley Cooper, the "elegant" Earl of Shaftesbury, who was a pupil of Locke.   Even in the best schools the admini-stration was chaotic, the school under-staffed, and the boarding arrangements most unsatisfactory.   The food was often scanty and ill-cooked.   After lesson-periods little supervision was exercised by the masters.   In some schools, after prep, the boys were driven into the dormitories, the doors locked and not opened until it was time to rise for morning meal and school.   Bullying and fagging were almost universal.   The latter custom, athough it seemed so objectionable to the outsider, does not seem to have been objected to by the boys themselves, who took it as part of the nature of things that the smaller boys should look after the wants of their seniors.   The picture of life at Rugby presented in *Tom Brown's Schooldays* is a true one.   Cowper, who had been educated at Westminster, once wrote: "Great schools suit but the sturdy and the rough."

Discipline was usually maintained by flogging.   Lamb's account of James Boyer, his old master at Christ's Hospital, presents a picture common to the age.   He concludes his description of Boyer's ferociousness and brutality with the words, "Perhaps we cannot dismiss him better than with the pious ejaculation of C— when he heard that his old master was on his death-bed; 'Poor J.B.!—may all his faults be forgiven; and may he be wafted to bliss by little cherub boys, all head and wings, with no bottoms to reproach his sublunary infirmities.' " Flogging was not the only form of punishment at Christ's. Lamb's descriptions of solitary confinement in fetters, and public scourging, fill the modern reader with horror. Without attempting to defend the disciplinary methods of the 18th and early 19th centuries we have to bear in mind that the universal practice of flogging in schools was part and parcel of the attitude to life adopted at that time. An age which began with the use of the pillory and stocks for minor offences and hanged the small pilferer, which later sanctioned transportation to Botany Bay and suffered the sight of the bodies of criminals hanging on gibbets, was not likely to be unduly disturbed by the flogging of schoolboys.

Locke was at Westminster as a pupil of Dr. Busby, whose name has been handed down the ages as the type of the flogging schoolmaster. Perhaps the flogging by Dr. Busby aimed at achieving something like the hardening and toughening process which Locke recommended in his *Thoughts on Education.* Two masters at Eton have been made famous by their flogging activities. One was George Heath, headmaster from 1792 to 1801. Tradition has it that on one occasion he administered ten cuts with two birches to each of seventy boys, and that as a result he was laid up with aches and pains for more than a week. This was probably his reply to the open defiance of his orders by the fifth form and some of the juniors who "shirked" the six o'clock absence and rowed up the Thames as far as Maidenhead. The other headmaster famous for his flogging was Dr. Keate. All kinds of legends have grown round the latter and it is difficult to discover how far they are true. There is, for example, very little foundation for the story that Keate, in explaining the meaning of the Beatitudes, said, "Blessed are the pure in heart. Mind that, it's your duty to be pure in heart. If you are not pure in heart, I'll flog you." A better-authenticated story is that of Keate flogging the boys who had been sent to him for instruction as Confirmation candidates. The mistake can be easily explained. The list of the candidates was on a piece of paper of the same size and shape as that which bore the names of offenders. Many of Keate's old pupils have recorded that at heart he was really a kindly man and that his ferociousness was assumed. Keate was called to the headmastership of Eton at a very difficult and critical time. His predecessor was Dr. Goodall, who was appointed Provost of Eton in 1809. During Dr. Goodall's time, discipline had become very relaxed and the boys had got completely out of hand. The school was ridiculously under-staffed, eight or nine masters for between five hundred and six hundred boys in the upper school. The average number of boys in the class of an assistant master was seventy. When Keate took over he had the tremendous task of creating order from chaos, and he employed the only means that the old-time schoolmaster knew. He was a first-class scholar, but he had the impossible task of teaching the upper fifth and sixth forms together, a total of 170 boys. His first problem was to enforce some kind of order, but he did not always succeed in this. On winter evenings, when the upper school was illuminated by the dim light of candles, the boys were able to hum tunes and throw bread pellets at one another without much chance of being discovered. No wonder that the masters were severe to cruelty under conditions such as these, and small wonder that the schoolboys regarded their masters as natural enemies and judged any form of escape, whether by lying or cheating, as fully justified. Keate took it for granted that every boy would lie to him, and so most of them did.

At times the pupils rose in actual revolt. Every great boarding-school has its story of schoolboy insurrection in the latter years of the 18th and the early years of the 19th century. Winchester led in rebellion, but was soon followed by Rugby and Eton. The school most affected by rebellions was Harrow. The great rebellion at Rugby in 1797 was so serious that the military were called out and the Riot Act read. It would not be true to say that all these revolts were caused by bad conditions. Even the most enlightened schoolmasters had to face them. Schoolboys have always been creatures of tradition, and when the school at Shrewsbury rose against Butler, although the reason given was bad feeding, it was really a protest against Butler's endeavour to tighten up discipline. James was troubled with two revolts at Rugby because he denied to his praepostors the right to flog. Keate had to face a very serious rebellion in 1818 when five boys smashed his desk to pieces with a sledge-hammer. He quelled this by his usual vigorous methods and was able to report in his diary that "the boys are as quiet as lambs." The last revolt at Eton took place in 1832.

Some writers, such as Gibbon and Goldsmith, wrote in praise of the public schools, but in spite of what they had to say, the fact remained that many of the schools declined noticeably in numbers. The prestige of an able headmaster temporarily resulted in a rise in numbers which began to fall immediately a less capable man took his place. Between 1610 and 1800, Winchester fluctuated considerably. Although the "scholars" remained at the original number of seventy, the "commoners," who were as numerous as 123 in 1734, fell to eight in 1751. James at Rugby, Butler at Shrewsbury, Barnard at Eton, and Thackeray at Harrow, are examples of outstanding headmasters. When James was appointed to Rugby in 1778 he found the school nothing more than an ordinary county grammar-school. He left it as a first-class school. Samuel Butler always declared, in his rather perverse way, that James was a much better schoolmaster than Arnold.

The foremost headmaster of this time was Dr. Samuel Butler of Shrewsbury. A great deal is known about him from the biography written by his better-known grandson. The latter's *Life and Letters of Dr. Butler* throws a remarkable light upon the 18th-century public schools. Butler was appointed to the school in 1798. It was practically a dead school; some accounts say that it had declined to three pupils. Butler was an accomplished scholar and a magnificent teacher. Through his inspiring headmastership, Shrewsbury turned out many scholars who were a signal success at the universities. Although he was a great believer in the classics, he encouraged his boys to read widely in private, and his teaching was of a kind that he "certainly did succeed in making us believe that Latin and Greek were the only things worth living for." [1] In the days when examinations, even at the universities, were a farce, Butler instituted regular examinations in the school and got to know his boys and their capabilities. He was a great believer in the competitive spirit and spent much time in making out order-of-merit lists from which he could ascertain which pupils were worthy of "merit" money.

Although he was a quick-tempered man, he thoroughly understood boys. He tried to break down the barrier between boys and masters and, unlike Keate, he trusted boys. The great Charles Darwin was one of his pupils. In spite of Butler's skill and enthusiasm, Darwin did not take kindly to classics. He was interested in chemistry and in collecting minerals and insects. He tells us that because of his interest in chemistry he was nicknamed "Gas" by his schoolfellows. Butler rebuked him for his interest

---

[1] Dr. Butler was the author of *Modern and Ancient Geography for the use of Schools*, and of *An Atlas of Modern Geography*, both of which were extensively used in the early 19th century.

in chemistry. In his autobiography, Darwin says: "Nothing could have been worse for my mind than this school, as it was strictly classical, nothing else being taught, except a little ancient geography and history. The school as a means of education to me was simply a blank. . . . The sole pleasure I ever received from such studies was from some of the odes of Horace, which I admired greatly."

Butler often tried to reason with his older boys, but he emphatically believed in flogging younger pupils, and he told parents that if they did not approve of his flogging small boys for idleness they could take their sons away from the school. In many ways Butler was limited by the traditions of the age in which he lived, but his strong and forceful personality raised Shrewsbury to the first rank of English schools.

The greater toleration of the 18th century allowed a few Roman Catholic schools to open. At first they were small institutions providing an elementary education. One of the best-known was "Dame Alice's School," taught by Alice Harrison at Fernyhalgh in the Fylde. Pupils came not only from the district but even from Liverpool, Manchester, and London, and these were lodged in the neighbouring cottages. One of the most prosperous preparatory schools was at Twyford, where the poet Alexander Pope received his early schooling. He distinguished himself by writing lampoons on the master and even scratched one on the window. It is said that he was flogged for this escapade and left the school. Meanwhile the Catholic colleges on the Continent had continued with varying fortunes. Douai entered upon the most flourishing period of its existence, while the college at St. Omer had just begun to prosper when the order expelling the Jesuits from France was promulgated. The French Government intended to hand over the whole institution to the secular clergy, but the Fathers and their pupils forestalled them by moving unexpectedly to Bruges which was then in Austrian territory. After the suppression of the Jesuits by Clement XIV the school sought refuge in Liége.

The two streams of Catholic education, that on the Continent and that in England, were brought together by the French Revolution. The thousands of refugees who fled to England had resulted in a great growth of tolerance, and when the Jesuits came to this country they were offered a home at Stonyhurst. The seculars had some difficulty in finding a permanent home, but in 1808 they were able to establish their college at Ushaw. The Benedictines opened a school at Ampleforth in 1806. The Catholic Emancipation Act of 1829 removed their difficulties with the exception of membership of the older universities.

The 17th century saw several important developments within the universities. The independent position which was being achieved by the colleges had been strengthened by the Elizabethan statutes of 1570, but the work of Archbishop Laud, whose name will always be associated with Oxford, put the finishing touch to this development. Laud became Chancellor of the university in 1630, and in 1636 gave it a set of statutes, under which it was governed until the middle of the 19th century. They superseded the confused collection of existing statutes, but strengthened the power of the colleges, and especially of the Heads of colleges, against that of the university. From this time, for about two hundred years, the government of the university was controlled by the Heads of colleges, who formed a close oligarchy. The new governing body consisted of the Heads of Houses, two Proctors nominated by the colleges in turn, and a Vice-Chancellor, who was always to be a Head. It was called the Hebdomadal Council, and its consent had to be obtained before any new statute could be discussed by the convocation of masters and doctors. Laud certainly improved the discipline of the university, and his detailed scheme of examination for the B.A. and M.A. degrees represented a considerable advance upon previous practice. Unfortunately, his statutes remained binding upon the university when conditions had greatly changed. The Laudian statutes did not affect Cambridge, which continued under the Elizabethan code until the middle of the 19th century. There the governing body was known as the *Caput Senatus* and was composed of the Vice-Chancellor, a Doctor from each of the three faculties, and a regent and non-regent Master of Arts respectively. The *Caput* was elected by the Heads of colleges, but the freedom of election became restricted, and at the beginning of the 18th century it was usual to vote only for those names on the Vice-Chancellor's list. Every grace had to be approved by the *Caput* before it could be submitted to the Senate.

Laud's work identified Oxford with the Royalist cause, and one of the first acts of the Puritans when they gained power in 1644 was to expel all those who were not in sympathy with the Parliamentary party. During the Civil War, Oxford had been the Royalist head-quarters, and it only surrendered to Fairfax when Charles was finally defeated. Needless to say, during these turbulent times the studies of the university suffered and only about fifty students graduated each year.

In the early part of the century, new colleges were founded, *e.g.* Wadham (1610) and Pembroke (1624) at Oxford, and Trinity at Cambridge was rebuilt. During the reign of James I the universities were granted parliamentary representation, which they retained until legislation in 1948 deprived them of this privilege.

At the Restoration, the Fellows and Heads of colleges who had been expelled by the Puritans came back. The Act of Uniformity, 1662, required Heads of colleges to conform to the Book of Common Prayer, and those who refused were expelled. It was because of this that the Nonconformist academies, described earlier in this chapter, were opened.

Wadham College, Oxford, played an important part in the founding of the Royal Society. The Puritans had expelled the Warden and many of the Fellows and appointed John Wilkins, brother-in-law to Cromwell, as Warden. Wilkins was a very distinguished scholar, and after the Restoration was made Bishop of Chester. Amongst his friends were John Wallis, who became Professor of Mathematics at Oxford in 1648 ; Sprat, afterwards Bishop of Rochester, the historian of the Royal Society ; and Seth Ward, who became Savilian Professor of Astronomy. These scholars were interested in the development of science, and held regular meetings at Gresham College, London, and Wadham College, Oxford. Other members of the "Invisible College" were Sir Christopher Wren, who had been a commoner at Wadham, and Sydenham, the founder of modern medicine. It was after a lecture by Wren in 1660 that the proposal to form what was later the Royal Society was made. Two of the most prominent members of the Royal Society in the Restoration period were Robert Boyle and Isaac Newton, who became Professor of Mathematics at Cambridge in 1669. It was owing to Newton that Cambridge gained a reputation in mathematics which has been maintained ever since.

During the 18th century the two universities, like the public schools and grammar-schools, reached their lowest point. Cambridge was a strong supporter of the Whigs, whilst Oxford was well known for its Jacobite sympathies. As mentioned earlier in this chapter, many members of the well-to-do classes preferred their sons to be in the charge of a private tutor rather than send them to the public schools and the universities. The admissions to Oxford and Cambridge fell rapidly, and an increasing number of students left before taking their first degree. A considerable number of new professorships had been established during the last century, but some Chairs were so poorly remunerated that they failed to attract men of learning and ability. Most of the actual teaching was undertaken by the college tutors. The Fellows have been described as lazy and self-indulgent, and were frequently compared with the monks of the 15th century. Gibbon's description of their habits is well known. "They were decent easy men, who supinely enjoyed the gifts of the founder ; their days were filled by a series of uniform employments ; the chapel and the hall, the coffee-house and the common room, till they retired, weary and well satisfied to a long slumber. From the toil of reading or thinking or writing they had absolved their conscience ; and the first shoots of learning and ingenuity withered on the ground, without yielding any fruits to the owners or the public. Their conversation stagnated in a round of college business, Tory politics, personal stories and private scandal ; their dull and deep potations excused the brisk intemperance of youth." The Fellows were in some respects to be pitied. Election to a Fellowship provided a poor student with what was relatively a good income for life, provided he remained celibate and lived in residence. Not all those obtaining election were such as to find fulfilment in a purely intellectual and academic life. The only escape was to obtain clerical preferment.

At the present day the Fellow has a choice of a considerable number of occupations. Teaching- or examining-work may be his preference, or he may take a part in the administration of his college, or become an active member of some of the boards and committees which regulate university affairs. He may engage in some line of research and record the additions he has made to the knowledge of his subject by publishing the results of his work. In the 18th century, however, no suitable outlet existed for his activities. His share in the management of his college was infinitesimal and was confined to acquiescence in the decrees of the governing body of the university. College tuition occupied only a fraction of his day, and even the most energetic must have found time hanging on their hands. If he wished to take part in activities outside the university his intentions were frustrated by the fact that non-residence might lead to the loss of his Fellowship. Occasionally the condition of residence might be waived to allow him to become tutor to some young nobleman. Small wonder, then, that many Fellows took the easiest way out of their difficulties by settling down to a comfortable life, which their modest competence allowed them. It was possible for a Fellow to live in a fair degree of comfort on an income of £100 a year, although quite a number received less than this. For the more active, a Fellowship was merely a stepping-stone to a more lucrative appointment in the future.[1]

Much has been said and written on the subject of professors who never lectured. Trevelyan tells us that "no lecture was delivered by any Regius Professor of Modern History at Cambridge between 1725 and 1773; 'the third and most scandalous' of the holders of that Chair died in 1768 from a fall while riding home drunk from his Vicarage at Over." [2] At Oxford, two-thirds of the

---

[1] That amusing publication known as the *Oxford Sausage* or *Select Poetical Pieces written by the most celebrated wits of the University of Oxford*, affords a commentary on what has been said above. Thus, in the parody on Gray's *Elegy* entitled *An Evening Contemplation in a College*, the following lines occur:

> "Within those walls, where through the glimm'ring shade
> Appear the pamphlets in a mouldr'ing heap,
> Each in his narrow bed till morning laid,
> The peaceful fellows of the college sleep.
>
> The tinkling bell proclaiming early prayers,
> The noisy servants rattling o'er their head,
> The calls of business, and domestic cares,
> Ne'er rouze these sleepers from their downy bed.
>
> No chatt'ring females crowd their social fire,
> No dread have they of discord and of strife;
> Unknown the names of husband and of sire,
> Unfelt the plagues of matrimonial life.
>
> Oft have they bask'd along the sunny walls,
> Oft have the benches bow'd beneath their weight:
> How jocund are their looks when dinner calls!
> How smoke the cutlets on their crowded plates!"

The poem called the *Progress of Discontent* relates how an undergraduate enters college and, "Our pupil's hopes, though twice defeated, Are with a scholarship completed." At length he obtains a fellowship, but he soon becomes discontented, and muses,

> "These fellowships are pretty things,
> We live, indeed, like petty kings;
> But who can bear to waste his whole age
> Amid the dullness of a college,
> Debarr'd the common joys of life,
> And that prime bliss—a loving wife?
> Oh! what's a table richly spread
> Without a woman at its head!
> Would some snug benefice but fall,
> Ye feasts, ye dinners, farewell all!"

The editor of the *Oxford Sausage* was Thomas Warton (1728-90), who was not only Poet Laureate but held the posts of Professor of Poetry and Camden Professor of History. He has been described as an accomplished critic of other men's poems.

[2] G. M. Trevelyan. *English Social History*, p. 366, Longmans Green, 1946.

professors never lectured, and those who did seldom had an audience. It is, however, only fair to mention that some Chairs were established for subjects not required for examination, and hence such studies only attracted a small number of students. There were some brilliant exceptions to the usual custom. Newton, the principal of Hertford, not only lectured, but insisted that his Fellows should follow his example. Blackstone was another exception, and his *Commentaries on the Laws of England* were based on lectures which he had delivered. Lowth, who was Professor of Poetry and Fellow of New College, became famous for his lectures on Isaiah.

The training of undergraduates was mainly in the hands of the college tutors. It is important to remember that, although the age of matriculation had been gradually rising, yet a large number of students matriculated at fifteen and a few at a younger age. Thus the bulk of undergraduates were boys in their early 'teens. They were too old for school discipline, but not old enough to take responsibility for their own conduct and studies. It was felt that they stood in need of a tutor and governor. One must not suppose, therefore, that the paucity of university lectures meant that no teaching of any consequence was done in the university. "The non-academic world, not interesting itself in the rather obscure relation between Colleges and the University, seldom takes the trouble to define its ideas as to different kinds of academic education. It rests for the most part content with a vague and incurious belief that University teaching is represented by the Professoriate; and if Professors do not teach, then there can be no University teaching, and therefore obviously no teaching in the University. This view ignores the College tutor: and although it is true that Colleges in general, as distinct from the University, have had their moments of educational inefficiency, it is by no means safe to assume that at any period within the last two centuries Oxford has been untaught because her Professors were silent or unheard." [1]   Examinations were a complete farce. Lord Chancellor Eldon describes his examination in 1770 for a first degree. He presented himself in Hebrew and history. The first question asked was: "What is the Hebrew for the place of the skull?" When he replied, "Golgotha," he was then asked: "Who founded University College?" In deference to the ancient legend, Eldon answered, "King Alfred," whereupon the

[1] A. D. Godley. *Oxford in the Eighteenth Century*, p. 38, Methuen, 1909.

examiner declared, "Very well, sir, you are competent for your degree."

Vicesimus Knox, who was admitted to St. John's College, Oxford, in 1771, describes how the forms of the mediaeval disputations were still maintained. The candidate for the B.A. degree was obliged some time during the four years he spent at the university to "oppose" and "respond." This process was usually known as "doing generals." The topics for disputation were handed down from generation to generation and consisted of "foolish syllogisms on foolish subjects, of the foundation or significance of which the respondent and opponent seldom knew more than an infant in swaddling cloaths." On the day of examination, the respondent and opponent took their places in a large, dusty room full of dirt and cobwebs. Here they had to sit opposite to each other for two hours. On rare occasions an examiner would enter, listen for a few minutes to a syllogism, and depart without saying a word. "The disputants would then return to the amusement of cutting the desks, carving their names, or reading Sterne's *Sentimental Journey* or some other edifying novel." To complete his test for the degree, the candidate was obliged to "answer under bachelor," a form of disputation similar to the earlier one, and to present himself before the examiners, who questioned him on the matter contained in a few little books of questions and answers which the candidate had spent three or four days in learning by heart. The examiners were Masters of Arts chosen by the candidate and were frequently his pot-companions. "If the vice-chancellor and proctors happen to enter the school . . . a little solemnity is put on." Otherwise, "the examiners and the candidates often converse on the last drinking bout, or on horses, or read the newspapers or a novel."

Cambridge never sank as deep in lethargy as Oxford, and was the first to begin internal reforms. "In 1747-48 the first 'Tripos' list was published, and the name had a mediaeval origin. In the 15th century, the 'ould bachelor' who disputed with the candidates had sat on a three-legged stool and was known as 'Mr. Tripos'. . . he had been in the habit of writing frivolous verses on the subject of disputation. These were known as 'Tripos Verses' and survived after the 'ould bachelor' had disappeared from the scene. In 1747 the custom was begun of printing the candidates' names in order of merit on the back of the sheet of verses, and hence the name Tripos came to be applied to the examination itself." [1] Cambridge

---

[1] S. C. Roberts. *Op. cit.*, p. 30.

introduced written examinations about 1722. At Oxford the Public Examinations Statute added a written examination to the oral and introduced the distinction between pass and honours. The reforms at Oxford were due to Dr. Cyril Jackson of Christ Church (1783-1809), Dr. Parsons, who was Master of Balliol from 1798, and Dr. John Everleigh, the Provost of Oriel. The *viva-voce* test was retained, but the written examinations began to carry more weight.

In spite of the prevailing deadness, however, there was still some life left in the ancient universities. Nearly twenty Chairs, chiefly in science and mathematics, were established during the 18th century, and at Oxford the Ashmolean Museum was founded about 1682, when Elias Ashmole bequeathed to the university his collection of natural-history curios, coins, and pictures. The exhibits were housed in the upper room, whilst the lower room and basement served as lecture rooms for the professors of philosophy and chemistry. Unfortunately, the endowment was small and the chemical laboratory was practically derelict by 1710.

At both universities, although certain reforms with regard to studies and examinations could be effected, any radical changes were frustrated by statutes, the Laudian at Oxford and those of 1570 at Cambridge, and both had long outlived their usefulness. In fact, nobody knew exactly what the statutes enjoined, but what little was known about them showed how impossible it was to obey them. Hence members of the university took a solemn oath to observe the statutes, knowing full well that they could not carry out their obligation.

The statutes of Trinity, Cambridge, ordered that "there are to be only three College washerwomen, one for the fellows, another for the scholars, and a third for the chaplains, etc. Undergraduates that miss a single chapel, if they are under 18, are to be publicly birched in Hall in the presence of all the fellows ; if above 18, they are to be fined one halfpenny. The College lectures are to be delivered in Hall at 6 a.m. Every member of the College is to repeat a barbarous Latin prayer upon his knees, before he leaves his bed-room in the morning to attend chapel, and likewise a similar one at night ; and there is to be a Prescribed Latin service in the College chapel, which, by the bye, is quite different from the ordinary Liturgy. Certain students are to be appointed under the name of 'Bible-clerks,' to read the Bible aloud during dinner-time in Hall, and all the students are in the meantime to remain perfectly silent. No person during term-time is to speak any other language than Latin, Greek, or Hebrew, except to a stranger. No student is to stand covered in the College court, or elsewhere in the College, when a M.A. is present; and they are not to drink together in Hall, except at breakfast. Bachelors as well as undergraduates are to wear violet-coloured gowns." [1] Until such obsolete statutes had been superseded, and that was accomplished during the 19th century, no substantial progress could be made.

[1] Quoted by Albert Mansbridge. *The Older Universities of England*, pp. 148-9, Longmans Green, 1923.

CHAPTER V

SCHOOL REFORM AND STATE INTERVENTION IN SECONDARY EDUCATION — 1805-95

The condition of the schools related in the previous chapter raised a whole crop of critics in the early 19th century. Their criticisms took two main directions; they were aimed either at the intellectual training provided by the schools, or at the moral effect of the schools upon the pupils.

The average educated Englishman of the time was not unduly worried about the restrictions resulting from a purely classical curriculum. The real criticism sprang from the radical reformers and, although at first based on educational grounds, it began to be mixed up with the views of the opposing political parties. The Edgeworths believed that even if the classics were efficiently taught, the school which confined itself to these studies was on the wrong lines. Jeremy Bentham and his followers objected to the way in which Latin was taught and the amount of time spent in learning it, which they thought could be spent more profitably in studying politics or law or science. Cobbett, as one might expect, complained of the bookish, unreal character of the education given in the schools and preferred to educate his own children at home. Writers of this school of thought contributed to the *Edinburgh Review* and *Westminster Review*, the leading Liberal periodicals of the country. The former started the attacks in 1809 by criticising the devotion of the schools to Latin and Greek, and called for the inclusion of, modern studies, languages, geography, mathematics, chronology, and experimental philosophy. In 1810 the *Review* turned its attention to the moral aspect, and Sidney Smith, himself an old Winchester scholar, violently attacked Winchester, Eton, Charterhouse, and all similar schools, charging them with tyrannical control of their boys. Bullying and fagging were the particular aspects selected by the critics. In 1830 the *Edinburgh Review* returned to the attack and, speaking of Eton in particular, said: "The most precious years are spent, not in filling the mind with solid knowledge; not in training it to habits of correct and patient thought; but in a course of half-studious idleness, of which the only lasting trace is the recollection of misspent time." The renewed attack was more prolonged than its predecessor, very largely because the unrest of the period of the Reform Bill displayed itself in the criticism of all accepted institutions.   The Fellows at the public schools were compared with the rotten boroughs which had been destroyed by the Reform Act.   The masters were called aristocratic dunces, and it was asserted that at Eton, "the most celebrated public school of England," a boy's classical studies were a complete failure because he was never trained to appreciate the literature of Greece and Rome.   He was confined to the study of a wretched textbook of selections and an even worse grammar book.   The consequence was that the boy left school absolutely ignorant of mathematics, science, modern languages, and history.   Unfortunately, party politics obtruded into the controversy, as it has done many times since, and there was a tendency for the Liberals to lose sight of the educational ends for which they stood.

The *Westminster Review* spoke of the aristocrat as a slave to the institutions which fashioned him.   "They render him as much as possible an instrument of misery, both to himself and to his fellow-beings."   The *Quarterly Journal of Education* compared the tone of Eton to the morals of the corrupt courts of Charles II and Louis XV.   The general conclusions of the opponents of the public schools were that these institutions were so hopelessly bad that it was not possible to reform them and suggested that experiments should be tried out in other types of school.

During this controversy, the attackers were met by a spirited defence which became identified with the Conservative party, just as the attack was due to the Liberals.   In 1821 a Bill was presented to Parliament to undo the effects of Lord Eldon's decision in the Leeds Grammar School case and to allow English, writing, and accounts to be included in the curriculum of the grammar-schools. The Bill was rejected mainly because of the opposition of Vicesimus Knox, who published a treatise entitled, *Remarks on the Tendency of Certain Classes in a Bill now pending in Parliament to Degrade Grammar Schools*.   In this he put up a vigorous defence of the grammar-schools.   In another of his works, *Liberal Education*, 1791, he had argued that the present system in the public schools was good because it had grown up as the result of the experience of many generations.   Canning declared that without her public schools England would never have reached the position she now held, for it was due to the schools and the universities that the great men of the past had received the training which enabled them to fill the prominent positions in Church and State so successfully. As the controversy became more acrimonious, the political sympathies of the opponents became the more obvious.

The Nonconformists, who had been allowed to enter the teaching profession in 1779, although still excluded from the universities and public schools, might have been expected to carry on the traditions of the academies of the 17th century, but they did not rise to the opportunity.   When the Congregationalists opened Mill Hill in 1807, it was modelled very largely on public-school lines, but its curriculum included mathematics and other subjects.   Thus French was taught by a Frenchman ; drawing, English reading, history, and geography, though included, were given a very small place in the time-table.   The Society of Friends founded a number of schools at this time, and Bootham School, York, opened in 1823, showed a desire to break away from a purely classical curriculum.   Mathematics and English were studied, and some attention was given to geography.   The school also possessed an observatory.   The most interesting experiment was that conducted at Hazelwood, near Birmingham, in 1819, by Thomas Wright Hill and his three sons: Rowland, who introduced the penny post ; Matthew Davenport, the reformer of the Criminal Code ; and Arthur.   Later the school was moved to Bruce Castle, Tottenham. At first the experiment was a great success.   Hill was influenced by the educational ideas of Pestalozzi and his plan was remarkable for the breadth of the curriculum and the scheme of self-government adopted in the school.

The Hills tried to avoid the harsh methods of obtaining class order that were usual in the older schools, and sought to enlist the co-operation of the pupils through interest.   Plenty of freedom was allowed the pupils in the choice of subjects for study, and the scheme of self-government adopted was based on a written constitution.   Offenders were tried and awarded punishment by the boys themselves and, in order to foster a sense of responsibility, older pupils were allotted important duties in connection with the running of the school.   In addition to the classics, the subjects taught included spelling, parsing, shorthand, geography, and mathematics. Special attention was given to French, and the boys of the top class were taught geography in French by the French master.   The physical aspects of education were not neglected and visiting masters taught fencing, dancing, and music. Boys were trained in gymnastics and swimming, and those who had a practical bent were encouraged to choose such activities as art and music, map-making, surveying, and printing. At first the school attracted much attention. Then public interest began to flag and it became almost forgotten. Adamson speaks of the school as "illustrating the neglect into which the ideas of English educators have sometimes been allowed to fall, until they have been revived as sheer novelties under a foreign cachet." [1] Its main practical importance lies in its influence upon Dr. Arnold. The almost complete failure of the scheme was due to two factors. One was the innate conservatism of the average Englishman of the middle classes, who, however much he might grumble and demand a change, desired one that was much more moderate and which did not involve a complete break with the past. Another cause of the decline in interest was the mistrust that the average Englishman has for theory. The scheme of the Hills was based upon scientific principles derived from the theories of Pestalozzi and the work of the Edgeworths,[2] and of Bell and Lancaster. It is generally true to say that the reforms in secondary education in the 19th century were due in no small measure to the work and personality of great schoolmasters like James and Butler and, later, Arnold and Thring.

[1] J. W. Adamson. *English Education*, 1789-1902, p. 51, C.U.P., 1930.
[2] The Edgeworths exercised a remarkable influence on educational ideas of the early 19th century. Richard Lovell Edgeworth (1744-1817) married four times and had eighteen children. Maria Edgeworth (1767-1849) undertook the education of her half-brothers, an occupation which lasted until she was fifty years of age. The father served as a Royal Commissioner on Irish Education, and in 1809 he proposed the formation of an association to establish secondary schools throughout the country. Their joint work was *Practical Education*, published in 1798. This book was a pioneer in child-study since it was based on a careful and systematic account of the development of her children kept by Edgeworth's second wife. The eldest member of the Edgeworth family had been brought up on the theories of Rousseau, but in his case the experiment was not successful. Hence, in *Practical Education*, Rousseau's theories were modified, but the influences of Locke, the American writer Benjamin Thompson, and Joseph Priestley are clearly discernible.
Maria was responsible for sixteen chapters of a theoretical nature, the father for six, mainly practical; and the sixth member of the family, Lovell Edgeworth, wrote the chapter on the teaching of chemistry. The book emphasised Rousseau's view that it is essential to study the child and adapt the curriculum and teaching methods to his ever-changing needs and interests. The writers contended that learning is an active process; that it should be rendered attractive, and that play and handwork occupations should be prominent factors in the education of children. Edgeworth himself was keenly interested in mechanical inventions; hence it is not surprising to find that he illustrates his exposition by examples from mechanics and that he stresses the utilitarian value of studies.
Practical Education was followed in 1809 by *Professional Education*. Maria was antagonistic to fairy stories. She preferred that the child's mind should be filled with useful knowledge presented through the medium of the story. In support of her belief, she wrote the six volumes of the *Parent's Assistant* and the *Moral Tales*, both of which had a wide circulation. Her literary reputation, however, rests on her novels dealing with Irish life.

They achieved a reform which was permanent but which was brought about by their high ideals, force, and earnestness of character, rather than by their views about the nature of public-school education.

Arnold's work at Rugby has been described by many writers, some who hold him up as the ideal schoolmaster, and others who, living in a later period, are severely critical.[1] Much that was once attributed to him as original is now recognised as being derived from other sources, but when due allowance has been made for the limitations which were a consequence of his upbringing and of the age in which he lived, there is no doubt that he was instrumental in creating the prestige which the public schools of this country now enjoy. There is no space in a work of this size and character to enter upon the details of Arnold's career, but certain aspects of his work were so important an influence that they cannot be passed over.

Thomas Arnold was a pupil of Winchester when the distinguished Dr. Goddard was headmaster. The latter exercised considerable influence upon his pupil and many of the ideas which Arnold put into practice at Rugby were the result of his early years at Winchester. From the college, Arnold passed to Corpus Christi, Oxford, where he gained a great reputation as a scholar, being placed in the first class in *Litterae Humaniores* in 1814, and winning successively the Vice-Chancellor's prizes for Latin and English essays. He was elected a Fellow of Oriel, and after his ordination and marriage settled at Laleham in Middlesex, where he undertook private tutoring for some years. While at Laleham, the headmastership at Rugby fell vacant in 1828 and Arnold's candidature was warmly supported by the Provost of Oriel, who wrote: "If Arnold were elected, he would change the face of education all through the public schools of England." Rugby, at the time of Arnold's election, had grown, under the able administration of James, from a typical free grammar-school to a large boarding-school. From the very start, its non-local character was emphasised and it developed as a boarding, rather than a day school. A few years before Arnold's election, the school buildings had been considerably enlarged. Arnold's reputation as a great schoolmaster was not due to his introduction of new methods of teaching nor to any attempt to widen the existing classical curriculum. Indeed, he firmly believed in

[1] *e.g.* Strachey in *Eminent Victorians*, and Bertrand Russell in *Education and the Good Life*.

the value of the classics as a sound foundation for any educational system, but in his hands the traditional studies gained a new significance. He looked upon them as opportunities for giving a truly liberal education. He once wrote: "The knowledge of the past is valuable, because without it our knowledge of the present and of the future must be scanty: but if the knowledge of the past be confined wholly to itself: if instead of being made to bear upon things around us, it be totally isolated from them and so disguised by vagueness and misapprehension as to appear incapable of illustrating them, then indeed it becomes little better than laborious trifling, and they who declaim against it may be fully forgiven." The classics were for Arnold the vehicle by means of which history, literature, philosophy, geography, ethics, and politics could be taught. He believed that: "Every lesson in Greek or Latin may or ought to be made a lesson in English: the translation of every sentence in Demosthenes or Tacitus is properly an exercise in extemporaneous English composition: a problem how to express with equal brevity, clearness, and force in our own language, the thought which the original author has so admirably expressed in his." Dean Stanley, who was one of his pupils, tells us that his lessons remained as ever-living memories to those who heard them.

"A black cloud was on his brow when he spoke of Tiberius or Augustus or Napoleon, of the soulless Epicureanism of Horace or the coarseness of Juvenal; and few of his pupils have lost his enthusiasm for the often misrepresented and vilified Cicero, or for the best and holiest of kings, St. Louis of France." Ancient history was not merely ancient history when taught by Arnold.   He thought of it as a means of bringing home to his Rugby boys those great lessons in citizenship which mean so much to our modern English civilisation.   Modern history was employed in much the same way.   It was not, however, as a teacher that Arnold became a lasting influence in English public-school tradition.   As an administrator he was greater still.   The evils of public-school life mentioned in the previous chapter were to be found at Rugby, but Arnold was distinguished as an administrator by his possession of that most precious gift of tact.   He realised that he could not transform the school at once and was content to move slowly but surely, building upon what was good in public-school life rather than introducing revolutionary changes.   He found fagging a universal custom, but instead of abolishing it he made use of it.

The introduction of the prefect system was not Arnold's invention, though some have spoken as though it was. At Eton, in Elizabeth's time, praepostors had been responsible for a good deal of the daily routine work of the college. Westminster and St. Paul's had also used older boys for a similar purpose. Charterhouse, at the beginning of the century, had adopted a monitorial plan based on that of Bell and Lancaster. It was Arnold's own experience at Winchester under Goddard that influenced him most. Goddard had used his older scholars to help in disciplining the younger, and, although he did not organise the system in the way that Arnold did, yet the root principle was there. Arnold built up his system partly upon the institution of fagging, partly upon the prestige enjoyed by the sixth form. He once told the sixth, "I want you to feel how enormous is the influence you possess here on all below you." On another occasion he said, "You should feel like officers in the army whose want of moral courage would be thought cowardice. When I have confidence in the VIth, there is no post in England for which I would exchange this; but if they do not support me, I must go."

Unlike Keate, Arnold's attitude to a boy was, "If you say so, that is quite enough for me ; of course I take your word." Eventually the tradition grew that it was a shame to tell Arnold a lie because he always believed it. Arnold's conception of a great school was essentially a Christian one, but, unlike some people with high ideals, he could be absolutely ruthless if the occasion and his duty demanded it. One boy whom he considered had a bad influence upon the rest was expelled immediately. He told the school, "It is not necessary that this should be a school for 300 or even 100 boys, but it is necessary that it should be a school of Christian gentlemen." Like Butler, he made use of the rod, but he never punished a boy unless his fault was a moral one. Arnold attached tremendous importance to the influence wielded by his prefects, and he took great pains in choosing them. Any abuse of their powers was severely reprimanded, but when their powers of giving punishment were questioned he gave them strong support. He held regular meetings of the prefects and discussed with them measures to raise the general tone of the school. Speaking of his use of the prefects, he said, "He, therefore, who wishes really to improve public education would do well to direct his attention to this point and to consider how there can be infused into a society of boys such elements as, without being too dissimilar to coalesce thoroughly with the rest, shall yet be so superior as to raise the character of the whole. It would be absurd to say that any school has as yet fully solved this problem. I am convinced, however, that, in the peculiar relation of the highest form to the rest of the boys, such as it exists in our great public schools, there is to be found the best means of answering it. This relation requires in many respects to be improved in its character; some of its features should be softened, others elevated; but here, and here only, is the engine which can affect the end desired."

Again, "Those who having risen to the highest form in the school, will probably be at once the oldest and the strongest and the cleverest; and if the school be well ordered, the most respectable in application and general character." Arnold's prefect system has since his day been introduced into countless schools, but it has only been a success when inspired by the same lofty ideals as held by its founder. Where prefects have been regarded as a kind of police force for the headmaster and the staff, the system has met with a well-deserved failure.

Perhaps Arnold's greatest influence was due to his truly Christian character and example. He thought of the school as a Christian community whose centre and inspiration was the school chapel. His own sermons had a far-reaching effect on his listeners. Dean Stanley said, "I never heard or saw anything which gave me so strongly the idea of inspiration." They were not dogmatic, but rather expressed an earnest desire to apply the teaching of Christianity to the problems of the schoolboy in his everyday life. Arnold's work came to an end by his sudden death in 1842, but his influence lived on. Not only did it leave a permanent mark upon Rugby School, but his reputation spread to other schools through pupils and members of his staff who accepted posts in other institutions. Thus many great schools continued the Arnold tradition and the prestige of public schools became higher than ever before. This led to a demand for more schools of a similar character, and a feature of this period of the 19th century was the opening of a number of large proprietary schools, which to a large extent took the public schools as their model.

The new schools reflected the changed political, economic, and social conditions which had come into existence after the Reform Bill. For the first time the middle classes achieved political power, and new careers were being opened to them. There were really three divisions within the so-called middle class. The upper division consisted of wealthy individuals who were not members of the old land-owning class—bankers, financiers, merchants, and factory owners who had been enriched by the Industrial Revolution. The middle section comprised the smaller manufacturers and merchants, professional men, clergy, and junior officers in the Services. The lower middle class contained shopkeepers, farmers, and even a number of skilled artisans. This tripartite division of the middle class exercised considerable influence on the educational provision of the latter part of the 19th century. Thus the recommendations of the Taunton Commission with regard to the grading of secondary schools were not only due to German influence, but were no doubt based on the actual structure of society at the time. Is it too fanciful to suggest that the present tripartite division of secondary education is a faint echo of earlier social conditions?

The middle classes were acutely aware of the advantages of education. As R. H. Tawney wrote: "They looked to the schools to provide . . . a common platform enabling their sons to associate on equal terms with those of families who, if increasingly outdistanced in income, still diffused a faint aroma of social superiority." [1] The middle classes, whose income largely depended on industry, looked to the schools to provide their sons with a sound intellectual training which would fit them for entry into industry, commerce, or the professions. In addition, they demanded an effective moral training. The public schools and the ancient grammar-schools, as the reports of the Clarendon and Taunton Commissions were to show, could not meet these requirements. The private schools, established in large industrial towns, did not offer a satisfactory alternative. The criticisms of the *Edinburgh Review* were really the reflection of middle-class feelings. To a certain extent, the reforms of Butler, James, and Arnold, provided a solution to the problem of the middle classes. The existing public schools, however, were unable to offer the number of places required, and in any case they were too expensive for the majority of the middle class. It became clear that more boarding-schools of the public-school type were needed. The development of the railway system solved the problem of communication and enabled the middle classes to send their sons quickly and cheaply to schools situated at a considerable distance from their homes.

The earlier schools of this type were day-schools, such as the Liverpool Institute, 1825, King's College School, 1829, University

---

[1] "The Problem of the Public Schools" in the *Political Quarterly*, Vol. XIV, 1943, p. 123.

College School, 1833, the City of London School, 1837, and the Liverpool College, 1840. It was due to Arnold's influence that the later schools were boarding-schools. Amongst them were Cheltenham College, 1841, Marlborough College, 1843, Rossall School, 1844, Wellington College, 1853, Epsom College, 1855, Haileybury College and Clifton College, 1862, Malvern School, 1863, and Bath College, 1867 These schools were less expensive than the large public schools and, although their curriculum was mainly classical, yet in most of them considerable time was given to mathematics, science, and modern languages.

The establishment of the schools of the Woodard Foundation was connected with the middle-class movement. Canon Woodard, when he became curate of New Shoreham in 1846, was impressed by the lack of educational facilities for the sons of local tradesmen and especially of sea captains, who lived there. In 1848 he published a pamphlet entitled *A Plea for the Middle Classes*. He urged the provision of "a good complete education for the middle classes at such a charge as will make it available for most of them." He was convinced that until the middle classes were educated it was wasteful to spend money on the education of the poor. Hence he conceived the idea of covering the country with a system of schools built and equipped through the generosity of wealthy benefactors. Woodard's appeal for funds met with a satisfactory response, and by 1849 his first two schools had been established. The first, St. Nicholas' Grammar School and Collegiate Institution, the future Lancing, was for the sons of the gentry. It removed to Lancing in 1857. St. John's was a middle-class school for the sons of well-to-do tradesmen. It eventually moved to Hurstpierpoint and became permanently established there in 1853. The school for the lower middle class was moved from Shoreham to Ardingly in 1870.

Canon Woodard regarded education as primarily religious education, and he believed that only in a boarding-school could religious ideals be developed. Although at one time he entertained the idea of founding day-schools, he eventually decided in favour of boarding-schools. He made little contribution to the problem of the curriculum. As Dr. K. E. Kirk writes: "Woodard's contribution to the cause of education was a contribution of bricks and mortar rather than of intellectual inspiration."[1] The demands of the middle classes for modern studies forced Woodard's hand and he founded

[1] K. E. Kirk. *The Story of the Woodard Schools*, p. 75, Hodder and Stoughton, 1937.

the Military and Engineering School at Leyton in 1850 for those boys of St. Nicholas' who wished to take up a career in the Services or to enter the engineering profession. Woodard had a strong admiration for Arnold and introduced the prefect system into his schools. Within a comparatively short space of time most of the new foundations reached a standard in public esteem not far below that of the older schools.

While Arnold was busy in transforming the life at Rugby, the controversy about the public and grammar schools was still continuing. One of the bitterest of the critics of the public schools was M. J. Higgins, who had been at Eton for a short time. He chose his old school as his special target. Higgins has been described as a genial giant in appearance but possessed of a most bitter tongue. He turned his energies to contributing articles attacking Eton to the periodicals, especially the *Cornhill Magazine*. Writing under the pseudonyms of "Mother of Seven" and later as "Paterfamilias" he wrote letters couched in bitter invective attacking the public schools in general and Eton in particular, and charging them with every fault imaginable. At the same time, Sir John T. Coleridge gave a lecture on Eton at Tiverton in 1860, and in the course of his address criticised the college along the same lines but in a far more reserved fashion than Higgins. The *Edinburgh Review* and the *Westminster Review*, on behalf of the Liberal party, once more joined in the attack, and the torrent of criticism, invective, and abuse, brought about a crisis. The Government realised that something had to be done, and in 1861 a royal commission, usually known as the Clarendon Commission because of its chairman, Lord Clarendon, was appointed to investigate the matter. Other members of the Commission were Lord Devon, Lord Lyttelton, the Hon. E. Twistleton, Sir Stafford Northcote, Mr. H. H. Vaughan, and the Rev. W. H. Thompson. The public schools complained that they were inadequately represented on the Commission, but the results of the inquiry do not show any antagonism on the part of the Commissioners. The field of reference of the Commission was to inquire "into the nature of the endowments, funds, and revenues belonging to or received by" a selected number of schools and colleges. It was also to inquire into "the Revenues and Management of Certain Colleges and Schools, and the studies pursued and instruction given there." The Commission pursued its work for three years and issued its report in 1864. Nine schools were chosen for the inquiry: Eton, Winchester, Westminster,

Charterhouse, St. Paul's, Merchant Taylors', Harrow, Rugby, and Shrewsbury. All of these except St. Paul's and Merchant Taylors' were boarding-schools. Other important schools such as the newer proprietary schools and Uppingham, already being made famous by Thring, were omitted.

The original intention of the Commissioners was to examine the schools themselves, but this raised a storm of protest. Only two of the schools allowed them to enter. The schools were very jealous of their autonomy, and they feared that to allow the Commissioners into them would be a step towards further Government interference. This attitude forced the Commissioners to adopt other methods of obtaining information. They addressed questionnaires to the headmasters, interviewed witnesses, and obtained the opinions of persons who had special knowledge of public-school education. The Commissioners reflected the views of the time and, with certain modifications, upheld the classical curriculum. They were very impressed by the Prussian Gymnasium with its idea of a general liberal education. The Gymnasium in Prussia corresponded to the public school of England in that it aimed at educating boys for the universities and the learned professions. It was due to the work of von Humboldt, who was the chief of the Prussian Bureau of Education, 1808-10. Humboldt was a distinguished classical scholar who saw the value of blending the Humanistic aims of the classical world with the ideals of the modern. Accordingly, he thought of Latin, Greek, mathematics, and German as the main subjects of the curriculum; but other studies and accomplishments, he believed, should find a place in school instruction. Thus some time would be given to history, geography, natural science, religious instruction, drawing, and writing. Hebrew and modern languages were regarded as optional subjects.

The Commissioners therefore were in agreement with the main classical courses provided by the schools, but they considered that the curriculum lacked breadth and flexibility. The teaching of the classics to the abler pupils was on the whole good, but the average pupil left school with a very low standard in classical knowledge, and an even lower one in English, arithmetic, mathematics, and general knowledge. Far too many boys left school at nineteen who could not construe a simple passage in Latin or Greek without the assistance of a dictionary, almost ignorant of the history and geography of their own country, and of modern languages, having great difficulty in writing correct English, unable to work the simplest example in arithmetic or an easy rider in Euclid, knowing nothing of physical science, and never having had any practice in drawing or acquaintance with music. In such cases their intellectual education must be considered a failure, though their principles, character, and manners might be everything that could be desired. "Of the time spent at school by the generality of boys, much is absolutely thrown away as regards intellectual progress either from ineffective teaching, from the continued teaching of subjects in which they cannot advance, or from idleness, or from a combination of these causes." [1]

In spite of recent improvements, the Commissioners felt that modern languages, mathematics, history, and geography still held an unimportant place in the curriculum because too little time was devoted to them and they were not counted for promotion. They pointed out that this was a very serious defect because a large number of men who have little aptitude or taste for literary subjects may show considerable interest and ability in science, especially if it deals with external and sensible objects. The fact that due weight was not given to modern subjects, mathematics, and science, was not altogether the fault of the schools. It was difficult to obtain good teachers of these subjects. This was especially true in the case of modern languages. The choice lay between English teachers whose knowledge was imperfect or foreigners who had difficulty in controlling their classes. The situation with regard to history was equally difficult, and the opinion expressed by Dr. Moberley, headmaster of Winchester, is well known: "I wish we could teach more history, but as to teaching it in set lessons I should not know how to do it."

On the constructive side, the Commission was influenced by the practice of the Prussian Gymnasium. The Commissioners recommended that the classical languages and literature should remain the chief studies in the schools, and emphasised that the main advantage in learning the classics was to gain a greater command over the English language. In addition, every boy ought to be taught arithmetic and mathematics, at least one modern language (French or German), one of the natural sciences, and either music or drawing. He should also leave school with a general knowledge of ancient history, have some acquaintance with modern history, and a command of pure grammatical English. When they reached

[1] *Report of the Public Schools Commission*, Vol. I, p. 26.

the higher classes, it was recommended that those pupils who wished might be allowed to spend less time on the classics and more on mathematics, modern languages, and science.   On the other hand some pupils might desire to specialise more fully in classics. The Commissioners spoke very highly of the work of the public schools in training character, in inculcating a love of healthy sport and exercise, and in fitting pupils both to control themselves and to govern others.

As regards administration, the Commissioners recommended the reconstitution of the governing bodies of the schools, the defining of the powers of the headmaster, and adequate representation of the assistant masters on the school councils.

The Report was followed by the Public Schools Act of 1868 which completely ignored the recommendations of the Commissioners as regards curriculum and confined itself to administrative matters.   It was felt by the Government that the inquiry had caused sufficient resentment and that reforms had better be left to the good sense of the schools themselves rather than be the subject of further Government intervention.   The Act ordered the schools either to accept a constitution framed by the Commissioners or to draw up one for their approval.   The new governing bodies were to include members nominated by the universities and the learned societies.[1] They were to possess considerable powers in fixing the amount of school fees, and the number of pupils, and in determining the curriculum and the kind of religious instruction to be given.   The headmaster was to be appointed by the governing body and he should have the power of appointing and dismissing the assistants.   The two day-schools, St. Paul's and Merchant Taylors', were left out of this scheme.

The Liberals were furious that the rest of the recommendations were not included in the Act, and fought tooth and nail against what they described as "one of the most delusive and reactionary measures ever put before the country."   They urged the inspection of public schools, to be met with the reply that to adopt Government inspection "would be to degrade the great public schools of England down to the level of village schools."   The Government was

[1] For example, the governing body of Charterhouse was to consist of the Archbishop of Canterbury, a member elected from each of the universities of Oxford, Cambridge, and London, one nominated by the Royal Society, one by the Lord Chancellor, one by the Lord Chief Justice, one elected by the headmaster and assistant masters, three by the governors of Sutton's Hospital, and four co-opted members.

probably wise not to press for further intervention but to leave the schools to put their own houses in order. The autonomy of the schools was saved, and in the following years many of the recommendations of the Commission were adopted and the curriculum became more varied and flexible. Thus, at Eton, Dr. Hornby introduced teaching in French, German, history, physics, chemistry, and zoology, and boys who were in the upper forms were given considerable choice in selecting the subjects they wished to study.

Perhaps the most striking effect of the Commission was to be seen in the developments at Harrow. There are records which prove the existence of a school at Harrow as early as 1384. It was flourishing at the time of Mary, and the records of Caius College, Cambridge, contain the names of three undergraduates who had attended the school at Harrow in the days of Elizabeth's reign. The school was refounded by John Lyon (*de novo erigere*) in 1572, and the Lyonian Statutes were drawn up in that year and elaborated in 1591 (*Orders, Statutes and Rules*).[1] The original statutes sufficed for the government of the school until 1868, by which time they had outgrown their usefulness. The Act of 1868 reconstituted the Board of Governors, and the out-of-date statutes were replaced by regulations more suited to modern conditions. The changes were not completed until 1874. The most important innovation was the establishment of a Modern Side under E. E. Bowen, who is best known to the general public as the writer of the Harrow School Song, *Forty Years On*. Boys allocated to the Modern Side studied Latin, but their curriculum included history, modern languages, mathematics, and natural science. Bowen was well supported by his headmaster, Henry Montagu Butler, who ensured that the Modern Side should not be a soft option by ruling that only boys who had a good record on the Classical Side should be admitted.[2] Butler's successor, J. E. C. Welldon, did not continue this policy, and much to Bowen's disgust treated the Modern Side as a refuge for those who had not been successful in their classical studies. Eventually, in 1893, this led to Bowen's resignation from the control of the Modern Side, though he continued to teach the upper forms until his death in 1901. Bowen's experiment had,

[1] The statutes of 1591 are given in full by E. D. Laborde in his *Harrow School*, Appendix A, Winchester Publications, 1948.

[2] Bowen's ideas on the Modern Side are given in the " Memorandum on the Modern Side," in W. E. Bowen, *Edward Bowen*, pp. 103-15, Longmans Green, 1902.

however, been entirely successful and it was imitated in other public schools.

The Clarendon Commission focused attention upon secondary education as a whole, and as a natural consequence the Schools Inquiry Commission of 1864, generally known as the Taunton Commission, was appointed. The object of the Commission was to inquire into the education given in those schools which had been included neither in the Clarendon Commission nor the Inquiry into Popular Education conducted by the Newcastle Commission, "and also to consider and report what Measures (if any) are required for the Improvement of such Education, having especial Regard to all Endowments applicable, or which can rightly be made applicable thereto."

The inquiry lasted four years and the report was issued in 1868. It was an exhaustive investigation of every type of secondary education and no pains were spared to make the report as complete and accurate as possible. Girls' as well as boys' schools were included, private and proprietary schools as well as endowed schools. The inquiry was conducted along three main lines: the oral examination of witnesses (religious denominations, examining bodies, representatives of the professions, school masters and mistresses, the legal profession, and any other persons having a special knowledge or interest in education), circulars of questions seeking for written information in detail from the school authorities, and finally, through assistant-commissioners, who personally investigated certain selected districts. Among the assistant-commissioners were J. G. Fitch and James Bryce. In order to obtain a comparison with the methods and results of the systems of education in some parts of Europe, Canada, and the U.S.A., Matthew Arnold was sent to inquire into secondary education in France, Germany, Switzerland, and Italy, and the Rev. James Fraser, afterwards Bishop of Manchester, performed a similar task in regard to the United States and Canada. Information about Scotland was obtained from an inspection of the schools in nine cities and towns by Mr. Fearon.

The work of the assistant-commissioners revealed an astounding state of affairs. The provision of secondary education was hopelessly inadequate, especially in the large centres of population. One of the districts selected for special study was the West Riding of Yorkshire, and the report of Mr. (later Sir) J. G. Fitch was typical of the situation,[1] and clearly showed the uneven distribution of secondary schools.

In 1861 the population of the West Riding and the city of York was 1,548,229, and it was estimated that the number of boys who should be receiving education above the primary stage was 20,533. The actual number in attendance at the endowed schools was 1,836, and Fitch recorded that in no instance was the available school accommodation fully occupied.   Large towns, such as Huddersfield, did not possess an endowed school and its inhabitants relied on private and proprietary schools. The number of grammar-schools in the area was given by the Charity Commissioners as sixty-five and of these five had ceased to exist. Of the remaining sixty schools, only twenty-nine gave some kind of classical education. The rest were in reality rather inefficient elementary schools. "Of the fact of the general decadence of the endowed grammar schools within the country there can be no doubt. The schools are not popular ; they do not possess the confidence of the parents . . . the class of parents whose children may be presumed to stay long enough at school to make any use of Latin, and who are above the status of the labouring poor, generally prefer private schools ; and that while these are numerous and well attended, the old foundations, with all their historical prestige and their wealth, do not attract the classes for whom they are intended." [2]

In the whole of the riding, "There are three grammar schools . . . which are conspicuously in advance of all the rest in numbers and reputation. They are St. Peter's in York, Leeds, and Doncaster. These Schools lay themselves out for higher education, and their curriculum is designed to prepare boys for the universities. All are under the care of accomplished and energetic men, are increasing in numbers, and are obtaining distinction at the universities." [3] There were a large number of reasons to account for the decay of the endowed schools. In the country towns the governing bodies had become nothing less than a small group of self-elected trustees who seldom met and who took insufficient interest in matters which concerned the schools. They had little control over the headmaster, who in turn had a minimum of control over his assistants.

Thus, at Normanton, there was a body of not less than twenty trustees who were responsible for the administration of an endowment of £10 per annum. Many of the members lived at a distance,

[1] *Schools Inquiry Commission*, Vol. IX, pp. 1-423.   [2] *Ibid.*, p. 109.
[3] *Ibid.*, p. 165.

and consequently the governing body never met and no supervision was exercised over the headmaster. Fitch found that worthy gentleman "leisurely reading *Bell's Life in London,* while eleven children were following their own devices. The vicar of the parish, who is absolutely powerless in the matter, has for years desired to get a good National School, but has found it impossible, because this worthless school already existed in the parish." [1]

In some districts the trustees were so satisfied with the shocking conditions of the school that they refused to make any improvements. The trustees of Haworth wrote to Fitch, saying: ". . . the trustees consider the present state of the school adapted for all classes of society in the township of Haworth. That the trustees are satisfied with the present state of the school, and do not contemplate any plans for its improvement." [2]

In the large towns the trustees often had many other duties which limited the time they could spend on the affairs of the schools. Sometimes the statutes required that the headmaster should be a clergyman, so that many competent teachers could not obtain promotion. "In another school in the district, the masterships are held by two clergymen, who have not been on speaking terms for fifteen years. Each of these gentlemen took me privately aside to assure me that the other was not to be trusted, and that it was impossible to work harmoniously with him. The headmaster accounted for the ignorance of the upper forms by complaining of the stupidity of the methods adopted in the lower classes, methods over which he, the headmaster, had no sort of control. The usher, on the other hand, assigned as a reason for the worthlessness of his own teaching, that it was of no use to prepare them for a course so absurd and useless as was pursued in the upper classes." [3]

Most of the schools had been free schools, but nearly all of them were now charging fees under some pretext or other. On the plea that the endowment was for Latin and Greek only, all other subjects had to be paid for. "The absurdest results follow from such arrangements as these. In one case I have seen a class of children, including some of nine or ten years of age, painfully employed in reading all day, and wholly unable to use a pencil or a pen, because their parents did not choose to pay the writing fee. In another there are children who reach a still greater age without ever receiving an exercise in arithmetic, for a similar reason. . . . Not infrequently,

---

[1] *Schools Inquiry Commission*, Vol. IX, p. 120.   [2] *Ibid.*, p. 122.
[3] *Ibid.*, p. 132.

when questioning the highest class of a school on geography, or history, or on grammar, I have noticed a number of children preserve a dead silence, and on inquiring further, have learned that these were the pupils who did not pay for the particular subject, and therefore did not learn it." [1]   In some schools an invidious distinction was made between the foundation scholars and those who paid fees.   "At Easingwold, I found a school along the middle of which was a partition breast high, dividing the scholars into two groups.   The master's desk was fixed in an elevated position and dominated both divisions of the school.   He explained to me that the free scholars were on one side and the paying scholars on the other.   He had erected the partition, he said, in defence of his own interests, for unless he kept the two classes of pupils—the 'sheep and the goats,' as he familiarly called them— habitually apart, the more respectable parents would object to pay, and perhaps remove their children altogether.   I learned that while he was bound to admit a certain number of free scholars, it had been his custom to receive others on the footing of private pupils, and that even in the playground there was no intercourse between them." [2]

The best schools worked to gain university scholarships and their curriculum was exclusively classical.   Some of them had created English departments.   "At Leeds there is an English depart-ment or lower school in which a reduced fee of £4 4s. 0d. per annum is charged.   There are, at present, 50 boys in it, the room being adapted for double that number.   The boys constitute an entirely distinct school, receiving no lessons in common with those of the classical school.   They learn a little Latin; and French is also well taught by the master, who is a clergyman, and has resided some years in France.   He has entire charge of the school, and is unassisted, except by a writing and arithmetic master, who gives lessons for certain hours in the week. . . . It is evident that an English department, thus constituted, has not a fair chance of success, and does not correspond to the needs of such a town as Leeds or to the resources and prestige of the great school of which it forms a part. It is impossible to have proper organisation in a school composed of 50 boys of all ages under one master." [3]

Even in those grammar-schools which had retained Latin and Greek, the teaching was of poor quality.   "On the whole, the

---

[1] *Schools Inquiry Commission*, Vol. IX, p. 144.   [2] *Ibid.*, p. 156.
[3] *Ibid.*, p. 168.

classical learning prescribed by statute in the large majority of the grammar schools may be safely pronounced a delusive and unfruitful thing. It is given to very few in any form. It is not carried to any substantial issue in the case of five per cent of the scholars. It is more often taught to keep up a show of obedience to founders' wills than for any better reason. It is so taught in the majority of cases that it literally comes to nothing. Finally, it furnishes the pretext for the neglect of all other useful learning, and is the indirect means of keeping down the general level of education in every small town which is so unfortunate as to possess an endowment." [1]

Small and old grammar-schools were handicapped by the conditions of their buildings. Some had no playgrounds and were without proper apparatus. "Maps and diagrams are rare, and blackboards rarer still. In all proper equipment and teaching apparatus the average grammar school is so deficient that an inspector under the Privy Council would generally withhold the grant on the ground that the room was insufficiently furnished. . . . Any money spent on improving the school fittings is necessarily deducted from the master's stipend, and therefore he has the strongest inducement to acquiesce in a state of things which otherwise he would think very unsatisfactory. Bare and dirty walls, shaky and inconvenient furniture, and outer offices which are not even decent, are rather the rule than the exception." [2]

The teaching of the subjects outside the classics was generally bad. Very little attention was given to oral reading which "is almost always slovenly, indistinct and tasteless." Arithmetic was taught in a formal and unintelligent manner. In most schools, very little attention was given to the study of English. Only rarely did physical science form any part of the curriculum. "It is excluded from the course of instruction in schools, because it was excluded from the education of the masters, who naturally think that alone to be worth knowing which they themselves know." [3] There are a few exceptions. "Leeds is the only grammar school in which I have found a resolute and systematic attempt to teach science. Here there is an excellent laboratory and a class is well drilled in chemical manipulation and analysis." [4] Even here, chemistry was taught rather because of its value to those boys entering the woollen industry than as a branch of liberal education.

[1] *Schools Inquiry Commission*, Vol. IX, p. 176.   [2] *Ibid.*, p. 177.
[3] *Ibid.*, p. 181.   [4] *Ibid.*, p. 182.

No adequate system of examinations existed to test the work of the schools. It is true that the Oxford and Cambridge Local Examinations and those of the College of Preceptors existed, but they tested a few selected individuals rather than the school as a whole.

Fitch found only one endowed school which had retained its grammar-school status and which admitted girls. This was at Rishworth, but although there were fifty-five boys and fifteen girls at the school, the boys remained until fifteen years of age and were prepared for the universities, but the girls were required to give up their schooling at fourteen. "It does not offer even to one of these girls, though some of them are children of professional men, and all of persons in a respectable position, the opportunity of qualifying herself as a governess or of proceeding to a place of higher education." [1]

The Commissioners found but twelve other schools in England where girls were admitted. It was only when a grammar-school sank to the status of a primary school that it catered for girls. Thirty-five of the West Riding schools were merely primary schools, and poor ones at that. "In regard to school appliances, as well as in organisation, method, and intelligence, the smaller endowed schools are generally inferior to National Schools. Nevertheless, their existence hinders the establishment of such National Schools, and thus deprives many towns and villages altogether of proper elementary teaching; of the advantages of inspection, and of the sympathy and experience of persons who would otherwise subscribe and feel an interest in the progress of the scholars." [2]

Fitch concluded that only three schools were in the first class: Doncaster, Leeds, and St. Peter's, York. Three others might be developed to become such: Ripon, Sheffield, and Giggleswick or Sedbergh. He did not think there was room for both the latter schools. "Giggleswick is the richer; it is more central; and it is in a far more hopeful condition, whether we consider the state of its buildings, its staff of teachers, or the zeal and intelligence of its governing body. It is not too much to hope that it may one day become for the North of England what Rugby is to the Midland districts. As to Sedbergh, I despair of putting it into any class at all. In its present state it simply cumbers the ground." [3] Fitch was right about Giggleswick, but he had gravely misjudged Sedbergh,

[1] *Schools Inquiry Commission*, Vol. IX, p. 197.   [2] *Ibid.*, p. 199.
[3] *Ibid.*, p. 214.

as those who know the splendid work done at the latter school can testify.

Twenty-six other schools, he considered, might be developed into good schools of the second class. Among these were the schools at Bradford, Rotherham, Sheffield, and Wakefield, and Archbishop Holgate's at York. The remainder he thought were unfit to be secondary schools. "Their only hope of usefulness lies in the acceptance of their position as primary schools, and in arrangements which will enable them to do that work well." [1]

A considerable number of exhibitions to the universities existed, but the Commissioners found that the value of these scholarships was restricted by obsolete conditions. Often the exhibition was confined to candidates from a particular district, and in many cases for a number of years none from the district had been forthcoming. This was a waste of a valuable endowment which could not be applied to any other locality on account of the founder's will. Some machinery was needed through which such exhibitions could be open to candidates from other schools, or even to the whole country.

"A rare instance of elasticity is afforded by the foundation of Lady Elizabeth Hastings in 1739, who left valuable estates for exhibitions, now ten in number, to Queen's College, Oxford, for scholars from 12 schools, viz., eight in Yorkshire,—Leeds, Wakefield, Bradford, Beverley, Skipton, Sedbergh, Ripon, and Sherburn ; two in Westmoreland,—Appleby and Heversham ; and two in Cumberland,—St. Bees and Penrith, and the foundress wisely provided that if any of these decayed, others might be substituted in their place. Though the foundation is only 130 years old, the need for such a provision has already been shown. Accordingly Beverley, Ripon, Sherburn, and Skipton have been replaced by Hipperholme, Giggleswick, Pontefract and York." [2]

The method of choosing the exhibitors was curious. Certain rectors and vicars were constituted as examiners and were to meet at the best inn in Aberford, Yorks, before 8 a.m. on the Thursday in Whitsun week. The candidates assembled at the same inn the night before, so as to be ready to sit the examination on the following day. The examiners chose the ten best papers and sent them to Queen's College, where the eight best of the ten were selected. These eight names were written on slips of paper, put into an urn by the

[1] *Schools Inquiry Commission*, Vol. IX, p. 216.
[2] *Op. cit.*, Vol. I, pp. 175-6.

Provost, and well shaken up. The first five to be drawn were awarded the exhibitions. Lady Hastings apologised for the method of selection, saying: "And though this Method of choosing by Lot may be called by some Superstition or Enthusiasm yet as the advice was given me by an Orthodox and Pious Prelate of the Church of England as leaving something to Providence . . . I will this Method of Ballotting be for ever observed!" Alas for Lady Hastings' wish! A modern age is averse to "leaving something to Providence" and therefore, in 1859, a new system of examination was introduced. The Hastings' Exhibitions (value £115 per annum and tenable for four or five years), are now awarded on the results of open competition between candidates from certain selected schools.

The findings of Fitch in the West Riding were comparable to those of the other assistant-commissioners in various parts of the country. "Thame had two masters receiving 300*l*. between them, one of whom had a good house also. Mr. Fearon found one boy in the school. . . . At Whitney the head master contented himself with teaching Greek to one boy. Reading had three scholars, and there was no hope of the school reviving under the then master. . . . At Whitgift's Hospital, Croydon, the late master (who died last year), Mr. Fearon was informed, found no pupils attending the school when he came, and never had any at all during the 30-odd years that he was master." [1] The value of the Whitgift endowment was £500 per annum.

Bryce made an unexpected find at Bispham. The school was an old house with thatched roof through which the rain penetrated, dropping upon the desks and leaving a pool upon the floor. The room measured $30\frac{1}{2}$ feet by $14\frac{1}{2}$ feet, and was $7\frac{1}{2}$ feet high, and the number of pupils on roll was seventy. When he visited the school, only twenty boys and twelve girls were present, but the air was so foul that he was obliged to keep the door open whilst he examined the children. No Latin was taught, and the reading and spelling were good, but the arithmetic was taught in an old-fashioned way. "But the characteristic feature of the school was one which I had least expected to find in such a place. The small and wretched room was filled in every available corner by stuffed beasts and birds; geological diagrams hung upon the walls: shelves were loaded and drawers filled with collections of fossils and minerals.

[1] *Schools Inquiry Commission*, Vol. I, pp. 225-6.

In answer to my look of surprise, the master explained that he was an ardent naturalist; he had collected all these things himself, and used them in his teaching, giving a lesson to the whole school four afternoons in every week." [1]

Bryce remarked that such a master would not be found in a government school. If he had been found there, he would certainly have taught the three R's better and would have had a more suitable schoolroom. "But his time would have been too completely absorbed in bringing the children up to the "Standards" of the Revised Code, to let him stray into the regions of natural history, which he taught so excellently well, and to the so great profit of the neighbourhood."

Among the private and proprietary schools—more than 10,000 in number scattered throughout England—the Commissioners found a few that were really excellent, but the general condition of the private schools was most unsatisfactory. They reported that "the account given of the worst of the endowed schools must be repeated in even more emphatic language to describe most of the private schools." [2]

The proprietary schools were of recent origin and included many first-class schools giving special attention to mathematics and modern languages, others were second-class boarding-schools for the sons of farmers; some had developed from Mechanics' Institutes, like the Leeds Boys' Modern School, founded in 1845; others were schools erected by religious denominations, such as Woodhouse Grove, near Bradford, founded by the Wesleyans, the Congregational School of Silcoates near Wakefield, the Friends' Schools of Ackworth and Bootham, York, and the Jews' College at Finsbury. A few schools were founded in the interests of certain professions —such as Epsom, opened for the sons of medical men. Some of the schools had been a failure and others had become endowed, like Marlborough College, the Woodard Schools, and Bradfield College. "The educational character of proprietary schools stands very high. Some of them rank with the most famous of the Grammar Schools as places of preparation for the Universities; and the military and civil department of Cheltenham College is equally distinguished in the competition for admissions to Woolwich." [3]

Mr. Bryce spoke highly of the Roman Catholic college at Stonyhurst, "Its teaching is avowedly directed to bring every boy

[1] *Schools Inquiry Commission*, Vol. IX, p. 692.   [2] *Op. cit.*, Vol. I, p. 285.
[3] *Ibid.*, p. 318.

up to a certain level rather than to raise a few to a very high pitch of excellence." [1]

Although Fitch condemned most of the Yorkshire private schools, he admitted, "I have wholly failed to discover any example of the typical Yorkshire boarding-school with which Dickens' *Nicholas Nickleby* has made us familiar. I have seen schools in which board and education were furnished for 20*l.*, and even 18*l.* per annum, but have been unable to find evidence of bad feeding or physical neglect." [2]

The Commission paid great attention to the reports of the assistant-commissioners who were sent to other countries. Fraser reported that the New England high schools could not compare with our best schools, but the Americans are well supplied with secondary schools of a lower grade. "Whatever be the defects of the system, it has the one great merit of being alive. The teachers have the gift of turning what they know to the best account; they are very self-possessed, energetic, fearless; they are admirable disciplinarians, firm without severity, patient without weakness; their manner of teaching is lively and fertile in illustration; classes are not likely to fall asleep in their hands. . . . They fall short of Prussia in completeness and culture. But they seem to have succeeded in supplying every citizen with as much education as is indispensable for the ordinary duties of life, and in opening to him the door for more if he desire it." [3]

Matthew Arnold's description of Prussian secondary education produced the greatest impression. The Commissioners reported: "When we view it as a whole, the Prussian system appears to be at once the most complete and the most perfectly adapted to its people of all that now exist. It is not wanting in the highest cultivation like the American, nor in dealing with the mass of middle classes like our own, nor does it run any risk of sacrificing everything else to intellectual proficiency like the French. It is somewhat more bureaucratic in its form than would work well in England, but it is emphatically not a mere centralised system, in which the government is everything. . . . In Prussia the education department is simply the instrument which the people use to procure the fulfilment of their own desires. The Prussians believe in culture, and who may have originally created the educational machinery, that machinery has now been appropriated by the people

---

[1] *Schools Inquiry Commission*, Vol. I, p. 321.   [2] *Op. cit.*, Vol. IX, p. 262.
[3] *Op. cit.*, Vol. I, p. 53.

themselves. . . . The result is an unrivalled body of teachers, schools meeting every possible need of every class, and a highly cultivated people." [1]

The Commission then outlined the organisation of the Prussian system of secondary education. The highest grade of school was the *Gymnasium,* which was more like our best classical schools than any other schools in Europe, or indeed in the world. Below these were the *Realschulen,* which existed in three grades. The first grade provided a nine-year course, without Greek, but with compulsory Latin. Special attention was given to French, mathematics, and natural science, and English was compulsory for boys entering business. In addition, the mother tongue, divinity, history, and drawing were taught, and in the school-leaving examination a boy had to pass in every subject. The second-grade *Realschulen* provided a seven-year course so that a boy could leave school at sixteen. Latin was not obligatory. The third-grade *Realschulen,* or *Burgerschulen,* had a shorter and less complete course.

The recommendations of the Commission followed very sound lines. They were willing to learn from other countries, but they felt that the system of secondary education adopted in England must have its roots in English institutions of the past and be suited to the English temper and character. "It would probably be both useless and impracticable to attempt simply to transplant into England systems that have flourished elsewhere. We have not the universal energy and restlessness of the Americans, nor the long training of the Scotch, nor the singular aptitude for organisation of the French, nor the strong belief in the value of culture which makes education so universal an object of desire in Prussia. But there is no reason why, if we cannot do precisely what our neighbours have done, we should not do something of a corresponding character. The wants of England are not exactly the same with those of America, France, or Prussia; nor even, where the wants are identical, will the proper means of supplying those wants always coincide. But without quitting the course usually observed in dealing with English institutions, we have no doubt that the right result in the matter of education may be defined now and reached hereafter." [2]

The Commission believed that a national system of secondary education could alone be adequate and that the nucleus of this already existed in the shape of the present endowed schools, because

[1] *Schools Inquiry Commission,* Vol. I, p. 72.   [2] *Ibid.,* p. 22.

of their long tradition and their public position. Hence, the first step should be to make the best possible use of the schools. They enunciated as a general principle that three grades of secondary school were necessary. This was based on the length of time that parents were willing to allow their children to attend school. From this point of view, schools could be classified according to whether the leaving-age was eighteen or nineteen, sixteen or fourteen. These distinctions would correspond roughly to the social divisions in the nation. The majority of boys who needed a third-grade course should have a day-school adapted to their needs in the immediate neighbourhood. Those who needed a higher type of education would attend a high school in their district with a boarding attachment. In this system it would be necessary to establish preparatory schools for the higher-grade secondary schools, but there was no need for this provision for the third-grade schools.

Special attention was directed to the curriculum of each grade, and vocational education was severely condemned. This did not imply the exclusion of practical subjects which, though useful in a vocational sense, could be made instruments for the general education of the intellect. The three main subjects in a liberal education were language, mathematics, and science; and the primacy was given to language. "Nor is equal clearness of thought to be obtained in any other way. Clearness of thought is bound up with clearness of language, and the one is impossible without the other. When the study of language can be followed by that of literature, not only breadth and clearness, but refinement becomes attainable. The study of history in the full sense belongs to a somewhat later age; for till the learner is old enough to have some appreciation of politics, he is not capable of grasping the meaning of what he studies." [1]

The Commissioners thought that Greek should be taught only in first-grade schools. French or German, or both, should be taught, and English literature and history should receive careful attention, but would hold a subordinate position in the time-table. Science could be a valuable discipline if pupils began with those sciences which depended largely on observation, e.g. botany, and then progressed through physical geography to elementary physics and chemistry.

The Commissioners were seriously disturbed about the meagre facilities provided for the higher education of girls, and they

[1] *Schools Inquiry Commission*, Vol. I, p. 546.

protested against the "long established and inveterate prejudice that girls are less capable of mental cultivation, and in less need of it than boys; that accomplishments, and what is showy and superficially attractive, are what is really essential for them ; and in particular, that as regards their relations to the other sex and the probabilities of marriage, more solid attainments are actually disadvantageous rather than the reverse." [1]   In forming their opinions about the education of girls, the Commissioners were greatly impressed by the evidence of Miss Buss and Miss Beale, of whom we shall hear more later.

Mr. Fearon summed up the situation by saying that "the appropriation of almost all the educational endowments of the country to the education of boys is felt by a large and increasing number, both of men and women, to be a cruel injustice." [2]   It was recommended that in the reorganisation of endowments, a fair share should be employed for the education of girls.

The recommendations of the Commission were very drastic.   In the first place, the constitutions of the endowed schools would have to be thoroughly revised.   In this revision, a school would not be treated as an isolated unit, but would be considered in its relations to other schools in its area.   New endowed schools should be created in areas where they were needed, and all the schools should be placed under permanent supervision.   To carry out these proposals new administrative machinery would be necessary. A central authority was the first requisite and this could best be supplied by an enlarged and reconstituted Charity Commission presided over by a Minister of Education.   The Charity Commission should have power to make schemes for the reorganisation of endowed schools and submit them for approval to Parliament. It should appoint inspectors, audit the school accounts, and convert all charities which are "mischievous, or intended for purposes now obsolete" to educational purposes.   As the machinery for local administration did not exist, it would have to be created.   The country would be divided into provinces corresponding to the divisions of the Registrar-General, and the Charity Commission would appoint an Official District Commissioner for each area. He would be one of the trustees for every educational trust and would personally inspect every secondary school at least once in every three years.   Associated with him would be six or eight unpaid District Commissioners appointed by the Crown from the

[1] *Schools Inquiry Commission*, Vol. I, p. 546.   [2] *Ibid.*, p. 567.

local residents.   The District Commissioners would prepare schemes for all the schools in their districts and submit them to the Charity Commission.   Towns with over 100,000 inhabitants could form their own boards if they so wished.

The governing bodies of schools were to be reorganised. Besides the Official Commissioner, they should include representatives of parents, ratepayers, or various public bodies, and members co-opted from the original governors.   The governors should be responsible for the school property, appoint or dismiss the headmaster, fix the salaries of the assistants, and have a certain amount of control over fees and the curriculum.   The headmaster should have power to appoint and dismiss the assistant masters.

The creation of an examining council was recommended.   It should consist of twelve members, two elected by each of the universities of Oxford, Cambridge, and London, and six appointed by the Crown.   The examining council would not only conduct examinations in the schools, but should draw up rules and appoint examiners to examine and issue certificates to candidates for the teaching profession.   "Lastly, the council would do a very great service to education by making an annual report, giving as complete a picture as possible of what was being done, and of what is still needed to be done." [1]

The Commission decided that the idea of a free grammar-school was obsolete and recommended a scale of fees according to the grade of the school, with a large number of scholarships awarded by competitive examination.

The Commissioners asserted that "the reorganisation of endowments is the beginning, but only the beginning, of a systematic provision of education above the elementary. When that beginning has been made, the largest part of the work will still have to be done." [2]   They had in mind the organisation of a national system of secondary education so that schools of different grades would be within reach of all classes of society.   It seemed as though at last England was to possess a thoroughly well-organised system of secondary education, but it was not to be so.   The time was not yet ripe and the opportunity created by the Schools Inquiry Commission was neglected.   One reason, according to Matthew Arnold, was the prevalence of class interests.   Probably a more potent influence was the almost universal mistrust of Government intervention, a legacy from the earlier part of the century.   Another cause

[1] *Schools Inquiry Commission*, Vol. I, p. 651.   [2] *Ibid.*, p. 652.

was one of administration; local authorities for the provision and administration of schools did not exist. It should be remembered that the School Boards did not come into existence until 1870, and the county councils were not created until the Act of 1888. The Commissioners were distinctly ahead of their time. The majority of educated people, including the schoolmasters, had no very clear ideas about the aims and purposes of secondary education, but were, rather, bound by the tradition of the past. It needed nearly half a century before the goodwill of the people, for which the Commissioners pleaded, was to be obtained.

The immediate result of the Commission was the passage of the Endowed Schools Act of 1869, which put into operation some of the administrative proposals of the report. Mr. Forster introduced in the Commons a Bill embodying the recommendations about examinations and the setting up of a body for the registration of qualified teachers. It won general approval, but the rush of legislation compelled the Government to drop it.

The Government postponed the proposal to create local authorities for administration and occupied itself entirely with the reorganisation of the central authority. This took the form of an Endowed Schools Commission created for three years only. In 1873 its life was prolonged for another year, and in 1874 its powers were merged with those of the Charity Commissioners.

This was partly due to the inconvenience of having two distinct bodies to deal with charitable trusts. The newly organised Charity Commission was not only concerned with secondary schools, but, after the Elementary Education Act of 1870, was busy with drawing up schemes for endowed elementary schools. This aroused considerable resentment and, by the Act of 1873, all elementary schools with an endowment of less than £100 per year were transferred to the jurisdiction of the Education Department. The seven public schools which were the subject of the Clarendon Commission's investigation were exempted from the control of the Charity Commission; also choristers' schools connected with cathedrals and those concerned with the professional training of ministers of religion. Schools founded after 1819 could be dealt with only by consent of their governors. With these exceptions, the Commission had power to prepare schemes for endowed schools. The usual procedure was to act on the invitation of the governors. If action were urgent, they could prepare their own scheme, but in such a case the governors, the corporation, or twenty ratepayers, had the right to petition Parliament against the action of the Commission.

The work of the Commission went on slowly. By 1884 only half the work was accomplished; 595 schemes had become law, but 660 schools were still unaffected. Even as late as 1895, the Leeds Grammar School was not working under a revised scheme drawn up by the Commission, and Huddersfield possessed no secondary schools at all.

One important part of the work of the Commission was to apply many endowments which had not specifically been designed by the founders for boys' schools, to establish girls' schools. "The Bradford Grammar School, for instance, in 1868 contained fifty-eight boys who were receiving a poor classical education in an atmosphere of 'general languor and feebleness.' 'I could see among the boys no evidence of interest in their work, or of desire to do it well.' Without adding any endowment, the new scheme was a means of transforming this institution into two schools of 530 boys and 300 girls, receiving the best education of the day. In the ten years previous to 1871 it sent only five boys to the universities and gained only one scholarship. 'In the ten years previous to 1893 it sent 108 boys, took 73 scholarships, 44 first classes, 4 fellowships, and 10 university scholarships and prizes. And a vast proportion of those honours were taken by boys who had been in public elementary schools.' " [1]

The Leeds Girls' High School is another example. The school was founded in 1876 through the efforts of the Yorkshire Ladies' Council of Education and the Leeds Ladies' Educational Association. The Leeds Girls' High School Company, Ltd., was formed with a nominal capital of £10,000. The aim of the company was "to establish and maintain a High Class Day School for the Girls of Leeds, which shall be to them what the Grammar School is to their brothers." In 1898 the Charity Commission turned its attention to the endowment of the Grammar School and decided that the term "young children, youths, and scholars" used by the founder included girls as well as boys. Hence, the Commission agreed to part of the Grammar School endowments being used for the education of girls. £12,000, and the interest upon it, was set aside to purchase the site on which the present school stands.

[1] Helen Wodehouse. *A Survey of the History of Education*, p. 198, Edward Arnold, 1929. Also see, W. Claridge, *Origin and History of Bradford Grammar School*, Chaps. ix and x, J. Green, 1882.

One feature of 19th-century development in secondary education was the increasing attention given to the provision of high schools for girls. Very few schools existed in the 18th century for the education of girls. Well-to-do parents either employed governesses to train their daughters or sent them to private schools where the main instruction was in languages, deportment, and accomplishments. The movement to provide good secondary schools for girls was really part of the much wider movement for the emancipation of women, and it began with the attempt to secure suitable training for governesses. About 1841 the Governesses' Benevolent Association was formed with the object of assisting private governesses who were in temporary difficulties. At first the Association did not make much headway until the Rev. David Laing accepted the post of honorary secretary. He at once set to work to reorganise the Association and added an employment agency and a teachers' registry. It was soon seen that many of the applicants were unfit for their work and it was proposed to award a diploma on the result of an examination. Professor Denison Maurice and his colleagues at King's College, London, volunteered to teach and examine women who wished to become governesses. In 1848 Queen's College, Harley Street, was opened for women, and Professor Maurice became its first principal. Miss Buss and Miss Beale were among the early students of the college.

As Queen's College gave instruction according to Anglican principles, it was felt that a similar institution was needed for Nonconformists. In 1849 Mrs. John Reid founded the undenominational college in Bedford Square, which in 1860 became the Bedford College for Women, of which George Eliot was one of the students. Queen's College received its charter in 1853 and Bedford College in 1869. Miss Buss and Miss Beale were the pioneers of secondary education for girls in the 19th century. The former became headmistress of the North London Collegiate School in 1850, and the latter principal of the Ladies' College, Cheltenham, in 1858. The North London Collegiate School was mainly a day-school and became the pattern on which the schools of the Girls' Public Day Schools Company modelled their schools. This company started in 1872 and opened its first school at Chelsea in 1873. By the end of the century, thirty-three schools had been built and provided high-school education for more than 7,100 girls.

Although the curriculum of the new girls' schools was to a great extent modelled on that of the boys' schools, the pioneers of the movement for secondary education for girls took advantage of the recommendation that modern subjects should be included. Thus, at the Cheltenham Ladies' College, Miss Beale included history in the curriculum and, although Latin was still retained, she emphasised the study of German on the ground that it was a good substitute for the classics because it had a complicated grammar. In the North London Collegiate School, Miss Buss introduced French, history, and natural science. It should be noted that the leaders of the movement claimed that girls were equal in intellectual ability to boys and insisted that they should sit for the same examinations on the same terms as boys.

Another pioneer was Miss Emily Davies, who had been a member of the committee of Bedford College. She presented to the Taunton Commission a petition signed by twelve prominent women teachers urging that the foundation for women of a college connected with one of the ancient universities was the greatest educational need of the time. The petition was supported by prominent educationists, scientists, and important figures in the worlds of literature, art, and politics. As a result, Miss Davies secured a house at Hitchin in 1869, and started off with six students. In 1873 the college removed to Girton, just outside Cambridge, and in 1880 Newnham College was established. Newnham will always be associated with the name of its first principal, Miss A. J. Clough (1820-92). Miss Clough had previously taught in schools at Liverpool and Ambleside. She was well known in the north of England where she was instrumental in organising classes for women, under the charge of university lecturers. In order to develop this work, the North of England Council for Promoting the Higher Education of Women was formed and held its first meeting in Leeds in 1867. During the seven years of its existence, Miss Clough was its secretary, and it was at the invitation of the Council that Mr. James Stuart lectured in the north and as a result the University Extension movement (described in Chap. xiii) was launched.

When Henry Sidgwick, the Cambridge philosopher, opened a house for women students at Cambridge, it occurred to him that Miss Clough, whose work in the north of England had become widely known, would be the most suitable person to take charge of it. She accepted the post in 1871 and threw herself whole-heartedly into the work. After the experience of occupying two temporary residences, Miss Clough planned the establishment of a permanent hall. Accordingly a company was formed, and in 1875 the new building was opened at Newnham. Within a few years it proved too small for the increasing number of students, and additional buildings became necessary. In 1880 the foundation was recognised as Newnham College. At first the policy adopted at Newnham was different from that followed at Girton. Miss Davies aimed at securing the admission of her students to the university examinations on the same terms as the men. Miss Clough, on the other hand, was content to arrange special women's courses. Eventually the policy of Girton prevailed and both colleges claimed admission to university examinations for their students.

Meanwhile, a similar movement was taking place at Oxford. In 1879 Somerville Hall and Lady Margaret Hall were both started, each with nine students. Miss Wordsworth, principal of Lady Margaret Hall, opened St. Hugh's Hall in 1886 for twenty-five students who were not able to afford the high fees of Lady Margaret Hall.

Miss Beale, Miss Buss, and Miss Davies were called as expert witnesses to give the Schools Inquiry Commission information about secondary education for girls. Another result of their work was the formation of educational associations of women in different parts of the country, such as the Yorkshire Ladies' Council of Education at Leeds, the Ladies' Educational Society at Liverpool, and the National Union for Improving the Education of Women in London. The work with private governesses was carried on by Miss Charlotte Mason in 1887 by the formation of the Parents' National Education Union, which later opened schools of its own. In 1892 she opened her "House of Education" at Ambleside, to be a training-centre for governesses and to provide courses for mothers in the theory and practice of education. Miss Mason was a prolific writer, and in her books expounds a complete system of instruction for children between the ages of six and twelve.

Yet another consequence was the admission of girls to university examinations. They were allowed to sit for the Cambridge Local examinations in 1865. In 1862 Miss Garrett applied to sit for the London Matriculation. The Senate refused her request, and it was not until 1869 that girls were admitted to the examinations of the University of London. Oxford opened its examinations to girls in 1870. The year 1880 saw women admitted as degree students in the University of London and the newly formed Victoria University of Manchester; in the latter university, for some years, women students could be admitted only after adequate provision had been made for male applicants.

So far, degrees were not open to women at the older universities, but in 1887 Miss Agnaton Ramsay of Girton was the only student at Cambridge to attain the first division of the first class in the classical tripos. This was followed by a memorial addressed to the Senate asking for the degree to be granted to women. The Senate refused, and later, when Miss Fawcett of Newnham was placed before the Senior Wrangler in 1890, it again rejected the proposal to admit women to full membership of the university. Oxford rejected a similar memorial in 1896 by 215 votes to 140. Women were admitted to full membership at Oxford in 1920 and to full membership of the University of Cambridge from the Michaelmas Term 1948. They had been admitted, at Cambridge, to the titles of degrees in 1921.

An extremely important influence upon secondary education in the later years of the century was the impact of the elementary system upon the secondary schools. In the words of the Spens Report, there was a tendency for elementary education to throw up experiments in post-primary education. In the early part of the century, the rapid development of elementary education, first under the National and the British and Foreign School Societies, resulted in experiments in providing instruction of a higher type than elementary. Sometimes this instruction was of a practical character, and at others it approximated to that envisaged by the Taunton Commission for the third-grade schools. Although the issue of the Revised Code of 1862 tended to check the movement in schools which received the Government grant, many voluntary schools organised a "higher top" to the elementary school or arranged for older boys to be sent to a central village school. The recommendations of the Taunton Commission in regard to the third-grade schools prepared the way for an extension of this tendency.

The first decade after the passage of the 1870 Act was chiefly concerned with the provision of elementary education in those districts where it was deficient, but the voluntary schools were still free to experiment, and two interesting examples of schools providing a higher top were to be found at Lancaster and Oswestry. The attempts made by the Education Department, between 1870 and 1880, to expand the elementary curriculum and to secure regular attendance, resulted in an increase in the number of children who remained at school after the age of thirteen. In 1882 a seventh standard was authorised to meet the needs of these children and later ex-standard classes had to be formed. For ease in administration, it became convenient to group these pupils together in one central school, which eventually became the Higher Grade School. Many of these schools organised a science course in order to earn grants from the Science and Art Department. In some districts, older pupils remained in the elementary school and attended a special science class within the school in order to obtain grants.

Certain School Boards in London and the larger towns displayed great interest in developing higher-grade schools. Sheffield opened a Higher Central School in 1878 and similar schools developed in London, Birmingham, Manchester, Leeds, and Bradford. Because of the grants from the Science and Art Department, all these schools developed with a definite science bias. Leeds presents a very good example of the movement described above. Some years before the Act of 1870, the headmaster of the Leeds Parish Church School began to develop his school as a higher-grade school. Science was introduced in order to earn the grants of the Science and Art Department, and this led to the erection of a separate school in 1870, known as the Church Middle-Class School. It was recognised as an Organised Science School by the Science and Art Department in 1895, and, after the 1902 Act, the Board of Education recognised it as a Secondary School. Owing to financial difficulties it was taken over by the Leeds Education Committee in 1907. The school was inspected by Mr. A. P. Laurie, assistant-commissioner of the Royal Commission on Secondary Education, 1895. He reported: "If this school is to regain its position in Leeds, the headmaster will have to reform the teaching both in science and in art, and in manual instruction, and the committee of the school will have to spend a considerable sum of money in proper equipments." [1]   From this school, Mr. Laurie went to the Leeds Higher Grade School, of which he says, "This school is the most interesting in Leeds in many ways, representing as it does the entering of a new power into the existing system of Secondary Education." [2]   This school was opened in temporary buildings in 1885 and transferred to a new building some four years later. Mr. Laurie spoke very highly of the work of Dr. Forsyth and his staff, but he made a criticism which was applicable to most schools of this type.

He wrote: "The school, however, is suffering from two grave defects, both of which are an inheritance from bad traditions, and are likely soon to disappear. In the first place, the school having

[1] *Royal Commission on Secondary Education,* 1895, Vol. VII, p. 158.
[2] *Ibid.,* p. 159.

been organised by the school board, has necessarily suffered from the traditions of elementary schools as to the size of classes, and we consequently find that the classes are much too large, sometimes numbering as many as 60 children. . . . The other serious defect is due to the fact that the school is depending for its income very largely on the grants it earns from the Science and Art Department. The result of this is, in the first place to give an undue bias to science as opposed to other subjects on which grants can be earned; in the second place, to require the children to store up an undue amount of information upon scientific subjects which they are too young to digest and which are necessary if grants are to be earned."

Later he said : "It is impossible to convey in a report the impression which this school makes upon one of efficiency, energy, and vitality, and I think no one who has spent some time inside it can fail to realise that we are here in the presence of a new educational force which has already developed to a vigorous and lusty youth and that it is impossible to say what may be the limit of its growth, or how soon, to quote Dr. Forsyth himself, 'the organisation which was originally devised for the elementary education of the country, passing with great strides across the realms of Secondary Education, may soon be battering at the doors of the ancient universities themselves'. . . this higher grade school represents a new educational movement from below, and a demand from new classes of the population for Secondary Education which has sprung up in a few years." [1]

Another factor was the influence of the reports of the Royal Commission on Technical Instruction, 1882-4. The result was that parents were encouraged to send their children to the higher-grade schools if they were able to keep them at school until fourteen or fifteen years of age. The Cross Commission of 1888 produced conflicting opinions about the higher-grade schools. Some witnesses, while stressing the importance of establishing an efficient system of secondary education, thought this would be better achieved by developing the endowed schools rather than by increasing the number of higher-grade schools. It was also argued that by withdrawing the "cream" of the pupils from the elementary schools, harm would be done both to the teachers and to the scholars of the latter. In reply it was stressed that practical convenience demanded the grouping of the older children in special schools in order to use the supply of available teachers economically. These differences

[1] *Royal Commission on Secondary Education*, 1895, Vol. VII, pp. 161-2.

of opinion were expressed through a majority and a minority report. The latter strongly encouraged the building of higher-grade schools "which would prepare scholars for advanced technical and commercial instruction." The majority, however, considered that the growing extension of elementary education into the secondary sphere would mean that "a portion of the cost of the education of wealthier persons would be defrayed out of the rates."

Bradford was also one of the pioneers in the provision of higher-elementary education. At the time of the Bryce Commission of 1895 the city possessed five higher-grade schools which, after the passage of the 1902 Act, became secondary schools of the town. The Leeds Higher Grade School also became a municipal secondary school under the name of the City of Leeds School. It was closed temporarily during the Second World War and afterwards reopened as the Central High School which provides for grammar-school, technical, and commercial streams. It is still in an experimental stage and may be altered considerably in the near future.

We must leave for a time the account of the progress of higher-elementary education to consider a further important influence upon secondary education in England. To do this it will be necessary to glance at educational progress in Wales.

The growth of Welsh secondary education in the Middle Ages was in many respects similar to that of England. Until the 15th century all Welsh schools were attached to the Church, but with the foundation of Oswestry Grammar School about 1407, the Welsh Independent Grammar Schools came into existence. In the following century a number of similar schools were founded or refounded by the Tudors, in pursuance of their policy of assimilating Welsh life, customs, law, language, and education, to those of England. Just as in England, song-schools and schools of an elementary character existed. The latter were often preparatory schools for the grammar-schools, but, again, as in England at the same period, some grammar-schools included an elementary department. Thus, in the statutes of Oswestry, 1577, the master is directed to provide "an able and efficient usher in the sayd schoole for the teaching of the younger sort to read the A.B.C., the English prymer and the gramer comonly called the King's gramer." During the 17th and 18th centuries a similar deterioration to that in the English schools occurred in the Welsh grammar-schools. The middle years of the 19th century saw an awakening of interest in secondary education. It began with the foundation in 1848, by

Sir Thomas Phillips, of the Collegiate School at Llandovery, which was followed in 1853 by the opening of the girls' schools at Llandaff and Denbigh.   Between 1850 and 1869, the year of the Endowed Schools Act, the Court of Chancery and the Charity Commission revived a number of old endowed schools.   The Taunton Commissioners investigated the state of secondary education in Wales and reported that twenty-four classical and semi-classical endowed schools existed and provided for the education of 961 boys.   As a result of the work carried out by the Endowed Schools Act, the number of schools in 1880 had risen to twenty-seven, with 1,540 boys.   Also three girls' schools had come into existence.   While this slow progress was being achieved, the Reform Act of 1868 produced a great wave of political enthusiasm which advocated Home Rule for Wales, or, at least, special consideration for Welsh affairs.   The result of the General Election of 1880 persuaded the Government that something would have to be done, and as a consequence they decided to appoint a Departmental Committee under the chairmanship of Lord Aberdare.

The terms of reference of the inquiry were "to inquire into the present condition of Intermediate and Higher Education in Wales, and to recommend the measures which they may think advisable for improving and supplementing the provision that is now, or might be made available for such education in the Principality." The inquiry revealed a lamentable state of affairs.   The population of Wales and Monmouthshire in the census of 1881 was 1,570,000. The number of boys receiving some type of secondary education was:—

In endowed grammar-schools	1,540
In proprietary schools	209
In private schools	2,287
Total	4,036

The only three girls' schools were those at Denbigh, Llandaff, and Dolgelly.   The grammar-schools were capable of accommodating 2,846 pupils, but the poorness of the attendance was due to their remoteness from the large towns, the inadequate instruction given, the apathy of the parents, and the prejudice of a population containing a very large number of Nonconformists against schools which were Church institutions.   Another factor which made for the unpopularity of the schools was that in many cases the headmaster was an Englishman with little sympathy for the Welsh language or culture. The endowments were very unequally distributed in relation to the population. Proprietary schools, which had been greatly developed in England, were rare in Wales, but private schools were fairly numerous. Seventy-three were girls' schools with a total of 1,871 pupils. The only county which had anything like sufficient endowments for its needs was Denbigh. To sum up, the proportion of educational endowments of Wales to those of England was as one to three.

The report was enthusiastically received in Wales and bore fruit immediately in the establishment of university colleges at Cardiff and Bangor. Some delay was experienced in regard to intermediate education (*i.e.* intermediate as being between elementary education and that provided by the university colleges), but at length the recommendations of the inquiry were embodied in the Welsh Intermediate Education Act of 1889. The Act created, as the local authority in education, joint education committees for every county and county borough. Each committee consisted of five members, three nominated by the county or county borough council, and two persons "well acquainted with the conditions of Wales and the wants of the people," who were selected by the Lord President of the Privy Council. The Charity Commission was represented on the committee by an assistant-commissioner who was without the power of voting. The duty of each local authority was to submit a scheme for intermediate and technical education for its area. They were to take into account the educational endowments that could be utilised and might levy a rate not exceeding $\frac{1}{2}$d. in the £ if recommended by the county council to do so. The Treasury would make a parliamentary grant not exceeding the contribution from the rates, and this would be paid on the results of an annual inspection and report on each school.

The schemes of the local authorities were to be approved by the Charity Commissioners and the administration of the schools was left in the hands of the governing bodies, on which the county councils were represented. The Act was well received and its provisions were being carried out within six months of its acceptance by Parliament. A number of general conferences of the joint education committees took place and led to the proposal for a central examining board to co-ordinate the work of the committees and inspect and examine the schools. It was not, however, until

1896 that the Central Welsh Board for Intermediate Education was instituted. Many of the endowed grammar-schools were adopted by the education committees, but some of the larger preferred to remain outside the county organisation. The results of the reorganisation were soon apparent. By 1898 the county schemes covered ninety-six schools, of which seventy-nine were newly constructed. Of these, twenty were girls' schools and forty-eight mixed. The number of girls receiving secondary education had risen from 263 in 1880 to 3,372 in 1898.

While affairs in Wales were being reduced to order and system, educational administration in England was growing more and more chaotic and unwieldy. The Education Department was responsible for elementary education as a whole, except for certain schools of an elementary character with endowments worth more than £100. The higher-grade schools, which were secondary schools in everything except name, also came under the authority of the Education Department except in so far as they received grants from the Science and Art Department. The great public schools were independent and the endowed grammar-schools were subject to the Charity Commission except in so far as they also received grants from the Science and Art Department. The Board of Agriculture and Fisheries made grants to certain universities and to one county council for agricultural education in its area. In all this multiplicity of departments there was little co-ordination, and constant overlapping. Nor was local administration in any better state. The endowed schools possessed their separate governing bodies. There were 2,568 different School Boards and 14,238 other authorities (school-attendance committees and boards of managers). It was felt that some kind of Government action was necessary to bring order out of confusion, but the extent to which Government intervention might grow was a matter for controversy. The waste and overlapping due to too many cooks led to an attempt in 1892 to introduce legislation enabling counties to organise secondary education as they had done in Wales. The attempt failed, but owing to the resolutions passed by the Bradford Independent Labour Party in 1893 and the recommendations of a conference on secondary education in England called by the Vice-Chancellor of Oxford, the Government resolved to appoint a Royal Commission on Secondary Education in 1894. Its chairman was Mr. (afterwards Viscount) Bryce and its report was published in 1895. Before we examine the Bryce Commission and its recommendations it will be necessary to turn our attention to the development of elementary education. But before leaving this period it will be of interest to consider the achievements of another outstanding headmaster, Thring of Uppingham.

Edward Thring was born at Alford in Somerset in 1821. From Ilminster Grammar School he was sent to Eton, then under the stern rule of Dr. Keate. As a foundation scholar of Eton, Thring went in due course to King's College, Cambridge, in 1841. He showed promise of exceptional ability, and after remaining at Cambridge until 1847 as a Fellow of King's, he was ordained and served as a curate at St. James's, Gloucester. His parochial experience led him to believe that a clergyman's parish work is an excellent apprenticeship to the profession of a schoolmaster. It was due to his teaching experience in the National Schools of Gloucester that Thring formed the opinion that the highest teaching skill is needed in the education of the younger children. After a breakdown from overwork, Thring took a curacy at Marlow, where he did some private tutoring. He declined the offer of an assistantship at Eton, but in 1852 he applied for the vacancy at Durham School. The headmaster of Uppingham was appointed and this led Thring to apply in turn for the vacancy at Uppingham. On being appointed in 1853, he said, "I think I have found my life work to-day." At the time of Thring's appointment, Uppingham was a small country grammar-school which had been founded by the Archdeacon of Leicester in 1584. A similar school controlled by the same governors had been founded at Oakham. Thring wanted to rebuild Uppingham and turn it into a large public school in which he could work out his own ideas of what a public school should be. He was definitely opposed to the large classes which were to be found in most public schools of the time. He considered that thirty boarders was the maximum a master and his wife could look after, and that a form should never exceed thirty. The ideal public boarding-school would not consist of more than ten or eleven houses, each containing about thirty boys. If the school were larger than this, the headmaster could not know each individual personally and would be dependent on others for his information. The idea of a multilateral school containing 2,000 pupils would have appeared to Thring as an educational monstrosity. He had definite ideas about the boarding arrangements. The long dormitory such as he had experienced at Eton was something to be avoided. He believed in each boy having his separate cubicle and study. In a large school a variety of interests, tastes, and abilities will be found amongst the boys. Thring firmly believed that every boy could do something well, and it was therefore the business of the schoolmaster to find out what this something might be, and of the school to provide a variety of studies and occupations. He was also convinced of the importance of games and physical education, and in 1859 he opened the first school gymnasium in England. Shops for woodwork and metalwork were built and the school was provided with a swimming-bath and opportunities given for school gardens. Like Arnold, he attached great importance to the school chapel. From the moment of his appointment, Thring was working for the realisation of his ideal, but he had to face enormous difficulties. He was not a wealthy man and he put every penny he could spare into the rebuilding of the school. In 1857 the debt on the school had grown to £2,680, but still he persevered with his schemes. He had to meet with opposition from his governors, who did not want Uppingham superior to Oakham.

When the governors refused to support him in building the school chapel, Thring set to work and raised the necessary funds through subscriptions, and the chapel was finished in 1865 at a cost of £10,000. The governors also refused to co-operate with him in the rebuilding of the schoolroom, but he obtained support from his staff, who believed in him to such an extent that they were willing to invest their savings in the venture. Even as late as 1858, only one of the governors had troubled to visit the school to see how the work was progressing. The result of this reconstruction daunted Thring in striving after his ideal. Then came a cruel blow. The Endowed Schools Act was passed in 1869 and the Commissioners claimed that Uppingham came under their jurisdiction. Thring fought this claim, for he believed that Government intervention in the affairs of the public schools would curtail their freedom and independence and prevent them from developing along their own individual lines. This led Thring to form the idea of presenting a united front to the threat aimed at the independence of the schools. Accordingly he suggested that a meeting of the headmasters of the most important endowed schools be held to consider what steps should be taken to meet the situation. The result was the constitution of the Headmasters' Conference in 1869. The first members of the Conference were Uppingham, Repton, Sherborne, Tonbridge, Liverpool College, Bury St. Edmunds,

Richmond (Yorks), Bromsgrove, Oakham, the King's School (Canterbury), Felsted, Lancing, and Norwich. The older public schools soon joined in and, as further schools asked to be admitted, certain conditions of eligibility for membership were drawn up.   The member schools had to be satisfactory from an educational standpoint, must send an adequate number of boys to the universities, and have a headmaster and governing body who were independent. At first the members were limited to 150 schools, but in 1937 the limit was increased to 200 and the rules for admission modified. Direct-grant schools were admitted, and even maintained schools, if "the Committee is satisfied on the general question of the freedom of the School and the Headmaster."   When the Fleming Committee inquired into the public schools in 1944, it accepted as a working definition of a public school a school represented on the Headmasters' Conference or on the Governing Bodies' Association. When the Government proposed a central examination council, the Conference in 1873 urged the universities of Oxford and Cambridge to form a joint board to inspect and examine schools and grant certificates.

Thring went through a very anxious time in 1875 when enteric fever broke out in the school. It seemed as though the school would be broken up, but he saved the situation by evacuating it to a site near Aberystwyth. The school returned to Uppingham in 1878, where Thring remained as headmaster until his rather sudden death in 1887.

Thring did much to broaden the curriculum of the school, as we have seen. He was not a musician himself, but he had a great belief in the refining and stimulating power of music, and with the assistance of one of the masters he built up a strong musical tradition at Uppingham. The mornings at Uppingham were given up to the compulsory subjects of the curriculum—classics, mathematics, and English—but in the afternoons the boys were granted a good many options and were encouraged to enter the workshops, referred to previously. Thring was also interested in the art and technique of the teacher, and to help new-comers to the profession he wrote his *Theory and Practice of Teaching* in 1883;   a book that for many years after was studied by intending teachers.

CHAPTER VI

ELEMENTARY EDUCATION IN THE AGE OF PHILANTHROPY

It is a great mistake to think that, before the work of the great philanthropic societies of the 18th century, England was unprovided with schools giving elementary instruction. On the other hand, one must not hasten to the opposite extreme and assume that the provision of primary education was in any degree adequate to the increasing population of the country. That many primary schools existed is certain, but we have no means at present of ascertaining their number.

Adamson writes, "The practice, by a few private persons in different parts of the country, of maintaining or founding purely elementary schools for the poor, which had been begun under Elizabeth, continued, and the number of such schools probably increased during the century which followed. For example, at Lambeth in 1661 Richard Lawrence, a Commonwealth soldier, founded a charity school for twenty boys. During the period 1671-81, Dr. Busby, headmaster of Westminster School, gave five or six pounds annually for instructing the poor children of the parish. The Blue Coat School, Westminster, founded in 1688 . . . educated and clothed, and, finally, apprenticed fifty boys. In 1697 Colonel Colchester, one of the five original founders of the Society for the Propagation of Christian Knowledge, was maintaining at Westbury on Severn a school in which sixty-seven boys and girls learned writing and reading, the horn book,[1] primer and New Testament." [2]

[1] The Horn Book was a development from the Prymer. The latter was originally the people's prayer book of pre-Reformation days, containing those parts of the Breviary suitable for the laity. The 15th- and 16th-century prymers not only contained instructions on the Creed, the Lord's Prayer, etc., but were generally prefaced by the alphabet, lists of vowels and consonants, and lists of syllables, *e.g.* ab, eb, ib, etc. The Horn Book appeared as early as 1450 as a kind of abridged prymer. The alphabetic preface to the prymer, together with the Lord's Prayer and the Creed, were printed on a card and attached to a wooden tablet. The card was protected by a sheet of horn. The handle of the tablet made the affair look like a bat, and no doubt schoolboys used it for this purpose as well as for learning to read. Girls often worked out their own little prymers with needle and coloured wools. These samplers contained the alphabet, vowels and consonants, texts, prayers, verses, and illustrations of various kinds. Eventually the name "prymer" was given to any type of introductory textbook.

[2] Adamson, J. W. *A Short History of Education*, p. 197, C.U.P., 1919.

At Leeds there was, in addition to the grammar-school, a Free School which was conducted in the chantry on Leeds Bridge until 1728. This chapel was bought by the trustees of the grammar-school in 1579 and used as a reading-school. It may have served the purpose of a preparatory school for the grammar-school. Thoresby states that he received part of his education from "the Reverend Mr. Robert Garnet, M.A. of Christ's Col. Cambridge," at "a private grammar school at the North-end of the Great Stone Bridge." This is generally accounted a reference to the Free School. He adds that "the higher Story is for Writing and Arithmetick lately taught by Mr. Robert Kettlewell." The Minutes of the Committee of Pious Uses at Leeds contain the following entries:—

"1675 Robert Kettlewell, gent., allowed and approved to keep a writeing school in the Schoole at Leedes bridge end . . .

"1676 John Moore, gent., ditto.

"1677 Joseph Pickles, gent., ditto.

"1694 Mr. John Rotton admitted vice Lawson [?] deceased but to keep it in good repair.

"1698-9 Mr. Robert Jackson to have use of the school and to agree with Mr. Hurst for such benches etc. as he has there." [1]

At Bradford in the 17th century there is evidence of the existence of a free endowed school which was distinct from the Bradford Grammar School and was probably the parish school.[2]

In the writer's own parish of Adel, Yorkshire, the registers contain the entry of the death of the schoolmaster, William Smith, 1627, and, towards the end of the century, the entry of the baptism of "Elizabeth Watson, daughter of Israel Watson schole-master of Eccup." Thus, in one small parish of Adel-cum-Eccup, which at that time had a population of less than 400, there were two distinct schools. The *Account of Charity Schools* for 1724 lists Adel (spelt as Addle) as containing twenty-five pupils.

For convenience, the primary schools which existed before 1698 may be divided into the following classes:—

(1) Pre-Elizabethan schools which had survived until the eighteenth century, *e.g.* the Clerk's School at Skipton.

---

[1] A. C. Price. *History of the Leeds Grammar School*, R. Jackson, 1919.

[2] Bradford Grammar School is an interesting example of a grammar-school which had a long life before the official date of its foundation. Its charter was granted by Charles II in 1662, but the school was probably in existence as early as 1547 at the dissolution of the chantries. The records show that Gervase Worrall was appointed master of the school in 1641.

(2) Schools originally of the grammar type which had become impoverished and were now primary schools.

(3) Petty schools functioning as preparatory to grammar-schools.

(4) Parochial endowed schools. Many of these were charity schools endowed by wealthy individuals living in the locality who were stimulated by the example of such institutions as Christ's Hospital.

(5) Private schools.

The first three classes have already received attention and the last will be considered later in this chapter. The fourth class merits a more detailed study. The *Reports of the Charity Commissioners* (1818-43) list 460 endowed non-classical schools as existing before 1698, but this total is known to be incomplete. Moreover, private individuals continued to endow schools in the 18th century, many of which at the time of their establishment had no connection with the philanthropic societies. The explanation of this educational activity in the 17th century lies partly in the new intellectual and social forces which were spreading and partly in the religious motive.

One of the earliest of 17th-century endowed schools for primary education is that of Henley-upon-Thames. Carlisle describes it as follows: "Dame Elizabeth Periam about the year of Our Lord 1609 founded and endowed a Charity School in . . . Henley upon Thames, for the education in writing, reading and casting accounts (but not in grammar learning), clothing and apprenticing twenty poor boys of the said town." [1]

In fact, the intention of the Long Parliament seems to have been to set up a system of primary schools which, if it had been carried out, would have created parochial schools somewhat on the model of Scotland. Thus the Act for the Better Propagation and Preaching of the Gospel in Wales and Redress of Some Grievances, 22nd February 1649, set up about sixty free schools in Wales. The schools were endowed by funds obtained through the disestablishment and partial disendowment of the Welsh Church. Later in the same year another Act allocated the first fruits and tenths, which since the Reformation had been in the hands of the Crown, to augment the stipends of preaching ministers and schoolmasters. It is of interest to note that this was the first grant ever made by the

[1] Carlisle. *Endowed Grammar Schools of England and Wales*, Vol. II, p. 307.

State to education in this country. The Restoration put an end to these schemes of State intervention, and until 1833 all schools were maintained by voluntary effort.

A good example of a 17th-century charity school in a town is afforded by the Green Coat School at Wakefield.[1] The school originated from two sources. In 1674 John Storie, a benefactor of Wakefield Grammar School, left the rent of his lands to enable twelve boys to proceed to the grammar-school and from thence to the university. This was known as the Storie Petty Gift. His wishes were carried out as soon as his will was proved, and the governors of the grammar-school named twelve boys and resolved "that John Pickersgill, Schoolmaster, be admitted to teach and instruct the twelve boys included in John Story, gent., his gift." The number twelve was obtained by nominating three boys over a period of four successive years. They were to be admitted as "free petty scholars to be taught by the foresaid Pickersgill, till they be fitt for the Free Grammar School." A room for the petty school was never obtained, so that the boys were probably educated on the grammar-school premises. In 1675 the Spokesman and another member of the Governors of Wakefield Grammar School were appointed to see if Pickersgill was actually teaching the twelve boys, and it seems they found that everything was in order.

Quite independently of this arrangement, the governors of the grammar-school decided to open a charity school in Wakefield in connection with the administration of the Elizabethan poor-laws. We find that in 1703 twenty-two boys and nineteen girls, scattered over seven different places, were receiving elementary instruction. This was an unsatisfactory and uneconomical arrangement, and it came to an end in 1705 when it was "then agreed with Mr. William Lambert to Bee Schoolmaister for teaching in the free petty Schoole in Westgate, sallery per annum Twenty pound; for a Dame after election to her place Tenn pound." We know that the estate of John Storie did not realise as much as was expected, so presumably the petty and charity schools were amalgamated.

At first the children were clothed in grey, but in 1737 orders were issued that white clothing should be bought and dyed green. Hence the name of the school. The account rendered in 1714 which follows gives some idea of the school at that period.

[1] Full details of the school were collected by M. H. Peacock, formerly headmaster of Wakefield Grammar School, and published in pamphlet form in 1928.

	£	s.	d.
For cloathing 70 boys and girls at 35s. each per annum	122	10	0
For Master and Mistress' Sallery per ann.	40	0	0
For Coals and Repairs to School House and the pavement in the Street per ann.	6	0	0
For Books, Pen, Ink, and Paper per ann.	10	0	0
	£178	10	0

The school continued to receive fresh bequests and, in 1839, weekly pence paid as fees were abolished. Fitch visited the school on behalf of the Taunton Commission and he advised against its closure and the diversion of the funds to erect a middle-class school. By that time the annual income had risen to £600 and there were 140 boys and 70 girls on roll. The school was closed in 1875 and the endowments used for the creation of Storie scholarships, twenty-four for boys and twelve for girls, to be held at the grammar-school and girls' high school. These scholarships are open to pupils who have been educated for at least three years in the schools of the Wakefield L.E.A., and are awarded on the results of the tests for grammar-school selection.

Many country primary schools owed their existence to the philanthropic activities of local gentry, but information about their location and the number of children educated in them is scanty. The returns made to the Charity Commissioners are incomplete and often inaccurate. A typical instance of an 18th-century school is provided by the Burnt Yates Endowed School, which is situated in the parish of Ripley in the district of the Claro Divisional Executive of the West Riding L.E.A.[1]

It is an illustration of how a particular benefaction could have widespread effects and create, as it were, a fashion in the neighbourhood for endowing schools. In this case the impetus was given by the establishment of Ripley Free School, through the endowment of Catherine and Mary Ingilby in 1702. They provided that a master, who should be a member of the Church of England, should be

[1] The writer is supervising a team of post-graduate research workers who are investigating the provision of primary education in the West Riding during the period 1550-1760. The area of the Claro Divisional Executive, which covers roughly the country between the Nidd and the Swale, seems to have been rich in private benefactors during the 17th and 18th centuries. No doubt other areas in the West Riding and in the rest of the country would yield similar results. The investigation involves much patient work in classifying and examining letters, deeds, parish registers, and other records, many of which are to be found in the libraries of the descendants of the original benefactors.

appointed at Ripley, "a layman of sober life and conversation, able to teach and instruct youth in reading English, writing, and the common and useful rules of arithmetic—and once every week cause his scholars to learn the Church catechism." The influence of the Ingilby family is clearly shown in the schools which were founded at Hampsthwaite, West Syke Green (before 1711), Hampsthwaite, Ridsdale's School, 1711, Hookstone's School, Menwith-cum-Darley, 1748, Burnt Yates, 1760, and Braithwaite, 1778.

The school at Burnt Yates, which had been opened in 1750, was endowed by Admiral Robert Long in 1760. The original building, which is now the head teacher's house, contained the schoolroom and a trustees' room on the upper floor. Admiral Long directed that as long as only one master was employed, the number of boys was not to exceed thirty, but if there was sufficient money a schoolmistress might be appointed for the girls. The boys were to be taught to read, write, and cast accounts: the girls to sew, knit, read, and write ; and both should be instructed in the catechism. The Ingilby influence was shown by the appointment of the Rector of Ripley as permanent chairman of the trustees.

The school received a most interesting bequest from a sea captain, William Mountaine. In 1778 he gave a sum of £140, derived from the tolls collected on the Wetherby-Grassington turnpike road. The gift also included his books and pamphlets, a bookcase, pair of globes, some charts, a telescope, some mathematical instruments, and portraits of his wife and himself. He also arranged for the sum of fifty shillings a year to be paid to a librarian to look after the books. At the close of the last century, the library was sold to a Leeds bookseller. The writer has only been able to discover one of the books, a pamphlet entitled *An Account of the Methods used to describe Lines, on Dr. Halley's chart of the Terraqueous Globe ; shewing the Variations of the Magnetic Needle, By William Mountaine and James Dodson, Fellows of the Royal Society, 1756.* Mountaine also left £100 to the trustees, the interest on which was to augment the stipend of the schoolmaster at Dacre Banks (founded 1695). An oak chest with three locks is in the trustees' room, and the letters, deeds, accounts, and minutes in it are sufficient to give a complete picture of the life and work of the school over a period of more than 150 years.

These documents provide interesting illustrations of the tendencies in primary education during this period. Thus there seems to have been a large number of Catholic children in the neighbourhood.

At first they attended the school, but a regulation of 1811 forbade their admission. This was rescinded at the time of Catholic Emancipation. The Charity Commissioners visited the school in 1819, and the letters of the trustees show that they approved the work carried out there, but they criticised the constitution of the governing body. Most of the trustees lived at a considerable distance from the school, and were elderly, and, because of frequent illness, the meetings were not as regular as they should have been. The chest contains a large number of letters from members of the trustees, apologising for absence owing to sickness. The unsatisfactory nature of the half-time system, the working of the Revised Code, and the pupil-teacher system, topics discussed later in this book, are all illustrated by the documents. The accounts show that the trustees' meeting was evidently a jovial affair, for such items as the following frequently appear:—

| 1798 | March 29th | Three bottles, port wine | 10s. 6d. |
| | May 31st. | Do   Do one Sherry | 15s. 0 |

Mountaine's Charity, following a common custom, provided for money prizes and for gifts of food and clothing to poor scholars. The following report of William Cockett, master from 1810 to 1856, refers to boys considered for prizes. The reader should note, in the light of the report of the Newcastle Commission, the ages of the scholars concerned. The report shows that even at this date the school was independent and stood apart from the charity-school movement co-ordinated by the S.P.C.K.

"1st. Thomas Pullen aged 15 or upwards has been regular in attendance at school for two years last past and has behaved well while there. He has gone through common Arithmetic. I think him eligible to partake of the bounty contemplated by the Trustees.

"2nd. John Andrew is 15 years old, he is now learning Barter and has behaved well at school, he has lost his father and his mother who is left with a large family would be thankful to have him put to a trade. I would recommend him to the notice of the Trustees.

"3rd. William Coverdale is 14 years old and was very regular in his attendance at school and at church till about two years ago when he was taken away and sent to a mill. A few months ago he came again and attention since that time has been paid to his writing and reading, and if three months more were allowed to go over his accompts again as far as the Rules of Practice, I should think him a fit object for the Bounty of the Trustees.

"4th.   William Thorpe is about 11 years old, his grandfather thinks his time would be better spent at school a year or two longer, otherwise he is a very active lad and has made good progress in his learning as his books will testify.

"5th.   John Maud is 14 years old, has been irregular in his attendance at school and his progress in learning as may be expected but indifferent but his father is very desirous that he should be put to a trade, as he has a large family and cannot afford to keep him much at school.

"The two first would have had Mr. Cracroft's recommendation if he had been present and I have to express to the Meeting his wish that the Trustees should become subscribers either to the Bible Society or to the Society for promoting Xstn Knowledge in order to obtain Bibles, Testaments and Prayer Books at the reduced prices for the use of the school and for reward books for the scholars. I have also to express his wish that three dozen of Hymn Books be purchased for the use of the school.

"I have also Mr. Cracroft's permission to say that he has observed that the walk leading to the school is rough and unpleasant and that a part of the school floor and the school-house floor are bad and he thinks that if the old flags were taken to amend the walk and new ones had for the floors, two benefits would be conferred with a little more than the expence of one.

"The school is in want of 3 doz: of Catechisms, 1 doz: Markham's Spellings, 2 doz: A.B.C. books, 2 doz. Scripture References, $\frac{1}{2}$ doz. Bibles and 2 Reams of writing paper—also—3 doz. Prayer Books and 3 doz. Hymn Books.

"The number of scholars upon the list

Boys	56
Girls	54
In all	110

Burnt Yates School
May 30th 1826
WILLIAM COCKETT." [1]

[1] The writer wishes to thank Mr. A. A. Ingham, B.Sc., M.Ed., Education Officer, Claro Divisional Executive, and Mrs. Kenyon, B.A., the headmistress of Burnt Yates School, for their courtesy in giving him access to the documents.   A detailed account of this School is given in *Researches and Studies*, No. 2, May 1950 ("The Endowed School of Rear-Admiral Long at Burnt Yates, Ripley, Yorks." S. J. Curtis), University of Leeds Institute of Education.

As an endowed school with an income of over £100 per annum, Burnt Yates came under the provisions of the Endowed Schools Act of 1869 and eventually received a new scheme of government. At present it is an infant and junior mixed school with about thirty-three pupils in attendance.

The closing years of the 17th century witnessed a remarkable revival of interest in elementary education. Professor Helen Wodehouse links the revival with the discovery of the idea of the joint-stock company. "Power, it was found, could be multiplied indefinitely, at any one point, if a number of persons put together their small sums of money and handed over the management to a chosen few. . . . Might it not be possible, some good people asked, to combat by this means the mass of carelessness, ignorance, and irreligion which they saw in the poor? Many Religious Societies and Societies for the Reformation of Manners, came into being in England, but all have been overshadowed by the greatest, the Society for Promoting Christian Knowledge." [1]

The S.P.C.K. was founded in 1698, and among its many aims was the foundation of schools to give a sound education, religious and secular, to the children of the poor. The first meeting of the new society adopted a resolution to "further and promote that good design of erecting Cathechetical schools in each parish in and about London." The society proposed to obtain funds for the erection and maintenance of Charity Schools by issuing lists to the parishes inviting people to subscribe. The money obtained in this way was supplemented by the preaching of special "charity" sermons at which a collection in support of the schools was made. The idea caught on and was received everywhere with great enthusiasm. Rich and poor hastened to give what they could afford in support of the movement. Wealthy individuals either contributed a lump sum or engaged themselves to pay a fixed amount each year. Some of the clergy undertook to teach a number of children gratis or contributed to the expenses of children attending school. In some parishes, certain individuals were appointed as parish clerks on condition that they, as part of their duties, would teach a number of children. At Warwick, a collecting-box was placed in the church with the inscription, "For the use and increase of the Charity School." In some districts the parents themselves applied the principle of self-help and themselves contributed towards the education

[1] Helen Wodehouse. *A Survey of the History of Education*, p. 141, Edward Arnold, 1929.

of their children.   The best-known example is that at Winleton, County Durham, in 1717.   Here "the workmen of an ironwork, who are about 400 or 500, allow one farthing and a half per shilling per week, which, together with their master's contribution, maintains their poor, and affords about £17 per annum for teaching their children to read etc."

The bishops preached many charity sermons which not only added to the funds of the society but helped to heighten the enthusiasm.   By 1754 the society claimed that its efforts had resulted in the establishment of 2,044 schools containing 51,161 children.

The committee of the S.P.C.K. took its work very seriously and realised that building schools was not sufficient unless trained teachers could be obtained and the efficiency of the instruction maintained.   Accordingly, they proposed the establishment of a training-college "to prepare young persons for the arduous and responsible work of instructing children."   This proposal did not come to anything, but in 1701 the Rev. M. Coghan was appointed inspector of the charity schools in the London neighbourhood at a stipend of £20 per annum.   Within a very short space of time the movement spread to all parts of the country.   In 1705 Ralph Thoresby was largely instrumental in establishing a school at Leeds. He was a corresponding member of the S.P.C.K., and in his diary shows considerable interest in the fortunes of the school.   In 1620 a workhouse had been erected near the Leeds Grammar School and part of the workhouse building was converted into a charity school where, we are told, forty poor boys and girls were maintained and "duly instructed in the Knowledge and Practice of the Christian Religion ; taught to read and write, with a competent skill in Arithmetick, as also to spin, sew, knit, etc."   The pupils were also taught to "Scribble, a new Invention whereby the different colours in the deyed Wool are delicately mixed."   The school was maintained by voluntary subscriptions which totalled £200 a year. Thoresby not only contributed to the funds but became one of the collectors for the school, persuading many of his friends to become contributors as well.   A seat on the north side of the parish church was allotted to the children "who decently cloathed in blue, first appeared in public, March 24th, 1705."   In 1726 the school was removed to another site, and in 1752 a room for spinning was added at a cost of £76.   In 1815 attendance at the school was restricted to girls only.

The Leeds Charity School is an illustration of a development which was common to the whole country. The schools gradually introduced industrial occupations (such as spinning), and gardening. Some were day-schools, but others, like that at Leeds, were boarding-schools and frequently provided a distinctive uniform for the pupils. Thus we hear of blue-coat, green-, grey-, or yellow-coat schools. It is noteworthy that most of the schools admitted girls as well as boys.[1]

The Dissenters had their own charity schools, and even claimed to have originated them. The first school is said to have been one founded in 1687 at Southwark. Originally it contained forty children, but soon the number increased to 130. In 1728 Dr. Watts published an *Essay towards the encouragement of Charity Schools*, particularly those which were supported by Protestant Dissenters.

In the S.P.C.K. schools, the schoolmaster was required to be at least twenty-five years of age, a member of the Church of England,

[1] The S.P.C.K. published the following tables giving the cost of clothing boys and girls in 1758:—

An ACCOUNT of the Rates of Cloathing the Poor belonging to CHARITY-SCHOOLS and WORK-HOUSES.

Charge of Cloathing a Boy, with Yorkfhire Cloth, or blue Kerfey.

	£	s.	d.
A Boy's Suit	0	11	6
A Shirt of Doulafs Cloth	0	1	10
A Pair of Stockings	0	0	10
A Pair of Wafh-Leather Gloves	0	0	7
A Knit Cap, with Tuft and String, of any Colour ..	0	0	9
A Band	0	0	3
A Pair of Buckles	0	0	1
A Pair of Shoes	0	2	7
The Total ..	0	18	5

The Charge of Cloathing a Girl.

	£	s.	d.
A Gown and Petticoat	0	8	0
A Coif and Band of fine Ghenting	0	1	0
A Shift of Doulafs Cloth	0	1	10
A White, Blue, or Checquer'd Apron	0	1	0
A Pair of Leather Bodice and Stomacher, 2s. 10d. or	0	2	8
A Pair of Woollen Stockings	0	0	10
A Pair of Shoes	0	2	4
A Pair of Buckles	0	0	1
A Pair of Wafh-Leather Gloves	0	0	7
The Total ..	0	18	6

N.B.

The different Stature of Children is allowed for in this Eftimate, and a Number may be cloathed at the above Rates, by John Hall and John Lodge, at the Acorn and Charity-School Warehoufe oppofite Gray's-Inn Gate, Holborn, London.

able to pass an examination in the principles of the Christian religion, a good disciplinarian, able to write a good hand, and to have an aptitude for arithmetic. One wonders how many really came up to this standard.

Both the Government and the S.P.C.K. were anxious that persons of Jacobite tendencies should be kept out of the schools. Hence all masters and mistresses were obliged to make the following declaration on being appointed to a school: "That they do heartily achnowledge his Majesty King George, to be the only lawful and rightful King of these Realms; and will to the utmost of their Power educate the Children committed to their Charge, in a true Sense of their Duty to him as such: That they will not by any Words or Actions, do anything whereby to lessen their Esteem of, or their Obedience to the present Government. That upon all publick Days, when their Children may be likely to appear among any disorderly Persons, they will do their best to keep them in, and severely punish them, if they shall hear of their running into any Tumults, or publick Meetings, contrary to the good Order of such Schools and Scholars."[1]

When one realises the number of schools said to have been established and the amount of money available, it became apparent that a great many of these schools must have been housed in existing buildings. No doubt some of them represented a revival of an earlier endowed elementary school which had closed through lack of funds. The boys were apprenticed to various trades and the girls usually entered domestic service.

Mandeville attacked the schools bitterly. He sneered at the "enthusiastic passion for Charity-schools" amongst the wealthy and argued that the education of the poor would result in discontent and rebellion. The poor occupied a position in society which had been assigned to them, and if they were to be labourers they should be used to their position from the very first. The enthusiasm for charity schools began to wane after the middle of the century. Some failed because of incompetent management; others lingered on until they were eventually incorporated with the National Schools of the 19th century.

Besides the charity schools and those endowed schools which had survived from the previous century, popular education was represented by private schools. These seem to have been fairly

[1] *An Account of the Society for Promoting Christian Knowledge*, pp. 37-8, London, 1758.

numerous, but we have no means of ascertaining their number. Some were "Dame" schools intended for very young children and are described in the oft-quoted verse of Shenstone in 1742.

> "In every village marked with little spire,
> Embower'd in trees, and hardly known to fame,
> There dwells, in lowly shed and mean attire,
> A matron, whom we schoolmistress name,
> Who boasts unruly brats with birch to tame."

Some of these schools attained a certain measure of efficiency, but for the most part they were very inefficient baby-minding establishments. Schools for older children were taught by schoolmasters. A few of these were really well-run schools, but in most cases the masters were drawn from the very dregs of society. Many were ignorant and brutal, much addicted to drink, and in numerous cases carried on at the same time some kind of artisan employment, turning their attention from their work at intervals to superintend the running of the school. Often the schoolmaster was a man who had tried and failed at every occupation in turn and had taken up the charge of a school as a last resort. For the majority of children the only education they received was that given in their own homes. The boys were often trained in their father's occupation and the girls learnt sewing, knitting, cookery, and domestic work from their mothers. In a few homes the parents taught their children the alphabet, reading and writing, and there are cases of boys who later attained eminence without any other training than that provided by the home. When, however, all these different agencies are considered, the fact remains that only a very small proportion of the child population received even the most elementary instruction. The proportion of literates amongst the population was probably much less than in Tudor days, and as the century wore on, owing to the industrial changes and the growth of the population, it became even smaller.

As early as 1675 Thomas Firmin had erected a spinning-factory where children of four or five years of age were taught to read and to spin. In 1697 Locke had suggested a similar type of industrial school for pauper children. A few industrial schools were set up in the early part of the 18th century, but it was not until the factories began to multiply that they became more numerous.

The boys were taught useful occupations such as gardening, carpentry, cobbling, and printing; the girls spinning, knitting, sewing, and straw-plaiting. The work done by the pupils was sold and the proceeds went to their maintenance. If the child's earnings exceeded the cost of his keep, he was given a cash payment. The idea was to make each school self-supporting. In some schools of industry the children were taught reading and writing, but there was always the temptation to emphasise the occupational aspect in order to cover expenses. The boys' schools were largely a failure as their products did not command as ready a sale as those from the girls' schools. As the change to factory conditions accelerated, the demand for child labour became so great that children of tender years could be found work in the mills and mines and bring home their earnings to augment the family wage. Even foundlings and orphans were insufficient to keep up numbers in the schools of industry. The guardians of the poor often apprenticed pauper children to masters whose only consideration was the amount of work they could obtain from them.

By 1780 the influence of the charity-school movement had practically ceased, and the schools of industry, never very numerous, were declining in numbers. The effects of the great industrial changes were becoming very noticeable in the drift from the country to the towns and in the rapid growth of population in the new industrial areas. In the age of domestic industries, children had been accustomed from their early years to working in the home or on the farms at occupations which were not wholly unpleasant and which to a certain extent were educational. Now, the demand for child labour brought them into the factories, but they still had one day of the week in which they were free. It was their wild and mischievous behaviour on Sundays that was the occasion of the Sunday School movement which for the first time had the object of extending education to the poor of the whole country. The movement is generally associated with the name of Robert Raikes of Gloucester. Raikes was not, however, the inventor of the Sunday School, nor are we certain that he was even the first to open a Sunday School in his own city of Gloucester. John Wesley had experimented with a Sunday School at Savannah in 1737, and about the same time one was opened at High Wycombe by Hannah Ball. The honour of opening the first Sunday School in Gloucester probably belongs to Raikes's friend, the Rev. Thomas Stock, who had started a school in his parish of St. John. It is possible that the idea resulted from a conference between the two, but we do know that, in 1780, Raikes opened his first Sunday School in Sooty

Alley, so called because it was the quarter in which the chimney-sweeps lived.[1]

Raikes was the descendant of an old Yorkshire family which had migrated to Gloucester. In 1722 his father had founded the *Gloucester Journal,* a paper which warmly supported philanthropic movements. Raikes was intensely interested in alleviating the terrible conditions of the prisoners in the Gloucester gaol. He met a kindred spirit in John Howard, and the result was that from 1773 onwards the *Gloucester Journal* did all it could in support of Howard's crusade.

Raikes was also acquainted with Wilberforce and his efforts to suppress the slave-trade. As Raikes's biographer says, "The Sunday School system with which the name of Robert Raikes will ever be inseparably connected may be said to have originated in the Gloucester gaols. It was there that he learnt the direct connection between ignorance and crime, and there he saw the futility of punishing the effect without removing the cause." [2]

At this time the chief industry in Gloucester was the manufacture of pins. Many children were employed in the industry, which was carried on partly in their homes and partly in factories. Sunday was a day of freedom for them, and their wild, lawless behaviour so horrified Raikes that he wrote in the *Journal*: "The misuse of Sunday appears by the declaration of every criminal to be their first step in the course of wickedness." He testified that "the farmers and other inhabitants of the towns and villages receive more injury in their property in the Sabbath than in all the week besides; this in a great measure proceeds from the lawless state of the younger class who are allowed to run wild on that day free from restraint." Whether this was exaggerated or not, it seemed to Raikes that the most effective way of preventing crime would be to keep the children occupied on Sundays and try to do something to improve them. One story relates that Raikes's attention was directed to the lawlessness of the children by the noise they made under his office window where he was preparing his Monday morning article for the *Journal*.

His friend Stocks opened his school on Sundays only, but from the start Raikes opened on week-days as well. He began by employing paid teachers. The first teacher received 1s. for Sundays and 2s. for teaching during the meal-time break on week-days. Parents

[1] In 1763 a Sunday School had been established at Catterick, Yorks, by the Rev. Theophilus Lindsey.
[2] A. Gregory. *Robert Raikes*, p. 27, Hodder and Stoughton, 1877.

who wanted instruction for their children during the week paid 1d. The scholars were obtained in various ways; sometimes by persuading the parents to send their children to Sunday School, sometimes by meeting the children in the street and bribing them with gifts of sweets and presents to attend. The first school remained open only for six months, but a little later Raikes restarted it under better conditions near his own home. He soon found difficulty in managing his little hooligans, e.g. one boy brought a badger to school and let it loose during the lesson. To maintain order he resorted to flogging, and on one occasion it is recorded that he punished a boy who told a lie by "pressing the tips of his fingers on the bars of the fireplace so that he was blistered a bit." [1] Raikes was neither a bully nor was he cruel, and he soon found out his mistake in resorting to harsh methods. At heart he was a most kindly man and experience showed him that the best way of controlling children was to try to understand them, win their liking, and discover the kind of things which interested them.

The result was that the school became increasingly successful and this led him to open three other schools. This experiment attracted a good deal of attention, and Raikes was able to publicise his work in the *Journal*. Soon the movement spread to the rest of the county and eventually to other parts of England. This diffusion was assisted by the formation, in 1785, of a Society for the Establishment and Support of Sunday Schools Throughout the Kingdom of Great Britain. At its commencement, the Sunday School movement was undenominational, but it fell in with other religious and philanthropic influences such as the preaching of John Wesley and George Whitefield and the Evangelical Revival in the Established Church. Popular interest and imagination were stirred: the movement grew at a phenomenal rate and both the Church and the Nonconformists opened Sunday Schools. By 1795 nearly 250,000 children attended the schools and when the Sunday School Union, with a committee half Churchmen and half Dissenters, was formed in 1803, there were 7,125 Sunday Schools with 88,860 teachers and 844,728 pupils. The scholars were taught spelling as a preparation for reading the Bible, but in many schools other items of secular instruction were given. As the movement grew, the tendency was to replace paid teachers by volunteers and for the instruction to become more religious and less secular. The influx of a large number of voluntary teachers, full of enthusiasm but

[1] Guy Kendal. *Robert Raikes*, p. 72, Nicholson and Watson, 1939.

with little knowledge and no idea how to teach the small amount they possessed, often rendered the instruction of small educational value. Nevertheless, there were individuals of outstanding personality and ability who discovered by experience the best methods to adopt and who were more successful in their efforts. Raikes met John Wesley, who was greatly in favour of the spread of the movement, and the latter recorded in his *Journal*, "I find these schools springing up everywhere." The authorities warmly encouraged Raikes at the beginning and he was able to tell a friend, in 1792, that for the first time on record there was no case to be tried at the Gloucester Assizes. Farmers and factory-owners joined in their praise of his work.

Opposition soon appeared from two distinct quarters. The events of the Reign of Terror frightened many people, who imagined similar things happening on this side of the Channel and that revolution would surely come to pass in this country if children were educated above the station in life in which it had pleased God to place them. Even the Bishop of Rochester in the House of Lords condemned Sunday Schools as fostering the views of the French Revolution, and some Dissenters accused Raikes of being a Sabbath-breaker because the schools were opened on Sundays. Opposition also came from the parents themselves. One of the persons most influenced by the movement was Hannah More who, with her sisters, left the society life of London to live in the Mendip parish of Cowslip Green in 1785. She records that when she tried to persuade parents to send their children to school, they believed she was trying to secure them to sell as slaves in the West Indies.

The movement, however, proved stronger than the opposition. Hannah More was shocked by the ignorance, filthiness, and depravity of the people in the Cheddar district. She relates that she saw only one Bible in the village and that was used to prop up a flower-pot. Wilberforce visited her and convinced her that her life's work lay in redeeming the people of Cheddar. He promised to supply the funds if she and her sisters would undertake the work. With this assistance, she opened a Sunday School, and obtained a teacher for £30 a year. She soon found that parents as well as children were in need of education and she formed a reading society for the parents and friendly societies for the women. Within her limitations she did magnificent work, but her good intentions were frequently marred by the narrow religious views she held and the spirit of condescending patronage that often accompanied her efforts. For example, she was strictly opposed to teaching writing on Sundays.

A sterner and perhaps more intelligent person of the Hannah More type was to be found in Mrs. Trimmer, who opened schools in Brentford in 1786. Her object was to rescue the poor from ignorance and barbarism, but at the same time to see that they kept their appointed place. In the circle of her aristocratic friends she was able to stir up enthusiasm for the schools and she busied herself with writing story-books and primers for young children. George III and Queen Charlotte visited the Brentford schools and Mrs. Trimmer wrote of the Queen: "It is impossible to do justice to the charming manner in which the Queen expressed the most benevolent sentiments and the tenderest regard for the happiness of the poor." Mrs. Trimmer was very particular about the behaviour of her children and issued the admonition, "Keep from swearing, lying, and stealing. Do not fight or quarrel, call nicknames or tell tales. Bow to gentlemen and ladies whenever you meet them. Do not take birds' nests, spin cockchafers or do anything to torment dumb creatures." In her book *Reflections upon the Education of Children in Charity Schools*, 1792, she differentiates between charity schools and schools of industry, and assigns to them their separate functions. She emphasised the opening of schools of industry where poor girls would be taught spinning, knitting, and plain needlework, or trained to be domestic servants. As Professor Frank Smith writes, her book "is an interesting example of the educational views of a kindly, energetic and devoted Churchwoman of the eighteenth century, written just before the wave of panic poisoned the minds of the governing classes." [1]

The Sunday School movement of the 18th century owes its importance not so much to what it actually achieved, as to the ideal towards which it strove, namely universal popular education. It pointed the way to the realisation of this ideal, not indeed through private effort alone, but through the co-operation of the State. No one saw the value of these philanthropic movements more than Sir James Kay-Shuttleworth, who wrote many years later, "It is also important to observe, that the development of Sunday Schools for the poor proceeded with gigantic strides. . . . The idea of education for the poor sprang from a religious impulse . . . it regarded the school as a nursery of the Church and congregation, and confided

[1] F. Smith. *A History of English Elementary Education*, p. 58, University of London Press, 1931.

its management to the chief communicants, to the deacons, elders, and class teachers. Thus the Sunday School became the type of the daily school." [1]

An example of a Sunday School in an industrial district is given in the *Reports* of the Society for Bettering the Condition of the Poor.[2] The school was situated at Kirkstall, then a village about three and a half miles from Leeds. A forge had been built nearby and the fathers of most of the children attending the school were engaged in the cast-iron industry. On Sundays the inhabitants spent their time wandering through the woods or in the ruins of Kirkstall Abbey. The school was opened in June 1801, and a workman who was the father of a family of seven was obtained as a teacher. He received no stipend, but was given a guinea at Christmas with clothes for himself and his children. Parents who sent their children to the school were expected to make a small contribution at Christmas towards running expenses. When the school was visited it contained about thirty children of both sexes who ranged in age from five to fourteen years. Some of the older people came to hear the reading of the Bible.

The Report significantly remarked: "The whole place has now a very different appearance on a Sunday ; and the hedges and birds-nests escape on that day, at least, from the depredations consequent to total idleness. A few books are occasionally given as rewards for regular attendance, and good behaviour. Some children come from so considerable a distance as two or three miles, and are remarkable for regular attendance."

The revival of schools of industry through the efforts of Mrs. Trimmer and similar individuals has already received mention. One interesting example of this kind of institution was the Industry School at Oakham. It was an English version of the spinning-school which had been so characteristic of certain areas in Scotland earlier in the century. The school was open to all the inhabitants of the parish. No poor person was eligible for poor-relief unless he sent his children to the school or could prove that he had set them to satisfactory employment. The instruction included spinning in wool and linen, and knitting. Those who wished were taught to read, and the girls were encouraged to bring their sewing to school. Instruction was free, and the children were allowed to keep the money they obtained for their work. The hours were eight to one

---

[1] Sir James Kay-Shuttleworth. *Public Education*, p. 34, Longmans, 1853.
[2] *Reports*, No. CXL, 18th April 1803.

and two to seven, and the school was closed on the Saturday afternoon.

It was originally opened in 1787 and the children used to go home for the midday meal. During the winter much time was lost through the inclement weather, and it was resolved to supply meals at the charge of 6d. per head per week. The children ate barley bread and as much as they required of pease-porridge, rice with milk, or broth and potato pudding. By means of wholesale buying and the use of Count Rumford's coppers,[1] the expense of providing the dinner was kept below 6d. per head per week.

During the 17th and 18th centuries, Wales, because of its widely scattered agricultural population, was far worse off than England in regard to the provision of primary education. The first name connected with elementary education in Wales is that of the Rev. Thomas Gouge, who in 1674 founded a society for the instruction of poor Welsh children in the English language. His efforts were supported by Dean (afterwards Archbishop) Tillotson and other prominent English divines. The society also aimed at circulating the Bible and Prayer Book in Welsh. Gouge found that Welsh Bibles were difficult to obtain, so that it was necessary to print a new edition of 8,000 copies. As there were but few large centres of population, he found that the only way of reaching the people was by personal visits. For a considerable number of years he travelled throughout the Principality, and it was claimed that, by his efforts, every year from 800 to 1,000 poor children were taught to read and several large towns were encouraged to open schools. Gouge died in 1681 and, although twenty years afterwards the society he had founded ceased to exist, his ideals lived on and inspired his successors.

The most important movement in Welsh education during the 18th century was the Circulating School associated with the name of the Rev. Griffith Jones, Rector of Llandown, Carmarthenshire. Jones had become a corresponding member of the S.P.C.K. in 1713, and he was appalled by the ignorance of the Welsh people, who had been largely unaffected by the very few schools so far established. He conceived the idea that the only practical solution of the problem consisted in the establishment of mobile schools, by means of which it would be possible to overcome the difficulty of reaching

---

[1] Rumford was one of the leading supporters of the Society for Bettering the Condition of the Poor, which was founded in 1796. He was a scientist who was interested in the application of science to cooking, heating, and ventilation. His connection with the Royal Institution is mentioned in Chap. xiii.

the scattered population of the country districts. Although his plan was in this respect similar to that of Gouge, yet it differed in at least two important particulars. The new Circulating Schools were to be for adults as well as for children, and Jones emphasised that the medium of instruction was to be Welsh and not English.

The first school was opened in Griffith Jones's own parish in 1730. It was so successful that the idea spread to neighbouring parishes, and within a few years to the whole of Wales. The work was carried on by means of travelling teachers who stayed from three to six months in one locality and then passed on to the next. Any kind of building available was used as a school, and people of all ages were instructed both in the day-time and in the evening. The following statistics published by the S.P.C.K. show the state of the Circulating Schools in 1758.

"An Account of the Circulating Charity Schools in Wales, from Michaelmas 1757, to Michaelmas 1758.

	Schools	No. of Scholars		Schools	No. of Scholars
Anglesea	21	1,003	Glamorganshire..	26	888
Breconshire ..	6	290	Merionethshire ..	10	354
Cardiganshire ..	15	1,100	Monmouthshire..	6	223
Carmarthenshire	68	3,509	Montgomeryshire	5	110
Carnarvonshire	31	1,262	Pembrokeshire ..	18	712
Denbighshire ..	10	319		—	—
Flintshire ..	2	64		65	2,287
			Brought over ..	153	7,547
	—	—		—	—
	153	7,547		218	9,834

N.B.

In many of the Welch Schools, the Adult People, Men and Women, (being ignorant of the English Tongue) are taught to Read the Scripture in the British Language: and most of the Masters instruct, for Three or Four Hours in the Evening, after School-time, twice as many as they had in the Schools by Day, who could not attend at other times.

N.B. Some English Charity Schools are included, set up of late for the Poor who did not understand Welch."

It is estimated that by the time of Griffith Jones's death in 1761, 150,212 persons between the ages of six and seventy had been taught to read the Bible in Welsh.

Griffith Jones left over £7,000 to his friend Madam Bevan, to carry on the work, and she was able to record that, by 1777, 6,456 schools existed. Madam Bevan died in 1779 and left her property to the use of the Welsh Circulating Schools. Her will was disputed by her relations and her estate was thrown into Chancery, with the result that the schools came to an end. The will was upheld in 1807, but for over a quarter of a century the work of the schools had been frustrated by the procrastination of the Court of Chancery. As Montmorency comments: "In 1779 education was in full swing in Wales; but when the Bevan schools resumed their work, the people of the Principality had forgotten once more the meaning of popular education, and so we find that in 1820 popular education in Wales was less effective than in any part of England." [1]

Meanwhile, the Sunday Schools had reached Wales. The pioneer in this movement was the Rev. Thomas Charles of Bala. He was ordained deacon in 1785, and when he took up parochial work he was deeply moved by the ignorance of his parishioners. Experience showed him that his own parish was typical of the decline in popular education which had followed the lapse of the Bevan schools. He was successful in raising sufficient money for his purpose, but he found himself handicapped by the lack of teachers. The only solution of the problem was to train a number of teachers in his own parish and then send them further afield. He found it necessary to publish his own catechisms and textbooks, but through perseverance he was able to establish his schools in all parts of Wales. The schools catered for children on the week-days, but were also open for adults on Sundays and in the evenings.

Charles's work led to a widespread demand for copies of the Welsh Bible, and to satisfy this he suggested, at a meeting in London, the publication of the Bible in the Welsh language. Not only was he successful in obtaining his desire, but his efforts were instrumental in bringing about the formation of the British and Foreign Bible Society. The day-schools tended to disappear, but the Sunday teaching was permanent and developed into the Welsh Sunday School which was so characteristic of the Principality. In spite of the fact that the origin of the Sunday School was due to the Established Church, the Church authorities failed to grasp the full possibilities of the development. It was left to the Methodist revival to make use of the opportunities created. The effect of the Methodist revival was to bring not only a new spiritual life into Welsh Nonconformity, but also to introduce a new principle of organisation. As a prominent Welsh member of Parliament declared in 1893: "The people in these Welsh villages have learnt,

[1] J. E. G. de Montmorency. *State Intervention in English Education*, p. 205, C.U.P., 1902.

during the last 150 years, the most valuable lessons of self-govern-ment. Their chapels have been to them a splendid education in self-government; they manage these chapels and manage their organisations with admirable skill and success." It must be said that Nonconformity rather than the Established Church has played the greater part in the shaping of Welsh education.

Despite the rapid growth and the marked success of the Sunday School movement, it was soon apparent that the problem with which they were grappling was too big for them, and that it could be solved only by the provision of a national system of day-schools. Already there were certain advanced thinkers who believed in a nation-wide system of day-schools, sponsored by the State, in which attendance would be compulsory. Adam Smith, Thomas Paine, and Malthus, for different reasons were of this opinion, but William Godwin, who clung tenaciously to his belief in the freedom of the individual, was strongly opposed to State intervention in the educational sphere. State intervention, however, was not to come for many years yet, and any scheme for general education would have to rely on philanthropy. The practical difficulties to be faced included the enormous numbers of children to be educated, the small amount of money available, and the scarcity of experienced teachers. Under the circumstances, any education provided would have to be cheap and would have to use the few teachers available to the best possible advantage.

It was for these reasons that the systems advocated by Andrew Bell and Joseph Lancaster attracted popular support. Bell seems to have been first in the field. In 1787 he went to India as a lecturer in science, and amongst the many offices he held was that of chaplain to the Military Male Orphan Asylum in Madras. At this establishment he found about twenty boys receiving rather ineffective tuition at the hands of a master and two ushers. While visiting a native school, Bell noticed the children learning to write by tracing with their fingers in a sand-tray. This appeared to him to be an ideal method of teaching and he resolved to introduce it into the asylum. The ushers resented his orders, and Bell selected John Frisken, a boy about eight years of age, and commanded him to take the class. Under Bell's instructions, Frisken taught the lowest class successfully and was made the permanent teacher. The experiment was continued by putting other boys in charge of the lower classes with Frisken as superintendent. When Bell returned to England, he published an account of his methods in a small book entitled *An Experiment in Education*. At about the same time, Joseph Lancaster (who, when in his teens, had tried to run away to Jamaica where he hoped to teach reading to the negro slaves) had opened a school in the Borough Road for about 100 pupils. Numbers grew rapidly and soon the school contained over 500 boys. In order to manage these large numbers, Lancaster hit upon the idea of teaching some of the older boys and setting them in turn to teach others.

Neither Bell nor Lancaster can be claimed as the inventors of the monitorial plan. Mention has already been made of some form of monitorial system in use at Winchester College, Manchester Grammar School, and other grammar-schools. Robert Raikes was using a similar idea when he taught a prisoner to read and then set him to teach another, and later he introduced a kind of monitorial scheme into his Sunday School. There is no evidence that Bell or Lancaster were aware of previous applications of their principle, so that for each of them it was an independent discovery. Lancaster lost no time in advertising his discovery, and claimed that a school of 1,000 boys could be taught at the expense of one master and that the more the numbers were increased the less became the expense per head. The cheapness of the scheme constituted its greatest appeal. George III, the Queen, and the Princesses, became subscribers to the Borough Road School, and the project aroused much popular enthusiasm. Churchmen and Dissenters alike supported it and a kind of monitorial plan was tried out at Charterhouse and at the High School in Edinburgh.

Unlike Lancaster, Bell did not found a school but introduced the monitorial principles into certain existing parochial schools. The plan was first used in 1798 at St. Botolph's, Aldgate, and a little later at Kendal. When, in 1801, Bell became rector of Swanage, he introduced the system into the school along with vaccination for the "cow-pock." Lancaster visited the school at Swanage and both men interchanged notes, though it seems that Bell obtained greater help from his opposite number than Lancaster did. A breach between the two was occasioned by a publication of Mrs. Trimmer, in which she proclaimed that Bell had discovered the principle and Lancaster had merely copied him. She also pointed out that in the Lancasterian school the Catechism was not taught (Lancaster was a Quaker), and that the religious instruction was undenominational. This was quite sufficient to withdraw the support of the Church of England. The controversy which followed

is not important in itself, but the fact that the Church supported
Bell, and the Nonconformists Lancaster, started that acrimonious
warfare between the Churches which was so disastrous to the cause
of national education.

Lancaster's great weaknesses were his love of display and his
lack of capacity for financial administration.   His extravagant
ways soon threatened money troubles, and, to save him from bankruptcy, the Royal Lancasterian Society was formed in 1808. His
mismanagement of money caused the committee to exclude him
from handling the finances of the school. He resigned from his
position as superintendent of the Borough Road School, and the
committee changed the name of the institution to that of the British
and Foreign School Society.   The Church of England formed in
1811 the National Society for Promoting the Education of the Poor
in the Principles of the Established Church, which took over much
of the work previously carried out by the S.P.C.K.   Both societies
established schools in all parts of the kingdom.   The National
Society kept careful records of the number of schools, teachers, and
scholars, and the statistics furnished show an amazing rate of
growth.

			Schools	Children
1812	...	...	52	8,620
1813	...	...	230	40,484
1815	...	...	564	97,920
1830	...	...	3,670	about 346,000

Unfortunately these figures include the number of scholars
attending Sunday Schools. Similar statistics for the British Schools
are not available, but the return of 1851 gave the number of Church
schools as 17,015, with 955,865 scholars and the British Schools as
1,500 with the estimated number of scholars as 225,000.[1]

While the Lancaster-Bell controversy was at its height, Mr.
Whitbread, in 1807, introduced into the Commons a Bill for
establishing parochial schools in England and Wales. He acknowledged that the success and cheapness of the monitorial schools had

---

[1] In Leeds, the Royal Lancasterian Free School was opened in Boar Lane in
1812.   The school accommodated 500 boys who were taught reading, writing,
and arithmetic, "in a mode the cheapest as well as the most effectual ever
devised."   A similar school for girls was opened in Call Lane.   In 1813 a
"handsome and convenient edifice" in Kirkgate was opened as a National
Free School. The school was built for 360 boys, and later was absorbed by
the Parish Church Schools. Dr. Hook, when Vicar of Leeds, encouraged the
National Schools, and during the period of his incumbency they grew from
three to thirty.

greatly impressed him.   But the time was not yet ripe for such
a measure.   The governing classes still viewed with suspicion any
attempt to diffuse education amongst the ranks of the poor, who
might be tempted to forget the position ordained for them in life,
and the Church was firmly opposed to any form of religious instruction of an undenominational character.   After encountering fierce
opposition in the Commons, the Bill was rejected by the House of
Lords.   Its importance lies in its being the first of a series of
attempts to secure State intervention in popular education.   The
same day that Whitbread's Bill was presented, the Commons voted
a sum not exceeding £23,270 for promoting English Protestant
schools in Ireland.

The differences in practice between the systems of Bell and
Lancaster were comparatively slight.   If anything, Bell's system
was the more flexible, while that of Lancaster tended to suffer from
over-organisation.   Both made use of the "factory" idea in their
attempt to instruct large masses of children by mechanical means,
and both were affected by the taint of cheapness.   They were
directly responsible for the large classes and the trail of cheapness
which haunted English elementary education until very recent
times.[1]

There were several other experiments during this period which
are of interest and importance.   Perhaps the most influential was
that connected with the name of Robert Owen, the founder of
British Socialism.   Owen was a self-made man who by the age
of thirty had reached the position of manager and partner in the
cotton-mills of New Lanark.   He found the conditions in the mills
deplorable.   The workers and the apprentices were "ignorant and
destitute—generally indolent and much addicted to theft, drunkenness, and falsehood."   Owen was a convinced believer in the
power of environment in shaping the individual's character and
personality.   Like Helvetius in the previous century he adopted as
his creed *L'éducation peut tout*.   He immediately set to work to
improve conditions in the factory.   Working hours were reduced
to a maximum of ten per day and he refused to employ children
under the age of ten.   Other reforms aiming at the establishment
of better and healthier working conditions and an increased level
of wages were inaugurated.   He provided free instruction for the

[1] For a detailed account of the teaching and organisation of the monitorial
school, see C. Birchenough, *History of Elementary Education in England and
Wales from 1800 to the Present Day*, pp. 242-54, U.T.P., 1938.

children of the workers up to the age of twelve, but it was his work with infants which was most successful. His infant-school, the first of its kind in Great Britain, was opened in 1816, and catered for children from one year upwards. This was consistent with his faith in the power of environment, for if the latter was to be effective it could not operate at too early an age.

For assistants, he chose James Buchanan, "a poor, simple-hearted weaver," and a young girl of seventeen, Molly Young, both of whom had impressed him by their sympathy with and understanding of small children. The accounts of the school reveal that the methods used were astonishingly modern. Harsh treatment and brutal punishment were never employed, and the aim of the teachers was to win the liking and respect of the children. Emphasis was laid on the use of illustration, the telling of stories suited to the age and interests of the pupils, and instruction in natural history based on observation of plant and animal life in the garden and the neighbourhood. Dancing and singing were taught and the children were encouraged to play games in order to improve their powers of conversation. Owen met Pestalozzi in 1818 and had visited Fellenberg's school, but his own ideas had been worked out in complete independence of these educationists.

Unfortunately for the acceptance of his schemes, Owen was a free-thinker and did not win the support from the Church and public personages that he might have done. His views on religion brought him into disfavour with his partners, upon whom he relied for the success of his experiment. One of these, William Allen, was a member of the Society of Friends. Allen was also a prominent philanthropist who was interested in the work of the British and Foreign School Society, and had been an active worker in the campaign for the abolition of slavery. As time went on, the rift between Owen and his partners grew wider, until in 1824 the school was placed under the patronage of the British and Foreign School Society. Owen relinquished active participation in the scheme and turned his attention to projects of social and political reform. The school at New Lanark continued to exist until the Scottish Education Act of 1872, when the School Boards were established.

The centre of interest now shifts to London. Owen's example directly influenced the establishment of an infant-school at Westminster, which was supported by Lord Brougham, James Mill, and Zachary and Thomas Babington Macaulay. Owen was approached

with a request for the services of James Buchanan. When he agreed
to the transfer, Owen wrote: "I had thought, from the daily instruction which, when at the establishment I had as it were drilled into
him for years, that he could now act for himself in a practice which
under my direction, with the aid he received from Molly Young,
appeared so easy to execute. But I found he could proceed no
further in the practice than he had done for some time." [1]

Some time later Owen visited the school at Westminster, and
his remarks about Buchanan and his wife were responsible for
the hitherto generally accepted idea that the latter were complete
failures. Owen described seeing Mrs. Buchanan standing over the
children, threatening them with a whip. On his appearance, an
unsuccessful attempt was made to conceal the whip, but the harsh
treatment meted out to the children was reflected in their sullen
and unhappy look. Buchanan was represented as being completely
under the domination of his wife. [2]

Owen seems to have been guilty of a cruel injustice in his dis-
paragement of Buchanan. Even as early as 1847, an anonymous
article in the *Westminster Review,* which undoubtedly was written
by Brougham, ascribed the origin of infant-schools to J. F. Oberlin
in north-eastern France in 1769, but credited Buchanan with founding the first English infant-school. Brougham spoke of Buchanan
as a person eminently fitted by natural gifts for teaching young
children, and attributed the success of the New Lanark school as a
consequence of his attractive personality and his understanding of
his little pupils. The facts, also, are in conflict with Owen's estimate. Buchanan remained teaching in London for twenty years
and was invited to open infant-schools in different parts of England.
In 1839 he received a request from the New Zealand Land Company
to go to New Zealand to take charge of an infant-school. All this
is strange if Buchanan was a failure.

When Buchanan reached Capetown, his eldest son prevailed
upon him to stay there. Later he was joined by Mrs. Buchanan
and he settled at Pietermaritzburg, where he died in 1857. Buchanan's reputation as a teacher has been cleared by the publication in
1923 of the *Buchanan Family Records.* They were collected by
his grandchild, Miss Barbara Buchanan, and the book was printed
for private circulation in Capetown. The picture it gives of Buchanan shows how wide of the mark were the statements made by

[1] *The Life of Robert Owen: Written by Himself,* p. 196, G. Bell and Sons,
Ltd., 1920.   [2] *Ibid.,* pp. 210-11.

Owen. In spite of certain weaknesses which belonged to the age in which he lived, and which were further exaggerated in the teaching methods of Wilderspin, we obtain an impression of Buchanan as a man who was entirely devoted to what he believed was his life's work. He possessed a wonderful influence over children and his simplicity of nature was displayed in the tenderness and sympathy which he showed in the management of infants. Mrs. Buchanan was a typical kind-hearted, thrifty, and practical Scots housewife. The idea that she was ever harsh or cruel is preposterous.

The evidence we now possess goes a long way towards vindicating Buchanan and his wife and, in modern phraseology, to "debunk" the reputation as a teacher previously enjoyed by Owen. There is no doubt that the latter was the originator of the scheme at New Lanark, but his ideas would have come to nothing without a James Buchanan and a Molly Young. Owen's account was written forty years later, and it is only charitable to assume that his memory played him false. Probably his disparaging remarks were due to a fault in his own psychological make-up. Owen was one of those men who possessed a great belief in himself and was quite unable to credit that anything could be successful unless he was responsible for every detail. Like many individuals of wide vision, he paid little regard to those whose indispensable aid rendered his schemes a reality.

A second infant-school was opened in Spitalfields by Samuel Wilderspin in 1820. Wilderspin's ideas closely resembled those of Pestalozzi, though he denied emphatically that the latter had ever influenced him. The *Buchanan Family Records* show conclusively that Wilderspin's connection with the infant-school movement began through a chance meeting with Buchanan. Miss Buchanan claims that her grandfather gave Wilderspin free tuition in his methods and then recommended him for appointment at the Spitalfields school. There is further evidence to support this claim, for at the beginning of his career Wilderspin acknowledged his debt to Buchanan, but when he became well known and successful he forgot all about it. When he gave evidence before the Select Committee on the State of Education in England, 1834-5, he asserted that he was the originator of the infant-school in this country. Wilderspin was undoubtedly an enthusiast and also a man of great energy and business ability. Buchanan was so engrossed in his work that he had no desire to advertise himself, and the field was left open for Wilderspin.

At first he encountered many difficulties in handling his large group of tiny children, but experience taught him that "the senses of the children must be engaged ; so that the great secret of training them was to descend to their level and become a child." Wilderspin's vanity led him to claim for himself many ideas, and the invention of apparatus, which had been used by others long before his time, but his success as a teacher was due to his rejection of the mechanical methods of the monitorial school. His weakness lay in too great a reliance upon memory methods, in learning by heart catechisms of questions and answers, and memorising rhymes and stories (of course with a moral) which marred the excellence of the rest of his approach. His work bore fruit in the formation in 1824 of the Infant School Society, the object of which was to found infant-schools and train teachers for them. Wilderspin's later years were occupied with travelling to all parts of the kingdom in order to spread his gospel. The new society was shortlived and was super-seded in 1836 by the Home and Colonial Infant School Society to provide trained teachers for infant-schools.

This society was founded by J. S. Reynolds of Manchester, but it derived its inspiration from Dr. Charles Mayo and his sister Elizabeth. It was in 1819 that Mayo, then in charge of a group of English schoolboys, visited Pestalozzi's school at Yverdun in French Switzerland. He was so affected by the outlook and methods of Pestalozzi that when he returned to England he opened, in 1821, a Pestalozzian School for the children of upper-middle-class parents. The school was eventually transferred from Epsom to Cheam, where Mayo continued to teach until his death in 1846. Mayo was an able scholar and, although he was full of praise for the merits of Pestalozzi's teaching, he was not blind to the defects and possible dangers of the system. Elizabeth Mayo, who had assisted him at Cheam, showed in her book *Lessons on Objects* that she was not equally discerning.

The book was a reaction against the verbalising tendencies of contemporary teaching, and was designed to direct attention to the actual qualities of common objects, the names of which were about all that children knew of them. It was intended to encourage direct observation and inference from what had been seen, but in the hands of an unskilful teacher there was the danger that it might lead children to see merely what they had been told existed, and so develop into a formalism as bad as that which it had been designed to replace. Later the same idea led to the craze for "object lessons," which incurred the well-merited criticism of Sir John Adams in his *Herbartian Psychology*.[1]   Miss Mayo's most important contribution to primary education was her work in the training of teachers, which she undertook at the training establishment of the Home and Colonial Society.   Bell and Lancaster had only been concerned with children above the ages of six or seven, but Miss Mayo concentrated on the training of infant-school teachers.

The most important influence upon primary education during this period was perhaps that of David Stow and John Wood.   The former had for some time been engaged in social work amongst the poor of Glasgow, and it was the experience gained that turned his attention to education.   He opened a Sunday School in 1816, and afterwards taught an evening school, but he soon felt dissatisfied with current educational aims and methods.   Above all, he was convinced that education suffered from lack of the right kind of teachers.   With these motives, he was led to devise what he termed the Training System.   Its primary object, he tells us, was to provide an antidote to the demoralising influence of large towns and manufacturing villages.   The fault of the prevailing systems of education lay in being concerned almost entirely with the cultivation of the intellectual powers.   In other words, Stow realised that training implied far more than either teaching or giving information.   A system was needed which would be "applicable not merely to the head of the child, but to the *whole man*—the moral being—a training up of" the child in the way he should go, "in his habits of thinking, feeling, and acting."[2]

Stow realised that the education given by the Sunday School was inadequate, since it only catered for the child on one day in the week.   In 1826 he founded the Glasgow Infant Society, and on meeting Wilderspin, adopted some of his methods.   Stow claimed no originality as regards administration or instruction and quite freely acknowledged his debt to Pestalozzi and practical teachers like Wood, Bell, and Wilderspin.   The novelty of his system consisted entirely in his belief that moral training was the fundamental aim of the school.   In his account of his work he tells us: "The Training System had its origin in a Sabbath School conducted by the author.   He afterwards embodied it in a Day School for infant children, and in 1831-2, in a Parochial Juvenile School, both serving

[1] A specimen of the method recommended in the book is given by C. Birchenough, *History of Elementary Education in England and Wales from 1800 to the Present Day*, p. 285, U.T.P., 1938.

[2] D. Stow. *The Training System*, p. 12, Glasgow, 1840.

as Models and as a Normal School for the training of schoolmasters. The success of this seminary in training children and students, induced the Glasgow Educational Society, in 1834-5, to adopt these schools as the basis of the present more extended Normal Seminary." [1]

Stow was firmly convinced that the correct training of the infant forms the basis of all future development of the child, and that, from the first days of schooling, boys and girls should both learn and play together. He was not impressed by the systems of Bell and Lancaster. "Monitors," he wrote, "cannot train, although they may teach facts, and are in use in some of the ordinary school exercises." He believed that "an apprenticeship is as requisite for the profession of the schoolmaster, as that of any other art ; and it appears extraordinary, that while we would not employ a gardener or mechanic who has not been trained, we should employ young men to experiment upon our children, who, however well informed themselves, have yet to acquire the art of communicating their knowledge to others. . . . Many teachers work out and arrive at a good system, it is true ; but no one man can possess all that may be concentrated and exhibited in a Normal Seminary, to which every student may be trained." [2]

Stow claimed that his Normal Seminary or Training College was the first institution of its kind in Britain, and his "trainers," as his teachers were called, were in much demand. In addition to Scotland, the "trainers" had been introduced into other countries. "From England and Ireland the society has received demands for four or five times the number of trainers they have been able to supply ; and the demand continues unabated till the present day. Sixteen trainers were sent to Australia in 1837, and more have been ordered since. Above twenty-four have gone to the West India islands, several to British America, and some have been ordered from other British colonies." [3]

Stow based school instruction on two main principles, which he termed the sympathy of numbers and the method of picturing out. By the phrase "sympathy of numbers" he understood the influence upon one another which is found in a suitably-sized group. To make use of this principle in moral training, there must not only be teaching of children in a gallery, but the teacher must know how to train children out of doors, in the playground or "uncovered

---

[1] D. Stow. *The Training System*, pp. 30-1, Glasgow, 1840.
[2] *Ibid.*, pp. 91-2.   [3] *Ibid.*, p. 114.

school." Stow anticipated Kay-Shuttleworth's criticism of the Revised Code. "Reading, writing and arithmetic are imagined to be sovereign remedies for the evils of the youth of large towns. Will anyone acquainted with the moral condition of this novel, *and to some a fearful*, state of society, for a moment conclude that the knowledge of these arts, with minds and *habits* totally untrained to the proper use of them, ever can morally elevate the sunken masses in such cities as Glasgow, Manchester, London, Liverpool, Edinburgh, Paisley, Birmingham and Dundee? . . . We require an entirely new machine for the moral elevation of society in towns and manufacturing villages." [1]

"Picturing out" was to be a substitute for meaningless repetition. "Never commit words to memory until the meaning is previously analysed and understood." It involved appealing to the child in simple language and using analogies with his everyday experience. The following example, which is an introduction to the study of the camel, will explain the process.

"Now, children, you see this picture (presenting the picture of a camel, if you have one, but if not, you must describe its comparative size with some animal they are acquainted with, noticing also the peculiar hunches upon its back), I shall tell you the name of this animal. It is called the camel. What did I say its name was? *The camel*. Camel is the name of this—*animal*. The camel, children, lives in hot countries such as Arabia. Arabia is a very hot —*country* in Asia, where there are hot sandy deserts, in which there are neither trees nor—*grass*. The camel, children, has feet and legs and (pointing to the parts)—a head, and—*a back*, as every animal has. *What a lump on its back, master!* This is a—*lump*. Do you remember the name I gave that lump? I called it a hunch. Remember it, a—*hunch*. A great—*hunch*, and that is a—*lump* or —*hunch*. How many hunches has it got? *Two*. It has got two hunches on its—*back*. This one is on—Where is this one near? Supposing this boy went on all fours, that is, suppose this boy walked on his hands and—*feet*, and a hunch were above this— *place*. What do you call this place? *Shoulders*. The camel, then, has a hunch upon its—*shoulders*, or close behind its—*shoulders*, and another upon—What is this? *Tail*. Is this the tail? *Back, sir*. It is upon its—*back*, near the—*tail*, close to the—*tail*, but not upon the—*tail*." [2]

[1] D. Stow. *The Training System*, pp. 32-3, Glasgow, 1840.
[2] *Ibid.*, pp. 245-6.

Stow believed in simultaneous answering, and in the above example the pupils' answers are in italics. Notice the mixture of direct questions and ellipses which are filled in by chorus-answering. One can imagine that in the hands of an indifferent teacher the lesson could become extremely mechanical.

Stow's ideas had considerable influence upon the elementary schools of the early 19th century. "By his elaboration of the thesis that education presupposes the interaction of mind upon mind, the cultivated upon the relatively uncultivated, he made a contribution of permanent value to the educational thought and practice of his time. Too little value had been attached to the living voice in elementary education, and too much to the printed page. Stow aimed at setting this right. In the sequel, teachers went to the other extreme, and teaching came to be too much associated with talking." [1]

A somewhat similar development had been taking place in Edinburgh, in 1813, where the Sessional School had grown from the Sunday School. A large number of pupils who were admitted to the Sunday Schools were unable to read or write, and the new institution was formed with the object of remedying this defect. At first the Sessional School adopted the plan of Lancaster, but when Bell visited Edinburgh his advice was sought and certain of his suggestions were put into practice. John Wood came into the picture by accident. During the winter of 1819-20, a number of weavers had become unemployed, and in order to assist them a fund was raised and placed in the charge of Wood. The managers of the fund decided that it would be advantageous to send the younger weavers to school, and the Sessional School, because of the high reputation it enjoyed, was selected.

Wood took upon himself the task of supervising these pupils, and in the course of frequent visits to the school he examined them in order to ascertain the progress they were making. The result .was that he became extremely interested in the experiment. He was led to investigate the work of other classes in the school, and he thus discovered the mechanical nature of much of the instruction. "The children were taught, indeed, to read, but the doubt was, whether they had been made such masters of their own language, as in future life to give them any pleasure in reading, or to enable them to derive much profit from it. They had learned their

[1] C. Birchenough, *op. cit.*, p. 270.

catechism, but were they much wiser with regard to the truths which it contained?" [1]

Wood's doubts increased until, at length, he was convinced that the prevailing methods of instruction were wrong. He described his own attitude thus: "We therefore felt an extremely strong anxiety to give the school more of an intellectual tone, not only in order to enable the pupils better to understand what they read there, but also to give them a taste for profitable reading, and make them understand whatever they should afterwards have occasion to read." Rather than trust his ideas to the execution of others, Wood began to take an active part in the teaching. He was gratified to discover that his methods aroused an active interest whatever the subject of instruction might be. In his reaction to drill and memory-work, he emphasised the importance of interest and understanding.

It should be realised that Wood was not aiming at the establishment of a new system of education. He was content to accept the organisation of Bell and Lancaster, but he wished to infuse fresh life into it. His outlook was quite different. Whereas they aimed at a kind of mass-production at the lowest possible cost, Wood, on the other hand, regarded the pupil "not as a machine, or an irrational animal, that must be driven, but as an intellectual being who may be led ; endowed, not merely with sensation and memory, but with perception, judgment, conscience, affections, and passions; capable, to a certain degree, of receiving favourable or unfavourable impressions, of imbibing right or wrong sentiments, of acquiring good or bad habits ; strongly averse to application, where its object is unperceived or remote, but, on the other hand, ardently curious, and infinitely delighting in the display of every new attainment which he makes." [2]

Wood warned would-be imitators that it is not the external arrangements and organisation of a school that matter, but the spirit in which the instruction is given. "The copyist may introduce precisely the same number and the same size of classes,—may place the master, the monitors, and the scholars, in the same respective positions,—may prescribe to them the same movements,—may put the same books into their hands,—and, in short, may give the whole the self-same external aspect. But, if he be not at least equally desirous to catch the spirit . . . let him not wonder, if, notwithstanding all the pains which he has bestowed on the externals

---

[1] J. Wood. *Account of the Edinburgh Sessional School*, p. 27, 1828.
[2] *Ibid.*, p. 2.

of his system, it should degenerate into as dull, cold, and lifeless a routine, as is exhibited in any of the most unproductive seminaries around him." [1]

Like Stow, he emphasised the value of a teacher who had been trained in his craft. Alexander Wilson, a future Prebendary of St. Paul's, was a pupil at the Sessional School in the evenings. Wood had noticed his ability and persuaded him to become a teacher. He obtained a post at Dalkeith. When Dr. Kay, whose work will be considered in the following chapter, was seeking a master for his Poor Law School at Norwood, he visited the Edinburgh Sessional School and was advised to see Alexander Wilson at Dalkeith. The result was that the latter was persuaded to come to England as headmaster of the school at Norwood. This was an important link between the work being done in Scotland and the future developments in England.

An interesting instance of individual philanthropy is afforded by the work of John Pounds of Portsmouth. At first a sailor, Pounds, as a result of an accident, was obliged to take up the trade of shoemaker. When, in 1818, he took charge of the child of a sailor friend, he started a school to provide companionship for the child. From this modest beginning, he extended his activities and divided his time between his trade and caring for the poorest and most uncared-for children of the town. He seems to have wielded an extraordinary influence over them. His workshop was his schoolroom, and as well as attending to his craft he managed to instruct the destitute boys and girls in reading and writing and also to give them lessons in cookery and cobbling. John Pound's example led to the formation of the Ragged Schools, which by 1858 numbered 192 schools with 20,909 pupils. The instruction was entirely free because the parents of the children were of a type who either could not, or would not, pay fees. Later, two such schools were opened in Leeds (1859) and did remarkable work in disciplining the slum children and fitting them for future employment. [2]

All these experiments and even the bitter controversies over the respective claims of Bell and Lancaster served to focus attention upon popular education. The fate of Whitbread's Bill had already been recorded. At Whitbread's death in 1815, the cause of popular education found a champion in Mr. (afterwards Lord) Brougham.

---

[1] J. Wood. *Account of the Edinburgh Sessional School*, pp. 10-11, 1828.
[2] The development of the Ragged School movement was largely due to the work of Lord Shaftesbury in England and Dr. T. Guthrie in Scotland.

As a result of his advocacy Parliament was persuaded to appoint a Select Committee on the Education of the Lower Orders. The inquiry revealed the growing demand for education and the inadequate facilities provided. The report placed on record the fact : "There is the most unquestionable evidence that the anxiety of the poor for education continues not only unabated, but daily increasing, that it extends to every part of the country, and is to be found equally prevalent in those smaller towns and country districts, where no means of gratifying it are provided by the charitable efforts of the richer classes." [1]

The great difficulty was to find the money for any extension of popular education. Brougham's attention was drawn to the numerous educational charities that existed, which either were not being used to the best advantage or which were in some cases actually useless. [2]   Could not these funds be redistributed? Accordingly, Brougham pressed and obtained an Act of 1818 appointing commissioners to inquire into the use being made of educational charities. The Act, however, was so whittled down in its passage through the Lords that it was deprived of any practical value. The universities and public schools deeply resented an inquiry into the way in which they used their funds, but in spite of its apparent failure the Act indirectly was of considerable value. The Commission came into being and collected a number of statistics, but its value was in providing a pattern for the Charity Commission of later date.

Brougham also introduced an Education Bill into the Commons in 1820. Speaking in support of the Bill, Brougham showed that the inquiry had revealed the utter inadequacy of the existing educational facilities and the unsatisfactory attendance of the children who were going to school. "It appeared . . . that there were now educated at unendowed schools 490,000 children, and that to these were to be added about 11,000 for 150 parishes from which no returns had yet been made. In the endowed schools 165,432

[1] *Third Report from the Select Committee on the Education of the Lower Orders*, 1818, p. 56.

[2] Kay-Shuttleworth wrote: "In other cases a small property may have been left for some use, which, though innocent, may be inconsistent with the appropriation of a greatly increased annual value. Mr. Fearon, secretary to the Charity Commission created in 1849, related to me the following facts:— A tobacconist left a field, with directions that the rental should be held in trust to supply six poor women with snuff at Barthelemy tide. The field became valuable building land, and the annual rent increased to a very large amount. To apply such an income to such a use was obviously absurd." (*Public Education*, p. 189.)

children were educated; making a total (exclusive of the 11,000) of 655,432. In England it appeared that on the average 1-14th or 1-15th of the whole population was placed in the way of receiving education. . . . Another deduction ought also to be made for the dame-schools, where 53,000 were educated, or rather not educated, for it amounted to no education at all, since the children were generally sent too young, and taken away just when they were competent to learn. . . . The average means of mere education, therefore, was only in fact one sixteenth in England ; yet even this scanty means had only existed since the year 1803, when what were called the new schools, or those based upon the systems of Dr. Bell and Mr. Lancaster, were established. These schools were in number 1,520, and they received about 200,000 children. Before 1803, then, only the twenty-first part of the population was placed in the way of education, and at that date England might be justly looked on as the worst-educated country of Europe. What a different picture was afforded by Scotland ! The education there was in the proportion of 1-9th or between 1-9th and 1-10th. Wales was even in a worse state than England; at the present day the proportion was 1-20th, and before 1803, it was 1-26th." [1]

The report praised the liberality of the National Schools where "the church catechism is only taught, and attendance at the established place of public worship only required, of those whose parents belong to the establishment; due assurance being obtained that the children of sectaries shall learn the principles and attend the ordinance of religion according to the doctrines and forms to which their families are attached." These words, which would not have been true a few years later, contain in germ the Conscience Clause of the 1870 Act.

The Education Bill aimed at providing schools in places where they were needed. The money for building the schools was to come from the manufacturers "who, while they increased the objects of the poor-rates, contributed but little towards them," and the masters' salaries from a tax on country gentry. Rates were to be levied by the parish officers twice yearly to support the school, and all parents who could afford to do so were to pay 2d. or 4d. a week in fees. The master must be a member of the Church of England, and should be approved by the incumbent of the parish, who had the power of dismissing him. The instruction to be given was to be fixed by the clergy, who would have authority to visit and examine

[1] *Hansard*, 1820, Vol. II, col. 61.

the schools. In order to appease the Nonconformists, Brougham suggested that the religious teaching should consist solely in the study of Scripture, and that no form of worship should be allowed except the Lord's Prayer. Every child should be taken by his parents to church or chapel on Sundays. The suggestion about religious teaching was in substance the same as the Cowper-Temple Clause of 1870.

The Bill was opposed by both Church and Nonconformists, especially the latter, and Brougham withdrew it after the second reading. Although no new education proposals were presented to Parliament for over ten years, a good deal of useful work was going on, mainly through the efforts of Brougham. In 1825 he published his pamphlet *Observations on the Education of the People,* and it is a commentary on the awakening interest in education that it had to be reprinted twenty times in the year. The pamphlet led to the formation of the Society for the Diffusion of Useful Knowledge. Brougham's support of the newly founded Mechanics' Institutes and the part he played in creating the University of London will be mentioned in later chapters.

The Reform Bill became law in 1832 and the new Parliament of the following year was packed with members eager for other reforms. Knowing the temper of the new House, petitions pleading for the creation of a national system of education flowed in from all parts of the country. Joseph Hume, Member for Middlesex, supported the petitions and attacked the Government vehemently. Suddenly, Brougham announced in the House of Lords his change of opinion about compulsory education. He argued that the great increase of the children in school did away with the need for compulsion. There were now 1,030,000 pupils receiving instruction in the non-endowed schools and 165,000 in the endowed schools. Brougham's former position was championed by Mr. J. A. Roebuck who moved that the House, "deeply impressed with the necessity of providing for a due Education of the People at large; and believing that to this end the aid and care of the State are absolutely needed, will, early during the next Session of Parliament, proceed to devise a means for the universal and national Education of the whole People." [1] The plan he proposed was greatly in advance of anything that had been suggested before, and in many ways showed a similarity to the Acts of 1870 and 1876. "In general terms, I would say, that I would oblige, by law, every child

[1] *Commons Journal,* Vol. LXXXVIII, p. 615.

in Great Britain and Ireland, from, perhaps six years of age to twelve years of age to be a regular attendant at school. If the parents be able to give, and actually do give their children elsewhere sufficient education, then they should not be compelled to send them to the national school. If, however, they should be unable or unwilling to give them such instruction, then the State should step in and supply this want by compelling the parent to send the child to the school of the State." [1]

Roebuck proposed three types of State school, infant, school of industry, and the normal school for training teachers. In addition, evening schools in the towns were suggested. Every county should be divided into school districts, in each of which a school committee should be elected. A member of the Cabinet would supervise and direct the national school system. On the financial side, the cost would be met by fees from those who could afford them, from additional taxation, and from a redistribution of existing educational endowments. An interesting debate followed which showed that many people had been earnestly discussing the problems of national education. The Government was unwilling to proceed with Mr. Roebuck's Bill, but on 17th August 1833, in an almost empty House of Commons, Lord Althorp's suggestion of voting £20,000 for the purposes of education was carried by fifty votes to twenty-six.

The grant was opposed on two widely different grounds. Hume objected that the amount was inadequate to establish a national system and would only have the effect of discouraging philanthropy. Cobbett, rather surprisingly, opposed the grant on the ground that education was not improving the condition of the country. The increase of educational facilities in recent years had been accompanied with an increase of crime. All education did was to produce a new race of idlers—schoolmasters and schoolmistresses.

The actual vote was worded, "That a Sum, not exceeding £20,000, be granted to His Majesty, to be issued in aid of Private Subscriptions for the Erection of School Houses, for the Education of the Children of the Poorer Classes in Great Britain, to the 31st day of March 1834; and that the said sum be issued and paid without any fee or other deduction whatsoever."

This historic occasion attracted very little notice in the Press. It was merely a fact the significance of which was not yet apparent. Only the *Quarterly Journal of Education* pointed out the defects of

[1] *Hansard*, 1833, Vol. XX, col. 153.

the grant. It was to be paid only when at least half the total cost of the building had been raised by private subscription. In giving grants, preference would be shown to large towns after an inquiry into the availability of already existing charitable funds. As there was no Government department to control the expenditure, the amount was divided equally between the National Society and the British and Foreign School Society. No conditions were made with regard to inspection, suitability of buildings, or curriculum.

The failure of organised philanthropy to solve the problem of elementary education in this country had resulted in State intervention. The latter, however, was not sufficient by itself, but the reason for this statement is usually implied rather than explicitly given. For nearly half a century England had been experiencing the change-over from the domestic system in industry to the factory age, a development which is generally summed up in the term "Industrial Revolution." The inventions which made such a change possible, the growth of factories, the use of machinery, the shifting of population from the country to the industrial towns, many of which were of recent origin, and the deterioration in the social, economic, and moral conditions amongst the poorer classes, are well known to readers of the history of this period. The Revolutionary and Napoleonic wars had sent up the price of food and other commodities with an alarming rapidity and, as numbers have learnt to their cost, in such times wages do not increase correspondingly. There was an urgent demand for labour, but it was labour of a kind different from that of earlier days. A small but increasing number of skilled workers and technicians was necessary, but the chief need was for the services of unskilled or semi-skilled workers to superintend the machines and to perform certain indispensable operations in the mines.

Families, which at an earlier age had been to a large extent self-supporting, now came to face penury and starvation. There was only one solution. As soon as the children were old enough, they had to become wage-earners. However much a parent wished to take advantage of the educational facilities provided by philanthropy, with or without State assistance, his first concern was to see that sufficient was being earned by himself, his wife and children, to gain the bare necessities of life. With State aid, it was possible to build schools, but without restrictions upon the hours of child labour it was impossible to fill the places provided. This fact explains the great progress made in attendance at Sunday Schools, since the majority of the poorer children could not attend school on the week-day.

In many cases, the nature of a child's employment was such that by Sunday he was so exhausted that he needed at least one day of rest to recuperate from his labours of the previous week. The modern age has marvelled at the blindness of those reformers who spent their whole effort in securing the freedom of the negro slaves but yet ignored the far more terrible conditions of serfdom which were common in their own country. Disraeli, in his novel *Sybil*, a work too seldom read at the present day, paints for us a terrible picture. "They come forth ; the mine delivers its gang and the pit its bondsmen ; the forge is silent and the engine is still. The plain is covered with the swarming multitude ; . . . troops of youth—alas! of both sexes—though neither their raiment nor their language indicates the difference ; all are clad in male attire ; and oaths that men might shudder at issue from lips born to breathe words of sweetness. Yet these are to be—some are—the mothers of England! But can we wonder at the hideous coarseness of their language, when we remember the savage rudeness of their lives? Naked to the waist, an iron chain fastened to a belt of leather runs between their legs clad in canvas trousers, while on hands and feet an English girl, for twelve, sometimes for sixteen hours a-day, hauls and hurries tubs of coals up subterranean roads, dark, precipitous, and plashy ; circumstances that seem to have escaped the notice of the Society for the Abolition of Negro Slavery. Those worthy gentlemen too appear to have been singularly unconscious of the sufferings of the little Trappers,[1] which was remarkable, as many of them were in their own employ.

"See too these emerge from the bowels of the earth! Infants of four and five years of age, many of them girls, pretty and still soft and timid ; entrusted with the fulfilment of most responsible duties, and the nature of which entails on them the necessity of being the earliest to enter the mine and the latest to leave it. Their labour indeed is not severe, for that would be impossible, but it is passed in darkness and in solitude."[2]

The apprenticeship system, which in the 16th and 17th centuries supplied the technical training of those days, had now almost broken down. Skilled training was necessary more than ever for the engineer who designed the machines, but the vast majority of the

---

[1] The trapper opened and shut the doors on which the ventilation of the mine depended.   [2] Bk. III, Chap. i.

work-people became operatives rather than craftsmen. What remained of the apprenticeship system often provided the employer with a means of obtaining semi-skilled labour at the cheapest possible rate. The apprentice of Elizabethan days learnt more from his master than the mere elements of his trade. Now the emphasis was on those operations alone which were needed for the particular task. Until something was done to restrict the employer's powers over the young who worked for him, it was useless to think of filling the day-schools. The clauses of the Factory Acts which dealt with the conditions of work for children were as much educational clauses as those which constituted the Education Acts of later days.

The first factories depended upon water-power for their operation, and even now one can still discover the remains of these mills in the dales of Yorkshire and Lancashire. Pauper children were drafted from all parts of the country to supply the labour, and were crowded together under conditions which favoured the spread of epidemics. At West End, a hamlet not far from the main road from Harrogate to Skipton, lies the remains of an old woollen-mill operated by water-power. Hundreds of children from the south of England were sent to it by the magistrates, and as they died at the looms their bodies were thrown into a pit dug on the opposite side of the road. When steam-power became more common in the 19th century, the mills were erected where coal could be more readily obtained, but the conditions of the children who worked in them were only slightly improved.

The first Factory Act was that of Sir Robert Peel (the elder) in 1802. It restricted the employment of apprentices to twelve hours a day, excluding meals, and abolished compulsory work between 9 p.m. and 6 a.m. It also included provision for their education. "Every such apprentice shall be instructed, in some part of every working day, in the usual hours of work, in Reading, Writing and Arithmetic, or either of them, according to the age and abilities of such apprentice, by some discreet and proper person, to be provided by the master or mistress of such apprentice, in some room or place in such mill or factory to be set apart for that purpose."

The Act became largely inoperative because employers quickly discovered a means of evading it. Since it only applied to apprentices, it was a simple matter to give up taking apprentices and make use of free child labour. From this point of view the Act was a further nail in the coffin of the old-time apprenticeship system. No adequate machinery, however, was set up to enforce it. It is true that a Justice of the Peace and a clergyman were to visit each mill to see that the provisions of the Act were being carried out, but such casual visitation was ineffective, and it was not until the establishment of an inspectorate that it became possible to enforce the law. From now on, the vital issue was that of securing a ten-hour day. Those who supported the subsequent factory legislation were mainly concerned with obtaining the ten-hour maximum for the adult worker, but they realised the strength of an appeal made on behalf of the children, and that the organisation of the factories was such that any reduction in the hours of work for those under eighteen would also apply to adults.

In 1815 Sir Robert Peel introduced a Bill to extend the provisions of the earlier Act to cotton, woollen, and flax, mills, and to prohibit the employment of children under ten. The educational clause of the Bill was to provide that young people should receive instruction in the three R's for one half-hour in each working day. Peel suggested the appointment of a Select Committee to inquire into the whole question of child employment. In his efforts he received the whole-hearted support of Robert Owen. The Bill was strongly opposed by the factory owners, and Peel was not sufficiently firm to prevent it from being watered down. Eventually the Bill became law in 1819 and, in its new form, the legislation only applied to cotton-mills. Once again there was no adequate machinery to see that it was obeyed and, as far as we know, only two convictions were obtained under the Act. J. C. Hobhouse, Radical member for Westminster, introduced several abortive measures dealing with the factory problem, but it was not until popular feeling had been organised that anything effective was accomplished.

The leaders of the agitation were almost all Tories and they received encouragement from the Tory country gentlemen who regarded the self-made manufacturers as upstarts. The rank and file of the movement were largely Radicals. The Short-Time Movement, as it was called, was inaugurated by Richard Oastler, a Tory land-agent in Yorkshire, who on 29th September 1830 wrote a letter to the Leeds *Mercury* which drew attention to the fact that the slavery prevalent in the woollen-mills was far worse than that in the British colonies. He accused Wilberforce and other members of Parliament of shedding sentimental tears over the sufferings of negro slaves while they turned a blind eye to the appalling conditions in the English factories. The letter concluded: "The very streets which receive the droppings of the Anti-Slavery Society are every morning wet by the tears of innocent victims at the accursed shrine of avarice, who are compelled, not by the cart-whip of the negro-slave driver, but by the dread of the equally appalling thong or strap of the overlooker, to hasten, half-dressed, but not half-fed, to those magazines of British infantile slavery—the worsted mills in the town and neighbourhood of Bradford. Thousands of little children, both male and female, but principally female, from seven to fourteen years of age, are daily compelled to labour from six o'clock in the morning to seven in the evening . . . with only thirty minutes allowed for eating and recreation. Poor infants! ye are indeed sacrificed at the shrine of avarice, without even the solace of the negro slave ; ye are no more than he is free agents ; ye are compelled to work as long as the necessity of your needy parents may require, or the cold-blooded avarice of your worse than barbarian masters may demand."

These words rang through the land, and, in the industrial areas of the north, Short-Time Committees were set up to bring pressure to bear on Parliament. Oastler was supported by John Fielden, a Todmorden manufacturer, and Michael Thomas Sadler, then Tory M.P. for Newark. Sadler became the spokesman of the movement in the House of Commons. He introduced a Bill in 1832, but before the Committee of the House, of which he was the chairman, had completed its work, a general election took place and Sadler, who contested Leeds against Macaulay, failed to be elected. His work was taken up by Lord Ashley, better known under his later title of the Earl of Shaftesbury. In the meantime, the mill-owners organised their opposition. They protested that the evidence brought before Sadler's Committee was unconvincing because the majority of the witnesses came from the neighbourhood of Leeds and was therefore not truly representative. Moreover, some of the evidence proferred was incorrect. The result was that the Government, by a majority of one, ordered the appointment of a Commission to inquire into the employment of children in the factories.

The investigations of the commissioners in some cases brought to light instances of cruel treatment and shocking conditions of work far worse than had been suspected. On the other hand, they revealed the existence of a considerable number of humane employers who interested themselves in their work-people. One of the most progressive mill-owners was John Marshall, who, with Macaulay, represented Leeds in Parliament. His father had begun the manufacture of linen in a flax-mill at Adel. Later a large factory had been erected at Holbeck, Leeds, in which as early as 1791 one of Savery's steam-engines was working. All children between the ages of nine and eleven worked half-time and attended the works' school for the other half. "We gave them 1/6 per week, out of which they had to pay 1d., 2d. or 3d. per week. The half fee for learning to read, 1d.; read and write, 2d.; or read, write and account, 3d., respectively." [1] Other employers commended were A. R. Strutt of Belper, Derby, and Thomas Ashton of Hyde, Lancashire.

The result of the Commission was that the Government amended the Bill sponsored by Ashley, and in its new form it was presented to the House by the Chancellor of the Exchequer, Lord Althorpe. Further amendments were made by the House of Lords, and it eventually became law as the Factory Act of 1833. The ten-hour day was not secured, but such important progress was made that Trevelyan speaks of it as "the children's charter of 1833." It was the first legislation by which a determined attempt was made to protect the children, and it applied to all textile factories except those engaged in the manufacture of silk. The Act distinguished between "young persons" between thirteen and eighteen years of age, who should not work more than sixty-nine hours a week, *i.e.* twelve hours a day with nine hours on Saturdays; children between nine and thirteen, who were restricted to a forty-eight hour week; and those under nine, who were not to be employed. Thus the younger children were able to attend the schools of the National and British and Foreign Societies until they were nine years of age.

After they had finished their eight hours of work, children between nine and thirteen were to attend schools provided by the employers. Each week the child was obliged to render to his employer a schoolmaster's certificate stating that he had attended school for at least two hours in the preceding week. To enforce the Act, four salaried inspectors were appointed, who were empowered to inflict fines for breaches of its provisions or to withhold payment of salary in the case of any schoolmaster or schoolmistress who was incompetent. This was only the first stage in the long struggle for the recognition of a universal ten-hour day and the raising of the age below which a child could not be employed. The later phases of the battle belong to the period discussed in the following chapter.

[1] Quoted by A. H. Robson. *The Education of Children Engaged in Industry in England*, p. 23, Kegan Paul, Trench, Trubner and Co., Ltd., 1931.

CHAPTER VII

FROM THE BEGINNING OF STATE INTERVENTION TO THE REVISED CODE, 1862

The advocates of a national system of elementary education were far from satisfied by the meagre grant made by the Government in 1833. The following year, Mr. Roebuck initiated a discussion when he put a motion for a committee to inquire into the means of establishing a system of national education. The ensuing discussion brought into relief several important points. Not only was the education given declared to be deficient in quality as well as quantity, but the need for the training of teachers was pressed. The sole training institutions available in England were the model schools of the National Society and the British and Foreign School Society. At the latter's school in Borough Road the course was of three months duration only. Lord Brougham advocated a plan for normal schools in London, York, Lancaster, and Exeter. The result of the debate was the grant of an additional £10,000 divided between the two great societies, who were obliged to raise further sums by subscriptions before the work could go forward. The National Society eventually opened the College of St. Mark's, Chelsea, in 1841, and the British and Foreign School Society opened the Borough Road College a little later. In 1838 Mr. Wyse moved in the Address to the Queen a request for a board of commissioners in education to consider the immediate establishment of training institutions for teachers. The indifference of the Government, and the hostility of the Church to certain points in his suggestions caused the motion to be defeated by four votes.

The antagonism between the Church and the Nonconformists was growing increasingly more bitter. Many of the clergy, influenced by the Oxford Movement, were insisting more vehemently upon the right of the Church to control education, and the more it asserted its claims, the greater grew the jealousy and antagonism of the Nonconformists. There was also a feeling in some quarters that the only solution lay in a purely secular education. In the midst of the controversy, Lord John Russell announced, in 1839, the creation by Orders in Council of a Select Committee of the Privy Council consisting of the Lord President, the Lord Privy Seal, the Home Secretary, and the Chancellor of the

Exchequer, "to superintend the application of any sums voted by Parliament for the purpose of promoting Public Education." The Church, especially that section affected by the Oxford Movement, sprang at once into opposition. Archdeacon Denison foreshadowed a change of front on the part of the National Society when he asserted that, since the society had been formed to promote the principles of the Church of England, Nonconformist parents who wished their children to attend National Schools must either agree to allow them to learn the Catechism and attend the services of the Church or stay away altogether. The vote of protest against the establishment of the new committee was defeated by a majority of only five, and the education grant of £30,000 was carried by the narrow margin of two votes.

The first act of the committee was to propose the establishment of a training-school at Kneller Hall for teachers. This proposal brought matters to a head. The idea had been to give the students a general religious instruction which was not distinctive of any denomination and to appoint a chaplain for each denomination having a sufficient number of students. The opposition was so great that the scheme was dropped. It is interesting to notice that both Mr. Gladstone and Mr. Disraeli were on the opposition side. The former declared that in practice the proposal amounted to a recognition by the State of all forms of religion. The really solid achievement of the committee in its first year of life was the appointment as secretary of Dr. Kay, afterwards Sir James Kay-Shuttleworth. Even this appointment was subject to criticism, and Dr. Kay was charged with being a Unitarian and with showing hostility to the Church. As late as 1905, a writer of the National Society inserted the following passage in his book: "Great changes were now intended; the Government, having found in Dr. Kay an able and accomplished Secretary (but as a Nonconformist one not likely to sympathise with Church-school teaching) to undertake the work of an Education Department." [1] Professor Frank Smith has shown conclusively that Dr. Kay was a communicant member of the Church of England.[2]

The small majority by which the grant of 1839 was carried suggested that at any moment a chance division might put an end to State intervention in education. That this did not happen was

[1] Dean Gregory. *Elementary Education*, National Society, 1905.
[2] Frank Smith. *The Life and Work of Sir James Kay-Shuttleworth*, note pp. 81-2, John Murray, 1923.

due entirely to the perseverance and tact of Kay-Shuttleworth, who realised in himself the dual role of an able administrator and an understanding and far-seeing educationist. Dr. Kay had been a physician in Manchester during the great cholera epidemic of 1832. His experience of the dirt and squalor and degradation prevalent in certain quarters of the city convinced him that the greatest evils to be fought were those of bad housing and unsatisfactory sanitary conditions, and that education would be one of the most important means of overcoming them.   Hence the value he attached to schools, libraries, and Mechanics' Institutes. He wrote: "The infant is the victim of the system. . . . He is ill-fed, dirty, ill-clothed, exposed to cold and neglect ; and in consequence, more than one half of the offspring of the poor die before they have completed their 5th year." There was no accurate knowledge about the state of education in the country. True, the Kerry Report of 1833 had professed to give this information, but it was well known that the statistics given in the report were unreliable. Dr. Kay's descriptions of conditions in Manchester, in his pamphlet *The Moral and Physical Condition of the Working Classes employed in the Cotton Manufacture in Manchester*, inspired a number of influential Manchester citizens to form the Statistical Society to investigate conditions in Manchester, Liverpool, and the surrounding neighbourhood.

Similar societies were formed in London, Leeds, and other provincial towns. The investigations of the Manchester society showed that the schools had deteriorated rather than improved. This was especially true of the private school. "In one of the Manchester dame schools eleven children were found, in a small room, in which one of the children of the Mistress was lying ill in bed of the measles. Another child had died in the same room, of the same complaint, a few days before; and no less than thirty of the usual scholars were then confined at home with the same disease." [1]

The conditions in other dame-schools and in private-adventure schools were almost too horrible to credit. The statistics collected for Manchester showed that the children of school age formed about a quarter of the total population. Of these, two-thirds received some kind of education and the remainder were absolutely untouched by any educational influence. In Liverpool the latter class included more than one-half of the child population. A

[1] Quoted by Frank Smith, *A History of English Elementary Education*, p. 150.

similar investigation of conditions in Leeds revealed that one-eighth of the population was receiving some kind of education, but if the pupils who only attended Sunday Schools were deducted, then only just over two per cent of the child population, or 1 in 49·5, attended day-schools. In 1839, owing to the influence of grants in aid of school building, the percentage had risen to 8·23. The result of such inquiries was to condemn the voluntary system and call for measures of State control.

But Dr. Kay was not to stay long in Manchester. The Poor Law Reform Act of 1834 stipulated that children in workhouses should receive three hours instruction each day. In 1835 he was appointed Assistant Poor Law Commissioner in East Anglia, and later transferred to London. He continued the work he had begun in Manchester and coupled it with a careful study of schools and methods of teaching in this country, in Scotland, and on the Continent. All this experience convinced him that the monitorial school was a complete failure. He entirely disagreed with the idea that one child who has been instructed in the subject of the lesson is capable of teaching another. At the same time, visits to Edinburgh and Glasgow, where he saw the work of Wood and Stow, impressed him with the superiority of their methods of class teaching. He found what he was seeking by pure accident. In a certain workhouse school the master had fallen ill, and when the chairman of the union visited it he found everything progressing favourably under William Rush, thirteen years of age, who was teaching a class with great success. Rush was left to continue the work, and the thought was raised in Dr. Kay's mind whether he had found what he was seeking. Kay allowed other boys to do the same in other workhouse schools. These assistants were called pupil-teachers. He saw the value of replacing the monitors by older boys who would serve, as it were, a period of apprenticeship in the art of teaching. When he was transferred to London in 1838, Kay was able to experiment further in the workhouse school at Norwood, which housed 1,100 children. He enlisted the help of the master and secured a grant of £500 a year from the Home Office. With the help of this grant he was able, as was mentioned in Chapter vi, to import teachers from Scotland. Alexander Wilson taught at Norwood for a year and a half, and then accepted the offer of the National Society to take charge of their model school at Westminster. At Norwood, a scheme of handicrafts was introduced and the idea of pupil-teachers given a trial. The experiment attracted a good deal of attention and Norwood received a constant stream of visitors. It was due to the excellent work and the all-round experience that he had gained in education that Dr. Kay was appointed Secretary of the Select Committee of the Privy Council.

Meanwhile, the terrible conditions prevalent in some of the private-adventure schools, which were largely unknown to the general public who rarely read reports, were brought home to them in a very vivid way through the publication of *Nicholas Nickleby*. The description of Mr. Squeers and Dotheboys Hall was based on certain schools in North Yorkshire which Dickens had actually visited.

Before he took office, Dr. Kay had realised that his most urgent problem was that of obtaining better teachers in adequate numbers. The monitorial system was not only mechanical ("monitorial humbug" as he once called it), but it ignored an educational influence of the greatest value, the interaction between the immature mind of the pupil and the mature mind of the teacher. Kay wished to replace the monitors by pupil-teachers, but his idea went further than the mere substitution of an older boy for a younger one. He thought that the pupil-teacher should serve an apprenticeship to teaching under the guidance of an experienced headmaster, and then proceed to a well-organised training-college to complete the training for his profession. Hence the most immediate necessity was the establishment of training-colleges for teachers. We have seen the fate of the proposal for opening a training-college in 1839. Kay was actually one of the most important influences behind the proposal, although at that time he had not accepted office. He would not acknowledge defeat and, if the Government was not prepared to open a training-college, he would carry through the experiment relying on his own resources. With the assistance of his friend Mr. Tufnell, he opened in 1840 a training-college in the old manor-house at Battersea. The college was a residential one, and the domestic side was in charge of Kay's mother and sister. Although he was fully occupied with his official post he managed not only to live at the college but to take a considerable share in the teaching. The students were of two types, pupil-teachers from institutions like Norwood, and older men between the ages of twenty and thirty. The religious instruction was based on the Anglican Church and the students were required to attend Battersea Parish Church on Sundays. Kay had recently visited the Continent in the company of Tufnell and he had been impressed by the schools of Holland and Switzerland—especially the latter, which had developed under the influence of Pestalozzi and Fellenberg. Hence Kay adopted as his model for Battersea the Swiss normal schools of Fr. Girard, Fellenberg, and Vehrli. Frank Smith describes the internal economy of Battersea as follows: "The pupils were required to make their own beds, scrub floors, clean their boots, lay the tables, prepare the vegetables; just as out-of-doors they had to look after two cows, three pigs, and three goats, which belonged to the establishment, to clear the neglected garden of weeds, and grow vegetables and fruit for the needs of the community. This healthy labour was to safeguard them from the danger of forming a false estimate of their position in relation to the class to which they belonged. They were Spartan days; all were up at five-thirty (including the tutors, except when prevented by sickness), and domestic duties and garden occupied them till eight o'clock. Meals, school, and garden, alternated through the long day until nine at night, making in all about fourteen hours of mental and bodily labour." [1] It must have been a tough time for some who were not used to such a life, but those who survived it gained in their general physical health and well-being. Many of the pupil-teachers were found to be very backward as regards their own education, so that the course began with teaching elementary subjects. The curriculum included mensuration and land-survey-ing, geography, elementary science, accounts, drawing, and music. Kay gave lectures on the theory and practice of education.

Unfortunately the struggle to keep the college going was more than the limited resources of Dr. Kay and his friends could stand, and by 1842 the deficit had reached over £2,000. Dr. Kay left the college on his marriage, when he took by royal licence the name of Kay-Shuttleworth. The Government made a tardy grant of £1,000 for one year only, and demanded in return the right of inspection in perpetuity. The founders of the college realised that the only way to obtain a sound financial basis for the work was to hand it over to the National Society. This was done in 1843, but the example of Battersea stimulated the Church to undertake a campaign for building training-colleges. The result was that by 1845 the Church of England had established twenty-two training-colleges containing at that date 540 students.

[1] Frank Smith. *The Life and Work of Sir James Kay-Shuttleworth*, p. 107, John Murray, 1923.

For many years after 1839 education was seriously hindered in its progress by the acute controversies which were based upon the sharp religious differences that existed in the nation. There was no reason—except the conflict between the Churches, which extended to a great extent to the political parties also—why a national system of education should not have been evolved in the early years of Victoria's reign. The bitterness showed by the antagonists is largely incomprehensible to the present-day Englishman, who has grown up in an atmosphere of understanding and toleration and who sees the relations of sympathy, goodwill, and co-operation, which now obtain between the Anglicans and the Free Churches.

Hence, to appreciate the difficulties with which Kay-Shuttleworth had to contend, it is necessary to try to estimate the very different religious situation of the 1840's. In the 16th and 17th centuries the Church of England claimed, with a good deal of justice, that it represented the English nation. Church and State were practically synonymous. The Puritan movement was not so much a movement of separation as a struggle taking place within the Church itself. The Separatists, who dissociated themselves from the Church, and the Roman Catholics, represented a very small minority of the people, and had no political power. We can view the Puritan Rebellion not only as an attempt to replace the personal government of the Crown by the supremacy of Parliament, but also as an endeavour to remodel the whole basis of ecclesiastical government and belief. During the brief years of the Commonwealth, the attempt had been successful, but the restoration of the monarchy in 1660 involved also the restoration of the Church, with the result that considerable numbers of people who were unable to fulfil the conditions of the Clarendon Code found themselves cut off from the Church and in actual hostility towards it. Nevertheless, it is true to say that until about the end of Anne's reign the Established Church represented, for practical purposes, the vast majority of the English people. As long as Church and State consisted of almost the same body of people, there was no serious opposition to the claims of the former to control education. During the Whig ascendancy of the 18th century, the Church had entered upon a period of deadness and apathy. Large numbers of the population, still nominally members of the Church, were growing up not so much in hostility to it as almost unaffected by it. The age of apathy came to an end through the Wesleyan revival, which began as a movement within the Church itself, but which, because of the lack of sympathy and understanding on the part of the clergy, culminated in the secession of thousands of members who had no special quarrel either with the services of the Church or with its organisation.

Thus the situation at the beginning of the 19th century had changed completely, and, although the Church still had a majority in the nation, it could now no longer claim to represent the whole population. Indeed, many writers considered that its day was done and the time for its disestablishment was at hand. But this view failed to reckon with the vitality which was already asserting itself in the Church. First the Evangelical revival, and then the Oxford Movement, had changed the conditions within the Church, and it began to recover in the north of England some of the ground it had lost to Methodism. The Tractarians, though a small minority, influenced great numbers of the clergy who did not follow them in doctrinal matters, and all schools of thought were united in asserting the ancient claim of the Church to the control of education.

The condition of the 1840's may be summarised thus. In the first place, while the Church represented the majority of the nation, the Nonconformists stood for a large and influential minority. The political parties on the whole were influenced by this grouping. The Tories were supporters of the Church and the Whigs showed an opposite tendency. There were of course many exceptions, but this represents the general layout of the political situation.

The Nonconformists resented the claims of the Church to control education, but at the same time most people, Churchmen and Dissenters alike, agreed that religion was an essential part of education. The secularists were as yet quite a small party. The majority of the schools were in the hands of the National Society. This did not cause a great deal of difficulty in the large towns which had National Schools and undenominational schools existing side by side. It was otherwise in the country villages, where as a rule the only available school was the National School, in which religious instruction was based on the Catechism. Attention has already been drawn to the liberal attitude of the National Society in the early days in providing what in practice amounted to a conscience clause for the children of Dissenters. One effect of the Oxford Movement was that its more extreme adherents insisted upon Church teaching as a condition of entrance to the schools. Thus Archdeacon Denison said on one occasion, "I cannot take one step in educating a child who has not either received, or is not, if of such an age as to admit of previous teaching, in a definite course of preparation, for holy baptism, and in the latter case I should not admit the child into the school until holy baptism had been received," and on another, "Under no circumstances whatsoever could I consent to admit a single child to a school of which I have the control and management, without insisting most positively and strictly, on the learning of the catechism and on attendance at church on Sunday."

The Dissenters, on the other hand, objected more strongly than ever to Church teaching which they thought was becoming, under the influence of the Tractarians, more and more estranged from the principles of the Reformation. The Church would not entertain any idea of undenominational teaching in the schools, while the Dissenters pointed out that in the division of the Treasury grant the National Society was getting the lion's share. The Church admitted this, but considered it as justified since the National Society's schools were far more numerous. They pointed with pride to the large number of schools and the Church training-colleges which had been built very largely with money subscribed by Church people. Thus any schemes submitted to Parliament which involved the building and maintenance of schools out of rates and taxes failed to receive the necessary support because undenominational teaching was not acceptable to the Church, and the Dissenters argued that if denominational teaching was provided, they would be contributing to the cost of doctrinal teaching with which they strongly disagreed.

One of the duties of the Committee of Council was "to determine in what manner the grants of money made from time to time should be distributed." In June 1839 the Committee issued a Minute which announced that all future building-grants would involve the right of inspection. "The right of inspection will be required by the Committee in all cases ; inspectors, authorised by Her Majesty in Council, will be appointed from time to time to visit schools to be henceforth aided by public money: the inspectors will not interfere with the religious instruction, or discipline, or management of the school, it being their object to collect facts and information, and to report the result of their inspections to the Committee of Council." (*Minutes of the Committee of Council,* 24th September 1839.)

The Church immediately objected to the right of inspection and the National Society claimed to inspect its own schools. Kay-Shuttleworth realised that the most practical solution of the problem was to work in co-operation with the Church, and in pursuance of this policy he reached what is generally known as the Concordat of 1840 with the National Society. The archbishop had the right of nominating persons as inspectors of Church schools. The instructions to the inspectors as regards religious teaching were to be given by the archbishops, and the instructions issued to them by the Committee of Council were to be shown to the archbishops before they received sanction. Duplicate copies of the inspectors' reports were to be sent to the archbishop of the province and the bishop of the diocese. Mr. Tremenheere had already been appointed as inspector, but the Concordat restricted his activities to the schools of the British and Foreign School Society. The Rev. J. Allen was made inspector of Church schools, and Mr. J. Gibson inspector for Scotland.

The real clash of the denominations came in 1843 and was occasioned by a Factory Bill introduced by the Home Secretary, Sir James Graham. The factory inspectors appointed to ensure that the legislation of 1833 was being observed had for some years reported that there was a wholesale evasion of the provisions of the Act. Not only did they wish to see the regulations concerning the employment of children extended to factories other than those specified in 1833, but they also urged upon the Government the necessity of defining when the eight hours work should take place. Many factories began the day's work at 5.30 a.m. and closed down at 8.30 p.m. Children could be employed at any eight hours of this period, and the practical result was that in many instances they did part of their work before, and the remainder after, dinner. They might be on or about the factory premises during the whole of the period and thus provide a temptation to an unscrupulous employer to make use of their services for more than the legal hours.

Lord Ashley obtained in 1840 the appointment of a Select Committee to inquire into the Act for the Regulation of Mills and Factories. The reports of the factory inspectors decided the Committee to recommend that children under the age of thirteen should not be employed for more than seven hours a day, and that this work should be performed either before or after the factory dinner-hour. It was thought that this amendment would enable many children to attend the National and British Schools on certain half-days during the week.

Some factory inspectors considered that employers should not be called upon to provide schools for the children in their factories.

They suggested that the Treasury might grant half the cost of the intended school and issue the other half as a loan, repayable with interest in five or seven years. If this principle were to be adopted, there would be no excuse under cover of which the employer could delay the building of a school.

The result of the recommendations of the Committee was the Factory Bill of Sir James Graham, the educational clauses of which had been discussed with Kay-Shuttleworth. Children between eight and thirteen years of age were to be prohibited from working more than six and a half hours per day, and those of thirteen not more than twelve hours a day. The Bill was intended to apply to all children employed in woollen, flax, silk, and cotton, factories. No child under eight was to be employed at all, and all children under thirteen were to be obliged to spend three hours a day in school. The new schools were planned to be built through Government loans, and were to be maintained by fees of not more than 3d. per head per week and through the local poor-rate.

So far these proposals met with general agreement, but when the question of the management of the schools was approached dissension flared up. The intention was for the school to be managed by a committee of seven persons. The local incumbent should be a member and should be empowered to nominate his two church-wardens as trustees. The remaining four, of whom two should be mill-owners, were to be elected by the magistrates. The headmaster was to be a member of the Church of England, and should be approved by the bishop. The religious instruction would be based on the Book of Common Prayer, and attendance at church was to be compulsory, though a conscience clause was included which it was thought would be acceptable to Nonconformists. The schools were to be inspected by the clerical trustees and the Committee of Council.

At the first reading the Bill received but few criticisms, but when it came before the House for the second reading the opposition of the Nonconformists had become organised. Numerous petitions to the House poured in, and in the provinces the opposition was led by Edward Baines, the editor of the Leeds *Mercury*. The Nonconformists objected that, whilst all inhabitants were required to contribute to the maintenance of the schools through the poor-rate, the management would be exclusively in the hands of the Church.

At the Committee stage, Graham suggested several amendments in the hope of pacifying his opponents. He proposed that denominational teaching should be voluntary and might be given in separate rooms. While the Church teaching was being given, the children of Nonconformists could receive instruction in other subjects, and their minister would be allowed to visit the school for three hours on one day each week to teach the tenets of the particular denomination. The clergyman should choose one trustee only ; the other should be elected by the subscribers to the school. The four remaining members of the management committee were to be elected by the ratepayers, but no ratepayer would be able to vote for more than two candidates. The headmaster alone should be approved by the bishop : the other teachers would be appointed by the trustees.

The concessions proposed by Sir James should have been sufficient to gain the consent of reasonable people, or at least to have formed the basis for further bargaining. The Nonconformists, however, were no longer reasonable people, but, elated by their success, they would listen to nothing less than an unconditional surrender by the Government. Graham was determined to give ground no further. He stated: "I say that as a Minister of the Crown—that Crown being the head of the Church established by law—I should betray my duty if I made any concession on this point." He felt that parents of Church of England children had a right to demand Church teaching in the schools for their boys and girls, although he had agreed that Nonconformists should also be able to obtain the kind of religious instruction they wanted. The Bill was dropped and a promise given that a new Bill would be introduced in the following session.

The abandonment of Graham's Bill was the most serious setback that education had so far received. If it had become law, there was a real possibility that it might have laid the foundation for a general provision of schools in the industrial areas and that in the course of time it might even have led to a national system of education. As it was, religious bigotry postponed the hope of establishing universal elementary education for another thirty years.

Sir James Graham's Factory Act of 1844 entirely abandoned the idea of aiding the provision of schools. The question of religious instruction was dropped and the main part of the Act was concerned with the hours of employment. In one respect it was retrograde, for the age at which a child could be employed was lowered from nine years to eight. It obliged children between the ages of eight and thirteen to spend either three whole days or six half days at school. The hours of work were limited to six and a half per day, either before or after the dinner-hour. Every employer was obliged to obtain a certificate from a schoolmaster testifying that the child had attended school for the prescribed number of hours during the preceding week. The factory inspectors were given further powers for inspecting schools and of disallowing the certificates given by incompetent schoolmasters. Twopence per week might be deducted from the child's wages to pay for his schooling. These regulations were extended to other factories and workshops in 1864 and 1867 respectively. Thus began the system of "half-timers" which, much to the hindrance of educational efficiency, lingered on to 1918.[1]

At a meeting of the Congregational Union, held at Leeds in 1843, Edward Baines repudiated State control in education and declared for a voluntary system on a religious basis. The Voluntaryists set about raising funds for schools, and by 1851 had opened 364 schools which were independent of State aid. They opened their own training-college at Homerton in 1846. The movement spread for a time, but then diminished and finally came to an end in 1867.

Kay-Shuttleworth now turned his attention to what he had always considered his most important aim, that of improving both the supply and the quality of the teachers. In the Minutes of 1846, his scheme of training was announced, and it formed the basis of training for many years to come. In the scheme he definitely introduced the pupil-teacher system. Certain schools which had received a favourable report from the inspector were to be recognised as suitable for the training of pupil-teachers. The young person entered upon a five-year apprenticeship at the age of thirteen. His stipend was £10 per annum rising by annual increments

---

[1] The unsatisfactory nature of the half-time system is illustrated from the following comments taken from the records of Burnt Yates School in the West Riding.

"1888, Sept. 26th. A list of Half-Timers' absences was sent to-day to Mr. Threlfall, Shaw Mills, who has promised to see into the matter.

"1890, May 1st. Sent note to the overlooker at Shaw Mills informing him of the irregular attendance of the half-timers.

"1891, March 10th. Sent note to Mr. John Threlfall, the Mill, Shaw Mills, respecting the absence from school of several half-timers.

"March 11th. Record reply from Mr. Threlfall saying he cannot stop the work of a batch of children.

"N.B. The half-timers' attendance book has been filled up regularly and returned to the Mill each week, the absences, as they occurred being specially noted therein. No notice has apparently been taken of these entries at the Mill. It is a growing evil."

of £2 10s. to £20 per annum.   One pupil-teacher was allowed for
every twenty-five scholars, and head teachers were required to
give them one and a half hours instruction each school day.   For this
work head teachers received an addition to their salaries of £5
for one pupil-teacher, £9 for two, and £3 for every additional one.
At the end of their apprenticeship the pupil-teachers presented
themselves for the Queen's Scholarship examination.   Those who
were selected were awarded exhibitions to the value of £20 or £25
at a training-college.   Annual grants were paid to training-colleges
for each of the three years of training.   The unsuccessful candidates
were to receive a preference for minor appointments in the Government Revenue departments.   Trained teachers were to receive
proficiency grants from the Government and old-age pensions were
to be provided for men and women teachers who had a minimum
of fifteen years service in approved schools.   Special grants were
offered in respect of field gardens and workshops.   This involved
a larger grant, and in 1847 the Government grant was increased to
£100,000.   The same year the Committee of Council offered grants
for school-books and maps on condition that two-thirds of the cost
was met by subscriptions.   The latter condition was mischievous,
since the schools which needed the apparatus most were those in
poor parishes where it was most difficult to raise money by fees
or subscription.   Thus, in London, four slum parishes with large
school populations received £12 0s. 8d. between them, whilst four
parishes in well-to-do districts obtained nearly £4,000.

Another important Minute dealt with management clauses which
were required to be included in the trust-deeds of schools.   Four
different types of management clause were decided upon for the
Church of England, Wesleyan, and Roman Catholic schools, and
the schools of the British and Foreign School Society.   In the case
of the Church schools the incumbent of the parish was to be the
chairman of the managers and was given the right to use the school
premises as a Sunday School.   The incumbent was responsible for
the religious instruction, and any case of dispute was to be referred
to the bishop.   The management and control of the school and
the appointment or dismissal of the teachers were the concern of
the management committee.   In Wesleyan schools the minister
took the place of the parish clergyman, and in Roman Catholic
schools the priest acted upon a faculty from his bishop.   In 1847
the Catholic Poor School Committee was formed, and after some
delay was recognised as an authority which could receive grants for

the building of schools. The priest nominated his committee of managers, but in Church schools the managers were elected from the subscribers. In the British Schools the whole committee was elected. The National Society objected to the management clause on the ground that it introduced a distinction between religious and secular education which they could never admit. Archdeacon Denison led the extremists of the National Society and at one time it seemed as though the society would dissolve into two opposing factions. Fortunately, moderate counsels prevailed and a working compromise was accepted.

One interesting proposal to end religious conflict was made by Dr. Hook, Vicar of Leeds. In a pamphlet published in 1846, entitled *On the means of rendering more effective the Education of the People,* he suggested a system of schools supported by the rates and under local management, providing secular education only. Religious instruction should be given by the clergy of the different denominations on Sundays and on two afternoons a week. The pamphlet attracted considerable attention, and some correspondence passed between Dr. Hook and Kay-Shuttleworth on the matter. After mature consideration, the latter decided to adhere to his original plan of the denominational school with a conscience clause.

Before the establishment of the Committee of the Council, very little attention had been paid to the important question of school buildings. It is true that both the National and the British Societies had drawn up building regulations, but far too frequently, especially in rural districts, schoolhouses were erected by rule of thumb by the village bricklayer and carpenter. The rooms were often low, dark, and ill-drained, with no other means of heating than a stove at one end. The floor was usually of brick, which wore into dust and was cold to the feet. There were rarely cloak-rooms for the children, and sanitation was universally neglected.

The Committee of Council, in the regulations of 24th September 1839, required that in order to receive a building-grant, "Every building . . . shall be of substantial erection, and that in the plans thereof not less than six square feet be provided for each child."[1] *Circular No. 1,* November 1839, consisted of forty-two questions which were to be answered by applicants for a building-grant. The questions included ones concerning the site, the nature of the tenure,

---

[1] *Minutes,* 1839-40, p. 2.

the names of the trustees, and particulars of the contemplated building, *e.g.* walls, windows, roof, floor, and ventilation. Instructions were also issued indicating how the questions should be answered. Detailed plans of the schoolhouse, the master's house, and children's playground were to accompany the answers to the questionnaire. "The mode of ventilating and warming the school is of such importance to the health of the masters and scholars, that it ought to be most carefully considered by the school committee, and a sketch of the air-grates and flues should be included in the sectional drawings. The school committee will find useful information on this subject, in the minute explanatory of the plans of school-houses published in the 8vo edition of the Minutes of the Committee of Council." [1]

The Minutes of 20th February 1840, included plans and specifications of different types of school. The arrangements of the schoolroom were described, first according to the system of mutual instruction, *i.e.* the system adopted in the schools of Bell and Lancaster, and then according to the mixed method, in which the monitorial system was combined with the simultaneous method advocated by Stow and Wilderspin. In the latter case, provision was made for the erection of a gallery. "In making arrangements for teaching on the simultaneous method, it is therefore necessary to provide for two somewhat conflicting objects: —

"1. The technical instruction of the children in classes, carefully arranged according to their intellectual proficiency.

"2. The general instruction of 100 to 120, or even more children, by the use of suggestion, ellipsis, and interrogation, either in the schoolroom common to all the classes, or in a gallery provided for that purpose." [2]

The building-plans of the Committee of Council brought into being a new profession, namely that of the school architect. Thus an architect, H. E. Kendall, produced an album of designs for schools and school houses in 1847, which included a number of plans and sketches of schools which he had built in accordance with the official requirements. The following specification represents a typical school of this period.

"The previous estimates of the number which a school will contain are calculated by allowing six square feet of the surface of the schoolroom floor to each child, a space recommended as sufficient by the Committee of Council on Education. According to

---

[1] *Minutes*, 1839-40, p. 11.   [2] *Ibid.*, p. 52.

this rule, the present design will accommodate eighty-five children only.

"The school should be faced with red bricks, which might be pleasingly varied by interlacings of black heading bricks, and in parts alternately with dark ochre coloured bricks. The porches, bay window, dressings round windows, the base of the plinth, the plinth weathered string course, the gable quoin-corbels and their acroteral ornaments, the gable coping and the apex acroteral terminations, the buttress consoles of the chimney shaft, and the bracketted chimney tops, would be best formed of Caen or Bath stone ashler; the belfrey and ventilator painted and sanded to imitate stone.

"The moulded window frames, mullions, and transoms, doors, and open side parapets of porch, to be fir, finished in imitation of oak. The roof timbers open to the school, and framed ornamentally, the floor boarded, and the glazing exhibiting an arrangement of geometrical forms. The slating plain—except to the ventilating turret, which should be scalloped with a moulded ferro metallic like coping. The roof of the porch and bay window to be covered with lead, laid with curved hip ridge rolls, as practised in the varied, picturesque, but fantastic medley manner of building in the time of James I; the style in the Author's eye when composing this elevation.

"The teacher's lodgings, as usual, consist of parlour, kitchen, pantry, two sleeping rooms over, and scullery, coal room, with a cellar under the stairs etc.; the school and house together would cost £350.

"In the designs which have been executed, the schools are generally heated by open fires; and the ventilation produced in the manner recommended in the Minute of the Committee of Council on Education. Open spaces are left at intervals in the external wall, between the sleeper joists, and openings are also made in different parts of the boarded floor, having valves to regulate their size. Through these valved openings a quantity of fresh air constantly flows into the school-room, and the warm breathed impure air rises to the roof, and escapes by a perforation in the ceiling, and through the valves or luffer boards of the ventilating turret, into the atmosphere. This Apparatus is found to act with precision in most states of the weather, and the air of the school-room to be incessantly renewed, without discomfort to the children placed on the floor."

The reader should note the following points about the above specification : —

    (a) The tendency to build a school after an ecclesiastical model or in a pseudo-Gothic, Tudor, or Jacobean style.

    (b) The low cost of the building.

    (c) The arrangements for ventilation.

    (d) No provision for playgrounds.

    (e) The arrangement of the forms in the classroom. The school was designed for the mixed method. The rear desks were to be occupied by children who were writing, whilst the front desks were used for children listening to an oral lesson. The cloak-rooms were in the porch, and in a school of this size, no gallery was provided.

Owing to the tremendous pressure of work, coupled with the reluctance of the Privy Council to increase his staff, and also to his anxieties about the religious question, Kay-Shuttleworth's health gave way in 1848. After a partial recovery in the following year, he tendered his resignation and the Queen in recognition of his great services to education conferred a baronetcy upon him. He was succeeded by Mr. (afterwards Lord) Lingen.

Kay-Shuttleworth's services to education cannot be better expressed than in Frank Smith's appreciation. "It is the literal truth to say that he had in those ten years, laid the ground plan of English elementary education. 'To him, more than anyone else,' says Sir Michael Sadler, 'we owe it that England is supplied with schools for the children of her people, and that this costly work has been accomplished without a breach between Church and State.' What had seemed impossible in 1839 was, by 1849, almost achieved in its main outlines, and the victory was on the side of tolerance and reason. . . . Under his guidance and by his directive force a silent revolution had been started in the schools, which in the end transformed them." [1]

The denominational disputes referred to above led to the rise of a Secularist party consisting of many able and thoughtful men who, despairing of reaching agreement in any other way, advocated purely secular instruction in the schools, leaving religious education to the clergy. Several ineffective attempts were made in Parliament in 1850 and 1851 to secure an Act setting up a national system of

[1] Frank Smith. *A History of English Elementary Education*, p. 211.

secular schools. The Secularists started from the Lancashire Public School Association which by 1850 had become the National Public School Association. They never succeeded in persuading Parliament or the nation, which was united in the belief that all education should rest on a religious basis.

During the period of religious controversy, the Committee of Council had been quietly issuing its Minutes and gradually asserting public control over education. Its work is a very interesting example of the use of delegated powers of legislation about which we hear so much at the present time. Most people, until the publication of Lord Hewart's *New Despotism*, had not realised the extent to which government is carried on through a bureaucracy by means of delegated powers, and even now it is thought that this is a recent innovation. The Committee of Council had been established in 1839 by an Act of the royal prerogative and its Minutes were usually issued without parliamentary authority, since the only time for discussing them was when the annual grant was submitted to the House.

The accumulation of power in the hands of the administrative officials did not pass without notice. For example, in 1852 the Committee ruled that in all schools receiving grants a conscience clause must be inserted in the trust deeds. This was bitterly opposed by the National Society and, when the matter was discussed in the House of Lords, Earl Derby pointed out that most of the important decisions made by the Committee of the Council were issued when Parliament was in recess and the education grant for the year had been passed. Again, it was an Order in Council that raised the Committee in 1856 to the status of an Education Department. The Lord President was to remain the chief of the new department, but he was to be represented in the House of Commons by a Vice-President who would be responsible to the House for the expenditure and administration of the department. The Vice-President was selected by the Prime Minister when he chose his Cabinet, and thus his term of office ended when the particular party in power, of which he was a member, ceased to have a majority in the House. Thus the progress of education became definitely linked with politics, and on many occasions the tendency has been to regard education from the point of view of the policy of the party in power rather than from its relation to the children of the country. The occasion of the formation of the Education Department was chosen by Lord Monteagle to express his belief "that the Committee of Council was in constitution and principle one of the worst modes of administration. The members were ill-assorted ; some could not attend for want of time; others had not the knowledge or opportunity of understanding the functions that nominally devolved upon them; and, as the result, the real power was in the hands of subordinate persons." [1]

In addition to differences between denominationalists and secularists, many people were alarmed at the increasing cost of education. The Parliamentary grant had risen from £150,000 in 1851 to £541,233 in 1857. Against this increase one had to set the cost of the Crimean War which amounted to nearly £78,000,000. Ought not the amount spent on education to be reduced ? Was the instruction given in the schools yielding satisfactory results for the money spent ? These thoughts led Sir J. Pakington to secure the appointment of a Royal Commission under the chairmanship of the Duke of Newcastle, " to inquire into the present state of education in England, and to consider and report what measures, if any, are required for the extension of *sound and cheap elementary instruction* to all classes of people." The words in italics sufficiently reveal the purpose of the inquiry. The report of the Newcastle Commission was issued in 1861, and on the whole was optimistic in character. The Commissioners professed to be content with the system by which schools provided by voluntary bodies received assistance through Government grants and they affirmed that universal compulsory education was neither attainable nor desirable. They were satisfied with the wide diffusion of education and ignored the fact that many areas were inadequately supplied with schools.

The Report classified schools either as public or private. The former were directed by the religious societies without regard to profit. The latter were conducted by individuals for profit. Although the Report included a section of 127 pages of statistics, the figures given are not wholly reliable since they were frequently based on estimates rather than accurate returns. It is possible, however, to form from them a picture of the diffusion of educational facilities. The diagram on page 250 summarises the relevant statistics.

The Commissioners, however, were not so happy about the attendance of the children. Even in the inspected schools, the attendance amounted to only 76·1 per cent of the pupils on roll and

[1] Holman. *English National Education*, p. 148, Blackie, 1898.

was distributed over about four years in the case of children between six and twelve years of age. Seventeen per cent of the pupils attended less than 50 days in the year, 19 per cent between 50 and 100 days, 23 per cent for 150 days, and only 41 per cent attended 176 days, the minimum period fixed for payment of a grant. In the inspected schools, owing to the fact that only a minority of the children remained at school after ten years of age, the Commission

NEWCASTLE COMMISSION   1858 - 1861

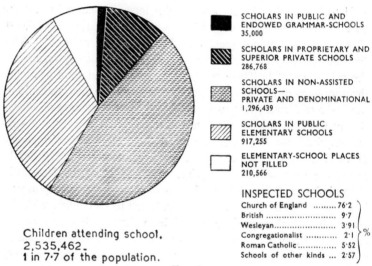

SCHOLARS IN PUBLIC AND ENDOWED GRAMMAR-SCHOOLS
35,000

SCHOLARS IN PROPRIETARY AND SUPERIOR PRIVATE SCHOOLS
286,768

SCHOLARS IN NON-ASSISTED SCHOOLS—
PRIVATE AND DENOMINATIONAL
1,296,439

SCHOLARS IN PUBLIC ELEMENTARY SCHOOLS
917,255

ELEMENTARY-SCHOOL PLACES NOT FILLED
210,566

INSPECTED SCHOOLS
Church of England .... 76·2
British .... 9·7
Wesleyan........................ 3·91
Congregationalist .... 2·1   %
Roman Catholic.............. 5·52
Schools of other kinds ... 2·57

Children attending school.
2,535,462.
1 in 7·7 of the population.

Fig. 1.

considered that not more than a quarter of the pupils were receiving a satisfactory education.[1]

While the Commissioners thought the basis of the existing system quite sound, they pointed to a number of defects. The instruction of the inspected schools was undoubtedly superior to that in other schools, but the inspectors' reports were not altogether reliable because they judged the achievements of the older rather than the younger scholars. Inspection tended to raise the standards of the school, but it also had an adverse effect in leading the teacher to

---

[1] The statistics for Leeds in 1857 were: average leaving age 9·59 years, average length of schooling 4·73 years, percentage who had previously attended an infant-school 51·75. Average rate of wages obtained on leaving school varied from 3s. 2d. to 5s. per week.

place overmuch reliance on memory at the expense of reason. The teachers were tempted to concentrate their efforts on the older children and to neglect the groundwork of the three R's amongst the juniors. The moral and religious influences of the schools were greater than their intellectual influence, and in many cases good schools had civilised the whole neighbourhood in which they were set.

They were very concerned with the large number of pupils who attended uninspected schools where little or no improvement had occurred since the early days of the century. Speaking of the dame-schools, they described the mistresses as "generally advanced in life and their school is usually their kitchen, sitting and bedroom." The room was "often so small that the children stand in a semi-circle round the teacher. Indeed, I have seen the children as closely packed as birds in a nest, and tumbling over each other like puppies in a kennel." [1] Speaking of the masters, Dr. Hodgeson reported, "None are too old, too poor, too ignorant, too feeble, too sickly, too unqualified in one or every way, to regard themselves, and to be regarded by others, as unfit for school-keeping. Nay, there are few, if any, occupations regarded as incompatible with school-keeping, if not as simultaneous, at least as preparatory employments.   Domestic servants out of place, discharged bar-maids, vendors of toys or lollipops, keepers of small eating-houses, of mangles, or of small lodging houses, needlewomen who take in plain or slop work, milliners, consumptive patients in an advanced stage, cripples almost bedridden, persons of at least doubtful temperance, outdoor paupers, men and women of seventy and even eighty years of age, persons who spell badly (mostly women, I grieve to say), who can scarcely write and who cannot cipher at all." [2] Again, "When other occupations fail for a time, a private school can be opened, with no capital beyond the cost of a ticket in the window.   Any room, however small and close, serves for the purpose; the children sit on the floor, and bring what books they please; whilst the closeness of the room renders fuel superfluous, and even keeps the children quiet by its narcotic effects.   If the fees do not pay the rent, the school is dispersed or taken by the next tenant." [3]

The reaction of the Commissioners to the reports of their assistants was astounding. They recommended that private schools should receive aid if the school were properly ventilated and drained

[1] *Report*, Vol. I, p. 29.   [2] *Ibid.*, p. 93.   [3] *Ibid.*, p. 94.

and if the inspector reported favourably on it. The reason given was that under these conditions most private schools would be ruled out and a better type of individual would be encouraged to open schools.

A further suggestion was to admit to the Teachers' Certificate examination any persons who had a good moral character and had kept a school for three years. The Commission ascribed the popularity of private schools to the fact that the parents thought the pupils more respectable, "that the teachers are more inclined to comply with their wishes, that the children are better cared for, and that they themselves, in choosing such schools for their children, stand in an independent position, and are not accepting a favour from their social superiors." [1]

The suggestions of the Commission may be summarised as follows: —

There should be no interference in the religious instruction given by the different denominations. All grants should be paid to the school managers, from whom the teachers should receive their salaries. They recommended the simplification of the system of grants and suggested that they should be reduced to two types: —

(a) A grant paid by the Government out of general taxation and dependent on attendance and the fulfilment of certain conditions by the managers and a satisfactory report from the inspectors.

(b) A sum derived from the county rates based on the result of an examination in reading, writing, and arithmetic, conducted by examiners appointed by county and borough boards of education.

The Government grant should be calculated on the average attendance and should not be more than 6s. or less than 5s. 6d. per head in schools having under sixty pupils, and not more than 4s. 6d. per head for larger schools. An additional grant of 2s. 6d. per child under the instruction of a qualified pupil-teacher or assistant teacher could be earned. Thirty children were allowed for each pupil-teacher and sixty for each assistant teacher. The amount of these grants would vary according to the inspectors' reports.

Aid from the county rate could be claimed for each child who had attended at least 140 days in the year and had passed the

[1] *Report*, Vol. I, p. 96.

prescribed examination in the three R's (with the addition of plain needlework for girls). The aid given by the county rate should range from 21s. to 22s. 6d., but children under seven would not be examined. A grant of 20s. would be paid on them based on the average number of children in daily attendance. The amount of Government grant and rate aid was based on the assumption that the total cost of educating a child would not exceed 30s. a year. Any deficiencies would be supplied from fees and the income yielded by endowments. The grants were dependent on an inspector's certificate that the school was healthy, properly drained and ventilated, and that the main schoolroom contained eight square feet of floor space per head.

The suggestions of the Commissioners were quite inadequate to meeting the urgent problems of education at that time. The Report was frankly a compromise, and its seeming unanimity concealed many divergent views. We know, for instance, that Matthew Arnold was not in agreement with some of the statements which he thought had been reached on insufficient evidence. We have already drawn attention to the large number of inefficient private schools. Another important problem, the fact that only a small proportion of scholars stayed long enough at school to reach higher classes, was complacently set on one side.

They accepted the fact that most children left school at the age of ten, and concluded that nothing could be done without raising the leaving-age. Hence they emphasised the two points of irregular attendance at school and the pupils' alleged lack of proficiency in the three R's.

During the session of the Commission, Mr. Lingen had complained that the regulations concerning grants and inspection were contained in the Minutes of the Committee of Council and in the reports of the Department and were not readily available. Mr. Robert Lowe, who had been appointed Vice-President of the Department in 1859, had them collected together and issued as the Code of 1860.

Robert Lowe's name will always be associated with the system of "Payment by Results" which he inaugurated in the Revised Code of 1862. Probably no man has been so universally condemned by educationists as Lowe.

Lowe was a product of Winchester and University College, Oxford, where he distinguished himself as a scholar. For some years he acted as a private coach and an examiner. Lord Bryce relates a story of Lowe in his capacity as examiner for Responsions. A friend visited him whilst he was conducting a *viva* and asked how the examination was progressing. Lowe is supposed to have replied, "Excellently. Five men plucked already, and the sixth very shaky." [1] Such a story reveals two important characteristics in his make-up, namely his love of efficiency and his impatience with the shortcomings of other people. After a visit to Australia, where he played a considerable part in politics, Lowe returned to take up a political career at home. He was a Liberal, but his ideas were more at one with the aristocratic Whigs of an earlier period than with the newer Liberals led by such men as Gladstone and Forster. Nevertheless, he had a great affection for Gladstone and, later in his career, when he was Chancellor of the Exchequer in Gladstone's first ministry, he achieved fame through his speeches in defence of his chief.

When he was appointed to the office of Vice-President of the Education Department, the idea of competition was in the air. Darwin's *Origin of Species* had familiarised the public with the notions of the "struggle for existence" and the "survival of the fittest." Lowe, as a convinced free-trader, firmly believed in the value of competition as a means of selection. Some time before accepting the office, he maintained that by throwing open certain minor Post Office appointments to competition, the cost of education could be reduced. The growing amount of the grant for education was a cause of concern in some quarters. Public expenditure on education had grown from £125,000 in 1850 to £836,920 in 1859. Lowe argued that if his suggestion were accepted the poor would thereby be encouraged to look after the education of their children for their own benefit.

Certain Civil Service appointments were already being awarded on the results of a competitive examination, and this development had received the warm approval of Horace Mann, who thought it would encourage parents to keep their children longer at school.

Examinations had also begun to enter the secondary schools, though their adoption was slow, as the Taunton Commission showed. The College of Preceptors began their school examinations in 1853, and the Oxford and the Cambridge Local Examinations started in 1857. Inspectors had been urging pupil-teachers and

[1] Lord Bryce. *Studies in Contemporary Biography*, p. 301, note, Macmillan, 1903.

assistant teachers to take London Matriculation. A few years later, the Taunton Commission recommended periodic examination of schools, supervised by a Council of Examinations, and the Rev. J. P. Norris, H.M.I., giving evidence before the Commissioners, stated: "The studies of the classroom must be those wherein progress can be definitely measured by examination. For examination is to the student what the target is to the rifleman; there can be no definite aim, no real training without it." [1]

At the same time a feeling was growing, especially amongst the business section of the community, that in spite of the enormously increased grants in aid of education, the nation was not getting value for money, though Lowndes warns us that too much emphasis must not be placed on this. Speaking of Payment by Results, he says: "The origin of the system does not, as some historians have too readily assumed, appear to have been entirely due to the blind demand of mid-Victorian parliamentary thought for a visible demonstration of value received for money expended. This demand no doubt played a substantial part." [2]

Lowe was primarily an administrator and a politician, and it was unfortunate in many ways that he was called upon to exercise the functions of Vice-President of the Education Department at this time. As an administrator he had many points to recommend him. His love of efficiency, his quick, logical mind, which led him to grasp the essential features of a situation but which frequently played him false by suggesting generalisations without counting all the relevant facts, and his ruthless determination to go ahead once his mind was made up, were characteristics that inspired the respect of some but the intense dislike of many more. Sidney Low, speaking of his work as Chancellor of the Exchequer, says: "He was a man of much intellectual power and dauntless energy . . . and he carried into his new office an aptitude for giving offence which almost amounted to genius. When Robert Lowe saw a head in his way he was pretty sure to hit it—especially if the head was a soft one." [3]

He never claimed to be an educationist. There is a story that when an H.M.I. went to consult him, Lowe said, "I know what you've come about, the science of education. There is none. Good morning." Any views he had about education were simply

[1] *Schools Inquiry Commission Report* .Vol. IV, p. 60.
[2] G. A. N. Lowndes. *The Silent Social Revolution*, p. 8, O.U.P., 1937.
[3] Sidney Low. *Political History of England*, Vol. XII, p. 223, Longmans, 1907.

the product of his political and economic outlook, which in some ways belonged to the end of the 18th century. In an oft-quoted passage in the pamphlet *Primary and Classical Education*, 1867, he wrote, "I do not think it is any part of the duty of the Government to prescribe what people should learn, except in the case of the poor, where time is so limited that we must fix upon a few elementary subjects to get anything done at all. . . . The lower classes ought to be educated to discharge the duties cast upon them. They should also be educated that they may appreciate and defer to a higher cultivation when they meet it, and the higher classes ought to be educated in a very different manner, in order that they may exhibit to the lower classes that higher education to which, if it were shown to them, they would bow down and defer." Note Lowe's reference to the shortness of time available at school. The people who should have known better, the members of the Newcastle Commission, had made no suggestions about prolonging the period children spent at school, but had complacently assumed that the economic system which encouraged an early school-leaving age was incapable of modification. It is therefore not surprising to find Lowe openly contemptuous of democracy and putting forth every effort to defeat the Reform Bill of 1867. When the Bill had become law, he realised that a democracy can only be successful if it is an educated democracy, and he coined the famous epigram generally misquoted as "We must educate our masters."

Was there anything else in Lowe's mind which helped to shape his policy? It is here that Lowe the administrator peeps out. The state of affairs in the Education Department was causing him some alarm. The increase in grants and the consequent growth of the number of schools from 46,042 in 1850 to 58,975 in 1859 had thrown more and more administrative work on an already over-burdened and under-staffed department. This had been one of the causes of Kay-Shuttleworth's illness and retirement in 1849. Since then the burden had increased and a parsimonious Treasury was always reluctant to sanction additional administrative staff and inspectors. As Lord Lingen pointed out many years later when he gave evidence before the Cross Commission, the Government grants had always been paid to individuals. Every pupil-teacher drew his stipend through the Post Office by means of an order made out to him personally, and assistant teachers received their grants in much the same way. One simplification of the administrative procedure would be to rule that in future all grants should be paid to the school managers, who would then be responsible for allocating them to the staff. Lowe's acute mind seized upon this as a desirable measure of decentralisation, and he made it a permanent feature of the method of paying the annual grants. Holman points out that the principle of Payment by Results was already latent in the Department as early as 1857. The Education Department had replied to an inquirer that teachers had no claim whatever upon the capitation grants, but "at the same time my lords would not disapprove of an arrangement whereby the teacher was given some interest in obtaining the capitation grant, *e.g.* a percentage upon it in addition to the salary otherwise assured to him. Any such plan, however, both in principle and detail, rests exclusively upon the discretion of the managers." [1]   There is therefore good reason to believe that Lowe had made up his mind before he read the report of the Newcastle Commission, but when he perused it his attention was attracted by the following paragraph—speaking of the means of securing increased efficiency of school instruction, the Commissioners had said: "There is only one way of securing this result, which is to institute a searching examination by competent authority of every child in every school to which grants are paid, with a view to ascertaining whether these indispensable elements of knowledge are thoroughly acquired, and to make the prospects and position of the teacher dependent to a considerable extent on the results of this examination." [2]

When he submitted the education estimates of 1861, Lowe proposed to cancel the Code of 1860 and to substitute for it his suggestions as contained in the Revised Code, which was presented to Parliament at the end of the session, 29th July 1861. The suggestion of the Commission about the establishment of county and borough education boards with power to contribute from the rates was rejected. Lowe concentrated on the two defects mentioned in the report, irregularity of attendance and the meagre accomplishment of the younger scholars in reading, writing, and arithmetic. In future all grants would be paid to managers on the principle of Payment by Results. "Hitherto," he said, "we have been living under a system of bounties and protection; now we propose to have a little free trade." Lowe's proposals raised a growing volume of protest from teachers, managers, clergy, and educationists. It is recorded that out of the thousands of petitions

[1] Holman. *English National Education*, pp. 136-7, Blackie, 1898.
[2] *Newcastle Commission Report*, Vol. I, p. 157.

sent to both Houses of Parliament, only one petition in favour of the proposals was received. As a result of the protests and the parliamentary criticisms, Lowe postponed the issue of the Revised Code until 1862. When it appeared, certain modifications had been made. Originally children from three to seven were to have been included in the examination, but now he had realised the absurdity of this proposal. The training-college grants which were to have been annulled were to continue for the time being. The Revised Code would not apply to Scotland, and certain modifications were made with regard to the amount and the conditions of grant. With these exceptions, however, Lowe retained his general principles.

As he told Parliament, "I cannot promise the House that this system will be an economical one, and I cannot promise that it will be an efficient one, but I can promise that it shall be either one or the other. If it is not cheap, it shall be efficient; if it is not efficient, it shall be cheap." In its final form, the Code made two conditions for grant: attendance, and results in examination. An attendance was reckoned as two hours instruction in the morning or afternoon and one and a half hours in the evening, but evening attendances only applied to pupils over twelve years of age. A grant of 4s. per scholar according to the average number in attendance throughout the year at the morning and afternoon meetings of the school would be paid, together with a grant of 2s. 6d. per scholar for the evening meetings of the school. For children under six, a grant of 6s. 6d. would be made subject to a satisfactory report from the inspector. The remainder of the grant was to be dependent on the result of the annual examination. Every scholar who attended more than two hundred morning or afternoon meetings of the school and passed the examination would earn a grant of 8s. Evening scholars who attended not less than twenty-four evening meetings and passed the examination would earn a grant of 5s.

If the scholar failed to pass the examination in reading, writing, and arithmetic, the amount of 2s. 8d. was forfeited for each subject in which he failed, and, in the case of evening students, 1s. 8d. for each subject failed in was deducted. The children were to be grouped in six Standards and no child could be examined a second time in the same Standard. The syllabus for the examination in each of the Standards is reproduced in the table on the page opposite.

All girls must receive instruction in plain needlework. The grant could be withheld or reduced if the inspector was not satisfied with the condition of the school, e.g. the school building must

	STANDARD I	STANDARD II	STANDARD III
Reading.	Narrative monosyllables.	One of the narratives next in order after monosyllables in an elementary reading book used in the school.	A short paragraph from an elementary reading book used in the school.
Writing.	Form on blackboard or slate, from dictation, letters, capital and small, manuscript.	Copy in manuscript character a line of print.	A sentence from the same paragraph slowly read once and then dictated in single words.
Arithmetic.	Form on blackboard or slate, from dictation, figures up to 20; name at sight figures up to 20; add and subtract figures up to 10, orally, from examples on blackboard.	A sum in simple addition or subtraction, and the multiplication table.	A sum in any simple rule as far as short division (inclusive).

	STANDARD IV	STANDARD V	STANDARD VI
Reading.	A short paragraph from a more advanced reading book used in the school.	A few lines of poetry from a reading book used in the first class of the school.	A short ordinary paragraph in a newspaper, or other modern narrative.
Writing.	A sentence slowly dictated once by a few words at a time, from the same book, but not from the paragraph read.	A sentence slowly dictated once, by a few words at a time, from a reading book used in the first class of the school.	Another short ordinary paragraph in a newspaper, or other modern narrative, slowly dictated once by a few words at a time.
Arithmetic.	A sum in compound rules (money).	A sum in compound rules (common weights and measures).	A sum in practice or bills of parcels.

be properly lighted, drained, ventilated, and supplied with offices, and must contain eighty cubic feet of internal space for each child in average attendance. The head teacher should be certificated, and various conditions as regards the number of pupil-teachers and assistant teachers had to be complied with. The documents such as the log-book had to be kept up to date.

When the inspector's report was sent to the managers by the Education Department, it was to be entered in the log-book by the secretary of the managers. Lay persons alone could be recognised as teachers in elementary schools. The examination syllabus for each of the five years of the pupil-teacher's apprenticeship was detailed in the Code, and the pupil-teachers were to be paid by the managers from the annual grant. The provision for granting pensions to teachers who retired after a minimum of fifteen years service was annulled for those who entered after the Revised Code, but the pension rights of existing teachers were to be respected. In the instructions to H.M.I.s on working the Code, the following paragraph occurred: "The grant to be made to each school depends, as it has ever done, upon the school's whole character and work. The grant is offered for attendance in a school with which the inspector is satisfied. . . . You will judge every school by the same standard that you have hitherto used, as regards its religious, moral, and intellectual merits. The examination under Article 48 does not supersede this judgment, but presupposes it. That Article does not prescribe that, *if this much is done a grant shall be paid* but, *unless this much is done no grant shall be paid.* . . . If you keep these distinctions steadily in view, you will see how little the scope of your duties is changed."

Detailed instructions about the method of conducting the examinations were issued to the inspectors, *e.g.* "You will begin with writing and arithmetic, and you will direct the teachers to see that all who are to be examined under Standard I, have before them a slate and pencil; under Standards II and III a slate, a pencil, and a reading book; all under Standards IV-VI, a half sheet of folio paper, a pen, ink, and the appropriate reading book. You will then call 'Standard I, stand up throughout the school.'" When the children had been checked, the inspector was to give the order, "Standard I, sit down, and write on your slates as I dictate." The same procedure was to be observed throughout the school. Then the examination in arithmetic and reading followed. The standard for a pass was the mark "fair." "The word *fair* means that *Reading* is intelligible, though not quite good; *Dictation* legible, and rightly spelt in all common words though the writing may need improvement, and less common words may be misspelt; *Arithmetic,* right in method, and at least one sum free from error."

How far was the Revised Code cheap and efficient? From the narrow point of view it was cheap. The cost to the country because of a diminishing annual grant was considerably lessened. The grant, which had reached £813,441 in 1862, fell steadily to its low-water mark of £636,806 in 1865. But cheapness cannot be considered apart from efficiency. Was the nation really getting

value for money?   Kay-Shuttleworth prophesied the results of
the Revised Code: a loss in grant to the schools of about £175,000
a year (actually it came to £190,000), a decrease in the number and
quality of the pupil-teachers (from 13,237 in 1860 to 8,937 in 1866,
but after this numbers began to rise), a lowering of the standards of
instruction in both the schools and the training-colleges, and a
reduction in teachers' salaries.   The number of certificated teachers
increased, but this was offset by the total number of teachers, which
remained stationary although the school population increased from
751,325 in 1860 to 871,309 in 1866.   This resulted in larger classes.
In 1860 the average number of scholars per teacher was 37·7, but this
had risen to 43·4 in 1866.   The new regulations certainly produced
a better average attendance; the pupils remained longer at school
and teachers concentrated on the younger and duller children with,
now, a neglect of the older and brighter ones.   The Code speeded
up the development of evening classes.   Before 1862 evening
schools were hampered because certificated teachers had not been
allowed to teach both in the day and in the evening.   When this
restriction was withdrawn evening classes grew more numerous,
but many of the students were of poor quality.   Most of the adolescents and the adults who attended were presented for examination in
Standards I and II.   Holman says, quite justly, "The author of
the revised code is far too often exclusively reviled by critics as
the author of payment by results, and no regard is paid to the
fact that he certainly made the best of a bad business.   He was a
strong man, a clear thinker, and a determined and inflexible ruler,
with a well-thought-out plan designed to secure definite returns
for large outlay.   And he was successful.   The results which he
demanded and obtained were at any rate better than the absence of
results in respect of three-fourths of the pupils, as had been
previously the case.   If for nothing else, Mr. Lowe deserves our
thanks for having perpetrated a blunder, which has been one more
step to our blundering out of blunders." [1]   Lowndes suggests an
aspect which has seldom been considered when he writes, "We can
now appreciate after 70 years' effort to build an educational system
fit to be the servant of the nation, not the servant of the political
state, that the infinitely diverse needs of modern civilisation can
never be met by one system of schools unified under rigid public
control, still less by a system at the mercy of successive party
machines.   Perhaps, Robert Lowe, in apparently doing a grave

[1] Holman. *English National Education*, pp. 170-1, Blackie, 1898.

injustice to a whole generation, in reality by this early measure of decentralisation saved English education once and for all from the pitfalls which have ensnared the systems of so many other countries; notably Germany, Italy, and to a less extent France." [1]

So much for the credit account; what is to be said on the debit side? Important evidence comes from the inspectors. Some, such as Sir J. Fitch, were favourable in their comments, but even he criticised the formal and mechanical spirit introduced into school work. Matthew Arnold's reports are most illuminating. In the report for 1863 he noticed certain changes after one year of the Code. One good effect was the improvement of the school reading-books. "At last the compilers of these works seem beginning to understand that the right way of teaching a little boy to read is not by setting him to read such sentences as these—'the crocodile is viviparous,' 'quicksilver, antimony, calamine, zinc, etc., are metals,' 'the slope of a desk is oblique, the corners of a door are angles'; or the right way of teaching a big boy to read better, to set him to read: 'some time after one meal is digested we feel again the sensation of hunger which is gratified by again taking food'; 'most towns are supplied with water and lighted by gas, their streets are paved and kept clean, and guarded by policemen'; 'summer ornaments for grates are made of wood shavings and of different coloured papers.' Reading books are now published which reject all such trash as the above, and contain nothing but what has really some fitness for reaching the end which reading books were meant to reach." [2]

Matthew Arnold thought the new examination compared unfavourably with the old inspection. Speaking of the latter, he said, "The whole life and power of a class, the fitness of its composition, its handling by the teacher were well tested; the Inspector became well acquainted with them, and was enabled to make his remarks on them to the head teacher, and a powerful means of correcting, improving, and stimulating them was thus given." [3] The examination did not afford this opportunity because the children were examined by Standards, which did not always correspond with the class. "I know that the aim and object of the new system of examination is not to develop the higher intellectual life of an elementary school, but to spread and fortify, in its middle and lower

---

[1] G. A. N. Lowndes. *The Silent Social Revolution*, p. 11, O.U.P., 1937.
[2] Board of Education. *Reports on Elementary Schools*, by Matthew Arnold, H.M.S.O., 1910.
[3] *Ibid.*, p. 92.

portions, the instruction in reading, writing, and arithmetic, supposed to be suffering. I am not contesting the importance of this subject, or the adequacy of the means offered by the new examination for attaining it. I am only pointing out the real value of a certain mode of operation on schools which the old inspection undoubtedly supplied, and which the new examination does not and by its nature cannot supply." [1]

Under the old system, the inspector's visit tested and quickened the intellectual life of a school, but the examination had changed the centre of interest. "Scholars and teachers, have their thoughts directed straight upon the new examination, which will bring, they know, such important benefit to the school if it goes well, and bring such important loss if it goes ill. On the examination day they have not minds for anything else." [2] The examination pressed heavily upon the younger element of the school which was affected by nervousness and therefore did not do itself justice.

Arnold had been investigating systems of secondary education on the Continent in 1865 for the Schools Inquiry Commission, so that his next report was in 1867. During his visit he had opportunities of seeing elementary schools in several European countries and he was now able to review the Revised Code in clearer perspective. His report was distinctly unfavourable. "I cannot say that the impression made upon me by the English schools at this second return to them has been a hopeful one. I find in them, in general, if I compare them with their former selves, a deadness, a slackness, and a discouragement which are not the signs and accompaniments of progress. If I compare them with the schools of the Continent I find in them a lack of intelligent life much more striking now than it was when I returned from the Continent in 1859. This change is certainly to be attributed to the school legislation of 1862." [3]

One change he regretted was the decline in number of pupil-teachers whom he had once described as "the sinews of English public instruction." He thought the real evil of English schools at that time was the irregular attendance and early leaving-age of the pupils and not the lack of intelligence, of initiative, and the prevalence of mechanical modes of instruction. "The mode of teaching in the primary schools has certainly fallen off in intelligence, spirit, and inventiveness during the four or five years which have elapsed since my last report. It could not well be otherwise. In a country

---

[1] Board of Education. *Reports on Elementary Schools*, pp. 92-4.
[2] *Ibid.*, pp. 94-5.   [3] *Ibid.*, pp. 102-3.

where every one is prone to rely too much on mechanical processes, and too little on intelligence, a change in the Education Department's regulations, which by making two-thirds of the Government grant depend on a mechanical examination, inevitably gives a mechanical turn to the school teaching, a mechanical turn to the inspection is, and must be, trying to the intellectual life of the school." [1]

In 1876 a complicated Minute designed to give aid to small schools, to increase pupil-teachers, and to add another subject to the three R's, had been introduced. Arnold remarked that this action revealed the decay into which the teaching of language, history, and geography, had fallen; and that the grant for the specific subject was so small, and saddled with such complications, that many of the schools in his district declined to have anything to do with it. Such a palliative could not cure the evils wrought by the Revised Code. "More free play for the Inspector, and more free play, in consequence, for the teacher, is what is wanted." He warned the Department, "In the game of mechanical contrivances the teachers will in the end beat us ; and as it is now found possible, by ingenious preparation, to get children through the Revised Code examination in reading, writing, and ciphering, without their really knowing how to read, write, or cipher, so it will with practice, no doubt, be found possible to get three-fourths of the one-fifth of the children over six through the examination in grammar, geography, and history, without their really knowing any one of these matters." [2]

Two years later he wrote, "I have repeatedly said that it seems to me the great fault of the Revised Code, and of the famous plan of payment by results, that it fosters teaching by rote; I am of that opinion still." He quoted the opinion of a colleague that, "Unless a rigorous effort is made to infuse more intelligence into its teaching, *Government arithmetic* will soon be known as a modification of the science peculiar to inspected schools, and remarkable chiefly for its meagreness and sterility." [3]   He summed up his criticism of the Code in the words, "It tends to make the instruction mechanical, and to set a bar to duly extending it. School grants earned in the way fixed by the Revised Code—by the scholar performing a certain minimum expressly laid down beforehand—must inevitably concentrate the teacher's attention on

---

[1] Board of Education. *Reports on Elementary Schools*, pp. 112-13.
[2] *Ibid.*, pp. 115-16.   [3] *Ibid.*, p. 128.

the means of producing this minimum, and not simply on the good instruction of his school." [1]

Kay-Shuttleworth found his prophesies were true. In his *Memorandum on Popular Education,* 1868, he wrote, "The Revised Code has constructed nothing. It has only pulled down. . . . It has not succeeded in being efficient, but it is not even cheap; for it wastes the public money without producing the results which were declared to be its main object." [2]

When the Code was being discussed in Parliament he had protested in his book *Four Periods of Education,* 1862, that an examination in the three R's was no real measure of the work that a school was doing. He selected two pictures of districts he knew well to illustrate his argument. One was the manufacturing areas of Lancashire and Yorkshire. Speaking of the children, he said: "They probably have never lived but in a hovel; have never been in a street of a village or a town; are unacquainted with common usages of social life; perhaps never saw a book; are bewildered by the rapid motion of crowds; confused in an assemblage of scholars." Such were the children who had migrated from their native moors to the industrial districts. "They have to be taught to stand upright—to walk without a slouching gait—to sit without crouching like a sheep dog. They have to learn some decency in their skin, hair, and dress. They are commonly either cowed or sullen, or wild, fierce, and obstinate. In the street they are often in a tumult of rude agitation. In the school they are probably classed with scholars some years younger than themselves. They have no habits of attention, and are distracted by the babel of sounds about them. The effort of abstraction required to connect sound with a letter is at first impossible to them. Their parents are almost equally brutish. They have lived solitary lives in some wild region, where the husband has been a shepherd, or hind, or quarryman, or miner, or turf-cutter, or has won a precarious liveli-hood as a carrier, driver of loaded lime ponies, or poacher. The pressing wants of a growing family have induced them to accept the offer of some agent from a mill. From personal experience of many years, I know that such children as these form a large portion of the scholars which the schools of the cotton and woollen districts have to civilise and Christianise." The other district was the East End of London. "A different kind of brutishness is shown by a

[1] Board of Education. *Reports on Elementary Schools,* pp. 134-5.
[2] P. 30, Ridgway, 1868.

large class of scholars in the most degraded parts of great cities. A London child living in a street of brothels and thieves' dens, with parents leading abandoned lives, spends his day in the kennel among sharp-witted, restless little creatures like himself. He is his own master. His powers of observation are singularly acute; his powers of decision rapid; his will energetic. He is known as 'the arab of the street.' He learns a great deal of evil. Perhaps he is an accomplished thief or beggar, or picks up a precarious living by holding horses, sweeping a crossing, or costermongering. Such children have of late years been netted in shoals—got into schools, have been won, tamed, and in some degree taught. But is it not a mischievous fallacy to say that the work done is to be measured by the proficiency of such children in reading, writing, and arithmetic? All that has been done has been done against wind and tide. At home—misery, drunkenness, sullen despair, or the irritability of a dissolute life drive the child into the streets. Bad example lends its corruption to the foulness of the street of stews and hiding-holes. Are twenty scattered weeks, even if repeated in three successive years, enough to get rid of the wild untamed barbarism of such children, and to graft on this civilisation that amount of knowledge of reading, writing, and arithmetic which the Commissioners say is so easy?" [1]

The effect of the Code upon the teachers was distressing. They were sorely tempted to falsify the register to make sure of earning their livelihood, and it is greatly to their credit that so few cases of dishonesty occurred. That this occasionally happened is shown by an Inspector's report of 29th January 1885:—

"The Headmaster has been guilty of false registration in order to keep boys from examination.

"1. By omitting until after the beginning of the 22 weeks the names of boys who entered before that time.

"2. By marking boys who had never left the school as having left a little before the beginning of the 22 weeks and been admitted a little later.

"3. By marking boys as absent when they were present so that the registers might show a continuous absence of six weeks."

The author remembers the exaggerated importance attached to attendance registers. When he was a student in school practice

[1] Kay-Shuttleworth. *Four Periods of Education*, pp. 583-5, note, Longmans, 1862.

some years after the Revised Code had disappeared, instructions were issued to the school with regard to action in case of fire. The first duty of the teacher was to secure his register, and then he would lead the children by the authorised exit, into the playground. Teachers and managers alike concentrated on the grant and ways of earning it. Some of the devices which Matthew Arnold hinted at are described in Lowndes's *Silent Social Revolution*.[1]

Teachers and managers were so eager to earn the grant that children were compelled to get up from the sick-bed and attend the examination. Inspectors reported instances where children suffer-ing from scarlet fever and other diseases presented themselves for the examination. "To hear paroxysms of whooping-cough, to observe the pustules of small-pox, to see infants wrapped up and held in their mothers' arms, or seated on a stool by the fire because too ill to take their proper places, are events not so rare in an inspector's experience as they ought to be."

The inspector was regarded by the teacher as his natural enemy, to be outwitted whenever possible. The Revised Code came to an end in 1897, but the unhappy relations between the teachers and the inspectorate continued for many years after and still survive in some places. When the Code had disappeared the older inspectors found it difficult to adjust themselves to new conditions, and it was not until a race of inspectors arose that knew not the Revised Code, that the mutual distrust of teacher and inspector died a natural death. The harshness of the Code was lessened by various Minutes from 1867 onwards, admitting first one subject and then another into the curriculum as grant-earning subjects, but the whole process proceeded piecemeal without any thought being given to the principles which underlay a balanced curriculum. All that can be said is that it worked out in practice better than one might have expected.

The Committee of Council on Education were greatly concerned with the progress of elementary education in Wales. That country presented two distinct but most important problems which had to be solved. During the 18th century Wales had been a purely agri-cultural country, with a sparse and scattered population in the mountainous districts. In the early years of the 19th century the southern part had been affected by an industrial change far more rapid in character than the corresponding development in England.

[1] See the account on p. 14, 1937 edition.

The opening up of the South Wales coalfield and the growth of the iron and copper smelting industries had completely changed the character of this district almost, one might say, overnight. The consequence was a sudden influx of population to the industrial districts of South Wales, which produced overcrowding, with all its attendant evils, on a scale hardly appreciated in England where the pace had been much slower. The workers suffered acutely, and the miserable conditions under which they laboured and lived led to wholesale discontent.

The Chartist agitation found willing supporters amongst the Welsh miners, and the riots at Newport in 1839 assumed so serious a character that the military were called in to quell the disturbance. A further cause of discontent was the toll-house system, and it manifested itself in the formation of secret societies antagonistic to law and order, and led to the Rebecca Riots of 1843. The latter resulted in the burning and breaking up of toll-houses amidst scenes of brutality and bloodshed. As soon as the authorities had disposed of one disturbance, another occurred in a different area, and even when comparative tranquillity had been restored a spirit of sullen resentment remained.

The second problem was that of bilingualism. A large proportion of the population was Welsh-speaking, but the authorities in London assumed that Wales possessed no national literature which could serve as a vehicle for culture, and that the solution lay in substituting English for Welsh. This view was often supported by the poorer people in Wales who believed that a knowledge of English would provide their children with opportunities for advancement. The teachers, whose knowledge of English was often defective, did their utmost to carry out this policy. One means adopted was that of the Welsh "note" or "stick." Thus one inspector reported: "My attention was attracted to a piece of wood suspended by a string round a boy's neck, and on the wood were the words ' Welsh stick.' This, I was told, was a stigma for speaking Welsh. But, in fact, his only alternative was to speak Welsh or say nothing. He did not understand English." [1] The Welsh stick could be transferred from the offender to any other pupil who spoke Welsh. The pupil in whose possession it was found at the end of the week was punished by flogging. It was not until the closing years of the century that the attempt to force English upon the

[1] Report of Henry Vaughan Johnson in *Reports of the Commission of Inquiry into the State of Education in Wales*, p. 452, H.M.S.O., 1848.

Welsh was finally abandoned and the Welsh language began to take its proper place in the school curriculum.

The first inquiry into the state of education in Wales was in 1839, when the Committee of Council instructed Mr. Tremenheere to investigate the situation as regards schooling in the mining area of South Wales. The parishes he visited were among those chiefly concerned with the Chartist riots of that same year. His description reveals the desolation which uncontrolled industrial development had brought to a once beautiful countryside. He wrote: "The people are for the most part collected together in masses of from four to ten thousand. Their houses are ranged round the works in rows, sometimes two to five deep, sometimes three stories high. They barely contain less than from one to six lodgers in addition to the members of the family, and afford most scanty accommodation for so many inmates. It is not unusual to find that ten individuals of various age and sex occupy three beds in two small rooms. Far worse instances might be given. The surface of the soil around is frequently blackened with coal, or covered with high mounds of refuse from the mines and the furnaces. The road between the rows is so imperfectly made as to be often, in wet weather, ankle-deep in black mud. Flat pavement is rarely seen, except in some new works now erecting. Volumes of smoke from the furnaces, the rolling mills, and the coke-hearths, are driven past, according to the direction of the wind. Gardens are few, and almost entirely neglected. Due attention to sewerage is also overlooked. The house of the master or resident director stands conspicuous amidst a small group of stunted and blackened trees." [1]

The educational facilities of the district were most inadequate. In a total population of 85,000 it was estimated that education ought to be provided at day-schools for 11,334 children. Actually, 3,308 were attending school, leaving 8,026, or more than two-thirds, who were not receiving any education. There were forty-seven schools in the district, of which four boys' and four girls' schools were conducted on the system of the National Society, and one boys' and one girls' school on that of the British and Foreign School Society. School attendance was most irregular; only ten of the teachers had received any training, and the instruction given was poor in quality. Only two schools admitted infants.

Mr. Tremenheere was of the opinion that the parents were largely to be blamed for this sad state of education. They were

[1] *Minutes of the Committee of Council*, 1839-40, p. 176.

completely indifferent since they had discovered that lack of education did not prevent their children from obtaining employment.
Frequently boys entered the mines at the age of eight or nine, and
the sixpence a day they earned represented a welcome addition to
the family income. "They leave their homes at an early age, if they
find they can be boarded cheaper elsewhere, and they spend the
surplus of their wages in smoking, drinking, and gambling. Boys
of 13 will not unfrequently boast that they have taken to smoking
before they were 12. All parental control is soon lost. Shortly
after the age of 16 they begin to earn men's wages." [1]

The 1840's began with a great educational revival, which was
significant because the impetus came from the Welsh people themselves. It was associated with the names of Sir Thomas Phillips of
Newport, Sir Hugh Owen, and the Rev. Henry Griffiths of Brecon,
and was supported by both Churchmen and Nonconformists.
Owen's work bore fruit in the formation of the Cambrian Educational Society in 1846, which advocated the establishment of undenominational schools. Owen, himself, supported the British and
Foreign School Society, but the National Society also turned its
attention to Wales. It was realised that one of the greatest defects
in Welsh education was the lack of trained teachers, and, to remedy
this, not only were Welsh teachers encouraged to enter the English
training-colleges, but in 1848 Carmarthen Training College was
opened. Unfortunately, the cause of Welsh education received a
serious set-back which turned the attention of Phillips and Owen to
secondary and higher education.

This reverse was occasioned by the publication in 1848 of the
*Reports of the Commissioners of Inquiry into the State of Education
in Wales.* The Commissioners, of whom Mr. Lingen was one,
reported very adversely on the condition of the Welsh schools, but
it was not this that roused popular resentment. They had been
instructed to send in their observations on the social and moral life
of the Welsh people. The result was that the Reports contained
numerous instances of drunkenness, dishonesty, and gross immoral-
ity, which conveyed to the rest of the kingdom the impression that
the Welsh were a most degenerate race.

The Reports called forth indignant protests from Welshmen in
all stations of life. For years after, the popular name of *"Brad y
llyfrau gleision* (the treason of the blue books)" indicated the
impression produced upon the national feelings. Sir Thomas

[1] *Minutes of the Committee of Council*, 1839-40, p. 183.

Phillips replied in 1849 by the publication of *Wales, the language, social conditions, moral character and opinions of the people considered in their relation to education*. This book was an exhaustive and accurate survey of social life and education in Wales, which did much to correct the erroneous ideas created by the Reports. Nevertheless, the damage had been done. The Reports had been intended as a prelude to comprehensive schemes of reform in Welsh education, but their effect was to arouse such popular antagonism that the Committee of Council resolved to proceed no further. The Welsh leaders turned their attention to the aim of instituting a national university, and elementary education attracted little notice until after the Cross Commission.

Among other influences which affected the progress both of elementary and higher education in Wales was the literary revival of the 18th century. Welsh scholars not only strove to encourage the study of the national literature of past ages, but also initiated the scientific study of the ancient language and the interpretation of mediaeval Welsh manuscripts. In 1751 a society for the encouragement of Welsh learning, known as the Honourable Society of Cymmrodorion, was founded and later gave rise to numerous local societies which contributed to the advancement of Welsh culture. A less satisfactory feature of such societies was that they tended to concentrate on antiquarian research, and many of their members were not Welshmen. The outcome of these different movements was the revival in 1819 of the Eisteddfod,[1] which has proved so potent an instrument of national culture. The more puritannical of the Nonconformists did not at first view the movement with enthusiasm, but when its achievements became fully realised the Welsh Sunday Schools began to give it their support.

[1] The Eisteddfod of 1819 was held at Carmarthen by *The Cambrian Society of Dyfed*. It exercised such an influence upon the Welsh people that by the middle of the century every town and most villages held their Eisteddfodau. After the Llangollen Eisteddfod of 1858, the National Eisteddfod was instituted.

CHAPTER VIII

FILLING THE GAPS — 1870-1895

The complacent spirit in which the Newcastle Commission declared itself satisfied with the diffusion of educational facilities throughout the kingdom was not shared by the nation as a whole. The Revised Code had slowed down the building of schools, but the population was now increasing rapidly, so that the proportion of children not attending school was almost as great as when the Manchester Statistical Society had made its investigations in 1834. Secularists and denominationalists in Manchester combined to form the Manchester Education Aid Society in 1864, which had for its object the provision of assistance to poor parents in paying their school fees. Similar societies sprang up in Birmingham, Nottingham, and Liverpool. Two Education Bills were presented to Parliament, in 1867 and 1868, in which rate-aid for the building of schools was suggested, but both were withdrawn in deference to the strongly expressed feelings of the Nonconformists against aiding denominational schools from the rates. The General Election of 1868 returned the Liberals to power with a strong working-majority. Mr. W. E. Forster, Member for Bradford, was given the post of Vice-President of the Education Department. Forster was well known in the North for his views on social and economic questions and his intense interest in popular education. He married the daughter of Dr. Arnold of Rugby, and was an intimate friend of Carlyle. Although a Bradford business man and a wealthy manufacturer, Forster found time to work for the social schemes he advocated, and one acquaintance described him as the only mill-owner he had ever heard claimed by the working men as a friend. He was an opponent of the Revised Code, and because of his great interest in education was chosen as a member of the Taunton Commission. In 1869 he was instrumental in securing the passage of the Endowed Schools Act. His views on national education were well known and on his appointment to the Education Department the country awaited with interest the Bill which it was now certain he would present to Parliament.

Forster found himself in a rather difficult political situation. The more extreme Liberals, or Radicals, were advocating free compulsory education on unsectarian lines, and in Birmingham the

Birmingham Education League, with George Dixon as Chairman, Joseph Chamberlain as Vice-Chairman, and Jesse Collings as Secretary, was formed in 1869 to secure these demands. This movement alarmed the supporters of denominational teaching, who formed in opposition the National Education Union. As a consequence of the agitation on the subject of education, Parliament ordered an inquiry into the condition of education in the four towns of Liverpool, Manchester, Leeds, and Birmingham, which might be taken as samples of the provision of educational facilities in the industrial areas. Sir J. Fitch and Mr. Fearon were instructed to furnish a return, not only of the number of schools, but also of the quality of the instruction provided. The diagram on p. 274 gives the relevant details as regards the attendance at school.

The Government inquiry showed that the unsatisfactory private schools of earlier ages still existed in the large towns. The following are three typical examples of schools that Mr. Fitch found in Leeds : —

1. "In a squalid little room 14 feet 4 inches by 8 feet, in a back street, I found, on descending to the basement floor of a small house, 33 children crowded together, of whom 16 were boys. The master is standing, in his shirt sleeves near the fire, over which some stew is preparing for dinner. The room is hot and close, and the children move with difficulty, owing to the clumsiness of the household furniture with which it is nearly filled. The master has been here for 30 years. . . . His own knowledge and qualifications are of the humblest kind, and his method of instruction is to hear the lessons of each child one by one, while the rest are 'learning off their spellings.'. . . The scholars are broadly divided into the 'fourpennies' and the 'sixpennies'; the latter, consisting of those who write in copybooks. . . . No other written or memory exercises are given, and the children are deplorably inactive and ignorant."

2. "A somewhat rude loft, to which access is obtainable by a ladder, is rented by a man of very humble pretensions, and used for the purposes of a school. There are about 25 scholars present. The master is hearing a task at a desk, the rest are playing, except a group who are watching with much interest the process of making ink, in which two of the elder boys, half-stripped for the purpose, are busily employed on the floor. Nearly all have said their tasks, and there is more to do. . . . One is writing this sentence, 'The imperfections of a believer's sanctification make him constantly

depend on Christ for his justification.'. . . . The master is spiritless and disheartened. . . . It is impossible to believe that any educational result of the least value can be obtained here."

3.   "In the front room of a small dwelling house, half-filled with dirty household furniture, I found 35 boys, all of whom were entirely unemployed, except eight who were writing in copy-books. The master . . . was a cloth-dresser by trade, and 'took to schooling because work was slack.'. . . . He regrets that he is not a 'bit of a singer,' for if he were, he would 'learn them a few ditties, and the

SCHOOL RETURNS 1870

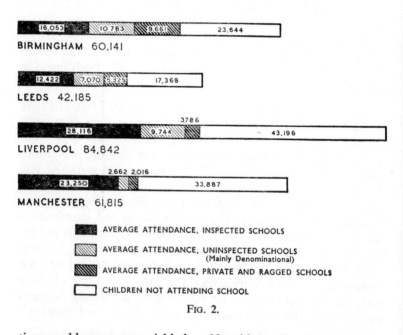

BIRMINGHAM 60,141

LEEDS 42,185

LIVERPOOL 84,842

MANCHESTER 61,815

AVERAGE ATTENDANCE, INSPECTED SCHOOLS

AVERAGE ATTENDANCE, UNINSPECTED SCHOOLS (Mainly Denominational)

AVERAGE ATTENDANCE, PRIVATE AND RAGGED SCHOOLS

CHILDREN NOT ATTENDING SCHOOL

Fig. 2.

time would pass away quickly.'. . . . Notwithstanding the prominence given to spelling lessons, all the elder boys failed to write an easy sentence without gross mistakes."

The Nonconformists, who had done such great work in the past, seemed to have lost interest in education, for Mr. Fitch writes: "My chief duty, however, is to place on record here the simple but significant fact, that, with the exception of the Wesleyans and the Unitarians, I have been unable to find a single Nonconformist congregation in Leeds, which is doing anything to help forward primary education, or is contributing money, or supervision to the permanent maintenance of a day school in any form." [1]

Mr. Fearon described a school in Liverpool where the mistress was assisted by her daughter, fourteen years old.   ". . . the mistress cannot write; she makes a mark for her name in signing it. . . . She said she was obliged to leave the school very much to her daughter, as she was 'a martyr to spasms.' There was a strong smell of some spirit or other, and she seemed in a maudlin condition. . . . For this 'education,' some of these children are said to pay 6d. a week."

Taking the country as a whole, the schools under Government inspection had accommodation for 1,878,000 children, which was a little more than half that which was required. Moreover, the schools were very unevenly distributed, the attendance irregular, and the leaving-age low. Something had to be done, but how was it to be done? Forster carefully examined the alternatives. The Education League had great hopes that he would support their scheme. To their disappointment Forster rejected their plan, partly because of the enormous expense which the country would have to shoulder, and partly because he feared a greater danger than money, namely that it would deprive the nation of those who really cared for education. He was in favour of an idea which had recently been put forward by Robert Lowe. The essentials of Lowe's proposals had been that the Government should survey the educational needs of each district and, where deficiencies existed, compulsion should be brought to bear, but the voluntary bodies should first be given an opportunity of making good the deficiencies.[2] Forster submitted a memorandum to the Cabinet on these lines.

When he introduced his Elementary Education Bill in 1870, he said: "The first problem, then, is, 'How can we cover the country with good schools?' Now, in trying to solve that problem there are certain conditions which I think hon. members on both sides of the House will acknowledge we must abide by. First of all, we must not forget the duty of the parents. Then we must not forget our duty to our constituencies, our duty to the taxpayers. . . . And thirdly, we must take care not to destroy in building up—not to

[1] *Report on Schools for Poorer Classes in Birmingham, Leeds, Liverpool, and Manchester*, p. 89, House of Commons, 1870.
[2] Robert Lowe in 1844 secured the appointment of a Select Committee by the New South Wales legislature to survey the existing facilities for education in the Colony. As a result, in 1848, State schools came into existence side by side with denominational schools aided by grants, a situation similar to that created by the 1870 Act in England.

destroy the existing system in introducing a new one. In solving this problem there must be, consistently with the attainment of our object, the least possible expenditure of public money, the utmost endeavour not to injure existing and efficient schools, and the most careful absence of all encouragement to parents to neglect their children. . . . Our object is to complete the present voluntary system, to fill up gaps, sparing the public money where it can be done without, procuring as much as we can the assistance of the parents, and welcoming as much as we rightly can the co-operation and aid of those benevolent men who desire to assist their neighbours." [1]

The country would be divided into districts and the wants of each duly ascertained. Thus, if in any one district the inspectors find "the elementary education to be sufficient, efficient, and suitable, we leave that district alone." Mr. Forster made it clear that he did not expect to find many such districts. The existing schools should be subject to three conditions for receiving public aid: they must be efficient; they must be open to undenominational inspection; and a conscience clause must be attached. In districts where there was a deficiency, time would be granted for voluntary agencies to supply the need. Mr. Forster suggested a year of grace for the voluntary bodies to make good deficiencies in their areas.

After the period of grace any gaps would be filled by means of School Boards elected by the town councils or, in the case of rural areas, by the vestries. School fees were to be retained, but parents unable to pay fees because of poverty could apply for a free ticket. The School Boards could provide schools themselves from rate aid or assist existing schools. Each Board should consist of a minimum of five and a maximum of fifteen members. Women might be elected and the system of cumulative voting should be adopted. A voter would have as many votes as there were vacancies and could give all to one candidate or distribute them as he wished. This was to safeguard the rights of minorities. Each Board would also be free to decide the kind of religious instruction to be provided, subject to a conscience clause in every school. The School Boards would also have powers of framing by-laws for the compulsory attendance of children between the ages of five and thirteen and for fixing the school-leaving age. Provision was made for the transfer of voluntary schools to the School Boards, but Mr. Forster over-estimated the number which were actually trans-

[1] *Verbatim Report of the Debate in Parliament during the Progress of the Elementary Education Bill*, pp. 7-8, National Education Union, 1870.

ferred. The by-laws could enforce the attendance of children by exacting from the parent a penalty not exceeding five shillings for non-attendance of his child, unless he could show reasonable excuse. The latter included "either education elsewhere, or sickness, or some unavoidable cause, or there not being a public elementary school within a mile" (later, not exceeding three miles).[1]

Mr. Forster summed up the object of the Bill by saying, "What is our purpose in this Bill?   Briefly this, to bring elementary education within the reach of every English home, aye, and within the reach of those children who have no homes. This is what we aim at in this Bill ; and this is what I believe this Bill will do."

The first reading of the Bill proceeded without difficulty, but in the interval between the first and second readings Mr. Dixon and the Education League had time to reflect and found that there were many things they did not like about it.   Their chief objections were : the period of grace allowed to voluntary effort would result in the building of numbers of new voluntary schools; the Bill did not insist on the universal establishment of School Boards and did not make attendance compulsory ; the conscience clause was ineffective and the principle of allowing each School Board to decide the kind of religious instruction to be given in its district would make it possible for denominational teaching to be financed by the rates. Accordingly, they attacked Forster and the Government with great bitterness, and gained the support of many Nonconformists.   Mr. Dixon opened the attack by proposing the amendment, "This House is of opinion that no measure for the elementary education of the people will afford a satisfactory or permanent settlement which leaves the question of religious instruction in schools supported by public funds and rates to be determined by local authorities."[2]   He pressed the House to declare that all rate-aided schools should be unsectarian and that in other schools the secular and religious instruction should be separate.   Mr. Forster did not agree, and replied: "The English people cling to the Bible, and no measure will be more unpopular than that which declares by Act of Parliament that the Bible shall be excluded from the school." Mr. Vernon Harcourt attacked the proposition that the question of religious instruction should be decided by the School Boards, and gave an amusing description of what would happen at the School Board

[1] *Verbatim Report of the Debate in Parliament during the Progress of the Elementary Education Bill*, p. 11.
[2] *Ibid.*, p. 42.

elections. "We all know something of municipal elections. We know that they are not very orderly at the best; but what will they be when the element of religious animosity is superadded? I suppose that there will be 'religious' public houses opened in every street; that blue and yellow placards will invite the voters to support 'Jones and the Thirty-nine Articles,' or 'Smith, and No Creed,' or 'Robinson, and down with the Bishops'; and cabs will be flying about advertising the theological merits of the different denominations, and rival divines will take the chair nightly at meetings in public houses and beer taps. There will be a great deal of religious discussion, and a good deal more of religious beer. Towards the afternoon of the polling-day there will be miraculous conversions of all kinds—next morning many people will find out that in the course of twenty-four hours they have held every known form of religious faith, while close upon four o'clock on the polling-day men will accept as many articles of faith as you may supply them with pints of beer, and the least sober will be the most orthodox." [1]

After a debate lasting three nights, Mr. Gladstone intervened to promise that the religious problem would be carefully considered at the Committee stage. Mr. Dixon agreed to withdraw his amendment and the Bill was read a second time, March 18th. When the Committee stage opened on June 16th, Mr. Gladstone announced some very important alterations which drew from Mr. Disraeli the remark that for practical purposes they amounted to a new Bill. A time-table conscience clause was proposed, which should apply to every grant-aided school, to the effect that parents were free to withdraw their children from religious instruction either at the beginning or at the end of the school day. The clause suggested by Mr. Cowper-Temple was accepted—"No religious catechisms or religious formulary, which is distinctive of any particular denomination shall be taught in the school." Although rate-aid would not be applied to maintain denominational schools, the Prime Minister promised that they should receive an increased Treasury grant. The election of the School Boards was to be by those whose names were on the burgess roll of the borough and, in the country, by the ratepayers. After a good deal of heated discussion, the Bill passed through the Committee stage. The Government cut down the year of grace allowed to voluntary effort to six months. London was to have its School Board immediately after the passage of the

---

[1] *Verbatim Report of the Debate in Parliament during the Progress of the Elementary Education Bill*, p. 106.

Act, and was given the power of paying its chairman. The Act received the royal assent on 9th August 1870.

The Elementary Education Act of 1870 was essentially a compromise. It did not abolish the voluntary system, but allowed it to remain, with the help of Government grants, alongside the schools erected by the School Boards. This was the beginning of the dual system which, with modifications, exists at the present time. Whilst affirming the principle that unsectarian religious teaching could find a place in the Board schools, the Act allowed individual School Boards to make their own decision about religious instruction, and a few decided in favour of secular instruction only. The vast majority followed the lead of the London School Board, which decided, "In the schools provided by the Board, the Bible shall be read and there shall be given such explanations and such instruction therefrom in the principles of morality and religion as are suited to the capacity of children; provided always . . . that no attempt be made in any such schools to attach children to any particular denomination." This decision was largely due to the influence of Professor Huxley. The Act gave power to the Boards to make education compulsory in their area if they wished, and the London School Board availed itself of this permission by inserting a by-law compelling the attendance of all children between the ages of five and thirteen, but granting exemption to children over ten who had passed Standard V and who were obliged to go to work to support their parents. Many School Boards did not make use of the powers given them under the Act.

The Leeds School Board was very progressive. The School Board was elected on 28th November 1870, and immediately set to work to fill the gaps. A return for the town showed that 48,787 children should have been attending school, but there was only accommodation for 27,329. Thirteen temporary schools were opened in Sunday Schools and public halls, and by-laws enforcing attendance were passed. Moreover, prizes were offered for regular attendance, and Leeds had the satisfaction of seeing the average attendance raised from sixty-four per cent to eighty-nine per cent of the number of children on the school roll. The first Board school was opened in Bewerley Street in 1873, together with fourteen evening schools and seven science and art classes. In 1885 the Board opened one of the earliest higher-grade schools of the country. The new kindergarten system based on Froebel was introduced into the Leeds infant-schools and instruction in cookery provided for the older girls and swimming and manual work for the boys. The School Boards of other large towns pursued a similar enlightened policy, but in some country districts progress was very slow.

In rural districts, it was many years before School Boards were set up where they were required, and many country Boards proceeded with the task of supplying schools in a very leisurely fashion. Mr. Pickard, H.M.I., reported to the Education Department in 1882 the example of the establishment of a public elementary school in the village of Hornton, near Banbury. "First notice, 30 December 1872; second notice, 25 September 1874; election of school board, 1875; my first visit, 24 March 1876; requisition threatened, 1877; my second visit, June 1877 . . . second school board elected 1878; my third visit, September 1878. The school board begins to talk about acquiring a site, 1879. A new clergyman comes and asks for six months' grace to enlarge parochial school, 16 September 1879; school board agree, October 1879; . . . plans forwarded to Education Department, January 1880; placed in hands of builder, April 1880; . . . building finished November 1881; school opened January 1882; to be inspected for the first annual grant, January 1883, more than ten years after the first notice of insufficient accommodation was issued." (*Report by the Committee on Education,* p. 415, 1882.)

Mr. Sneyd-Kynnesley described the School Board of the small village as sometimes a farce and sometimes a tragedy. He sent a letter to one Board making an appointment, but he received no answer. Nevertheless, he kept his appointment and arrived at the Board meeting. When he asked why they had not acknowledged his letter, they began to make excuses. Afterwards, he discovered, "There was not a man on the Board who could read and write, and they had to take all their correspondence to the market town to get the advice of the clerk to the Guardians before they could reply. They were in too small a way of educational business to have a clerk of their own." [1]

There were some rural districts where a penny rate brought in less than £10, and one Board in Norfolk had an average attendance of five children in its school. "They cost £26 apiece, and it took a 3d. rate to pay the clerk; its total rate was 13d. in the pound." [2]

---

[1] Sneyd-Kynnesley, *H.M.I.*, p. 173, Macmillan, 1908.
[2] *Ibid.*, p. 177.

Dixon and the League did not take their defeat lying down. They centred their opposition on Clause 25 of the Act, which empowered a School Board to pay the whole or part of the fees of children who could not otherwise afford them. In the heat of the debate on the Bill nobody had realised the significance of the clause, but in practice in most districts it meant that the voluntary schools were the only ones which received this money. Manchester, which did not erect Board schools for some years, contented itself by paying large sums of money out of rates to voluntary schools under this clause. At Birmingham, the influence of the League was so strong that the School Board refused to apply the clause. The controversy grew more heated still when some of the Nonconformists refused to pay the education rate on the ground that some part of it was going to support denominational teaching, and the League started a campaign for purely secular instruction in 1872, but this policy did not receive the whole-hearted support of the Nonconformists, who favoured non-sectarian religious teaching. The result of the agitation was a serious division in the ranks of the Government, which contributed considerably to their defeat in the election of 1874.

The six months period of grace stimulated the denominations to tremendous efforts. Most of the new voluntary schools which were built were Church of England schools, but the Roman Catholics, although a much smaller body, showed equal zeal. 3,342 applications were made to the Department for building-grants. Of these, 376 were refused and 1,333 afterwards withdrawn. The Church of England made 2,885 applications, mainly through the National Society. Churchmen showed great liberality in increasing their subscriptions to the schools, and by 1880 had added over a million school places to those which had existed in 1870. In the race between the Church and the School Boards to provide extra school accommodation, the Church accomplished an amazing feat, whilst the Boards, with rate-aid, were only able to add an equal amount. Even at the end of the century, in spite of the unequal competition, three-fifths of the available places in schools were in Church of England schools. Since then the number of Church schools has steadily decreased so that in 1939 the Church had 8,478 schools out of a total of 22,000. The growth of State schools should not blind us to the debt England owes to the efforts of the denominations, and in particular to the Church of England and the National Society. Before 1870 the National Society had contributed

£6,270,577 in building schools and £8,500,000 in their maintenance. Between 1870 and 1893 the society spent £7,125,402 in erecting 5,838 schools having accommodation for 1,328,761 children. All this money had been freely given by Church people, who often made great sacrifices for the sake of their schools.

One of the reasons why the Church found it so difficult to keep abreast of things was the constant rise in the cost per child. At the time of the 1870 Act, Mr. Forster had reckoned that a 3d. rate would be quite sufficient for school purposes, and the cost per head would not be likely to increase beyond 30s. In Church schools in 1871 the average cost per child in average attendance was £1 5s. 9¼d., but it had risen to £1 14s. 10¼d. in 1880. At the same time the voluntary subscriptions from Church people for the maintenance of their schools had increased from £372,350 to £762,162. The average cost per head in the Board schools was £2 1s. 11¾d. Lord Sandon's Act of 1876 provided some relief to managers of Church schools by raising the grant from 15s. per child to 17s. 6d., and allowing a still larger grant if local subscriptions equalled the sum that could thus be obtained. This roused the Nonconformists, who once again raised the cry that public money was being used to foster denominational teaching.

There is a very widespread idea amongst the general public that the Act of 1870 inaugurated universal free compulsory elementary education. Nothing is further from the truth. It is one thing to provide school places, but a very different thing to see that they are filled, and much of the interest of the next twenty-five years lay in the efforts made to secure regular attendance, to make the schools free, and to raise the average leaving-age. Because so many School Boards did not avail themselves of the powers of compulsion granted under the Act, although the numbers in average attendance rose, they were not by any means satisfactory. Parents had still to be convinced that it was their duty to see that their children received a satisfactory education. Lord Sandon's Act of 1876 declared that it was the duty of every parent to see that his child received adequate instruction in the three R's, and that if the parent failed in his duty, he became liable to certain penalties. Employers were forbidden to employ children under ten, and children between ten and fourteen were obliged to attend school half-time. Unfortunately there were loopholes in the way of exemptions. For instance, if the child had passed Standard IV, or made a certain number of attendances each year during the past five years, he could be exempted from further attendance.[1] Parents neglecting the attendance order were liable to a fine not exceeding 5s., and employers who contravened the Act to a penalty of 40s. Parents not able to afford school fees could apply to the Guardians to have them paid. In many areas where no deficiency had existed in 1870, School Boards had not been constituted. In such districts School Attendance Committees were formed having the same compulsory powers as the School Boards. Children who were out of parental control and refused to attend school could be committed to industrial schools.

Mr. Mundella's Act of 1880 went a step further and made the framing of by-laws compulsory on all School Boards and School Attendance Committees. Moreover, a child of thirteen could gain exemption on attendance alone, apart from proficiency. Thus the question of compulsion was definitely settled. The school-leaving age was raised to eleven in all cases in 1893, and to twelve in 1899.

The Act of 1870 did not contemplate the abolition of school fees, but limited them in the case of public elementary schools to 9d. per week. In 1891 parents were given the right to demand free education for their children, with the result that the majority of schools became free. Fees in elementary schools were not entirely abolished until 1918.

From 1870 progress had been rapid. The number of schools and pupils had increased, the cost of maintenance had risen, and the education rates had become heavier each year. It was now felt that the time had arrived for an inquiry by an impartial authority into elementary education as a whole. This desire was met by the Royal Commission of 1886, generally known as the Cross Commission from its chairman Lord Cross.

The Commission reported in 1888, and, although on many points the Commissioners were unanimous, they differed on others, and as regards these, fifteen members submitted a majority, and eight a minority, report. The former were well disposed to the denominational schools and were of opinion that they should receive rate-aid. The latter held that such a course would upset the equilibrium established by the 1870 Act. Both agreed that there was an urgent need for more and better-trained teachers and that to extend the facilities for training, the creation of day training-colleges connected with the universities and university colleges was recommended. The

[1] This was generally known as the Dunce's Pass.

majority were greatly impressed with the system of denominational residential training-colleges. Both recommended the admission to the inspectorate of elementary-school teachers and the majority were in favour of the appointment of women inspectors. We have already seen, in Chapter v, the attitude of the majority and minority towards the growth of the higher-grade schools. Both thought that the respective spheres of elementary, higher-grade, and secondary schools should be defined. They also agreed that a more liberal curriculum was necessary for the schools, and emphasised the importance of science and technical instruction, manual instruction, and drawing. They thought that the latter should be compulsory for boys and that Government grants should be paid to aid the erection of manual workshops.

The system of Payment by Results was very severely criticised, especially by the minority, who believed in its complete abolition and the substitution of a fixed grant together with a variable grant for such subjects as drawing, cookery, and elementary science. The minority expressed the view, "We are of opinion that the best security for efficient teaching is the organisation of our school system under local representative authorities, over sufficiently wide areas, with full powers of management and responsibility for maintenance, with well-graduated curricula, a liberal staff of well-trained teachers, and buildings sanitary, suitable, and well-equipped with school requisites." The Commissioners recommended a stricter application of the school attendance regulations and the minority were of opinion that "No Child should be allowed to leave school before fourteen unless he or she is profitably employed either at home or at work." They recommended a revision of the regulations for evening schools. Under the Revised Code these schools had been chiefly concerned with teaching the three R's, since the pupil had to satisfy the examination requirements before he could earn a grant. After 1870 there had been a considerable falling off in attendance at evening schools, and, even when the age-limit was raised to twenty-one in 1876, they still continued to decline. Although other subjects in addition to the three R's were admitted in 1882, every pupil was obliged to satisfy the original requirements in order to earn grant. The Commission considered that the mistake consisted in regarding the evening school as an elementary school. Its real function should be that of an evening continuation school, and a place should be made for instruction in science, art, and technology, besides giving opportunities for recreation and social life. The age-limit should be abolished, and freedom should be given these schools to adapt themselves to varying conditions.

It was fortunate for the report that, when it was presented to Parliament, the Secretary of the Education Department was Mr. (afterwards Sir) G. W. Kekewich, who had wide and liberal views on the subject of education, and who was in sympathy with the teachers. The report bore fruit almost immediately in the Code of 1890, which abolished the grant for the three R's, raised the fixed grant, and retained the grants only for class and specific subjects. This was the beginning of the end for the system of Payment by Results. More subjects were added to the curriculum by the Codes of 1893 to 1896, and encouragement was given to teachers to plan class visits to museums and art-galleries and to historical buildings. As Sir G. Kekewich said, "My creed was that the children came first, before everything and everybody."

As was mentioned above, the Cross Commission paid special attention to the training of teachers. Before describing the changes which came about as the result of the Commission's report, it will be convenient at this point to summarise the developments which had taken place in regard to pupil-teachers and training-colleges between 1846 and the Cross Commission. Kay-Shuttleworth had been faced by the urgent problem of providing a sufficiently large teaching staff in the schools, and his solution had been the adoption of the pupil-teacher system. The only alternative would have been to have attracted young people of eighteen to twenty years of age to the teaching profession and to have organised a scheme for training them. These candidates would necessarily have been selected from those who had spent several years in industry and business, and their lack of academic attainments would most certainly have created an insuperable obstacle. Though it is easy from a present-day standpoint to criticise the arrangement adopted, it was at that time the only workable solution of the problem.

High hopes for the new scheme were entertained. The Minutes of 1846 described it as follows: "Every boy of character and ability who is first among his fellows, may select this career, and in the majority of cases will do so. In his whole course he will be in vigorous competition with the pupil-teachers of other schools; and thus the Queen's Scholars, who after a public trial, are selected for admission into the Normal Schools, will be naturally the most gifted, and by persevering application, the best instructed and most skilful youths, which the elementary schools of the country can rear. . . .

Their skill in conducting a class will have been developed by five years' experience as assistants in a common school. . . . The Normal Schools, therefore, will be fed with a class of students much superior to that which now enters them." [1]

These anticipations, however, were not realised. It had been hoped that the majority of pupil-teachers would enter a training-college for a professional course extending over three years. In fact, a great many pupil-teachers did not enter a college and either left the profession at the end of their apprenticeship or continued as uncertificated teachers. Of those who entered a training-college, only a small number offered themselves for more than one year of training. The conception of a three-year course of training was premature and the ideal has not been realised even at the present time, except in the case of a comparatively small number of students. The Committee of Council vainly endeavoured to lengthen the usual course by giving twice the grant for the completion of a third year of training.

In 1856 the Education Department resigned itself to the inevitable. The training-college course was fixed at two years, and those students who left at the end of the first year were regarded as uncertificated teachers. Two other modifications were made. Young people above eighteen years of age, who had not served as pupil-teachers, were allowed to sit for the Queen's Scholarship examination.[2] Also, the "pledge" was introduced. Intending entrants to a training-college were required to declare that it was their bona-fide intention to become teachers in a recognised school. Although the declaration was signed before witnesses, in reality it had no legal validity, though of course the student incurred a moral obligation.

The work of the training-colleges suffered from a number of defects which could hardly have been avoided. They drew their students from the pupil-teachers who had left the elementary school at thirteen years of age to begin their apprenticeship. Although each student was required to spend 150 hours in practical teaching, the necessity of providing him with an adequate academic background left little time for a purely professional training. The colleges were attempting an almost impossible task. Although the competition was so keen that only the most promising of the

---

[1] Reprinted in the *Report of the Board of Education*, 1912-13, pp. 15-16.
[2] Samples of the examination questions are given in the *Report of the Board of Education*, 1912-13, pp. 19-20.

pupil-teachers were selected for training, yet because it was the exception for any of these to have passed through a secondary school, the training-colleges had in fact to do the work which at a later period was part of the normal secondary-school course.

Candidates for the Queen's Scholarship were required to pass in practical teaching, reading and recitation, arithmetic, music, English grammar (with a small amount of literature), geography, and history. Boys offered mathematics, and girls needlework. Certain additional subjects could also be offered, for which extra marks might be obtained. The syllabus for the first year of training was of a similar nature, but a higher standard was demanded and students were examined in school management. The second-year syllabus was also similar, but science, political economy, and languages could be substituted for certain sections of it. The examinations of the Science and Art Department could also be taken. Specialisation was never contemplated. The student was expected to be a class-teacher ready to teach all the subjects of the elementary-school curriculum.

At the conclusion of his training each student gave a lesson in the presence of an inspector, and was tested in oral reading and recitation. Most training-colleges possessed a Practising or Model School attached to them. Thus the school at York, in which students received their practical training in teaching, is still often referred to as the Model School. A serious limitation was that students were restricted to teaching in the practising schools under rather artificial conditions and no arrangements could be made for them to visit other schools to extend their experience. The colleges themselves were residential, and lively descriptions of the student and his daily routine have been given by old students who were in training before 1884.[1]

The witnesses examined by the Cross Commission, while generally expressing satisfaction with the existing system of teacher-training, in some cases criticised severely its limitations. It was urged that the policy of segregating men and women who intended to become teachers, by having special training establishments, was quite wrong. The students had been scholars in elementary schools, had taught in them as pupil-teachers and then completed their teaching practice in the same type of school, lived in company with others who had the same limited experience, and spent the rest of

[1] *Report of the Board of Education*, 1912-13, pp. 47-69. These accounts are too lengthy to be quoted here, but they will well repay study.

their lives in the elementary-school environment. Under these conditions they had no opportunity of broadening their ideas or of coming into close contact with those who had chosen quite different professions.

Some witnesses believed that the denominational tests imposed by the majority of colleges often debarred the most promising candidates from the profession. The staffs of the training-colleges were severely criticised. In both men's and women's colleges the principal was usually a man who had graduated, and was often in holy orders. In women's colleges there were certain lecturers in addition to the principal. The senior woman official was the Lady Superintendent, who was responsible for supervising the discipline of the students, but took little part in the training itself.

Most of the colleges, because of the difficulty of obtaining well-qualified and experienced lecturers, suffered from inbreeding. As a rule, the principal was the only person who had received a university training. He was sometimes responsible for lecture courses, but more often he confined himself to religious instruction and the administrative work of the college. Higher education for women had only recently been made possible, so that there was no pool of well-educated women to supply the needs of the training-colleges. Consequently, able students were offered posts as junior lecturers. Eventually they became senior lecturers, and in this way the colleges trained their own staffs. Although many of these lecturers were thoroughly efficient within narrow limits, they knew little of education outside the elementary school and their own college. The men's colleges were not handicapped to so great an extent and were able to call upon the services of lecturers who were better qualified and who possessed a wider experience. In both men's and women's colleges, however, the residential system encouraged staff and students to form "little worlds of their own, cut off almost entirely from other educational thought and activity."

The majority report of the Cross Commissioners suggested the foundation of non-residential colleges and advocated setting up day training-colleges attached to the university colleges. The minority report was in favour of day training-colleges, aided by local rates and under local authorities, in addition to those connected with university institutions. It attached greater importance to residence than did the majority report, and considered that a certain number of the students attending day training-colleges should be boarders.

In the regulations of the Education Department for 1890, although the minority report was not entirely ignored, the recommendations of the majority report were favoured. Day training-colleges attached to universities and university colleges were recognised and day students were permitted to attend residential colleges. The total number of day students was restricted to two hundred. In addition, a third year of training was authorised for selected students. It was not long before three-year students were allowed to read for university degrees, and the Education Department accepted the university examination as equivalent to its own examination in academic subjects. The professional examination in the principles and practice of teaching was still conducted by the Education Department.

The original day training-colleges were King's College, London, and Owens College, Manchester, for men ; Mason's College, Birmingham, for women ; and Durham College, University College, Nottingham, and University College, Cardiff, for both sexes. In 1891-2 the restriction with regard to numbers was changed and these colleges were recognised for double the number of students. At the same time, Cambridge University, the Yorkshire College, Leeds, and University College, Liverpool, were recognised for men, and Firth College, Sheffield, for men and women. The following year Oxford University, University College, Bristol, University College, London, and University College, Aberystwyth, were added to the list. Before the end of the century, training-departments were recognised at Bangor, Reading, Southampton, Exeter, and Southampton Street, London, and most of the colleges mentioned opened their doors to both men and women.

The new colleges became an integral part of the universities and university colleges, and contributed to widening the intellectual background of those preparing to enter the teaching profession. At the same time the residential training-colleges were greatly improved and began to build up their staffs from men and women who possessed higher qualifications and more varied experience. The new system, however, revealed certain defects. Many students admitted to the day training-colleges were anxious to obtain university degrees, but were not intellectually capable of the work required. As a result, the number of failures in the intermediate and final degree examinations was unduly high.

Another serious difficulty was the fact that university degree courses had not been planned for intending teachers. To obtain a degree, a full three-year course of study in certain academic sub-jects was necessary, and those students who were training for the teaching profession had to take their professional course and com-plete their practical teaching within the same period. This threw a much greater burden upon them than upon the private student reading for a degree. Moreover, there was always the tendency to attach greater importance to the academic studies and to belittle the professional training. Eventually, some universities achieved a fairly satisfactory compromise. Thus, at Leeds, recognised students were allowed to offer education as a subject in the final examina-tion for the ordinary degree. Honours students, however, had to complete the honours course, with education as an additional sub-ject. It was not until a four-year training-course was introduced that a really satisfactory solution was reached.

Another disadvantage suffered by day students was that many of them lived at a distance from their college, and thus spent a considerable time in travelling. At Leeds, students travelled in from the surrounding district, sometimes covering more than fifty miles in the day. The other alternative was for them to live in lodgings. University College, Reading, was unique in being planned as a residential college from the start, so that all students except those actually living in the town of Reading were accommodated in halls of residence. Although the other modern universities and university colleges eventually began to develop the hostel system, in most cases there is much lee-way to be made up and, at the present time, at a university like Leeds far too many students are faced by the alternatives of travelling or of living in lodgings.

It was only towards the close of the century that attention was paid to the training of teachers for secondary schools. It was thought sufficient that the teacher had obtained a university qualifi-cation in academic subjects. In 1854 the College of Preceptors began to grant diplomas for secondary teachers, and in 1873 started courses of lectures for teachers. In 1878 the Teachers' Training and Registration Society founded the Maria Grey Training College, in which special courses were provided for those intending to enter a secondary school. Towards the end of the period, the universities began to cater for the secondary-school teacher. The Teachers' Training Syndicate was formed at Cambridge in 1879, and the Oxford Delagacy for the training of secondary teachers in 1896. The University of London had instituted a secondary-teachers' diploma in 1883.

The Cross Commission criticised the pupil-teacher system, but, believing that there was nothing to put in its place, suggested improving it. Already the wisdom of entrusting the training of the pupil-teacher to the head teacher of a school had been questioned. Very few head teachers possessed the qualifications necessary for this task. The realisation of this fact led to the development of Pupil-Teachers' Centres after 1881. At first the pupil-teacher taught at school in the day and attended the centre for academic instruction in the evening. This was felt to be too great a burden, and in 1884 pupil-teachers were required to teach only half-time and were able to attend classes at the centre during the remainder of the day. The establishment of Pupil-Teachers' Centres was really a sign that the system was beginning to break down. The minority report of the Cross Commissioners was very emphatic on this topic. It declared that the pupil-teachers taught badly and were badly taught. The outcome was an inquiry into the whole system by the Education Department, 1896-8. The committee reported that, while it did not suggest complete abolition of the pupil-teacher system, it recommended raising the age to fifteen of pupil-teachers entering their apprenticeship, and eventually to sixteen. At the same time it was of the opinion that the Pupil-Teachers' Centre should approximate to a secondary school. Another improvement, in 1899, was the permission to substitute London Matriculation or the Senior Local examinations of Oxford and Cambridge for the Queen's Scholarship examination.

The Cross Commission's recommendations concerning evening schools resulted in a new evening-school Code in 1893. The requirement that students should pass in the three R's was abolished, and adult students over twenty-one were recognised for grant. The new Code offered grants based on the total number of hours of instruction given and not on the achievements of individual pupils. Moreover, the encouragement of scientific and technical studies, about which more will be said in a later chapter, made the evening institutes more popular, and as a result the number of students increased rapidly.

Our large towns still possess far too many schools which were built as a result of the 1870 Act, and which, with certain modifications, are yet in use. The typical school of this period consisted of a large classroom with one or two smaller classrooms leading off from the main room. The younger children often had the privilege of being in one of the smaller classrooms whilst the upper part of the school used the main room, which housed several classes. The latter served also as an assembly-hall for the school. Town schools were often built near the junction of busy streets, where the roar of traffic and the babel within the room, owing to one teacher having to make himself heard above the rest, interfered with the concentration of the pupils and played havoc with the teacher's voice and nerves. The author has vivid memories of one such school which abutted immediately on to a main road and tram route and in which the smell of the nearby gas-works was never absent. The windows were frequently placed behind the scholars, and heat was supplied by open fires or stoves, so that those near the fire were scorched whilst the remainder shivered with cold. Ventilation was achieved by vertical flues assisted by a gas-light burning in the flue. Lighting was by means of gas and there are still quite a number of schools being used at the present time in industrial towns where incandescent gas mantles are employed in lighting. High galleries were in the fashion and the entrance lobbies contained hooks for hats and coats, and lavatory basins. The playgrounds were usually inadequate in size and paved with flagstones or gravel. The main room was divided by sliding partitions which could be opened out to convert it into an assembly-hall. These schools were often double-storey buildings to accommodate boys and girls separately. One floor communicated with the other by a stone staircase, and often an iron fire-escape was attached to the outside of the building.

The London School Board experimented with what was known as the Prussian model, a large schoolroom with separate classrooms for each teacher, each accommodating as many as eighty children under a certificated teacher.[1]   The next development was the central-hall type introduced about 1890. Classrooms led off from a central hall and were much smaller and better lit. The open fire was replaced by central heating, and separate cloakrooms and lavatories were provided. A later improvement consisted in having the classrooms on one side of the hall only, which was lighted from the other side. Separate buildings for infants were erected and additional rooms provided for handicraft and domestic science. These schools were two- or three-storey structures ; boys on one floor and girls on another, or juniors on one and seniors on the other.

---

[1] The London School Board was the first to appoint its own school architects. The development of school buildings in London is illustrated by plans in the *Final Report of the School Board for London*, 1904.

It is difficult for anyone at the present day to realise how unsatisfactory were the conditions under which some schools had to work. The following extracts from school log-books are revealing, and show, in the words of Mr. G. A. N. Lowndes, how great has been the "Silent Social Revolution" accomplished by our elementary schools. The extracts refer to schools in the London district and are taken from a collection made by Mr. H. G. Carr, who kindly placed it at the author's disposal. Mr. Carr has been connected with London schools as pupil, student, and teacher, since 1895.

One head teacher wrote of a school: "Many of the children are so poor and dirty in their clothing that the work is sometimes very dirty. The class of children now in the school is very poor indeed, in fact each year sees a poorer and more careless class of children. The teachers are all overpressed by work in trying to maintain discipline and cleanliness among their scholars. To teach the children under our present circumstances is simply disheartening and depressing."

Parents in the poorer districts were distinctly unco-operative.

"1884. Feb. 1. Mrs. B. called and was exceedingly abusive about her boy being kept back to do his work. She went so far as to threaten personal violence with a dinner fork which she kept in her hand. The boy was suspended till apology was made by mother.

"1886. A boy having been punished, 'I received a note from his mother saying that she would take the nose out of my face.'"

Sometimes organised hooliganism interfered with the work of the schools, e.g.: —

"1872. Sept. 16. Large stones, pitched through the broken windows at intervals. No means of detecting the culprits.

"1884. June 12. About fifty or sixty boys from neighbouring schools came to the playground of this school at a quarter to one o'clock and attacked our children by throwing stones."

In the poorer districts children were sent to school in an unfit condition, and attendance was most irregular.

"1891. Nov. 30. Mrs. S. sent her daughter to school absolutely naked except for an old gown—the child complained of cold—the teacher found her a jacket to keep her warm.

"1889. Mrs. C. states that her children often have to come to school without any breakfast. The Doctor informs her that her boy in Std. IV is likely to go out of his mind through studying and having no nourishment. Mrs. G. states her children are often sent to school without breakfast. The two lads D. are often fed at school by the teachers. I have frequently seen them eagerly devouring a loaf of bread.

"1883. June 1. Organised a systematic cleaning of all dirty boys in the school. 80 cleaned this morning and 60 cleaned this afternoon.

"1884. Nov. 18. A note was sent enquiring as to the reason for a boy's absence. The reply was, 'Fetching the gin and no boots.'

"1871. Aug. Roll 244. Average attendance 164. Master and two pupil-teachers.

"1884. Numbers in classes starting with Std. I were 81, 66, 59, 67, 63, 51, 71.

"1884. In Miss W.'s division of Standard III, 82 were present out of 83 on the roll.

"1883. Nov. 5. To-day being Guy Fawkes Day our attendance was exceedingly bad, only 182 present in the morning and 158 in the afternoon out of 350.

"1879. April. Attendance still very irregular. . . . An impression is abroad among the parents that children are allowed to absent themselves twice a week."

Sometimes H.M.I.s were quite outspoken, as witness the Inspector who wrote: "1896. Dec. 23rd. With much pleasure I give up the charge of this very undesirable little school, where the mistresses come and go, bringing with them years of good reports and leaving with none, due to the many disadvantages and muddling under which they work, it being the practice of the schoolmaster to pick from his school the biggest child-dunce and send in here as 'Teacher' six months prior to my time of Inspection when the numbers are higher. This has been the case for the last two years. The school was condemned when I took charge and earning the lowest grant; it is now taking the higher grant to which I raised it."

Teachers were frequently outspoken about the examinations given by Inspectors, e.g. 1890, "The Examination throughout was the most unpleasant examination this school has had during the last five years, the children having to endure a great deal of harsh scolding through the giving of incomplete orders. On the last day, especially, they were expected to be very much on the alert in oral work, long after their usual dinner hour." 1890, "The following sums were given on Card No. 200 Std. III and the attention of the Inspector was drawn to them as being above the capacity of the children in that standard. No. 2. What is that number which contains six hundred and four, one hundred and thirty-seven times? No. 4. Fifty hens laid an egg each day every other day for 28 days. What profit would be made by selling the eggs at three half pence each if the hens cost a half penny each day for their food?"

At times the entries are definitely humorous, *e.g.* 1893, June 15, "One of the seats is broken in consequence of the Teetotallers' Concert held here on Monday night. The schoolroom was in a bad state on Tuesday morning." One wonders what was the composition of the mineral water which caused such high spirits.

Teaching methods in the 1880's were largely mechanical, partly owing to large classes, partly to the influence of the Revised Code. As additional subjects found their way into the curriculum, teaching methods improved, but very slowly. Elementary science was represented by the object lesson which was lauded as a means of developing the pupil's powers of observation. Frequently they resulted in the pupils repeating after the teacher long strings of technical terms or memorising perfectly obvious facts in a set form of words. Professor Armstrong's Heuristic Method was a protest against the method of teaching science which ignored the child's activity and relied on the memorisation of strings of facts.

Professor Armstrong was convinced that if the pupil were placed in the position of the original investigator and faced with problems similar to those encountered by the pioneers of scientific knowledge, he would understand science and grasp scientific principles more readily. Hence the title of his method—Heuristic—that is, a method of discovery. The method "caught on" and produced both critics and enthusiastic advocates. There is no doubt that Armstrong did good service to the cause of education by drawing attention to certain points which had been sadly neglected by the schools. Instead of lessons consisting mainly of "chalk and talk," he insisted that the learning process should be one of progressive discovery involving observation, experiment, and the use of inference ; but, like many reformers, in his zeal he lost sight of a very important principle. The child is still a child with the child's background of knowledge and experience, and an outlook on life different from that of the adult. In strictness, he cannot be equated with the original investigator, and before he can use the method with profit his background must be widened and deepened by certain facts and ideas, which must be presented to him. Also, the method should be regarded as being supplementary to class teaching and not as a complete substitute for it. Nevertheless, the Heuristic method sounded the death-knell of the old object lesson and emphasised that the teaching of science is an affair of the laboratory and workshop rather than of the classroom. The teaching of elementary science became more practical, and oral lessons and demonstrations were superseded by laboratory work in which the pupils handled apparatus, carried out experiments, and drew their own conclusions from the observations and experiments they had made. Too often, however, the practical work assigned to pupils was conceived in a most unintelligent manner. For example, in some higher-grade schools, pupils spent a whole year in manipulatory exercises and in learning how to measure directly and indirectly, without really understanding the purpose of accurate measurement.

In the middle of the century the influence of Pestalozzi, or more accurately Pestalozzi as interpreted by Fellenberg, was predominant. We have already seen its effect in the importance attached to the object lesson and the emphasis placed on analysing subject-matter into its simplest elements. It seems that the English followers of Pestalozzi had imperfectly grasped his principles. They were attracted more by the external aspects than by the spirit of his system. Unfortunately, they tended to exaggerate certain weaknesses.[1] Andrew Bell, when he visited Pestalozzi at Yverdun, was impressed by his personality, but he was quite unable to grasp the ideals which lay beneath the system of the great Swiss reformer. Bell found no trace of the elaborate machinery which he believed necessary for the smooth running of a school, and he was led to make the rash prophecy that the monitorial system would still be flourishing when Pestalozzi was forgotten.

Another of Pestalozzi's visitors understood more fully what was implicit in the system. This was Froebel, who, although he realised the weaknesses of the system, recognised its merits and gained

---

[1] The absurdity to which the principle of analysis was carried can be seen in the work entitled *Calisthenics or the Elements of Bodily Culture on Pestalozzian Principles* by Henry de Laspée, Charles Griffin and Company, 1865. The writer advertises his method by saying, "My book was the only one on Physical Training, admitted on the list issued by H.M.'s Committee of Council on Education." The method consists in analysing all the possible positions of the head, eyes, trunk, and limbs. Each of the elementary positions is numbered, and more complicated movements are built up from a combination of the elementary positions.

inspiration from them. Pestalozzi was essentially an empiricist, but Froebel brought a trained philosophic mind to bear upon his problems. Froebel's idea of the Kindergarten at first made a greater appeal to the German and American educationists than to the English. Like Pestalozzi, Froebel had his English imitators, but they failed to grasp the deeper meaning of his teaching and concentrated upon his Gifts and occupations, believing these to be the essential parts of his system. It was only much later that the true spirit of Froebel was understood. Even Sir Joshua Fitch considered that the Froebelian methods were useful only for children under seven, and then as supplementary to the more formal teaching of the infant-school.

The kindergarten idea was introduced into England in 1851 by the Baroness von Marenholtz-Bülow, who had become a great admirer of Froebel's work. The Society of Arts held an educational exhibition in London in 1854 and for the first time teachers were able to see the Froebelian apparatus and samples of the work done by pupils of Bertha Ronge, the teacher of the first English kindergarten. Charles Dickens, in an article published in *Household Words*, 1855, entitled "Infant Gardens," helped to popularise the idea. Dickens issued a warning, which was largely unheeded, that it would be all too easy to allow Froebel's system or any similar system of training to degenerate into a mechanical routine.

Unfortunately the new ideas had commenced to take root in this country only when the Revised Code, with its insistence upon the three R's, put an end, for a time, to further progress. The kindergarten idea began to revive after the Elementary Education Act of 1870. Emily Shirreff and her sister, Maria Grey, were instrumental in forming the Froebel Society in 1874. Its aims were to popularise the Froebelian principles and to provide training for Froebelian teachers. In the same year the London School Board appointed Miss Bishop to lecture on the system, and the British and Foreign School Society chose Miss Heerwart as principal of the kindergarten college and practising school established at Stockwell. After four years' work, Miss Bishop had to report that the kindergarten system was still widely misunderstood in England. It was regarded as a subject rather than a principle which should pervade the whole life of the infant-school. Also, in 1874 Madame Michaelis, the friend and pupil of Baroness von Marenholtz-Bülow, was appointed head of the kindergarten department of the Croydon High School, a foundation of the Girls' Public Day School Company.

In spite of all this, the Froebelian principles made only slow progress in England, and the existence of the kindergarten was practically ignored by the Cross Commission. English people did not take kindly to educational ideas which came from foreign sources. There was a lack of teachers who had been trained in kindergarten methods. Perhaps the most important reason for the tardy acceptance of Froebel's ideas was the firmly established view that schools for young children were places in which the elements of reading, writing, and counting were inculcated. Added to this, Froebel's works were not translated until the years 1885-93. There was, however, some progress. Froebel societies sprang up at Croydon, Bedford, and Manchester. These were independent associations, and it was obvious that much was to be gained if they coalesced into a national association. This came to pass in 1887, when the National Froebel Union was constituted for the work of examining and certificating teachers. The local societies carried on with propaganda. Meanwhile, the Froebelian movement had made more rapid progress in the United States, and it was a Froebelianism reformed and reconstructed by the critical mind of John Dewey which brought new life into the English kindergarten in the early years of the present century.

Another feature of the 1890's was the increasing attention given to the physical development of the child through games and physical exercises. The Code of 1871 recognised military drill, which was frequently taught by the sergeant of the local volunteers. The boys were instructed in marching in different military formations in the school-yard, and many School Boards arranged an annual contest between the schools of the area, in which banners were presented to the schools which distinguished themselves. This kind of drill made no pretence of giving scientific physical training; its main object was to inculcate a sense of discipline and prompt obedience to orders amongst a large group of children. Indian-club and dumb-bell exercises furnished the only variety from the marching and turnings. The table on p. 299 gives an idea of the type of physical-training work carried out by Standard VI boys under the Birmingham School Board. The table for girls was a slightly less strenuous version of the same course.

Swedish drill was introduced by the London School Board, who in 1879 invited Miss Löfving to give a course of instruction to schoolmistresses. In 1882 an attempt to popularise Swedish drill in boys' schools failed. The Board then instituted a series of courses

Marching	General Drill	Exercises
(a) March at a uniform rate, at even distance, and with a good carriage. (b) Change step, and do the right-about turn on the march. (c) Counter-marching. (d) March in line backwards and forwards. (e) First simple figure march. (f) Marching in fours. (g) Running.	(a) The turns. Right turn; left turn; half-right turn; half-left turn; right-about turn. (b) Dressing of lines. (c) Wheeling in fours forwards and backwards. (d) Opening and closing of ranks for exercises.	(a) Indian-club exercises, or (b) Stave exercises, Nos. 1 to 9.

in physical training on the English system which involved free body and limb movements. Lectures on the theory of physical training were given to teachers. A certain amount of military drill was retained on the ground of its value "as a means of maintaining discipline; obedience and promptness are secured; the tendency to roughness and noise is counteracted." Musical drill was also advocated because "it secures a more interested and consequently a more satisfactory execution of the work." Horizontal and parallel bars were erected in asphalt playgrounds, but owing to the large number of accidents were subsequently removed from the majority of schools.[1]

Leeds adopted Swedish drill in 1880 and musical drill in 1890. Special courses in physical training were arranged for teachers, and evening classes for young men in business, and instruction in gymnastics was given at two schools specially equipped for the purpose.

In the 1880's, school football clubs were formed in various London schools, but the idea of forming a school football association was due to Mr. W. J. Wilson of Balham, who, with the help of several other teachers, inaugurated the first elementary-schools football association under the name of the South London Schools F.A., 1885. This was the beginning of a national movement, and by 1895 nearly every important town had a school organisation for the promotion of football and cricket. Competitions between teams in the same town and between towns were organised. One of the earliest inter-town matches was played between the Sheffield

---

[1] The London School Board introduced dancing into twenty-four of its schools, but owing to the unfavourable comment of the Vice-President of the Education Department in 1901 it was dropped from the school curriculum.

Schools F.A. and the South London Schools F.A. at Bramall Lane, the famous Yorkshire ground, in 1890. In 1894 Manchester and Sheffield schools played before 40,000 spectators. The Sheffield F.A. organised a number of matches for charities, and in ten years raised over £1,000.

Cricket was much more difficult to organise owing to the lack of suitable practice grounds, but in London, Liverpool, and Brighton, park pitches were set aside for the schools on Saturday mornings. Athletic associations were formed for promoting annual school sports, and girls and boys were included. Swimming instruction also received attention. Leeds formed an Elementary Schools F.A. in 1896, and adopted the association game in spite of the fact that Leeds was even then a great rugby centre. The reason given was that association football was a better game for boys who wanted to practise during the midday break and had not time to change. Arrangements were made in 1875 for pupils from elementary schools to obtain swimming instruction, and in 1895 it became part of the ordinary school course.

In many districts the public libraries were made available to school-children. The first municipal rate-supported public library was established at Warrington in 1848 and the earliest Public Libraries Act (Ewart's Act) was passed in 1850. The movement to set up public libraries grew slowly, and in 1870 only about forty places in the kingdom had established public libraries. After 1870, public libraries became more numerous. In 1865 the Birkenhead librarian reported that 743 juvenile books had been borrowed during the year, and the first separate children's library was begun at Nottingham in 1882. The first free public library authority to work in unison with the schools was at Leeds in 1877, and by 1894 sixty-three juvenile libraries had been established in Board schools and six in voluntary schools.

The central library and twenty-one branch libraries in Leeds had special juvenile departments. In one Leeds Board school special lesson-periods were assigned on the time-table for library reading and every pupil above Standard III was supposed to have a library book which he was reading. In some towns every school was supplied with a number of book boxes, the contents of which were changed from time to time. The Education Department urged teachers to make their instruction lead up to an appreciation of art galleries, museums, and public libraries. In 1896 the Cardiff School Board tried out a new experiment. It was arranged that every class above Standard III should visit the public library at least once a year for an illustrated lesson on a definite subject. The lesson for the first year was the History of a Book, and the library staff organised a most interesting exhibition. Pupils were shown examples of the clay tablets of the Assyrians, the papyrus of Egypt, mediaeval MSS., the Horn Book, early English printed books, books made by the Japanese, and special books for the use of the blind. Other towns repeated the Cardiff experiment.

School apparatus became more plentiful. The early lesson-cards and wall-sheets were replaced by black-boards. Wall-maps and atlases made their appearance and attention was given to the seating arrangements. The London School Board replaced the long, backless forms by dual desks, but in many country schools little improvement took place.

So far in this account of the development of English education we have been considering the provision made for the education of the normal child who comes from a normal home. There is, how-ever, the problem of satisfying the needs of those children who, in some way or other, have been less favoured and cannot take their place in the ordinary schools. Such children fall into the following classes : —

(1) Those who have been deprived of one or both parents, or whose parents by reason of poverty or sickness are unable to support them. These children require maintenance as well as education.

(2) Those who come from homes where they have not experienced a happy home life. They may have been ignored and neglected, or actually ill-treated.

(3) Those living in a criminal environment, or who have by begging or by petty offences infringed the law.

(4) Children who by reason of some physical or mental defect are unable to take advantage of the education provided for normal children.

The problem arising with the first three categories of children has been that of providing them with an environment which, as far as possible, would supply the training conditions found in a good home and, at the same time, giving them adequate instruction in the subjects of the elementary school. Attention was first directed towards those who had actually transgressed the law. In the early days of the century, quite young children who had been convicted by the magistrates were sentenced to transportation for periods varying from five to ten years. As in the case of normal children, the first efforts in reform were made by philanthropic societies. The Marine Society, founded in 1756, and the Philanthropic Society in 1788, aimed at receiving and treating juvenile offenders who had been released from imprisonment or transportation under a conditional pardon. The latter was granted if the child entered a "Home" or "Charitable Institution" and remained there for a number of years. The work of the Philanthropic Society in reclaiming young offenders was so highly thought of that the Society was incorporated by an Act of Parliament in 1806.

When the voluntary societies showed signs of being unable to solve the problem, the Government intervened. The first Government experiment was at Parkhurst Prison in 1837. All juveniles sentenced to transportation were lodged in the prison and an attempt was made to reform them through outdoor industrial training, religious teaching, and school instruction. As Parkhurst remained a prison, the experiment was not successful and it was abandoned in 1864.

Those of us who remember the two world wars will also recollect the enormous increase in juvenile delinquency which followed them. Such developments were not the result of war conditions only, for at several periods during the 19th century popular attention was directed to the growth of juvenile crime. Thus in the 1840's public opinion was so outraged by the growth of juvenile delinquency that a Select Committee of the House of Lords was instituted in 1847 to consider the operation of the criminal law in respect to children. Statistics produced before the committee showed that the number of criminals under twenty years of age who had been convicted had increased from 6,803 (or 1 in 449 of the juvenile population) in 1835, to 11,348 (or 1 in 304) in 1844. Some witnesses quite illogically connected the increase with the growing number of children attending the Ragged schools. Such children were generally referred to as those belonging to the "perishing and dangerous classes."

The result of the inquiry was the institution of reformatory schools by an Act of Parliament of 1854. By 1860 there were forty-seven reformatory schools, which were training 2,594 juvenile offenders. In the early days the training was not altogether successful, since the atmosphere of such institutions resembled that of a prison rather than a school. The initial mistakes were eventually corrected, and when a reformatory school was opened at Adel, Leeds, in 1857, its object was declared to be "to promote the reformation of boys convicted of crime by training them up in habits of industry, in outdoor and other employment, imparting to them an education of a plain character, and especially by an earnest endeavour to bring them under the influence of religious principles and also by placing them in suitable situations on their discharge from the institution." This particular school has long enjoyed the reputation of treating the boys as human beings, of trying to discover and develop their individual interests, and of providing a sound basis of religious instruction. The school stands in extensive grounds, and the boys are employed in horticultural work. There is a large carpenter's shop for instruction in woodwork, and special attention is given to physical exercises and games. The boys have taken a great interest in chess, and not only is the game played indoors, but on several occasions they have given demonstrations of living chessmen, in which each boy represents a bishop, knight, or some other piece.

In addition to institutions which dealt with actual offenders, efforts were made to prevent children from unsatisfactory homes from developing into delinquents. The Ragged schools had done good work in this respect, but it was felt that the problem ought to be attacked in a much more systematic way. In some towns Ragged schools developed into industrial schools under the control of the Boards of Guardians. The Industrial Schools Act of 1857 empowered magistrates to commit to industrial schools children who had been found begging or who had committed some minor breach of the law. The Committee of Council gave 3s. a week towards the maintenance of each child who had been committed, but parents who could afford to contribute to the child's keep were expected to do so.

Two kinds of industrial school were recognised: certified and uncertified. The former received children who had actually been committed by the magistrates. Other children who suffered from neglect or who came from destitute homes might attend either type of school. These schools were residential, and it was hoped that by bringing the children into a wholesome environment and teaching them a trade, they would become respectable, self-supporting members of the community. The number of residential industrial schools aided by the Committee of Council was thirty-six in 1858, and 2,822 children were in attendance.

The Elementary Education Act of 1870 created an additional problem. Many parents refused to send their children regularly to school. This difficulty gave rise to the day industrial schools which were instituted by the Education Act of 1876. Children who did not attend school could be committed by the magistrates either to a residential or a day industrial school. In some cases parents complained that they could not prevent their children from playing truant. Such children could attend an industrial school on a voluntary basis, but the parent was expected to contribute a small amount towards the child's maintenance. The day industrial schools looked after the children between the hours of 8 a.m. and 6 p.m. They were fed at school, and it was hoped that the training given would counteract the influence of the home and the streets. Unfortunately, in most cases the effect of the training was not sufficiently strong to overcome the adverse influences, and in this respect the residential schools were more successful. As a result of this experience, day industrial schools were abandoned in the early years of the present century.

Until the latter part of the 19th century little attention was given to those children who, because of some physical or mental defect, were unable to benefit from the instruction designed for the normal child. The worst cases never attended school, whilst those suffering from slighter defects formed the dull and backward members of the school The problem of such children grew more acute when, after 1870, schooling was becoming universal. A common device was to form a Standard 0 in which were grouped all those who could not take their places with normal children, but no attempt was made to discover the cause of their backwardness; whether it was physical, (*e.g.* defective eyesight or hearing) or mental, or whether it was due to accident or to some defect which entailed special treatment.

The earliest attempt to deal with the problem of mentally defective children was by means of the Education (Defective and Epileptic Children) Act of 1899, which empowered School Boards to provide special accommodation for defective children, but this duty was not made obligatory until 1914. Nevertheless, the School Boards in London and the large towns turned their attention to providing the necessary accommodation. A special curriculum was prepared for these children, and individual and practical modes of instruction were emphasised. Bradford, which for many years was a pioneer of this kind of work, opened a special school for mentally defective children in 1894. The Leeds School Board opened a temporary school in 1900 until a special building for mental defectives was erected in the following year.

As early as 1883 the Leeds School Board instituted a class for deaf and dumb children. The blind were cared for by a voluntary agency: the Leeds Institute for the Blind. The work of the latter body was transferred to the School Board in 1890, and a separate classroom was allotted to blind children. In Bradford, day classes for the blind and deaf were opened in 1885. The Elementary Education (Blind and Deaf Children) Act of 1893 empowered School Boards to provide for the education of blind and deaf children. The Leeds School Board opened a residential school for these children in 1899. The provision of accommodation for crippled children was considered by certain School Boards, but nothing definite was accomplished until after the Education Act of 1902. Some School Boards began to take an interest in the health of the school-child. School medical inspection was started in London in 1890 and in Bradford in 1893. For many years the latter city was the pioneer of school medical services. Some School Boards, like that at Leeds, employed a part-time medical officer, but his duties were mainly confined to certifying children for admission to special schools and examining teachers in accordance with the regulations of the Education Department. The rapid extension of the services rendered by the special schools and the school medical service belongs to the first decade of the present century.

CHAPTER IX

THE FOUNDATION OF A NATIONAL SYSTEM
1895-1902

The point has now been reached where the two streams of secondary and elementary education meet and their development can be considered together. At the end of Chapter v, the reason for the appointment of the Bryce Commission was given. The Bryce Commission is noteworthy because for the first time it included women amongst its members, and had wider terms of reference than any previous commission. Its object was "to consider what are the best methods of establishing a well-organised system of secondary education in England, taking into account existing deficiencies, and having regard to such local sources of revenue from endowment or otherwise as are available or may be made available for this purpose, and to make recommendations accordingly." This Commission, like the Taunton Commission, employed the usual means of obtaining information, and, through Sir J. Fitch, Mr. (later Professor) Findlay, and Mr. (later Sir) M. E. Sadler, secured reports on the progress of secondary education in various countries of Europe, Canada, and the United States.

Certain districts were selected for special study: Devonshire, including Exeter and Plymouth; the north of England, including Leeds, Bradford, Keighley, Manchester, and Liverpool; Bedfordshire, and other counties. After a brief review of the work of the Taunton Commission and the Endowed Schools Act, the Commissioners emphasised with regret that four important recommendations of that Commission had not been carried out: the establishment of a central authority for secondary education, the creation of local authorities, the institution of a register of schools and teachers, and the authorisation for local authorities to apply rate-aid to secondary education. The benefits gained by the Endowed Schools Act were only a fragment of the system the Commission had elaborated with so much foresight and patient statesmanship. Since the Taunton Commission, events had moved rapidly and the Commissioners referred to the establishment of new agencies in the field of education; School Boards for elementary education, which were now financing higher-grade schools, a type of secondary school of the third grade; the Science and Art

Department, whose grants were given to what was virtually secondary education; the university colleges for the higher education of men and women, the University Extension movement, which had brought instruction of an advanced type to people outside the normal university courses, and the recent development of technical education. The latter had been financed from the funds created by the Local Taxation Act of 1890, funds which were being applied by the county councils, who had gained valuable experience in educational administration. The Welsh Intermediate Education Act of 1889 provided a new source of suggestions. The report then emphasised the hopelessly chaotic state of educational administration shown by the variety of authorities and the constant overlapping of their functions and lack of co-ordination. The teaching profession was now organised and had given rise to such bodies as the Headmasters' Conference, 1870, the National Union of Teachers, 1870, the Association of Headmistresses, 1874, the Association of Assistant Mistresses, 1884, the Headmasters' Association, 1890, the Association of Assistant Masters, 1892, and others. All this was a sign of the growth of a strong professional spirit which would tend to raise the influence and the status of the teaching profession. Another tendency noted was the growth of the proprietary schools and the better provision of secondary schools for girls. Yet one more agency had appeared in the field of secondary education in the Board of Agriculture, which, since the Act of 1889, had powers of inspecting the teaching of agricultural subjects given in secondary schools and institutes for higher education. In addition to the endowed schools and schools receiving grants from a Government department, there were still numerous private schools. All this added to the confusion into which educational administration had fallen, so that the pressing problem to be solved was that of organisation.

Although not strictly within the terms of reference, the report considered that little progress could be made until the meaning of the term "secondary education" had been defined. "In every phase of secondary teaching, the first aim should be to educate the mind, and not merely to convey information. It is a fundamental fault, which pervades many parts of the secondary education now given in England, that the subject (literary, scientific, or technical) is too often taught in such a manner that it has little or no educational value. The largest of the problems which concern the future of Secondary Education is how to secure, as far as possible, that in all schools and in every branch of study the pupils shall be not only instructed but educated." [1]

The changes of recent years had resulted in the breaking down of the barriers between cultural and practical subjects. Hence secondary education "is the education of the boy or girl not simply as a human being who needs to be instructed in the mere rudiments of knowledge, but it is a process of intellectual training and personal discipline conducted with special regard to the profession or trade to be followed." [2] Therefore technical instruction cannot be separated from secondary education.

The report recommended certain steps that were necessary for establishing an efficient system of secondary education in England. The primary need was the creation of a central authority to organise and co-ordinate all the different agencies supplying secondary education. The past record of the Education Department had raised suspicions in the minds of certain members of the Commission as to what the establishment of a central authority might entail. "Greater variety and freedom in secondary schools than the old uniform codes allowed in elementary. Teachers . . . have shown a proper and becoming fear lest the hard reign of these codes, which has, indeed, of late years been, with happiest results, gradually made lighter, should be introduced into secondary schools, or lest all spontaneity should be ground out of them by the iron machinery of 'payment by results'." [3]

That these fears were not altogether groundless has been borne out by the tendencies of recent years. On the whole, however, the Commission thought that by combining elementary and secondary education under the same department, the general results would be beneficial because the central authority would be obliged to think of education as a whole and not simply of its several parts. Another advantage would be the greater ease with which teachers and pupils could pass from one type of school to another. The bureaucratic tendencies of centralisation would be checked by the existence of local education authorities, and the policy of the central authority would have a larger and more liberal spirit when it had to reckon with secondary education than when it had to deal with elementary education alone. The central authority should not occupy the position of a dictator. "So far from attempting to induce uniformity, we trust that a free and spontaneous variety, and an open field

---

[1] *Report of the Commission on Secondary Education*, 1895, p. 80.
[2] *Ibid.*, pp. 135-6.   [3] *Ibid.*, p. 103.

for experiment and enterprise of all kinds, will be scrupulously observed. . . . Some central authority is required, not in order to control, but rather to supervise . . . not to override or supersede local action, but to endeavour to bring about among the various agencies which provide that education a harmony and co-operation which are now wanting." [1]

Professor Archer summed up the difficulty which presented itself to the Commission when he wrote, "Educationalists were undoubtedly groping for some arrangement by which secondary education could be controlled and financed by the State without becoming subject to the party system. . . . It has always been regarded as an integral part of the Constitution that departments which spend the public money should be represented by a minister responsible to Parliament. Under the party system this means that the Education Minister comes into office with his party, goes out with it, however efficient he may be, and is rarely likely to be turned out however inefficient he may be. The system, which was designed to secure parliamentary control, works out in a manner quite the reverse. The minister himself is responsible to Parliament, that is to the party whips, who have no interest in real educational efficiency, with the result that the permanent officials, who are the real authors of educational policy, are responsible to nobody." [2]

The Commission recommended the following solution to the problem. The first necessity would be the creation of a central authority as a Government department, having a Minister of Education responsible to Parliament and charged with the supervision of both elementary and secondary education. He should be assisted by a permanent secretary. But some of the work of the department would be "so purely professional, as to belong rather to an independent body than to a Department of State." Therefore the creation of an Education Council to advise the Minister was recommended. It would act as an executive body and take charge of the compilation of a teachers' register. The Minister would be responsible for general policy and the control of administrative details, "but we believe that the unwillingness which doubtless exists in some quarters to entrust to the executive any powers at all in this branch of education would be sensibly diminished were his position at once strengthened and guarded by the addition of a number of

---

[1] *Report of the Commission on Secondary Education*, 1895, p. 257.
[2] R. L. Archer. *Secondary Education in the Nineteenth Century*, pp. 311-12, C.U.P., 1921.

independent advisers." Unfortunately for future generations, this recommendation was only partially carried out when the Board of Education was established.

The Commission thought that the Education Council should be a small body of twelve members—one-third appointed by the Crown, one-third by the universities of Oxford, Cambridge, London, and Victoria, and one-third selected by the rest of the Council from experienced educationists. The term of office should be six years, and arrangements should be made to prevent all the members retiring at the same time and so breaking continuity. Additional members might be co-opted when necessary. The existing authorities, the Education Department, the Science and Art Department, and the educational functions of the Charity Commission, would be merged in the new central authority.

The local administration should be in the hands of authorities established by the county councils, the county boroughs, and other boroughs having a population over 50,000. These local authorities would carry out the functions of securing a due provision of secondary education in their areas, co-ordinating existing schools, administering sums provided by the rates or the national exchequer, initiating schemes for endowed and public schools, and providing for the inspection of schools. The local authorities should also have the power of granting recognition to private and preparatory schools provided they reached a certain standard as regards buildings and efficiency, and should organise scholarships and exhibitions for deserving scholars, including those being educated in the elementary and higher-grade schools of the district.

The Commission called attention to the anomalous aspect of the higher-grade schools as being under the management of the elementary School Boards and yet, for practical purposes, providing secondary instruction. It suggested that they should be treated as secondary schools, but this recommendation implied the assumption that the School Boards would continue and that the new local authorities would be responsible for secondary education only.

The work of the Bryce Commission had shown the value of having accurate and up-to-date information about education in different parts of Britain, in the Colonies and Dominions, and in other countries. The following year the Department of Special Reports and Inquiries, under the charge of Mr. (later Sir) Michael Sadler, was created and unwittingly became one of the agencies that was to help in laying the foundation of the national system.

The central authority recommended by the Commissioners was created by the Board of Education Act of 1899. The powers of the Education Department, the Science and Art Department, and the Charity Commission, as regards its educational work, were merged in the Board of Education. Legally the Board consisted of the President, the principal Secretaries of State, the First Commissioner of the Treasury, and the Chancellor of the Exchequer. During its long history of forty-five years the Board never met, and for practical purposes it consisted of the President, a permanent Secretary, a Parliamentary Secretary, and senior administrative officials.

The Board was to superintend educational affairs in England and Wales, and at the same time a Consultative Committee was established to advise the Board on any matter referred to it. The Committee consisted of eighteen members, men and women, who held office for six years. Another duty of the Committee was to prepare a register of teachers. Thus the Consultative Committee was shorn of most of the powers which had been recommended by the Bryce Commission for the Education Council. The former could not proffer advice to the president of the Board until asked to do so. This was not rectified until 1944, but meanwhile the Consultative Committee had done much valuable work in the issue of reports such as the report on *The Primary School,* the *Education of the Adolescent,* etc.

A Registration Council was set up in 1902, but the National Union of Teachers objected to the division of the register into two columns, one for elementary teachers and one for secondary. The Board withdrew the register, and it was not until 1907 that a new Teachers' Registration Council was established. The new register contained the names of teachers in alphabetical order representing teachers in all kinds of schools, including the universities. Registration was voluntary, and those teachers whose names appeared on the register were entitled to add the letters M.R.S.T. (Member of the Royal Society of Teachers) to their names. A large number of teachers did not avail themselves of the register, mainly because neither the central nor the local authorities made any use of it when candidates offered themselves for educational appointments. In 1948 the Ministry of Education decided to abandon the idea of registration and the Royal Society of Teachers came to an end. No further registrations can be accepted, but those who are already registered are entitled to use the letters M.R.S.T.

The second main proposal of the Bryce Commission in regard to the institution of local education authorities took seven years to materialise. The first move was due to the difficulties in which the voluntary schools found themselves. In the unequal competition with the Board schools they found themselves left more and more behind because of the rising costs of education. The Conservative party were strong supporters of the denominational schools and when they were returned to power in 1895 the archbishops of Canterbury and York drafted a memorial which was presented to the Government. It prayed that in the framing of a new Education Bill the religious character of education should be preserved by retaining the voluntary schools. Parents should have the right to determine the religious instruction given to their children and no school should be penalised because of the religious views held by the teachers or the pupils. The memorial emphasised the value of variety in the type and management of schools and asked for the abolition of the limits on the grants to schools and that the grants should be rearranged so as to assist the poorer schools. They asked for increased exchequer grants, the provision of facilities for separate religious instruction in both voluntary and Board schools, and power to establish denominational schools where parents demanded them.

The Government presented a Bill in 1896 closely following these proposals. The Bill had been prepared by the Vice-President of the Education Department, Sir John Gorst, assisted by the Secretary, Sir George Kekewich, and Mr. Sadler. It suggested making the county and county borough councils the local education authorities controlling elementary, secondary, and technical schools. This was an advance on the proposals of the Bryce Commission which had contemplated retaining the School Boards for elementary education. The grant limit of 17s. 6d. per head was to be abolished and a special grant of 4s. per head was to be paid to the county authority for distribution among the voluntary schools in its area. A clause was inserted to enable separate religious instruction to be given in Board schools to those children whose parents desired it. This amounted to the repeal of the Cowper-Temple clause. The new proposals were assailed from two directions. The School Boards were not inclined to a voluntary surrender which would result in their ceasing to exist, and the Nonconformists and the Liberal party were up in arms against the idea of giving rate-aid to the voluntary schools. The Lord

President, the Duke of Devonshire, decided to drop the measure and broke the news to Sir John Gorst by bursting into his room with the remark, "Gorst, your damned Bill's dead." However, the following year the Government passed a Voluntary Schools Act abolishing the 17s. 6d. limit on grants, freeing the schools from payment of rates, and providing an aid-grant of 5s. per head paid through the Association of Voluntary Schools. The same year a similar Act gave aid to necessitous School Boards.

It seemed that the recommendations of the Bryce Commission would be entirely neglected. That they were not was almost entirely due to the work of one man, Mr. (later Sir) Robert Morant. Morant's career opened with a series of crises. He was born of middle-class parents in 1863, and it was intended that he should enter Rugby. The death of his father when Morant was ten years old seemed to close the door to his mother's hopes of sending him to a public school, but he was fortunate enough to secure the nomination of the headmaster of Winchester. His great ambition in his early years was to take Orders and with this in view he went up to New College, Oxford, in 1881. On account of his poverty he had to take up coaching in order to keep himself at Oxford, and he had just secured a First in Theology when the news came that his mother, to whom he was devoted, was seriously ill. For a time he accepted a teaching post in a preparatory school, but in 1886 he applied for appointment as tutor to the children of the Siamese Minister in London, who had just returned to Siam. In 1888 he became tutor to the Crown Prince of Siam and remained in that country until the end of 1893, when the crisis caused by the French attempts at annexation brought about his dismissal. During his stay in Siam he had worked earnestly for the cause of reform in Siamese education and had been the advisor of the king and his ministers. Now on his return to England he had to look for another appointment. He applied to the Education Department and was given the post of Assistant Director of Special Inquiries and Reports in the newly created department of which Sadler was chief.

Morant made himself familiar with the reports of the Cross and the Bryce Commissions, and assisted his chief and Sir George Kekewich in preparing memoranda in connection with Sir John Gorst's ill-fated Bill. During 1896 he was absent in France studying the French system of Higher Primary Schools. The results of his work were published in the first volume of *Special Reports on Educational Subjects*, 1897. Morant's next visit was to Switzerland, where he made an exhaustive study of the Swiss educational system, and he was struck by the careful organisation of Swiss education, which contrasted strongly with the administrative muddle in England. When he wrote his report on Swiss education he inserted the following paragraph. "The Central Authority has not, as with us, any voice in limiting any additional efforts that the Commune may desire to make out of its own funds, towards extending the educational advantages of its members, or towards making any higher developments of its educational supply. This at once suggests a vital difference between Swiss and English conceptions. For instance, in England many School Boards have desired to improve their higher Elementary Education and to extend its scope by providing Day Schools of a Higher Grade; but they have been frequently told by the Central Authority that they cannot take any such steps as would involve the School Board in any expense for this purpose, that it would be illegal to spend their rates in such a manner, inasmuch as they were only empowered by the Act of 1870 to use the rates to provide Elementary Education." [1]

At this time a dispute had been going on between the London School Board and the London Technical Education Board because the latter had applied for recognition as the authority responsible for secondary education. The county council supported their Technical Education Board and the two bodies appealed to the Science and Art Department. Dr. Garnett, the secretary of the Technical Education Board, was given the task of preparing the case for the county council. Morant contrived to bring to Garnett's notice the paragraph in his Swiss report, and followed it up by giving him evidence of the illegality of the London School Board in using the rates to support what was secondary instruction given through the higher-grade schools. Sir John Gorst was astonished at the evidence collected by Morant, and, after giving a decision in favour of the county council, asked Dr. Garnett to

---

[1] *Special Reports on Educational Subjects*, Vol. III, p. 47, H.M.S.O., 1898. Morant expressed his views quite clearly in the last paragraph of his report. "Surely it is not too much to hope that England may yet learn to value and to create for herself a true and complete organisation of her schools not merely of her Primary Education, but also of that most valuable asset of the national welfare—her Middle and Higher Schools; so that each and every grade of education, and each and every type of school may have a clear presentment before it, both of the function which it is intended to fulfil, of the results which it is framed to produce, and of the area which it is created to supply. Thus, and thus only, can each and every school, and each and every grade of education, have its due share of national interest and assistance, and be enabled effectually to play its due part in national development."

challenge the legality of the London School Board's position at the next meeting with the Government Auditor, Mr. T. B. Cockerton. The latter was satisfied with the evidence and surcharged the School Board.   The School Board took the case to court and lost.   On appeal to the Master of the Rolls the court of appeal upheld Mr. Cockerton's view.   Sir John Gorst followed this up by relating to Parliament instances of other School Boards which had been acting illegally.   A special Act, 1901, was passed to allow the School Boards to carry on until the Government had prepared the Education Bill that everyone now knew was inevitable.

The delay caused by the South African war necessitated the renewal of the Act of 1901, and it was not until the end of March 1902 that the Government was ready to present the new Bill to the House of Commons.   Morant, who for some time had been busy with the drafting of the Bill, was present during the debate.[1]

The Act carried out the second main proposal of the Bryce Commission and brought education under municipal control. "The Education Act of 1902 . . . brought administrative order where there had been chaos, and set up an organised system of elementary, secondary, and technical education."[2]   In place of the School Boards and School Attendance Committees, the Act constituted the county and county borough councils as the local education authorities.   This in itself was a great administrative simplification, since instead of over 2,500 School Boards and nearly 800 School Attendance Committees, about 300 new local authorities took their place. As the county councils and county borough councils were concerned with Part II of the Act, which dealt with higher education, they were generally known as Part II authorities.   In addition, the councils of boroughs with a population of over 10,000, and urban districts with over 20,000 inhabitants, were constituted as authorities for the purposes of Part III of the Act, which dealt with elementary education only.   Hence the latter authorities were known as Part III authorities, and both were entitled Local Education Authorities, generally abbreviated to L.E.A.   The L.E.A. was empowered, for local administration, to set up a Local Education Committtee to which it could delegate the exercise of its powers under the Act, with the exception of the power of raising a rate or borrowing money. This ensured that the local finances were under public control.   The

[1] The work of Morant in connection with the drafting of the Act is described in detail by Dr. B. M. Allen in *Sir Robert Morant*, pp. 151-71, Macmillan, 1934.

[2] F. Smith.   *A History of English Elementary Education*, p. 347, University of London Press, 1931.

majority of the members of an education committee were to be appointed by the council from its members, unless, in the case of a county, the council should determine otherwise. The council also appointed to the committee persons with experience in education or those who had intimate knowledge of the needs of the various kinds of schools in the district. This enabled teachers to become members. Women as well as men were able to be members of the education committee. If it seemed desirable, persons who had been members of School Boards at the time of the passing of the Act might be appointed as members of the first committee. Separate education committees could be formed for areas within the county, or two or more boroughs or urban districts could amalgamate to appoint a Joint Education Committee. All L.E.A.s took over the duties of the School Boards and the School Attendance Committees with regard to the control of secular education within their areas.

The Board schools now became council schools, and because the buildings were provided by the L.E.A., such schools were known as provided schools. The voluntary schools, because the buildings were not provided by the L.E.A., were termed non-provided schools. Provided schools under a county L.E.A. had six managers, four of whom were appointed by the education committee. In the case of a borough or urban district, the L.E.A. could appoint the number of managers it considered necessary. Non-provided schools also had a board of six managers, four foundation managers appointed under the provisions of the trust-deed, and two (who might possibly be Nonconformists) appointed by the education committee. The foundation managers would preserve the denominational character of the school and the presence of two managers representing the public authority would act as a check to innovations in religious teaching introduced by a too zealous vicar. This clause was inserted to appease the Nonconformists, who feared that Anglo-Catholic teaching might be introduced into a school against the wishes of the majority of the parishioners.

The managers of a non-provided school were to provide the building free of charge, and undertake all repairs except those due to fair wear and tear. As regards secular instruction, the managers were obliged to carry out the directions of the L.E.A., who would decide the number of teachers required and their educational qualifications. The L.E.A. had the power to dismiss a teacher on educational grounds. The managers appointed the teachers subject to the consent of the L.E.A., which had a veto on educational grounds, but the managers did not need to obtain the consent of the L.E.A. to dismiss a teacher on grounds connected with the giving of religious instruction. In a provided school the latter had to be undenominational as prescribed by the Cowper-Temple clause, but in a school maintained but not provided, religious instruction was to be in accordance with the trust-deeds of the school, subject to a conscience clause. In secondary schools and colleges provided by the authority a new clause governed the nature of the religious instruction. "No pupil shall, on the ground of religious belief, be excluded from or placed in an inferior position in any school, college, or hostel, provided by the council, and no catechism or formulary distinctive of any particular religious denomination shall be taught in any school, college, or hostel, so provided, except in cases where the council, at the request of parents of scholars at such times and under such conditions as the council think desirable, allow any religious instruction to be given in the school, college, or hostel, otherwise than at the cost of the council; provided that in the exercise of this power no unfair preference shall be shown to any religious denomination." (Pt. II, para. 4 (i).)

Elementary education was limited to pupils under sixteen years of age, except in the case where no suitable higher education was available within a reasonable distance of the school, when the L.E.A., with the consent of the Board of Education, could extend the age-limit. Evening schools were considered as belonging to the sphere of higher education. Besides aiding secondary and technical education, the L.E.A. possessed the right to train teachers.

As non-provided schools were now supported by the rates, the Government grant was rearranged to ease the burden on the poorer districts.[1]

[1] The rearranged grant consisted of a fixed grant equal to 4s. per scholar together with a variable grant. This consisted of $1\frac{1}{2}$d. per scholar for every complete 2d. per scholar by which the amount which would be produced by a 1d. rate fell short of 10s. a scholar. This complicated arrangement was intended to ease the burden on a poor district where the product of a 1d. rate was not as large as that in a wealthier district having a smaller school population. A district which raised less than a 3d. rate lost from the grant an amount equal to half the difference between the amount raised from a 3d. rate and that raised by the actual rate.

Thus, in a district where the rate was 2s. and which fell short of 10s. by 8s., the grant would be 4s. + $\frac{3}{4}$ of 8s., i.e. 10s. If the rate was 5s. the grant would be 4s. + $\frac{3}{4}$ of 5s., i.e. 7s. 9d.

The Bill received its first reading without encountering any fierce opposition, but in the interval before the second reading a spirit of bitter animosity towards the proposals developed. Bryce, the chairman of the Commission of 1895, moved the rejection of the Bill when it came before the House for a second reading. Sir Edward Grey criticised the proposal to put the voluntary schools on the rates, but the most determined attack was led by Mr. Lloyd George. The second reading was passed by a vote of 402 to 165, but everybody realised that there would be a hard fight at the Committee stage. In the country, the Nonconformists were aroused by Dr. Clifford by means of letters to the *Daily News* which he later embodied in a penny pamphlet. In Parliament, the Liberal Opposition made capital out of the Nonconformist hostility and Mr. Lloyd George's bitterest invective was employed to defeat the Bill. It was fortunate for Mr. Balfour that he had secured the services of Morant, whose detailed and accurate knowledge of educational administration and statistics provided the ammunition for the support of the Government.   Joseph Chamberlain had been injured in a street accident and was not present for the debate.   In the midst of the struggle, Lord Salisbury felt he should, on account of age, resign the premiership, and was succeeded by Mr. Balfour.

The Cabinet was reconstructed and Lord Londonderry was appointed president of the Board of Education, with Sir William Anson as parliamentary secretary. Mr. Balfour felt that Sir George Kekewich, the secretary to the late Education Department, was not a strong enough man to carry out the Government's policy and he agreed with Lord Londonderry that it was necessary to have someone who was thoroughly acquainted with all the intricacies of the Bill. The latter suggested that Morant should be the successor to Kekewich. Accordingly, Morant was appointed acting secretary, to become permanent secretary to the Board of Education when Kekewich retired in 1903. Thus in seven years Morant had risen from the rank of junior civil servant to be the head of the Department. Balfour was ably assisted by Morant, and although certain modifications, such as the clause moved by Colonel Kenyon-Slaney to the effect that the religious teaching of a non-provided school must be in conformity with the trust-deed, were adopted on Morant's advice, the Bill became law on December 20th, the second anniversary of the Cockerton judgment, with all its main proposals intact.

The Act of 1902, like most Education Acts, presented many features of compromise. The dual system was maintained and the Kenyon-Slaney clause, adopted to appease the Nonconformists, roused the anger of the Anglo-Catholics. The creation of the Part III authorities was a concession to the supporters of the School Boards and may have been of value in stimulating local interest in education. It led, however, to a number of anomalies (*e.g.* Birchenough quotes the example of Canterbury, a county borough with a population of 25,000, which became an authority for both elementary and higher education, whilst Part III authorities like Leyton, Willesden, Rhondda, and Tottenham, with populations ranging from 99,000 to 114,000, had powers over elementary education only [1]).

The Act of 1902 opened a new chapter in the history of English education. It created local education authorities empowered to co-ordinate elementary and higher education, and provided what at the time was described as "the ladder from the elementary school to the university," because it rendered possible the award of scholarships for promising pupils from the elementary school. It gave the denominational schools a definite place in the system and ensured that the pupils in these schools received an education up to the standard of that provided in the council schools. It led to the provision of an adequate supply of secondary schools to which parents could send their children on payment of moderate fees. Eventually it made other developments possible; the pupil-teacher system was changed and later the secondary school ousted the pupil-teacher centre; it produced a marked increase in the number of teachers' training-colleges ; and important developments with regard to evening and technical instruction followed. At the same time, the delegation of power to local authorities made for variety and elasticity. One thing was not achieved by the Act. All through the 19th century, secondary education had been regarded as different in kind from elementary education. The idea that secondary education should be restricted to a certain class in the

[1] C. Birchenough. *History of Elementary Education in England and Wales from 1800 to the Present Day*, p. 163, U.T.P., 1938. The following example will show the difference between Part II and Part III authorities. Harrogate was a Part III authority, and its education committee was responsible for the elementary schools in the town. There were also the Harrogate Grammar School and Technical and Art schools. These came under the control of the Part II authority, the Education Committee of the West Riding of Yorkshire at Wakefield. In many cases friction was avoided by the custom of appointing the Director of Education of the Part III authority as secretary to the governors of institutions for higher education.

community gradually broke down when the scholarship system was extended as a consequence of the Act. But the Act of 1902 still regarded the secondary school as an institution of a different character. It was perhaps too much to expect, at that time, that education should be viewed in stages so that the secondary stage would be a natural sequence to the primary. The Balfour-Morant Act did not go so far as to create a national system of education, but it laid the foundation on which others would be able to build.

Strong support had been given to the Act by the Fabian Society, owing to the influence of Mr. Sidney Webb, who, whilst criticising some of the details, supported its main proposals. London had been left outside the operation of the Act, and it was largely due to the work of Sidney Webb that in 1903 the London County Council became the authority for all types of education in its area.

The Liberals were not content to acknowledge defeat. The rate conflict prophesied by Dr. Clifford and Mr. Lloyd George began. Many Nonconformists refused to pay their rates and distraint was made on their property. This campaign of passive resistance continued for many years. Looking back, one always wonders why the passive resisters did not also refuse to pay their taxes as well, since the latter provided the money from which the Government grant to the voluntary schools was paid. In Wales, certain towns refused to have anything to do with the Act and some counties decided not to pay any money from the rates to the voluntary schools. In 1904 the Government passed the Education (Local Authorities Default) Act which stated that if the L.E.A. did not make adequate grants to the voluntary schools in its area, the Board of Education would deduct an equivalent sum from its grant to the L.E.A. and pay it direct to the managers of the voluntary schools. Lloyd George threatened that if the Government put the Default Act into operation, the whole of Wales would be thrown into educational chaos, since the Welsh authorities would refuse to carry on elementary education and would close the council schools. Mr. Balfour called his bluff and applied the Act to two defaulting authorities. No action of any importance followed since it was realised by Mr. Balfour's opponents that the general public was unlikely to tolerate an action which made the school children victims of a political wrangle. When the election of 1906 was fought, the Liberals included the repeal of the Education Act of 1902, along with the Chinese Slavery and the Big and Little Loaf propaganda, as part of their political programme. The result of the election was a great landslide in favour of the Liberals and the new Prime Minister, Campbell-Bannerman, appointed Mr. Birrell as president of the Board of Education. Within a few months, Mr. Birrell presented a Bill to Parliament which was designed to meet the grievances of the Nonconformists. One of its principal clauses proposed the abolition of the voluntary schools by transferring them to the L.E.A.s. After a stormy debate the Bill went to the Lords, where it was amended so drastically that the Government refused to proceed any further with it.

Dr. Clifford wanted to force a constitutional issue with the Lords—to mend or end the House—but the Act had now been working with great success for four years and the Government thought it unwise to follow this line of action. A further attempt to reverse the 1902 policy was made by Mr. McKenna, who was president of the Board in 1908. His proposals did not satisfy the Nonconformists and roused the intense opposition of the Anglicans and Roman Catholics, who threatened in turn a campaign of passive resistance if it became law. The Government, in view of the storm it had aroused, withdrew the Bill but made a concession to the Welsh Nonconformists by establishing a Welsh Department of the Board which would be concerned with all matters of educational administration in Wales. Yet another attempt at reversal was made the same year by Mr. Runciman, who had succeeded Mr. McKenna, but the combined opposition of the Church, the Roman Catholics, and this time the teachers, who were beginning to have their say in matters which concerned them more even than the political parties, convinced him that it would be wise to withdraw his Bill. By this time Mr. Runciman and the Government realised that the Education Act of 1902 had come to stay.

CHAPTER X

THE DEVELOPMENT OF THE NATIONAL SYSTEM
1902-1944

The main educational problem during the period which began in 1870 and culminated in the Education Act of 1902, had been that of providing sufficient elementary-school places for the child population and seeing that they were filled. In the period 1902 to 1944, the centre of interest shifted to secondary education. During the last decade of the 19th century, two well-marked tendencies had been operative ; the school-leaving age had gradually risen and experiments had been carried out in the provision of new types of post-primary schools (higher-grade, higher-elementary). So far little had been done to improve either the quantity or the quality of secondary education given in endowed schools. The number of pupils attending these schools has been estimated at about 30,000 in 1895. A small proportion of elementary-school children had, by means of scholarships, entered the secondary schools ; about 2,500 in 1894 and 5,000 in 1900. Most of these scholarships were offered by local government authorities using the powers given them by the Technical Instruction Act of 1889 and the Local Taxation Act of 1890. Secondary education was still regarded as something quite distinct from elementary education, even though the emphasis on class distinctions was not quite so sharp as formerly.

The first step in the expansion of secondary education was to make more schools available. In 1903 many of the former higher-grade schools and pupil-teacher centres were taken over by the new local education authorities. When they had been under the control of the School Boards, these schools had qualified for the grants of the Science and Art Department and as a consequence had developed a curriculum with a decided scientific bias in contrast with the classical and linguistic studies of the endowed schools. Unfortunately, the Board of Education, influenced by Morant, in looking for a model for the new secondary schools of the future, decided that the public schools and the traditional grammar-schools supplied what was needed. Hence the experience gained during the previous twenty years in regard to curriculum and teaching methods was largely ignored. In the *Regulations for Secondary Schools,* 1904, the Board attempted a definition of a secondary school. Curiously enough, the only definition of an elementary school had been that given in the Act of 1870, where it was described as a school in which elementary education was the principal part of the education given and the fees did not exceed 9d. per week. In the Act of 1902, secondary and technical education was referred to as "education other than elementary." In the 1904 Regulations, a secondary school was defined as "a Day or Boarding School offering to each of its scholars up to and beyond the age of sixteen, a general education, physical, mental, and moral, given through a complete graded course of instruction, of wider scope and more advanced degree than that given in Elementary Schools." In the absence of a clear definition of an elementary school and the aims and purposes of elementary education, the above does not offer a great deal of guidance in regard to the secondary school, but when the content of secondary education is examined, it is soon apparent that the new schools were conceived along traditional lines.

The Regulations stated that to achieve a sound general education a secondary school must offer a four-year course, at least, in certain groups of subjects. These were: (1) English language and literature, with geography and history ; (2) at least one language other than English; (3) mathematics and science, both theoretical and practical ; and (4) drawing. Girls were to receive training in practical housewifery, and both boys and girls were to take some kind of manual work and physical exercises. The influence of tradition is clearly seen in the following paragraph, "Where two languages other than English are taken, and Latin is not one of them, the Board will require to be satisfied that the omission of Latin is for the advantage of the school." Thus, from the start, the secondary course was planned according to the needs of the minority who were eventually entering either the university or one of the professions, and it proved a difficult task—and one not by any means fully accomplished even now—to shake off this tradition. Indeed, the recognition of a secondary grammar type of school by the Act of 1944, tends to perpetuate the tradition for a large number of pupils. This kind of school has done valuable work in the past and still has a very important function in the future, but a more realistic and practical approach to its studies would prove an inestimable boon even to those of its scholars who have a university career in view. The description of Sanderson's work at Oundle given later in this chapter shows what may be accomplished successfully without any loss in the standard of scholarship.

The Spens Report indicates two other errors: an unreal and unnecessary division was introduced between secondary and technical education (the Bryce Commission had emphasised that in a sense all secondary education is technical), and a confusion in the meaning given to the term "general education." The latter reflected the influence of the now discarded "faculty psychology" in which Morant was a firm believer. Finally, the school course was graded according to the demands of the subject-matter rather than based upon the needs, abilities, interests, and outlook, of the pupils at different stages of their development. The schools themselves at first showed little inclination to depart from the academic tradition, and the introduction of the School Certificate Examination in 1917 which gave, under certain conditions, exemption from matriculation, tended, in spite of its many obvious advantages, to confirm them in their view.

Morant was much happier in his dealings with the elementary school, and the *Code for Public Elementary Schools* in 1904 struck an entirely new note. The introduction was written by Morant himself and shows that he had thought deeply and to good purpose. The introduction is too lengthy to quote in full, but the opening paragraph shows a completely fresh conception of the meaning of elementary education. "The purpose of the Public Elementary School is to form and strengthen the character and to develop the intelligence of the children entrusted to it, and to make the best use of the school years available, in assisting both boys and girls, according to their different needs, to fit themselves, practically as well as intellectually, for the work of life." Morant followed its publication by issuing new Regulations for training-colleges and for evening schools and technical institutes. In the former he described his ideal of the elementary-school teacher and the influence he should have. "The influence of a body of thoroughly competent, zealous, and conscientious teachers in our Public Elementary Schools may plainly be an immensely important factor in our national life, and, apart from their professional work, the teachers as a body of well-educated men and women may render services, out of all proportion to their number in the population, in the performance of the common duties of citizenship." The truth of these words was exemplified in 1939 when the teachers of both elementary and secondary schools, by their efforts and their high sense of public service, saved the evacuation scheme from the chaos into which it was falling.

Apart from efforts, already described, to secure the repeal of the Act of 1902, the events of the first five years were not spectacular. All the partners in the work of education were new and had to learn their job and get to know each other. The Board of Education soon realised the limitations of its powers and chose the path of leading rather than dictating. The new L.E.A.s got down to the business of surveying their areas and preparing schemes to remedy deficiencies, and the managers of the non-provided and endowed schools took their responsibilities seriously and did much to improve the schools under their charge. Sir Michael Sadler, who was then Professor of the History and Administration of Education in the Victoria University of Manchester, rendered most valuable service in gathering detailed information concerning the progress of education in six large boroughs and three counties.[1]

The General Election of 1906, which was a great land-slide in favour of the Liberals, for the first time brought forty members of the Labour party into Parliament. With their assistance, the Education (Provision of Meals) Act was passed which empowered L.E.A.s to arrange for the feeding of those school-children whose education was suffering because of lack of food. Where the parent was able to pay, a moderate charge was made, but in cases where the parent could not afford the cost the L.E.A. could meet the expense by levying a rate not exceeding $\frac{1}{2}$d. in the £. The following year Mr. McKenna's Education (Administration Provisions) Act introduced some very important changes.

[1] Sadler had resigned his post as Director of the Office of Special Inquiries and Reports in May 1903. This step was taken because of an irreconcilable clash between his outlook on educational matters and the views of Morant. The latter was regarded with awe and even with dislike by some of his colleagues, as Dr. Allen relates (*Sir Robert Morant*, Macmillan, 1934). He was certainly a brilliant administrator who was quite sure what he wanted, but in the achievement of his aims he displayed a certain ruthlessness and an inability to understand and sympathise with points of view other than his own. Sadler was infinitely broader in his outlook and was not prepared to tone down his reports to fit in with Morant's preconceived ideas in administration. When he was told that the work he was doing must be carried out "for the benefit of the Board, at the instance of the Board, and under the direction of the Board," he felt that the only course for him was to resign. Those, like the writer, who had in later years the privilege of serving under Sadler, realise the breadth of vision, the intimate knowledge of educational problems, the ready sympathy and power of inspiration which made Sadler the greatest educationist of his day. The two men, their characters and achievements, are described by John Graves in *Policy and Progress in Secondary Education*, 1902-24, Chapter iv, "The Clash of Ideals," Thomas Nelson and Sons, Ltd., 1943.

(1) The Act empowered the L.E.A.s "to make such arrangements as may be sanctioned by the Board of Education for attending to the health and physical condition of children in Public Elementary Schools." Morant took immediate advantage of the opportunity given. He had always been a convinced believer in the importance of the physical development of the school-child, and in the Code of 1906 had introduced organised games. Using the powers conferred by the Act, he established a medical department and succeeded in obtaining the services of Mr. (later Sir) George Newman as the Chief Medical Officer to the Board of Education. Anyone who has read Sir George Newman's annual reports until he became Chief Medical Officer to the Ministry of Health in 1919 will realise the wonderful work he accomplished through the school medical service. The Act of 1907 instituted a compulsory system of medical inspection in elementary schools, but so far the parent was not obliged to carry out the recommendations of the school doctor.

(2) A clause in the Act empowered L.E.A.s to acquire land compulsorily for the building of new secondary schools, and the raising of the secondary-school grant to £5 per head encouraged the opening of new secondary schools. By 1910 there were 980 schools on the Board's grant-lists.

(3) The provision for the establishment of a Teachers' Registration Council was referred to in Chapter ix.

(4) Last, but perhaps most important, the Board's regulations insisted that in all fee-paying secondary schools in receipt of grant, twenty-five per cent of the admissions each year were to be free places for children from elementary schools. In order to maintain the standards and efficiency of the secondary schools, candidates for free places were to be selected on the result of an attainment test designed to discover whether they were able to profit by a secondary-school education. This was the beginning of the "Scholarship Ladder to the University." In 1906 the number of scholarships was 23,500, of which 11,500 were for intending teachers. This number grew to 60,000 in 1913 and to 143,000 in 1927.

In 1911 the blow fell which deprived the Board of Education of the services of Sir Robert Morant. The circumstances were briefly as follows. Mr. E. Holmes was H.M.I. in the north of England in 1903, where he found that many of the conditions produced by the era of Payment by Results were still prevalent. Some of the inspectors of the local authorities were appointed from the ranks of elementary-school teachers who had grown up during the period in which the Revised Code was in operation and who were cramped and narrow in their outlook upon school education. When Mr. Holmes was promoted to the chief inspectorship of elementary schools in 1905, he found that the conditions of the north of England were not confined to that region alone. In a confidential report to Morant, he expressed his views at some length. He wrote, "Apart from the fact that elementary school teachers are, as a rule, uncultured and imperfectly educated, and that many—if not most—of them are creatures of tradition and routine, there are special reasons why the bulk of the local inspectors in this country should be unequal to the discharge of their responsible duties." The report was placed at the bottom of a pile of memoranda on Morant's desk and by mistake he signed it, authorising publication. The Holmes circular found its way into outside hands, including those of Sir Samuel Hoare, who saw in it an opportunity for launching an attack on the Liberal Government. The N.U.T. quite naturally resented what they considered a slur on the teaching profession, and Dr. Clifford joined in with glee to crush his old enemy. Holmes had retired before the storm burst. Morant was bitterly attacked from all sides but the Government were too conscious of the value of his services to lose him, and he was offered by Mr. Lloyd George in 1911 the appointment of chairman of the National Health Insurance Commission. Mr. Holmes, on his retirement, wrote a book, much discussed at the time, *What Is and What Might Be.* The first part, "What is, or the Path of Mechanical Obedience," embodies much of his experience as an inspector.[1]

The policy of the Board of Education before the First World War encouraged the developments already latent in the Act of 1902. It would have been a simple matter for the Board, following the routine of its predecessor the Education Department, to have issued detailed instructions concerning the syllabus of the elementary school and the methods of teaching to be employed. Morant realised the value of encouraging teachers to display initiative and to experiment with new methods of teaching. In place of attempting to impose a set syllabus on all schools, he issued, in 1905, a *Handbook of Suggestions for the Consideration of Teachers and others engaged in the Work of Public Elementary Schools.* The title was a deliberate choice, and although from a present-day

[1] Edmond Holmes. *What is and What Might Be,* Constable, 1911.

standpoint much of the book would be considered out of date, based as it was upon a faculty psychology, yet its issue was momentous because for the first time it gave the teacher freedom to try to work out his job in his own way.[1] This purpose was distinctly stated in the preface: "The only uniformity of practice that the Board of Education desire to see in the teaching of Public Elementary Schools is that each teacher shall think for himself, and work out for himself such methods of teaching as may use his powers to the best advantage and be best suited to the particular needs and conditions of the school. Uniformity in details of practice . . . is not desirable even if it were attainable. But freedom implies a corresponding responsibility in its use.

"Teachers who use the book should therefore treat it as an aid to reviewing their aims and practice, and as a challenge to independent thought on such matters."

One of the most important consequences of the Education Act of 1902 was the attention given to the training of intending teachers. The pupil-teacher system, even as amended by the establishment of pupil-teacher centres and the reduction of the period of apprenticeship to three years in 1900, was still the target for a good deal of criticism. The Board of Education raised the minimum age for pupil-teachers to sixteen (fifteen in rural districts) and reduced the normal period of apprenticeship to two years. Half of the pupil-teacher's time was to be spent in receiving instruction at a centre, which might be attached to a secondary or higher-elementary school. This stipulation was to ensure a more liberal education for him and to prevent cramming for examinations. The remainder of his time was to be spent in teaching or observing teaching. No school was normally permitted to receive more than four pupil-teachers at a time, and each school employing pupil-teachers had to be certified by an inspector as fit for training them.

The Board proposed an alternative to the pupil-teacher system. Any secondary-school pupil who had received instruction in the school for not less than two years (raised to three in 1910) and who

---

[1] The influence of faculty psychology may be seen in such phrases as the following: "The process of teaching, therefore, involves a careful development of the faculties of the child"; "enforcement of attention and training of memory are among the essentials of education"; "in the lower classes teaching about common things will be directed mainly to cultivating exact observation. . . . In the higher classes . . . the main purpose of the lessons is to exercise the scholars in reflecting and reasoning upon the results of their own direct observation"; "the search for natural laws belongs to a later stage of mental discipline."

A comparison of the *Suggestions* of 1905 with those of 1937 will reveal a complete change of attitude.

wished to become a teacher, could claim a bursary for a year and then either serve for another year as a student-teacher or pass direct to the training-college. Many L.E.A.s adopted this alternative scheme, and the number of pupil-teachers declined sharply after 1907. The whole problem of intending teachers was raised again in 1923 when Lord Burnham's Committee gave the opinion that the normal means of entry to the profession should be through the secondary school. In urban districts, pupil-teachers' centres were to be abolished, but they might be allowed to continue provisionally in rural areas where no secondary school was available. By 1938 the number of pupil-teachers in centres had fallen to 51, and rural pupil-teachers to 287. There were also 545 student-teachers recognised by the Board. In 1907 the King's Scholarship examination, which had been the entrance examination for all training-colleges except those which were an integral part of an institution of university status, was abolished. Its place was taken by the preliminary examination for the elementary-school teachers' certificate. Bursars disappeared after 1921 and, with the decline in the numbers of pupil and student teachers, the usual practice was for the intending teacher to pass direct from the secondary school to the training-college.[1]

By the end of the 19th century the training-college accommodation, even when supplemented by the day training-colleges connected with university institutions, had become quite inadequate. By 1902 the number of children in average attendance at elementary schools had risen to 5,030,219, but the annual output of trained teachers was only 2,791. In 1904 separate *Training-College Regulations* were issued. They had formerly been part of the Code. This was an opportunity for the Board to tighten its control over the training-colleges and to raise the standards of the staff and the curriculum. At the same time, the declaration signed by the entrant was made more specific. Each student gave an undertaking that, in the case of a man, he would serve, for seven years in the first ten after leaving college, in a school which received grants from the state, or in a training-college. The woman student pledged herself to serve five years in the first eight after leaving college.

For the first time, L.E.A.s were encouraged to develop their own training-colleges and received a building-grant in aid. Later, the grant was extended to cover erection of hostels in connection

[1] In 1938 ninety-three per cent of training-college students came from secondary schools.

with the training-departments of the universities and university colleges. L.E.A.s quickly took advantage of this offer, and the first municipal colleges to be opened were those at Sheffield, Hereford, Graystoke Place, Avery Hill, and Southampton Row. The last three were erected by the London County Council. Following these, the City of Leeds Training-College, the Bingley Training-College for the West Riding, and the Hull and Swansea Municipal Colleges were opened. The City of Leeds Training-College is now one of the largest in the kingdom. By 1938 there were twenty-eight colleges provided by local authorities, including seven for domestic subjects. Some of the new colleges were wholly residential; others partly residential, or similar to the day training-colleges.

These changes have resulted in the widening of the curriculum of the training-colleges, the raising of standards, and the increased attention that can now be given to the professional training of the teacher. There was, at first, a danger that the bulk of the students in the municipal training-colleges would be drawn from the locality, but this was avoided by the local authorities themselves, who only allowed a proportion of their own students to occupy places, and encouraged those from other districts to apply for entrance. The Act of 1902 placed the "Model" schools under the control of the L.E.A.s instead of the training-colleges. In 1909 a regulation of the Board required every training-college to have a "demonstration" school for "the purpose of illustrating the most approved and successful methods of school organisation, discipline, and instruction." The scheme was not always satisfactory. In some districts the L.E.A. co-operated with the college and allowed its authorities considerable power in choosing the staff and planning the curriculum of the demonstration school. In other districts such co-operation was lacking and the so-called demonstration school was of little value for the purpose of training.

One of the most important developments in the training-college curriculum was the introduction of such studies as hygiene, physical training, art, handicrafts, gardening, music, and needlework (for women). In many of these subjects it was difficult to assess the progress of students by means of a written examination, and colleges were instructed to group them according to their proficiency. The inspector could sample the work displayed in different groups and ensure a uniform standard of grouping. The number of students reading for degrees in university departments of education increased rapidly, and training-colleges were encouraged to select their most able students for a third year of training. Those chosen specialised in the study and teaching of one or more subjects. In 1908 the Board began to pay grants for the training of secondary-school teachers. The majority of teachers in secondary schools had hitherto been untrained. The usual system was to award a fourth year of training to those graduates who wished to enter the teaching profession. After 1921 the four-year course became the normal at universities, and the handicap the graduate student suffered by having to read for his degree and take his professional training all in the space of three years was removed.

Such students fell into three classes: (1) recognised four-year students, who received a grant for the whole period they spent in the university training-department; (2) recognised one-year students, who receive a grant for their post-graduate year only ; and (3) recognised fee-paying students, who did not receive a grant, but were certificated if they passed through the training-course successfully. In most universities all these students were prepared for the university diploma in education, success in which included the award of the Teachers' Certificate. At Cambridge a certificate was awarded in place of a diploma. The result of these changes was that the number of trained teachers in secondary schools rose rapidly, and at the present time they greatly outnumber those who have not been trained. Many of the graduate teachers entered elementary and higher-elementary schools, so that it became common for these schools to have a number of graduates on their staffs.

The Cockerton judgment had revealed the illegal position occupied by higher-grade schools, and, in order to legalise schools giving advanced forms of elementary education, the Board, in a Minute for the year 1900, recognised the existence of higher-elementary schools for pupils attending a four-year course between the ages of ten and fifteen. Such schools were the forerunners of the central schools established some years later. At this time the policy of the Board was to discourage the development of higher-elementary schools, and most L.E.A.s preferred to experiment along other lines. Thus London (1911) and Manchester (1912) adopted the central-school system into which higher-elementary schools were absorbed. The central school provided a full-time general education for pupils up to the age of fifteen, with the object of enabling them to enter trade and industry immediately after leaving school, without the necessity of undergoing any additional course of

training. The curriculum of the central school had a commercial
or industrial bias without being technical in the narrower sense.
Some authorities preferred to develop day trade schools or junior
technical schools.

At the same time, experiments were being carried out with
regard to the education of younger children. Although the Code
of 1905 contained many progressive suggestions concerning the
work of the infant-school, the Board on the whole deprecated the
attendance of children under five and left L.E.A.s free to refuse
them admittance. In 1907 the Consultative Committee was asked
to investigate the problem of schools for children under five. In
their report in 1908, the Committee submitted evidence from France,
Germany, and Switzerland, and, although they concluded that on
account of industrial and social conditions in various parts of
England nursery schools in such districts were a necessity, they
did not think it advisable to change the lower limit of school
attendance. No action was taken to carry out the proposals of
the report until the Education Act of 1918, and nursery schools
were not eligible for grant, although grants were given to day
nurseries in 1914. Meanwhile, nursery schools were opened by
voluntary effort in several large towns. The best-known example
was the school established at Deptford in 1911 by the sisters Rachel
and Margaret McMillan, who may justly be regarded as the founders
of the nursery-school movement.

Margaret McMillan had been a member of the Bradford School
Board which, as the reader will remember, had been a pioneer in
the provision of the school medical services. She believed so
thoroughly in the necessity of this work that she did all in her power
to convince the public that compulsory medical inspection of school-
children was essential to the creation of a healthy nation. Dr.
Allen, in his life of Sir Robert Morant, tells us that when the school
medical service was instituted in 1907 Morant had consulted Margaret McMillan before he decided upon the details of the scheme.
He wrote to her on the occasion of the publication of Sir George
Newman's first report, "This is the *first* clear proof of the *first*
Annual Report of the *first* National System of School Medical
Inspection that this country has known ; and I cannot resist giving
myself the pleasure of sending it, in confidence, to yourself ; for
you are to me the person who has most signally and most successfully embodied in a private individual the best enthusiasm and the
most warming faith both in the possibilities of a Medical Inspection

and in the potentialities of a real honest preventive conscience in the state and in the people." [1]

Rachel and Margaret McMillan opened their first school clinic at Bow in 1908. The example they set was imitated in all parts of the country, and the school clinics were instrumental not only in dealing with minor ailments but also in giving treatment for more serious afflictions of the nose, ears, and throat. From the beginning the McMillan sisters welcomed children under five at their clinic. The clinic was moved to Deptford in 1910. The experience of the McMillans convinced them that to obtain the optimum benefit the clinic should concentrate on preventive measures rather than treat ailments when they had fully developed, and gradually the idea came to them that the conditions of the open-air nursery school provided what they were seeking. With the aid of voluntary subscriptions they started their first nursery school at Deptford in 1911. The London County Council was interested in the experiment, and provided them with a site for a larger school in the early months of 1914.

Unfortunately, progress was seriously hampered by the outbreak of war. Staff was difficult to obtain, and financial difficulties absorbed the time and the strength of the sisters. These eventually brought about Rachel McMillan's illness and death in 1917. She lived long enough to see her principles approved by Mr. Fisher, the president of the Board of Education, and it was he who a few months after her death formally opened the enlarged premises.

The McMillans firmly believed in Locke's dictum that one of the principal aims of education is the creation of a healthy mind in a healthy body. Hence there were two aspects of the nursery-school movement. On the one hand, the services of a band of trained nurses and doctors were considered essential. On the other, the children would be under the care of a trained teacher who would make use of what was best in the Froebelian and Montessori principles. The nursery school was an open-air institution. Margaret McMillan wrote: "Children want space at all ages. But from the age of one to seven, space, that is ample space, is almost as much wanted as food and air. To move, to run, to find things out by new movement, to 'feel one's life in every limb,' that is the life of early childhood. And yet one sees already dim houses, behind whose windows and doors thirty or forty little ones are penned in

---

[1] *Sir Robert Morant*, p. 233, Macmillan, 1934.

'Day Nurseries.' Bare sites and open spaces are what we need today." [1]

Great importance was attached to the garden, in which there were trees and shrubs, a flower garden and lawn, a herb and kitchen garden, and a greenhouse. Children were in the garden whenever the weather was fine, playing and engaged with their simple occupations. In winter and during stormy weather the children were in shelters; the McMillans avoided using the term "classroom." The shelters were open to the air, but could be closed on the rare occasions when the weather made it absolutely necessary. The open sides of the shelter faced away from the wind, the effects of which were broken by carefully arranged terraces.

Children arrived at the nursery school at 8 a.m., and were given three meals a day. They remained until 5 or 5.30 p.m. After lunch came a rest-period and each child lay on his tiny stretcher-bed to rest and sleep. The McMillans realised the value of sleep in a child's life. Unless the weather was inclement, the rest-period was passed in the open air. Inside the shelters there was little which resembled the formal classroom. Low tables and chairs took the place of desks, and everything was arranged to give the maximum amount of space. When not in use, the stretchers were packed away in built-in cupboards. The whole atmosphere of the shelter was to be "home life, not school life as we know it. Low chairs for the nurse, who is mother and sister for the time; pictures and prettily coloured walls and light, musical instruments, flowers, and an atmosphere of joy and love." [2]

The McMillans did not agree with the Consultative Committee's Report of 1908 which recommended nursery schools for children from poorer homes only. They believed that such institutions were necessary in an equal degree for those who came from well-to-do homes. "Nurseries and Nursery Schools are wanted simply because little children want nurses. They, being children, need that very important kind of early education called nurture. Can this be given, and given entirely by, let us say, the average mother? The well-to-do mother never attempts to do it alone. She engages a nurse, perhaps also a governess, perhaps a schoolroom maid; a great many engage a cook, also a housemaid. All these mother-helps work in a spacious house, with probably a free garden." [3] Hence, Rachel McMillan wrote: "The open-air Nursery School is

[1] Margaret McMillan. *The Nursery School*, pp. 10-11 (revised edition), J. M. Dent, 1930.   [2] *Ibid.*, pp. 20-1.   [3] *Ibid.*, p. 6.

here for rich and poor. It is here, the thing, lacking which, our whole educational system was like a house built on the sand."[1]

Progress had also taken place in infant-school methods through a more intelligent use of the Froebelian conception of free activity and the introduction of individual occupations due to the influence of Dr. Montessori. The latter had been an assistant in the clinic of psychiatry in the University of Rome, and later she came to develop an interest in the education of mentally defective children. She had been influenced by the ideas of J. Itard and E. Seguin, two Parisian physicians of the first half of the 19th century who had paid special attention to the treatment of feeble-minded children. It was from these sources that Dr. Montessori obtained the suggestions which led to the construction of her didactic apparatus. The results she obtained, when teaching mental defectives, convinced her that similar methods would be equally beneficial in the training of normal children. She had the opportunity of testing this in 1906, and, as a consequence of the success which followed her methods, opened the first of her "children's houses" in the following year. Her chief work was translated into English in 1912, under the title of *The Montessori Method,* and brought her ideas to the notice of the English and American publics.

It is not the function of a work of this kind to give a detailed account of the didactic apparatus. The aim of this material was to provide a thorough and scientific training in sensory discrimination. Unfortunately, Dr. Montessori was a believer in the faculty psychology and its corollary that formal sense-training is both necessary and possible and can be carried out by special exercises designed for the purpose. If this had been Dr. Montessori's only contribution to education it would have been of very doubtful value. It is now generally agreed that sensory training is best carried out through play and through activities and occupations which naturally occur in the daily life of the child.

The essence of her system was the importance which she attached to the concept of freedom, although even in this she has been misunderstood. In her view, freedom is not to be confused with anarchy. The principle of freedom in the Montessori system "appears to include (1) that we are to provide full opportunity for the exercise of the child's motor activities so far as they are not anti-social, and (2) that while we are to repress anti-social activities,

[1] Margaret McMillan. *The Nursery School,* p. 113 (revised edition), J. M. Dent, 1930.

we are to do so with as little conflict as possible between the child's will and our will. . . . The child is to develop his own powers through his own experience, as free as possible from the domination of a superior mind. This is not only because we thus avoid the conflict of wills with its antagonisms and emotions, but also because we get the child into the habit of depending on his own mental powers rather than on the assistance of the teacher."[1] Hence the teacher is to be regarded, not as an instructor, but as a source of guidance, direction, and inspiration.

The Montessori school, like the McMillan nursery school, took a more complete charge of the children than the ordinary school. The children were taught to wash themselves, brush their teeth, and generally to keep themselves tidy. As they attended school for the whole day, lunch was provided, and the children learnt valuable lessons in setting tables, in behaviour during meals, and in clearing away and washing up. The desks of the ordinary classroom were replaced by light tables and chairs which could be easily moved by the children themselves so as to make a space for their spontaneous activities. The didactic material and toys were stored in low cupboards within easy reach of the children, and each child was free to select his own material and play with it how and as long as he liked, provided that he did not interfere with the freedom of other children to do the same. The role of the teacher was to suggest rather than to command.

During the period we are reviewing, the social and moral welfare of the child received much attention. The earlier factory legislation has already been mentioned. During the Victorian era, more than a hundred Acts of Parliament were passed (excluding Education Acts) which directly or indirectly were concerned with the protection or welfare of the child. Thus in 1878 children under ten were debarred from employment in factories, and those under thirteen who were employed were under an obligation to attend school either one session per day throughout the week or one full day on alternate days. The age of employment was raised to twelve in 1901 and remained so until the Education Act of 1918. The Employment of Children Act of 1903 empowered local authorities to fix the minimum age at which children could be employed out of school-hours and the total number of hours per day and per week beyond which employment was illegal. The Act also

---

[1] E. P. Culverwell. *The Montessori Principle and Practice*, p. 174, G. Bell and Sons, Ltd., 1913.

regulated the conditions under which children could engage in street trading, *e.g.* selling newspapers, and it empowered local authorities to fix a minimum age for this. The Prevention of Cruelty to Children Act of 1904 still further restricted the employment of children and fixed heavy penalties for adults who evaded the Act.

Perhaps the most important legislation of the pre-war period was the Children's Act of 1908, which for a long time was known as the Children's Charter. It was a very comprehensive piece of legislation which dealt with such subjects as the prevention of cruelty to children, juvenile smoking (it was made illegal for any young person under sixteen to smoke), reformatory schools, industrial schools, and children's courts. Before this time, juvenile offenders had been tried in the ordinary police courts. The idea of special children's courts was first tried out in the United States, where such a court was established in Chicago in 1899. Several experiments were attempted in England, and the Children's Act provided that all juvenile offenders who were charged should be dealt with in a different building or room from that in which ordinary court proceedings were held, or at different times, or on different days. The idea was to prevent children from coming into contact with adult offenders. Only persons directly concerned with the case were allowed to be present, unless specially authorised by the magistrate. Liverpool was the first English city to provide a special children's court. A further Act, the Juvenile Courts Metropolis Act of 1920, provided for the appointment of special magistrates in London who had experience and qualifications for dealing with juvenile offenders.

The Probation Act of 1907 gave power to magistrates to use their discretion with regard to dismissing cases when the offence was trifling or the age of the culprit, or other circumstances, rendered this the most suitable way of dealing with the offender. Such cases were to be placed under the supervision of a Probation Officer for not more than three years. The latter might be a salaried official or a volunteer probation officer associated with some religious or philanthropic institution, *e.g.* an officer of the N.S.P.C.C., a leader of a boys' or girls' club, a Church worker, or a Sunday School teacher.

The Children's Act instituted "remand homes," which served the dual purpose of accommodating those children who were awaiting trial and those who were waiting until a suitable school could be found for them. The maximum time for which a child could be retained in a remand home was one month. No child could be sentenced to imprisonment, and a young person could only be committed if he was so badly behaved that it was impossible to keep him in an ordinary institution. Juvenile offenders, on conviction, might be sent by the court to an "industrial" or a "reformatory" school. The former fulfilled the double function of acting as a reformatory for those who had committed less serious offences and had not become habitual delinquents, and as an institution for providing a training for children whose home life, because of the criminal or intemperate habits of the parents, was deemed unsuitable. The reformatory provided for young persons between fourteen and sixteen who had been convicted of an offence that in the case of an adult would have been punished by a term of imprisonment. Children between twelve and fourteen who had been convicted of a similar offence for the second time, and industrial-school children whose behaviour was such that they could not be retained in the school might also be committed to a reformatory.

Such institutions might be certified or uncertified. The Home Office encouraged private persons to experiment with schemes for re-educating delinquents. One of the best-known private institutions was the Little Commonwealth in Dorsetshire, which was under the charge of Homer Lane. The Little Commonwealth was a co-educational community which aimed at developing in its members the ideal of self-discipline. Homer Lane insisted that the community should have freedom to make and enforce its own laws. The disapproval of the community was the only sanction which the law-breaker encountered, and when he found that there was no authority but that of his fellows, the anti-social child discovered that no glory was to be gained by defying rules he had helped to make. Thus, instead of breaking, he made and enforced laws. Such communities had been established in the United States, and it was their success that induced Mr. George Montagu (afterwards the Earl of Sandwich) to experiment with the idea in this country. Mr. Lane, who had acquired a successful reputation for his work in the Ford Republic in America, was asked to come to England in 1913 to take charge of the experiment. Its failure in 1918 was one of those unfortunate circumstances which casts no reflection upon Homer Lane or the ideals which inspired the community. In fact, similar ideals have proved most successful with younger children in such experiments as those carried out by the Caldecott Community.

The Children's Act of 1908 represented a considerable advance in dealing with the problem of delinquents, but it left certain important questions untouched. Thus the distinction between industrial schools and reformatories was fast losing all meaning and value. It was also felt that the question of supervision when the young person had left school, and the finding of suitable employment for him, had not received sufficient attention. These defects were remedied by the Children and Young Persons Acts, 1933 and 1938. Children were defined as those persons under fourteen years of age, and young persons as those between fourteen and seventeen. The courts were given power to remove from their homes all children who had broken the law, or who were out of control, or who stood in need of care and protection. No child under eight years of age could be charged with an offence. The juvenile court was given authority to order that young people in the above categories could either be sent to an "approved" school, *i.e.* a school approved by the Secretary of State for the purposes of education and training, or they could be committed to the care of a fit person who was willing to receive them. Local authorities were recognised as fit persons for this purpose. They were empowered to maintain their own approved schools, which were to be classified, according to the age of the pupils, into "junior," "intermediate," and "senior" schools. Further developments under the Children Act of 1948 will be mentioned in the following chapter.

These experiments were held up for four years by the outbreak of the First World War in 1914. As increasing numbers of men were needed for the Forces, the schools became gradually depleted of their men teachers. Some women teachers also obtained leave of absence to serve in nursing units or in the women's auxiliary services. As a consequence of under-staffing, classes became larger and many boys' schools were taught almost entirely by women teachers. Conscription was introduced in 1917 and all men under thirty-one and in medical categories A-1 and B-1 were called to the colours. Teachers of a lower medical category who were on home service were released to take up their school duties again. The severe fighting of 1917-18 stepped up the service demands so that all men in A-1 category under forty-five, and B-1 men under thirty-six, were called upon to serve. Approximately half the male teachers in the country were absent on war service. Retired teachers, married women who had previously been teachers, clergy, and others who had sufficient educational attainments, volunteered to teach in the schools during the emergency. Further dislocation was caused by the requisition of school premises as billets for the troops, and many schools had to use places of worship, Sunday Schools, and public halls, as school accommodation. Certain schools and colleges were used as hospitals or for the accommodation of refugee children from the Continent.[1] It is idle to pretend that the efficiency of the schools did not suffer under these straits, but both teachers and scholars made a magnificent contribution to national service. The children assisted in the War Savings effort through the Elementary Schools Savings Associations. There had been a penny bank in connection with most schools for a large number of years. In School Board days a school bank had existed in Leeds since 1874. In 1891 the Leeds School Board entered into an arrangement with the Yorkshire Penny Bank whereby a bank was established in every school. Similar arrangements were working in most areas by the end of the century. The purpose of the school bank was to encourage the children in habits of regular savings. Pupils brought their contributions to school each Monday morning and accumulated deposits which could be drawn upon for holidays and in emergencies.

In Leeds, in 1890, there were 9,915 school accounts, and the sum deposited from 1890 to 1926 amounted to £1,747,143 8s. 10d. In 1916 War Savings Certificates were introduced and could be purchased through the school bank. During the war, Leeds children bought Savings Certificates to the value of £52,233 9s. 0d. The War Savings Associations were continued as a permanency and thus were able to render valuable service once more during the Second World War.

During the war of 1914-18, encouragement was given to the establishment of school gardens and allotments, which produced valuable food at a time when supplies were restricted by submarine warfare. Teachers and pupils collected wild fruits for jam, and horse-chestnuts which were used in the manufacture of anti-gas masks. Through the Scouts and Guides, older children were able to perform some important public services. The shortage of food was so great towards the closing stages of the war that the Board allowed children of school age to be excused attendance for a limited period to assist in agricultural and other work. The absence of fathers on military service and of many mothers on munition work resulted in a relaxation of parental control and the growth of hooliganism and juvenile delinquency. The Government encouraged

[1] Thus in both World Wars the Leeds City Training-College was used as a military hospital.

education authorities and voluntary associations in the establishment of play-centres for children in order to keep them off the streets and out of mischief and to provide them with opportunities for organised play and healthy recreation.

Well before the conclusion of hostilities the Government had been giving serious thought to the work of post-war reconstruction, and in 1916 the Ministry of Reconstruction was constituted to prepare schemes for the transition from war to peace. Education occupied a prominent place in the deliberations of the Ministry because the war had revealed many of the inadequacies of the national system. When Mr. Lloyd George considered the time ripe for a reorganisation of national education, he decided to secure the services of a well-known scholar as president of the Board of Education. Mr. H. A. L. Fisher, a distinguished Oxford historian who had been appointed Vice-Chancellor of the University of Sheffield, was chosen for this position and given the services of a number of men who possessed expert educational knowledge and technical experience. For the first and only time in our history a distinguished scholar was given the opportunity of overhauling the national system, and the results of his planning, as seen in the Education Act of 1918, justified the Prime Minister's choice.

The striking feature of the Act of 1918 was the attempt to place the onus of reconstruction on the local authorities and to rely on their public spirit and initiative to carry through the proposals in the way that was intended. Mr. Fisher had thought of increasing the powers of the Board of Education so that laggard and reluctant authorities could be compelled to put the Act into operation. At the same time he considered that some of the Part III authorities should be merged with the county councils. These proposals had appeared in the Bill of 1917, but they awakened so much opposition that Mr. Fisher did not consider it worth while imperilling the acceptance of the measure by insisting on the administrative clauses. Thus the administrative framework of 1902 was retained, but the powers of the local authorities received a definite extension. Much of the legislation was permissive instead of being mandatory, and therein lay the weakness. It was possible for certain educational services to be obligatory in one district and not in another; thus the provision of continuation schools was compulsory in the area of the London County Council, but not in some of the surrounding districts. Barnard blames post-war financial stringency as the cause of the ineffectiveness of the main provisions of the Act.[1] The "Geddes Axe" is, however, only part of the story, and the clean sweep it made was facilitated by administrative weaknesses in the Act itself. The powers of the L.E.A.s had been augmented, but those of the Board of Education remained as nebulous as before. Another weakness of the Act was that the dislocation caused by the war prevented its main clauses from coming into operation immediately. The reconstruction contemplated involved building a large number of new schools and obtaining an adequate supply of trained teachers suitable for the particular work they would be required to undertake. The author remembers being present at a discussion of officials of the Board, where the main objects for consideration were the extent to which existing buildings could be improvised for continuation schools until new buildings were ready, and what potential supplies of teachers existed to carry on the work until a sufficient number of new entrants to the profession could be obtained and trained. He recollects well the enthusiastic spirit with which major difficulties were attacked and demolished. The fact remained, however, that the dates on which the various clauses of the Act would come into operation could not be stated.

The purpose of the Act, as given in its opening clause, was to establish a national system of education available for all persons capable of profiting thereby. Hence "It shall be the duty of the council of every county and county borough, so far as their powers extend, to contribute thereto by providing for the progressive development and comprehensive organisation of education in respect of their area, and with that object any such council from time to time may, and shall when required by the Board of Education, submit to the Board schemes showing the mode in which their duties and powers under the Education Acts are to be performed and exercised, whether separately or in co-operation with other authorities" (Clause 1). The L.E.A.s were directed to use the powers conferred on them by the Act of 1902 to provide by means of central schools or classes, practical instruction suitable to the ages, abilities, and requirements of the children, and to organise advanced instruction for the older and more intelligent pupils who remained at school after the age of fourteen; to provide for adequate attention being given to the health and physical condition of children

[1] H. C. Barnard. *A Short History of English Education, 1760-1944* p. 274, University of London Press, 1947.

attending public elementary schools; and to co-operate with other authorities with regard to the preparation of children for further education in schools other than elementary and their transference at suitable ages to these schools, and to make arrangements for the supply and training of teachers.

It was evident that the term "elementary education" was becoming obsolete, since, to avoid the repetition of anything resembling the Cockerton judgment, the definition of the elementary school as given in the Act of 1870 was not to apply to the above advanced courses of instruction.

The period of compulsory full-time attendance at school was to be from the age of five to fourteen. A pupil could not leave school until the last day of the term in which his fourteenth birthday occurred. A local authority had the power to enact a by-law to raise the school-leaving age to fifteen. The system of "half-timers," which had been gradually disappearing, was to be abolished from 1st July 1922.[1]

Pupils who left school at the age of fourteen would be required to attend a continuation school for 320 hours in each year. The distribution of the hours was left to the discretion of the local authorities, who would have regard to the circumstances of the district. Thus it might be convenient in an urban district for pupils to attend for one whole day or two half days a week, but in a rural area a block attendance of several weeks at a time might be desirable. L.E.A.s would be required to submit to the Board schemes for the progressive organisation of a system of continuation schools in their areas. Pupils in full-time attendance at secondary or technical schools were exempt from this part of the Act provided they remained at school until sixteen and passed matriculation or an equivalent examination. For the first seven years after this part of the Act came into operation, attendance at a continuation school would be required until sixteen years of age, but after that period compulsory attendance would be extended to eighteen. All fees in elementary schools were abolished.

The Act amended the law in regard to the employment of children. No child under twelve could be employed, and the employment of those over twelve was limited to two hours on Sundays, and on school days a child could not be employed before

---

[1] Half-time scholars in Leeds numbered 1,264 in 1860. The number had fallen progressively: in 1890 there were 846; in 1900, 61; in 1902, 44; and in 1915 there were only five.

the close of school, nor on any day before six o'clock in the morning, nor after eight o'clock in the evening.   Local authorities were empowered to enact by-laws permitting children over twelve to be employed on a school day before 9 a.m. for one hour, provided also that the same child should not be employed for more than one hour in the afternoon.   In many towns the by-law enabled news-agents to employ children for the delivery of the morning papers.   No child of school age was permitted to be employed in factories, mines, or in street-trading.   This clause put an end to the selling of newspapers by boys in the streets.   Children might be employed to take part in entertainments, e.g. in a pantomime, under a licence issued by the L.E.A.   The powers and duties of L.E.A.s were extended with regard to the provision of facilities for physical training and organised games, holiday camps, and facilities for social and physical training in the day or evening. In provided schools, medical inspection and treatment was extended to secondary pupils, but was to be optional in aided schools. Permission was given to local authorities to open nursery schools or classes where they were necessary and desirable, and such schools, if open to inspection, would be able to receive a grant.

The Elementary Education (Defective and Epileptic Children) Act of 1914 had made the provisions of the Act of 1899 obligatory. Accommodation was to be provided for mentally defective and epileptic children.   The Act of 1918 extended this to include physically defective children.

Power was given to local authorities to pay maintenance grants to pupils holding scholarships at secondary schools, so that a child who had the ability to profit from a secondary education should not to be held back through poverty.   The dual system was retained but managers of non-provided schools might group them if they found it desirable.   All private schools were to be registered and open to inspection by the Board and the L.E.A.   The worst abuses of private-adventure schools had disappeared, largely through the progressive enlightenment of public opinion, but there still remained a number of private schools which were inadequate either as regards buildings or in the quality of the instruction they gave.

The system of grant payment to L.E.A.s was entirely revised. In the 19th century, grants had been made for specific purposes or for specific subjects taught in the schools.   The grant procedure had been simplified in 1902, but since that time the rapid increase of education expenditure had been throwing a heavy burden on the rates, and a percentage plan was introduced. It depended on the principle that the State and the L.E.A. should each pay half of the net approved expenditure of the L.E.A. on higher education. The income of the L.E.A., mainly from fees and sale of work and produce, was first deducted from the gross expenditure. Half of the expenditure was met from the rates and the other half by a grant which was termed the Deficiency Grant. As the State was already paying more than half of the expenditure on elementary education, the grant only applied to higher education. A more complicated percentage formula was devised for calculating the elementary grant. In order that administrators would be able to apply the existing law on education more easily, a consolidating measure, the Education Act of 1921, was passed. It included the Act of 1918 and clauses of earlier Acts which had not been repealed.

Mr. Fisher realised the importance of attracting to the teaching profession the right type of person. As long as the salaries of teachers were inadequate, people of ability and character would be attracted elsewhere. Some people believed that teachers should be civil servants, but it was considered that the withdrawal of the control of teachers from the local authorities would destroy the whole framework of the system developed since 1902. Teaching had always been poorly remunerated as compared with other professions, although the average salary of certificated teachers had been gradually improved.

The cost of living in 1918 was more than double that of 1914. There was no standard scale, and wealthy and progressive authorities, by paying higher salaries, were always able to attract the best-qualified teachers. In secondary schools graduate assistant masters might receive anything between £120 and £200 per annum. The salaries of elementary school certificated assistants averaged £167 (men) and £123 (women) in 1918. This represented an increase on 1870 when the figures were £94 and £57 respectively, but it was not sufficient to meet the cost of living under post-war conditions. The Board issued a minimum scale of salaries in 1917 and gave a supplementary grant for elementary education to improve the salaries of teachers. As a result of the report of a departmental committee and of negotiations with the teachers' associations, the Burnham Committee of 1919 was constituted. Under the chairmanship of Lord Burnham, it comprised representatives of the education authorities and the National Union of Teachers. Three standard scales were authorised for different areas, and later a fourth scale for London and a number of metro-politan authorities, which was higher than the provincial scales owing to the additional cost of travel and living in the metropolitan area. Similar scales were constructed for teachers in secondary and technical schools, and all the new scales came into force in 1921. The scales cannot be said to have offered a generous remuneration, but they eased the teachers' financial problems considerably. Thus the average salaries of men and women certificated teachers had risen in 1923 to £310 and £254 respectively. Extra increments on the scales were given for additional years of training and for a first degree, but one major criticism was that no reward was available for the teacher who obtained further qualifications. Immediately the scales came into operation, the serious condition of the national finances called for reduction of expenditure, and in 1922 the teachers agreed to a five per cent voluntary cut in salary. Other small adjustments, such as the abolition of Scale I in 1936, were made, but the principles of the original Burnham Scale remained in operation at the outbreak of the Second World War.

The superannuation of teachers was bound up with the problem of salaries. The pension scheme instituted by Kay-Shuttleworth had been withdrawn at the time of the Revised Code, and teachers in endowed schools had never received any form of State pension. The Teachers' Superannuation Act of 1898 offered a contributory deferred annuity scheme, and after 1902 some authorities allowed teachers to participate in the superannuation schemes devised for their officials. Mr. Fisher's Superannuation Act of 1918 included all teachers in grant-earning schools except those in universities and similar institutions which had adopted their own federated schemes. At first the scheme was a non-contributory one, but the financial stringency of 1922 necessitated an amendment by which teachers were obliged to pay five per cent of their salaries towards superannuation. To benefit under the scheme the teacher must have reached the age of sixty and have spent thirty years in approved service, of which at least ten years must have been recognised service. Other forms of teaching, e.g. in a university, counted as qualifying but not as recognised service. The superannuation consisted of an annual pension equivalent to one-eightieth of the salary in respect of each complete year of recognised service or a half of the average salary of the last five years, whichever was

less, and a lump sum calculated on a similar basis.   Further Superannuation Acts in 1925 and 1937 dealt with certain anomalies and
extended the provisions to include recognition of service in Scotland
and overseas.

The slump in trade, the increase in unemployment, and the
financial difficulties which followed the boom years immediately
after the war, caused the appointment of the Geddes Committee on
National Expenditure.   Education was one of the services which
came under review, and various measures of economy were introduced which called a halt to forward progress.   The developments
planned by the author of the 1918 Act were curtailed or postponed,
and in particular the scheme for establishing continuation schools
on a compulsory basis was left to the local authorities to make
attendance voluntary or compulsory as they wished.   The L.C.C.
and some other authorities went ahead bravely enough with a
compulsory scheme.   They soon found themselves pitted against
immense difficulties in the way of obtaining the necessary buildings
and suitable teachers.   Many buildings designed for other uses
were employed as schools, and the author remembers one case where
a working-men's club was utilised as a school, the bar being carefully covered up in the day-time.   Further difficulties were created
by the attitude of some employers.   Some saw the benefits of
further education and, in voluntary areas, encouraged their boys and
girls to attend school.   Others grudged the time the young people
were absent from employment in order to attend school.   Thus,
for some distance, the Edgware Road constituted the boundary
between London and Middlesex.   Young people applying for posts
were often asked where they lived.   If their homes were in the
London area where attendance at a continuation school was compulsory, some employers refused to consider their applications
further.   One by one, the local authorities dropped compulsion
and established the schools on a voluntary basis.   After some years
the majority of authorities abandoned the idea altogether, although
some large industrial undertakings established continuation schools
for their employees.   Rugby was the only district in which the Act
was fully carried out, and continuation schools have been retained
until the present time.

In 1924 the Labour party came into power for a brief period
and progress was resumed.   Dr. Tawney had for some years
advocated "secondary education for all" but had carefully defined
what he meant by secondary education.   He wrote: "The Labour

Party is convinced that the only policy which is at once educationally sound and suited to a democratic community is one under which
primary education and secondary education are organised as two
stages in a single continuous process; secondary education being
the education of the adolescent and primary education being education preparatory thereto." [1] This view had been gaining support
after the war, and many teachers and officials emphasised the
meagre provision made for the training and instruction of the
majority of our adolescents at a period which was perhaps the most
important and critical of their lives.

The problem appeared such an urgent one that the Consultative Committee, under the chairmanship of Sir W. H. Hadow, was
asked to inquire into "the organisation, objective, and curriculum
of courses of study suitable for children who will remain in full-
time attendance at schools, other than secondary schools, up to
the age of fifteen." The report of the Committee, *The Education
of the Adolescent,* appeared in 1926, and its publication inaugurated
a new era in education which culminated in the Act of 1944.

The report drew attention to the essential nature of the problem
under investigation. "There is a tide which begins to rise in the
veins of youth at the age of eleven or twelve. It is called by the
name of adolescence. If that tide can be taken at the flood, and a
new voyage begun in the strength and along the flow of its current,
we think that it will move on to fortune." The Committee advocated a clean break in the education of children between the ages of
eleven and twelve. All those who did not go forward to "secondary"
education in the traditional meaning of the term, should receive a
secondary education in a truer and broader sense in selective and
non-selective central schools and senior departments. This newer
form of secondary education would differ from the older in two
main ways; it would be shorter in duration on account of the existing school-leaving age of fourteen, and it would be characterised by
a practical and realistic rather than by an academic bias. In order
to clear the ground for the new proposals, the Committee recommended the adoption of a new terminology. The word
"elementary" had become misleading and the term "primary"
should be substituted for it. This would apply to all education up
to the age of eleven or twelve. Education after this age should be
termed post-primary, or secondary, and would include that given
in the existing secondary schools and that given in the schools now

[1] R. H. Tawney. *Secondary Education for All,* p. 7, Allen and Unwin, 1924.

called central.   Hence secondary education would be given in schools of two different types, one in which the leaving-age would be over sixteen—the grammar-school—and one with a leaving-age of fourteen-plus to fifteen-plus—the modern school.

This would necessitate a complete reorganisation of the existing elementary schools into separate departments catering for infant, junior, and senior pupils respectively.   The report expressed the hope that the school-leaving age would soon be raised to fifteen to secure an adequate course of instruction for the adolescent.   The ideals behind the scheme were, "the forming and strengthening of character . . . the training of boys and girls to delight in pursuits and rejoice in accomplishments—work in music and art; work in wood and metals; work in literature and the record of human history—which may become the recreations and the ornaments of leisure in maturer years.   And still another is the awakening and guiding of the practical intelligence, for the better and more skilled service of the community in all its multiple business and complex affairs."

The modern schools would be of different types corresponding to the existing selective and non-selective central schools or, where this was not possible, senior classes or departments would be established in the elementary schools.   In addition, the Committee believed that certain children would benefit by being drafted from these schools at the age of thirteen-plus to trade or junior technical schools.

The next problem was that of deciding upon the types of post-primary education suited to the abilities and interests of the individual child.   The report made suggestions concerning the methods of selection which, with certain minor variations, were put into practice by L.E.A.s.   The author's experience at this period as senior external examiner for the City of Wakefield Education Committee may be quoted as typical of the procedure adopted. An examining board consisting of the Director of Education, members of the education committee, and representatives of the teachers in primary and post-primary schools, was constituted as the body for controlling administration, receiving the examiner's reports, and recommending the awards to the education committee. Every child in the junior schools between the ages of ten and twelve who had passed through Standard IV sat for a preliminary examination consisting of written papers in arithmetic, English, and composition, together with an intelligence-test.   The papers were set by the external examiners and marked by a panel of head teachers according to a marking scheme submitted to the board by the examiners. Those who reached a minimum standard of attainment were permitted to enter the second examination, which was the scholarship examination proper, and consisted of tests similar to those in the preliminary examination. The papers in the second examination were marked by the external examiners and the marks were adjusted by the addition of an age-allowance. All borderline cases were examined orally and the reports of head teachers taken into consideration. The examiners presented their recommendations to the board. Candidates were classified into three groups: those considered suitable for secondary grammar-schools, those fitted for selective central schools, and the remainder who entered non-selective senior schools. Additional examinations were provided for pupils in central and senior schools between the ages of twelve and fourteen, and for those in secondary schools of twelve to sixteen years of age who for some reason stood in need of a free-place award. At first the weakness of the system was due to the allotment of a fixed number of free places in grammar-schools by the Board of Education. This was obviously for administrative reasons, but it had the effect of producing slight variations of standard each year. Later, when the fixed allotment of free places was withdrawn, a more uniform standard could be maintained. Some authorities did not employ an intelligence-test, and others dispensed with a preliminary examination.

The Hadow Report expressed anxiety lest the modern school should become an inferior "secondary school" and deprecated any attempt to ape the academic outlook and curriculum of the grammar-school. It was thought desirable that some type of school-leaving certificate should be provided, but the presentation of pupils for such an examination should be optional. The curriculum of the modern school was considered under its respective subject-heads, but the principle on which it should be based is that it should be suited to the needs, outlook, interests, and ability, of the pupil and not *vice versa*. Thus "There is no question that among the pupils of the new post-primary schools the desire and the ability to do and to make, to learn from concrete things and situations, will be more widely diffused than the desire and the ability to acquire book-knowledge and to master generalisations and abstract ideas. Accordingly, ' practical work ' in its several forms must fill a large place in the curriculum. But this does not mean that the pupils' intellectual training is to be regarded as of secondary importance.

It has been amply shown that for many children the attainment of skill in some form of practical work in science, handwork, or the domestic arts may be a stimulus to higher intellectual effort. . . . Moreover, apart from the question of stimulus, boys and girls with the type of interests we have in view can grasp concepts through practical work much more easily than by devoting long periods to the abstract study of ideas."

The report on the *Education of the Adolescent* was a notable step in educational progress, but its full implementation depended on certain requisites, such as the whole-hearted effort of local authorities to reorganise, as soon as possible, the raising of the leaving-age to fifteen, and the necessity of convincing parents that the modern school was different from, but not inferior to, the grammar-school. The school-leaving age was not raised, so that the number of pupils who remained at school after fourteen years was extremely small. The examination system had the unfortunate effect of persuading parents that the children who were passed on to modern schools were of an inferior type. Many education authorities pressed on vigorously with their schemes of reorganisation, but in some cases authorities made no move until pressure was applied by the Board of Education. Those like the West Riding authority, who went ahead with the building of new schools, accomplished much of the work before the next economic slump slowed up developments, and were on the way to carrying out the requirements of the Act of 1944. Less progressive authorities found themselves with large numbers of unsuitable schools, so that in consequence they have an enormous building programme in front of them.

The clean break at eleven-plus has been criticised on the ground that it was adopted for administrative reasons to ensure a full three-year course of post-primary education and that from a psychological point of view twelve-plus or even later would have been more suitable. The answer is that it was necessitated by the conditions of 1926. As long as the official school-leaving age remained at fourteen it was necessary to make the transfer to a post-primary school at eleven-plus in order to ensure that every child would have a three-year course. The Report might have admitted this more boldly instead of trying to justify the decision of the committee by bringing in psychological arguments. In England a child of eleven-plus is rarely an adolescent, and the psychological evidence quoted by the Report is more pertinent to the thirteen-year-old age-group. The impression that gained ground was that as soon as the child reached the age of eleven-plus new characteristics had begun to appear which necessitated different treatment for him. Another criticism was that, logically, the Committee should have considered the education of infants and juniors before that of the adolescent. It must be admitted that the order was unfortunate, since in most areas priority was given to the needs of the adolescent.[1] The report on the junior school appeared in 1931, whilst that on the infant and nursery schools was not issued until 1933. Meanwhile, a good deal of damage had been done. The scholarship examination had taken possession of many junior schools and the whole of their work was orientated to obtaining as many entrants to grammar-schools as possible.

The report on the junior school emphasised that the curriculum should be considered in terms "of activity and experience rather than knowledge to be acquired or facts to be stored," and laid stress on the working out of suitable projects rather than a rigid division of the time-table into subjects. In quite a number of cases the free-place examination turned schools away from this wise advice and there was a considerable danger of a new form of Payment by Results controlling the junior schools.

During 1931 the economic condition of the country became so alarming that the Labour Government called into being Sir George May's Economy Committee to advise the Chancellor of the Exchequer about reducing national expenditure. The Committee recommended a number of drastic reductions which were accepted by the new National Government. The fifty-per-cent Exchequer grant made for building purposes was withdrawn, teachers' salaries were cut, and other economies were made. No new buildings could be erected except in cases of necessity, such as providing school facilities for a new housing estate. Many progressive schemes were abandoned, and in some cases economy was carried to such an extent that from a long-term point of view it became an extravagance. The worst aspects of the slump began to fade after 1933, and the work of reconstruction began once more, but more slowly and steadily, and perhaps with greater practical wisdom and foresight. The economy campaign produced a change in the free-place system. The free-place examination became a special-place

---

[1] The Government approved in principle the recommendations of the *Education of the Adolescent* and urged the re-organisation of the Elementary schools into Junior and Senior Departments. The pamphlet *The New Prospect in Education* explained the principles of re-organisation and gave as illustration a number of areas in which it had been completed.

examination. Parents of children selected for entrance to grammar-schools were required to pay fees on a sliding scale according to their incomes. Only those whose income was below certain limits, fixed according to the number of children in the family, could obtain a free place for their children. The amount of grant paid to students in training for the teaching profession depended upon a similar "means-test" and still does.

The dual system presented difficulties to reorganisation, especially in rural districts, owing to lack of transport facilities. When an all-standard school was converted into a junior school, the distances children had to travel to a senior school were greatly increased. If the school happened to be a Church of England school, the senior pupils either had to be drafted to a council school or a new senior non-provided school would have to be built by the Church authorities, thus throwing a heavy burden on their finances. The Education Act of 1936 was meant to answer this and other problems.

This Act raised the school-leaving age to fifteen, to take effect on 1st September 1939. Exemptions were allowed where it could be proved that the child was proceeding to "beneficial employment," but so many loop-holes were left that it was feared that the provision would become ineffective on account of the number of exemptions which might be granted. This was not tested, as the outbreak of the Second World War postponed the scheme. The Act empowered L.E.A.s to make grants to managers of non-provided schools up to seventy-five per cent of the cost of the school buildings for senior children. Such schools were to be known as "special-agreement" schools, and managers were given a time-limit in which to make up their minds. Altogether, 519 schemes were submitted, and at the outbreak of war thirty-seven had materialised. The Act of 1944 honoured this "gentleman's agreement." In return for the grant, managers surrendered the appointment of teachers to the L.E.A. Denominational teaching could be given by reserved teachers, but undenominational teaching was to be given to those children whose parents desired it. This was to be in accordance with an agreed syllabus.

By the close of 1938, about sixty-four per cent of school-children were attending reorganised schools, but further progress came to an end with the outbreak of the Second World War in September 1939.

One of the marked features of the period 1914-38 was the rapid increase both in the number of secondary schools and in the number of the pupils attending them.[1] In 1937 the total admissions to grant-aided secondary schools was 97,115, and of these 78,912 were from elementary schools.

In 1911 the Consultative Committee of the Board of Education was asked to investigate the question of external examinations for secondary schools because of the increasing confusion owing to the multiplicity of examinations and examining bodies. As a consequence of the Committee's report, the Board, in consultation with the universities and a number of professional bodies, produced a scheme to limit the number of examinations. It was proposed to recognise the universities as the responsible bodies for conducting such examinations, and to co-ordinate the work of the eight examining bodies, an advisory committee consisting of representatives of the universities and L.E.A.s was to be formed.[2] The advisory committee was constituted in 1917 under the title of the Secondary School Examinations Council. Two standard examinations were proposed. The first was the School Certificate examination, taken at about sixteen years of age, which was to test the results of a four-year course of general education. The second was the Higher School Certificate examination which allowed for a degree of specialisation and would be taken about two years later. The latter was intended for the pupils who remained in the VIth Form to follow an advanced course in arts or science for which the Board of Education gave a special grant. It was intended that both examinations should be in groups of subjects and that in the School Certificate, drawing, music, handicrafts, and housecraft (for girls) should be included. The form and not the pupil was to be the unit for examination. The examinations were not to be purely external, and it was thought that this could be achieved by bringing teachers, through their representatives, into touch with the examining bodies, by allowing them to submit alternative syllabuses for examination

---

[1] This is illustrated in the following table:—

Year	No. of Grant-aided Schools	No. of Efficient Schools (Non-grant-aided)	No. of Pupils in Grant-aided Schools	No. of Pupils in Efficient Schools*
1913	1,027	121	187,647	22,546
1921	1,249	233	362,025	46,610
1937	1,397	397	484,676	73,421

* Excluding preparatory schools.

[2] Originally seven and eventually eight, the recognised examining bodies were the Joint Matriculation Board of the Northern Universities; the universities of London, Bristol, and Durham; the Central Welsh Board; the Oxford and Cambridge Schools Examination Board; the Oxford Delegacy for Local Examinations; and the Cambridge Local Examinations Syndicate.

and by obtaining from heads of schools their estimate of the mei
of candidates from their schools in each of the examination subjects.
The examinations came into operation in 1917. Although the
Board of Education had emphasised that it should be "a cardinal
principle that the examination should follow the curriculum and
not determine it," that precept was largely ignored. This was partly
due to the fact that the School Certificate examination was made to
serve a double purpose. On the one hand, its function was that of
a Vth-Form examination for those who would leave school about
the age of sixteen, but, on the other, since universities accepted the
certificate under certain conditions as providing exemption from
matriculation, it also was considered a university entrance examination. In the same way a Higher School Certificate was looked upon
as a qualification for entry to a university honours course. Quite
erroneously, employers regarded the possession of a Matriculation
Certificate as something very much superior to an ordinary School
Certificate. Thus, as the Spens Report showed, the examinations
reacted upon the schools in a fashion that those who framed the
original regulations had never contemplated. The School Certificate examination began to control the curriculum of the schools and
often caused overstrain and excessive anxiety to some of the pupils.
The requirements for exemption from matriculation narrowed the
choice of subjects already restricted by the group system. Thus
pupils who had received instruction in scripture, art, music, and
handicrafts in the lower forms often relinquished these subjects on
approaching the Vth, since only art or music was originally recognised for purposes of exemption from matriculation. In view of these
unfortunate results the Spens Report considered that a Matriculation Certificate should no longer be awarded on the results
of the School Certificate examination. This recommendation was
accepted, but the outbreak of war interfered with the amendments, and for a time the original regulations were in force as a
special concession.

The Spens Committee thought that in many ways the examinations had been a valuable influence in raising the general standard
of attainment in each of the school subjects, but this had been offset
by the narrowing effects of the group system and the tendency to
regard those subjects which were not recognised for matriculation
requirements as inferior. In 1941 the president of the Board of
Education appointed the Committee of the Secondary School
Examinations Council, under the chairmanship of Sir Cyril Norwood,

to consider suggested changes in the secondary-school curriculum and the problems of school examinations. The Norwood Committee recommended that "in the interest of the individual child and of the increased freedom and responsibility of the teaching profession, change in the School Certificate Examination should be in the direction of making the examination entirely internal, that is to say, conducted by the teachers at the school on syllabuses and papers framed by themselves." (P. 140.) Such a drastic reorganisation of the examination called for a transitional period during which the School Certificate examination would be carried out by the existing examining bodies and supervised by a Standing Committee of eight teachers, four members of L.E.A.s, four university members, and four H.M.I.s acting as assessors. The schools should be encouraged to offer their own syllabuses, and some of the present ones should be lightened. No restrictions should be placed on the subjects pupils wished to offer, but such changes would require two years notice given by the examining bodies. It was suggested that the transition period should be seven years, at the end of which the whole problem would be reviewed to decide whether conditions were such that a change to a wholly internal examination would be possible.

The Norwood Committee thought that a school-leaving examination should be conducted twice a year for pupils of eighteen-plus to meet the requirements of university entrance and of entry into the professions. Pupils should take in this examination the subjects required for their particular purpose. The present Higher School Certificate examination should be abolished and State and Local Education Authority scholarships should be awarded on another basis. The winning of a scholarship at a university "should constitute a claim upon public funds for assistance towards the cost of living at the university, subject to evidence of the need." The university examining bodies should hold an examination in March for the award of State and Local Education Authority scholarships. Recommendations would be made to L.E.A.s by the examining bodies and would be considered by specially appointed boards, who would take into account performance in the examination and the school records of candidates. The State would make the final award and bear the cost of the scholarships. It was thought that the amount of the scholarships should be sufficient to enable the holders to take a full part in university life and activities. Many L.E.A.s had for some years assisted university candidates by loans, a system which the Committee deprecated, since the repayment of the loan threw a heavy burden on the student.

The report on *The Education of the Adolescent* had been concerned with those types of post-primary schools (senior, selective, and non-selective central schools) which are now included under the term "secondary-modern." It had omitted from consideration two other important forms of secondary education, the secondary grammar-school and the junior technical school. This omission was rectified by the Spens Report, 1938, which took for its terms of reference "to consider and report upon the organisation and interrelation of schools, other than those administered under the Elementary Code, which provide education for pupils beyond the age of 11 + ; regard being had in particular to the framework and content of the education of pupils who do not remain at school beyond the age of about sixteen." Although the report was not specifically concerned with the modern school, yet the Committee found it impossible to discuss the problems with which they were dealing without some reference to other types of post-primary school. It was felt that the schools covered by the terms of reference should retain a special character and must retain a special importance, though this did not entail the enjoyment of specially favourable conditions. The Committee had carefully considered the possibility of multilateral schools which, by means of separate streams, would offer all types of secondary education. For two or three years there would be a common core to the courses provided, but at the age of thirteen or fourteen pupils would be able to follow courses suited to their individual needs and capacities. These would include grammar, modern, technical, and perhaps other courses. The idea was an attractive one in that it would bring together pupils of different abilities, interests, and objectives, and would ease the transference of pupils from one type of course to another. The Committee, however, did not favour this solution. The multilateral school would of necessity be a large institution with at least eight hundred pupils, and it would involve the difficulty of finding a head who would be competent to control and inspire to the same degree each side of the school.

Great importance was attached to the influence of the VIth Form upon the rest of the school. In the multilateral school, the VIth would be mainly recruited from pupils on the grammar side and would therefore be too small to exert an appreciable influence on the life of the school. There was also the risk that the grammar side, because of its traditional prestige, would have an undue effect on the modern side. Moreover, the value of a technical school would be diminished unless it was closely associated with the staff of a technical college and able to use the equipment of the latter institution. For these reasons the report considered it best for grammar and modern schools to exist and develop independently, though there was some scope for experiment with the multilateral idea.

The report envisaged secondary education under three forms, grammar, technical, and modern, so that every child could receive that kind of education for which he was fitted. As soon as the national finances permitted, admission to both the grammar and technical high schools should be on the basis of one hundred per cent special places. "If parity of schools in the secondary stage, so generally advocated by our witnesses, and regarded by us as essential, is to be established, payment of fees in one school and not in another becomes incongruous." (P. 309.) The technical high school would offer a five-year course to its pupils from eleven-plus, and would thus be distinguished from the existing junior technical school with a two- or three-year course from thirteen-plus. In view of the difficulty of ascertaining at eleven-plus whether a child was more fitted for a grammar than a technical high school or *vice versa*, the curriculum of each type of school should be broadly of the same character in the first two years. The technical high schools should be housed in the premises of technical colleges or institutes, and, although they would have their own headmasters, they would secure the benefit of the teaching staff and special equipment of the parent institution. "Whilst we do not recommend that every Junior Technical School should as a matter of course be converted into a Technical High School, we do consider that a generous provision of such Technical High Schools should be made by the conversion of existing schools and the establishment of new schools." (P. xxx.)

The technical high school should have its own leaving-examination. "We recommend that a new type of leaving certificate should be established for pupils in Technical High Schools on the basis of internal examinations founded on the school curriculum, and subject to external assessment by assessors appointed or approved by the Board of Education. . . . We recommend that these certificates should be given an equal standing with School Certificates as fulfilling the first condition for Matriculation." (P. 373.) The criticisms of the School Certificate examination have already been mentioned.   The existing grammar-school curriculum was "still coloured by obsolete doctrines of the faculties and of formal training; and the endeavour to teach a wide range of subjects to the same high level to all pupils has led to the overcrowding of the time-table." (P. xxii.)   Although eighty-five per cent of the pupils left the grammar-school at about sixteen, the curriculum was still planned in the interest of the minority who looked forward to a university career.   Up to sixteen, the courses provided should be complete in themselves and this need not prejudice the interests of those pupils who wished to proceed to the university.

In a few places experiments were carried out on the lines suggested by the Spens Report, but the outbreak of war put an end to new developments for the time being.   However, many of the ideas suggested were incorporated in the Act of 1944.

The Hadow Report of 1926 had considered the types of post-primary education which are now included under the term "secondary modern."   Later, in 1938, the Spens Report had been concerned with other forms of post-primary education, the secondary grammar and the technical high school.   The relation between these different types of post-primary education was the concern of the Norwood Report.

The Norwood Committee accepted the view that secondary education is the stage following that of primary education.   "At the primary stage the main preoccupation lies with basic habits, skills, and aptitudes of mind, using as data the veriest elements of knowledge which all children should be put into the way of acquiring. . . . In the secondary stage, on the other hand, the attempt is made to provide for such special interests and aptitudes the kind of education most suited to them; they may have begun to indicate themselves at least roughly in the last phases of primary education, or they may not declare themselves in such degree as to deserve attention till a different kind of education is encountered.   It is the business of secondary education, first, to provide opportunity for a special cast of mind to manifest itself, if not already manifested in the primary stage, and, secondly, to develop special interests and aptitudes to the full by means of a curriculum and a life best calculated to this end." (Pp. 1-2.)   This would mean that secondary education should meet the needs of three main groups of pupils, and to achieve this there should be three types of education, secondary grammar, secondary technical, and secondary modern. The ideal would be a relation of parity between the types, but the

Committee added significantly, "Parity of esteem in our view cannot be conferred by administrative decree nor by equality of cost per pupil ; it can only be won by the school itself." The age of eleven-plus or even earlier was chosen as the beginning of the secondary stage in education, and pupils would pass into the type of school which seemed to meet their needs. As the selection in a number of cases would be tentative, it was recommended that the pupil should pass into what may be described as the "lower school" of one of the three types of school and should spend three years there. During this period the child would be carefully studied to see what special interests developed and, if found necessary, a transfer to another type of school should be arranged. This would entail a curriculum which in its broad lines would be common to every type of school for the first two years. From thirteen-plus to sixteen-plus the pupil would pursue a course of study suited to his abilities and interests in the type of school which could offer it. At the end of the course he might enter employment and pursue a part-time education, or remain at school to take a more advanced course leading to the university or some other institution for further study. The secondary grammar-school course was envisaged as extending to eighteen-plus, but it was thought that pupils from secondary technical schools should have more opportunities than at present of proceeding to institutions providing advanced study.

The report then makes a very important statement. "On educational grounds we are in favour of a break of six months, in which boys and girls between the ages of eighteen and nineteen years would render public service interpreted in a broad sense. . . . Before this break comes, pupils going on to universities and other places of advanced study would have taken the examinations necessary to secure admission and financial aid, and would take up residence after the period of service." (P. 16.) This recommendation has materialised for quite a different reason. The needs of national defence in these post-war years have necessitated the retention of a form of conscription for, at any rate, some time ahead. Boys intending to enter a university usually receive defer-ment of service until they have completed the university entrance requirements. At present they have the option of doing their two years service before entering the university or of deferring it until they have completed their degree course. Opinion is divided as to which of these options is the more advantageous. Some claim that the loss in academic knowledge during the period of service is compensated by the greater maturity of mind and the fuller know-ledge of the world in general and human nature in particular, that they bring to their university studies.

The problem of selection at eleven-plus was carefully considered by the Committee. The difficulties were acknowledged and the value of effective school record cards, showing the history of the child's progress through the school, was stressed. The judgment of the teachers in the primary school might be supplemented by intelli-gence or other tests. In order to make transfer to another type of school at thirteen-plus easier and more effective, the establishment of multilateral schools had been suggested. The attitude of the Norwood Committee on this matter is similar to that expressed in the Spens Report. The Norwood Report also adds: "The phrase ' multilateral school ' has frequently been used in evidence offered to us orally and in writing. It is a phrase which few of our witnesses have used in the same sense. To some of them the larger secondary schools of to-day are already 'multilateral' in the sense that they offer alternative courses of study; others would carry further the diversity of courses so as to include curricula which would offer specialised courses in preparation for particular occupations ; others again would extend the range of a multilateral school to include technical work such as is now undertaken in a Junior Technical School and also the curriculum appropriate to the existing Senior School. The vagueness of the phrase has in our opinion been responsible for much confusion of thought and statement." [1]

The relation of a technical high school to local industry was deemed an essential one and the Committee doubted whether that relationship could be maintained unless the school were free to direct its own destiny. A more satisfactory arrangement seemed to be that of a "bilateral" school in which a grammar-school and a modern school were combined. The separate sides of such a school should not fall in number below a certain limit if variety of courses was to be offered. "On the other hand the tradition of English education has always valued human contacts and is not favourable to large schools in which the Head Master cannot have sufficient knowledge of each boy ; thus a maximum figure is imposed beyond which expansion is undesirable, and in this connection it must always be remembered that there are far more pupils for whom a Modern School is appropriate than there are pupils for whom a Grammar School is appropriate." [2]

[1] pp. 18-19.   [2] p. 19.

Owing to the work and influence of such outstanding head-masters as Arnold and Thring, the public schools had risen high in public esteem, but by the last decade of the 19th century they showed a tendency to rest upon their laurels. They were shaken out of their complacency by the challenge issued by Mr. F. W. Sanderson, headmaster of Oundle, who in his conception of the function of the public school was a lineal descendant of Thring. Many of his own generation regarded Sanderson as an innovator and were sceptical concerning the developments which were taking place at Oundle, but his contribution to education is perhaps the greatest made by any headmaster of a public school, since it has influenced many secondary schools outside the circle.

Sanderson never claimed to be a philosopher or psychologist, nor had he made any serious study of the theory of education. He arrived at his conclusions because he felt profoundly dissatisfied with the outlook and the teaching of the public schools. He was an earnest student of science and social affairs and he saw school problems through the eyes of a social reformer.

At the end of the last century Oundle School was an ancient grammar-school which had been developed by the Grocers' Company into a public school with accommodation for about 500 boys. It had dwindled, partly because of its proximity to Rugby and Uppingham, but more so because it adhered to the stereotyped traditions of the past. Sanderson was appointed in 1892 to bring new life to the school, which had fallen to about 100 pupils. At first he met with violent opposition to his reforms both from the older boys and from the masters. He persevered and wore down the opposition and succeeded in carrying out his reforms to a degree he never imagined possible at first. All through the period of his office, he was continually progressing and experimenting with new ideas. At the time of his sudden death in 1922, the school had grown to over 500 pupils, with a long waiting-list, and parents all over England were only too anxious to enter their sons for a place at Oundle. As the school increased in numbers, it grew in material equipment. This growth consisted not only in classrooms and boarding-houses, but, to fulfill Sanderson's educational aims, the school was equipped with workshops for joinery and engineer-ing, a machine-shop, a forge, a foundry, and an experimental farm. Sanderson added laboratories for physics, chemistry, and biology, art rooms, an observatory, a large library, and a museum. In these respects, the school became one of the best-equipped educational institutions in the country. As a consequence of Sanderson's changes, Oundle not only continued to win university scholarships but its scholars gained interests and developed an enthusiasm for work and study of a kind unknown to the average public-school boy.

Sanderson was essentially a practical teacher. Hence we find certain weaknesses in his understanding of educational aims. He had little experience of the class-teaching which had developed in our elementary and secondary schools. We find in him, therefore, a violent dislike of classroom studies, which he considered merely as a drill. Also, as a scientist he failed to appreciate fully the value of cultural studies in the service of humanity, and thought of science as affording the best example of creative thought in the service of mankind. The last phrase indicates that his breadth of view helped him to a large extent to overcome his limitations. Science for itself, apart from its service to humanity, had, in his eyes, little value in school.

As a form-master at Dulwich, and in his early years at Oundle, he became increasingly impressed with the futility of methods of teaching and learning in which pupils were passive, receptive, and generally bored. He found that the average boy disliked school lessons and only worked if there was an incentive in the way of examinations, marks, and punishments. Sanderson regarded such as artificial incentives which, if relied upon, destroyed the true spirit of work and study. It was not a question of the subject-matter of instruction. The evil was as rampant in science and mathematics as in classics and literary studies. As he said, "Education must be fitted to the boy, not the boy to Education." He further realised that the education of the schools was out of touch with the natural tendencies of youth and failed to prepare the pupils for entering into the life and work of the community in the right spirit of work and service. He said repeatedly that the traditional spirit of school learning was individualistic, acquisitive, and possessive, when it should be social, co-operative, and creative.

He thought of the ordinary methods of teaching boys mathematics, languages, and elementary science, as the gaining of the tools of knowledge. Too much time was spent on learning the tools without using them, and he spoke of the classrooms where boys go to be taught, as tool-sharpening rooms, necessary but subsidiary. For creative work, other types of room and other occupations were needed. Sanderson visualised the school as preparing the boy for complete living, not merely for making a livelihood, but for entering into the work and life of the world with wide and active interests and in the spirit of progress and service. For this reason he thought that practical work similar to the real work of the world was essential in school. Thus he introduced workshops, a foundry, and a farm. But nothing was further from his purpose than the training of engineers and farmers. He believed in putting boys to these subjects because their abilities or tastes showed that by means of them he could train their powers. In other words, he sought to satisfy the needs of each individual. He considered that the aim of the school was to stimulate a life, not to acquire possessive knowledge but one which would develop more intense interests in work and thought. At the same time, he did not despise scholarship or knowledge. He held, however, that these were secondary, by-products of creativeness. Given interests and creative power, these would follow.

So, too, with examinations. He did not despise them, but he realised that his schemes would not be sound if they did not produce thorough learning, and examinations acted as an incentive and a test of this. But he also realised that if the school produced nothing else but examination results, then the learning was empty and profitless.

Sanderson believed that the schools should be in the closest and most intimate touch with the life and work of the community. As he said, "Work in schools should be for service and should be turned to the practical and social needs of the community." Again, "Adult life should not be a breaking away from school, but a continuation and a development of school." Like Dewey, he conceived schools as miniature copies of the community. They should exercise boys in the same kinds of activities and interest as they would be called upon to use when they left school to enter life. Hence he was not afraid of the term "vocational." He saw vocation as the centre about which a boy's interests were moving, and he wished to seize this natural interest and turn it to good account, to develop it in the right atmosphere into a right spirit of true work in the service of the community.

In his last lecture at University College, London, a lecture followed by his sudden collapse and death, Sanderson told his audience, "When I became a headmaster I began by introducing engineering into the school—applied science. The first effect was that a large number of boys who could not do other things could do that.   They began to like their work in school.   That led on to introducing a large number of other sciences, such as agricultural chemistry, horse-shoeing (if that is a science), metallurgical chemistry, biochemistry, agriculture;   and of course, these new sorts of work interested a large number of other boys of a type different from the type interested by the old work, so we got an exceptional number of boys, curiously enough, unexpectedly liking what they had to do in school.   Then I ventured to do something daring; it is most daring to introduce the scientific method of finding out the truth—a dangerous thing—by the process of experiment and research.   We began to replace explicit teaching by finding out. We did this first with these newly introduced sciences.   Then we began to impress the aims and outlook of science on to other departments of school life.   History, for instance: we began to replace the old classroom teaching and learning by a laboratory for history, full of other books and other things required in abundance, so that boys in all parts of the school could, for some scientific purpose (not to learn;   to go into schools to learn was egotistical), find out the things we required for to-day.   We set them to find out things for the service of science, the service of literature, modern languages, music." [1]

Sanderson despised the formal mechanical measurements which often masqueraded under the name of practical science.   He believed that the work in laboratories and workshops in the school must be real work.   "Sanderson was always strongly in favour of the work done in the shops being 'real,' something that boys would realise at once was of genuine value;   models and toys and petty jobs were all useful enough in giving a certain manual dexterity, but genuine commercial work could be made much more truly educational.   The whole process from drawing-office to the final erecting and testing, he held, should be followed, if possible, and a real insight gained into the reason for the design, into the properties of various materials used, and into the way in which each part fulfilled its purpose." [2]   Thus when the First World War broke out the workshops at Oundle were sufficiently well equipped to take a valuable part in the manufacture of munitions.   "The plan was adopted of sending into shops each form for a complete week, and this arrangement seemed so satisfactory that it has been retained.   It was soon found that the regular work of the school

---

[1] *Sanderson of Oundle*, p. 357, Chatto and Windus, 1924.
[2] *Ibid.*, p. 36.

did not suffer. In fact the life and elasticity given by these calls for help seemed to have the effect of invigorating the regular work. There is no doubt that the opportunities provided for creative work make a strong appeal to most boys, and many who might be voted dull in the classroom show themselves to be possessed of exceptional powers in other and no less important directions. Such boys frequently find that a problem they have met in the classroom or laboratory is presenting itself to them again in a form which evokes a much readier response from their understanding." [1]

Sanderson's work was carried out in the environment of a great public school, but it has lessons for other types of school. Those who are concerned with the curricula of secondary modern schools can learn much from a study of what he accomplished at Oundle.

The years 1902 to 1939 were very important for Welsh education. The Board of Education, by creating a separate Welsh Department in 1907, recognised that the Principality had special educational problems of its own. The attempt to force English upon a Welsh-speaking population was finally abandoned, and the new department set to work to encourage the use of Welsh and English side by side. Where Welsh was the language of the home, it was considered that it ought to be taught in the schools and used as the medium of instruction in other subjects. Whenever possible, the teaching of both English and Welsh was encouraged so that pupils would become acquainted with two languages and two literatures. Emphasis was also placed on the study of Welsh history, traditions, and institutions. In secondary schools where a language other than English was taught, it was recommended that the second language should be Welsh, and instruction in other subjects might be given wholly or partly in Welsh. In training-colleges, provision was to be made for the teaching of Welsh. Since that date, in appointing inspectors the policy has been to select those who have a knowledge of the Welsh language and of social and economic conditions in the Principality. The intentions of the Board were set forth by the publication in 1927 of the *Report on Welsh in Education and Life.*

During this period, almost revolutionary advances were made in regard to school buildings and equipment. The central-hall type of school in its many modifications, which was popular at the beginning of the century, suffered from certain grave disadvantages. It was difficult to ensure adequate ventilation of the classrooms, and

[1] *Oundle School Commemoration Book*, 1927, p. 54.

although attempts were made to overcome this by the use of artificial means of ventilation the results were not entirely satisfactory. Moreover, when the central hall was being used for music, or for physical training as was often the case in bad weather, the occupants of the classrooms on either side were seriously disturbed.

A marked improvement was afforded by the introduction of the pavilion type of school after 1907. In this type the classrooms led off from a veranda or corridor, and it was a simple matter to arrange for windows on each side of the classroom to give cross-ventilation. The assembly-hall was apart from the classrooms, either at one end of the building or in the centre of the line of classrooms. The new arrangements for ventilation could be very troublesome in cold and boisterous weather. Experiments made to avoid this resulted in semi-open-air schools in which the provision of folding glazed doors, which could be closed or opened according to the state of the weather, effected a great improvement. Whenever possible, the classrooms were built to face south. Most pavilion types of school are one-storey buildings and take up a good deal of ground, an important consideration in districts where land is limited and expensive.

An alternative arrangement was provided by the quadrangle type of school, in which the classrooms were sited on the long sides of the quadrangle, and on the shorter sides the assembly-hall and rooms for art, science, and handicrafts were located respectively. In towns, where land is expensive, the quadrangle type of building is in greater favour. Many variations of each type exist. Corresponding improvements were made in the lighting and heating of school premises in areas where electric light and power were available.

The modern tendency has been to abolish the rigid-desk accommodation, either by providing single or dual desks with chairs and lockers, or by substituting chairs and tables for desks. The emphasis has been upon arrangements which allow greater freedom of movement to the children. As the value of practical occupations became more widely recognised, special rooms for activities began to be provided. Attention was also paid to the provision of adequate playground space, playing-fields, and school gardens. All these features have been made compulsory by the *Building Regulations* which followed the Act of 1944.

Between 1902 and the outbreak of the Second World War there was a corresponding development in methods of instruction.

This was closely connected with the development of educational psychology. Many American critics of the earlier part of the century expressed their surprise that so little attention was given to the study of educational psychology in English training-colleges. The small amount of psychology taught consisted of a simplified version of the adult psychology of the associationist school, and was marked by a definite intellectual bias. There were, however, brilliant exceptions to the prevailing tendency, *e.g.* Professor Sully and his studies of childhood. Attention had been drawn to the importance of the child's innate endowment, by the American psychologist William James, and his *Principles of Psychology*, *Text Book of Psychology*, and *Talks to Teachers*, became popular in England. Perhaps the writings of William McDougall were principally responsible for popularising the new outlook in psychology. His *Social Psychology*, first published in 1908, ran through an amazing number of editions and reprints. His views on the nature of instinct were criticised by the biologists, and this led him to restate the principles of the Hormic psychology in the *Energies of Men*, 1932.

Immediately prior to the outbreak of the First World War the works of the psycho-analysts were becoming known in England. At first, many people were inclined to accept the conclusions of the psycho-analysts uncritically, and by their very enthusiasm aroused opposition. Time has shown, however, that many of their conclusions have been of the greatest value, not only in connection with the problems occasioned by the difficult and delinquent child, but also as leading to a better understanding of the development of the ordinary pupil.

The employment of tests of general and special ability, and standardised tests of attainment, was another important development. The germ of this is to be found in the works of Sir Francis Galton and Karl Pearson, but the first workable intelligence-tests were those of Alfred Binet, published in 1905 and revised in 1908 and 1911. They were adapted to English conditions by Sir Cyril Burt. The Binet tests were originally compiled for the discovery of dull and defective children. Moreover, they were individual tests, and to apply them to a class was a lengthy procedure. During the war the American army made use of group tests (the well-known Alpha and Beta tests), and similar group tests were introduced into England, first as an additional paper in the Civil Service examinations, and then as a means of selecting pupils for entry to secondary schools. In the latter capacity, group tests were first used by the

Bradford L.E.A. in 1919, and their employment soon became widespread.

Important contributions to the theory of intelligence testing were made by Professor Spearman, Sir Cyril Burt, and Professor Godfrey Thomson. The first-named made considerable use of the correlation method and originated the two-factor theory (s and g). Modern tests show a high degree of reliability and possess considerable prognostic value, though recent criticism seems to indicate that some of the assumptions made in the early days of intelligence testing need to be revised.

All these developments have had a striking repercussion on classroom practice. Their practical applications were brought to the notice of teachers through the publications of a number of well-known educational thinkers, many of whom were connected with the university departments of education. It is not the purpose of this book to discuss the development of educational theories, but among those who have influenced educational practice may be mentioned the names of Sir John Adams, Sir Percy Nunn, and Professors Bompas Smith, Valentine, Campagnac, Olive Wheeler, and Frank Smith.

The result has been that the schools, at the outbreak of war in 1939, were far different places from those of 1902. Many were still hampered by inadequate buildings and unsuitable sites, but on the whole it may be said that they had become bright and pleasant places, pervaded by a friendly atmosphere, in contrast with the formal, repressive conditions of the 19th century. The modern school has become "child-centred," that is it no longer tries to mould the pupil to a preconceived curriculum, but in the matter and method of its instruction it endeavours to suit its teaching to the abilities, experience, natural interests, and outlook upon life, of the child at different stages of his development. The capacities, needs, and interest of the individual child are now considered, and the old idea that all children have the same interests and learn in the same way has been abandoned. This change not only affects the curriculum, but also the methods of teaching. Group and individual methods have come to supplement traditional class teaching, *e.g.* the Dalton and other plans of supervised study. The idea that education means learning from books has given place to a wider interpretation, and the project method and activity methods have replaced the meaningless grind of earlier days. In this respect the ideas of John Dewey have had a strong influence, and the value of practical occupations in the school has become widely recognised. There has been a great improvement in the standard of school textbooks, and the importance of visual means of presentation is now acknowledged. The danger, some think, is that the pendulum may have swung too far in the direction of freedom and activity, so as to be detrimental to sound discipline and the acquirement of the fundamentals of knowledge.   All agree, however, that the development of physical training and games, and the work of the School Medical Service, have resulted in a generation of healthier, cleanlier, better-nourished, and better-clothed children.   To gain the full benefit of these developments, classes will have to be much smaller than in years past.   Although the absurdly large classes common in the 19th century are seldom seen, there are still many cases in which numbers present an insuperable obstacle to the employment of the individual methods advocated by modern educationists.

CHAPTER XI

THE OVERHAUL OF 1944 AND THE FUTURE

The extension of the school-leaving age proposed by the Act of 1936 was not realised because the beginning of hostilities in September 1939 brought an end for the time being to all schemes of educational development. Since Munich, it had been realised that if war did come the air-power of the enemy would constitute a greater threat to this country than had hitherto been experienced in our long history. The general impression was that the war would begin with air-raids of unparalleled severity. For some time before the outbreak of hostilities the Government had been preparing a scheme for the evacuation of children and expectant mothers from London and those large cities which were considered to be in the danger area. These plans were put into operation at the end of August.

Unfortunately, the authorities lacked the courage to make evacuation compulsory from the start. Even if it was to remain voluntary, the Government should have realised that the majority of pupils came from homes where the parents were not accustomed to be separated from their children. Nation-wide publicity would have been necessary to bring parents to accept the scheme and to con-vince them that they were not justified in exposing their children to the perils that the danger areas might present. The publicity came too late. In addition, the scheme had been planned on paper but little in the way of general rehearsal seems to have been attempted. A rehearsal would have tested the efficacy of the plans and would have been excellent propaganda in persuading parents that the evacuation could be carried out smoothly and efficiently. Although the schools knew their destinations, there was little time for head teachers to visit the reception areas to discover conditions for themselves and to establish friendly relations with the schools there. The consequence was that when the time for evacuation came, only a proportion of parents was willing to allow its children to be moved; in some towns less than twenty per cent of children were evacuated.

In justice to the authorities one must say that practically everybody anticipated air-raids which might begin while the evacuation was in progress. Hence, the chief concern of the authorities was to get the children to the railway stations, put them on the trains and move them as expeditiously as possible. The marvellous part of the whole business is that thousands of children were transferred with only minor and occasional hitches. The difficulties began when the children arrived in the evacuation areas. The first thing to be done was to settle the children in their temporary homes and then to arrange for their schooling.

Information about billeting facilities in the reception areas was by no means complete. For example, householders at the receiving end were asked about their preferences, but little more seems to have been done to ascertain if they wished to have boys or girls, children or adults. Billeting officers worked in terms of numbers. If billets had to be found for thirty children, then thirty places were allocated without reference to the important factor that children could not feel at home if they were sent to families in which the standards of behaviour and living and outlook on life were greatly different from those to which they had been accustomed. "The sole consideration was to get everyone under a roof without delay. So slum-bred children were bustled off to lordly mansions and opulent country houses, delicately nurtured youngsters bundled into labourers' cottages, boisterous young 'toughs' thrust upon elderly folk of retiring habit, sensitive and introverted adolescents dumped into the midst of loud and hearty families of the 'Good Companions' type, pregnant women landed with confirmed spinsters or presented as an additional burden to already overburdened working house-wives. Every possible kind of sociological and psychological misfit was made in abundance."[1] Later came the sorting out, but in the meanwhile considerable damage had been done.

Probably the fact that the expected air-raids did not start for a considerable period saved the situation from degenerating into one of the utmost confusion and chaos. This allowed time for teachers and voluntary helpers, etc., to complete the sorting-out process, and one cannot speak too highly of the magnificent work they accomplished. Teachers, education officials, inspectors, and voluntary helpers worked wonders in ensuring that mistakes were rectified as quickly as possible. Most of the teachers accompanied the children and spent the first few days of evacuation tramping the countryside to find children who had been mislaid and to send

[1] H. C. Dent. *Education in Transition*, p. 15, Kegan Paul, Trench, Trubner, 1944

them to their proper destinations. Mistakes about billeting had to be corrected immediately.

The next step was to arrange for the schooling of the evacuees. This produced a fresh crop of difficulties. The school accommodation in the reception areas was, naturally, not sufficient for the flood of young people who came pouring in. Schools, therefore, had to be split, and one found instances of head teachers whose pupils were scattered over a wide area of several villages, perhaps a considerable distance from one another. The usual plan was that of a double shift, whereby the same school buildings were used, say, in the mornings by the original school and in the afternoons by the evacuated children. The hours of instruction were cut down and recreational and practical activities in the open air were arranged for pupils during the periods in which they were not receiving instruction in the school. In some places, public halls and Sunday Schools were available for additional accommodation.

Teachers and inspectors worked without thought for themselves to produce some kind of order out of chaos. A good deal of the muddle was caused by the contradictory instructions issued by directors of education, especially in areas administered by Part III authorities. The following example is typical of the kind of difficulty that had to be faced. Although parents had been given a list of the clothes and other articles which were necessary, many children arrived lacking essential things. Sometimes the parent was at fault through not acquainting himself with the instructions. In other cases the children came from homes where the parents were too poor to supply their children with the requisite clothes. One teacher relates that he found three of his boys tramping the village street with no soles to their shoes. A rainy spell had started and the country lanes were thick with liquid mud. He immediately applied to the local Part III Education Office for authority to obtain suitable shoes for the boys. The office informed him that it was not within their power to issue the authority but it must be sought from the major education authority which had sent the boys. This authority in turn denied that it was their responsibility and suggested that he applied to certain voluntary agencies. For a week he was referred from one body to another. At last, in desperation, he took the boys into the local shoe shop, explained the situation, and had the boys fitted out with suitable footwear. He expressed his willingness to foot the bill himself if no public body could be found to take responsibility. Fortunately for his own pocket, he found that at the end of a fortnight the bill had been settled by the major education authority.

Eventually, by dint of much hard work and improvisation, a tolerable educational organisation was constructed. The Dominions and the United States showed their practical sympathy by inviting children to their countries. Many parents who could afford it sent their children out of England, especially to Canada and the United States. In September 1940, the *City of Benares*, which carried a number of evacuee children, was torpedoed in mid-Atlantic during a storm and nearly eighty children lost their lives. This at once put an end to overseas evacuation.

When the expected air-raids did not materialise, parents were allowed to visit their children. This step was on the whole unwise because of the unsettling effect produced by the visitors. Those who did not accompany their parents back home obtained marked benefit from the fresh air and more healthy conditions of life. They came into contact with a kind of life they may have read about but had never before experienced. The impact of town upon country was beneficial not only to children from the towns but also to country dwellers. There were, of course, the grumblers who complained about the absence of trams, cinemas, and fried-fish shops, but on the whole the children who had been evacuated led a happy existence.

There is much truth in the saying that one half of the world does not know how the other half lives. Some of us remember stories which revealed the shocking conditions prevailing in the homes of some of the city children. Certainly some of these reports were exaggerated, especially by some selfish well-to-do people who unpatriotically seized upon any excuse to rid themselves of the care of the children who interfered with their time and pleasure. The accounts which found their way into the newspapers intensely shocked large numbers of people. One always knew that filthy and verminous children existed; that there were homes in which the sanitary conditions were terrible and in which there was little sense of either decency or discipline. Social workers knew of these defects but the general public was only dimly aware of them. Hence the shock when it began to learn from friends in the country and from reports in the press about the low standard of life and behaviour which was characteristic of a large section of the community. The result was a widespread feeling that this state of affairs ought to be remedied as soon as possible and that a general overhaul of the educational system of the country should be put in hand at the earliest possible moment.

When the "Battle of Britain" started in the early autumn of 1940, thousands of children who had returned to their homes came back into the evacuation areas. In those districts which had been designated as danger areas, the Government closed all schools, and many of the buildings were used as billets for the forces or to accommodate the different civil-defence organisations. The children who were left behind received no form of education whatever, and the withdrawal of control from the school, and, in many cases, from the home, left them to roam the streets and fall into mischief. In some towns the teachers visited the children in their homes and attempted to supply at least a minimum of education. The Education Department of the University of Leeds decided to organise a voluntary scheme. In conjunction with many of the local clergy classes were held at the University and in local churches and halls, and the teaching was given by volunteers from the teachers left behind and by the staff of the department and students in training for the teaching profession. This was a help but under the circumstances attendance could not be made compulsory so that only the fringe of the problem was attacked. Eventually the Government changed its policy. Air-raid shelters were built at the schools, the windows of the schools were covered with gummed paper strips, and blast-walls were built. The schools started again, but thousands of children had lost precious months of schooling.

In those towns which experienced large-scale bombing, the actual damage to schools was relatively small, and as a considerable proportion of the children had been evacuated, the casualties were but slight. In London, children had to spend night after night in shelters during air attacks, and it was thought this would play havoc with their nerves and their work. Strangely enough, they suffered little physical or mental damage, but, naturally, their school work was affected. There was also a shortage of schools, for some buildings had been handed over to the service authorities for billets, stores, or as hospitals and training establishments, and considerable pressure had to be exercised to induce the military authorities to part with them.

The evacuation had its redeeming feature. Schools could only take part of their equipment into the reception areas, and often the accommodation used as schoolrooms was practically bare of conventional educational apparatus. Teachers were compelled to provise, and to their astonishment, many of them found they could dispense with the aids which they had previously considered as indispensable. Work in the open air and of a definitely practical character took the place of formal class studies. Subjects like arithmetic, geography, and history began to have new meaning for pupils when studied at first hand. Handicrafts, art, and all kinds of physical activities became invested with a new importance, and the experience of these war years influenced the curriculum and teaching methods when peace followed.

It is significant and characteristic of the British people that before the crisis of the war had been reached, serious thought was being given to the problems of post-war reconstruction, and amongst them, education received considerable attention. Lester Smith considers that the stimulus was the speech of the Prime Minister, Mr. Churchill, made to his old school, Harrow. "When the war is won, it must be one of our aims to work to establish a state of society where the advantages and privileges which hitherto have been enjoyed by the few shall be more widely shared by the men and youth of the nation." [1]

The first active move was made by the religious bodies. The two Anglican Archbishops, the Roman Catholic Archbishop of Westminster, and the Moderator of the Free Church Federal Council joined in drawing up a memorial at the end of 1940, entitled, *A Christian Basis for Peace*, and at the commencement of the following year, Archbishop Temple, Chairman of the Anglican Conference at Malvern, made a number of proposals, some of which were incorporated in the Education Act of 1944. In August 1941 Dr. Temple led a deputation of Anglican and Free Churchmen to interview the President of the Board of Education, and lay before him their proposals about religious education. Discussion of the proposed educational reconstruction had now become nation wide. It has not often happened that educational matters have been regarded with such interest that they have become one of the main topics of discussion, but during this period feeling in all sections of the community ran so strongly that the Board of Education was inundated with suggestions for reform which came from bodies of widely different interests.

The Government showed itself sympathetic and ready to consider representations which were made. The Board of Education,

---

[1] *To Whom do Schools Belong?*, p. 166, Blackwell, 1943.

through its President, Mr. Ramsbotham, indicated that the Government was considering far-reaching changes in the national system. The next step consisted in the preparation of a memorandum on post-war education, which was sent as a confidential document to local authorities, teachers' associations, and to other bodies or individuals who were associated with the service of education. Although it was supposed to be a confidential document, the "Green Book" of 1941 (so called from the colour of its cover) was, in the words of Lester Smith, "distributed in such a blaze of secrecy" that its contents quickly became public property. This was perhaps unfortunate because through a mistaken interpretation of the President's reference to it, everybody thought it was intended as a public document, and those who considered that they were entitled to receive a copy and did not obtain one, were disappointed and offended. Its publication was designed to collect the opinions of educationists on such subjects as the raising of the school-leaving age, the abolition of secondary-school fees, the recruitment and training of teachers, and other important problems. The Government was anxious not to introduce legislation until it had thoroughly sounded the views of those who possessed first-hand experience of the working of the present system.

The publication of the "Green Book" stimulated lively interest throughout the nation. In civilian life, in the Forces, and through the B.B.C., discussion groups minutely examined every aspect of educational reconstruction. The Board received an enormous amount of information contributed not only by individuals but from such important bodies as the N.U.T., the T.U.C., the W.E.A., and the Association of Directors and Secretaries for Education. Although views about details differed considerably, there was a general concensus of opinion about the lines on which reform should take place. Mr. R. A. Butler, who succeeded Mr. Ramsbotham, felt that now the information had been digested, it was time to take a further step. In July 1943 he issued the White Paper on *Educational Reconstruction* which forecast the contents of the proposed Education Bill. Apart from a few items, the proposals of the White Paper were generally acceptable. The Labour Party asked for the announcement of a definite date for raising the school-leaving age to sixteen and demanded that in all secondary schools which received grants from public funds fees should be abolished. Mr. Butler believed that the time was inopportune for fixing a definite date and he was not willing to free all secondary schools from fees.

The favourable reception accorded to the White Paper encouraged Mr. Butler to go ahead with the drafting of the Education Bill. It was introduced into the House of Commons on 16th December 1943, and received Royal Assent on 4th August 1944. Its main principles were accepted by all parties and criticisms were largely directed to administrative matters. It was an agreed measure in so far as anything in this world can be agreed. Mr. Butler was fully aware that all the clauses of the Act could not be brought into operation immediately, and by his description of the day on which the first of its proposals would become effective as "D" Day in Education, he negatived the idea that it would be a final answer to all the problems of national education. Hence, the Education Act of 1944 which had as its avowed aim the complete overhaul of the statutory system of education, was designed to come into operation in stages. Thus Parts I and V came into operation at once, but Part II, which dealt with universal free secondary education, was postponed until 1st April 1945. Some sections of the Act have not yet come into force.

In regard to administration, central and local, the Act may be regarded as the fulfilment of the recommendations made by the Bryce Commission in 1895. The Board of Education disappeared and its place was taken by a Ministry of Education. The Minister was given the powers which the Bryce Commission thought were necessary. Thus the Minister now has the duty of directing the national policy in education and ensuring that it is carried out by the local authorities. The change was not made without certain criticism. Some members of the House thought that too much power was being placed in the hands of the Minister. Mr. Butler replied that it was the function of the central authority to provide leadership and to initiate rather than follow timidly. He also emphasised that the partnership between the central and the local authorities which had been built up after 1902, was to be maintained. The Minister would not be a kind of educational dictator, but he would possess statutory power to compel backward or laggard authorities to carry out their duties.

In his Message to education authorities, he told them: "The Education Act is now the law of the land. To convert legal phraseology into a living force will call for great and sustained exertion. I look, therefore, with confidence to authorities to join with the

Ministry in tackling the new responsibilities which the new Act lays on us. "Let us see to it that the children and young people of our country derive real profit from this, the first measure of social reconstruction which has been passed in these historic days, and is born of a faith in the part that education has to play in shaping the future destinies of our country.[1]

The Act itself provides safeguards against the abuse of the Ministerial powers. The Minister is responsible to Parliament for his department and is obliged to present an annual report which can be criticised by any member. He has authority to frame Regulations (Statutory Rules and Orders), but these must be laid before Parliament and may be annulled by a resolution of either House. Any member of the House of Commons may ask a question in the House on any matter concerning the public service of education, and members frequently exercise this right. Also, any private citizen can communicate with the member representing his own constituency and request him to take up any point about which, in the public interest, he thinks an inquiry should be made. Everything depends upon the vigilance and sense of public duty of Members of Parliament and the citizens of this country. If they are watchful and alive to their responsibilities there should be no fear of an educational dictatorship.

The Consultative Committee of the Board of Education was replaced by two Central Advisory Councils for Education, one for England and the other for Wales. These councils are entrusted with the powers recommended by the Bryce Commission. They can advise the Minister, as they think fit, on matters connected with the theory and practice of education. This constitutes another limitation of the powers of the Minister. The chairman and members of the councils are appointed by the Minister, but since he is required to report their composition and proceedings to Parliament, he is liable at any time to become the target for hostile criticism. The councils must include "persons who have had experience of the statutory system of public education as well as persons who have had experience of educational institutions not forming part of that system." A glance at the composition of the councils as announced by Mr. Butler in December 1944, shows that this principle was observed. The President was the late Sir Fred Clarke, and the membership of the councils included representatives of primary and secondary schools (including the public schools),

Trade Unions, the Universities, the religious bodies, industry, science, agriculture, and adult education.

The number of local education authorities was reduced by the abolition of the Part III authorities. The present L.E.A.s are the county councils and county borough councils. The 315 L.E.A.s created by the Act of 1902 became 146, and the first schedule of the Act provided an opportunity for further reduction. Where it would be to the public advantage because of economy or increase efficiency, the Minister may order the areas of two or more councils to be combined through the establishment of a Joint Education Board which will be the L.E.A. for that district. Thus the Soke and the City of Peterborough, which were areas of small population, were combined to constitute a Joint Education Board. The L.E.A. may delegate its functions (except those of raising a rate or borrowing money) to an education committee. The majority of the members of the committee must be members of the L.E.A., but the committee should also include persons of experience in education and those who have special knowledge of the educational conditions of the locality.

The proposed abolition of Part III authorities occasioned most debate. The White Paper selected two extreme examples to illustrate the kind of anomaly which existed: Harrow U.D.C., which had a population of 183,000 in 1938 but was not an education authority because its population was under 20,000 in 1901, and Tiverton, Devon, which with a population in 1938 of under 10,000, was still a Part III authority. The Local Authorities (Education) Act of 1931 had prohibited the establishment of any new L.E.A.s. In opposition, the Part III authorities canvassed their local M.P.s and in many instances were able to demonstrate that they were among the most progressive and efficient authorities, and that some county authorities had been extremely remiss in putting forward schemes of reorganisation. All this may have been true, but they failed to realise that a new educational scheme based on the principle of secondary education for all would entail a complete revision of local administrative units.

The White Paper proposed a solution which was afterwards materially modified in the Act. It suggested the abolition of Part III authorities and the division of counties into areas under district sub-committees. This had been the practice of some counties for a considerable number of years, e.g. Lancashire, Durham, Cheshire, Kent, and the West Riding. It should be noted that these are large counties, and one could say that delegation had been thrust upon them. The reasons advanced for handing the control of education to the county councils were: unification of the educational system; the adoption of larger units would spread the cost, and matters would be facilitated when it came to framing educational policy. In addition, the reduction in the number of educational units would be a distinct advantage for the Ministry.

When the White Paper was discussed in Parliament, the Part III authorities, through their local members, put up a strenuous opposition. It must be admitted that in most cases the driving force was fear of loss of power, but this was not necessarily a selfish motive. Consider the case of a member of such an authority who had worked conscientiously for twenty years or more for the cause of education in his district and who had freely given his time and advice with genuine enthusiasm. He had acquired an accurate and detailed picture of his area and its peculiar problems, and possessed first-hand knowledge of the schools, the teachers, and the different bodies of managers. The abolition of the Part III authorities might mean the end of his usefulness. He may have been chairman of his particular committee, but now, at the best, he would only be a member of a much larger Education Committee and would lose the power of determining lines of policy which perhaps he considered to be vital. His activities would be largely limited to giving advice. No wonder, as H. C. Dent remarked: "The controversy over units of educational administration blew up in a white heat on the publication of the White Paper."

In his reply for the Government, Mr. Chuter Ede admitted that the arguments in favour of the Part III authorities had impressed him, and he hoped that they would send their representatives to discuss the matter with the Government. The result was the publication of the Explanatory Memorandum to the Education Bill (Cmd. 6492) which contained the following significant paragraph:—

"Instead of the proposal that district committees should be entrusted with the general duty of keeping the needs of their areas under review and of making recommendations to the County Education Committee, there is substituted a system of delegation of functions to divisional executives representing individual county districts or groups of them. The divisional executives will . . . prepare and submit their own annual estimates of expenditure."

It was not obligatory for counties to set up D.E.s for all districts. Some counties or parts of counties could continue to be administered directly by the County Education Committee. The D.E.s were to be concerned with both primary and secondary education and also further education, if the county authority agreed to delegate such powers and the approval of the Ministry was obtained. Altogether, 171 D.E.s were constituted. In regard to their concern with all stages of education, the D.E.s were given a wider reference than the Part III authorities they replaced.

The White Paper had also mentioned excepted districts, which can be regarded as D.E.s in which the borough or urban district council constitutes the executive power, and after consultation with the county authority, prepares its own schemes for primary and secondary education. According to the original draft of the Education Bill, the condition for recognition as an excepted district was that the area should either have possessed a population of 60,000 or over at the census of 1931, or a public elementary school roll of not less than 7,000 on 31st March 1939. Pressure from Part III authorities produced some modifications in the Act. Originally, only thirty-nine areas could claim excepted district status, some by a very small margin. Most of these were in the London area. The Act changed the first condition to allow an area to claim excepted district status if its population was more than 60,000 on 30th June 1939 according to the estimate of the Registrar-General. This was to admit areas which had grown rapidly between 1931 and 1939. The result was that eight more districts, all round London with the exception of Worthing, were brought in. Some areas did not claim or withdrew their claims (e.g. Watford), thus leaving thirty-seven excepted districts.

Yet another provision was made to meet exceptional circumstances. Sixty-seven authorities applied but only seven were admitted: Cheltenham, Stretford, Keighley, Solihull, Nuneaton, Wallsend, and Lowestoft. Some of the claims were ridiculous, e.g. Richmond, Yorks., with a population of 7,000. This raised the number of excepted districts to forty-four. Like the divisional executive, the excepted district has no power to raise a rate or to borrow money.

Divisional executives vary in composition in different parts of the country. They possess both executive and advisory functions, and the actual power they wield depends upon the amount of delegation the county authority is willing to grant. In general, they include three types of member: representatives of the county authority, representatives of local authorities, e.g. an urban district

council, and added members chosen on account of thei
knowledge and experience or representing important intere:
as the religious bodies, industry, the teaching profession,
university.

The overhaul of the national system of education which was
the aim of the Act of 1944 was the logical outcome of the lines
of thought which had been expressed in the Hadow and the Spens
Reports. The Act regarded education as a lifelong process organised in the three progressive stages of primary, secondary, and
further education. It placed upon L.E.A.s the duty of contributing
towards "the spiritual, moral, mental, and physical development
of the community by ensuring that efficient education throughout
those stages shall be available to meet the needs of the population
of their area." Thus, reorganisation became compulsory and the
initiative no longer remained with the local authority. Every
authority was required by 1st April 1946 to survey its area in
order to ascertain its present and future needs as regards primary
and secondary education, and to submit its development plan to
the Ministry. Most authorities found that the time allowed was
insufficient, and on their request an extension of three months was
granted. The London County Council was given an extra year for
this purpose, and even by the end of 1947 there were still twenty
plans to be completed. Before development plans were submitted
to the Ministry, the governors and managers of voluntary schools
had to be consulted. After he had approved the development plan
the Minister issued a local education order. A period of two months
was allowed during which objections could be submitted.

The Act continued the Dual System in a modified form. Voluntary schools fall into three categories. The smallest class consists
of the special agreement schools sanctioned by the Act of 1936.
If the governors or managers of a voluntary school were both able
and willing to contribute half the cost of improvements or alterations to the school buildings to bring them up to the standard
required by the building regulations of the Ministry, they could
apply for aided status. If this was granted, the school retained its
right to provide denominational religious instruction according to
the trust deed, and the appointment of the teachers would be made
by the governors or managers. If the governors or managers were
unable or unwilling to contribute fifty per cent of the cost, the
L.E.A. was empowered to take over the maintenance of the school
as a controlled school. In such a case, two-thirds of the governors

or managers are appointed by the authority, and the religious instruction is based on an agreed syllabus. Parents who request denominational religious instruction for their children can obtain their wish for not more than two periods a week. This instruction is given by reserved teachers except in those schools where the staff (including the head teacher) is less than three. This means that in many small village schools the whole of the religious instruction is according to an agreed syllabus, though parents who wish can withdraw their children to obtain the kind of religious instruction they desire. All schools maintained by a local education authority are known as county schools; county primary or secondary as the case may be.

This compromise was the result of consultation with the religious denominations. From one point of view, the retention of a modified Dual System marks the recognition by the State of the part the religious denominations played in education for many centuries and the connection they have with it at the present. On the other hand, it has saddled them with a heavy burden. Few voluntary schools conform to the standards laid down by the building regulations; in fact, many of them had been for years on the "Black List" of the Board of Education. The majority have to be rebuilt or drastically altered. When the L.E.A. received the Ministry's approval of the development plan, the governors or managers of the voluntary schools were informed and were granted six months in which to decide whether they wished the school to be aided or controlled.

The modifications of the Dual System were carefully considered by the Churches. The Roman Catholics favoured a scheme similar to the Scottish solution of the dual control problem, but this was not acceptable to the Ministry. In the Anglican Church, each diocese explored the situation in its area to decide how many schools it could afford to keep as aided. The number of Church schools in January 1947 was 8,678, but this number, because of the closure of small schools, had fallen to 7,935 in January 1955, and consisted of 3,428 aided and special agreement schools, 4,032 controlled schools, and 475 whose status had yet to be determined. Dioceses and parishes made great efforts to keep as many aided schools as possible, and the National Society recommended the Barchester Scheme to enable managers to accumulate a building fund. The National Society had revised its Charter in 1934 and declared that the primary objects of the Society were: "The promotion, encouragement, and support of religious education in accordance with the principles of the Church of England among all our subjects living in England and Wales, irrespective of age or degree." In 1947 the duty of promoting and supervising the educational work of the Church became the responsibility of the Church Assembly acting through a Board for Education, which is at present organised into five departments: the Schools' Council, Children's Council, Youth Council, Adult Council, and the Council of the Church Training Colleges.

The Council for Education has estimated that in the future there will be about 2,500 aided and special agreement schools, 3,150 controlled schools, and about 2,350 schools scheduled for closure, some of which may be continued permanently because of the Ministry's drive to encourage the reorganisation of rural schools. Approximately £3 million is considered necessary to maintain these schools, and that two-thirds of this sum would eventually be found by dioceses and parishes. In the light of these estimates, the Church Assembly, in November 1956, approved the Church Schools (Assistance by Church Commissioners) Measure, which authorised the Church Commissioners to provide financial aid to the schools to the extent of £1 million by way of grants or loans extending over a period of twenty-five years. This financial assistance will enable the present position to be maintained and will encourage dioceses and parishes to do all they can to retain their aided schools.

The Act made religious instruction and worship obligatory in every school, county or voluntary. Parents still retain their right of withdrawal, and no teacher is compelled to give religious instruction. The Act prescribes that every school day must begin with collective worship attended by all the pupils. It will usually take place in the assembly hall, but if the school has no hall, worship may be held in the classrooms. In county schools the worship may not be distinctive of any particular denomination and the religious instruction will be based on the agreed syllabus that has been adopted by the L.E.A. The first agreed syllabus, the Cambridge-shire, was published as early as 1924. Other authorities followed suit, with the result that a number of agreed syllabuses were available. The earlier syllabuses were little more than outlines, but it soon became evident that teachers would welcome more detailed guidance with regard to teaching method, illustration, and background information. To meet their needs, most authorities revised their syllabuses and added to their contents.

The Fifth Schedule of the Act prescribes the procedure for bringing an agreed syllabus into operation. The L.E.A. convenes a conference consisting of representatives of the Church of England, the Free Churches, the teachers' associations, and the education authority. The conference can either draw up a syllabus or recommend the adoption of a syllabus prepared by another education authority. When the syllabus has been completed it must be approved by the conference. Each of the four panels constituting the conference has one vote and all four must be unanimous in their recommendation. If the conference is unable to agree, or the L.E.A. fails to adopt a syllabus, the Minister may appoint a conference to draw up a syllabus.

The religious instruction provided through agreed syllabuses differs widely from the Scripture teaching of the earlier part of the century. Mr. Chuter Ede declared that most parents "desire that their children shall have a grounding in the principles of the Christian faith as it ought to be practised in this country." Modern agreed syllabuses, therefore, concentrate on presenting the fundamentals of the Christian religion. Some people have expressed a doubt whether in the present divided state of Christendom a syllabus which has been approved by all the denominations can give doctrinal teaching which is sufficiently definite to be of value. An examination of agreed syllabuses reveals the astonishing fact that the body of doctrine about which there is dispute is comparatively small when compared with the bulk of Christian belief which is common to all denominations. Most dioceses of the Anglican Church have prepared syllabuses which may be used in conjunction with an agreed syllabus and which provide the supplementary instruction that is deemed necessary.

The changes mentioned above represent distinct progress when compared with the situation at the time of the Elementary Education Act of 1870. Religious instruction is no longer limited to the beginning or end of the school session. In county schools it is open to inspection by H.M.I.s. This should do much to impress both children and teachers with the importance of religious education. The religious instruction in aided schools and that given in controlled schools by reserved teachers is inspected, as in the past, under arrangements made by the denominations. One problem, namely that of securing a sufficient number of teachers who are both anxious and qualified to give religious instruction, is prominent. Much has been accomplished by the training-colleges and the vacation courses held by the Ministry. The Institute of Christian Education has provided lectures and courses, and publishes each term a journal entitled *Christian Education*, which contains articles designed to assist the teacher. Many University Institutes of Education organise special study courses on the agreed syllabuses, and the attendance at them shows that teachers welcome such assistance. These efforts lead one to hope that there will be a constant rise in the standard of religious education in our schools.

The Education Act of 1944 established the principle of secondary education for all. This necessitated the abolition of fees in all maintained secondary schools from 1st April 1945. It is extremely important to notice that the Act says nothing about a tripartite or any other form of organisation for secondary education. It viewed education as a continuous process in which the three stages of Primary, Secondary, and Further Education are demarcated. The Act stated the fundamental principle that the education given at any stage must be in accordance with "the age, ability, and aptitude of the pupil." It is the parent's obligation to see this is carried out in reference to his own children. Lord Sandon's Act of 1876 had defined the parent's duty as that of causing "his child between the ages of five and fourteen to receive efficient elementary instruction in reading, writing, and arithmetic." As ideas about the scope of education have become broader, the obligations placed on parents have developed. Contrary to popular belief, there is no such thing in this country as compulsory school attendance. If he wishes, a parent who has the time, the knowledge, and the skill, can undertake the instruction of his own children. Alternatively, he can provide a private tutor for his child or pay fees to have him educated at an independent school. Failing these, he must send the child to a school within the national system.

The Act enabled parents to obtain the benefits of a boarding-school education for their children. Some authorities have experimented by placing pupils in independent or grant-earning boarding-schools. Middlesex L.E.A. has recently experimented with their own maintained boarding-school. In other areas, the L.E.A.s have taken over grammar-schools which already possessed boarding attachments and have encouraged their development, *e.g.* the Grammar-Schools of Ripon, Skipton, and Drax, in the West Riding.

Many of the clauses of the Education Act ultimately became inoperative because they were permissive rather than mandatory. The Act of 1944 remedied this defect. It is no longer optional but is the duty of the L.E.A to provide nursery schools or classes wherever they are considered necessary. The continuation schools of the Fisher Act are to be revised under the name of County Colleges. It will be a duty of each L.E.A. to establish County Colleges for the part-time education of those pupils after the age of sixteen who do not remain at the secondary school or attend an institution for higher education. Every young person who is not exempted from this provision will receive a college attendance notice directing him to attend at a county college. The minimum attendance until eighteen years of age will be 330 hours a year, arranged as half-days, whole days, or continuous periods as is most convenient. Suggestions in regard to the curriculum of the colleges are given in the Ministry's pamphlet No. 3, *Youth's Opportunity*, 1945. The date for the opening of county colleges was not to be later than 1950, but problems connected with the supply of buildings and teachers, the critical financial position of the country, and the increased birth-rate in the war years have delayed the establishment of these institutions indefinitely. Only Rugby which still maintained the continuation schools of the Fisher Act was ready to switch over immediately to the county college.

The Act envisaged the raising of the school-leaving age to fifteen from 1st April 1945. As we were still at war, this was postponed for two years. As soon as conditions permit the leaving age will be raised to sixteen. Mr. Butler was pressed by Labour Party to name a definite date for the raising of the leaving age, but because of the uncertainty of the position, he very wisely refused to do so. He stated that not more than slightly over half the schools had carried out the Hadow reorganisation in urban districts, and that in the country the proportion was no more than twenty per cent. When the school-leaving age was raised to fifteen, about 391,000 additional school places would be required. To raise it to sixteen would entail another 406,000 places, and neither buildings nor teachers were available. Moreover, the schools had lost 150,000 places as the result of enemy action, and the first task was to replace these.

The Labour Government which came into power in 1945 was not inclined to be put off lightly, but it was not until 1947 that it was possible to raise the leaving age to fifteen, and in the words of Miss Ellen Wilkinson, the then Minister of Education, this was "an act of faith rather than an act of wisdom." By 1949, the Government had reluctantly decided that a further raising of the school-leaving age and the opening of county colleges would not be possible for some years.

Fees were retained in direct-grant schools. In 1926, grant-aided schools not maintained by local authorities had been given the option of receiving a capitation grant in respect of pupils over eleven direct from the Board of Education instead of through the L.E.A. In 1942, the Fleming Report gave the number of direct-grant schools as 232 with 85,681 pupils. Direct-grant schools were required to accept a minimum percentage of free or special-place pupils. When fees were abolished in maintained secondary schools all direct-grant schools were asked to re-submit their claims. Some were struck off the list even when they had previously enjoyed direct-grant status, e.g. Archbishop Holgate's School, York. Many schools feared the curtailment of their freedom, and those who had sufficient endowments raised their fees and decided to continue as independent schools. Some regretted their decision, and when faced with the burden of enlarging their accommodation, although it was understood that no additions could be made to the list, they renewed their application for direct-grant status.

In November 1956, the Minister of Education, Sir David Eccles, decided to reopen the direct-grant list. His argument was that these schools were essential to the national system because they combined the best features of the maintained and the independent schools. The conditions for direct-grant were published on 9th January 1957. Before considering applications, the Ministry will consult the L.E.A.s concerned, and only schools with high educational standards will be admitted. Factors which will count are the qualifications of the staff, the staff-pupil ratio, the average leaving age and the proportion of school-leavers who enter the universities.

Schools with fewer than sixty in the VIth Form, or less than 300 pupils in the main school, or with less than twenty-five per cent of day pupils, will not normally be considered. The school must not be one conducted for gain, and no pupil unable to profit by the education provided shall be admitted or retained.

The Labour Party criticised the decision to retain direct-grant schools as conferring privileges on certain sections of the community. Those in favour, have argued that education will benefit. The maintained schools have discovered what it involves to be deluged with forms and returns. Many head teachers complain that attention to administrative details is drawing them away from the really important aspects of school life and turning them into glorified clerks. One solution is to provide head teachers with more clerical assistants and other helpers. It may be that a new profession will arise, that of clerical administrators for the schools. The heads of direct-grant and independent schools are spared a great deal of the "red tape" and, consequently, have more time and freedom to experiment in different directions.

The Act required each L.E.A to establish and develop facilities for school playing-fields, camps, swimming-baths, gymnasia, and other forms of recreation. They are empowered to provide clothes and books for children, but the cost can be recovered from parents who can afford to pay. School medical inspection and treatment have been extended, and the continuation and extension of the school meals and milk service was provided for. A small charge is made, for those who can afford it, for pupils taking school meals, but when there are sufficient numbers of canteens, the intention was to provide these free of charge. So far, the rise in the cost of living has resulted in small increases in the money demanded for school meals.

One important feature of the Act should not be omitted, viz the position of the independent schools. This term includes all those institutions which are outside the statutory system and do not receive grants from the Ministry. They range from private and proprietary schools to the larger public boarding-schools, such as Winchester and Eton. Private schools, or as they were once termed, "private adventure schools," had for many years presented a problem. One should not jump to the conclusion that all private schools are inefficient. Many are excellent institutions, and in the past took advantage of the offer of inspection made by the Board of Education, and so were able to include in their prospectuses, the words, "Inspected by the Board of Education." There was, however, no compulsion on a school to open its doors to the inspector, and the machinery for closing an inefficient school was cumbrous. No register of them was kept so that it was only possible to guess at their number. It was estimated that there were nearly 10,000 such schools, of which over 4,000 had never been inspected. The Education Act of 1918 had required all private schools to be registered, but this clause had never been enforced.

Mr. Butler explained that he had no intention of closing the independent schools, for he believed that a variety of institutions for the education of children was not only an advantage from a national point of view but parents would be able to choose the school to which they desired to send their children and to pay fees for them. It was, however, the duty of the State to guarantee to parents that the school they selected gave a sound and efficient training. The Minister was directed to appoint a Registrar of Independent Schools who should keep a register of them. They would also be open to inspection. Certain schools which were already recognised as efficient secondary schools, and some preparatory schools which had previously been inspected, would be exempted from registration. If a school, because of inadequate buildings or an unqualified staff, or for any other reason, was found to be inefficient, it could be removed from the register. The proprietor was allowed the right of appeal to an Independent Schools' Tribunal consisting of a chairman appointed by the Lord Chancellor from the legal profession and two other members appointed by the Lord President of the Council from persons who possessed teaching or administrative experience. No officials either of the Ministry or of a local authority would be eligible for appointment.

It was not possible to bring this section of the Act into immediate operation on account of the shortage of H.M.I.s and the difficulties in regard to building materials and labour, and the supply of teachers which made it unreasonable to expect schools to remedy their deficiencies within a fixed time. When, after March 1949, the situation had eased, the inspection of independent schools began and was continued at the rate of about 150 a month. Contrary to expectations, the legislation of 1944 did not greatly decrease the number of private schools, and in some districts new schools were opened. The reason for this was that some parents were faced with a difficult problem. Their children could not obtain entry to a grammar-school unless they had been selected by the tests used for grammar-school entrance. The only other way of obtaining a traditional secondary education was through a public or a direct-grant school. Many of these schools had long waiting lists, and competition was so keen that a child who failed to pass the selection test for a grammar-school would not be likely to satisfy the requirements for entry into a public or direct-grant school. Hence a number of private schools which offer an education similar to that provided by a grammar-school have come into existence. Their efficiency is guaranteed by the necessity of registration and inspection.

Section 76 states the governing principle of the Act: "In the exercise and performance of all powers and duties conferred and imposed on them by this Act the Minister and local education authorities shall have regard to the general principle that, so far as is compatible with the provision of efficient instruction and training and the avoidance of unreasonable public expenditure, pupils are to be educated in accordance with the wishes of their parents."

Every local authority is now required to appoint a fit person to be the chief education officer of the authority. In most cases this had already been done, but it now becomes obligatory for every authority to make such an appointment. The Burnham Committees are maintained by the Act and are recognised as a Main Committee to deal with the salaries of teachers in primary and secondary schools and county colleges, and a Technical Committee is concerned with teachers in technical schools and colleges. Any award made by either committee is now binding on all local authorities.

The 1944 Act authorised the Minister to issue regulations dealing with the grant paid to L.E.A.s. They were to receive grants from the Ministry of Health in respect of their functions relating to the medical inspection and treatment of pupils. These obligations were extended, and the continuation and extension of school meals and milk were ensured. The Ministry of Education issued new grant regulations (*S.R. and O. 709* of 1945-6 and *1215* of 1946) under which the Government grant was to be comprised under six heads: a main grant; an additional grant; school milk and meals grant; training college grant; emergency training of teachers grant; and a grant for the removal of air-raid shelters. The main grant represented an average of 54·36 per cent of net recognisable expenditure. The additional grant was drawn from a sum of £1,500,000 to £2,000,000 to give extra assistance to poorer L.E.A.s. The main grant was to be calculated on the following formula: Main grant = sixty per cent of net recognisable expenditure, plus a capitation grant of £6 for each unit of average attendance, minus the product of a 2s. 6d. rate. The idea was to equalise the burden on poorer areas. The school milk and meals grant applied to all maintained, voluntary, direct-grant, and independent schools. In 1947 the school meals grant was amended to provide a premises grant and a dinner grant of 100 per cent, and a grant for meals and refreshment other than dinners at the rate of 54·7214 per cent.

The main provisions of the 1944 Act have been in operation for over a decade and one is now in a position to take stock. In spite of certain flaws which could only be apparent in the course of its administration, one is justified in saying that the Act constitutes what is possibly the greatest single advance made in the development of English education. Unfortunately events have prevented some of the important clauses of the Act from being put into force. The delay in raising the school-leaving age to sixteen has already been explained. The date when it will be possible to inaugurate the county colleges is still very much in the future.

The Education Act of 1944 has been amended by several subsequent Acts, and its educational policy has been developed through a large number of Statutory Rules and Orders (S.R. and O.) and Ministry of Education Circulars. The first amending Act came into force on 22nd May 1946.

Section 7 of the Act is a very important one. It states that the collective worship with which the school day in county and voluntary schools begins must take place on the school premises. The managers or governors of an aided or special-agreement school may desire that on special occasions the collective worship should take place elsewhere, *e.g.* in the parish church. They can make arrangements for this, but *Circular 111,* dated 24th May 1946, reminds managers that "it is important that parents should be given adequate notice of any proposal to hold the collective act of worship off the school premises in case they should wish their children to be excused from attending, under Section 25(4) of the 1944 Act. The method of informing parents will be affected by local circumstances, but it will not be sufficient only to make the time-table entry required by the regulations. Notice should be prominently displayed in the school, if possible not less than fourteen days beforehand, and the children instructed to inform their parents." This concession does not apply to controlled schools.

The Education (Miscellaneous Provisions) Act, 1948, amends certain provisions of the principal Act.

Section 3 is perhaps the most important of the Act. It amends the definitions of primary and secondary education as given in Section 8, Subsection 1, of the principal Act. Primary education is now defined as that which is suited to the requirements of junior pupils who have not attained the age of ten and a half years, or of pupils over that age whom it is expedient to educate in the junior school. Likewise, secondary education is that suited to pupils who have attained the age of ten years and six months whom it is deemed expedient to educate together with older children. This authorises the promotion of exceptionally able children to a secondary school six months earlier than the accepted age. The amendment has been accorded a very mixed reception. Those who held strongly that eleven-plus was too early an age to decide the abilities and aptitudes of the majority of children emphasised that all the objections to the previous age of transfer applied with the more force to those of ten and a half, who could not by any means be considered as even approaching adolescence.

In February 1947 the Minister of Education, Miss Ellen Wilkinson died suddenly and was succeeded by Mr. George Tomlinson. The General Election of October 1951 resulted in the return of Mr. Churchill and a Conservative Government. Miss F. Horsbrugh was appointed Minister of Education. She found it necessary to make further amendments to meet the changing conditions.

The Government's Education (Miscellaneous Provisions) Bill received its first reading on 14th November 1952. The object of the Bill was to give some measure of financial assistance to voluntary schools and to clarify certain points arising from the Education Acts of 1944 and 1946. These Acts had provided for the payment of grants not exceeding fifty per cent towards the building of new aided schools on new building estates. To claim the grant it was necessary to prove that one or more of the schools which pupils of the proposed new school had attended had suffered a "substantial" reduction in numbers as a result of the transfer. The grant would then be paid on the displaced pupils transferred to the new school. The phrase "substantial" is a relative one. Thus twenty might be considered a substantial reduction in a school where the number on roll had been about fifty, but this could not be claimed in the case of a large school of three hundred. It was soon discovered that most of the new denominational schools on the housing estates drew their pupils from a number of different districts so that it was difficult to prove a substantial reduction. In these circumstances, no grant would be paid. This had not been envisaged when the Act of 1944 was passed. The remedy suggested was a revision of the definition of "displaced pupil" to allow the religious bodies to claim grant for them. The cost to the Exchequer would be about £200,000 a year and the religious bodies would benefit to this extent.

The Minister stated that she had no intention of interfering with the main structure of the Act of 1944.

At the second reading of the Bill some members proposed that the grant should be made retrospective to 1944. Also a clause which gave the L.E.A. the duty of naming the school to which a child was directed by a school attendance order was criticised on the ground that it interfered with the responsibilities of parents in spite of the fact that they had the right of appeal. These points were discussed in standing committee. The Minister was opposed to an amendment which, by making the grant applicable to schemes in progress or for which accounts had not been closed, would include about six Roman Catholic schools. In the division, denominational interests were predominant and the amendment was carried against the Government by twenty-six votes to eighteen.

One important proposal of the Bill is to amend Section 40 of the Act of 1940 to enable L.E.A.s to bring truants directly before a juvenile court in place of the present practice by which they are obliged to go first to a magistrate's court. Their misdemeanours will now be considered by persons who have had experience in dealing with children. It is also made clear that it is the duty of L.E.A.s in England and Wales and in Scotland to provide their own school dental service instead of relying upon the National Health Service. Miss Horsbrugh proposed certain drafting amendments which were accepted and the Bill became law in 1953.

Considerable criticism has been directed to the system ot divisional administration, and sufficient time has now passed to allow one to ask if the scheme has been successful in practice. It was quite a new experiment in local government and was frankly a compromise to satisfy the claims of the former Part III authorities. It has been argued that although the divisional executive contains a large element of representatives of elected bodies, it is not democratically elected and so does not conform to the tradition of English local government. This fact would not condemn the system provided it worked efficiently. Much depends upon the amount of responsibility delegated by the county authority and the calibre of the Divisional Officers. Some authorities have been more generous in their delegation than others. Thus the county authorities of Lancashire and the West Riding of Yorkshire have not only delegated large powers in regard to primary, secondary, and further education, but have frequently urged the divisional executives to make use of them.

The divisional executives have, on the whole, served the original purpose of providing for the expression of local views and of stimulating local interest in education. The bulk of the criticism has focussed on the administrative efficiency of the arrangement. It has been said that considerable delays have occurred in respect of urgent matters and that the system is expensive in money and manpower. Some counties, such as Devon and Somerset, have adopted a policy of discontinuing divisional executives. Lancashire has reduced the number by amalgamating some of the smaller districts. The West Riding is cutting administrative costs by a regrouping of the divisional offices and their staffs.

Another problem has arisen in regard to the organisation of secondary education, a point on which the Butler Act was silent. Most local authorities were influenced by the Norwood Report and chose the tripartite arrangement of secondary-grammar, secondary-technical, and secondary-modern schools, each housed in a separate building. On the other hand, some L.E.A.s, including the L.C.C. and Middlesex, decided in favour of multilateral or comprehensive schools,[1] which to be effective would have to contain at least 1,200 pupils. One reason advanced in support of this policy was that by accommodating all the different types of pupil in one building or on one site, a breaking down of class distinctions would follow. Whether this is a fact is open to doubt, and some reports from similar schools in the U.S.A. strengthen this doubt. Many educationists believe that it is premature to come to a decision until further experience of different types of organisation has been gained and that the rational procedure would be to experiment in different districts with various types of organisation and to formulate a policy in the light of the knowledge so acquired.

Another argument for the comprehensive school is that it simplifies the problem of selection for secondary education. A pupil can be transferred from one type of work to another which is more suited to him without uprooting him and sending him to another school. Unfortunately, the discussion of the organisation of secondary education has become a party political controversy. The main support for the comprehensive school comes from the Socialist Party, but it is interesting to note that several divisional executives in South Yorkshire have clung tenaciously to their grammar-schools,

---

[1] Multilateral and comprehensive were generally employed as synonyms until they were defined by the Ministry in Circular 144 (*Organisation of Secondary Education*), 16th June 1947. A multilateral school differs from a comprehensive by being organised in three streams.

largely because of the outstanding personalities of individual members of the committees who were unwilling to lose the schools for which they had fought so vigorously in the past.

One criticism of the Butler Act is that it accepted without question the recommendations of the Hadow Report as regards the clean break at eleven-plus. This had been severely criticised by many well-known educationists and psychologists on the ground that it is not possible at such an early stage to ascertain with an exactitude the special interests, aptitudes, and abilities, of children. It should be noted in this connection that the Scottish Advisory Council has recommended the age of twelve-plus for transfer, which fits in with the practice followed in many parts of Scotland.

In the years which followed the conclusion of the war, one of the most serious problems was caused by the shortage of building materials and labour. This was complicated by the raising of the school-leaving age and the "bulge" which was the popular name for the increase in the birthrate after the war. At the time of writing, the "bulge" has passed through the primary school and has entered the secondary, and will eventually have a somewhat diminished influence on the universities. Immediately after the war the first priority was housing, and until the nation was supplied with an adequate number of houses, the building of schools could only proceed at a very modest rate.

The upward movement of the birthrate and the extension of the school-leaving age have added nearly a million children to the school population. A serious breakdown would have occurred but for the successful working of the plans devised by the Ministry of Education to meet the emergency. The large-scale construction of permanent buildings was at the time quite out of practical politics, and Miss Ellen Wilkinson arranged for the Ministry of Works to supply and erect prefabricated classrooms which could be delivered at the request of L.E.A.s and to equip them with suitable furniture. These were the well known HORSA huts and SFORSA furniture.[1] Many authorities remembered the wooden Army huts supplied after the First World War and hesitated to take advantage of the offer which was made in September 1945, and it required a strong reminder in the following year to speed up acceptances. The Government made it quite clear that new school buildings would be restricted to the replacement of premises

[1] HORSA—Hutting Operation for the Raising of the School Age. SFORSA—School Furniture Operation for the Raising of the School Age.

destroyed by enemy action, provision of schools for the new housing estates, and for the increasing number of school children who from 1947 onwards would be in need of school places.

Among the numerous Statutory Rules and Orders made by the Ministry, No. 345 of 24th March 1945 (*The Regulations prescribing Standards for School Premises*), was important because it laid down building standards for all primary and secondary schools. They apply to existing as well as to new schools, and are based on a school-leaving age of sixteen. The majority of existing schools fall far short of the prescribed standards, and many of them cannot be brought up to the new standards by alteration and extensions.[1] They must be replaced, and L.E.A.s have had to decide, in their development plans, not only which schools must be replaced, but also their relative urgency. The *Regulations* are too detailed to summarise, but some idea of them may be gained from the following example. The minimum size of a site for a three-class primary

---

[1] The following extracts from inspectors' reports provide examples of unsatisfactory buildings which are still in use:—*

(*a*) A North-Country manufacturing town.

"The predominant impression made by the schools is of one- or two-storey red-brick buildings, whose architects, uncertain as to whether their model should be a church, a barracks, or a railway station, created something solid, serviceable and ugly, which is unmistakably labelled 'late nineteenth century school.'". . . Other schools in the oldest part of the town are described as "not only ugly but also inconvenient and in constant need of renovation. Indeed, so dilapidated had one of these schools become that a few weeks ago the authority were obliged to close it as it was no longer safe, and to house its 800 children temporarily in other schools, in canteens, and church halls."

(*b*) An unreorganised all-age school.

"The building dates from the 1840's, and though said to have been remodelled in 1894, is still a fine specimen of Victorian Gothic. The rooms, though high and fairly spacious, are separated by partitions, and most of them are passage ways. They are dimly lit either naturally or by gas. There are no practical or store rooms, no hall, no library, no dining-room, no hot water, and no drying facilities. Sanitary arrangements are archaic. The staff lack all amenities. In fact, conditions have not changed since the last century. A new HORSA hut is the brightest thing on these premises." (HORSA = Hutting Operation for the Raising of the School Age.)

(*c*) A secondary-technical school.

"Most of the rooms now in use must date from that time (1825), though adaptations of a minor sort have been carried out. . . . There are about 280 pupils. Most of the rooms are of good size—but are horribly dark. Gas is still the means of artificial light and has, in some rooms, to be used during the whole day. There are dark dungeon-like passages. One of the rooms used as a laboratory has to serve as an assembly-hall and as a dining-room. The dust and grime that collect in the rooms seem to dishearten the cleaners, who tend to give up the unequal struggle. There is no playground at all; thus there can be no mid-session recreation breaks."

* *Education in* 1948, H.M.S.O., 1949, pp. 16-18.

school is two acres, without gardens. A three-form entry secondary-modern school would require a site of twenty acres, with two or three acres for gardens. The playground is included in the site, but it should be noted that playing-fields are additional to the site. A playing-field must be provided for every primary and secondary school or department. Thus the secondary-modern school given as example would need another fourteen acres for playing-field accommodation.

Many existing classrooms will eventually have to be used for other purposes, since they do not conform to the classroom accommodation prescribed. A five-class school, or over, must have an assembly-hall of at least 1,800 square feet, and every primary school of seven to twelve classes must have a dining-room. In schools of more than twelve classes, two dining-rooms will be required. All secondary schools must have, in addition to the assembly-hall and dining-room, a gymnasium, library, art and craft rooms, and practical rooms. All schools should have arrangements for film projection and the use of episcopes, and some classrooms should be wired for wireless reception. The assembly-hall must have a stage or platform, a projection-room, and be wired for wireless reception. There must be sufficient cloak-room, lavatory, storage, drying-room, staff-room, and kitchen accommodation. All large schools should have a separate room for medical inspection and a waiting-room for parents.[1]

The Minister deplored any attempt to lower the proper standards of teaching or to employ inadequate teaching staffs. The supply of books, stationery, and essential apparatus should be maintained at an adequate level. She also deprecated any move which would impair the efficiency of the school medical and dental services or restrict the facilities for the development of technical education. The *Circular* suggested certain ways in which local authorities might be able to effect economies. They were called upon to review their anticipated expenditure on administration. Thus the Hertfordshire Education Committee has proposed a reduction of divisional executives from seven to one. It is estimated that this would effect a saving of about £15,000 a year with the possibility of a further saving of about £4,000. This is equivalent to nearly one-tenth of the authority's expenditure on administration. It is also urged that there is nothing which the

---

[1] Because of the urgent need for economy, the Ministry in 1950 made certain modifications as regards buildings.

divisional executive can do which cannot be carried out as effectively by the managers and governors of schools.

The expenditure on Main Grant services had already been limited by *Circular 210*, September 1951, and the Minister could not approve any increase on this amount. Transport of school children was an item which called for serious consideration. Its cost had risen to over £4,000,000 a year and in many cases the statutory minima required by the Act of 1944 had been ignored. In normal cases, transport could be provided for children living two miles from the school if they were under eight years of age, and three miles for children over that age. Handicapped children could be considered as exceptional cases. Where, for various reasons, parents were sending their children to schools which were not the nearest to their homes, they might be asked to pay part of the fares.

The Minister recommended an increase of fees for further education and that recreational classes should be self-supporting. She did not expect drastic economies with regard to the provision of playgrounds, physical education, national camps, or the youth service, but efforts should be made to avoid unnecessary spending on these items. As regards capital expenditure, *e.g.* school building, separate suggestions would be made. These were the subject of *Circular 245* on capital investment in 1952-3. The revised programme for educational building set forth in the *Circular* was rendered necessary by the acute shortage of building materials, especially steel. The Minister promised guidance on the economic use of steel, but for the time being a halt would have to be made in all but essential building. Local authorities were asked to consider alternative forms of construction in which the use of steel would be reduced to the minimum. Plans for rebuilding out-of-date schools would have to be temporarily postponed and the fullest use be made of spare places in primary schools. This might mean the postponement of the age of transfer for not more than a year. The reduced building programme, coupled with the present shortage in the number of teachers, would prevent for some time any marked reduction in the size of classes.

In February 1953, Miss Horsbrugh announced a reduction in the grants for adult education which would effect a saving of about £30,000 a year. This met with widespread criticism on the ground that the amount of public money saved was almost negligible but the work of university extra-mural departments would be seriously restricted. In view of these protests, the Minister reversed her decision on the ten per cent cut in the adult education grant.

It will be some years before all out-of-date and inadequate buildings can be replaced. One principle, however, has been agreed, namely, that flesh and blood are more important than bricks and mortar. The outstanding problem remains that of the supply of teachers. During the war, various estimates ranging from 50,000 to 120,000 were made in regard to the number of teachers who would be required for the post-war period. The Ministry decided on a minimum of 70,000, and to secure this the Emergency Training Scheme was launched in 1943 to obtain men and women teachers from the Forces and from other forms of national service. In co-operation with L.E.A.s, arrangements were made to open emergency training-colleges in different parts of the country. The initial difficulty which confronted the Ministry was the fact that most of the suitable buildings were occupied by Service personnel. As the demands of the latter decreased, more colleges could be opened. The emergency training-colleges offered a one-year course of intensive training, and after its completion the student was expected to follow a course of directed reading in order to improve his academic background. Many head teachers have warmly praised the enthusiasm, character, and personality of these new entrants to the profession.

The chief criticisms of the scheme were that the period of training was unduly short and that in some cases the academic background of the teachers was slender, but this fault has been partially remedied by the provision of suitable refresher courses. The scheme was regarded as a temporary expedient which came to an end in October 1951. Some of the colleges were retained as two-year training-colleges, but the majority were closed. A full account of the scheme is given in *Challenge and Response* (Ministry of Education Pamphlet No 17, H.M.S.O., 1950). Out of 124,000 applicants, 54,000 were accepted for training. Taking into account withdrawals and transfers to two-year training-colleges, the scheme provided about 35,000 teachers, of whom 23,000 were men. In addition, the training-colleges and the university departments of education were urged to increase the number of entrants they could undertake to train.

These measures served their purpose for the first few years after the war, but it soon became obvious that a permanent solution of the problem had not been reached. In order to attract the right types of man and woman to the teaching profession it was realised that salary conditions should be at least equal to those in other walks of life. The whole question of recruitment and training of teachers had been considered by an important committee which met towards the end of the war under the chairmanship of Sir Arnold McNair. It was also concerned with the training of youth leaders. The McNair Committee reported in 1944.

Until 1930 the examination for the Teachers' Certificate had been conducted by the Board of Education. In that year an important modification took place which foreshadowed future developments. The training-colleges were organised in groups and each group was associated with the university or university college of its region. The aim was to develop a closer relationship between the universities and the training-colleges. Joint Examination Boards and Boards of Studies which contained representatives of each university and the training-colleges were established. Their function was to draw up and approve syllabuses and to appoint examiners. The Board of Education still retained the right to examine practical teaching, physical training, and other practical subjects. The high hopes of the scheme were only partly realised, and the McNair Committee came to the conclusion that the Joint Board system was not working as efficiently as could be desired. It neither brought about the effective co-operation between the universities and the training-colleges nor between the colleges themselves.

The McNair Report, in its review of the whole question of teacher training, proposed the establishment of a Central Training Council for England and Wales consisting of three to five members who should have the duty of advising the Board of Education about bringing into being that form of training service which the Report recommended and which it was hoped the Board would adopt. The Committee was agreed upon the policy of establishing Area Training Organisations (A.T.O.), but there was a sharp division of opinion about the form they should take.

One half of the Committee favoured what is generally known as Scheme A, which involved the establishment of University Schools or Institutes of Education. The supporters of this view admitted that it involved a "major constitutional change" in the organisation and administration of the training of teachers. They stated that the establishment of University Institutes of Education "will demand of the universities a richer conception of their responsibility towards education; it will also involve additional staff, both teaching and administrative. On the other hand, we are not proposing that the universities should burden themselves with detailed administration, but rather that they should accept responsibility for the general supervision of the training of teachers and that in that task they should have the active partnership of those already engaged in the work and of others who ought to be engaged in it."[1]

Some universities were seriously concerned about the major change involved by accepting Scheme A, and preferred as an alternative the extension and development of the Joint Board system which was generally known as Scheme B. Various modifications of Scheme B were suggested which could be grouped under a third category, Scheme C. Institutes of Education set up under Scheme A are financed by the University Grants Committee; the others by the Ministry of Education. When the Minister of Education agreed to allow the universities to choose which scheme they wished to adopt (*Circular 112*, 11th June 1946), it was found that whilst, on the whole, the universities preferred Schemes B or C, the L.E.A.s and the teachers were in favour of Scheme A. The first to make up their minds were Birmingham and Bristol, and the University Colleges of Nottingham and Southampton, in 1947. In the following year, Durham, Leeds, London, Manchester, Sheffield, and Wales, and the University Colleges of Exeter, Hull, and Leicester, also chose Scheme A. Reading, Cambridge, and Liverpool preferred Scheme C. For a time, Oxford remained outside the system, but eventually decided to come in during 1951.

The Institutes of Education are by no means uniform, but differ in various ways. Some cover a wide area, *e.g.* London and Leeds, and have a considerable number of member institutions. Others, such as Oxford, have a more restricted area and the number of member institutions is correspondingly less. The constitution of each of the Institutes also varies. Thus, at some universities the Director of the Institute is also the Head of the University Department of Education, but in most universities the Head of the Department holds a post which is separate from that of Director of the Institute. The University Department is a member institution but not a member college of the Institute. The post of Director of the Institute is often of professorial status.

An Institute of Education has two main responsibilities. In the first place, as the Area Training Organisation, it co-ordinates the provision for the training of teachers within the university area.

[1] *Report on Teachers and Youth Leaders*, p. 50, H.M.S.O., 1944.

It is responsible for awarding certificates in education to candidates of the member colleges who have satisfied the examiners and recommends each successful candidate to the Ministry for the status of Qualified Teacher. In accordance with the recommendation of the McNair Committee, the Ministry of Education recognises one grade of teacher, that of Qualified Teacher. The Report had also suggested that the Diploma in Education issued to graduate students in the University Departments of Education should be discontinued and be replaced by a certificate or graduate certificate. Some universities strenuously opposed the recommendation. They resented the abolition of the Diploma which they had granted to their successful candidates for more than a quarter of a century. In one university a compromise was arranged so that the graduate certificate was awarded under the authority of the Board of the Faculty of Arts. Another university, after accepting the certificate, decided to restore the Diploma.

The second responsibility of the institutes is that of providing facilities for study and research in the field of education. Thus the institutes not only organise refresher courses for acting teachers but provide instruction of a more advanced nature which lead to diplomas in primary, secondary, and religious education, and for teachers of backward children. These courses extend over one, two, or three years. The one-year courses are usually full-time, and the three-year courses part-time. Many of the two-year courses are also part-time, but include a full-time period of study of one or two terms. They are intended for teachers who have had several years' experience, many of whom do not possess the initial degree qualification which would enable them to undertake research for the degrees of M.A. in Education, M.Ed., or Ph.D. Most institutes have a full-time teaching staff and also make use of the staff of the university departments. In order to carry out these functions effectively, it is essential that the institute should be housed in suitable buildings equipped with a library, lecture, conference, and seminar rooms. Up to the present, because of lack of accommodation, this has often not been possible, and many institutes have had to make do with what premises were available and then to move into more commodious quarters as these become vacant.

The Board of the Institute constitutes the governing body on which the university, the training-college and member institutions, and the L.E.A.s are represented according to a scheme contained in the ordinance which constitutes the institute. The actual day-by-day work is the function of the Professional Committee, and the discussion of syllabuses of instruction takes place at the various Boards of Studies. The teaching profession is represented on the Board, and the Professional Committee and two assessors are appointed by the Ministry of Education, who can contribute to the discussions but have no voting powers. The Board and the Professional Committee have numerous sub-committees which deal with such matters as lectures and courses, the library, research apparatus, and school textbooks. Many institutes offer fellowships for more advanced research in the educational field, and the results are often published. In addition, most institutes issue a bulletin which discusses matters of contemporary interest and a quarterly journal containing longer articles concerned with research.

It is still somewhat early to make a full assessment of the value of these changes as regards teacher training. At first, the institutes were regarded with some suspicion by the training-colleges and other departments of the universities. Such has been the fate of many new ventures. The institutes are now settling down to a *modus vivendi* with other departments and the training-colleges, and there is a growing spirit of co-operation between them. On the side of teacher training, the results have been most promising. Without interfering with the autonomy of the member institutions, standards have been maintained, and in many cases raised, and the feeling of isolation which some of the smaller training institutions had formerly experienced is fast disappearing. They feel that they have now a centre in the institute of their regional university. They come to know their colleagues in other training institutions and also the staff of the university. There is no doubt that the Institutes of Education will develop considerably in the future and will enhance the status of the teaching profession.

The McNair Committee also grappled with the problem of the recruitment and supply of teachers in the post-war period. It recommended that the work and prospects of the teaching profession should be brought to the notice of pupils in the upper forms of the grammar-schools and that older men and women should also be attracted to the profession. In order to secure the services of the latter it would be essential that initial salaries should be based on the age and previous experience of the entrants. A basic scale of salaries should apply to teachers in all types of school, and special qualifications and experience should be rewarded by additional increments at the minimum and maximum of the scale. Special

allowances should be made to teachers holding posts of responsibility.

The "Pledge" system, under which entrants to training-colleges
and university departments received a two- or four-year grant on
condition that they declared in writing that it was their intention
to enter the teaching professions, should be discontinued as soon
as possible. It was felt that the undergraduate on entering upon
his academic course should not be earmarked for a particular profession. The Ministry adopted these recommendations, and in
1951 the four-year system was abolished. Students were not obliged
to declare their intention of becoming teachers until near the end
of their degree course, and in 1956 the signed declaration was no
longer demanded. The salary recommendations were considered
by the Burnham Committee and a new scale came into force from
1st April 1945. Because of the continual rise in the cost of living,
several revisions of the scale have taken place since that date.

The Government has now agreed to the principle of equal pay
for men and women teachers. It was felt that to make a sudden
change would place too great a burden upon the finances of the
country, and the policy of bringing the salaries of women teachers
to the level of men by seven stages to be completed by 1st April
1961 was adopted. The new scheme came into operation on 1st May
1955. Another financial problem was caused by teachers' pensions.
It was calculated that the superannuation fund would be in danger
of becoming insolvent in the near future, and Miss Horsbrugh proposed to raise the teachers' contributions to six per cent. This was
strongly opposed by the teachers' associations. When Sir Winston
Churchill re-shuffled the Cabinet in 1954, Sir David Eccles became
Minister of Education. The pension controversy was eventually
settled by the compromise of taking the increased contribution into
consideration when fixing the revised salary scales which came
into operation from October 1956.

The maintenance and increase of the supply of teachers is still
a serious problem. At the end of 1954, the Ministry returned
the number of teachers in maintained and assisted schools as
241,300, which was an increase of 7,600 over the number at the
end of the previous year. The estimate for 1955 included a further
increase of about 7,000. These figures, however, conceal the real
problem, which is that of supplying the teachers needed to cope
with the increased number of pupils now entering the secondary
schools, and the provision of teachers in scientific and technical
subjects. The latter point will be considered more appropriately

in Chapter XIII. The revision of the salary scales, which has narrowed the gap between the remuneration possible in industry and that in the teaching profession, may increase the number of entrants to the training-colleges and the university departments. It is significant that the number of applicants for training for the session 1957-8 shows a definite increase.

The relation between the State system and the schools outside it were the object of consideration of the Fleming Committee, which presented its report on the Public Schools and the General Educational System in 1944. During the war period the public schools had been the subject of much criticism, some justifiable but much of it misinformed. The most general criticism was that the public schools had little contact with the State system and ought to be brought into line with it. As Professor Barnard says, the public schools form "a closed private system, running parallel with the national system but having few points of contact with it."[1]

The public-school question has been debated so frequently in recent years that it is worth while recapitulating some of the points discussed in earlier chapters of this book in order to gain a clear picture of the issues involved. We saw that in their origin the public schools differed in no respect from other free grammar-schools which drew their scholars from all parts of the country. In fact, the terms "grammar-school" and "public school" were frequently interchangeable, but even in the later Middle Ages, Winchester and Eton, because of the scale of their foundations and their connection with the older universities, were becoming pre-eminent amongst English schools. The number of these "great" schools was swelled in Tudor times by the foundation or refoundation of certain others, both day and boarding schools, such as Harrow, Rugby, Westminster, Charterhouse, Shrewsbury, Merchant Taylors', and St. Paul's. Towards the end of the 17th century the distinction between these schools and the rest of the grammar-schools began to be more marked, and the divergence had become accentuated in the 18th century when the term "public school" began to be applied in the narrower sense.

The general state of stagnation in the public schools resulted in the critical attacks of the early 19th century and eventually led to the appointment of the Clarendon Commission. We saw that the Commission made certain suggestions about the curriculum of the

[1] H. C. Barnard. *A Short History of English Education*, 1760-1944, p. 282.

public schools, but they were largely left to reform themselves. That work had already begun with the efforts of Butler and Arnold. Other ancient foundations, such as Uppingham and Oundle, were added to the number of the public schools through the ability and personality of such headmasters as Thring and Sanderson. Moreover, the rise of a wealthy middle class, as distinct from the landed gentry, after 1832, led to the demand for more public schools, which was met by the establishment of new schools such as Marlborough, Haileybury, and Wellington.

The next extension of the term was to include under it a number of large schools of modern foundation and grammar-schools whose heads were members of the Headmasters' Conference, founded in 1869 and incorporated in 1909. This usage was recognised in 1942 when the President of the Board of Education, in an official answer, defined the public schools as those "which are in membership of the Governing Bodies' Association or Headmasters' Conference." The Association of Governing Bodies of Public Schools, founded in 1941, represents the governing bodies of those schools which are either independent or in receipt of direct grant. Certain maintained schools, for special reasons, have also been admitted to membership. The association was formed to create a means by which questions of common policy outside the sphere of those discussed at the Headmasters' Conference might be decided.

The reforms in the life, curriculum, and teaching methods of the public schools had raised them by the end of the 19th century to an exceedingly high position in public esteem; and their contributions to the nation, especially during the First World War, had increased their popularity, as was evidenced by the founding of new schools such as Stowe and Canford in 1923 and Bryanston in 1928. It was felt, however, that the central problem had not been solved. Much of recent criticism follows the line that the closed system of the public schools is open only to the sons of the well-to-do and that, in public and industrial life, too great a share of the senior appointments is given to ex-public-school boys. In short, the existence of a number of schools which charge high fees is a contradiction in a democratic community. Some critics assert that the public schools are hotbeds of snobbery, while others are opposed to the boarding-school system and prefer day-schools for all but a few abnormal types of children. The unfortunate point about the controversy is that political considerations seem to have greater weight than educational ideals. So much of public opinion is so ill-informed about the schools in question that it may be worth while to mention a few facts.

On the whole, though it is true to say that the public schools constitute an independent system in contrast with the State schools, one should remember that many direct-grant and maintained secondary schools enjoy membership of the Headmasters' Conference and the Association of Governing Bodies. The two systems, however, have other points of contact. The earliest associations between the public schools and the State were a result of the Clarendon and Taunton Commissions. The Charity Commissioners drew up schemes under the Endowed Schools Act, some of which applied to schools now recognised as public schools, and in some cases their action rescued the schools from oblivion and decay. Although the Headmasters' Conference owed its origin to the apprehension felt in regard to possible government interference, it was foremost in urging upon the Bryce Commission the appointment of an Educational Council with powers similar to those now possessed by the Central Advisory Councils created by the Act of 1944.

The Board of Education was given permissive power to inspect any secondary school which expressed a desire to be inspected. Many public schools asked for inspection, and as a result were recognised by the Board. Thus, by 1914, nine had been inspected and recognised, and since that date Harrow, Rugby, Eton, Shrewsbury, and Oundle have been added to the list.[1] Since 1917 the schools belonging to both the State and the independent systems have entered their pupils for the same School and Higher School Certificate examinations, and both compete for open scholarships at the universities. Whilst many public schools are controlled by independent governing bodies, quite a number have representatives of publicly-elected authorities on their boards of governors. The public schools shared with many direct-grant schools the privilege of furnishing contingents of the Junior Division of the Officers' Training Corps. The State schools have been influenced by the public schools in many ways, *e.g.* in the development of organised games, the prefect and house systems, the experiments of Sanderson at Oundle, and the work of Dr. Rouse and his colleagues at the Perse School, Cambridge. Many masters from public schools have become heads of State grammar-schools, and there have been

---

[1] The number of independent secondary schools recognised by the Ministry in 1948 was: England 491, Wales 21. These figures include many private schools.

instances of members of public-school staffs accepting the headship of secondary-modern schools. There is a greater two-way traffic between the systems than the general public imagines.

The criticism that the public schools form a closed system is more true of the schools fifty years ago than at the present time. A fundamental mistake is that of regarding the public schools as though they all conformed to one pattern. In fact, they present a large variety of types, and thus sweeping generalisations about them are apt to be erroneous. The criticism that owing to their high fees very few pupils from the State schools can enter them is a case in point. It is a generalisation true of some schools but not of others. Thus a large proportion of boys at Christ's Hospital have always come from the elementary schools; at Rendcombe College in Gloucestershire nearly half the pupils were admitted on the results of the special-place examination; and at Giggleswick nearly a third of the scholars come from the locality and are admitted on the results of a scholarship examination. Winchester, under Canon Spencer Leeson, established a generous scheme of scholarships.

It is less well known than it should be that in 1919 the schools represented on the Headmasters' Conference offered places to elementary-school children. Mr. Graves gives the details of negotiations which took place.[1] Mr. (later Sir) Frank Fletcher of Charterhouse, who was chairman of the H.M.C., put forward from the chair a proposal which met with acceptance, "that the schools which could afford to give pensions without applying for State aid should voluntarily accept the same conditions of State service as those which applied for and received it. We were prepared to offer as a voluntary service, or rather to claim as a privilege, that share in the education of ex-elementary-school boys which was demanded by the State from other schools." One of the conditions for State aid was that a school should offer from ten to twenty-five per cent of its entry to boys who had attended elementary schools. The offer was sent to Mr. H. A. L. Fisher, who replied that there was at present no demand for places from elementary school boys and added: "It is full of encouragement for the future of English education. It represents a sincere desire to make the public system of education as comprehensive, as accessible, and as effective as possible. . . . I think that we recognise as clearly as you do the importance of diversity and individuality both inside and outside the State-aided system of education, and the value of tradition."

[1] J. Graves. *Policy and Progress in Secondary Education, 1902-42*, pp. 188-9, Thomas Nelson and Sons, 1943.

An increasing number of people believe that the public schools have something to offer to the nation that is valuable and worth while preserving, but they differ in regard to the policy they would adopt. They are of opinion that the existence of a small number of fee-paying schools is a strength rather than a weakness in a democratic State by providing a variety of types and giving freedom of experiment that is more difficult to achieve under the State system. They also urge that, if parents are willing to save in order to provide for their children the type of education they wish them to have, there is no reason why they should not be permitted to do so. Thus, Donald Hughes writes, "The Public School system is part, and no insignificant part, of that decent British life and society which has been slowly and patiently built up, and I cannot believe that we shall allow it to be swept away in the days when our need for enlightened and effective education will be so urgent. We shall want, in future, not fewer but more and better Public Schools."[1] Mr. E. H. Partridge, headmaster of Giggleswick, claimed that the typical public boarding-school is a truly democratic institution representing a wider cross-section of the public than any other type of school, and that it reconciles and abolishes class distinctions rather than perpetuates them.[2]

One of the practical difficulties which has to be taken into consideration when it is proposed that boys from the primary schools should be admitted to the public schools is the age of entry. Pupils are transferred from the primary to the secondary school at eleven-plus, but during the latter part of the 19th century the age of entry to the larger boarding-school became settled at thirteen. Because of the importance assigned to the classics the general curriculum of the public schools is not completely parallel with that of the State grammar-schools. Again, because of the later age of entry to the public schools, a large number of preparatory schools have developed. The preparatory schools accept pupils at the age of eight upwards and prepare them for the Common Entrance examination which was established in 1903. Most of the preparatory schools are in private hands, but a few public schools, such as St. Paul's, have their own preparatory establishments. The difference in the method of preparation for entry to the two types of school accentuates the gulf between them.

[1] D. Hughes. *The Public Schools and the Future*, p. 71, C.U.P., 1942.
[2] E. H. Partridge. *Freedom in Education*, Faber and Faber, 1943.

These difficulties, however, are not insuperable. Various suggestions have been made for overcoming them. One of the most reasonable solutions seems to be the provision of residential preparatory schools for boys and girls who seem likely to profit from a public boarding-school education. Such preparatory schools would have an age-range of eleven to thirteen and would be part of the State system. The pupils would be introduced to the additional subjects studied at public schools and their progress watched carefully. Those who were not able to make headway with their studies could be transferred to one of the types of secondary school within the State system. Pupils chosen for the public schools would not be selected on account of their intelligence and attainments alone. Due consideration would be given to character, temperament, and powers of leadership. At the present, too much importance is attached to intelligence and attainment, to the neglect of other factors, possibly because the latter are more difficult to ascertain. The suggestion that suitable pupils should be transferred from the secondary grammar-schools at the age of thirteen is one that is not likely to find favour with grammar-school headmasters, who would rightly object to their schools being "creamed" in this fashion. Such problems as we have outlined were the object of the considerations of the Fleming Committee.

The Fleming Report stated the belief of the Committee "that the education given by the Public Schools includes elements of very high educational value, especially but not entirely on the boarding side. It would, therefore, be wrong to destroy them as the more extreme of their critics desire (by the appropriation of their endowments and the diversion of their buildings to other purposes) or to refuse to associate them in any way with the general system of education, provided that the number of boys admitted to them from Primary Schools is sufficient to avoid the dangers which have been discussed," e.g. the fear that boys from poorer homes would not be able to adjust themselves.[1] The Committee believed that opportunities of education in such schools should be made available to boys and girls capable of profiting from them irrespective of the income of their parents. It was recommended that the Board of Education should compile a list of associated schools, and that the terms of admission to the list and the conditions under which they would work should be of two types, described respectively as

[1] *The Public Schools and the General Educational System*, p. 56, H.M.S.O., 1944.

Scheme 'A" and Scheme "B." Both schemes should apply equally to boys' and girls' schools. Scheme "A" schools would consist mainly of the direct-grant schools. To be accepted as associated schools they would be required either to abolish tuition fees or "to grade them according to an approved income scale which shall provide for total remission if a parent's income requires it."[1] L.E.A.s should have the right to reserve at such schools a number of places, day and boarding, for pupils for whom they are responsible. The number of local places should be settled between the governors and the L.E.A.s, with reference to the Board of Education if necessary, and the L.E.A.s should pay to the school the cost of tuition and boarding at the approved rate for all pupils they send. The Board of Education would pay direct grant for the remainder of the pupils.

Scheme "B" would apply to "such Boarding Schools or schools taking a substantial number of boarders as the Board may accept, being schools recognised by the Board as efficient and not being conducted for private profit."[2] The Board of Education would grant bursaries to qualified pupils who had been educated for at least two years at a grant-aided primary school to enable them to proceed to such a boarding-school. The amount of the bursaries would be graded according to an approved income scale with total remission where necessary. It was recommended that the number of bursars should not be less than twenty-five per cent of the school's annual admissions and that the admission schemes should be reviewed every five years. As in Scheme "A," L.E.A.s should be empowered to reserve places at particular schools for pupils from their areas. Parents desiring a bursary would apply through the L.E.A. to the Board of Education and candidates would be interviewed by a Regional Interviewing Committee of four persons, one of whom would be the head of the associated school, another the head of a primary school, and the third a member or officer of an L.E.A.

The Fleming Report was so patently a compromise that it failed to satisfy the extremists on either side, and its value consists in indicating a possible way by which the relations between the public schools and the national system might be developed and strengthened. The State secondary schools were obviously not content with a proposal whose implementation would deprive them of some of their most promising pupils.

[1] *Ibid.*, p. 100.   [2] *Ibid.*, p. 101.

This brief sketch of post-war education would not be complete without a reference to two important social developments which are having a profound influence upon English education. One is the development of the youth service and the other the Curtis Report which has resulted in the Children Act of 1948.

The youth service, like so many of the important movements in this country, began with voluntary effort. Space forbids all but the mention of the Y.M.C.A., founded in 1844; the Y.W.C.A., in 1835; the Boy Scout movement, originated by Lord Baden-Powell in 1908; and the Girl Guides, founded in 1910. All these voluntary organisations, together with youth-clubs in connection with the churches, did most valuable work, but they extended their influence to only a section of the adolescent community. The State did not actively concern itself with young people above school age until the uneasy period between the two world wars. King George's Jubilee Trust was formed in 1935 and funds were accumulated for the purchase of playing-fields. The Government began to make grants for physical training and the provision of recreational facilities and in 1937 the National Fitness Council was formed to administer the money. This was merged into the National Youth Committee at the outbreak of war. The Board of Education *Circular 1486,* of 1939, emphasised that, in spite of all that had been accomplished by voluntary organisations and the L.E.A.s, the social and physical development of adolescents who had left school was being neglected. If the clauses of the Fisher Act dealing with continuation schools had been in operation, many of the problems would have been solved. The Circular recommended that L.E.A.s should set up youth committees to survey, encourage, and co-ordinate the youth services in their areas. Existing voluntary organisations should be represented on the local committee. A further Circular (*1503*), issued in March 1940, announced that the Board of Education was prepared to make grants covering fifty per cent of the expenses incurred by L.E.A.s in their youth services. In June 1940, *Circular 1516,* entitled *The Challenge of Youth,* recognised the youth service as part of further education. The State declined to create a compulsory youth service and defined its function as one of filling the gaps by supplementing the resources of existing voluntary organisations. A later Circular (*1577*) of December 1941, entitled *Registration of Youth,* dealt with boys and girls who became liable for registration by the Ministry of Labour and National Service. Boys and girls were interviewed by the Youth Committees of L.E.A.s and those who were not already members of a youth organisation were urged to join one. They were also encouraged to take up some kind of pre-Service training.

Owing to the war new types of pre-Service training were coming into existence. When Lord Haldane reorganised the Army and created the Territorial Force in 1907, the Officers' Training Corps was formed. It was divided into a Senior Division attached to universities and a Junior Division attached to certain public and secondary schools. Junior cadets were prepared for Certificate "A," and the seniors for Certificate "B." The aim of the O.T.C. was to provide officers for the Territorial Army and the Special Reserve. During the Second World War the demand for officers was so great that the O.T.C. was reorganised and greatly extended. The two divisions became the Senior and Junior Training Corps respectively, and all university students who were of military age were compelled to join the S.T.C. The establishment was increased and students were given a preliminary training to enable them to pass eventually to an O.C.T.U. if they were suitable. Compulsory service ended in November 1944, and as a consequence the numbers of the S.T.C. fell rapidly. The S.T.C., renamed the U.T.C. (University Training Corps) was brought into line with the new National Service scheme, and on 1st April 1948 it became an integral part of the Territorial Army. Undergraduates who joined became eligible for the same bounties and benefits as other members of the T.A. Recently, the original title of O.T.C. has been restored.

The O.T.C. had been mainly restricted to undergraduates and the pupils of a small number of schools. The war greatly increased the demands for pre-Service training and, in 1941, the Air Training Corps was formed. This was followed by the institution of Sea Cadets and the Army Cadet Force. Similar pre-Service organisations were available for girls and at present the War Office is considering the re-creation of some of them. All these organisations were educational in so far as they gave attention to the social and recreative needs of their members.

The National Youth Committee was replaced by the Youth Advisory Council in 1942. The latter was created to advise on problems submitted to it by the Board of Education and also to bring new suggestions to the notice of the Board. One of the most important problems in connection with the youth service is the training of those who, for want of a better name, have been called youth leaders. This problem received special attention at the hands of the McNair Committee. The report considered youth leaders under the broad classification of full-time workers, such as organisers, wardens, and heads of large institutions, who received a salary, and part-time workers, who might be paid or unpaid. The contribution of voluntary workers was warmly praised and the Committee hoped that any augmentation of the numbers of the professional youth leaders would not diminish the assistance given by the voluntary workers. It was recommended that those preparing to take full-time posts should receive a three-year course of training. People who already possessed experience of the work might enter upon a shorter course, but in any case the course of training should not be less than a year. It was considered that there should be a close association between service in youth organisations and teaching. To achieve this the suggestion was made that the salaries of youth leaders should be comparable with those given in the teaching profession and that service should be pensionable. To enable a person to transfer from one service to the other a linking of superannuation arrangements and the provision of short courses of training would be necessary.

For some time public feeling had been shocked at the revelation of certain cases where children who had been boarded out under the care of foster-parents had lived under most unsatisfactory conditions. As a consequence, the Care of Children Committee, under the chairmanship of Miss Myra Curtis, was constituted, and reported in 1946. The Committee inquired into the existing methods of providing for children who for various reasons had no home of their own, and recommended legislation to ensure that they would be brought up under conditions which would compensate them for the lack of parental care. These children included those maintained by local authorities under the Poor Law Act of 1930, evacuated children who for some reason were unable to return home,[1] children brought before the courts as delinquents or in need of special care and protection, children cared for by voluntary organisations, those maintained by foster-parents, adopted children, handicapped children educated away from home, those orphaned by the war, and mentally defective children. Altogether, these classes included 124,900 children.

The Clyde Committee conducted a similar inquiry for Scotland. The recommendations of the two committees were included in the

[1] On 31st March 1946 there remained in the reception areas 5,200 children unable to return home. Some were orphans; others had a parent or parents who could not provide a home for them.

Children Act of 1948. The Act lays upon the councils of counties and county boroughs in England and Wales, and of counties and large burghs in Scotland, the statutory duty of caring for every child under seventeen without parents or guardians, or who has been abandoned or lost, or whose parents are unable to provide for his upbringing. By making provision for children formerly dealt with under the Poor Law, the Act was complementary to the National Assistance Act, which proposed the abolition of the Poor Law and formed part of the new social legislation which came into operation on 5th July 1948. Each local authority is required to appoint a Children's Committee and an approved officer to carry out the functions which devolve upon the committee. The local authority should provide for a child in their care by boarding him out with foster-parents or, where this is not practicable or desirable, by accommodating him in a home provided under the Act or in a voluntary home. Local authorities are empowered to provide children's homes in which there will be the necessary facilities for the observation of the physical and mental condition of the children. Regulations governing the conduct of homes are made by the Home Secretary. The person in charge of a home, unless suitably qualified, must be approved by the Home Secretary. Already a course of one year has been arranged at universities to prepare sixty young women as supervisors and one hundred women have been selected for training as house mothers. Local authorities are also empowered to open hostels for young persons between fifteen and twenty-one who are or have been in the care of a local authority. The hostels will be close to the places where the young people are being employed or trained. Certain financial powers are given to local authorities for training or maintaining such young persons. The only persons liable to pay contributions towards the upkeep of these young people are the parents, whose liability will cease when the child reaches the age of sixteen.

The Act includes important provisions affecting voluntary homes and organisations. Every voluntary home must be registered by the Home Secretary, who can refuse or withdraw registration if he considers the home unsatisfactory. All homes are to be open to regular inspection, including that undertaken by local authorities. An exchequer grant not exceeding fifty per cent of the expenditure incurred by local authorities in the discharge of their functions will be made. An Advisory Council on Child Care will assist the Home Secretary in his administration and there will be a separate Advisory

Council for Scotland.   The Home Secretary, the Minister of Education in England and Wales, and the Secretary of State for Scotland,
are empowered to make regulations defining the spheres of responsibility of local authorities and L.E.A.s

It should be noted that the Act following the Curtis Report
gave a preference to private foster-homes or small corporate houses
rather than large institutions.   The principle was that of providing a real home life for children without homes.   Another feature
of the Act was the attention given to after-care by provision of
hostels and the award of financial assistance to those over eighteen
who need to complete their education and training.

To conclude this chapter, a reference must be made to the
Report of the Secondary School Examinations Council, 1947.   Its
recommendations modify and extend the Norwood Report.   They
were based on the following principles: (a) All secondary-school
courses should be designed with appropriate variety of subjects and
treatment to suit the ages, abilities, and aptitudes of the pupils.   In
the later years the future careers of pupils should have some bearing on the courses provided.   (b) Those children who can profit by
an extension of full-time education should be encouraged to stay at
school beyond sixteen.   (c) The conception of "sixth-form" work
should be maintained and specialisation should never be premature
or excessive.

It was recommended that on leaving school, each pupil should
be provided with a school report giving the fullest information
about him and his abilities and potentialities.   Different types of
objective tests should be given periodically and the results preserved
in school records and used to guide pupils towards suitable courses
of study or types of employment.   Each school should carry out
systematic internal examinations based on its courses of study.
External examinations serve to maintain national standards, and,
for pupils who do not need an external examination, some form of
internal examination would be necessary.

External examinations for pupils who wish to compete for
university scholarships or secure exemption from professional
examinations should be taken as late as possible in their school
career.   They should also be accessible to candidates who have
ceased to be full-time pupils at a secondary school.

An examination at Ordinary, Advanced, or Scholarship level
should be available each year to candidates who are at least sixteen
on September 1st of that year.   The Ordinary papers should provide

a reasonable test in the subject for pupils who have taken it as a part of a wide and general course up to the age of sixteen or for those who have studied the subject in a non-specialist way in the sixth form. The Advanced papers are for candidates who have taken the subject as a specialist study for two years in the sixth form. Scholarship papers should provide specially gifted pupils an opportunity for showing distinctive merit and promise. The group system should be abolished so that all subjects at all these levels should be optional. Satisfactory candidates are awarded a General Certificate of Education on which is recorded the subjects and the levels at which they satisfied the examiners. Once the certificate has been granted it can afterwards be endorsed for subsequent successes. No grant should be payable in respect of a candidate under sixteen on September 1st in the year of examination. Ordinary and Advanced papers in the same subject are not to be taken in different years, so that a single certificate takes the place of the present School and Higher School Certificates. The Pass in the Ordinary papers should be approximate to a Credit standard in the School Certificate, and a Pass at Advanced level should be roughly equivalent to a Pass in the Higher School Certificate.

The Council recommended that the examinations should be held at such a time as will enable the results to reach the Ministry of Education by August 1st. This would probably involve the holding of the examinations in May. The Ministry of Education approved the main recommendations of the Report and announced on the 26th April 1948 that the new system would be introduced by stages. The first examination under the new scheme was held in 1951. The Minister agreed with the principle that external examinations should not be taken before the age of seventeen, but until the number of pupils remaining at school after seventeen has substantially increased, he provisionally fixed the minimum age for candidates at sixteen. The Minister's decision was severely criticised by members of the staffs of certain schools and univerities, on the grounds that the minimum-age requirement unduly handicaps the brilliant pupil who is ready to sit for the examination before he is sixteen.

The recommendations of the Council should be compared with those of the Scottish Advisory Council described in Chapter XV. The "new" examination provoked considerable controversy especially in regard to the minimum age of entry and the abolition of the mark of distinction for candidates who showed exceptional knowledge and ability. Many of these criticisms came from the grammar-schools and the universities, the institutions which were most closely concerned with the changes. The Minister of Education, Miss F. Horsbrugh, considered the representations made to her and announced in the Commons 24th April 1952, that certain modifications would be made in 1953 and after. In the light of the experience of the examinations of 1951, she considered that while the existing age limit should be retained as a general principle, heads of schools should not be debarred from entering a pupil at an earlier age if the candidate is up to the required standard and it is educationally right for him to sit for the examination. She also approved the suggestion that a distinction mark should be awarded to exceptionally able candidates at the Advanced level.

Consequent on the resignation of Sir Anthony Eden in January 1957 and the appointment of Mr. Macmillan as Prime Minister, there was a Cabinet re-shuffle. Lord Hailsham, the grandson of Mr. Quintin Hogg (p. 495), succeeded Sid David Eccles as Minister of Education. Sir Edward Boyle was appointed Parliamentary Secretary to the Ministry of Education.

CHAPTER XII

THE MODERN UNIVERSITIES AND THE ANCIENT UNIVERSITIES IN THE MODERN WORLD

Until the end of the first quarter of the 19th century, Oxford and Cambridge had been the only two English universities. It is true that in 1575 Sir Thomas Gresham, a wealthy London merchant, had bequeathed his City mansion to be the home of a college, and had endowed seven professorships—in divinity, civil law, medicine, rhetoric, astronomy, geometry, and music. Gresham College was opened in 1596 and, as we have related, played a part in the movement which led to the formation of the Royal Society; but it was never a university. During the Commonwealth, Parliament petitioned for the establishment of a university at London, but it was not until 1825 that the movement for the founding of the University of London became practical politics.

As we have seen, membership of the ancient universities was restricted to adherents of the Anglican Church and the wealthier section of the population. The studies of the universities were predominantly classical and mathematical; and those who were interested in sciences, and manufacturers who desired a practical and technical education, were convinced of the need of a new institution for higher education. Thus there came about an alliance of all the dissatisfied elements, which included Liberals, Nonconformists, Roman Catholics, Jews, and all those who supported the scientific and secularist movements. The only way of satisfying so many diverse points of view was the establishment of a new university from which religious teaching would be excluded.

The opening move was made by the poet Thomas Campbell, who contributed a letter to *The Times,* 9th February 1825, in which he pleaded for the establishment of a "great London University." Campbell had visited, in 1820, the German University of Bonn and had been impressed by its constitution and its programme of studies. The letter was addressed to Henry Brougham, who supported the idea with great enthusiasm. It was also welcomed by Dr. Birkbeck, Francis Place, Zachary Macaulay, Joseph Hume, and other members of the "education-mad" party. In his letter Campbell conceived the proposed university as a means of educating the "middling rich." Great strides had been made in providing education for the working classes, and he thought the time was now ripe to attend to the educational needs of the middle classes. He considered that £100,000, which could be raised by 2,000 families subscribing £50 each would be a sufficient sum for building and endowing the new university.

A large number of the supporters of the proposed university had been educated in Scottish universities and therefore had clear ideas about the kind of institution they wished to establish. They were in favour of a non-residential university at which the fees would be moderate and thus make it available for the middle classes. The leading article of *The Times* published on the same day as Campbell's letter was not sympathetic towards the proposal. The writer stigmatised the scheme as "crude in conception and meagre in development." The promoters of the plan were full of enthusiasm and a joint-stock company was formed under the name of the Proprietors of the University of London, and subscriptions were invited. The tuition fee in all subjects except medicine was to be £25 per annum and, taking Bonn and the Scottish universities as a model, it was to be non-residential; but, unlike them, it was to be purely secular. A plot of land in Gower Street was purchased and the foundation-stone of the London University was laid by the Duke of Sussex in 1827, and by October of the following year the new institution started its life. Classes were formed in arts, law, and medicine. So far, the foundation was without a charter, and its efforts to obtain one were successfully resisted by Oxford and Cambridge.

Its secular constitution provoked much opposition. Thomas Arnold denounced it as "that godless institution in Gower Street," and many Nonconformists, among them the headmaster of Mill Hill, agreed with him. When the council of the university considered approaching the Crown for the grant of a charter, the Anglican party was roused to action. The initiative was taken by Dr. George D'Oyley, rector of Lambeth. He proposed the establishment of a second university in which religious instruction should be an essential part of the education provided. At a public meeting held on 21st June 1828, presided over by the Prime Minister, the Duke of Wellington, a resolution was passed which agreed to the foundation of a new college in which the doctrine and form of worship of the Church of England should be recognised. George IV had promised his patronage, and the new institution received the

name of King's College. It was granted a royal charter of incorporation in 1829, and the college was opened in the Strand near Somerset
House in October 1831. It was anticipated that the endowments
of the new foundation would be on a considerable scale, but
Wellington's support of Catholic emancipation offended many of
the subscribers who withdrew their patronage, and the college was
left rather meagrely endowed.

As a consequence of these events, London was provided with
two rival colleges based on different principles. The older college
was supported by the Whigs and the Nonconformists, but was
unchartered. King's College received the support of the Tories and
the Established Church. Neither college had the power of granting
academic degrees. The situation was felt to be extremely unsatisfactory. Efforts were made to unite the colleges, but all proposals
for union were rejected by King's. The older institution petitioned
Lord Melbourne's Government for a charter, which was granted in
1836. It received the title of University College. A compromise
was reached on the same day as the charter was granted. A royal
charter of 28th November 1836 created the University of London
as a body with power "to perform all the functions of the Examiners
in the Senate House of Cambridge."

At the time, University College and King's College were quite
satisfied with the compromise, but it was not long before its defects
became apparent. The University of London was merely an organisation for examining candidates and conferring degrees. It was
not a teaching body, and its affiliated colleges in which the instruction took place possessed no organic relationship with the university.
The first Senate of the University was appointed by the Government
in 1837, and included in its membership Dr. Thomas Arnold of
Rugby, who later became one of the foremost critics of the university, and Michael Faraday the distinguished scientist. The
former was responsible for framing the curriculum in arts.

The original charter had granted power to the University of
London to affiliate other colleges. This policy was actually carried
out in 1850, when a large number of institutions, some of which
were nothing more than secondary schools, were affiliated to the
university. Eight years later this practice was abandoned and the
university proclaimed "the comprehensive principle of testing
acquired knowledge by strict examination, with reasonable evidence
of antecedent continuous study." The latter point, it was thought,
would be secured by the establishment of Intermediate examinations

in arts and science. With the exception of the examinations in the Faculty of Medicine, the university was prepared to examine any candidate, whether he had pursued a recognised course in some institution of university rank, or whether he had been prepared by private tuition. At the same time, a Convocation consisting of graduates of the university was formed and given a share in the administration of the university.

The new arrangement provoked much criticism. Matthew Arnold described the University of London as "a mere *collegium*, or Board of Examiners," which gave no teaching itself but only examined for degrees. He believed that the teaching function of a university was far more important than that of examining, and urged that University College and King's College should be brought into full relationship with the university. Arnold's criticisms were but the forerunners of others which were more bitter in tone.

The first move towards reform came from Convocation, which in 1877 asked the Senate to consider means of strengthening the connection between the affiliated colleges and the university, and promoting in an efficient manner the ideals of sound learning and a liberal education. It should be remembered that it was at this time that the question of admitting women to the examinations and degrees of the University of London was being discussed. In the following year, Convocation adopted a number of resolutions which they presented to the Senate. These included a recommendation that the courses of study at those institutions which furnished candidates for London degrees should be brought into closer connection with the Senate. Convocation also urged the foundation of university Chairs in certain studies and the development of post-graduate work and research. The Senate, unshaken in its belief in the examination system, showed little sympathy towards the proposals.

In the Faculty of Medicine, events were moving to a crisis. London provided a number of famous hospitals in which students from the medical schools could obtain excellent training in practical medicine and surgery. Unfortunately these institutions were unable to provide an equally effective training in general science. The candidate who wished to obtain a medical degree at London had first to show, at the matriculation stage, that he had reached a good standard in his general education, and then the preliminary examination demanded from him a considerable knowledge of general science. The scientific training given in the endowed grammar-schools was so unsatisfactory that very few candidates were able to reach the standards demanded by the university. The majority of students found these conditions made it impossible for them to read for a university degree in medicine, and preferred to seek the professional qualifications given by the Royal College of Physicians or the Royal College of Surgeons. Moreover, the Scottish universities granted medical degrees without such stringent requirements in science, though they could not provide opportunities for clinical work on a scale comparable with London.

The result was a gradual drift of medical students to the north. The university authorities refused to change their policy, for they considered that this would lower the standard of the medical degree.

Another storm was appearing from a different quarter. The first member of Parliament for the University of London was Robert Lowe, whom we have already encountered in connection with the Revised Code. He had not changed his opinions with regard to examinations, and he believed that a university was essentially an examining body. This view was warmly opposed by such people as Lord Playfair, Professor Hales of King's College, and Professor Karl Pearson. University College considered that its position with relation to the university was so unsatisfactory that its governing authority contemplated affiliation to the Victoria University.

The controversy eventually led to the formation in 1884 of the Association for Promoting a Teaching University for London. It was suggested that there should be two universities, with the respective functions of teaching and examining. There might be one Chancellor, but each university should have its separate Vice-Chancellor. The relations between the examining and the teaching university were not fully worked out, but it was suggested that there should be an intimate association between the teaching university and the professional bodies in law and medicine which granted professional qualifications. Convocation approved the scheme, and a draft constitution of a reconstructed University of London was drawn up. It was impossible, however, to obtain the general agreement of all parties concerned, and it seemed as though the university would break up because of the threatened secession of its constituent members.

In 1887 there was a new turn to events. King's and University Colleges decided to petition the Crown for a charter giving them authority to grant degrees in all faculties. This move, once more, did not secure universal agreement, and a third of the members of the Council of University College resigned. The petition asked for the formation of a new institution, to be known as the Albert University. King's and University Colleges were to be constituted as colleges of the university, and power was to be given to admit other colleges. The Royal College of Physicians and the Royal College of Surgeons were to be affiliated to the university. The Senate of the University of London raised strong objections to the scheme. In particular, they disliked the idea of the power to confer degrees being in the hands of the teachers of the university. The dispute reached such dimensions that the Government found it necessary to intervene and to appoint a royal commission under the chairmanship of Lord Selborne. The Selborne Commission met in May 1888 and published its report in the following April.

The report suggested that the University of London should be reconstituted as a teaching university. The external examining system should be retained, but should be subordinated to the internal work of the university. The constituent colleges of the university should be institutions within the County of London, and neither the colleges nor the medical organisations ought to have the power of conferring degrees. This was the right of the university alone. A scheme for adequate representation of the constituent members of the university on the Senate was devised, and it was suggested that the university should appoint professors and lecturers of its own and receive endowments for this purpose. The Senate and Convocation were to be allowed a reasonable time in which to implement this policy and to apply for a new charter.

The Selborne Commission, however, did not bring about the agreement of the conflicting points of view. As Professor Archer wrote: "The problem of producing order out of chaos in London was, from the point of view of sheer organisation, the most complex that has ever presented itself in academic history. There were more students in London than in any city in the Empire, yet they were scattered amongst a host of utterly dissimilar institutions. . . . All these existed without any organic connection, with totally different histories, and many of them almost unconscious of each other's existence. We are not altogether surprised that the university entirely failed to devise a scheme of union. Public opinion came to look on London University as a steam-roller that had broken down and stuck in the mud, if we take a metaphor suited to its unwieldy bulk, or as Humpty-Dumpty after his fall, if we think rather of its fragmentary condition." [1]

[1] *Secondary Education in the Nineteenth Century*, pp. 266-7, C.U.P., 1932.

The scheme evolved by the university was not acceptable to University and King's Colleges. They objected to the size of the Senate (sixty-nine members, eventually reduced to fifty-two) and to what they considered the inadequate representation of the constituent colleges. The medical faculty criticised the scheme severely, but the final blow was dealt when Convocation rejected it in 1891. Convocation resolutely opposed a clause in the scheme which admitted provincial colleges on the same terms as London colleges. This clause was contrary to the views of the Selborne Commission. Meanwhile the Privy Council was busy drafting a charter for the university. The Committee of the Privy Council announced that it was favourable to the petition of University and King's Colleges to found a new University of London. All manner of objections were urged by other institutions which considered that the two colleges were being given a predominant position in the university. Public meetings were called; petitions against the charter were presented to Parliament; and the Victoria University and the provincial medical schools joined in the opposition. Bedford College for Women claimed the right of admission as an original constituent college. A powerful press campaign was organised by the opponents of the charter.

In face of this, University and King's Colleges decided to leave the existing university and to found a new teaching university which should be named the Gresham University. Their decision received the support of the authorities of the City of London and the professors of the Gresham College. The House of Commons asked the Queen to delay her consent to the charter until a new royal commission had investigated the situation and reported. The Gresham Commission, with Earl Cowper as chairman, was appointed in 1892. The Commissioners were in favour of a single university for London, and generally supported the conclusions of the Selborne Commission. They considered that legislation would be necessary to authorise the changes that had been recommended. After two abortive attempts, the Government passed the London University Commission Act in 1898, and the new statutes of the university were sealed in February 1900.

The next problem was that of finding administrative headquarters for the reconstituted university. The solution of this problem was provided by the Imperial Institute, the foundation-stone of which had been laid by the Queen in 1887 and which had since encountered serious financial difficulties. The greater part of the building was assigned to the University of London, whilst the Imperial Institute continued its work of research and propaganda in the remaining portion. The headquarters of the University of London in the Imperial Institute at South Kensington were set in the midst of a large collection of institutions for higher education which had been administered by the Science and Art Department. When the latter came to an end under the Board of Education Act of 1899, its work was merged into that of the Board of Education. On the same estate as the Imperial Institute were the Victoria and Albert Museum, the Science Museum and Library, the Royal College of Science, the Royal College of Mines, and the Royal College of Art. In addition, as near neighbours were the Royal College of Music, the Royal School of Art Needlework, the Natural History Museum, and the City and Guilds of London Institute for the Advancement of Technical Education. When, in 1907, a royal charter established the Imperial College of Science and Technology, the Board of Education transferred to the governing body of the Imperial College the administration of the Royal College of Science, the Royal School of Mines, and the Central Technical College of the City and Guilds of London Institute, renamed the City and Guilds (Engineering) College.

The reader may well wonder how the University of London came into this complicated organisation. It seems that in 1903 Lord Rosebery announced a scheme for establishing a College of Applied Science at South Kensington to work in close co-operation with the colleges already established there. In 1904 a Departmental Committee of the Board of Education, of which Lord Haldane was chairman, proposed that the new college should be a member of a federation of the colleges mentioned above, under a common scheme of government and administration. The details of the negotiations which followed are too lengthy and complicated to be dealt with in a work of this type. It is sufficient to say that proposals were made to incorporate the Imperial College in the University of London. Mr. McKenna, the then president of the Board of Education, decided in 1907 to advise the grant of a royal charter to the Imperial College as an independent institution, but he also suggested the appointment of a royal commission "to consider whether the amalgamation of the new institution with the University is desirable and feasible, and, if so, on what lines it can best be carried out."

The Haldane Commission was appointed in 1909 and its final report was issued in 1913. The Commission recommended a faculty organisation of the university, and the University of London Act (1926) created a new constitution for the University of London. University and King's Colleges had already been incorporated into the university in 1907 and 1910 respectively. Other institutions were now recognised as "schools of the university" in one or more faculties. Thus the medical schools of the hospitals are included in the faculty of medicine. The women's colleges, such as Bedford College, the Royal Holloway College, and Westfield College, are schools in the faculties of arts and science. The Imperial College of Technology, the London School of Economics, Queen Mary College, the Birkbeck College, and other institutions are also schools of different faculties. This organisation was rendered possible because of the specialist teaching given in the different institutions.

The problems of the University of London are by no means completely solved. The Haldane Commission drew attention to the need of providing a permanent building for the university. The Imperial Institute was no longer adequate for the purpose. In particular, a great hall, accommodation to promote the social interests of members of the university, lecture rooms, and a central library, were urgently needed. Violent controversy broke out on the question of a suitable site, but in 1920 the Government offered a site of about eleven and a half acres behind the British Museum in Bloomsbury. The refusal of King's College to remove from the Strand threatened to wreck the whole scheme, but it is to be hoped that the new university building next to the British Museum in Bloomsbury will succeed in drawing together the varied institutions that comprise the University of London.

The University of London is the only British university which is organised to grant degrees to candidates who are not resident students of the university. Candidates may be classified into three categories: students from university colleges which have not the power to grant degrees, students following day or evening courses at technical colleges and other institutes for higher and technical education, and private students who prepare for the degree examinations by their individual study, with or without assistance obtained from classes, private tuition, or correspondence courses.

The practice of granting external degrees has frequently been criticised. It was urged that institutions preparing candidates for the external examinations of the university had little control over the examination syllabus. Moreover, a large proportion of the candidates were private students who, because they were not members of any recognised educational institution, missed two of the most important influences of a university training, namely the daily contact with other students from different faculties and the close association with eminent teachers who possessed a rich and valuable experience. Against these objections the reply was made that, although the external system had its defects, it also possessed two advantages that outweighed them. The development of the university colleges would have been much more difficult if they had not been able to enter their students for degree examinations at London, and the external system made it possible for thousands of individuals to obtain a university qualification which otherwise would have been for ever beyond their reach. A further criticism was that many external students were ill-prepared for the examination test, so that the percentage of failures was unduly large. In recent years the university has introduced certain modifications so as to meet as far as possible these objections. Attention is paid to representations made by external teaching institutions in regard to the syllabuses, and an advisory organisation has been created to guide the reading of candidates and to attempt some supervision of their studies.

Following the establishment of University and King's Colleges, a movement began to provide university education for the north of England. The idea was no new one and dates back at least as far as the reign of Elizabeth. The people of the north did not take kindly to the religious changes of the 16th century, and the Rising of the North in 1569 convinced the Government that something ought to be done to bring the parishioners of Yorkshire to regard the Prayer Book and the reformed services more favourably. It was thought that this object might be attained through education. After several representations had been made to the Queen that the endowments of the collegiate church at Ripon might be applied to an educational foundation, a scheme was prepared in 1596 for the establishment of a university in that town. The prospectus, or broadsheet, giving details of the proposed university can be inspected in the library of Ripon Cathedral.

The Queen promised an annual subscription of £100, and several prominent members of the clergy and the nobility agreed to contribute. It was suggested that lecturers might be appointed to lecture to the populace on market days and that students should visit the villages in the dales to instruct the country folk in religion. The broadsheet gives details about the professors and lecturers, their duties, and their salaries. One surprising suggestion, in view of the monopoly enjoyed by the classics in the older universities and grammar-schools of the period, was the appointment of "Sixe Associates Professors of the vulgar tongs" (Italian, French, Spanish, Dutch and Flemish, Polish, and Hungarian). Each was to receive a yearly stipend of thirty marks, rising eventually to forty marks. In spite of the powerful support it received, the scheme came to nothing. It was revived in 1604 when a petition to James I was presented. The King decided not to grant it, and the result was the issue of letters patent reconstituting the church at Ripon as a collegiate foundation.

In 1641 Lord Fairfax asked his brother Ferdinando, the second Lord Fairfax, to petition the Long Parliament on behalf of a university at Manchester. The petition opened with the following preamble: "That whereas the want of an university in the northern parts of this kingdom, both in this and former ages, hath been apprehended a great prejudice to the kingdom in general, but a greater misery and unhappiness to these countries in particular, many ripe and hopeful wits being utterly lost for want of education, some being unable, others unwilling, to commit their children of tender and unsettled age so far from their own eyes, to the sole care and tuition of strangers; We therefore humbly crave leave to offer unto your pious care and wise consideration the necessity of a third university, and the convenience of such a foundation in the town of Manchester, for the future advancement of piety and good learning amongst us." In support of the petition, the long distance of the north from Oxford and Cambridge, the expense of life at the older universities, the necessity of confuting papists, the existence of a number of potential benefactors, and the "honour that might hence arise to these parts of the kingdom," were urged. In particular, a case was made out for Manchester as the most favourable town in which to establish a university.

The petition arrived at an unfortunate time, when both King and Parliament were about to enter on a trial of military strength. Moreover, news of the intention had spread across the Pennines, and Yorkshire was not content to allow a rival county to gain an advantage. The City of York sent two petitions to Parliament, couched in somewhat the same terms as Lancashire's, and added as a further reason for a northern university that Scotland "had long gloried in the happiness of enjoying the literature of four universities." The result of the rivalry was that neither petition was granted, for Cromwell was more inclined to favour Durham as a seat for a university. Conditions at Durham were also more favourable. An Act of 1649 had dissolved all cathedral and collegiate chapters, and Durham cathedral and the houses of the chapter stood empty. All that was needed was to obtain a grant of the endowments. Accordingly, when Cromwell was at Edinburgh in 1651, a deputation went over from Durham to meet him. Nothing came of the interview, for Cromwell was far too busy with other matters, and it was not until 1656 that the Privy Council issued an order founding a college at Durham. In May 1657 letters patent set forth its constitution. It was to be in charge of a master or Provost. The corporate body was to consist of two senior Fellows, twelve other Fellows (four professors, four tutors, four schoolmasters), twenty-four scholars, and twelve exhibitioners. It was to be known as the Provost, Fellows, and Scholars of the College of Durham, and its revenue was to be drawn from the cathedral chapter-lands. Permission to establish a printing-press was also given. At the end of 1658 the college authorities petitioned Richard Cromwell for a charter to turn the college into a university. This was opposed by Oxford and Cambridge, but before anything could be settled the Restoration occurred and the dean and chapter returned to the cathedral.

The idea of a University of Durham was raised at the beginning the 19th century. The University of Durham began as an ecclesiastical foundation and was endowed from the revenues of the see and cathedral chapter. It was established by an Act of Parliament in 1832 which enabled "the Dean and Chapter of Durham to appropriate part of their church to the establishment of a university in connection therewith." The charter was granted in 1836. The university was of the residential type and its curriculum was modelled on that of the ancient universities. Its students resided in residential colleges within the bishop's palace.

In 1832 also, a College of Medicine was founded at Newcastle-on-Tyne and it became associated with the university in 1852. The highly industrial Tyneside felt the need for advanced scientific and technical training, and this was met by the institution of a College of Physical Science in Newcastle in 1871. The college was affiliated to the university in 1874. The College of Science received increased endowments in 1904 and began to develop an arts faculty. From this date it became known as Armstrong College. Thus, at the beginning of the present century, the University of Durham was a federal university consisting of three practically autonomous institutions, each of which had full control of its own finances, of the appointment of its staff, and of its own teaching and discipline. With its strong clerical and arts element the older section of the university, situated in Durham itself, was reminiscent of Oxford and Cambridge. The inclusion of Armstrong College and the Medical College brought the university into close touch with modern life and industry.

In 1908 the University of Durham Act reconstituted the university into the Durham division containing University College, Hatfield, St. Chad's, and St. John's, and the Newcastle division containing Armstrong and the Medical College. A new Senate was created and the powers of the dean and chapter were modified. The Bishop of Durham was still retained as the Visitor. The new set-up was not altogether satisfactory, and certain controversies in the Newcastle division produced a good deal of resentment. As a result, a royal commission was appointed which reported in 1935. It found a number of defects in the constitution of the university. The university had insufficient control over its constituent members. For example, the colleges appointed their own professors, and the university had only a limited power in formulating the conditions for matriculation and the granting of degrees. Under the federal scheme the Durham division could not take full advantage of its opportunities, and in the Newcastle division the instruments of government were not satisfactory. Thus Armstrong College was constituted as a limited-liability company and this was not suited to university administration. As a result of the recommendations of the commission, the constitution of the University of Durham was remodelled. In 1937 Armstrong College was renamed King's College. Another result was the end of the federal constitution of the university by grouping its constituent members under a single control for administration and finance.

In the latter half of the 19th century, as a consequence of the increasing demand for scientific and technical education, university colleges developed in some of the larger towns in England and Wales. Another influence was at work, and in Chapter xiii the growth of universities and university colleges from the University Extension movement will be described. Other institutions owed their origin to the generosity of local benefactors. The earliest of the new provincial colleges was Owens College at Manchester. It originated from the benefaction of the merchant John Owens, who left the sum of £97,000 for its foundation. The college was opened in 1851 and accepted students who wished to read for external degrees of the University of London. In its earliest days the college had a hard struggle to maintain itself. During the session 1857-8 its numbers fell to ninety-three, including evening students, and in a leading article the *Manchester Guardian* referred to it as "a mortifying failure." An attempt to associate the schools of medicine, which already existed in Manchester, with the college, came to nothing. The main reason for the paucity of numbers was the unsatisfactory state of secondary education in Manchester at that period. Hence the students who came to the college were inadequately prepared to receive the benefits of higher education. As the number of entrants declined, there was a great temptation to lower the standards of the college, but fortunately the governing body decided against this course. The result was that though for some years numbers continued to grow less, the policy of maintaining a high standard was successful in the end and Owens College did much to raise the quality of the secondary schools in the district.

The tide turned in 1861 when the Working Men's College was absorbed, and by 1864 it had 127 day and 312 evening students. When the Taunton Commission visited the college, they found an institution "organised somewhat after the fashion of the Scotch universities, having a principal and nine professors teaching classics, mathematics, natural philosophy, chemistry, natural history, history and English literature, mental philosophy and political economy, jurisprudence, oriental and modern languages. As day and evening classes are held in these subjects, and periodical examinations conducted both by the professors themselves and by the University of London degree examiners, it may be easily seen that Manchester people enjoy opportunities of obtaining the higher education for their sons, and of thus filling up what may have been lacking to a short school training such as are scarcely to be found elsewhere in England, at any rate out of the metropolis." [1] The Commissioners thought that the college was not sufficiently well supported by Manchester people and should have at least four hundred to five hundred day students. "The buildings of the college are in every way unsuited to its need; they stand in one of the most obscure

[1] *Schools Inquiry Commission*, Vol. IX, p. 719, H.M.S.O., 1868.

parts of the city, and consist of small rooms in a private house, roughly adapted to their present purpose. Lying thus out of sight, the college has in a manner been out of mind also. I found people in Manchester who did not so much know of its existence, while in some quarters its very newness and unsectarian character seem to have created against it an unworthy and groundless prejudice." [1] Mr. Bryce, who wrote this report, recommended the reorganisation and extension of the college.

This had already been in the minds of the college authorities, and a campaign was launched to raise funds for rebuilding. The appeal met with a generous response, and by 1870 a Bill was presented to Parliament to obtain authorisation for extension and the grant of a new constitution. After considerable opposition, the Bill became law and the new constitution was in force from 1871. One of the objections had been to the admission of women students. They were accepted from 1874, but in the meantime another important development had occurred. Negotiations had been opened once more with a view to amalgamating the School of Medicine with Owens College. This time the discussions came to a successful conclusion and the two institutions were amalgamated in 1873. The new buildings for the college were opened in the following year. By this time the number of students had increased to 1,004, made up of 337 day, 533 evening, and 134 medical students. The growth of the college suggested a further development. For some time the Senate of Owens College had been dissatisfied with the external examinations of the University of London, and thought it was now time to transform the college into a local university with the power of conferring its own degrees. Accordingly, a memorial was sent to the Privy Council for the grant of a charter to Owens College, giving it the status of a university, to be called the University of Manchester.

This, however, was not to be granted for many years, since events were happening on the other side of the Pennines which were to have repercussions on the fortunes of Owens College. As early as 1826, proposals had been made for the establishment of a university in Leeds, but the funds were not forthcoming to give them practical effect. There were, however, in Leeds, three sources from which the present University of Leeds sprang. The oldest of these was the School of Medicine. Its beginnings were in the Old Infirmary, where medical instruction was being given as early

[1] *Schools Inquiry Commission*, Vol. IX, p. 720, H.M.S.O., 1868.

as the year 1800.   Shortly after this a private school of anatomy was opened which was superseded in 1831 by the Leeds School of Medicine.   The school had grown to a considerable size and import-ance by the middle of the century through the work of the prominent medical men associated with it.

The second institution was the Yorkshire College of Science, which began its life in rented buildings in 1874.   There were many causes to account for the establishment of the college: the growing appreciation of the value of a scientific and technical education which had been stimulated by the Great Exhibition of 1851 ; the influences of the Leeds Mechanics' Institute and the Philosophical and Literary Society ; and the revival of secondary education in the endowed grammar-schools, all of which contributed towards creating a suitable atmosphere.   A Yorkshire Board of Education had been formed with the objects of fostering the teaching of science in day-schools, establishing evening classes in science, and bringing into existence a central science college.   By 1869 the Board con-sidered the time was ripe for launching the third project, but they immediately came up against the difficulty of lack of money.   At one time the Board, in despair of gaining the necessary funds, almost decided to give up the idea, but the more adventurous spirits gained the day, and, with the hope of ultimately owning their own premises, the college was started under the circumstances related above.

The original purpose of the college was "to supply instruction in those sciences which are applicable to the Manufactures, Engineering, Mining and Agriculture of the County of York ; also in such Arts and Languages as are cognate to the foregoing pur-pose."   When the inauguration ceremony took place in 1875, there were several prominent speakers who saw much further than the utilitarian aims of the founders.   Amongst these was Mr. W. E. Forster, M.P., who prophesied that the college would be the beginning of a provincial university.   The *Bradford Observer*, in a leading article, urged that Yorkshire should not be content with an institution which aimed at imparting some branch of technical or professional knowledge.   "We hope that no one will be finally content until literary is added to scientific culture, until the College of Science has grown into a great Yorkshire university."   The opportunity for further development was soon to come.   A Univer-sity Extension Committee in connection with Cambridge University had been set up in Leeds, and it decided that the best way of putting its work on a firm basis was to hand over its functions to the College of Science.

Meanwhile, the three professors of the college, although appointed to teach science, soon discovered that it would be advantageous to include arts studies in the curriculum. The students were also asking for this kind of teaching, but the authorities were so hampered by lack of funds that they were unable to grant the request. When, however, in 1877 the Extension Committee proposed to hand over its work to the college and to guarantee sufficient funds to carry it on, the offer was gladly accepted. In consequence, the college changed its name and was known from 1878 as the Yorkshire College. A working arrangement was also made with the medical school to allow its students to attend classes in scientific subjects at the college.

Such was the situation on the eastern side of the Pennines when Owens College presented its memorial for the grant of a charter. The request met with formidable opposition from Yorkshire. The authorities of the Yorkshire College also presented a memorial to the Lord President of the Council, asking that the Queen should be advised not to grant a charter to Owens College, Manchester, but to create a new foundation in which Owens College and other institutions might be incorporated, and that such a university should not bear the name of any town or person which would localise it. Negotiations between the two colleges began, and it was agreed that, if Manchester abandoned the idea of a local name for the new university, Owens College should be named as the first college constituting the university and the president and principal of that college should be its first chancellor and vice-chancellor respectively. The Government favoured this proposal, but the Yorkshire College raised a further point. It protested against the power of the university to grant degrees in the faculty of medicine. The Government agreed, much to the disappointment of Manchester, which possessed a strong medical school, and the Victoria University received its charter in 1880 and Owens College was immediately incorporated in it.

University College, Liverpool, was founded in 1881 with the intention of its becoming a college of the Victoria University. In 1884 it was amalgamated with the Liverpool School of Medicine, and its inclusion in the Victoria University took place in the same year. In the meantime, the Leeds School of Medicine realised that unless it received university status it would compare unfavourably with other schools of medicine. The Yorkshire College likewise realised that as a separate institution it would not possess a strong claim to be included in the Victoria University. As both institutions agreed on this point, amalgamation took place in 1884, and the Yorkshire College became a member of the confederation in 1887.

The University of Birmingham sprang from two separate colleges. The first was Queen's College, which at the start was a theological and medical school. The latter prospered but the theological side disappeared. The second, Mason College, was opened in 1880 by Josiah Mason, who had been a pen manufacturer. Mason intended his college to offer a purely scientific and utilitarian education. Its title was the Mason Science College, and it was designed to give instruction "adapted to the practical, mechanical, and artistic requirements of the manufactures and industrial pursuits of the Midland district." It was to have nothing to do with literary education, and theology was to be rigidly excluded. As the students were reading for London degrees which demanded literary subjects, Mason was obliged to modify his position. In 1881 he admitted courses of study which would qualify students for degrees at London and in the Victoria University. Hence the word "Science" disappeared from the title of the college. The civic pride of Birmingham prevented the college from entering the Victoria University as a junior partner; and, through the efforts of Joseph Chamberlain, Birmingham received in 1900 its charter as an independent university and was the first provincial university to bear the title of a particular city.

Meanwhile, events were taking place which ultimately led to the dismemberment of Victoria University. The first rift appeared in connection with a proposal to institute a faculty of theology. When Owens College was founded, the controversy about the abolition of religious tests at the older universities and at Durham was at its height. Owens College not only shared with University College, London, a decided antagonism towards dogmatic theological teaching, but even viewed with suspicion any attempt to give undenominational religious instruction. The abolition of religious tests in 1870 had completely changed the atmosphere, and within a few years many considered that there were fair prospects of establishing a faculty of theology in the Victoria University. The first proposal came before the Court in 1890 and excited violent opposition. The constitution of University College, Liverpool, expressly prohibited theological teaching ; the Yorkshire College was definitely hostile to the proposal ; and even at Manchester opinion was divided. Dr. Bodington, the principal of the Yorkshire College, led the opposition, and the proposal was defeated. Subsequent attempts to provide theological teaching were made, and eventually in 1900 a resolution to establish a faculty of theology was accepted. The Yorkshire College refused to take any steps in the matter, and the controversy showed that the constituent members of the Victoria University were hopelessly divided. Another grievance was that meetings of the Court and of examiners took place at Manchester and this involved considerable travelling for members from the other colleges.

The foundation of the University of Birmingham brought matters to a head. It was immediately asked that if Birmingham had its own university, why should there not be separate universities for Manchester, Liverpool, and Leeds. Liverpool was the first to move. For some years it had been accumulating a sufficient endowment, and by 1901 it made its claim to the status of an independent university. The Yorkshire College was strongly opposed to the impending dissolution, but the course of events depended upon the attitude adopted by Owens College. After some time the Court decided that the establishment of a separate university for Manchester was desirable. The Yorkshire College was convinced of the merits of a federal university, and at a meeting in 1902 its governors passed a resolution to the effect that they "came with reluctance to the decision that the establishment of a University for Yorkshire appeared to have become a necessity." Liverpool and Manchester received their charters in October 1903, and the Yorkshire College was left as the sole constituent member of the Victoria University. The Privy Council was not favourable to the idea of a Yorkshire university and preferred the title of University of Leeds. On 25th April 1904, the University of Leeds came into existence by royal charter. The successors of the colleges which originally constituted the Victoria University with the Universities of Sheffield and Birmingham still co-operate through the Northern Joint Matriculation Board.

Sheffield had possessed a People's College founded in 1842 by the Rev. R. S. Bailey. This formed the nucleus of what was afterwards the arts side of Sheffield University. There was also a Mechanics' Institute and a Medical School that had been opened in 1828. The Firth College at Sheffield was founded by a wealthy ironmaster, Mr. Mark Firth, in 1879, who gave a site, a building of the value of £29,000, and a further endowment of £10,000. An additional £12,000 was raised by donations. In 1880 the Sheffield School Board built the Central Higher School, which provided evening classes in engineering and applied science. The school was opened on a piece of ground adjoining the Firth College. The Royal Commission on Applied Science and Technical Instruction, 1881, suggested that a fund should be raised to found a technical college. The latter was opened in 1886 and was attached to the Firth College, but, when the Technical Instruction Act of 1889 was passed, the municipal authorities separated the technical school from the college and raised a rate to support it. This was a great blow to Firth College, but because of its medical school and its University Extension work it managed to carry on. It derived much-needed assistance from the Government grant to university colleges and from the municipal authorities. The medical school became a definite part of the institution in 1897, and in the same year Firth College became University College, Sheffield. The endowments were increased, and its governing body thought of applying for admission to the Victoria University. The latter at this time was in a state of disruption. Sheffield had raised money by subscription to provide new buildings, and in 1905 the college received its charter. University College, Bristol, was founded in 1876 and became an independent university in 1909. The latest English provincial universities to be constituted were Reading, in 1926, and Nottingham, in July 1948. Both Reading and Nottingham were in certain ways unique in their development.

Reading is a fair-sized town situated in the midst of an agricultural district. This geographical factor exercised a twofold influence on the growth of the university. In the first place, since Reading, unlike the larger cities of the north, had no densely peopled district surrounding it from which it could draw its students, it has always been less provincial in character than the other modern universities. With the exception of students living in Reading and the immediate neighbourhood, the college recruited its undergraduates from all parts of the country. In consequence, Reading developed its system of halls of residence from the very beginning and is now the most completely residential of the modern universities. Even the "town students" are members of St. David's Hall. As a further consequence of its position, Reading has always paid attention to agricultural studies and research.

University College, Reading, was opened in 1892. It originated from the University Extension work which was being organised in the town by the University of Oxford. For some years it was known as Christchurch Extension College. As a university college the institution made steady progress. Its finances were assisted by local benefactors, and it had high hopes of obtaining its charter as an independent university. Unfortunately, the First World War intervened and the grant of a charter did not materialise until 1926.

Nottingham, like Reading, owed its origin to the extension classes carried out in that city by Cambridge University. The lecture courses began in 1873, but the leaders of the movement in Nottingham quickly saw that a permanent centre was needed for the work. An anonymous benefactor offered the sum of £10,000 for the erection of a building in which lectures could be given. The corporation were at this time considering the building of a free library, and it was suggested that the two projects might be combined. The endowment was offered to the corporation on condition that they would provide the necessary accommodation within a reasonable space of time. In 1877 the foundation-stone of a building which comprised the free library, the museum, and the lecture rooms for University Extension and science classes. The building was opened in 1881, and hence Nottingham is an example of an English university which started life under municipal control. In this respect it may be compared with Edinburgh. University College, Nottingham, developed rapidly as a college of applied science, but progress in pure science and the arts was much slower. By the outbreak of war in 1914 it seemed as though the college had reached the limit of its development, and the ambition of attaining university status would have to be shelved indefinitely. The brake on its progress was its association with the town council, which was limited in its outlook. It is only fair to say that without the aid of the council there would have been no college at all, but if the institution was to develop further it would need a greater measure of independence.

The college struggled valiantly to obtain a wider basis for its government, but until it had sufficient endowments it was bound to the municipal authorities. It was the generous benefaction of Sir Jesse Boot (afterwards Lord Trent) which enabled the college to move to a new block of buildings in 1928. In 1938 a supplemental charter was granted by which the constitution of the college was changed and it was given greater freedom in the management of its own affairs. Numbers had grown considerably, and the attempts of the college to obtain university status succeeded in 1948. As Nottingham had always been a prime mover in adult education, it is not surprising to find that it possesses the oldest university department in adult education. This was created in 1920, soon after the publication of the Report of the Adult Education Committee of the Ministry of Reconstruction. A Chair of adult education was created in 1923, and later a residential college for adults was acquired.

The remainder of the English institutions of university rank are the university colleges of Exeter (1901), Leicester (1918), and Hull (1928). The latest to receive university status are Stoke-on-Trent (1950), Southampton (1952), Hull (1954), and Exeter and Leicester (1957). At present, arrangements are going ahead for the establishment of universities at York, Norwich, and Brighton. That at York will specialise in history and the arts. The late Lord Lindsay was appointed principal of Stoke-on-Trent. The college was authorised to grant its own degrees instead of preparing its students for the external degrees of the University of London. The University of Leeds has abolished the traditional distinction between the ordinary and honours degree. Undergraduates read for a special or a general degree and can obtain honours in either.

Wales is the only country of the British Isles which possesses no ancient university ; Trinity College, Dublin, was established in 1592. In spite of their Welsh descent, the Tudor sovereigns never entertained the idea of founding a university in the Principality. Welshmen studied at Oxford where, in Elizabeth's reign, Dr. Hugh Price of Brecon founded Jesus College. For years Jesus was regarded almost as a Welsh college, and many grammar-schools were connected to it by means of exhibitions. The University of Wales came into being as a result of a national movement led by those men who had accomplished so much for Welsh elementary and secondary education.

When we considered in an earlier chapter the development of elementary education in Wales, attention was drawn to the prominent part played by the Welsh Nonconformists. As the 19th century wore on, the Established Church was rapidly losing ground and the situation grew so serious for Church people that leading members of the Anglican communion decided that something would have to be done to enable it to hold its own. Dr. Burgess, who

became Bishop of St. David's in 1803, was convinced that the solution lay in providing a Welsh college at which candidates for holy
orders could obtain a liberal education at a moderate cost. As a
result of his efforts, St. David's College, Lampeter, was chartered
in 1828. Sir Thomas Phillips, who had been so bitterly incensed
by the Commissioners' Report of 1846, was a staunch supporter
of Lampeter. He saw in it the foundation on which a national
university for Wales might be built, and he urged the necessity of
giving the college the authority to confer degrees.

In 1852 the college obtained a charter enabling it to grant the
degree of B.D., and in 1865 it was empowered to confer the degree
of B.A. But Lampeter was not destined to become the University
of Wales. It was too closely associated with the Established Church
to commend itself to Welsh Nonconformity, and, if anything, it
proved an obstacle to the establishment of a national university.
Strange to say, the idea of a Welsh university originated in the
West Riding of Yorkshire where, in 1821, a society called "The
Association of Welsh Clergy in the West Riding" was formed.
The society sent a petition to Parliament in 1852, which, while it
approved the granting to Lampeter of the power to confer degrees,
thought that the real solution was a national, free university which
would include amongst its members both Churchmen and
Dissenters.

The following year a pamphlet was published by B. T. Williams,
afterwards M.P. for Carmarthen Boroughs, in which he pleaded
for a Welsh university modelled on the University of Glasgow.
This pamphlet was described by Lord Aberdare as striking "the
first note" in the university movement. Sir Hugh Owen, who also
supported the movement, suggested the establishment in Wales of
a number of colleges similar to the Queen's Colleges which had
just been founded in Ireland. He pointed out that these institutions, like the colleges in England and Scotland, received Government grants, but Wales got nothing. The result of all this ferment
of idea was the series of meetings in 1863 in Mitre Court and in
the Freemasons' Tavern, near Fleet Street in London, at which the
campaign for a national University of Wales was started.

A provisional committee was formed to further the scheme,
but it came into practical politics when a lucky accident provided
a means for its accomplishment. In 1867 a huge hotel was being
built at Aberystwyth. After £80,000 had been spent on it, the promoter of the scheme became a bankrupt. The provisional committee

seized the opportunity, bought the hotel for £10,000, and opened it in 1872 as University College, Aberystwyth. From the start, residential accommodation was provided, with the result that Aberystwyth is still more fully residential than any other Welsh college. The students of the college read for external degrees of the University of London. Negotiations to work in association with Lampeter came to nothing, and St. David's is still outside the federation of colleges which constitutes the University of Wales.

The new college had a hard struggle to make ends meet and the Welsh members of Parliament pressed for Government aid. The result was the Commission of 1880 under the chairmanship of Lord Aberdare, which recommended the foundation of two colleges, both of which should receive Government grants. The problem was to decide the position of these two colleges. Whilst matters were under consideration, a separate grant was given to Aberystwyth in 1884 which served as a precedent for the grants subsequently made to the English university colleges. An interesting situation developed. Both Cardiff and Swansea claimed the right of having a university college for South Wales. Cardiff was successful and its college was opened in 1883. North Wales was not satisfied with Aberystwyth and claimed a college of its own which was opened at Bangor in 1884. This, however, resulted in the Government grant being taken away from Aberystwyth and being given to the two new colleges, an action which roused Aberystwyth to fight for its existence. A compromise was effected by which the Government agreed to give a grant to all three colleges.

So far, Wales had obtained three isolated university colleges and the Anglican foundation at Lampeter. The creation of a University of Wales still seemed a long way off. The effect of the Welsh Intermediate Education Act of 1889 was to produce a large number of pupils who were fitted to enter upon a university course. Once more the agitation for the establishment of a Welsh university began. In 1888 a conference of the three colleges had already suggested the creation of a federal university on the lines of the Victoria University. Eventually, owing to the support of Lord Aberdare and Viriamu Jones, the Welsh gained what they wanted, and in 1893 the University of Wales came into existence. It consisted of the three constituent colleges of Aberystwyth, Bangor, and Cardiff, to which later were added the Technical College at Swansea and the National School of Medicine at Cardiff.

Whilst London University and the provincial universities were developing, great changes were taking place in the ancient universities which fitted them to take a leading place in the modern world. In Chapter iv it was pointed out that no great changes could be expected in the older universities until their constitution and government had been reformed. The Public Examinations Statute of 1800 added a written examination at Oxford to the oral and introduced the distinction between pass and honours. The separation of the classical and mathematical honour schools making it possible for a candidate to gain a "double first" took place in 1807 at Oxford, whilst at Cambridge, in 1824, a second Tripos was established in classics. The original had been in mathematics. Reform of the examination system, however, moved very slowly on account of the resistance of the heads of colleges who were opposed to change. By 1851 Cambridge had instituted the Triposes in moral science and natural science, and by 1850 the Oxford honour schools included mathematics, natural science, law, modern history, and theology.

The men who were mostly responsible for the Public Examination Statute at Oxford were Cyril Jackson, Dean of Christ Church, John Everleigh, Provost of Oriel, and John Parsons, Master of Balliol. Jackson enjoyed a tremendous reputation. In his time Christ Church was packed with undergraduates, and, according to De Quincey, there was not a dog-kennel left untenanted. Several future statesmen, notably Canning and Peel, were amongst Jackson's pupils. When the classical and mathematical honour schools were divided, Peel was the first graduate with a "double first." Later both Keble and Gladstone achieved the same distinction. Many of Jackson's undergraduates were young noblemen, and he became famous for the tact and ability he showed in handling such a difficult class of pupil. His authority was unquestioned, and, although some considered that he was cold and aloof, in reality he was most kind and sympathetic towards those whom he had in charge. His dignified behaviour and even his mannerisms lived on for a generation. C. H. Hall, who was Jackson's successor in the Deanery, copied his mannerisms even to the extent of wearing his cap perched upon the bridge of his nose.

Everleigh, although he did not possess such a striking personality as Jackson, nevertheless had unbounded influence both in the university and in his college. Keble once remarked that he was "a man to bring down a blessing on any society of which he was a member." Parsons raised the intellectual standards of Balliol to such a degree that he was frequently referred to as the second founder of the college. Amongst his pupils were Southey, Coleridge, and William Hamilton who later became one of the severest critics of the university.

Reform was in the air, but it did not stop at the improvements effected in the public examination, and every aspect of university life was subjected to severe criticism. In addition to the reforming party within the university, pressure was being exerted from outside. The *Edinburgh Review,* which had been attacking the public schools, also turned its attention to the older universities, especially Oxford. Its criticisms were at first directed against the curriculum of the university. It was asserted, that Oxford professed an excessive veneration for Aristotle and treated his doctrines as though they were infallible decrees, that the infancy of science was mistaken for its maturity, that the mathematical sciences had never flourished, and that the scholar had no means of advancing beyond the mere elements of geometry.

Oxford was not lacking in defenders. In 1810 there appeared *A Reply to the Calumnies of the Edinburgh Review against Oxford, containing an Account of Studies pursued in that University.* The work was produced anonymously, but Newman had no doubts in claiming Edward Copleston as the author. At this time Copleston was a Fellow of Oriel, and he succeeded Everleigh as provost in 1814. The original *Reply* was followed by a second and a third, and Copleston, by his moderate tone and by the understanding of Oxford which he displayed, won general approbation. The first charge made by the *Edinburgh Review* was easily refuted. Copleston was able to state with assurance that "for more than a century, the Physics of Aristotle have been set aside, and, except for the sake of satisfying liberal curiosity, and of tracing the progress of science, they are never even consulted." (*Op. cit.,* p. 17.)

The criticism that only the mere elements of geometry were taught at Oxford was likewise denied. Copleston was able to state that the mathematics course included plane and spherical trigonometry, the properties of conic sections, of conchoids, cycloids, the quadratix, spirals, fluxions, and all branches of natural philosophy and astronomy.

In an article on Edgeworth's *Professional Education,* the *Edinburgh Review* attacked the classical studies of the universities and asked how they could be defended on the ground of utility.

It asserted that the ascendancy of classical learning in English education "is preposterous, and the mode of teaching it in English Schools and Universities, utterly absurd. . . . A young Englishman goes to school at six or seven years old: and he remains in a course of education till twenty-three or twenty-four years of age. In all that time, his sole and exclusive occupation is learning Latin and Greek." Copleston's reply constitutes one of the noblest vindications of literary studies, and of classical literature in particular, that has ever been penned. "In the cultivation of literature is found that common link, which, among the higher and middle departments of life, unites the jarring sects and subdivisions in one interest, which supplies common topics, and kindles common feelings, unmixed with those narrow prejudices with which all professions are more or less infected. The knowledge too, which is thus acquired, expands and enlarges the mind, excites its faculties, and calls those limbs and muscles into freer exercise, which, by too constant use in one direction, not only acquire an illiberal air, but are apt also to lose somewhat of their native play and energy. And thus, without directly qualifying a man for any of the employments of life, it enriches and enobles all." (*Ibid.,* pp. 111-12.)

Speaking of classical literature, he wrote: "The relics of Grecian and Roman literature contain some of the choicest fruits of human genius; that the poets, the historians, the orators, and the philosophers of Greece especially, have each in their several lines brought home and laid at our feet the richest treasures of invention; that the history of those early times presents us with a view of things 'nobly done and worthily spoken'; that the mind and spirit which breathed then, lives still, and will ever live in the writings which remain to us." (*Ibid.,* p. 113.)

Copleston was not so effective in his answer to the criticism of the undergraduate's course at Oxford. He discussed at great length the details of the subjects studied in the honour schools of the university, but this was largely beside the point. The criticisms of the *Edinburgh Review* were mainly directed at the studies of the pass man, and it is common knowledge that at this period the attainments demanded of him were distinctly modest.

The next line of attack was upon the exclusive position held in the universities by the Established Church. Several attempts had been made in the latter half of the 18th century to open the universities to those who were not members of the Church of England, but the events of the French Revolution and the Napoleonic Wars turned men's minds in other directions. The most unflinching opponent of religious tests was Sir William Hamilton, and his views seem to have been widely supported, judging from the petitions sent to Parliament from all parts of the country. A petition from Skipton added the name of Durham to those of the ancient universities.

One petition, signed by some eminent members of Cambridge, earnestly pleaded for the abolition of religious tests. Connop Thirlwall, Fellow of Trinity College (later Bishop of St. David's), suggested that the rule of compulsory attendance in college chapels might be discontinued. Christopher Wordsworth, master of Trinity from 1820 to 1841, violently opposed this plea. He demanded that Thirlwall should resign his fellowship. Whewell, who was also a Fellow of Trinity, successfully intervened, but the affair rendered Wordsworth unpopular with his fellows. This was no doubt one of the reasons why he resigned and was succeeded by Whewell as master of Trinity.

A Bill to remove the disabilities of Dissenters who wished to proceed to degrees was presented to Parliament in 1834. It passed the House of Commons, but was rejected by the Lords. The *Oxford University Magazine* rejoiced to see the fall of the first reformed House of Commons, "which carried by a large majority, in the midst of disgraceful uproar raised to drown remonstrance and surpass arguments which could not be answered, a bill to force upon the Universities persons of all, any, or no religious communion—a measure of Church and State, and which involved a violation of private rights and a tyrannical interference with private conscience, to a degree unequalled except in the ultimate stages of revolution." [1]

Although defeated in the first round, the fight for the admission of Dissenters was reopened by Hamilton in the *Edinburgh Review*. The question was once more raised in Parliament and a motion was moved in both Houses to institute a commission of inquiry. These motions were withdrawn on the understanding that the Government would consider the matter further and that the universities themselves intimated they were ready to introduce reforms. Nothing, however, was done by either party. In addition to his advocacy of the rights of Dissenters, Hamilton attacked the statutes of the universities and the collegiate system, and Professor Archer remarks that the language used in the controversy "frequently went

[1] *Oxford University Magazine*, No. IV, March 1835, pp. 116-17.

beyond what would now be considered seemly in academic discussion." [1]

Hamilton's accusations were answered by Dr. William Whewell, who was then tutor of Trinity College, Cambridge. Whewell was the son of a carpenter, and by his intellect and personality he eventually rose to be head of a college. He is chiefly remembered at the present day as a noteworthy logician and expounder of the inductive sciences. In spite of his humble origin, Whewell was a firm defender of the dignity of his position. He was Vice-Chancellor in 1843 and again in 1855. At this later period of his career he was not altogether popular amongst his colleagues. "Whewell's foible of omniscience might have been more easily forgiven by his colleagues if it had not been combined with an overbearing temper and an impatience of opposition which sometimes made him almost intolerable. He possibly might have been very successful as the leader of a totalitarian state, but the defects in his character prevented him from acquiring that influence in the University which was really his due." [2] There is a story to the effect that when he was caught in a sudden shower, he sought refuge under the umbrella of an undergraduate and quenched in advance any attempt at conversation by remarking that all communications to him must come through a tutor.

In his younger days Whewell represented the reformers within the university. In 1835 he published *Thoughts on the Study of Mathematics as a part of a Liberal Education,* in which he declared that the teaching at Cambridge was solely concerned with pure mathematics and neglected the applications of the subject in

[1] The tone of the attacks on the universities may be judged from the following extracts from Sir William Hamilton's article in the *Edinburgh Review,* "On the Right of Dissenters to Admission into the English Universities," January 1835: "Oxford is now a national school of perjury. The Intrant is made to swear that he will do, what he subsequently finds he is not allowed to perform. The Candidate for a degree swears that he has done, what he has been unable to attempt; and perjures himself, by accepting, from a perjured Congregation, an illegal dispensation of performances indispensable by law. The Professor swears to lecture as the statutes prescribe, and he does not. The reverend Heads of Houses, the academical executive, swear to see that the laws remain inviolate, and the laws are violated under their sanction; they swear to be vigilant for the improvement of the University, and in their hands the University is extinguished; they swear to prevent all false oaths, and for their own ends, they deliberately incur the guilt of perjury themselves, and anxiously perpetuate the universal perjury of all under their control. The academic youth have thus the benefit of early practice and high example. . . . Is it marvellous that England is a by-word among the nations, when the fountains of English morality and religion are thus poisoned at their source? How long is this to be endured?"

[2] D. A. Winstanley. *Early Victorian Cambridge,* p. 139, C.U.P., 1940.

mechanics and hydrostatics. This work was followed in 1837 by the *Principles of English University Education.* Whewell distinguished between two forms of teaching which he termed the "practical" and the "speculative," respectively. Practical teaching was what we should now call the "lesson" in distinction from the "lecture," and since it involved the constant interplay between the minds of the teacher and the taught, it was only possible in small classes and was best adapted to such studies as mathematics and classics. The lecture, delivered to a large audience and which does not demand as an essential that the student be called upon to do something which depends upon the knowledge he has acquired, is ill suited to these studies.

Whewell wrote: "He may follow with the clearest apprehension, and it may be, with full and well-founded conviction, the views which are presented to him by the teacher; but still he is passive only; he is a spectator, not an actor, in the intellectual scene. He does not interpret and employ a peculiar acquired language, as he does in his classical reading, or his algebraical calculations." [1] Whewell's dissatisfaction with the lecture method is being re-echoed at the present day in the modern universities in which reliance upon the efficacy of multitudinous lectures is waning, and demands come from tutors and undergraduates alike for fewer lectures and more tutorial classes. Whewell thought that the older universities struck the happy medium by providing both kinds of teaching, practical teaching in the colleges, and speculative lectures delivered by the professors in the university.

His views on examinations are interesting. He regarded them not only as tests, but also as a means of instruction. The latter was true of the college examinations which introduced the study of subjects into the college course which had no reference to the public examinations of the university. He was, however, well aware of the dangers of the examination system. He wrote: "The University must, in the discharge of its proper functions, have tests of proficiency to be applied before her degrees and honours are granted. There must, therefore, be University examinations. On the other hand, it must always be recollected that examinations are a means, not an end;—that a good education, a sound and liberal cultivation of the faculties, is the object at which we ought to aim; and that examinations cease to be a benefit, where they interfere with this object" (p. 56). Whewell had in mind "the strong disposition . . .

[1] *Op. cit.*, p. 7, John W. Parker, 1837.

in the University of Cambridge at least, to give a complete prepon-
derance to the indirect system : —to conduct our education almost
entirely by means of examinations, and to consider the lectures
given in the Colleges as useful only in proportion as they prepare
the student for success in the examinations" (p. 55).

Although Whewell did not mention the University of London
by name, there is no doubt about his reference to the external examination system. "The establishment of a board of examiners independent of the teachers, converts the system from one of direct to
one of indirect teaching ; and must be avoided or modified, except
we are prepared to give up direct instruction altogether. If, we do
this, and trust entirely to the force of examinations, using only the
honour and disgrace which they bring, as the means of stimulating
indolence and calling forth exertion, we come to an intelligible
system, but one very different from any which has ever prevailed
in the English Universities. We need then make no demand for
attendance at lectures, nor even for residence. One final examination, or several examinations at certain intervals, must be all the
evidence we require of the student's proficiency, and of his fitness
to receive the stamp of University approbation. In this system,
all the influences of our direct College teaching . . . are entirely
abandoned. There may be persons who would think this an advantage ;—who would prefer the uncollegiate system of foreign universities to ours ; or who would think that we might sufficiently supply
any deficiencies which may exist in them, by university examinations
properly devised. Such a system is quite intelligible ; but it behoves
us to understand what it is, before we decide in its favour. It is
right that we should see clearly that it never has been our system ;
and that when we talk of its establishment among us, we propose,
not the improvement, but the destruction of our College practices ;
—not a modification, but a revolution in our English University
education" (pp. 66-7).

The most important influence at Oxford in the second quarter
of the 19th century was the Tractarian or Oxford movement. Its
early leaders were Keble, Pusey, and Newman. In spite of the
controversies it caused in the university, which reached a climax
in Newman's secession to Rome in 1845, the Oxford Movement
was responsible for giving a new direction to the English Church
and for transforming it from the deadness into which it had fallen
to become a great living spiritual force. The effect of the Oxford
Movement upon the supporters of the national schools has already

been discussed, but it also had considerable influence in the university itself in developing ideals of life and conduct. When Newman published, in 1852, his lectures to the "Catholic University of Ireland" under the title of *The Idea of a University*, he included in them the ideals which were potent at Oxford in his day and skilfully blended them with Catholicism.

Although in 1835 the Duke of Wellington had announced that the universities were reforming themselves, progress was very slow and met with constant opposition. At Cambridge, the movement was less hampered than at Oxford. At the beginning of the century, Cambridge was given an opportunity of seeing what would be the result of a college with statutes that were fitted to the age. Downing College owed its foundation to the will of Sir George Downing in 1717. He directed that if his issue failed, the trustees of his estate should establish a college at Cambridge, named after him. When his heir died in 1764 without issue, the university put forward its claim. A lawsuit followed which dragged on for years until at length, in 1800, the Lord Chancellor pronounced in favour of founding a college. Now was the opportunity to draw up college statutes which should be free from the defects belonging to those of the more ancient colleges. Downing College was incorporated and received its statutes in 1805. They provided for a master, two professors, one of law and the other of medicine, and sixteen Fellows. Only two of the fellowships were for life ; the remainder were tenable for twelve years and were to be held by laymen who intended to enter the legal or medical professions. There was a definite lack of serious legal and medical studies at the university. The arrangements for the award of scholarships were a marked improvement on the practices of other colleges. Since statutes eventually became out-of-date, provision was made for amending the statutes of Downing, when and if required. Winstanley describes "the constitution of Downing . . . as an experiment in college reform."

The opportunity of demonstrating the advantages of possessing a modern set of statutes was lost because of a neglect of duty on the part of the Court of Chancery. It approved a very ambitious building-scheme which could not be completed for lack of funds. The Crown refused to appoint more than three Fellows, and the statutes did not allow any scholarships to be awarded until the buildings were finished. Thus Downing stood alone in the university as a college with no scholarships, prizes, or exhibitions, to award, and only three fellowships. The result was that it failed to attract undergraduates in any number.[1] "Thus what was intended to become an encouragement of reform became a warning against it ; and the other colleges were strengthened in the belief that the old ways were best or, at least, less dangerous. When urged to put their houses in order, they could point to Downing as an object lesson on what might happen if they drastically revised their statutes ; and they seldom failed to draw such a convenient moral. This was by no means the only argument used against college reform, but the others might possibly have been less effective if it had not been available."

Nevertheless, Trinity (largely due to the efforts of Whewell) in 1848, and St. John's in 1849, obtained new statutes. Also, in 1850 a committee was appointed to revise the university statutes. At Oxford, the Examination Statute of the same year remodelled the public examinations. The pace was far too slow to please the more ardent reformers, and in 1849 a memorial was presented to the Prime Minister, Lord John Russell, urging him to ask the Queen to appoint a royal commission to inquire into the state of affairs at the older universities. The memorial was signed by a number of Oxford and Cambridge men and by Fellows of the Royal Society. The Commission was issued in August of the following year and reported in 1852.[2]

Both universities protested against interference with what they considered were their internal affairs, but, when the Commissioners visited Cambridge, they were received, if not with warmth, at least with some show of cordiality. Those who visited Oxford encountered organised opposition, and every possible obstacle was placed in their way. The Vice-Chancellor announced that he would contest the legality of the Commission. Four well-known advocates declared it illegal, but the Government's law advisors pronounced the exact opposite, so that the question of the Commission's legality was dropped. Heads of colleges and university officials gave as little help as possible, though some, as at Corpus Christi, All Souls',

[1] D. A. Winstanley. *Early Victorian Cambridge*, p. 7, C.U.P., 1940.

[2] The Oxford Commissioners were Dr. Hinds, Bishop of Norwich, Dr. Tait, at that time Dean of Carlisle, Dr. Jeune, Master of Pembroke College, Dr. Liddell, Headmaster of Westminster, Baden Powell, the Savilian Professor of Geometry, the Rev. G. H. S. Johnson, a former Savilian Professor, John Dampier; and A. P. Stanley and Goldwin Smith as secretary and assistant-secretary respectively.
The Cambridge Commissioners were Dr. J. Graham, Bishop of Chester, Dr. Peacock, Dean of Ely, Sir John Herschell, Sir John Romilly, and Professor Adam Sedgwick, the geologist. The Rev. W. H. Bateson acted as secretary.

St. John's, Merton, and Lincoln, were more co-operative. Jeune, the Master of Pembroke and a member of the Commission, was enthusiastic for reform. Many members of the university feared that they were going to be brought under Government control, and even thought that Kay-Shuttleworth would rule the universities as he ruled the elementary schools.

The Commissioners were greatly concerned with the question of the expense of a course at the older universities. Just as the Newcastle and Taunton Commissions considered that elementary and secondary education, respectively, were not available for all those who needed them, so the University Commission feared that many members of the upper middle classes could not take advantage of the opportunities afforded by the older universities because of the expensive character of the courses, the restrictions of out-of-date statutes, and the religious tests. The Commisioners were instructed not to force the latter issue.

The report on Oxford, although written in a much superior English style by Stanley, was more drastic than that on Cambridge. The recommendations made were the basis of the Oxford University Act of 1854 and the Cambridge University Act of 1856. The Hebdomadal Board at Oxford, which the Commissioners discovered was extremely unpopular, was replaced by the Hebdomadal Council which contained a large number of elected members. The Laudian Statutes were repealed, and a new Congregation composed of resident members of the Convocation was created. Private halls or hostels were once more permitted and the university was given power to make statutes and regulations for them. The colleges were given new constitutions which freed them from the ties which had previously bound them to particular families, places, or schools. College revenues were reapportioned and the professorial system was reorganised and strengthened. Fellowships were to be awarded on merit and scholarships thrown open to free competition. Nonconformists were to be allowed to enter without a religious test and to take the degree of B.A., but the M.A. was still withheld. The Cambridge University Act followed similar lines. The *Caput* or Council of the Senate became to a great extent an elected body. In both universities, ordinances were to be discussed by Congregation or Convocation in English instead of Latin. The obligation for Fellows to take holy orders was removed.

One interesting point referred to the Cambridge Commission was the long-standing controversy between the university and the municipal authorities. The Cambridge Borough Council petitioned the Commissioners to have their grievances removed. The town authorities complained that the university exercised certain antiquated privileges and did not take its proper share in the burdens which fell upon the citizens. A compromise agreement might have been effected long before this, except for the fact that both parties were not inclined to yield any ground. The university tried to annoy the town and the latter always sought a chance to humiliate the university.

Since the days of Edward II, the mayors and bailiffs of Cambridge had been required to take certain oaths which suggested that the town was inferior to the university. The university claimed the right to license ale-houses in Cambridge and Chesterton and to grant licences for the sale of wine. As a result of an Act of 1836, the town claimed similar rights, but the university insisted that it possessed an exclusive right in these matters. Both parties continued to issue licences and complained that the other was doing so illegally. In order to prevent undergraduates piling up debts, the Heads of Houses ordered that any tradesman who instituted legal proceedings against an undergraduate without having previously informed his tutor, should be discommuned, *i.e* students were forbidden to deal with him. In addition, every tradesman to whom an undergraduate owed more than £5 was to inform the tutor.

An Act of 1843 had forbidden any theatre to be licensed in Cambridge or within fourteen miles of the town without the Vice-Chancellor's permission. The latter also had the power to forbid other kinds of entertainment. The town thought this was unreasonable, since it would have been a simple matter for the university to put such entertainments out of bounds for undergraduates. The university had also the right to supervise weights and measures, and appointed Taxors to examine and seal them. A person who used weights and measures which had not been sealed was liable to a fine. The Vice-Chancellor was authorised to be present when the university proclaimed the Cambridge markets and fairs at Barnwell and Stourbridge. The mayor and corporation also proclaimed the fairs.

Perhaps the most important grievance suffered by the town was that connected with the Chancellor's court. The latter was empowered by the Elizabethan statutes with jurisdiction within a mile of the town over most civil and all criminal proceedings. It was also felt that the distribution of financial burdens between the university and the town was unequal. The university only paid £100 per annum land-tax, and the town £2,700. Most university buildings were not assessed for rates. On the other hand, the university paid two-fifths of the expenses of paving, cleaning, and lighting the town.

Similar powers had been granted to the University of Oxford by a royal charter of 1525. They had been resisted by the towns-folk and a compromise agreement had been arrived at by arbitra-tion in 1542. As a result of the great riot on St. Scholastica's Day in 1354, the mayor and bailiffs of Oxford had each year to perform a humiliating penance. They were not finally released from this until 1825. By a decree of Henry III, 1248, the municipal authori-ties had to swear an oath "to keep the liberties and customs of the university," and this was discontinued only in 1859. Many of the outstanding differences between the town and university had already been settled by compromise.

At Cambridge the town authorities made the most of their grievances to the Commissioners, as was quite natural. The result was a temporary truce brought about by the curtailing of some of the privileges of the university. Others, however, were still maintained, e.g. licence for theatrical entertainments ; issue of wine-licences by the Vice-Chancellor, but no charge was to be made for them ; the jurisdiction of the Chancellor's court to extend to those cases where one party was a member of the university ; the university to be assessed for local rates ; the land-tax arrange-ments were not altered, but the university was now only respons-ible for a quarter of the expenses involved in paving, cleaning, and lighting the town.[1]

[1] The dispute between the town and the university flared up again in the later 19th century. The controversy centred round the powers wielded by the Vice-Chancellor's court. The latter was deemed necessary in order to protect the morals of the undergraduates. The court not only had the power to inflict fines but the university had its own prison, the Spinning-House. The town authorities regarded the existence of the court as a slur on their own ability to maintain order. The dispute came to a head as a consequence of a number of cases which had been decided in the Spinning-House Court. The press made much of what was styled "academic tryanny." Discussions on this matter, and also on the Vice-Chancellor's right of issuing wine-licences and his power of veto on entertainments, took place between the university and town authorities. The latter insisted upon the abolition of the university's authority over townsmen. A deadlock ensued and the town authorities appealed to the member of Parlia-ment for the borough. A Bill was promoted by the town authorities of Cam-bridge in 1892, but through pressure of business it failed to obtain a second reading. Further negotiations took place, and finally both parties agreed to a Bill which would bring about a satisfactory arrangement. The Bill became law in 1894 under the title of the Cambridge University and Corporation Act. The grievances of the town were removed (the Vice-Chancellor retained the right of issuing wine-licences) and amicable relations were restored between the university and the borough authorities.

The campaign for the complete removal of religious tests continued. Perhaps the events which did most to secure the abolition of the tests were the resignation of Sedgwick from the Fellowship of Trinity College, Cambridge, in 1869, and the accusation of heresy brought against Benjamin Jowett at Oxford. Sedgwick resigned because he felt he could no longer be a faithful member of the Church of England. Jowett, as Regius Professor of Greek, received a statutory salary of £40 per annum, and this was not augmented for years because of his views on the Atonement and his contribution, in company with Temple and Pattison, to *Essays and Reviews* in 1860. Jowett was actually brought before the Vice-Chancellor's court on a charge of heresy, but the proceedings were eventually dropped. In 1863 Dr. Pusey, to the dismay of his more extreme followers, proposed that Jowett's salary should be raised to £400 a year. This proposal was rejected by Convocation, and their action met with intense disapproval amongst undergraduates and in the public press. Eventually, in 1865, Dean Liddell persuaded the chapter of Christ Church to fix the salary at £500 per annum.

Such incidents as these convinced the Government that the time had come to abolish religious tests. Mr. Gladstone, who had previously thought such action dangerous, now changed his mind. The disabilities suffered by Dissenters were illustrated at Cambridge when the Senior Wranglers of 1860 and of 1861 were refused fellowships because they would not subscribe to the Thirty-Nine Articles. Liberals and Nonconformists had long been waging war on privilege and, when the Liberal Government came to power in 1868, Mr Gladstone announced his intention of abolishing the tests at Oxford, Cambridge, and Durham. The Bill became law in 1871, and all degrees with the exception of those in divinity were thrown open to Dissenters. Compulsory attendance at college chapel was also abolished. In 1915 Cambridge took the further step of removing all religious restrictions on degrees and fellowships, and Oxford followed suit in 1920.

The reforms brought about by the Acts of 1854 and 1856 bore fruit in the new life and vigour that appeared in university life and studies. The number of undergraduates grew rapidly and the distinctions between noblemen, gentlemen commoners, and commoners disappeared. The servitors at Oxford and the sizars at Cambridge, poor men whose presence at the university was only tolerated because of the menial duties they performed, likewise disappeared and their emoluments became exhibitions.[1] New studies were introduced and new Chairs established, especially in scientific subjects. New honour schools arose in natural science, law, history, oriental languages, English language and literature, and mediaeval and modern languages. It was felt, however, that in spite of these advances, certain important problems had not been solved. Although the requirements of residence in a college had been withdrawn, many of the ablest scholars were still unable to afford a university education. The solution advocated was the provision of halls in which the living expenses would be cheaper than the cost of residence in any of the colleges.

The system of private tutors, which had been roundly condemned by Whewell, was left untouched, and Mark Pattison urged that too little attention was being given to research. He believed that Fellows should be allowed to marry and that appropriate quarters might be provided for them. College revenues should be used more freely for university purposes, such as the creation of a common university fund, the foundation of new Chairs, the erection of new buildings, and the establishment of additional scholarships and prizes. The abuse of prize fellowships[2] still continued, and funds which might have been used for college teaching were absorbed in this way. It was important, too, that the lay Fellow should have an opportunity of making university teaching his profession for life.

These ideas and criticisms resulted in another Commission, with the Duke of Cleveland as chairman, and it was charged to conduct a most searching inquiry into the finances of both the colleges and the universities. It was appointed in 1872 and reported in 1874. As a consequence, the Oxford and Cambridge Act of 1877 appointed commissioners for both universities, with considerable executive powers. The commissioners soon got down to work. They were empowered to frame statutes for the colleges (the Acts of 1854 and 1856 had been concerned with university statutes), and to compel

---

[1] Many of these poor scholars rose to positions of eminence. Samuel Wesley entered Exeter College in 1683 as a servitor, and George Whitefield, who graduated in 1736, became a servitor at Pembroke. Isaac Newton was sub-sizar at Trinity College, Cambridge, and Richard Bentley and Richard Watson began their careers in the same way. The position of servitor at Oxford was more menial than that of sizar at Cambridge. The latter owed his name to the fact that he was granted a free "size" or portion of bread and ale.

[2] The prize fellowship was a non-resident fellowship awarded for exceptional merit in the examinations. It involved a life income of from £200 to £250 a year, and at Oxford between twenty and thirty such fellowships were given each year.

the colleges to contribute to university purposes from their revenues. Life fellowships were abolished and prize fellowships for research were established. At Oxford a common university fund was created, to which all colleges were expected to contribute. Fellows were allowed to marry; teaching duties were given them; their stipends were standardised, and a pension fund was set up. All these changes freed considerable funds which could be applied to the establishment of new Chairs, readerships, and lectureships, and for the maintenance of buildings. At Cambridge, the colleges contributed a fixed percentage of their incomes to the common fund. The obligation to deliver lectures was laid upon the professors, but attendance at lectures was not compulsory for students.

One interesting result of the abolition of religious tests was the establishment of new colleges and halls on a denominational basis. In association with the Church of England, Keble College was founded at Oxford in 1870 and Selwyn College at Cambridge in 1882. The Free Churches and the Roman Catholics established halls, although they were not part of the university constitutionally, the residents of which were able to benefit from university teaching.

To this period, also, belongs the founding of colleges and halls for women, a topic which was considered in Chapter v. The general effect of this legislation was to transform the older universities into institutions well organised and equipped to take a prominent place in the life and culture of the modern world. Although the following was written about Oxford, it applies equally to Cambridge: "Old defects had been largely remedied. New standards of work and order had been introduced. The 18th-century Don, with his easy conscience and unexacting duties, had been replaced by a generation of high-minded Tutors whose chief danger lay in the risk of over-work. An important movement had begun for the better organisation of studies. The whole field of instruction had been usefully enlarged. Science had asserted her right to a place beside Philosophy, Modern History, Modern Literature, even Modern Languages were putting forward claims which could not be ignored. The classical tradition could no longer maintain its monopoly, even by the stubborn retention of compulsory Greek. It is true that the throwing open of Scholarships had to some extent diminished the chances of boys brought up at humble schools. The abolition of the old servitorships had closed another avenue to the poor student. And the Non-Collegiate system had failed as yet to solve the difficult problem how to secure in an atmosphere so charged with comfort and enjoyment a fair and equal opportunity for men of narrow means." [1]

In the later Victorian period, Oxford was dominated by Benjamin Jowett of Balliol, and Dean Liddell of Christ Church. Balliol became a centre of intellectual and moral influence, and served as a training-ground for many famous men. Amongst Jowett's pupils were such well-known statesmen as Asquith, Milner, Curzon, and Grey. This was also a period of expansion and building reconstruction. Liddell set the example at Christ Church, and this was followed by many other colleges, such as Balliol and Exeter. New examination-schools were built in the High Street, and the Bodleian Library, which had outgrown its original quarters, overflowed into the old Jacobean schools. The core of the Bodleian was the 15th-century library of Duke Humphrey. This had suffered during the religious quarrels of the following century and was practically denuded of books. Sir Thomas Bodley (1545-1613) restored and endowed it and presented it with a collection of books. He drew up statutes for its government, and, by his agreement with the Stationers' Company, the Bodleian acquired the right to a copy of every new book that is published in the kingdom. Other libraries which are entitled to a similar privilege are the British Museum, Cambridge University, the National Library of Wales, the Scottish National Library, and Trinity College, Dublin ; but the Bodleian was the first to be granted this right. If the Bodleian is one of the glories of Oxford, Cambridge is no less proud of the Cavendish Laboratory, named after Henry Cavendish, the famous chemist and physicist. It is one of the greatest research laboratories of the world and is associated with the names of such eminent scientists as Clerk Maxwell, Lord Rayleigh, Sir J. J. Thomson, Sir Ernest Rutherford, and Sir William Bragg.

The beginning of the present century saw new problems confronting the ancient universities. The Education Act of 1902 resulted in the growth of municipal and county secondary schools, whose pupils came into competition with those from the public schools and older grammar-schools. Education authorities offered scholarships tenable at the older universities, at London, and at the provincial universities. For the first time it became possible for the children of working-class people to obtain university training.

[1] Sir Charles Mallett. *A History of the University of Oxford*, Vol. III, p. 352, Methuen, 1927.

In spite of scholarships, the expense of a course at Oxford or Cambridge often proved an insuperable obstacle to them. Another barrier was that caused by the insistence upon Greek as a condition for matriculation. Cambridge was the first to abolish compulsory Greek in 1919 and Oxford followed a year later.

In 1907 Bishop Gore of Birmingham moved in the House of Lords the appointment of a royal commission "to inquire into the endowment, government, administration, and teaching of the Universities of Oxford and Cambridge, in order to secure their best use for all classes of the community." In the same year Lord Curzon became Chancellor of Oxford and quickly identified himself with the movement for reform. He was foremost in suggesting the abolition of compulsory Greek and the granting of degrees to women. He also succeeded in reducing the number of members of Congregation, thus making it a less unwieldy body, and in 1912 he established a Board of Finance. At Cambridge the reform movement was mainly supported by the younger members of the university.

Before further changes could be effected, the First World War broke out and the idea of a royal commission was dropped for the time being. Immediately after the armistice, the universities became crowded by undergraduates returning from national service. The modern universities found themselves becoming overwhelmed by financial difficulties since the increase in expenses, coupled with the fall in value of money in the post-war world, was making it impossible for them to maintain their establishments at all adequately. The president of the Board of Education considered that their needs could only be met in relation to circumstances at Oxford and Cambridge, and he agreed to receive a deputation if the older universities, and also those of Scotland and Ireland, were represented on it. Oxford and Cambridge asked for financial aid, and their governing bodies agreed that the granting of it should be preceded by a royal commission.

The Commissioners were received quite differently from those of 1850. They were cordially welcomed and every effort was made to supply them with the information they required. The report was made in 1922, and its recommendations were embodied in new statutes which came into force in 1926. No drastic changes were suggested. Its chief concern was with the financial aspect. More staff was required; lecturers needed improvements in their salary position and more adequate pension schemes; additional funds were necessary for libraries, museums, new buildings, and the development of women's colleges and extra-mural activities.

The powers of Convocation were reduced at Oxford, and membership of Congregation was limited to those engaged in teaching or administrative work in the university. Cambridge had no body corresponding to Congregation and it was recommended that a similar house should be established. The administrative work of the universities was overhauled and placed on a modern footing. Professors were attached to colleges as Fellows and became members of their governing bodies. The question of salaries and pensions was adequately met and retiring-ages were introduced for all members of the universities. Many of the remaining restrictions on the marriage of Fellows were removed. The number of women students was not to exceed a fourth of the men, and women could be admitted as full members of the University of Oxford. This did not take place at Cambridge until 1948. Certain developments as regards the teaching staff and buildings were recommended, and for the first time each of the older universities received a large annual subsidy from the State. At the same time a guarantee was given that the acceptance of this grant would not in any way prejudice the independence of the universities.

Before leaving this sketch of events in the older universities, something should be said of an interesting development which had taken place at Oxford. This was the institution of the Rhodes scholarships for students from the British Empire, the United States, and Germany. Rhodes made altogether seven different wills. In the final will, twenty annual scholarships, tenable for three years, *i.e.* sixty in all for the British Empire, were established. These were to be divided in the proportion of eight for South Africa, six for Australia, two for Canada, and one each for New Zealand, Newfoundland, Jamaica, and Bermuda. In addition, each State or Territory of the United States was given two scholarships, making the total for that country one hundred. This will was dated 1899, but two years later he added a codicil which established fifteen scholarships for Germans. Rhodes believed that friendly relations between the three countries would be a potent factor in securing the peace of the world. The German awards were suspended in 1914, but in 1929 two German scholars were admitted each year. The original allocation of scholarships has been modified. Since 1939 the German scholars have again been suspended, and in 1947 two awards were granted to India. Other scholarships have been given to colonies and dominions not provided for in Rhodes's will, so that the numbers allocated to the British Commonwealth and the United States are now roughly equal.

The financial problems of the older universities, which resulted in the giving of a government subsidy, had their counterpart in the modern universities. All the modern universities in their early stages were severely handicapped by lack of funds. In many cases local donors made them large gifts which enabled them to extend their buildings and their work, but it was not until 1889 that the Treasury contributed to their upkeep. In that year the House of Commons voted the sum of £15,000 per annum to be distributed among the university colleges. The condition for participation in this grant was that colleges performed "an appreciable amount of advanced University work." This has generally been interpreted to mean the provision for post-graduate research as well as of courses for undergraduates. The annual grant continued to rise until, in 1919, a body known as the University Grants Committee was constituted. Thus the universities, except in the case of their teacher-training departments, do not receive funds direct from the Ministry of Education. The members of the University Grants Committee are people with wide experience of the work and needs of the universities.[1] The grant for the year 1948-9 reached an amount over £17,500,000. This arrangement has worked very well, since it has preserved the autonomy of the universities. Every university is free to decide what it will teach, draw up its own syllabuses, and organise its own examinations for degrees and diplomas. Thus the disasters which have overtaken some of the State-controlled universities of the Continent are avoided. Most local education authorities also make grants to institutions of university status in their areas.

The British universities of the post-war era are faced with a number of serious problems. Perhaps one of the most urgent is a consequence of the phenomenal increase in the number of full-time students, from 50,246 in 1938-9 to 85,421 in 1949-50. It is true that the return of ex-service students is to a great extent responsible

[1] The present terms of reference of the University Grants Committee are: "To inquire into the financial needs of university education in Great Britain; to advise the Government as to the application of any grants made by Parliament towards meeting them; to collect, examine, and make available information on matters relating to university education at home and abroad; to assist in consultation with the universities and other bodies concerned, the preparation and execution of such plans for the development of the universities as may from time to time be required in order to ensure that they are fully adequate to national needs."

for these numbers, but even when the flow of such entrants has been exhausted it can be assumed that the numbers of students will be permanently at least half as large again as the total of pre-war days. The universities are faced by an ever growing demand from a variety of sources, and it must be expected that further claims on their services will be made in the future.   There are many reasons to account for the increasing demand for university education.   On the one hand, the professions (medicine, dentistry, science and tech-nology, agriculture, commerce, education, architecture, and law), the Civil Service, and local government are all appealing for an increased number of graduates.   Thus the Barlow Report suggested that the present output of qualified scientists should be doubled at the earliest possible moment, and the Percy Report considered that the annual number of graduates in engineering should be half as large again.   On the other hand, the grammar-school population from which the universities draw the larger number of their entrants has grown from 342,000 in 1925-6 to 574,000 in 1945-6.   It is significant that the number of passes in the Higher School Certificate examination rose from 5,100 in 1926 to 20,600 in 1948, and the award of State scholarships increased from two hundred in 1925 to eight hundred in 1948.

This numerical increase in the total of university entrants, how-ever, only gives part of the picture.   When the intake of the different faculties is examined, the important fact comes to light that some faculties and departments are expanding more rapidly than others, and that this ratio is not the same for every university.   This is due to the demands of sectional interests.   One vital factor, however, emerges.   Thus, supposing the number of students reading for a degree in engineering suddenly increases, unless there is a propor-tionate growth in other departments there is a danger that the balance of university studies may be permanently altered.   All universities anticipated a period of expansion after the war and, at the request of the University Grants Committee had produced post-war development schemes to meet the situation.   It has also to be realised that expansion involves a large increase in the teaching and administrative staffs of the universities and a much greater income to meet such necessary items as salaries, new classrooms and laboratories, libraries, halls of residence, common-rooms, and sports facilities.

The need for a larger income has been met by increased Govern-ment grants.   Thus the annual grant, which was less than £800,000 in 1920-1, was approximately £17,500,000 in 1948-9, and rose to over £70,600,000 in 1961-2. Parallel with this, the amount contributed by the local authorities has increased. These facts raise a number of problems. In the first place, money is not everything. "Money is necessary, and more money will accelerate the expansion, but by itself it will not produce the teachers and research workers on whom everything depends."[1]

Secondly, the above figures may be regarded from another quite different point of view. In 1920-1 the universities received twenty-nine per cent of their income from the State. The participation of Oxford and Cambridge in the Treasury grant raised this percentage to thirty-two. This percentage continued to rise until it was 70·4 per cent in 1960-1, and, in addition, the universities received grants from other Government Departments and the local authorities. The non-recurrent grants for capital expenditure in 1960-1 amounted to nearly £22,200,000. The remainder or universities' income came from fees, endowments, and gifts. Thus the major part of university incomes is contributed by the State. At present, the University Grants Committee makes a block grant to each university for a five-year period. How far the autonomy of the universities can be balanced with their growing dependence on State aid is a problem that may occur in the future. Tradition in the past has generally been opposed to Government control and hence it is important that the delicate adjustment which has worked so well for the last quarter of a century should be maintained. The creation of the standing Committee of Vice-Chancellors and Principals performs the essential function of close liaison between the different universities and Government departments. Although at present it is not a fully authoritative body, its function can be regarded as supplementing that of the University Grants Committee.

The third problem is that of the financial position of the students as individuals. The proportion of would-be undergraduates who themselves are able to pay for a three or four year course is rapidly diminishing. The heavy incidence of taxation and the rising cost of essential commodities has considerably reduced the number of parents who are able to bear unaided the expenses of a university education for their sons and daughters. Hence there is an ever increasing body of students who are dependent on financial assistance either from the State or from local authorities. At present

[1] *The Problem Facing British Universities*, a Nuffield College Survey, p. 88, O.U.P., 1948.

about sixty-eight per cent of university students receive grants of one kind or another, and at Oxford and Cambridge this proportion is about eighty-two per cent. The majority of the grants were those made to ex-service men and women under the scheme for further education and training. These have now come to an end and the Ministry of Education working party (April 1948) considered what other grants should take their place. It recommended a large increase in the number of State scholarships and in the aid given towards university scholarships and exhibitions.[1] In addition, the number of students in receipt of teacher-training grants has grown considerably.

The result is that both the universities and the students are becoming more and more dependent on assistance given by public authorities. In the last century the universities and university colleges often owed their very existence to the munificence of local benefactors. Although it is to be hoped that similar public-spirited individuals will appear in the future, yet it must be acknowledged that, because of the changing economic and financial conditions, they will become fewer and fewer.[2]

The increasing number of students has raised the problem of accommodation. Not only are more rooms required for teaching and administrative purposes, but the question of hostel accommodation has become an urgent one. A large proportion of students in the modern universities have been obliged to live in lodgings because of lack of halls of residence. The advantages of a corporate life are becoming increasingly recognised. In the early days of the University Grants Committee, little attention was given to the provision of hostels. By 1936 the Committee was actively interested in the problem, but still thought it might be solved by the gifts of private benefactors or by the universities themselves. Since the war the housing shortage has made matters acute and the Committee has earmarked considerable sums of money for building halls of residence. In spite of priorities and shortages, the universities are going ahead with their plans for providing adequate hostel accommodation.

[1] It was considered that State and local scholarships should be increased to a point where two-thirds of the entrants to universities and university colleges could expect aid from public funds.

[2] One of the more recent benefactors has been Lord Nuffield, who not only endowed the medical school at Oxford with £2,000,000 as a research centre, but also gave £900,000 in 1937 for the foundation of Nuffield College for the development of social studies. The outbreak of war held up the building of the college. It was forced to carry on its work in temporary premises. The foundation-stone of the new college was laid in April 1949.

CHAPTER XIII

ADULT EDUCATION AND THE DEVELOPMENT OF SCIENTIFIC AND TECHNICAL EDUCATION

Adult education, in the modern meaning of the term, did not exist before the closing years of the 18th century, and it was not until the industrial changes had made considerable progress that serious attempts were made to grapple with the problems of adult education.

The history of adult education falls into two well-marked periods, with the year 1850 as a convenient dividing point between them. Before that date, adult education was promoted solely by voluntary agencies. Three main factors influenced the line of development of adult education during this period. It began with what may be called a religious-philanthropic inspiration; it was greatly influenced in the early years of the 19th century by the growth of interest in physical science ; and, finally, its course was shaped by the social and political agitation which later found expression in Chartism. After 1850, changing social and economic conditions altered the whole outlook. Revolutionary agitation had ceased by 1848 and the country entered upon a period of rising wages and falling prices. Moreover, by this time two new agencies had entered the field of adult education. The universities were showing an interest in the movement, and the State was concerning itself with the provision of primary education and was later to take into account the sphere of further education. In the earlier period, the majority of adults had been untouched by primary education and the adult agencies had to make good that deficiency. As more schools were opened for the children, the education of adults tended to become an extension of primary education.

The religious-philanthropic movement was responsible for the first attempts to teach adults. Before the adult-schools were established there were three interesting but isolated experiments. The earliest is that mentioned in the Minutes of the S.P.C.K. for 8th March 1700, and concerns two individuals, John Pierson and John Reynolds. The former, as well as teaching children to read, "twice in the week meets another Company of adult persons (about

467

8 in number) in the town, and hears them read, and trains them up in Bp. Williams' Exposition of the Church Catechism. The latter Instructs Gratis another Company every night at his House, in the Catechism, in Reading and Serious Principles, and endeavours to bring them to an awful sense of God and man." [1]

The second experiment was more than three-quarters of a century later and was connected with the Sunday Schools of Birmingham. It was an attempt to retain young men who had previously attended the Sunday School and had now become too old for that type of teaching. To achieve this end, the teachers of Sunday Schools in that city formed, in 1789, the Birmingham Sunday Society. It aimed at teaching reading, writing, and arithmetic ; and later geography, bookkeeping, drawing, natural science, and moral instruction were added. The instruction was not confined to Sundays, but was also extended to certain evenings of the week. Eventually the Sunday School Society was renamed the Brotherly Society and a new constitution was drawn up. One member of the society, Thomas Clarke, frequently assembled these young men at his own house. They were known as the "Cast-Iron Philosophers," and it was quickly discovered that they included some of the best artisans of the town. Hudson describes the objects of the society as "Reading, Writing, Arithmetic, Drawing, Geography, Natural and Civil History, and Morals, or in short, whatever may be useful to a manufacturer, or as furnishing principles for active benevolence and integrity." [2] It will be noted that in these early experiments there was no distinction drawn between adult and technical education. Hudson also adds that every member was expected to attend a place of public worship, and the rules contained a provision for excluding those who did not do so. One result of the classes was the formation of the Birmingham Artisans' Library to disseminate knowledge among the working classes by the aid of books.

The third example is that of the first adult-school which was opened in Nottingham in 1798 by William Singleton, a Methodist, and Samuel Fox, a member of the Society of Friends. The object of the school was to teach adults to read the Bible and to give them instruction in writing and arithmetic. This experiment is worthy of note because the school continued throughout the century, and

[1] Quoted by Helen Wodehouse. *A Survey of the History of Education*, p. 142, Edward Arnold, 1929.
[2] J. W. Hudson. *History of Adult Education*, pp. 29-30, Longmans, Brown, Green, and Longman, 1851.

although it did not immediately have imitators, yet nearly fifty years later it served as a stimulus to the school which had been founded in Birmingham.

The work of Hannah More and her sister has already been mentioned in connection with the philanthropic agencies of the 18th century. The early adult-school movement really began at Bristol in 1812 when William Smith, a door-keeper of a Methodist chapel, assisted by a merchant of the name of Stephen Prust, established in that town an *Institution for Instructing Adult Persons to read the Holy Scriptures*. Dr. Pole, who became a member of the Bristol committee, was the historian of the early adult-school movement. He was born in the United States and came to England when quite a young man. He was a member of the Society of Friends and became a promoter of the work of the British and Foreign Bible Society in Bristol. Pole had qualified as a physician and was also an able lecturer. When he settled in Bristol in 1802 his philanthropic nature urged him to deliver a series of lectures on chemistry, the economy of nature, and mineralogy. Pole's lectures were well attended and he enlivened them by his own pencil-sketches and models. When a local meeting of the British and Foreign Bible Society was held in Bristol, William Smith was amongst the audience. He was struck by the statement that in many instances the Bible was useless to poor people because they were unable to read it. He spoke to Stephen Prust about this and the result was that he undertook to carry out an experiment. Accompanied by two friends, Smith set out to sell Bibles in a poor district of the town. When he was told that the Bibles were useless because people could not read them, he arranged to give instruction in reading to those who were willing to attend. He secured two rooms for his evening school, and his first two pupils were "William Wood, aged sixty-three, and Jane Burrace, aged forty. Thus the first school fore-shadowed the present-day development in that women were granted equal privileges with men. The sexes were taught separately, under the guidance of two teachers, who had previous experience in charity schools for children. . . . Within three weeks the schools were opened, eleven men and ten women being enrolled on the first day." [1]

As the work developed, it became necessary to organise it on definite lines, and the Institution for Instructing Adult Persons to

[1] G. Currie Martin. *The Adult School Movement*, pp. 26-7, National Adult School Union, 1924.

Read the Holy Scriptures was formed. Dr. Pole, as previously mentioned, was a member of the committee, and it is through him that we possess the details about the spread of the movement. By 1816 there were in Bristol twenty-four schools for men and thirty-one for women, with a total membership of 1,581. Adult-school societies were formed at Plymouth, in Wales, at Salisbury, and at Bath. Evidently William Smith met with misfortune, for we read that in 1822, "This year Wm. Smith of Bristol, connected with the Adult Schools, being indisposed, and in want of assistance, we raised £5 15s. for him by subscription, which was given at various times for his support." [1]

Dr. Pole's History played an important part in the growth of the schools. It was circulated in all parts of the kingdom and was excellent propaganda for the movement. By 1820 schools had been opened in London, the Midlands, Sheffield, Leeds, Manchester, Liverpool, Newcastle, Yarmouth, and Ipswich, and in the rural districts of Berkshire and Buckinghamshire. The adult-school movement was entirely due to the efforts of the religious denominations—in particular the Society of Friends. It met with opposition from many people who believed that education would make the working man discontented with his lot and lead him to accept the doctrines of the French Revolution. Mr. Giddy, the president of the Royal Society, echoed the fears of the upper classes when in 1807 he said, in reference to Whitbread's Bill, "However specious in theory the project might be of giving education to the labouring classes of the poor, it would in effect be found to be prejudicial to their morals and happiness; it would teach them to despise their lot in life, instead of making them good servants in agriculture, and other laborious employments to which their rank in society had destined them; instead of teaching them subordination, it would render them factious and refractory, as was evident in the manufacturing Counties; it would enable them to read seditious pamphlets, vicious books, and publications against Christianity; it would render them insolent to their superiors; and in a few years the result would be that the legislature would find it necessary to direct the strong arm of power towards them, and to furnish the executive magistrate with much more vigorous laws than were now in force." [2]

[1] G. Currie Martin. *The Adult School Movement*, p. 39, National Adult School Union, 1924.
[2] *Hansard*, 1807, IX, p. 798.

One of the most interesting adult-schools was that of Severn Street in Birmingham, founded in 1845 by Joseph Sturge, one of Birmingham's most prominent citizens. At first the school was not a success and the number of scholars dwindled until there were more teachers than pupils. Sturge remembered having visited the school of Singleton and Fox many years earlier, and he resolved to send a deputation to Nottingham to interview Fox and discover the secret of his success. The result was that Sturge made a number of important modifications in the Severn Street school, and thus it was that the isolated experiment at Nottingham entered many years later into the main stream of the adult-school movement.

Hudson tells us that by 1850 many adult-schools had been discontinued and the numbers of scholars had everywhere declined. The three reasons he gives for the decline were the lack of good teachers, the effect of introducing children into adult-schools, and the objection raised by many of the well-to-do classes against teaching the poor to write. More potent causes, however, were the increasing number of primary schools, so that the need for teaching the three R's to adults was diminishing, and the influence of political views during the period succeeding the Reform Act, which tended to divert the working population in other directions. The rise of Mechanics' Institutes and other forms of adult education also accounted for the decline. The worker wanted more than the three R's and these other institutions could supply his need. The adult-schools, however, were to experience an astonishing revival later in the century.

When the use of steam-power and machinery became more widespread, factory owners who had previously been opposed to popular education began to encourage their workmen to take an interest in the machines they operated and the industrial processes in which they were engaged. They argued that this kind of learning would not encourage workmen to be dissatisfied with the station of life into which they had been called by a wise Providence. This explains the rapid progress of the Mechanics' Institutes in the first half of the 19th century.

The idea of the Mechanics' Institutes originated in Scotland. In 1760 Professor John Anderson, who taught natural philosophy in the University of Glasgow, gave some lectures in practical physics which were attended by a number of workmen. In 1799 Dr. George Birkbeck was appointed Professor of Natural Philosophy and Chemistry in the "Andersonian Institution" at Glasgow. In the course of visiting the workshops where apparatus for his classes was being constructed, he was astonished to find that the workmen showed great interest in what they were making. This experience suggested to him the happy idea of inviting the men to a special mechanics' class. The university authorities were sceptical about its success and told him that the men would not come; if they came they would not listen ; and if they listened they would not understand. The first meeting proved a great success. Those who came told others and, by the fourth meeting, the attendance had risen to 500. Birkbeck was astonished at the orderly behaviour and the keen interest shown by the students. In 1804 he left Glasgow for London, but his successor, Dr. Ure, continued the classes. Although Birkbeck practised in London as a physician, he still retained his interest in adult education, and he was the moving spirit behind the foundation of the London Mechanics' Institute which was opened in 1823. The same year, the workmen who attended the lectures in the "Andersonian University" at Glasgow seceded and founded a separate Mechanics' Institute. The Manchester Mechanics' Institute started in 1824, and this was followed by the rise of similar institutions at Leeds, Huddersfield, and other large industrial towns. Unions of Mechanics' Institutes followed, the first association being that of the West Riding of Yorkshire.

The Leeds Mechanics' Institute, at one time the largest in the country, is typical of the movement. The object of its foundation was "to supply at a cheap rate, to the different classes of the community, the advantages of instruction in the various branches of science which are of practical application to the various trades or occupations." Although the industries of Leeds involved many processes requiring a knowledge of chemistry, for a long time the response was poor. This was mainly due to the lack of elementary knowledge which prevented the students from getting full advantage from the scientific instruction. This was common to most Mechanics' Institutes and largely accounted for their decline after the middle of the century. In 1842 the number of students at Leeds had risen to 143, but by 1850 it had dwindled to seventy-three. Another cause of the slow growth of the science class was the fact that it was housed "in a dark, damp, dingy cellar." The institute had other activities, and included a reading-room and library, but all works of fiction and general literature were excluded from the latter. To supply this "pleasurable mental relaxation," the Leeds

Literary Society was founded in 1834, and in 1842 the two institutions were amalgamated.[1]

Hudson, the historian of the early adult movement, estimated that in 1850 there were 610 Literary and Mechanics' Institutes in England having a membership of 102,050 and possessing 691,500 books in their libraries.[2] The movement was supported by the weekly issue of the *Mechanics' Magazine,* and such well-known advocates of popular education as Lord Brougham, Cobbett, and Place, did much to encourage it. The decline of the Leeds Institute was typical of what happened throughout the country after 1850.

The Mechanics' Institutes were, however, an important step in the development of scientific and technical instruction. Some of them, as in London, Manchester, Birmingham, and Leeds, developed into important technical institutes and colleges. The London Mechanics' Institute eventually became the Birkbeck College; and at Leeds, Huddersfield, Bradford, and other large centres, they developed into important technical colleges. Although in many districts working men were replaced by middle-class members, this was not true of the Yorkshire Union. The annual report of the Yorkshire Union of Mechanics' Institutes, 1859, stated: "It is a prevalent opinion that Mechanics' Institutes are only so in name, their original purpose having been superseded by the rejection of them by the class for whom they were intended, and their adoption by the middle classes. But this is not true of the majority of those in Yorkshire, however it may apply elsewhere. Some of the most flourishing Institutes are composed almost wholly of the labouring class, and in most of them they form a considerable majority." In 1861 the Union asked for returns from the Institutes giving the number of working-class members. It was discovered that 70·7 per cent were working men. Others were clerks and shop-assistants.

[1] The Leeds Institute founded two schools for the sons and daughters of members, in 1845 and 1853 respectively. Fitch visited the schools as an assistant commissioner of the Taunton Commission and spoke very highly of their work. Nevertheless, he reported, "The name 'Mechanics' does not fairly represent the social position of the persons who avail themselves of such institutions. It is not men of the labouring class, but the more intelligent shopmen, clerks, warehousemen, and travellers of a great town like Leeds, who compose the Mechanics' Institute. And it is for children of this class that the committee have made ample provision in their day schools." (*Schools Inquiry Commission,* Vol. IX, p. 245, H.M.S.O., 1868.) These schools are now controlled by the Leeds Education Authority under the names of the Leeds Boys' Modern School and the Lawnswood High School. They represent, with their modern buildings and spacious playing-fields, two of the most up-to-date grammar-schools in the city.

[2] J. W. Hudson. *History of Adult Education,* Longmans, Brown, Green, and Longman, 1851.

At Huddersfield in 1876, out of 1,000 members all but 105 belonged to the working class and these were bookkeepers and clerks.

By 1862 the popularity of lectures was waning, largely because funds were not available to pay the fees of really able lecturers. Where a sufficient number of lecturers who would give voluntary service could not be obtained, the lecture was replaced by the Penny Reading. The latter seems to have originated at Ipswich in 1859 and was often given by members of the elocution class connected with the Institute. There was evidently no lack of fluent and expressive readers, since the readings became very popular and continued to attract audiences until the growing numbers of literates produced by the elementary schools rendered such readings superfluous.

The Mechanics' Institutes had been intended for artisans and skilled workers, but many supporters of the movement wished to attract unskilled workmen. It was obvious that if this scheme was to be successful the form of instruction given to the latter would have to be of a more popular character. This desire led to the establishment of the Lyceums. In these institutions there were reading and news rooms and libraries, whilst the lecture programme was of a type that had a wider appeal than the work of the Mechanics' Institutes. Discussions, concerts, and recreations, were added as additional attractions. The charges for admission were low and both men and women were welcomed. It was hoped that the social attractions would draw many people from the beer-houses and gin-palaces. The effort was not very successful. Many of those in charge of the Lyceums were too impatient with the programme offered and tried to make it more intellectual and an approximation to that of the Mechanics' Institute. The class of people it was hoped might be induced to attend preferred the public houses and the singing-rooms, and the Lyceums never attained the influence of the Mechanics' Institutes.

The upper and middle classes were not to be left out of the scheme of adult education. It was hoped to cater for them by the establishment of Athenaeums. The attractions of these institutions were on a more lavish scale. The main feature was the library and the courses of public lectures which were often delivered by eminent men of the literary and scientific worlds. On the social side the soirée was the great attraction. It was often organised on a grand scale and gave opportunities for listening to music and for social intercourse. According to the drawings in *Punch* of that period, it was the latter which proved the greater attraction. For a brief period the soirées were popular with the well-to-do. A more successful institution amongst the middle classes was the Literary and Philosophical Society, and many of these are vigorous institutions at the present time. In many towns, as at Leeds, the Mechanics' Institute and the Literary and Philosophical Society were closely connected.[1]

Birkbeck College was one of the most interesting and important of the institutions which sprang from the Mechanics' Institutes. It owed its foundation to a meeting held at the Crown and Anchor Tavern in the Strand in 1823, at which it was decided to establish a London Mechanics' Institute. The leading supporters in addition to Dr. Birkbeck were Thomas Hodgskin, who had been a naval officer, and J. C. Robertson, a journalist and patent-agent. The latter two were advocates of reform who were bitterly opposed to the industrial policy of the age. Dr. Birkbeck, as a scientist and educationist, shrank from anything that might engender revolutionary tendencies, and he acted as a sobering influence upon the more radical aspirations of his colleagues. They would have liked the constitution to have been on more democratic lines than it actually was, though from the start the members of the Institute were given a large share in its management.

[1] Great pains were taken to ensure that the soirées should have as wide an appeal as possible. In 1852 the Directors of the Skipton Mechanics' Institute decided to incorporate their soirée with the meeting of the Yorkshire Union of Mechanics' Institutes which on that occasion was being held in the town. Two of the committee were asked to find out if the Skipton Brass Band would play at the soirée in return for a free tea. The band demanded a fee of £3 15s., a free tea, and free conveyance on the trip to Bolton Abbey that was to follow the meeting of the Union. The directors suggested a fee of £1 10s., but the band refused to lower its fee and the idea was abandoned.

The soirée was held in the Great Hall of Skipton Castle. Arrangements were made for vocalists and the Skipton Quadrille Band was engaged. The prices of admission indicated that the soirée was designed to attract the middle classes—reserved seats 3s., front seats 2s., and back seats 1s. The combined soirée and meeting was widely advertised and arrangements were made with the L.N.W.R. to run a special stopping train from Settle to Skipton. The railway company offered to run the train for a guaranteed cost of £5 or to allow the Institute to run the train for £6. The latter offer was accepted.

Tea was provided for the soirée and wives of members undertook to bake the following:—

1¾ stones of Bath buns.	1¼ stones of cracknels.
1 stone of brown bread.	1½ stones of tea-cakes.
1 stone of currant loaf.	1 stone of seed loaf.
2½ stones of plain loaf.	

The shopkeepers agreed to close their shops at 2 p.m. on the day of the meeting and soirée. The author is indebted to Mr. J. Macgregor for the above information. Mr. Macgregor undertook a post-graduate research under my supervision into the History of Adult and Technical Education in Skipton-in-Craven during the 19th century.

The original object of the Institute was to provide instruction in the physical sciences and in economics. The curriculum was to be practical in the sense that it would have a direct bearing upon the daily work of the members. The inclusion of economics excited the suspicion of the Tories, who were afraid that it would prove to be a school for agitators. The new foundation was enthusiastically supported by Francis Place, Henry Brougham, T. C. Hansard, and the editor of the *Morning Chronicle,* on whose staff was Thomas Hodgskin, but it was severely criticised by a section of the press which thought it was a means of fomenting revolution.

The institution soon encountered dissension within, which was an anticipation of the differences in outlook which existed between the National Labour Colleges and the more orthodox adult-education movements in recent times. The Institute could not pay its way by relying on the subscriptions of the mechanics. Was it to avail itself of the aid freely offered by philanthropic members of the more wealthy sections of the community ? Hodgskin and Robertson thought not, and they withdrew from the committee. When Robertson, who had been secretary, resigned, it was thought necessary to appoint a paid official to do the work. The latter overspent his income and bolted to avoid arrest. The Institute, however, survived its early difficulties, and it moved into permanent quarters in Southampton Buildings in 1825.

The scope of the instruction given in the London Mechanics' Institute gradually widened and literary studies were added to the scientific. A class in landscape-painting was started. This was taught by B. R. Haydon, whose chief propensity seemed to be that of borrowing cash from his friends and forgetting to pay it back. On one occasion he implored the loan of £5 to take his dress-coat out of pawn to enable him to wear it at the classes of the Institute. Haydon was a much-liked teacher and an artist of ability. When he left the Institute in 1836 he presented his palette to remain in the Committee-room. "The palette, which is still preserved at Birkbeck College, bears the following inscription : 'Presented to the London Mechanics' Institute, May 16, 1836, by B. R. Haydon as a memento of respect for the conduct of its honourable President, Dr. Birkbeck, and its Members in opening their doors to him when every other institution had the moral cowardice to close them.'" [1]

[1] C. Delisle Burns. *A Short History of Birkbeck College,* p. 53, University of London Press, 1924.

After Dr. Birkbeck's death in 1841, the Mechanics' Institute was affected by the general decline. It had its own financial difficulties which eventually grew so great that it had to appeal to the Government for assistance This resulted in a complete overhaul of the institution and its teaching, and in 1866 it became the Birkbeck Literary and Scientific Institution. An important part of its work became the preparation of its pupils for the external examinations of the University of London. The successful reorganisation of the institution was due to the secretary, G. M. Norris (later the first principal), F. Ravenscroft, a member of the well-known firm of robe-makers and founder of the Birkbeck Bank and Building Society, and J. C. N. White. In 1907 the institution became the Birkbeck College and, as a result of the Haldane Commission, it became recognised in 1920 as a school of the University of London for evening and part-time students.

The period from the end of the Napoleonic wars to 1848 is remarkable for the intense interest displayed by the masses of the people in social, economic, and political problems. The works of the radical reformers, such as Tom Paine and Cobbett, were being widely read and discussed by groups of working men. The repeal of Pitt's repressive legislation had made the growth of the trade unions possible, but, when they seemed to offer little hope of improvement in their conditions, working men pinned their faith to the prospect offered by parliamentary reform. When they found that the Reform Act of 1832 had merely transferred political power to the middle classes, the workers sought guidance from other sources Robert Owen attracted much attention, and, on account of the emphasis he placed on education as a means of social regeneration, the large number of Owenite Societies of the 1830's made adult education one of their chief aims. The principal motive force, however, was not that of the co-operative societies, which had sprung up as the result of Owen's teaching, but the political agitation which was associated with Chartism. The ablest of the Chartist leaders was William Lovett. "Like his friends, Francis Place and Thomas Cooper, he was one of the workmen of whom it may be said that amid heart-breaking discouragements, poverty, and failing health and political persecution, the hunger for knowledge 'haunted them like a passion.' " [1] Lovett's views on education were expressed in his *Address on National Education*, 1837, in which he outlined an educational programme more than two

[1] *Final Report of the Adult Education Committee, Ministry of Reconstruction*, p. 18.

generations in advance of his time. His proposals, with one exception, came to nothing in his lifetime, but they were carried out by others at a later stage.

In 1842 the first People's College was opened in Sheffield through the initiative of an Independent minister, the Rev. R. S. Bayley. Before he came to Sheffield, Mr. Bayley had been instrumental in founding the Louth Mechanics' Institute in 1835. On his appointment to Sheffield he began to lecture to the Mechanics' Institute in that city, and when he proposed his scheme for a People's College he suggested eleven classes which would meet daily for one hour before the men started work and for two hours in the evening. One class was to be concerned with the three R's, but the others would study geography, moral knowledge, English and general history, English composition, science, logic and algebra, philosophy and natural history, English literature, Latin, and Greek, respectively. A public lecture on a topic of general interest would be delivered Tuesday evenings at a fee of 3d. a lecture. The fee of 4s. entitled a student to his class ticket, and he paid 6d. a week for the classes and an extra 2d. for borrowing books from the college library.

Bayley decided to enrol both men and women, and so great was the response that in a short time he had to increase the number of classes to fifty a week. The college received no aid from the Government and depended entirely on its own resources. A good deal of its success was due to the personality and high standard of scholarship of the founder. Mr. Bayley not only ran regular courses of study, but he tested the progress of the students by means of periodic examinations. For some years the college prospered and it was able to move from temporary to permanent premises. Then came the usual financial difficulties, which were aggravated by internal disputes. The college nearly came to an end, but when Mr. Bayley was appointed to a London chapel he urged his friends to maintain the institution whatever difficulties they had to face. During the time he was at Sheffield, Mr. Bayley had, amongst his pupils, Samuel Plimsoll who became member of Parliament for Derby, 1868-80, and became famous for the adoption of the Plimsoll line on the ships of the Merchant Navy.

Bayley's friends took his exhortation to heart and resolved that they would keep the college alive. In order to place it on a firm basis, they reorganised it under a committee and drew up a new set of regulations which put the government of the college into the hands of the students. The faith of the sixteen who carried out

Bayley's wish was amply justified and the college received a new lease of life. By 1850 the number of students had risen to 630, but after 1860 a decline set in once more. The college still continued its work until 1879, when the corporation demanded its premises for street improvements, and when it finally closed it finished solvent with a balance of £28 19s. 1d. The end of the college coincided with the opening of Firth College, which was destined to become the University of Sheffield.

The importance of the Sheffield college, apart from the work it carried out in that city, lies in the influence it had upon F. D. Maurice and his friends. Some years previously they had experimented with the co-operative movement, which they regarded as an application of Christian Socialism. The example of the Sheffield People's College inspired them to open in 1854 the London Working Men's College in Red Lion Square. Although Maurice believed that the college ought to be governed to a large extent by the students themselves, he was not prepared to allow them, as at Sheffield, to determine the methods and curriculum. He wrote in the *Working Men's College Magazine,* 1860: "I would not let the pupils have the least voice in determining what we shall teach or not teach, or how we shall teach. We may have social meetings with them individually; but no education will go on if we have general tumultuous assemblies to discuss what has been done or what is to be done. We who begin the instruction must claim authority over it, and not hastily resign our authority, however we may admit others by degrees to share it, and however willing we may be to creep out of it when the institution can stand without us." [1]

Maurice owed a good deal to the principles of the Chartist movement. The general belief in the first half of the nineteenth century was that education was a gift or benefit which the well-to-do conferred upon the less happy sections of the community. [2] Lovett and

---

[1] Quoted by M. E. Sadler. *Continuation Schools in England and Elsewhere,* p. 42, Manchester University Press, 1907.

[2] Hudson reflected the spirit of the age when he wrote: "The unexampled efforts now making in every part of the kingdom for the intellectual and physical improvement of the lower classes of the community distinguish the present, as an age of philanthropy and good will to all men. The middle classes vie with the rich in promoting the great and good work of education. The brightest minds in literature and science direct their talents to its development; preparing the ignorant by addresses, by lectures, and by their writings, to receive and understand the great and interesting truths which the Creator unfolds before them. The beloved Sovereign of these realms lends her fair and royal name in behalf of Bazaars to increase the stores of Institution Libraries. The lawned Divine and the ermined Duke feel a pleasure in presiding over the festivals of the artizan and the day labourer." (*Op. cit.,* Preface, page v.)

Place insisted that adult education would make little headway until the spirit of patronising philanthropy was stamped out. Maurice believed, as Dr. Yeaxlee points out, in beginning at both ends. Work must be raised so that it can become fit for association with learning, and the latter must be brought to bear upon work.[1]

The London Working Men's College was intended for manual workers. Any working man over sixteen who could read and write and who understood the first four rules of arithmetic was eligible for membership. The first class to be opened was a Bible class and it continued to be one of the best-attended. Maurice had been forced to resign his chair at King's College, London, because his religious views were thought unorthodox, and this left him free to throw himself heart and soul into the movement. He gathered round him a band of men with ideals like his own, and the London College became famous for its association with such outstanding personalities as Charles Kingsley, Dante Gabriel Rossetti, Lowes Dickenson, Tom Hughes, and John Ruskin. The secular side of the instruction was characterised by its liberality and, although after Maurice's death the religious aspect became less emphasised, the tradition of liberal education was maintained.

The example of the London Working Men's College was followed in other parts of the country, but only one other college has survived to the present day and retained its original name and purpose—the Vaughan College at Leicester, which was founded by Canon Vaughan in 1862.[2] The contribution of Maurice and such men is not to be measured by the number of institutions which they founded, but rather by the intellectual and spiritual stimulus that they transmitted to later generations. Sir Michael Sadler admirably summed it up when he wrote, "The great work which Maurice and his friends accomplished was the setting up of a new and more liberal ideal of adult education for men and women engaged during the day-time in the duties of the workshop, the office, or the home. This new ideal has had a far-reaching influence both on University opinion and on educational effort in its different forms throughout the country. The thoughts to which the founders of the Working Men's Colleges in London gave expression both in their writings and in their practical work as teachers were the outcome of a new social movement. . . . The same current of thought and feeling

[1] Basil A. Yeaxlee. *Spiritual Values in Adult Education*, Vol. I, p. 190, O.U.P., 1925.
[2] The Vaughan Memorial College is now associated with University College, Leicester.

affected the work of the Young Men's Christian Associations and many of the Mechanics' Institutes. It appeared later in the University extension movement." [1]

The modern period in adult education opens with the development of University Extension, due to the inspiration of a young Scotsman, James Stuart, who had been lecturing in the north of England at the invitation of the North of England Council for Promoting the Higher Education of Women. These lectures were followed by an invitation from the Rochdale Co-operative Society to lecture to the members, and it was here that an incident occurred which suggested to Stuart the idea of University Extension work. "One day I was in a hurry to get away as soon as the lecture was over, and I asked the hall-keeper to allow my diagrams to remain hanging until my return next week. When I came back he said to me, 'It was one of the best things you ever did leaving up these diagrams. We had a meeting of our members last week, and a number of them who were attending your lectures were discussing these diagrams, and they have a number of questions they want to ask you, and they are coming to-night a little before the lecture begins.' About twenty or thirty intelligent artisans met me about half an hour before the lecture began, and I found it so useful a half-hour that during the remainder of the course I always had such a meeting." [2] In 1871 Stuart persuaded several bodies for whom he had lectured to appeal to the authorities of Cambridge University, asking them to organise lecture-centres. The idea was approved, and the first University Extension lecture-courses were provided at Derby, Leicester, and Nottingham, in 1873. In 1876 the University of London formed its University Extension Society, and Oxford made similar arrangements in 1878.

The University Extension movement was a curious combination of failure and success. From the point of view of working-class education, it was not an unqualified success. The cost of providing the lectures was heavy, and the fees, though often reduced for them, were more than most working men could afford. This could not be remedied so long as the universities were left to bear the whole burden of the finance themselves. As the cost of the lectures had to be met by fees and local subscriptions, large audiences had to be attracted to make the courses self-supporting. In order to

[1] *Op. cit.*, p. 45.
[2] Quoted by A. Mansbridge, *An Adventure in Working-Class Education*, p. 6, Longmans, Green, 1920.

achieve this, the lectures had to have the widest possible appeal, and this often led to superficiality. Moreover, the lectures tended to be discontinuous and unsystematic. It was not until University Extension courses became eligible for grants under the Adult Education Regulations of the Board of Education that this handicap was removed. Like the Mechanics' Institutes, the lectures began to appeal more and more to the middle classes and to provide them with the higher education which for many had hitherto been impossible.

University Extension had a most important influence in another direction. It was the origin of many of our modern universities and university colleges. Thus Firth College at Sheffield, 1879, and University College, Nottingham, were directly due to the extension work carried on in those cities. In the previous chapter the effect of University Extension upon the development of the Yorkshire College was mentioned. University College, Reading, was founded in 1892 as a University Extension college, and University College, Exeter, originated in the extension work carried on in that city by Cambridge University.

As University Extension developed, other forms of adult education appeared or were revived. The work of Sturge at the Severn Street School in Birmingham has already been mentioned. It was very ably seconded by William White, a Reading man who settled in Birmingham in 1848 as a bookseller and printer. With Sturge, he urged upon the Society of Friends the necessity of educational work amongst adults. The Friends' First-Day School Association, founded by Sturge in 1847, had chiefly been concerned with children in Sunday Schools, but it was White who turned the attention of the association to adult-schools. Side by side with the development of the Friends' adult-schools a large number of non-Quaker schools sprang up. At first these schools were isolated units, but eventually the value of association became recognised. The rapid increase in their numbers after 1874 led to the formation of local adult-unions (Midland, Leicestershire, Somerset, London, and Norfolk). A further development was the idea of a National Council of Adult School Associations which took shape in 1899 with White as its first president. The Council became the National Adult School Union in 1914.

The revival of adult-schools was followed by the establishment of residential colleges—such as Woodbrooke, 1903 ; Fircroft, 1909 ; the Co-operative College, Manchester, 1919 ; Hillcroft College for

Women at Surbiton, 1920; the Catholic Workers' College at Oxford, 1921; the Avoncroft College for Agricultural Workers at Bromsgrove, Worcestershire, 1925: and by educational settlements such as Swarthmore at Leeds, 1909; St. Mary's at York, 1909; and the Homestead at Wakefield, 1913. Some of the educational settlements are closely linked with the universities. The pioneer settlement of this type is Toynbee Hall, opened in 1884 to commemorate the work done by Arnold Toynbee in the East End of London. Toynbee had been a friend and frequent visitor at Canon Barnett's vicarage in Whitechapel, where he had given up his vacations to deliver extension lectures to audiences of working men. Canon Barnett formed the settlement after Toynbee's death. University men and women came to spend part of their time living in working-class districts with the idea of understanding at first hand the conditions of life amongst the workers and sharing their knowledge and experience with them. The Society of Friends played a prominent part in settlement work, and T. E. Harvey, member of Parliament for the Northern Universities, was for a time Warden of Toynbee Hall. The settlements at Leeds and York were non-residential. Local education authorities are also taking an increasing part in the provision of residential colleges for adults. Thus the West Riding L.E.A. has recently acquired Grantley Hall, near Ripon, and has opened it as a residential adult-school providing shorter and longer courses in a variety of subjects.

In 1899 three Americans, Mr. and Mrs. Vrooman and Professor Beard, founded Ruskin College, Oxford, to give working-class students "a training in subjects which are essential for working-class leadership, and which are not a direct avenue to anything beyond." The idea of the founders was "to take men who have been merely condemning our institutions and teach them, instead, to transform these institutions, so that in place of talking against the world they will begin methodically and scientifically to possess the world."

The initial confusion of aims led to dissatisfaction amongst the students and in 1909 those who had Marxist sympathies seceded to form the Labour College. The latter has now been closed, but the work is being carried on by the National Council of Labour Colleges. Because the Adult Education Regulations demand an unsectarian and non-political approach to studies, the Labour Colleges do not receive grants from the Ministry of Education. Ruskin College was reorganised in 1910 and its management is entirely in the hands of the trade unions and the working-class societies which support it.   Wales had no adult residential college until the establishment of Coleg Harlech in 1927.

As University Extension was growing, the Co-operative movement developed its educational policy, but unfortunately it suffered at first from the lack of clear ideas about the function of adult education.   It is important, however, because, with University Extension and the trade unions, it was one of the factors which brought into being the Workers' Educational Association.   The founder of the W.E.A. was Albert Mansbridge, whose idea was to bring together the Co-operative Societies, the trade unions, and University Extension.   In 1897 Mansbridge was a clerk employed by the Co-operative Wholesale Society, and in a number of articles to the *Co-operative News* he ventilated his scheme for bringing about an active working partnership between the universities and the people.   His fellow co-operators did not at first see eye to eye with him, but he persevered, and, in an article contributed to the *University Extension Journal* in January 1903, he developed his plan.   It received support from a number of working men, and later in the same year the Association to Promote the Higher Education of Working Men came into existence with Mansbridge as honorary secretary.   This was the first national movement for adult education which worked in partnership with the universities and the national system of education.

In October 1904 the first branch was formed at Reading, followed a few months later by the establishment of another at Rochdale.   In 1905 the association changed its name to the Workers' Educational Association.   The movement spread rapidly. In 1906 there were thirteen branches; in 1907 forty-seven; and this number increased to fifty in 1908.   The first W.E.A. district was Manchester.   At the first national conference, held in 1905, the W.E.A. resolved to ask the Board of Education "how far and under what conditions employer and employed in their respective areas, would welcome legislation having for its ultimate object compulsory attendance at Evening Schools."[1]   A deputation from the W.E.A. was received by Sir Robert Morant and resulted in the publication of a report by the Consultative Committee of the Board of Education in 1909.   This was one of the factors which led to the day continuation schools of the Fisher Act.

William Temple (later Bishop of Manchester and Archbishop of Canterbury) attended this conference and became a whole-hearted

---

[1] A. Mansbridge. *An Adventure in Working-Class Education*, p. 17, Longmans, Green, 1920.

supporter of the W.E.A. Later, he was elected as the first president of the association. At first, the W.E.A. adopted every kind of educational method until it found that which best suited the kind of work it was attempting. The idea of tutorial classes had been suggested by Canon Barnett as early as 1900, but the first was not formed until 1906, at Rochdale. The University Extension Committee at this town found themselves in difficulties and consulted Mansbridge, who asked Rochdale to obtain thirty students to attend for two years and write regular essays. In return he promised the services of one of the foremost scholars in England. As a consequence, Mr. R. H. Tawney was appointed tutor. A similar experiment was tried at Longton in Staffordshire, where Mr. Tawney also acted as tutor. These were the first tutorial classes to be held in England, and the experiment was made possible by means of a grant from New College, Oxford.[1] This action had the strong support of Bishop Gore of Oxford and of Sir Robert Morant. The example of New College was followed by other Oxford colleges, and within a short space of time every university college in England and Wales was supporting tutorial classes. A permanent joint committee of the W.E.A. and the university was set up in each university and university college, and a central committee, known as the Central Joint Advisory Committee for Tutorial Classes, was established.

The next step involved the co-operation of the Board of Education, which for some time had been keenly interested in the movement. The Final Report of the Ministry of Reconstruction on Adult Education, published in 1919, recommended the granting of Government aid. This was followed in 1924 by the issue by the Board of Education of the Regulations for Adult Education. These regulations have been amended and expanded several times since that date.[2]

L.E.A.s make contributions to the work of the W.E.A., and in some cases take full financial responsibility for the classes, e.g. the West Riding of Yorkshire and in Kent.[3]

[1] The Rochdale class was the first to be organised, but the Longton class was the first actually to meet.

[2] Some aid had previously been given by the Board of Education under the Regulations for Technical Schools, Schools of Art, and other Forms of Provision for Further Education in England and Wales, 1918. Assistance had also been received under the provisions of the Act of 1902.

[3] The relations between the W.E.A., other agencies supplying adult education, and the L.E.A.s was the subject of a special report: Adult Education and the Local Education Authority, H.M.S.O., 1933.

In 1947 there were nearly nine hundred W.E.A. branches in the country, federated into twenty-one districts. The total number of branch members was approximately 39,000, and about 100,000 men and women were attending classes. The latter represented a fair cross-section of the population. The statistics for 1946-7 show that twenty-one per cent of students were manual workers, sixteen per cent clerks, draughtsmen, travellers, foremen, teachers, civil servants, and postal workers, five per cent professional and social workers, and twenty-six per cent engaged in home duties and nursing. The remainder consisted of students drawn from miscellaneous occupations and those whose occupation was not declared.[1]

The classes range from university tutorial classes of three years duration, to short courses of six months to a year, and provide for a wide range of subjects. Economics, history, and literature are the most popular, though in recent years psychology has been much in demand. The tutorial class has twenty-four meetings each year, the usual duration of which is two hours. The first hour is usually a lecture-period which is followed by a class discussion or, in classes studying science subjects, practical work. Subjects such as foreign languages, mathematics, etc., which are provided by L.E.A.s in their evening institutes, are not encouraged in W.E.A. classes. Book boxes are supplied to classes, and students are encouraged to read and are required to do some written work.

During the late war many W.E.A. classes were run under difficulties. The writer will never forget the experience of holding a class discussion in a cellar, while overhead, bombs were dropping and the barrage maintained by our anti-aircraft guns was deafening. The black-out created further difficulties for tutors and students who came from a distance, but the astonishing thing was the way in which most classes maintained their attendance. After the war, attendance was affected by the introduction of "staggered hours of work," but the Ministry of Education took account of this in its conditions for the award of grant.

Most of the universities have now reorganised their machinery for dealing with adult education in their areas. Extra-mural departments have been set up with a Director of Extra-Mural Studies as the academic head, and the work is usually organised by means of a Tutorial Class and an Extension Committee. Arrangements vary in different universities, but usually the two committees work

[1] *The Future in Adult Education*, pp. 11-12, W.E.A., 1947.

under the general direction of an Extra-Mural Board on which the university, the W.E.A., the L.E.A.s, and other agencies supplying adult education are represented. The tutors, who are employed in a full-time capacity, have formed an Association of Tutors in Adult Education, and in many cases are represented on the Extra-Mural Boards and Committees.

There have been two interesting developments in adult education in the period between the two wars. The first was the formation of the Cambridgeshire village colleges, which constitute at one and the same time schools for children, and educational, social, and cultural centres, for adults in the rural areas. The earliest of the centres was at Sawston, 1928, and owing to the active encouragement of Mr. H. Morris, County Education Secretary, and the Carnegie United Kingdom Trustees, they were extended to other districts in the county.

The other was in connection with the new housing estates built after the First World War, and was initiated by a conference, held in 1929, at which the National Council of Social Service and other bodies were represented. The New Estates Community Committee (later the Community Centres and Associations Committee) was created with the object of providing community centres to promote a healthy social life on the new housing estates. In 1944 the Ministry of Education issued a pamphlet entitled *Community Centres,* in which it was stated that the general responsibility for the development of community centres now rested with the Ministry of Education and the L.E.A.s. The centres themselves may be provided in a number of different ways, *e.g.* by an L.E.A. exercising its powers under Sections 41 and 53 of the Education Act, 1944 ; by a local authority acting as a housing authority under section 80 of the Housing Act, 1936; by a local authority exercising its powers under the Physical Training and Recreation Act, 1937, or by voluntary effort aided by the L.E.A., the National Council of Social Services, or the Ministry of Education. The Ministry of Education, in the pamphlet referred to above, expressed its opinion that it was desirable that all villages, especially those with a population over four hundred, should be provided with a village hall.

The Women's Institutes, which have been organised in a large number of villages, are an important educational influence in rural districts. During the last war they made a noteworthy contribution to the national effort. Each county has its own local federation of Women's Institutes, and these are united in the National

Federation of Women's Institutes. In addition to social activities, they engage in various types of educational work, mostly of a practical character. They have also developed an interest among their members in music and drama. Each month the National Federation issues its magazine *Home and Country*, which includes a supplement dealing with the special activities of each county federation.

In urban districts the Townswomen's Guilds perform functions similar to those of the Women's Institutes in rural areas. The individual gilds are federated in the National Union of Townswomen's Guilds. Members of the gilds are keenly interested in civics and social studies and in choral and dramatic activities. Classes providing instruction in handicrafts and homecrafts have a wide appeal.

The agencies for the promotion of adult education are at the present day so numerous that space only allows a brief mention of some of the more prominent associations which place education more or less among their principal aims. The Y.M.C.A. and the Y.W.C.A. have always taken an important part in adult education and their activities in forces education will be mentioned in the last chapter of this book. The Y.M.C.A. started from a meeting of a few young men for prayer and the reading of the Bible in 1844 in a bedroom on the premises of Hitchcock and Rogers, retail silk mercers of Ludgate Hill. The leader of the group was George Williams (later Sir George Williams) who was the son of a Somerset farmer. He realised the value of these devotional gatherings in the case of his own small group, and this suggested to him the idea of extending the Young Men's Society to every drapery business in London. He estimated that there were about 150,000 shop-assistants who were living in houses of retail trade. In those days hours of business were much longer than at present, and it was not unusual to start work at seven in the morning and continue until late at night, especially at the week-end. These young people were, to a large extent, outside the sphere of influence of the churches and there was no organisation to look after their spiritual and intellectual interests.

The new association was given the name of the Young Men's Christian Association, and it put as its chief aims comradeship, united prayer, and the study of the Bible. Williams received enthusiastic support from Lord Shaftesbury. The scope of the Y.M.C.A. was extended to men engaged in other trades than the drapery, and the Great Exhibition of 1851 provided an opportunity for it to interest visitors from all parts of the world. The movement grew rapidly and the American Y.M.C.A. was founded in the same year. At the jubilee of the association in 1894, delegates attended from all countries of the world. The Y.W.C.A. was founded for similar work amongst women. The Y.M.C.A. is not only active in the large towns, but its influence extends to remote rural districts. Red Triangle Clubs have been formed in many small villages and have co-operated with L.E.A.s, University Extension, and other organisations for providing adult education.

Albert Mansbridge was a keen Churchman and he was instrumental in establishing the Church of England tutorial classes. These were started in 1917 and were organised on a pattern similar to those of the W.E.A. There are numerous associations connected with the religious denominations, such as the Church of England Men's Society, the Mothers' Union, the Girls' Friendly Society, the Catholic Social Guild, the Brotherhood Movement, and the Men's Fellowships connected with the Free Churches. One of the most influential of these bodies is the Mothers' Union, founded by Mary Sumner in 1876. Like the Y.W.C.A., it arose from small beginnings—a group of mothers meeting at her husband's rectory at Old Alresford in Hampshire. From being a parochial organisation, it first grew to a diocesan union, then a national, and finally a world-wide association. At the present time the main association has over 4,000 branches with more than 570,000 members. The three objects of the Mothers' Union are (1) to uphold the sanctity of marriage, (2) to awaken mothers to a sense of their responsibility in the training of their children, and (3) to organise a band of women who are pledged to develop a Christian atmosphere in their homes. The association started with a hired room in Church House, Westminster. As it grew, another room was taken; then, in 1917, a house known as Mary Sumner House; and, after the founder's death in 1921, the present Mary Sumner House was opened by the Princess Royal in 1925. The Mothers' Union is interested in all matters which concern marriage and the home, the upbringing of children, training for motherhood, and sex education on Christian principles, and has frequently been consulted by Government departments on these subjects.

Other voluntary bodies connected with adult education include the British Drama League, the Co-operative Guilds, the Welsh Eisteddfod, and the English Folk Dance and Song Society.

A later comer in the field of adult education is the British Broadcasting Corporation. For some years, the B.B.C. had organised school broadcasts designed to meet the needs of both primary and secondary schools. Apart from entertainment, the B.B.C. has paid special attention to the interests of adult listeners, and the symphony concerts, recitals, and courses on musical appreciation have done much to raise the standards of musical taste. The latest feature, the introduction of the Third Programme, should be a very potent educational stimulus to the more serious-minded among adults. The programme was designed "for the alert and receptive listener, who is willing first of all to make an effort in selection and then to meet the performer half-way by giving his whole attention to what is being broadcast." Broadcast lectures and discussions are able to penetrate to lonely parts of the country and to people living under conditions where the formation of ordinary classes would be impracticable.

The Arts Council of Great Britain developed from the war-time organisation known as C.E.M.A. (Council for the Encouragement of Music and Arts), and it received a royal charter on 9th August 1946. It aims at providing the public with increasing opportunities of enjoying, and the artist of practising, achievements of the highest standard in music, drama, and the plastic and graphic arts. It has eleven regional offices and separate committees for Scotland and Wales. One of its achievements has been the establishment of arts clubs in different parts of the country. The council has also helped symphony orchestras to give concerts in industrial areas, arranged exhibitions in the visual arts, and sponsored a large number of dramatic ventures. Its work is carried out through its Advisory Panels for Music, Art, and Drama.

Although the adult-education movement may be said to have been born in Scotland through the work of Anderson and Birkbeck, yet the W.E.A. and University Extension in that country are of comparatively recent growth. Tutorial classes were not started in Edinburgh until 1913, and it was not until after the First World War that the universities gave serious attention to extra-mural activities. One reason for this late development is that until recently no grants were made for extra-mural education in Scotland by the Education Department, and classes could not receive aid from the local authorities unless they were organised by the School Boards (after 1918, by the Local Education Authorities). Another reason is that the democratic tradition in Scotland had rendered the ordinary university courses more accessible to the population than in England and the benefaction of Andrew Carnegie materially assisted poor students in the payment of their fees. Newbattle Abbey, at Dalkeith, was opened as an adult residential college in 1937, and is recognised by the Scottish Education Department.

Sir Richard Livingstone, in his book *The Future of Education,* makes an eloquent appeal for the establishment of a system of residential colleges for adults, run on the lines of the Scandinavian countries, which have provided about 200 such colleges for their 16,000,000 inhabitants. Speaking of our pre-1944 system of education, he says: "I am not criticising our elementary schools or their teachers, or denying the necessity of elementary education for all. But unless it leads on to something else, it is as useless as a ladder which has no rungs beyond one or two at the bottom or as a railway from Oxford to London which ends at Didcot. To cease education at 14 is as unnatural as to die at 14. The one is a physical death, the other intellectual death. In fact, we have left the vast majority of the population without any kind of liberal education. We have provided for the minority who attend secondary school and university. We have shown the rest a glimpse of the promised land, and left them outside it." [1]

He does not believe that the problem can be solved by raising the school-leaving age to sixteen or even eighteen; education must be lifelong. Moreover, many of the studies which are essential to the making of an educated nation—literature, history, philosophy, economics, and politics—cannot be fully appreciated by schoolboys because of their inadequate experience of life. He speaks highly of the accomplishment of the W.E.A. and kindred agencies, but he reminds us: "In 1938-39 there were 66,966 students in W.E.A. classes. The figure is remarkable, till we remember that there are forty-three millions in this island, and that the crowd at a cup-tie final is twice as large." [2] The only solution, in his view, lies in creating a system of residential colleges for adults analogous to the Danish People's High Schools. Alongside these colleges, a system of non-residential educational settlements is necessary. He writes: "Opportunities for systematic adult study . . . must not be limited to lectures or classes given in any hall or schoolroom that happens to be available. They must have a 'local habitation,' a focus in the Latin sense of the word, a hearth where the fire remains continually

[1] R. Livingstone. *The Future in Education,* pp. 3-4, C.U.P., 1942.
[2] *Ibid.,* p. 40.

lit, and where education can be more than isolated individual study and becomes a life shared with others. The Educational Settlements which have grown up during the century show how such a hearth can be provided." [1]   The Education Act of 1944 envisages a national system of adult education when it places upon L.E.A.s the duty of providing adequate facilities for full-time and part-time education and leisure-time occupation for persons in their areas who are able and willing to profit by the opportunities provided for that purpose. In preparing their schemes for further education the L.E.A.s have the further duty of consulting other agencies, such as the universities, the University of Wales Council of Music, and the W.E.A.

Technical education has made such strides during the past hundred years and has now so many ramifications that it is an impossible task to do it justice in a few pages.   Space limits our selection to some of its most important aspects.   References have already been made in other chapters to certain features of technical instruction, chiefly in connection with the higher-grade schools, the junior technical schools, and the Spens Report. This section is largely concerned with the provision of technical instruction for students above compulsory school age.

During the Napoleonic wars, Britain had established an industrial and commercial supremacy over all other countries, since her island position gave her the opportunity of developing her mines and manufactures undisturbed.   Thus she had a definite lead as a manufacturing nation, but in the years of peace which followed, other countries began to develop their industrial resources. Even before Britain's industrial supremacy was challenged, the value of technical and scientific instruction was beginning to be officially recognised.   In 1836 a Select Committee of the House of Commons recommended the establishment of a Normal School of Design for which the sum of £1,500 was voted.   From 1841 onwards, annual grants were made for promoting provincial schools of design. The supervision of these schools was given to a public office which later became the Board of Trade.   By 1852 there were seventeen provincial schools of design, situated in the more important industrial centres, such as Manchester, Birmingham, Glasgow, Leeds, and Paisley.

The Great Exhibition of 1851, which was in many ways a triumph for British industry and craftsmanship, gave indications

---

[1] R. Livingstone, in foreword to *Citizen Centres for Adult Education,* Educational Settlements Association, 1943.

that in certain aspects we were falling behind our Continental competitors. This led to a demand for the provision of scientific and technical instruction for workpeople. In 1852 the Normal School of Design became the Department of Practical Art in the Board of Trade, and the following year a Science Division was added. Its name was then changed to that of the Science and Art Department of the Board of Trade, and it was housed at South Kensington. When, in 1856, the Select Committee of the Privy Council became the Education Department of the Committee of Council, the Science and Art Department was put under its wing. The Royal College of Chemistry had been opened in 1845 and the Government School of Mines and Science applied to the Arts was established in 1851. These two were amalgamated for some years, but were again separated in 1890 under the titles of the Royal College of Science and the Royal School of Mines, South Kensington. The Normal School of Design eventually became the Royal College of Art which was established in 1896.

In order to encourage the teaching of science and art, the Science and Art Department instituted examinations and made grants to schools which presented successful pupils. In 1851 the number of science classes in the country was thirty-eight, with 1,300 pupils. It had risen to seventy schools with 2,543 pupils in 1861. The main problem was that of obtaining an adequate supply of suitably qualified teachers. Common sense would have suggested the foundation of a School of Science at which teachers of science could be trained. The official mind, however, did not work in this way; and the Department fell back upon the traditional method of encouraging a subject, and in 1859 instituted a special examination for teachers of science. The remuneration of the teachers who qualified depended upon the number of their pupils who passed the special examinations held by the Department. No arrangements, however, were made for ensuring that the teachers were properly prepared for the examinations. The influence of this policy was thoroughly bad. Teachers, in order to qualify, got up information from textbooks and afterwards crammed their pupils so as to obtain the maximum amount of grant from the Department. It was possible to pass the examinations without doing any practical work and many candidates obtained certificates who had never seen or handled any scientific apparatus. "Many self-taught students collected South Kensington certificates by the dozen. There is a legend that the highest number of certificates in Agriculture were gained by earnest young men who had never stirred beyond the precincts of Whitechapel." [1]   When the Revised Code came into operation in 1862, many teachers augmented their salaries by obtaining a South Kensington certificate and then giving science instruction in evening classes.   In Chapter v it was mentioned that after 1872 higher-grade schools presented pupils for the examinations of the Science and Art Department and were recognised as organised schools of science receiving grants for their successful candidates.   Also, endowed secondary schools and private schools followed this example, so that science began to take a more prominent place in the school curriculum.

Another factor which encouraged the teaching of science was the report of the Duke of Devonshire's Commission which recommended that in all public and endowed secondary schools, not less than six hours a week should be given to instruction in science and the requirements of the different examining bodies should insist on candidates offering mathematics and at least one science in order to pass.   Unfortunately, much of the preparation of boys for examinations in science consisted of lectures and the reading of textbooks.   Professor Armstrong, by his advocacy of the Heuristic method, did much to encourage more practical methods in science teaching.

The claim for the inclusion of science in schools was strengthened by the popular interest shown in such works as Darwin's *Origin of Species* and the articles written by Herbert Spencer, and afterwards, in 1861, collected into book form, entitled *Education—Intellectual, Moral and Physical*.   Spencer's advocacy of science was readily accepted not so much because of the cogency of the arguments in his book—for indeed it is a work riddled with inconsistencies and fallacies—as because of the prestige of his name. A more reasonable plea was put by T. H. Huxley who, in his *Essays,* emphasised the widening of outlook which resulted from the study of science.   Unlike Spencer, Huxley realised the value of humanities in education, if they were properly taught.   Although his *Essays* were not as widely read as Spencer's book, his personality as a teacher and lecturer, and the administrative work which fell to him as a member of the first London School Board, probably gave him the greater influence.

---

[1] D. M. Turner.   *History of Science Teaching in England*, p. 76, Chapman and Hall, 1927.

At the Paris Exhibition of 1867, British products were in many cases classed below those of the craftsmen of other countries and this caused considerable uneasiness in Britain.[1]   The usual remedy was attempted.   In 1871 a royal commission under the chairmanship of the seventh Duke of Devonshire was appointed to inquire into the conditions under which scientific instruction was being given in all types of English educational establishment.   The Devonshire Commission reported in 1875 and included in its report a survey of the technological advances made in foreign countries.

The latter stimulated the London City Livery Companies to appoint, in 1877, a committee to draw up a national scheme of technical instruction.   The result was the foundation of the City and Guilds Institute in 1880.   The Institute encouraged the teaching of applied science in schools and evening classes and organised a system of examinations in technical subjects.   It was responsible for the establishment of the Finsbury Technical College in 1883.   This was intended to be "a model trade school for the instruction of artisans and other persons preparing for intermediate posts in industrial works."   The college held both day and evening classes, the latter specialising in cabinet-making, which was one of the leading industries of the district.   Instruction was given in practical mathematics, mechanics, chemistry, physics, electrical technology, machine drawing, and workshop practice.   In the evening classes, besides cabinet-making and joinery, bricklaying, drawing, modelling, and design, were taught.   This college was an important influence in the development of similar institutions in different parts of the country.   As we have already seen, many of the new technical colleges developed from the existing Mechanics' Institutes.   In 1884 the City and Guilds Central Technical College was opened at South Kensington with the aim of training technical teachers, works managers, engineers, and industrial chemists.

One of the most interesting developments was due to Quintin Hogg.   His interest in education began with a reading-lesson given to a couple of crossing-sweepers in a street near the Strand.   In 1864 he was teaching a ragged school ; in 1868 he was in charge of a boys' home in Drury Lane ; and in 1878 he opened an evening institute.   His Working Lads' Institute outgrew its premises and he acquired in 1880 the building known as the Polytechnic in Regent

[1] At the Great Exhibition of 1851 there were one hundred different departments, in nearly all of which British manufactures were superior.   In 1867 there were ninety departments, and Britain was only able to excel her competitors in ten of them.

Street. The latter had been a place of popular and semi-popular entertainment, but after some years it was unable to pay its way. Hogg retained the name for his new institution. The Polytechnic movement owed its rapid progress to the City Parochial Charities Act of 1883. The movement of population away from the City of London had made a redistribution of the charitable endowments of the city parishes highly desirable. A royal commission reported that the property, yielding about £80,000 per annum, was being wasted, and it recommended that the income should be used for purposes which would benefit the whole metropolis. When the necessary authority had been obtained by the above Act, a scheme was drawn up for establishing throughout London a number of institutions, similar in character to the Regent Street Polytechnic. The Drapers', Goldsmiths', and Clothworkers' Companies made generous contributions to the scheme. When the London County Council was established by the Local Government Act of 1888, it took over the supervision of the polytechnics. The polytechnics have a wide range of activities and, whilst retaining their original functions of promoting social intercourse and healthy recreation, they have developed into educational centres of prime importance. In addition to running secondary and technical schools and day technical classes for more advanced students, they provide evening classes for apprentices and workmen which give instruction of a practical character in connection with the building, engineering, furniture, bookbinding and printing, clothing, and other trades. There are also commercial and foreign-language classes, and some of the students are prepared for degrees of the University of London.

The alarm caused by the industrial progress of the German Empire and the competition of the United States led to the appointment of yet another Royal Commission on Technical Instruction, in 1884.

The report of the Commission reviewed the facilities for technical education in this country and contrasted them with those available on the Continent and in the United States. The Commission not only investigated the training given in technical institutions, but science teaching from the elementary school upwards. The provision of an adequate number of secondary schools of a "modern type," probably similar to the third-grade schools of the Taunton Commission, was urged. The report stimulated the authorities to realise the need not only of first-class technical institutions, but also of an adequate supply of secondary schools in which the instruction given would lay the foundation for later technical training. The result of the inquiry was the Technical Instruction Act of 1889. The Act was permissive and gave power to local authorities (the new county and county borough councils) to levy a penny rate in order to supply technical instruction by founding schools and appointing teachers, to aid the supply of technical education by making grants to institutes supplying such education, and to promote technical education by the establishment of exhibitions and scholarships. A fortunate accident encouraged the local authorities to make use of these powers. In 1890 the Government passed legislation reducing the number of public houses. To compensate the dispossessed publicans, an additional duty was placed on wines and spirits, but many members of Parliament were opposed to any scheme for compensating the publicans. The Act imposing the tax had been passed and the Government found itself in the unique position of having a considerable surplus and not knowing what to do with it. Arthur Acland suggested that the money should be given to the county councils either for assisting technical education or for reducing the rates. The majority used it for the former purpose and were able to finance technical instruction without the necessity of levying the rate authorised by the Act. The experience thus acquired by the councils stood them in good stead when in 1902 they were required to take over the administration of education in their areas in place of the School Boards. This annual sum was known as "Whiskey Money." "So curious a source of revenue, however, entailed one unfortunate result; the funds available for technical education increased whenever drinking increased and diminished with a spread of temperance, so that, if the total abstainers could have persuaded the whole country 'to go dry,' there would have been no funds left." [1] Much of the money was spent on the education of pupils in secondary schools, and aided the teaching of science rather than technical instruction.

At this point it is perhaps well to give a short account of three bodies which exercised an important influence upon the teaching of science and technical subjects. The earliest in order of formation was the Society of Arts of London, which was founded in 1754 "for the encouragement of arts, manufactures and commerce in Great Britain." The society offered medals and prizes for useful

[1] R. L. Archer. *Secondary Education in the Nineteenth Century*, p. 308, C.U.P., 1921.

inventions and arranged for exhibitions of scientific curiosities. The great Exhibition of 1851 was largely due to the efforts of the society, whose president at that time was the Prince Consort. In 1854 the Society of Arts introduced its system of examinations, and the emphasis it gave to the importance of drawing in connection with trades and industries anticipated the recommendations of the Cross Commission. The examinations included such subjects as chemistry, physiology, botany, mathematics, and mechanics. In 1872 the society extended its examination system to technological subjects. The examinations were afterwards confined to commercial subjects. In 1908 the society received the title of the Royal Society of Arts.

The Royal Institution was founded by Count Rumford in 1800. Its object was stated to be that of diffusing knowledge and facilitating the general introduction of useful mechanical inventions and improvements, and, through teaching by means of lectures, the application of science to the purposes of daily life. Count Rumford was interested in domestic economy, and he lectured and wrote on ventilation, cooking apparatus, and fire-places. It was due to Rumford that in 1801 Humphry Davy was appointed lecturer in chemistry and head of the laboratory of the Royal Institution. When, in the following year, Rumford left for Munich, the policy of the Royal Institution was completely changed. His cooking apparatus was put on one side and his plans for the training of young mechanics were dropped. In future, the Royal Institution concentrated on the teaching of science. Davy secured an international reputation for the work accomplished in the laboratory of the Institution. After Davy's death in 1828 the fortunes of the Institution declined, but they rose to an even greater height when Michael Faraday became director of the Laboratory. His Friday evening lectures became famous and his Christmas talks were known and appreciated throughout the country. His researches laid the foundation of modern electrical science. In more recent years the Royal Institution has been associated with the names of Lord Rayleigh, J. J. Thomson, Rutherford, and Bragg.

The British Association for the Advancement of Science was founded in 1831. It had always shown an interest in schools, especially as regards the teaching of science, and in its report of 1889 it advocated the Heuristic method of Professor Armstrong. In 1901 educational science became a recognised part of its activities.

The reorganisation of the central institutions for advanced scientific and technical education at South Kensington has been described in Chapter xii. The Cross Commission had noticed the decline in the number of students attending evening schools and had suggested that the remedy was to regard these institutions as continuation rather than elementary schools. This recommendation was carried out in the Code of 1890, and as a result the evening schools began to give instruction in languages, science, art, handicrafts, and domestic work. A further advance was the issue in 1898 of a separate Code for evening continuation schools. The upper age-limit for students was abolished and grants were given for attendance instead of being based on examination results. The subjects of instruction were extended by the addition of technical instruction, physical training, and commercial subjects such as shorthand, bookkeeping, and typing. The object of the new Code was to provide opportunities to students to study subjects not included in the elementary-school curriculum and which did not receive grants from the Science and Art Department, and also to give a preparatory course for those wishing to proceed to more advanced studies in technical schools.

Although there was a marked increase in the number of evening students—from 298,724 in 1896 to 474,563 in 1899—much of the instruction still remained at an elementary-school level. Students were able to select the subjects they wished to study, and this led to a difficulty. A young man might elect to study mechanical engineering, but he soon found that he could not make satisfactory progress unless at the same time he advanced in his knowledge of such subjects as mathematics, physics, and machine drawing. The solution of this problem was the introduction of the group system, first adopted by the Halifax evening continuation schools in 1902. The Board of Education supported this policy and, in 1907, students were required to select a group of related subjects for study.

The students of the evening continuation schools fell into two main classes—those who intended to enter a technical school and those who would not carry their studies beyond the range of the evening school. As the former of these classes was considered the more important, the grouped courses were organised according to the occupations of the pupils or the industries they hoped to enter. There were usually five main groups: industrial, commercial, rural, domestic, and general. The first two attracted the largest number of students, but the general courses made a greater appeal as time went on, while the domestic courses naturally interested girls and women. In all the courses instruction was given in English in addition to the subjects peculiar to the course.[1]

The evening technical schools developed side by side with the evening continuation schools. When the Regulations of the Board of Education in 1904 made it possible for a class in almost any subject to receive a grant, the range of instruction extended as more highly trained teachers in different subjects became available. The courses provided by the evening technical schools were classified into junior, senior, and advanced, according to the age and experience of the pupils. The junior course was intended for pupils from fourteen to sixteen years of age and was taken in the evening continuation school. The senior course, taken in a technical school, was planned to extend over three years from the age of sixteen. Before they entered, students were expected to have received suitable education either in a secondary or an evening continuation school. The course was more specialised and was framed according to the different branches of industry or commerce. The advanced course, usually planned for two years, was held in the larger technical schools and gave the student greater freedom in the choice of subjects.

At the beginning of the century the traditional English view that the school should concentrate on the theoretical aspects and the workshop on practice was universally accepted. Thus the Technical Instruction Act of 1889 defined technical instruction as that given "in the principles of science and art applicable to industries and in the application of special branches of science and art to specific industries and employments." It was expressly stated that the instruction should not include the practice of any trade or industry. This attitude was in contrast to the work done in similar schools on the Continent where the importance of workshop apprenticeship was emphasised.

The traditional view is still generally accepted, but after the First World War it began to break down with regard to certain industries. The first to be affected was the building industry. ". . . it was in connexion with the teaching of plumbing that instruction in the actual practice of a craft first started on any considerable scale. When once the principle of giving workshop instruction to a particular type of workers had been admitted, there was no valid

---

[1] In some towns, *e.g.* Reading, the L.E.A. and the university college organised between them a complete scheme of education for evening students.

reason for refusing to permit the practical training of other crafts-men, and accordingly classes in carpentry and joinery, plastering, pattern making, acetylene welding, and other crafts exist in a number of technical schools." [1] This has given rise to the distinction between a Minor and Major course. The former denotes a training in craftsmanship or in workshop operations, whilst the latter is concerned with the principles which underlie those operations. Obviously there can be no hard and fast distinction between the two. It was found necessary to include certain theoretical sub-jects, such as mathematics and science, in the Minor course and in many cases the latter was planned in view of a subsequent Major course.

In the 19th century, technical and scientific instruction was largely moulded by the examinations of the Science and Art Depart-ment and the City and Guilds of London Institute. The Board of Education discontinued the science examinations of the lower grade in 1911 and followed within a few years by abolishing all these examinations except those used for awarding certain scholarships. The City and Guilds Institute followed suit and abandoned their lower examinations in 1918. There was, however, a widespread demand for tests which should be applied to students at different stages of their work, and it was felt that such examinations should have a national standing. The demand was at first met by exami-nations conducted by unions of L.E.A.s and schools, such as the Union of Lancashire and Cheshire Institutes, the Union of Educa-tional Institutions, the East Midland Educational Union, and the Northern Counties Technical Examinations Council.

This practice was not completely satisfactory since the unions did not cover the whole of the country and their certificates were those of regional bodies and not of a national one. This has led to the development of national certificates given as the reward of three to five years systematic study. The first move came in 1921 when the Institute of Mechanical Engineers, in conjunction with the Board of Education, developed a scheme to issue national certificates and diplomas in mechanical engineering. The certifi-cates were issued to students who passed with success through approved grouped courses of instruction at certain technical colleges and schools and satisfied the examiners in the final examination. The latter was held by the school or college authorities and assessed

[1] A. Abbott. *Education for Industry and Commerce in England*, p. 62, O.U.P., 1933.

by assessors appointed by the Institution.   The certificates were on two levels: the Ordinary National Certificate awarded on the results of a senior part-time course of three years, and the Higher National Certificate awarded on the results of an advanced part-time course to those who had already gained the first certificate and had covered another two years work.   For full-time students in technical colleges, the Ordinary and Higher National Diplomas were available.   Within the next few years, national certificates and diplomas were available in electrical engineering, chemistry, building, naval architecture, textiles, and commerce.   The certificate in the last-named subject is sponsored by the Royal Society of Arts, the London Chamber of Commerce, and other bodies.

The introduction of the national certificates and diplomas has entirely revolutionised the work done in senior technical institutes. The student can gain a qualification approximating to a university degree in his subject, and the standards of teaching in technical institutions have advanced considerably.

During the last war the importance of a high standard of technical education, beginning with the evening institutes (the name by which the evening continuation schools have been known since 1926) and extending to the senior technical colleges and the universities, was brought home to everybody.   That importance has not diminished in time of peace, and in the present production-drive it is everywhere realised that the recovery of our pre-war economic status is dependent, amongst other factors, upon the efficiency of our technical training and research.   A distinction is usually made between "technical training," which applies to the work of the evening institutes and technical schools, and "technological training," which denotes the higher study and research appropriate to the universities and central technical institutions.

So far we have been considering the work accomplished by the evening institutes and evening technical schools.   During the same period full-time courses of technical education were developed. Reference has already been made in an earlier chapter to the emergence of junior technical schools.   As a result of the operation of the Education Act of 1902 the majority of the organised science schools became secondary schools.   This left a gap of two or three years between the leaving-age of the elementary school (thirteen to fourteen) and the lowest age at which young people could be received as apprentices (sixteen).   Pupils who intended to become apprentices did not usually enter the secondary schools, but as their earnings were often essential to their parents, they tended to drift into blind-alley occupations, finally ending up as unskilled labourers. To prevent this wastage the Board of Education announced in 1905 that grants could be given to day technical classes provided for pupils who had left elementary schools.

The new junior technical schools fell into two groups: those which prepared pupils for particular trades and occupations (trade schools), and those which gave an education to pupils wishing to enter a particular industry but not a specific occupation within that industry (pre-apprenticeship schools). The latter represented the normal junior technical school. The trade school was closely allied to the French "écoles d'apprentissage" and the German "Fachschullen." The junior technical school was essentially an English development. It was a fee-paying school, the usual fee being £3 per annum. Under the provision of the Act of 1902, these schools formed part of the system of higher education and were aided by the county and county borough education authorities. Most of them were part of the larger technical colleges, shared their premises, and utilised the staff of the institutions which carried on technological work in the evenings. Thus the school at Halifax was housed in the premises of the Halifax Technical College. At Leeds the junior technical schools were carried on in buildings which had originally belonged to the Mechanics' Institute.

In 1913 the Board of Education issued Regulations for Junior Technical Schools. The grant payable for pupils who entered at thirteen or fourteen was £5 per head (£7 per pupil in exceptional cases). Permission was given for the schools to accept some pupils at the age of twelve, but in such cases the grant was only £3 per head. No pupil could be admitted unless the parent gave an undertaking that the boy would enter an occupation for which the school gave a preparation. Where possible, practical work would be given in all suitable subjects, and the teaching staff had to include a reasonable number of people with trade experience. All schools were to "provide for the continuance of the moral, intellectual and physical education given in Public Elementary Schools." It is important to note that these schools were not recognised as secondary schools until 1938.

These regulations remained in force until 1926, during which time a number of junior commercial schools appeared. Other schools not recognised under the regulations were opened, e.g. schools of nautical training and junior housewifery schools. By

1929 the number of recognised schools was 108 and they contained 18,000 pupils (including 4,600 girls). A report of the Board of Education issued in 1930 surveyed the progress made by junior technical schools. It described their growth as steady but not spectacular, and pointed out that in most cases each school had less than two hundred pupils; some less than one hundred. Such schools were expensive to staff, and their equipment was costly. On the other hand, the schools were popular and there was no difficulty in filling the places by fee-paying pupils. Moreover, they were successful in placing their pupils in suitable occupations, and the curriculum was less restricted by academic considerations than in the ordinary secondary school. This was because they did not prepare pupils for the School Certificate examination.

"Finally, the Junior Technical School is pervaded by an 'atmosphere' readily perceived by the visitor, but difficult to convey in words. The pupils attack their work with a seriousness and satisfaction not always found in schools for pupils of their age. They concentrate because they are interested, they are interested because they have no difficulty in realising the direct bearing of their work on their future life. They have the air of knowing exactly what they are doing, and exactly why it is worth doing."[1] In spite of this commendation the Board still continued to look upon the junior technical school as a poor relation. The views expressed by the Spens and Norwood Reports were discussed in Chapter x. The view of the Spens Report that every junior technical school should be part of a senior technical institution, although it tended to ease of administration, was severely criticised by many experienced teachers. As a result of the Education Act of 1944, the technical schools are being absorbed into the statutory system of secondary education.

One of the features of the period we have been considering was the slow growth of full-time courses in senior technical institutions. The Board of Education *Report on Education for Industry and Commerce*, 1928, showed that in Prussia only about ten per cent of technical schools provided evening classes; in the United States, less than thirty per cent; whilst in England, evening classes accounted for between eighty and ninety per cent of the total number of students. The Report urged the development of part-time and full-time day courses as a matter of national importance. The moving spirit behind the Report was Lord Eustace Percy who,

[1] *The Junior Technical School*, pp. 20-1, H.M.S.O., 1930.

when he became president of the Board of Education, displayed a special interest in the problems of technical education. He wrote : "The wastage of human material is, of course, only one aspect of the problem of technical education. The other aspect is that of industrial efficiency in a scientific and severely competitive age, which calls for continual improvement in the technical equipment of the individual worker." [1]

Lord Eustace Percy was responsible for a number of special inquiries into education for industry and commerce. They included not only a regional inquiry in one of the main industrial areas of England, but also an investigation of particular branches of industry and commerce. The results of the latter were embodied in the reports of the Goodenough Committee on Education for Salesmanship, 1931, and the Clerk Committee on Education for the Engineering Group of Industries, 1929. The former committee included a large number of directors of important firms, and it investigated the methods which should be employed for recruiting persons who would be engaged in buying and selling, and the means of providing them with suitable training. The Clerk Committee spoke highly of the work performed by the junior technical schools, and stressed the value of obtaining recruits to the engineering industry from those who had received a full-time education in them or in secondary schools.

The Second World War not only emphasised the value of technological education for the nation, but it also revealed the lack of co-ordination between the different agencies in the same region whose function it was to provide such training. An article in the *Times Educational Supplement,* 8th April 1944, pointed out that in the Midland region the major technical colleges at Birmingham, Wolverhampton, Coventry, and Rugby, worked in practical independence of the technological departments of the University of Birmingham. There was little liaison between the University of Leeds and the Leeds College of Technology, and none at all between the university and the technical colleges at Bradford and Halifax. On the other side of the Pennines, the University of Manchester possessed a complete faculty of technology in the Municipal College of Technology, but its relations with the Royal College of Technology at Salford, the Bolton Technical College, the Wigan Mining and Technical College, and the College of Further Education at

---

[1] In the preface to Mr. Abbott's book *Education for Industry and Commerce,* p. viii, O.U.P., 1933.

Stockport, were slender. The University of Liverpool had no liaison with the technical colleges in its area. In the north-east the University of Durham had no connection with the Rutherford College at Newcastle, and the University of Wales had but slight liaison with the colleges at Swansea and Newport. In London the situation was quite different because of the inclusion of the South Kensington group of science and technological colleges within the faculty organisation of the University of London.

In order to link up all the bodies concerned with higher technological education so that their work might be closely co-ordinated, the Ministry of Education appointed, in 1944, a special Committee on Higher Technological Education. The Report which was issued in 1945 is usually known as the Percy Report (from the chairman, Lord Eustace Percy, who had been chosen on account of his interest and wide knowledge of the problems of technological education).

The Report fully realised the issues involved. "The evidence submitted to us concurs in the general view: first, that the position of Great Britain as a leading industrial nation is being endangered by a failure to secure the fullest possible application of science to industry; and second, that this failure is partly due to deficiencies in education. The annual intake into the industries of the country of men trained by Universities and Technical Colleges has been, and still is, insufficient both in quantity and quality. We believe that the industrial demand for such men will increase in quantity after the war; and that the demand for higher quality, especially in certain categories, will become more insistent as the nation becomes more conscious of its need for technical efficiency. In particular, the experience of war has shown that the greatest deficiency in British Industry is the shortage of scientists and technologists who can also administer and organise, and can apply the results of research and development." [1]

Attention has already been drawn to the traditional British view that technical education which is concerned with the principles of the industry and their application should be quite distinct from works training. The Percy Report considered that the two aspects should be intimately related and that there ought to be a closer liaison between the technological institutions and the leaders of industry. "Technological education must be conceived in terms of of a combined course of works training and academic studies; and both the course as a whole and the period allotted to academic

[1] *Report on Higher Technological Education*, para. 2, H.M.S.O., 1945.

studies must be long enough to give full scope to the student's development. Full co-operation between industrialists and educators must be based upon a recognition, by both parties, of the supreme importance of increasing the efficiency of manufacturing processes, and of initiating new branches of technology, as a means of expanding the nation's export trade and advancing its standard of living." [1]

In order to achieve the necessary co-ordination, it is essential to understand quite clearly the division of function between universities and technological institutions. In some aspects of the work the division is clear enough ; the universities are expected to train scientists and research workers and to produce teachers of science ; the technical colleges aim at training technical assistants and craftsmen. In the future, both institutions will be expected to educate students who will become senior administrators and managers of industry. This necessitates a joint arrangement for consultation and planning, which at present scarcely exists. The Committee thought that in districts where Regional Councils of Further Education had been established, something of this kind had been accomplished, but much more was needed.

The report was mainly concerned with the three branches of engineering—mechanical, electrical, and civil—because these were the chief studies common to both universities and technical colleges. In 1939 the output of mechanical, electrical, and civil engineers was slightly above 2,000, of which the universities supplied thirty-five per cent. War conditions necessitated an increase, and in 1943 the output rose to about 3,000, out of which about forty-five per cent came from the universities, and this number would be required annually to meet post-war conditions.

The Committee agreed that, on the whole, the division of function between the universities and the technological institutions was sound, that the former should emphasise the science aspect and the latter the works training, but such a division could easily be exaggerated. They recommended that a limited number of technological colleges should be selected in which technological courses of a standard comparable with those of the universities should be developed. The selection of the colleges would have to be left to the Ministry of Education. In addition to the normal courses, provision should be made for post-graduate studies in special branches of technology available for both full-time and part-time

[1] *Report on Higher Technological Education*, para. 3, H.M.S.O., 1945.

students.   One aspect of the work would be research into specific problems of local industry.   Such colleges would be performing a national rather than a local function.   They should be organised to provide accommodation for a considerable number of residential students and should be given the greatest possible degree of self-government and responsibility.   The Government should assist them by capital grants in a way similar to that contemplated for universities, and the salaries of the staff should be comparable to those of university teachers.   It was important that colleges which were not selected under the scheme should not be regarded as of inferior status.

It was recommended that regional advisory committees should be established, working in co-operation with a National Council of Technology.   The work of the regional councils would be to further the co-ordination of technological education in the university and technical colleges of the region, and that industry should be fully represented on the regional organisation.   Eight regional councils were suggested;   London and the Home Counties;   the Southern and Western counties;   East Anglia and the East Midlands;   the West Midlands;   Lancashire and Cheshire;   Yorkshire;   the four Northern counties;   and Wales.   There should also be arrangements for consultation between central bodies in England and Wales and in Scotland.

The question of the recruitment of students was also discussed. The Committee believed that "the best material is not being offered . . . in sufficient quantities.   In a word, industry, and educational institutions training for industry, are not getting their fair share of the national ability." [1]   The solution lay in a national campaign to increase the prestige of the technical professions, and it should be specially directed to the public schools where a bias against technology existed.   There should be close co-ordination between the Ministry of Labour and its appointments department, the Juvenile Employment Bureaux, and the University Appointment Boards.   Industry, too, would have to take part in the recruitment drive.   Much could be expected from the State bursary system which should be continued and extended.   It was hoped that the expansion of secondary education, envisaged by the Education Act of 1944, would also be a potent factor.

The question of the qualifications to be awarded by colleges of technology caused some division of opinion amongst members of

[1] *Report on Higher Technological Educational*, para. 41, H.M.S.O., 1945.

the Committee. All agreed that it was desirable that the colleges should conduct their own examinations and award their own qualifications, but there should be some national body to guarantee national standards.

Such a body would be found in the National Council of Technology, which should work through an academic board. This would not mean the formation of an external examining body. Its function would be that of approving and moderating courses of study, suggesting standards of staffing and equipment, and selecting external examiners to co-operate with the staffs of the colleges, The technological qualification given by the major institutions should be equivalent to a university first degree. When the exact title of the qualification was discussed, disagreement became apparent.

Some members of the Committee thought that the title should be that of a degree which might be called the B.Tech. This would assist in attracting students to the major colleges and would present a parallel with the junior technical schools. The latter had become secondary technical schools and had taken a place in the system on an equal footing with the grammar-schools. The new technical schools would be a source of recruitment for the technological colleges, and it would be damped from the start if the idea got abroad that the ultimate qualification for students who followed this path was inferior to that given to those who proceeded to a university. It was also suggested that the degree of Tech.D. should be awarded for post-graduate research.

This view was not favoured by other members of the Committee. They argued that industrialists, in engaging a man, were concerned with the kind of training he had received rather than the exact title of his qualification. They preferred a diploma instead of a degree. Lord Eustace Percy did not agree with the former view and added a Note to the Report, in which he pointed out the difficulties that would arise if it were adopted. If the power to grant degrees were given to technological institutions there would be no end to the process. The same privilege would have to be offered to university colleges, the Royal Colleges of Art and Music, and to other institutions for further education. "In all civilised countries the power to confer degrees is the distinguishing mark of a University. In this country the power can be exercised only if it is granted by an act of Government, and the Government has jealously restricted such grants. Government policy has been based on the principle that a

University should be a fully self-governing community of teachers and students, working together in one place, with substantial endowments of its own, mature enough to set its own standards of teaching and strong enough to resist outside pressure, public or private, political or economic." [1]

The Chairman suggested that the selected colleges should be given the title of Royal Colleges of Technology and should be granted the power of conferring, at the graduating stage, an Associateship of the Royal Colleges of Technology and, at the postgraduate stage, a Fellowship. His recommendations were accepted with the others made by the Committee and endorsed by the Minister of Education in *Circular 87*, February 1946. This was followed by the establishment in 1948 of the National Advisory Council on Education for Industry and Commerce. The functions of this body were to co-ordinate the work of the regional councils and to advise on national policy.

This advice was given in the Council's Report, *The Future Development of Higher Technological Education*, 1950. The main proposals were that increased financial aid should be given for selected colleges and courses and that a College of Technologists should be established by Royal Charter. The latter proposal was not accepted by the Government. There was some discussion about the establishment of a technological university but in 1954, the Parliamentary Scientific Committee recommended that about twenty of the larger technical colleges should become Royal Chartered Colleges of Technology with the power of awarding a technical degree. Once again the Government did not agree with this policy and explained that it favoured an evolutionary to any sudden change. It did not agree with the removal of the colleges from the control of the L.E.A.s and looked ahead to the time when thirty of the technical colleges would develop into advanced regional colleges.

The increasing demand for more and more technicians and technologists to serve an atomic age has raised further problems. The first is concerned with the staffing of technical schools and colleges. Although by 1955 the number of teachers in all types of school in the national system had increased, yet the increase in the number of highly-qualified teachers of mathematics, science, and technical subjects was very slight. The graduate who had obtained

[1] *Report on Higher Technological Education*, Chairman's Note, para. 4, H.M.S.O., 1945.

a good honours degree in pure or applied science found that the rewards offered by industry and commerce were more adequate than those to be gained by teaching. As we said in Chapter XI, there are signs that the supply of science and technological graduates offering themselves for training as teachers is improving.

Another aspect of the problem is the augmenting of the number of highly trained men and women who are equipped to take responsible posts in industry, trade, and the professions. Even if the facilities which the universities could offer were expanded to the full, the supply would still fall short of what is required and it will be necessary to utilise to the maximum the contributions which the senior institutions for teaching technology, commerce, and art are able to make. With this idea in mind, the National Advisory Council recommended the establishment of an independent National Council to create and administer the awards to students who are pursuing approved courses in technology. The general view was that the awards should be equivalent in value to a first degree. It was proposed that the Council should be assisted by two Boards of Studies, one in engineering and the second in other technological studies. The Council was not to undertake the functions of an examining body. Its duty would be to decide the character of the new awards and to approve the courses which were proposed by the colleges. It would be assisted in this work by the Boards of Studies. In July 1955, the Minister of Education, after a discussion with the L.E.A.s, the colleges, and the relevant professional bodies, decided to adopt the proposals. Lord Hives, Chairman of Rolls Royce Ltd., was appointed as Chairman of the National Council which consists of five members appointed by the Minister and three nominated by each Board of Studies.

Another development has been the opening since 1946 of National Colleges which are intended to give advanced instruction in certain specialised technological subjects which it would be difficult to provide through the universities or the local authorities. The colleges so far established are those in Horology, Foundry Work, Heating, Ventilating and Fan Engineering, Rubber Technology, Food Technology, Leathersellers College, and Aeronautics. At the same time, the Royal College of Art, which developed from the Normal School of Design and which was established in 1896, was completely reorganised as a National College in 1949. It had been diverted from the original purpose of its foundation and had concentrated on the training of students and teachers of the fine arts.

The emphasis placed on technical and technological education in recent years has raised the further problem of the balance of the curriculum in the universities and in the regional and national colleges. Thus in November 1956, the Government proposed that by the mid-1960s, the number of students in institutions financed by the University Grants Committee should be increased from 84,000 to 106,000 and that two-thirds of them should be scientists or technologists. Will this policy result in a neglect of the human studies? How far can a technological course be humanised so as to bring out its cultural as well as its utility values? This problem is quite rightly attracting considerable attention.

CHAPTER XIV

EDUCATION IN SCOTLAND TO 1872

The history of education in Scotland deserves a book to itself, and in the two chapters which deal with this subject there is only space to consider the development of the Scottish educational system in broad outline and to indicate some of the main ways in which it has both influenced, and been influenced by, events in the southern part of the kingdom.

There are three main characteristics, amongst others, which have been distinctive of Scottish Education from a very early period: —

1. The people of Scotland have for centuries attached great value to education, especially university and secondary education, and have consequently made considerable sacrifices in the past to obtain the best that was possible for them. In England the majority of the poorer classes never appreciated the value of education, even when it was offered cheaply or freely. The Act of 1870 filled the gaps and covered the land with elementary schools, but, for over twenty years, compulsion had to be applied to fill them.

2. In Scotland there has never been the wide gulf separating primary and secondary education that existed in England until very recent times. The popular schools, *i.e.* the parish schools, not only provided an elementary education but frequently trained their bright pupils in classics and mathematics to enable them to proceed direct to the universities.

3. The Scottish people have never been class-conscious to the degree that the English were in the 18th and 19th centuries. In other words, in both the schools and the universities there has been a strong democratic tradition, so that the right of the clever child, the "lad o' pairts," the earnest, industrious, and capable student, to obtain the highest forms of education provided, has never been denied because of his lowly birth or his station in life. The Scottish parochial school of the last century was a common school in the sense that pupils of all creeds and of all degrees of society sat at the same benches side by side. This characteristic of the parochial school has been noticed by many observers. Thus, speaking of the 18th century, Graham writes: "They gave access to instruction to the lowest and the poorest as well as the highest,

for the laird's and the ploughman's son, the sons of the carpenter and of the lord of session, met together; they opened to them professions and posts in which so many rose to distinction; they effected an unequalled diffusion of education to every class in the country, and the teaching of the schools formed an easy stepping-stone for all to the highest training of the universities." [1]

The reputation of the parochial schools was maintained untarnished in the middle of the 19th century. Sir James Kay-Shuttleworth, weary of the incessant denominational disputes in England, was able to point in contrast to the tolerant character of the parish school in which members of all religious denominations and of all social classes could join. He wrote: "The Scotch Parochial School has been distinguished by one beautiful feature. Upon its benches the children of every rank in life have met, and have contended for honours, earned only by higher natural gifts, or superior moral qualities. Those whom the accidents of rank and fortune have not yet separated have here formed friendships, which have united the laird and the hind through life, by mutual service and protection. Thus, sentiment has overleaped the barriers which divide society into classes, to acknowledge the claims of personal feeling, and to lift humble merit from obscurity." [2]

There is practically no documentary evidence before the 12th century to prove the existence of specific schools in Scotland, but, as in England, organised education began with the coming of Christianity. St. Ninian left the shores of the Solway to visit Rome, and after training there he stayed some time at Tours before returning to Scotland. Here he met St. Martin, whose influence had contributed greatly to the spread of monasticism in Gaul. When Ninian returned to his home district he began to preach Christianity to his fellow-countrymen. He won many converts for the new faith and, with the help of masons sent by Martin, the first Scottish church of white stone—*Candida Casa*—was built at Whithorn about 397. Associated with this church was the first of many monasteries in Scotland bearing the name of St. Ninian. Using the monastery as a base, Ninian made journeys to carry the Gospel to the Picts who dwelt north of this district. It is a reasonable conclusion that the monastery of Whithorn was a centre for both religious and secular education.

[1] H. G. Graham. *The Social Life of Scotland in the Eighteenth Century*, p. 433, A. and C. Black, 1909.
[2] Sir James Kay-Shuttleworth. *Public Education*, p. 535, Longman, Brown, Green, and Longmans, 1853.

We are, however, on surer ground when we come to the work of Columba, who settled his headquarters in the island of Iona in 563. The monastery of Iona became the centre from which Christianity spread not only to other parts of Scotland, but also, as we saw in the first chapter, from which it was carried by Aidan to northern England. The monastery of Iona was modelled on abbeys in Ireland, from which country Columba had come. In Ireland the monasteries were centres of civilisation and learning to which students came, not only to receive training for the work of the Church, but for secular learning as well. In Scotland the Celtic Church differed in its organisation from the Roman Church which had been introduced into southern England by Augustine. The ancient Irish and Scottish Churches, owing to their long isolation from the Continent, had not only developed customs of their own, but had organised themselves on a monastic basis. Each Scottish monastery looked to the Abbot of Iona as its head. As yet there was no diocesan and parochial organisation such as was growing up in England. As a consequence, whilst the early English schools grew up in association with the cathedrals and collegiate churches, those in Scotland developed in connection with the monasteries.

Each monastery was a centre of learning and civilisation, and young people entered them not only to be trained as novices, but also to gain a general education. The work of the monasteries in education was especially stressed by the disciples of Columba. We can picture the Celtic Church gradually extending southwards into Northumbria, founding here and there a monastery to be the religious and educational centre of its district and, at the same time, the Roman missionaries moving ever northwards, bringing with them the traditions of order and organisation derived from the Continent. The two streams of Christianity met in the northern Midlands and the problem as to which should be supreme in England was settled at the Synod of Whitby in 664. In Scotland the better organisation of the Roman system prevailed only after many years, but by the time of Malcolm II, 1018, the Celtic Church was fast being merged into the Roman.

Much as one admires the piety and zeal of the Columban Church, its assimilation to the Roman brought Scotland into the main stream of European civilisation from which it had so long stood aloof. The old tribal organisation of the Celtic Church disappeared, and Scotland, like England, was eventually mapped out into dioceses and parishes. The great monastic orders of the

Western Church entered into possession of the Celtic monasteries, and many new abbeys founded by the Benedictines and Cistercians sprang up in different parts of the kingdom. From the time of this assimilation we have increasing documentary evidence of the rise of specific schools associated with the monasteries, cathedrals, and churches. Thus there are definite references to the existence of schools at Abernelly, Perth, Stirling, Roxburgh, and Lanark, in the 12th century. "Schools for Latin, to which were subsequently added 'Lecture' schools for English, existed in the chief towns of Scotland from a very early period. We have authentic notice of a school in Aberdeen in 1124. The schools of Perth and Stirling were in existence in 1173." [1]

The history of these mediaeval Scottish schools is analogous to those in England of the same period. They were under the control of the Church and were directly connected with the cathedrals, monasteries, and collegiate churches. The original dioceses were St. Andrews, Dunkeld, and Moray, but new dioceses were created subsequently, and by the end of the 12th century there were eleven bishoprics organised on English models, *e.g.* Dunkeld and Glasgow were modelled on Salisbury, and Elgin on Lincoln, as regards their constitutions. As in England, two types of school developed from the cathedrals and collegiate churches, the Grammar School, and the Sang (Song) School. Grammar-schools, distinct from schools of the monks, grew up in connection with the monasteries and, where the abbey was in or near a town, the grammar-school was often to be found in the town itself, as in Edinburgh. The division of the country into parishes resulted in another type of school connected with the parish churches. The church building was often used for the purposes of a school. The instruction given in these parish schools was probably very elementary and was connected with the services, and especially the music, of the church. Most of these schools were smaller versions of the sang-school attached to the cathedrals. A well-known story of the village school at Norham-on-Tweed is related by Reginald of Durham in the 12th century.

A certain boy named Haldane tried to escape the rod for idleness by stealing the key of the church, locking the door, and throwing the key into a deep pool of the river. The master and his assistants were unable to break open the church door, but Providence intervened to help them. St. Cuthbert appeared in a dream to the

[1] *Third Report of the Schools Commission (Scotland)*, Vol. I, pp. 1-2.

master and instructed him to go to the fishermen early next day and buy their first catch. When he awoke, he carried out the saint's instructions and received an enormous salmon which contained the missing key in its gills.

Grant illustrates the work of the sang-school of Aberdeen in the contract signed by the master, in which he "obliges himself by the faith of his body, all the days of his life, to remain with the community of the burgh, singing, keeping, and upholding mass, matins, evensongs, completories, psalms, responses, antiphonies, and hymns in the parish kirk on festival and ferial days, for a salary of 24 merks Scots annually. The town council further appoints him master of their sang school to instruct burgesses' sons in singing and playing on the organs, for the upholding of God's service in the choir, they paying him his scolage and dues." [1]

The Scottish Church, like the English, claimed a monopoly of education and occasionally schoolmasters set up private schools without the permission of the ecclesiastical authorities. For instance, in Glasgow, the control of education was in the hands of the Chancellor of the diocese. In 1494 a priest who had attempted to teach grammar without authority from the Chancellor was brought before the Bishop and ordered to give up his school. The claims of the Church, however, were not always successfully maintained. In Brechin, in 1485, a dispute on the right of presentation as preceptor of Maisondieu, to which office was attached the duties of schoolmaster, arose between the bishop and the Earl of Ross.

The King decided in favour of the latter and gave warning that none of his subjects should "take upon him to make any manner of persecution or following of the said matter at the Court of Rome since it pertains to lay patronage."

The 15th century was a very important one for Scottish education. In the first place it furnished the first attempt in any European country to make education compulsory by means of legislation. An Act of Parliament, 1496, in the reign of James IV, ordered all barons and freeholders who were of "substance" to send their eldest sons to school at the age of eight or nine and to keep them at the grammar-school until they "have perfect Latin." On leaving the grammar-school, they were to spend three years at the school of Art and Law, so as to obtain knowledge and

[1] J. Grant. *History of the Burgh and Parish Schools in Scotland,* p. 66, William Collins, 1876.

understanding of the laws.[1]   The penalty for disobedience was a fine of £20 to be paid to the King.   Some writers suggest that this statute is a proof of the high level in education reached in Scotland at this time.   It is true that it presupposed the existence of grammar-schools, but it more probably emphasised the backward state of education and endeavoured to improve it by legal enactment.   The Act applied only to the wealthier people, "men of substance," and there is no evidence that it was ever enforced.

In the Middle Ages it was one thing to enact a law but quite another to get it obeyed, and the complaint of John Major in 1521, "the gentry educate their children neither in letters nor in morals— no small calamity to the state," shows that the Act was not universally observed.   The Act, however, foreshadowed the line of development of the national education in later years.

The second important development in 15th-century Scottish education was the foundation of the universities.   Before this time Scotland had no institution for higher education, and scholars, after leaving the grammar-schools, were forced to travel abroad to continue their studies.   Many Scottish students were to be found in the universities of Bologna, Geneva, Pisa, Louvain, and Padua. In the latter, the Scottish students formed a "Nation" and later, at Paris, the Bishop of Moray founded a Scots college in 1326.   Other students pursued their studies at Oxford and Cambridge.   Those who travelled overseas ran the risk of attack by pirates, and because of the almost continual warfare between England and Scotland, it was not an easy matter for Scottish students to enter England. James I fell into the hands of the English and remained a prisoner for a considerable time.

Yet in spite of the difficulties, quite a number of students found their way to the English universities, and, to maintain poor Scottish students at Oxford, Sir John Balliol founded a college there.   His work was completed by his widow, Devorgilla, the founder of New Abbey (Sweetheart Abbey) in Kirkcudbrightshire.   There was, however, a strong feeling that the needs of Scottish students could only be met by a university in Scotland.   Bishop Wardlaw of St. Andrews obtained from Benedict XIII a Bull of foundation for a *studium generale* in 1411.   The university was modelled upon Paris and Bologna and its members were divided into Nations according to the district from which they came.   (Fife, Lothian,

---

[1] The reference to schools of Art and Law ("sculis of Art and Jure") refers to higher monastic schools where the art of charter-writing was taught.

Angus, and Alban.   The last included all students who were not in the first three Nations.)

The arrival of the Papal Bull was the occasion of great rejoicing, and even James I, still a captive in England, heartily approved of the new foundation.   When he was released from captivity, he confirmed the privileges of the university by a royal charter and did all in his power to ensure its successful development.[1]

At the beginning, the University of St. Andrews had few students and teachers.   There were no colleges, and students lodged in the town.   Shortly after its foundation, Robert of Montrose provided a house for the students of theology and other benefactors began to add to the buildings of the university.   In the early days the teaching was carried on in buildings lent or hired for the purpose and the professors had no salary.   By the time of the Reformation, St. Andrews possessed three colleges: St. Salvator's, 1450, founded by Bishop Kennedy, the successor of Wardlaw; St. Leonard's, 1512, founded by Archbishop Alexander Stuart; and St. Mary's, founded by Archbishop James Beaton in 1537.   The distinguished scholastic, John Major, was the principal of St. Salvator's.

Glasgow was the next university to be established, and its foundation in 1450 was due to the influence of William Turnbull, Bishop of Glasgow, who persuaded James II to petition Pope Nicholas V for a Bull authorising its inception.   The royal charter was received in 1453.   Glasgow University was modelled on Bologna and Louvain.   Like St. Andrews, Glasgow had no buildings for teaching purposes and students were obliged to attend classes in the cathedral and other churches.   Later, a tenement in the High Street with four acres of land was given by Sir Gavin Hamilton.   It seems he had some doubts about the success of the institution, for in the charter he asserted the right of his heirs to take back the land into their possession.   His Scottish caution was perhaps justified, for Glasgow had a very chequered history for a number of years, and it was not until the time of Andrew Melville that it was in a flourishing condition.

Scotland's third university was founded at Aberdeen in 1494, when Alexander VI issued a Bull to James IV and Bishop Elphinstone.   The King had sent a petition to the Pope asking for his authority to establish a university, and he urged its foundation on the ground that owing to the geographical features of the Highlands and their remoteness from seats of learning, the people were

[1] One of the privileges was that its members were exempt from all taxes.

ignorant and almost barbarians. As a consequence it was difficult to find suitable priests to preach and administer the sacraments. The King was probably referring not so much to Aberdeen itself, which was provided with schools and had already produced some well-known scholars, as to the wild country to the north and west. In any case, he no doubt thought it worth while to colour his petition highly to ensure its success. Elphinstone, who had been Rector of Glasgow University, fully realised from his experience the vicissitudes resulting from an institution which is unendowed, and he took good care that Aberdeen had sufficient endowments to pay the salaries of its teachers. Hence, in its early days, the University of Aberdeen had a more flourishing career than the earlier foundations.

The foundation of three universities (the fourth, Edinburgh, was founded in the next century) was a marvellous achievement in those days for a country such as Scotland. Her population was scanty,[1] and the land was disturbed both by constant warfare with England and by rebellions of the nobles against the King. Moreover, compared with England, Scotland was a very poor country, and remained so until the expansion of trade in the 17th century and the industrial changes of the 18th. Her largest towns were not much more populous than English villages. Glasgow in 1450 had about 1,500 inhabitants, and Aberdeen as late as 1572 had a population of less than 3,000. Edinburgh itself was not much larger. We may suspect that much of the teaching in the early days of the universities was little in advance of that given in the grammar-schools, and a good deal later the schools complained that the functions of the grammar-school and university overlapped to a considerable extent, to the detriment of the former. The importance of the universities at this period lay in the fact that from the beginning they provided the basis from which future development could spring, and after the Reformation they were able to play a leading part in the intellectual life and cultural progress of the kingdom.

The effects of the Renaissance reached Scotland almost a century later than in England, with the consequence that they had barely time to be felt before the country was thrown into turmoil owing to the Reformation. At the end of the 15th century, the Renaissance was represented by the works of such men as William Dunbar and Gavin Douglas, and the introduction of printing and the dissemination of books led to the growth of lecture-schools in

[1] Even by 1560 it was probably not more than half a million.

the burghs for teaching reading and writing.[1] Another effect was the increasing interest in education shown by the town councils, and their claim to have a share in the patronage of schools. The first recorded appointment to a school by a burgh was that at Peebles in 1464. The claims of the burghs led them into conflict with the Church and we shall see that the Reformation speeded up the process by which the burghs obtained control over their schools. Dr. Strong illustrates this development by the following example.[2]

In 1418, at Aberdeen, the master of the school was presented for examination to the Chancellor by the Provost and the community of the burgh. In 1509 John Merschell was appointed by the "provost, bailzeis, counsale, and communite" without reference to the Chancellor. This occasioned an appeal to Rome by the Church, but the quarrel concerning the patronage of the school broke out again in 1538. The town council appointed Hugh Munro, but the Chancellor had already selected Robert Skeyne. The council prevailed, but when Munro retired in 1550 the new master, James Chalmer, was appointed by the burgh council and sent to the Chancellor for admission "as vse hes bene tharrof in tymes bigane." The claim of the town councils was a reasonable one since in many cases they had undertaken the provision and upkeep of the school buildings and even the payment of the master's salary. There are also instances where the Church authorities and the council combined to exercise supervision over the school.

The earliest known teaching of Greek in Scottish schools is 1534, when Andrew Melville was taught the language by a French teacher in the grammar-school of Montrose and later surprised the masters at the University of St. Andrews by being able to read Aristotle in the original. Greek was introduced into the schools of Aberdeen about 1540, and, as in England, a few schools taught Hebrew. Owing to the close friendship between Scotland and France, the teaching of French was fairly widespread, and shortly after the Reformation the town council of Edinburgh licensed a schoolmaster to keep a school for the teaching of French.

The supporters of the Reformation had grown so powerful by 1543 that they influenced Parliament to enact that the Bible might be read in English or Scottish translation. In 1557 the lords of the congregation, inspired by John Knox, drew up their covenant,

---

[1] Grant (*op. cit.*, p. 63) thinks that the earliest lecture-school was that in Edinburgh in 1479.

[2] J. Strong. *A History of Secondary Education in Scotland*, pp. 33-4, Clarendon Press, 1909.

and by 1560 the Protestant party became supreme in Parliament and an Act was passed abolishing the Mass and the Papal authority, adopting the Confession of Faith drawn up by Knox and his supporters. The Reformed Church asserted the control over education claimed and exercised by the Catholic Church, and John Knox thought the time was ripe for a complete reorganisation of Scottish education. He realised the decay into which the rural parish schools had by now fallen. The burgh and the grammar schools were fairly efficient largely due to the zeal and interest displayed by the town councils, which not only had the patronage of the schools in their hands, but were also financially concerned in them. The universities, especially Glasgow, were not in a flourishing state, and many students preferred to seek higher education in England or on the Continent. It was to meet these conditions that Knox prepared for the consideration of Parliament a scheme in which he was assisted by his colleagues Wynram and Douglas. The organisation proposed forms part of his *First Book of Discipline,* which was mainly concerned with religion, education, and the poor, and his scheme was so clearly thought out, so masterly in its conception, and so comprehensive in its scope, as to be several hundred years in advance of the time.[1]

Knox proposed the establishment of a school in every parish or associated with every kirk. Its function was to supply primary education for children up to the age of eight. Grammar and Latin might be taught, but in rural districts where a competent schoolmaster would be difficult to obtain, the minister or reader should be responsible for seeing that the village children were instructed in elementary subjects and the Catechism, *i.e.* the Catechism of Calvin, translated in the *Book of Common Order.* Those who could afford it would be compelled to educate their children at their own expense, but the children of the poor would be paid for by the Church and maintained at school, either to proceed to a university, if capable of higher studies, or be set to a trade. From the elementary school the pupil would go to a grammar-school. No scholar of ability was to be barred from the grammar-school on account of poverty. This involved the establishment of a grammar-school in every important town where, under a master appointed by the Church, the pupil would learn "grammar and the Latine toung" for a

[1] The title *First Book of Discipline* was adopted to distinguish it from a later Book of Discipline written by Andrew Melville. Although Knox was the chief author of the *First Book of Discipline,* there is no proof that he wrote the section on Education. The book was issued in 1560.

period of three or four years. In every notable town there was to be a higher grammar-school, or college, where a four-year course in logic, rhetoric, and languages, would be provided. Finally, those who could produce a satisfactory certificate from the master of the school and the minister might enter one of the three "great Schollis callit Universities." At each stage, the pupil's progress would be supervised and tested each quarter by the minister and other learned persons, and if, at the end of any course, a pupil was found not to be fitted for further study, he would be sent to craft or other suitable occupation. At whatever stage a pupil's education ceased, it was to be ensured that he had received sufficient religious and moral instruction to enable him to become a responsible member of the kirk. The scheme was meant to be compulsory.

"No father of what estate or condition that ever he be, can use his children at his own fantisie, especially in their youth-head," wrote John Knox, "but all must be compelled to bring up their children in learning and virtue." The reason for compulsion was the claim of the State, "that the Commonwealth may have some comfort by them." The pupil who was unfit to proceed to the next stage in his education was, as we have seen, to be put to handicraft. "It is pretty certain that Knox did not intend that the embryonic handicraftsman who was to make a profitable exercise of his life, should waste his time in grinding at Latin grammar. He knew that there were pupils for whom university training would be of no benefit either to themselves or to their country, pupils who were intended by nature to be hewers of wood or drawers of water, and whose proper and unalterable sphere of action was handicraft or other functions subordinately intellectual." [1]

The scheme of John Knox presented a magnificent ideal far in advance of anything that had been worked out at that period and, if it had been adopted in its entirety, it would have revolutionised the whole of Scottish history. It was, as Dr. Kerr says, "a national misfortune" that it was not fully carried out. John Knox knew that his scheme would require a great deal of money, but he had carefully provided for this. He proposed that the money used by the Catholic Church for education, and the incomes of the abbeys and chantries which had been suppressed, should be given to the building and maintenance of schools and colleges, and teachers and professors. What happened in England in the 16th century took place on a more thorough scale in Scotland. The greed and

[1] J. Kerr. *Scottish Education, School and University*, p. 78, C.U.P., 1910.

rapacity of the nobles knew no bounds and only a small proportion of the money found its way to the Scottish Church which, in the view of John Knox, should provide the funds for education. When Knox put his proposals to Parliament, Maitland, the Queen's Secretary, styled them "a devout imagination." Knox was bitterly incensed, but he could do but little to prevent the nobles from seizing the spoils of the Catholic Church. A small amount of money did indeed find its way to the funds of the Kirk, but the result was that for generations both religion and learning had to contend with insufficiency of money.

It is easy to criticise Knox's scheme in detail as being too bound to mediaeval scholastic learning, or its policy of handing over the control of education to the Church, but it is important to remember that every man is limited by the age in which he lives. Knox's views have proved a living ideal to which the Scottish nation, step by step, through many generations, has striven to attain.　Dr. Strong summarises the great principles of his scheme as follows.[1]

(a) It was a national system; (b) education was graded from the primary school to the university; (c) all schools were to be periodically examined; (d) promotion depended upon successful effort; (e) provision was made for the free education of poor but clever pupils.　One could add that the very point on which Dr. Strong criticises the scheme is perhaps one of its greatest features, namely Knox's clear perception and firm conviction that all sound education must rest on a religious basis and that the Church at that time was the only organised body that could or would superintend education.

The graded course from the elementary school to the university did not come into existence and pupils passed to their higher studies, not only from the grammar-school, but also from the parochial schools.　It was this association of the parochial schools of Scotland and the universities that was distinctive of Scottish education for so many generations and which resulted in a less rigid line of demarcation between elementary and secondary education than in England.　The support which the Church was unable to give was partially provided by the efforts of the town councils.　Indeed, it was largely the poverty of the Church that accounts for the ease with which the burgh schools passed into municipal control.　The Church at first opposed the claims of the municipalities, but eventually a concordat was established whereby both bodies were able to

---

[1] J. Strong.　*A History of Secondary Education in Scotland*, p. 61, Clarendon Press, 1909.

work harmoniously together. The parish schools, which became the backbone of the Scottish educational effort, remained under Church control, with the result that in no other country was the power of the Church over elementary education so complete as in Scotland.

In pursuance of its claim to control education, the Church enacted in 1565 that nobody should have charge of schools, colleges, or universities, or teach privately, unless he was "tried" by the Kirk, *i.e.* examined by the Presbytery, or admitted by the Kirk. The decree of the Church was supported by an Act of Parliament in 1567. The power thus gained was freely exercised. We read of the dismissal of schoolmasters who refused to conform to the Confession of Faith, the suspension of masters and tutors for teaching Popery, the fixing of age-limits for university students, and the making of the provisions for bursars. The schoolmaster was also expected to take a leading part in the parish work of the kirk, such as reading prayers on Sundays or acting as precentor or session clerk. This was partly due to the fact that a large number of priests had refused to accept the changes in religion. An interesting case is provided by William Robertson, master of the grammar-school at Edinburgh. He remained an adherent of the old faith and the town council wished to remove him. Robertson refused to resign and appealed to Queen Mary, and the council was obliged to retain him and pay his salary. It was not until twenty years later (1584) that Robertson agreed to give up his post on consideration of the payment of a generous pension.

The people who resented most the introduction of the new religion were the schoolboys. They had been accustomed to holidays on the feast days of the old Church, but the Reformers abolished the holidays at Easter and Christmas because they thought the keeping of these festivals savoured of Popery. The schoolboys demanded the holidays as a right, and in Edinburgh, Aberdeen, and other towns, frequent riots and rebellions occurred. At Aberdeen, the scholars took possession of the school and held it by armed force against the masters. In 1587, at Edinburgh High School, a similar event occurred, and in 1595, when the council refused their petition for a holiday, the scholars took possession of the school and barred out the master, Mr Rollock. He applied to the magistrates for assistance and John Macmorran, a member of the town council, was shot through the head and killed when he was trying to force open the door.

During the latter part of the 16th century and most of the 17th century there is evidence to show that the town councils made great efforts to procure the best qualified masters for the burgh schools, and that the Church authorities, as far as their financial resources would allow, made an honest attempt to put into practice the recommendations of John Knox.   As Grant shows, they frequently protested to the King and Parliament against the behaviour of the nobles in regard to their "wrangous using of the patrimony of the Kirk to the great hurt of scullis." [1]

The schoolmaster's lot in these times was not a happy one. He suffered from insecurity of tenure; it was not until the 18th century that the custom became common of appointing the master for life, *ad vitam aut culpam*.   There was no provision for pensions, and since endowments were few and slender, the schoolmaster largely depended on his fees.   If at the quarterly examination of the school the results of his teaching were not considered satisfactory, he was liable to dismissal.   He sometimes had a house provided, but his finances were frequently so straitened that he gladly availed himself of goodwill gifts from the parents.   One source of profit, as in England, was from cock-fighting, and the pupils either supplied the cocks or compensation in money. [2]   Before the Reformation, the schoolmaster was high in the social order but his position had now declined.   However, it is surprising how efficient the average schoolmaster was in spite of his handicaps.   Political changes caused him a great deal of concern.   When the Presbyterians were in power, he had to sign the Covenant, but when, as in the reign of Charles II, the Episcopalians were supreme, he had to accept the Prayer Book. [3]

The University of Glasgow, which had nearly ceased to exist in the middle of the 16th century, received some help from Queen Mary, who assigned the monastic property of Glasgow to the town council.   On the advice of James VI, this was presented to the university, but owing to maladministration and fraud, the property yielded a yearly income of only £300 Scots.   When

[1] J. Grant. *History of the Burgh and Parish Schools in Scotland*, p. 80, William Collins, 1876.

[2] Sometimes the council supplied the master with coal or a money equivalent, and parents often sent a load of peat to the schoolhouse.   Grants to buy clothes were made and one town council subscribed half a guinea to buy the assistant a new hat.   This may have been on account of his poverty, or, quite likely, it was due to the fact that the wearing of a hat added to his dignity.

[3] When Presbyterianism was suppressed in 1662, the schoolmaster had to be licensed by the bishop as in England, but in 1690 William III once again recognised the Presbyterian form of Church government.

Andrew Melville returned from the Continent in 1574 with a great reputation as a scholar, he found Glasgow University in what has been described as a state "of suspended animation." He accepted the post of principal and began with determination to revive the university.   Although after six years he was transferred to St. Andrews, yet in this short time he brought about revolutionary changes which placed Glasgow on a sound footing.   He began by abolishing what was known as the "regenting" system in which all students who entered in any one session were placed under the same regent or tutor, who took them through their studies until they graduated. Obviously this did not conduce to sound scholarship since it would be rare to find one man who was equally good at every subject.   Melville substituted for this a system whereby a separate lecturer became responsible for each main subject of the university course.   Lack of staff forced him to train a number of promising young men himself, which speaks much for his wide range of scholarship.   He instituted four new Chairs—in languages, science, philosophy, and divinity, which last he held himself—and he insisted on Latin and Greek being continued throughout the university course instead of being dropped at an early stage. In 1577 James VI granted to the university a new charter which recognised the reforms.   Melville introduced similar reforms into Aberdeen in 1575 and St. Andrews in 1579.   His transfer to St. Andrews was in order to supervise the working of the reforms there.   The latter part of Melville's life was devoted to opposing the attempt of James VI to impose Episcopalianism on the Scottish people.

The original college of Aberdeen was King's College, but in 1593 Marischal College was founded by George, Earl Marischal of Scotland, and the two colleges were united under the University of Aberdeen in 1641.   This union broke up later and the two colleges again became separate institutions until 1860.

The University of Edinburgh is an example of a foundation due to the efforts of the municipality.   The accounts of its foundation differ considerably, but we do know that from 1582 the college carried out the work of a university in granting degrees.   In 1621 an Act of Parliament granted Edinburgh the full privileges of a university, but it still remained under the control of the Town Council and did not gain its full independence until the Universities (Scotland) Act of 1858.   In 1592 Sir Alexander Fraser made an attempt to found a fifth university, at Fraserburgh, but the institution was shortlived.

It will perhaps be more convenient to consider the later developments in education under separate heads and begin with an account
of the Parochial Schools.   When the Church, in the 17th century,
was unable to achieve its policy by direct means, it endeavoured
to carry it into effect by securing Acts of Parliament.   Thus in
1616 the Privy Council directed "that in every parish of this
kingdom, where convenient means may be had for entertaining a
School, a School shall be established, and a fit person appointed to
teach the same upon the expense of the parochinares, according to
the quality and quantity of the parish."   This decree was ratified
by Parliament in 1633 and was the first Act authorising the establishment of Parish Schools.   Another Act for founding schools was
passed in 1646 which ordered the heritors[1] to provide a school
house and a stipend for the master in every parish.   Once again
the law was largely disregarded, and in 1662 it was repealed.   These
early Acts were incorporated in the important Act for Settling
Schools, 1696.   This law ordered "that there be a School settled
and established, and a Schoolmaster appointed, in every parish
not already provided by the advice of the heritors and ministers of
the parish."   The schoolmaster was to be provided with a commodious house which should be used for a school and that the "stent"
(assessment) should come half from the tenants and half from the
heritors to pay his salary.   If the heritors refused to act, the
Presbytery could apply to the Commissioners of Supply[2] to carry
out the provision at the expense of the heritors.

The Presbyteries did their best to compel the heritors to carry
out their obligations, but many parishes still remained without
schools.   Progress in establishing schools was slow and by 1732
only 109 new schools had been built.   "Notwithstanding the inadequacies of the parish school system after the 1696 Act, and the
difficulties which presbyteries had during the eighteenth century in
arousing, sometimes through vigorous measures, the heritors of the
country and magistrates of the towns to understand and to fulfil
their legal obligations toward education, it exercised a profound

---

[1] *Heritor* = Scottish freeholder.
The Act of 1646 authorised the Presbyters to nominate "twelve honest
men" to carry out the law if the heritors neglected their duties.   Graham
remarks, "It was all very well to appoint 'twelve honest men' to look after the
heritors; but who was to look after the twelve honest men?"   H. G. Graham,
Social Life of Scotland in the Eighteenth Century, p. 419, A. and C. Black,
1909.
[2] The Commissioners of Supply were similar to the Commissioners of Land
Tax in England.

influence upon Scottish character and education.   During the eighteenth century it was not only instrumental in satisfying the desire for education on both the primary and secondary levels, but it was also an influential agency in cultivating further interest in education. . . . By opening an educational highway to the universities and the learned professions, the parish school encouraged boys with ability and determination to pursue their studies beyond the primary school level." [1]

One important defect of the Act was the stipend laid down by law for the schoolmaster. A minimum of one hundred merks (£5 9s. 0d.) and a maximum of two hundred merks (£10 18s. 0d.) was provided for.

At the beginning of the 18th century this represented a stipend which would just keep a married man and his family. Owing to the rapid fall in the value of money, by the end of the century schoolmasters were in dire poverty, and it was not until 1803 that another Act of Parliament raised the schoolmaster's salary to a minimum of 300 and a maximum of 400 merks and provided a dwelling-house and a fenced garden. The man who enjoyed this princely salary was expected to have graduated and to be capable of teaching the elementary subjects together with Latin, Greek, French, and mathematics.   He was exceedingly fortunate if he received the whole of his statutory salary. It often had to be collected in petty sums from the heritors and tenants and frequently he was put off by stories of bad harvests and disease amongst the cattle.[2] No wonder that the schoolmaster sought other means of augmenting his income. Cock-fighting has been mentioned previously. One custom which added to his salary was the payment of "bent silver." The schoolroom often had an earthen floor which was covered with rushes or bent. In early times the children were given a holiday to collect the bent but later, once in a quarter, the bent silver was handed in as a substitute. The children continued to have holidays to mark the occasion. In many parishes where no schoolhouse existed, classes

[1] N. A. Wade. *Post-Primary Education in the Primary Schools of Scotland, 1872-1936*, p. 22, University of London Press, 1939.

[2] At Prestonpans there was an endowment of 70 merks a year. This furnished the heritors with an excuse, and in 1725 they refused to contribute on the grounds that the endowment produced a sufficient sum to pay the master's salary.   In Kirkcudbright in 1696, the schoolmaster was paid £7 Scots from the fines which had been imposed for misdemeanours. The pound Scots amounted to 1s. 8d. and became obsolete after an Act passed in the reign of Queen Anne.

were taught in the kirk or in any barn or stable which happened to be vacant.[1] In others, the schoolhouse was often in a semi-ruinous condition with leaky roof,[2] small windows, often unglazed, and very little in the way of furniture.[3]

Children travelled miles over the moors to start school at seven o'clock in the morning. On winter days, the only means of warmth was a peat fire which filled the small room with dense clouds of smoke. In the Highlands, where pupils lived at small farms widely separated from each other by moors and hills, a system reminiscent of the Welsh Circulating Schools was in vogue. The master travelled from house to house and stayed a short period in each filthy, verminous hovel, instructing the Gaelic-speaking children in the English language. Probably in no modern State has education been carried on under such difficult and heartbreak-ing conditions and our admiration increases when we realise how efficiently the schoolmasters carried out their duties and the remarkable influence which the parish school exerted upon the Scottish people. As in England, order was maintained by a free use of the birch or tawse (strap). In Aberdeenshire, a curious piece of school furniture known as the "queelin" or cooling-stone was in use in many schools even until the beginning of the 19th century. When a boy had been flogged he was made to sit upon a smooth, flat stone. It is uncertain whether this was an act of mercy designed to assuage his pain or part of his punishment.

Reference has been made to the Act of 1803 which raised the stipends of the parish schoolmasters. In the Highlands and Western Islands, parishes were of such extent that often two school-houses were needed for a single parish. In such cases, the heritors might provide a salary of 600 merks without a house and divide the money between two or more parishes. The additional school was known as a Side School. The Act laid down that the school-master should be elected by the minister and the heritors; after

---

[1] At Strathblane, the school was held in the kirk until 1731 and then was transferred to a stable at the inn.

[2] Frequently the Kirk-Session ordered the pupils to bring straw to thatch the roof. At one school it was found that straw was so scarce that season that only half of the school roof could be covered.

[3] In 1677 Mr. Thomas Kirke of Cookridge, Yorks, and his friend Ralph Thoresby, the historian of Leeds, toured Scotland on horseback. The former wrote an account of his journey, *The Journal of Thomas Kirke, Esq. of Cookridge, An. 1677, Through Most Parts of Scotland.* At Burntisland he found that there were no forms in the school. There was a seat for the master but the scholars sat on the heather and grass covered floor "like pigs in a stye."

examination and approval by the Presbytery, he was required to subscribe to the Confession of Faith.

The Act did not apply to the large towns where great deficiencies in school accommodation existed,[1] and it was ineffective in dealing with the large scattered parishes of the Highlands and the Islands in which John Knox's proposals for a school in every parish were seldom carried out. These regions presented a special difficulty on account of the obstacles to communication, the barren nature of the soil, the poverty of the inhabitants, and the fact that a large proportion of the population was Gaelic speaking. The government made every effort to extirpate the speaking of Gaelic. Thus an enactment of the Privy Council decreed that the "Irishe language [Gaelic] which is one of the chieff causes of the continuance of barbaritie and incivilitie among the inhabitants of the Isles and Highlandes should be abolished." The people were strongly attached to their language and therefore it is not surprising that they generally disobeyed the injunction.

The conditions of this part of the country had acutely disturbed a number of nobles and gentry, and at their instigation the Society in Scotland for Propagating Christian Knowledge was formed. It was not necessary that members of the Society should be Presbyterians, indeed most of the London members were Episcopalians, but they had to be Protestants. The early years of the Society's work were marred by the attempt to suppress Roman Catholic schools and to prohibit the use of Gaelic. It should be remembered that many of the inhabitants of the Highlands clung to the old faith, and that Catholicism and the speaking of Gaelic were regarded with suspicion as intimately associated with Jacobitism. Later in the century, the S.P.C.K. changed its policy and actually provided copies of the Scriptures and religious books printed in the Gaelic language. Encouragement for the Gaelic-speaking people was also provided by the establishment of Gaelic Societies at Edinburgh, Glasgow, and Inverness, in the early years of the 19th century.

The S.P.C.K. received letters patent in 1709, and with the help of the General Assembly it set about the business of establishing schools. One of the earliest schools erected by the S.P.C.K. was in the remote island of St. Kilda. George I gave an annual grant of £1,000 for the work in the Highlands and the S.P.C.K. received £2,000 from the estates forfeited as a result of the 1715 Rebellion.

[1] Even as late as 1873 the deficiency of elementary-school places was about 30,000 in Glasgow and over 4,000 in Edinburgh.

It was due to the work of the society that, in conjunction with the Presbytery, the school at Stornoway in Lewis was reopened after a closure of some years. The S.P.C.K. was instrumental in establishing a spinning-school at Stornoway in 1763. It was at first difficult to persuade the women to attend, as a story had been circulated that it was part of a scheme to send them to the plantations.[1] When they had been reassured, the school became a great success. The Scottish spinning-schools form an interesting feature of this period.[2]

The first two Stuarts had encouraged the development of the Scottish woollen and linen manufactures and the earliest school of which we have record was opened at Peebles in 1633, but the disturbed conditions of the mid-17th century did not encourage the development of further experiments. Spinning-schools were established in the early part of the 18th century by the Board of Trustees for Manufactures and later by the S.P.C.K. One of the expressed objects of the society was "To Erect and Maintain Schools, to Teach to Read, especially the Holy Scripture and other good and pious books; As also to Teach Writing, Arithmetict, and such like degrees of Knowledge in the Highlands, Islands, and remote Corners of Scotland." At first the S.P.C.K. kept strictly to this curriculum but later, as in the case of the similar movement in England, instruction was given in industrial subjects. New letters patent issued in 1738 allowed the society to do this, provided it did not neglect its former work. Thus, in the Minutes of the society from 1753 to 1767, we find encouragement given to the teaching of Gaelic and the establishment of spinning-schools. Nearly 100 dame-schools for girls were built. In some of the schools the curriculum was expanded to include such studies as mathematics, Latin, Greek, music, and bookkeeping. Raining's School, founded by the S.P.C.K. in Inverness in 1757, provided a definite secondary education. At the beginning of the 19th century, the S.P.C.K. had about 290 schools with nearly 16,000 scholars.

The philanthropic movements of the late 18th and early 19th centuries, *e.g.* Sunday Schools, Infant Schools, and Monitorial Schools, affected Scotland and have already received attention in Chapter vi in connection with the work of Bell, Stow, Wilderspin, Wood, and Owen. The Ragged School movement was also an

---

[1] The rumour may have started from the fact that in the north a type of linen (Harns) was manufactured to supply clothing for the negroes in the plantations.

[2] A full account is given by Irene F. M. Deans in *Scottish Spinning Schools*, University of London Press, 1930.

important influence in Scottish educational effort amongst the poor. Three years before the London Ragged School Union was formed, Sheriff Watson opened the first Ragged School in Aberdeen in 1841. A similar school for girls was opened in 1843, and a mixed school in 1845. The movement spread to Dundee and other towns, but the great apostle of the movement was the Rev. Thomas Guthrie. Through his pamphlets he kindled a fire of enthusiasm, and the schools founded through the efforts of Dr. Guthrie saved hundreds of children from a life of crime and poverty.

When in 1833 the Government voted a grant of £20,000 for building schools in England, Scotland did not receive any money, but from 1834 to 1839 an annual grant of £10,000 was paid. An Act of 1838 set aside part of the grant for endowing schools in the Highlands for which the heritors were to provide a schoolroom, a master's house, and a garden. These schools were afterwards known as Parliamentary Schools. In 1837 and 1839 the respective sums of £6,000 and £4,000 were set aside from the grant for this purpose. In 1839 the Committee of the Privy Council was formed, and as far as State intervention is concerned, the Scottish schools came under the same system of grant and inspection as the English schools. Part of the annual grant of £30,000 was allocated to Scotland. As was the case in regard to some denominational schools in England, quite a number of Scottish parochial schools did not avail themselves of the increased income provided by the grant.

In 1843 came the Great Disruption, when 470 ministers left the Established Church and formed the Free Church. Sectarian bitterness was rife for a time and the Free Church began to build its own schools, often in places where a parochial school already existed. Thus in some districts there was overlapping, whilst in others the deficiency in school places still remained. These years were the only period in which the religious difficulty which had proved so formidable a problem in England, invaded Scottish education, but the disturbance was mainly confined to competition between the Established and Free Church schools in certain districts. In 1829 the parochial schools had been opened to all denominations, including Roman Catholics, and parents were able to withdraw their children from religious instruction they did not approve.

The Revised Code was intended to apply to Scotland. The parochial schools, with a wider and more liberal tradition than the English elementary schools, resented its introduction bitterly, and in 1864 the most injurious part of the Code, Payment by Results, was withdrawn, although the examination in the three R's was retained.   One of the chief grounds for the opposition to the Revised Code was that it introduced class distinctions into the schools and tended to destroy the democratic tradition.   Shorn of its most vicious feature, the Code produced certain beneficial results.   There had always been a tendency for the schoolmaster to concentrate on his able pupils with the hope of sending them to the university.   Inspection and examination forced him to spend more time and effort on the less able who thus became better grounded in the elementary subjects.

The Parochial and Burgh Schoolmasters' Act of 1861 increased the stipends of the parish schoolmasters to a minimum of £35 and a maximum of £70 per annum, and gave them certain advantages as regards their accommodation.   Women teachers were recognised, with a salary of not more than £30 a year.   The examination for teachers was taken out of the hands of the Presbyteries and put under the control of the universities.   The schoolmaster was no longer obliged to subscribe to the Confession of Faith, but merely had to make a declaration that he would not teach anything contrary to the doctrine of the Church of Scotland.   The power of dismissal for inefficiency or neglect of duty rested with the heritors and minister of the parish after consideration of the report of the H.M.I.   A teacher charged with a moral offence came under the jurisdiction of the sheriff of the county in place of the Presbytery. In burgh schools, teachers were no longer required to sign a Confession of Faith or submit to the discipline of the Church of Scotland, or be subject to the Presbytery as regards their qualifications.   These conditions really recognised what had been common for some time.   Thus, in 1861, only fifty out of 113 burgh school teachers were members of the Church of Scotland.   The Act of 1861 is important not only for the benefits it conferred on members of the teaching profession, but chiefly because it represents a step in the transfer of the control of education from the Church to the State, a change which was accomplished in 1872.   We can now leave the parochial school for a time and turn our attention to the progress of the other educational agencies prior to 1872.

According to Dr. Strong, the progress of the burgh or grammar schools from the Reformation to 1872 falls into three well-marked periods.[1]   In the first, which extended well into the 18th century, the dominant subject of the curriculum was classics, especially

[1] *A History of Secondary Education in Scotland*, pp. 135-6, Clarendon Press, 1909.

Latin. The second period, which began about the middle of the 18th century and continued to the early years of the 19th, was characterised by a reaction against the exclusively linguistic outlook of the schools. This produced in turn a state of confusion in regard to both educational aims and organisation.

The scheme proposed by John Knox had failed to materialise through lack of funds. The burgh or grammar schools still continued to supply the bulk of secondary education, especially in the towns, and like the grammar-schools of the same period in England, their curriculum was almost entirely classical. The Scottish Parliament in 1607 tried to follow the example of England and attempted to prescribe a national Grammar to be used in all schools. Fortunately the attempt met with failure.[1]

Already by the beginning of the 17th century, certain schools in the larger towns, because of the number of their scholars, and the ability of their masters, were taking the lead in secondary education. The outstanding examples were the grammar-schools of Edinburgh and Glasgow. The classical curriculum of the schools and the demand that pupils should be grounded in the reading and writing of English before admission to the grammar-school led Edinburgh and Glasgow to the establishment of separate preparatory schools not unlike the petty schools of England. The grammar-schools in non-university towns taught the elementary subjects in the grammar-school itself and in this way approximated to the parochial schools. In fact, some parochial schools, such as that at Kilmarnock, eventually became grammar-schools. As in the case of England, we occasionally find other subjects than the classics taught in grammar-schools, e.g. bookkeeping, navigation, mathematics, drawing, and French. In large schools such as those of Edinburgh and Glasgow, the regenting system mentioned in connection with the universities was adopted. Thus at Edinburgh there was a staff consisting of a principal master and four regents or doctors, who kept their classes through each year until they handed them over to the principal master. As the schools were financed by the town councils, it naturally followed that the council would take a prominent part in the affairs of its grammar-school.

At Peebles in 1649 the council drew up a set of regulations for the conduct of the school, and in most burghs the council visited the school at regular intervals. They were very proud of their

---

[1] Ruddiman's *Rudiments* appeared in 1714 and was universally used for 150 years, but this was by consent and not by legal enactment.

grammar-schools and did all they could to promote the efficiency of the instruction. In some towns the council insisted upon compulsory attendance and inflicted fines for disobedience. In the 17th century the councils prohibited the opening of other schools in the district without a licence, but towards the end of the next century this discipline was relaxed and some councils even encouraged private-adventure schools.

About the middle of the 18th century a reaction against the classical curriculum set in. The trade and industries of Scotland were quickly developing and a demand for a type of education of a more practical character which would help the pupil in his career began to show itself. This movement was not altogether unconnected with changes that were taking place in the universities. The ideas of educationists like Comenius, Locke, and, later, Rousseau, were beginning to be known in Scotland. The pioneer of the reform movement was the town council of Ayr. In 1746 it introduced into the grammar-school instruction arithmetic, geometry, algebra, natural philosophy, navigation, surveying, and literature, and announced that their aim was to give the scholars a preparation "for business in the most expeditious and effectual way possible." The example of Ayr inspired Perth to go a stage further. This town took the lead in the teaching of science, and in 1761 opened the first academy, an innovation soon followed in other towns. Many of the grammar-schools were housed in ancient and dilapidated buildings, and, instead of reconstructing these, the councils often preferred to erect academies. The latter not only taught classics but included mathematics, modern languages, and commercial subjects, in the curriculum.

A curious state of affairs came into existence. In some towns the academy and the older grammar-school continued their existence either in co-operation or, more generally, as rivals; in others the academy superseded or absorbed the grammar-school. This explains why some schools which were originally grammar-schools have since been known as academies. In Edinburgh and Glasgow, where the grammar-schools had a great reputation, they continued in their original role. New endowed schools, proprietary schools, and high-class private schools were established. Some of these new institutions have since become so well known that they deserve special mention.

The foundation of the Dollar Academy constitutes a romance in itself. Dollar is a village or small town of about 1,500 inhabitants situated between Stirling and Perth. It possessed a parochial school of which, in 1800, Mr. M'Arbrea was the master. One day he received a visit from an old gentleman who discussed with him in detail the subject of the state of education in the parish of Dollar. The visitor hinted that he knew of an anonymous donor who was prepared to augment the educational facilities of the parish. Nothing more of this was heard until two years later when Mr. Watson, the minister, received a copy of the will of Captain John McNabb of the parish of St. Dunstan, Stepney, Middlesex, by which a large sum was left to the parish of Dollar. After mentioning some personal legacies, the will continued, "the other moiety or share, I would have laid in the public funds, or some such security, on purpose to bring one anualy income or interest, for the benefite of a charity or school, for the poor of the parish of Dollar and shire of Clackmannan, whier I was born, in North Britain or Scotland." The parish minister and the Kirk Session were nominated as trustees.

No steps seem to have been taken to carry out the will of the founder until 1807. The delay was caused by an objection raised by a cousin of John McNabb, and the Court of Chancery ordered a scheme to be prepared for the disposal of the legacy. Mr. Watson thought that a hospital, school, or almshouse should be erected for the poor of Dollar. The heritors refused to carry out his wishes in view of the fact that Mr. M'Arbrea declared on oath that he remembered the visit of the old gentleman, who was none other than John McNabb himself who had received his baptism in the old parish church of Dollar. No mention of a hospital or almshouse had been made during the conversation. The result was a lengthy Chancery suit which was finally decided in favour of Mr. Watson. Before the decision could be enforced Mr. Watson died, and the scheme for a hospital was abandoned. This long delay was actually beneficial, for in the meantime the original sum had grown, by the addition of interest, to £92,345 in 1819.

Dr. Mylne, Mr. Watson's successor, arranged for the management of the legacy to be brought under the control of the Court of Session. The scheme for building a school was approved and the statutes and rules for the Dollar Institution were drawn up. The building was planned by Playfair, the most famous of Scottish architects, and he produced what has been described as "one of the finest Grecian structures to be seen and admired anywhere." The school building was completed in 1821, but for some time teaching had been carried out in temporary premises.

Dr. Mylne had to endure a good deal of opposition to his plans, but he was determined to go ahead. His ideas were much in advance of the age. Thus the first two appointments he made were those of a school doctor and a nurse. When an infant-school was opened in 1831 and put under the charge of Mr. Russell, two conditions were made regarding the admission of pupils. All pupils were required to be vaccinated, and parents promised that they would ensure that their children came to school clean, with hands, faces, and necks washed each morning. The school prospered and numbers increased so that in 1867 additional accommodation was added. As a consequence of the Endowed Schools Commission of 1887, the infant and junior schools were handed over to the School Board and the Dollar Academy was able to concentrate on secondary education. It is now a secondary school recognised for direct grant. A new junior school was opened in 1937.

The St. Andrews Madras School owed its origin to Dr. Bell, who gave a sum of £50,000 to the town council in 1831 on condition that the old grammar-school should be transferred to the trustees of Dr. Bell and the monitorial system of instruction adopted.[1] In such cases, the town council lost most of its control over the school. The new acadamies had their own governors elected by the subscribers.

Perhaps one of the most widely known Scottish schools is Loretto, which rose to fame on account of the work of its great headmaster. Hely Hutchinson Almond is one of those names in the history of schools that one couples automatically with those of Butler, Arnold, Thring, and Sanderson. Loretto School is at the east end of the town of Musselburgh, near Edinburgh. The origin of its name is often a puzzle to English people, but it has quite a simple explanation. At the beginning of the 16th century, Thomas Doughtie of Musselburgh, who had left his home land to fight the Turks, decided to return to Scotland. On his way back he passed through Loretto, and from the famous shrine he carried back a statue of Our Lady of Loretto. The provost and council of Musselburgh granted him land on which he could erect a chapel for his image. The shrine of Our Lady of Loretto attracted numbers of pilgrims, but in 1544, when the Earl of Hertford (later Protector Somerset) invaded Scotland, the chapel was entirely destroyed. By 1550 it had been rebuilt, only to be razed to the ground when Scotland accepted the Reformed faith.

[1] The Cupar Academy was founded in a similar way by Dr. Bell.

The Loretto land came into the hands of Maitland of Lauderdale, who built his house on it. This was entirely rebuilt early in the 18th century and still forms part of the school. After several changes of ownership, the house was eventually bought in 1829 by the Rev. Dr. Langhorne, the Episcopal clergyman of Musselburgh, for the school which he had started and which had outgrown its premises. At first Loretto was a preparatory school. Pupils left before the age of fourteen to proceed to the Edinburgh Academy (founded 1824), or to the Merchiston Castle School, or to some English public school. It had, however, gained a good reputation. Almond was appointed mathematics master in 1857, but he soon left to become second master at Merchiston under Dr. Harvey, later Rector of the Edinburgh Academy. Almond purchased Loretto from the sons of Dr. Langhorne in 1862.

When Almond took over Loretto, he found the school almost extinct and he began his first year with only twelve of the old pupils and two new ones. His aim was not only to build up numbers, but to make Loretto a distinctive school, one that would compare with the public schools of England. The first few years were difficult and he was beset with financial worries, but eventually the fine training given by the school was recognised and its success was assured. Almond learnt much from the writings of J. S. Mill, Herbert Spencer, and John Ruskin. Many people spoke of him as unconventional, but this was a complete misjudgment of him. From Mill he had learnt that life should be guided by reason; in Spencer he found ideas that supported his own practice, and Ruskin had shown him the importance of teaching and practising the laws of health. Thus Almond chose physical education as the guiding principle in building up Loretto School. He was a firm believer in the virtues of cricket and football, and was the originator of the inter-school matches beween Loretto and such schools as Merchiston, the Edinburgh Academy, and Fettes College; and this was at the time when physical training and games were practically unknown in Scottish schools.

Almond was opposed to any form of coddling. In defiance of prevailing ideas he insisted that bedroom windows should be open at night, and he saw that all classrooms were well ventilated. The next step was regarded as scandalous by many of his contemporaries. Considering that boys wore too many clothes to be healthy, he introduced the custom of wearing knickers, and, later, shorts and open-necked shirts and going bare-headed. In hot weather, boys were allowed to take off their coats in school. Every class-room was furnished with a thermometer, and when the temperature reached 60° it was considered warm enough for a boy to discard his coat. All this, be it remembered, was entirely contrary to the conventions of the 1860's. Almond also paid attention to the feeding of the boys. In contrast to many of the boarding-schools of the period, he insisted that growing boys should have plenty of good food and that a variety in the diet was an acceptable thing.

Before long, numbers began to grow and pupils had to be accommodated in houses outside the main school-building. Like all great public-school masters, Almond regarded the school chapel as essential in the life of the school. He was a music lover, and as a result the choir-singing at Loretto gained a well-deserved reputation. The first chapel was an iron structure, but an appeal was launched and sufficient funds were acquired to build the present chapel in 1893. Almond instituted the anniversary of the founding of the chapel as Commemoration Day, and this became the most important festival of the school year. After Almond's death in 1903, a foundation scheme was organised. Funds were raised by subscription, and a company was formed and its directors became the governing body of the school. By this Loretto was placed upon a permanent footing and carried on under a regularly constituted board of governors.

Fettes College, in one respect, is unique amongst Scottish schools. It was opened in 1886 under the trust deed of Sir William Fettes, Lord Provost of Edinburgh. The trustees considered that the education of the poor was being well cared for by numerous hospital schools, and like Canon Woodard in England, they thought it was time that something was done for the children of the middle classes. Fettes is entirely a boarding-school, and it has a generous scheme of open scholarships and a number of foundation scholarships available for competition only by boys who have attended State-aided schools. The college is run on English public-school lines and its pupils are prepared for the examinations of the English universities.

The new developments resulted in what may be called a state of educational chaos. A fresh type of school had appeared which affected the older grammar-schools considerably. The curricula of schools were expanding in different directions and staffs began to increase. Unfortunately there was no clear idea about the aims of secondary education and experiments were being made in the dark. In many schools there was no controlling authority, but often several departments existed, each independent of the rest. Dundee High School presented a good example, with eight departments each having its independent headmaster, but no rector to exercise co-ordination. The universities, if they had been constituted on the English model, might have had some influence in controlling matters, but as they had no external examinations or even entrance examinations, their effect on the schools was negligible. Later we shall see that this state of affairs produced the Royal Commission on the Universities in 1826, and the University Act of 1858. Dr. Strong speaks of Dundee as "a little republic without a chief magistrate." At Edinburgh, the rector was in absolute control of the school, and in other towns the administration varied between these two extremes. As a rule there were no compulsory studies. Each subject taken was paid for separately and the parent made the choice for his child. It was quite possible for a pupil to attend a grammar-school for some subjects and a private-adventure school for others. The reader will recollect that in England the great problem was to bring some flexibility into the rigid classical curriculum of the public and grammar schools. In Scotland it was the opposite problem of introducing order and organisation into the chaos and confusion into which misguided, or rather unguided, zeal had led the grammar-schools.

One more type of institution calls for mention. In the matter of educational endowments, Scotland was very unfortunate as compared with England. Very little money or property was left to the Reformed Church to endow schools, and until later years few benefactors appeared to help the cause of education. Practically the only bequest of importance for education until the middle of the 17th century was a modest sum given to Dunfermline by Anne of Denmark, the queen of James VI. In 1639 George Hutcheson of Glasgow left land for the erection of a hospital for poor and aged men. Two years later his brother Thomas left money and land for the building of a "commodious and distinct house" associated with the hospital to house and educate twelve orphan boys who were sons of the citizens of Glasgow. Similar hospitals were founded in Aberdeen, Stirling, and other towns. Some of them were for the aged and infirm and only partially concerned with education. In course of time, the hospital system became obsolete and the trustees sought powers from Parliament for their reorganisation. As a result various Acts, including the Education Act of 1872, were passed which put the hospitals on a new footing, and they were able to play their part in the secondary education of

Scotland. Thus the Hutcheson Hospital at Glasgow came under the administration of the Hutcheson Trust which erected a number of first-class schools for boys and girls.

One of the most famous endowed institutions was the George Heriot Hospital at Edinburgh which originated from the bequest of George Heriot, a jeweller and goldsmith to James VI. He became a very wealthy man, and when James became King of England, he followed his sovereign to London. Heriot died in February 1623/4 after he had invested the bulk of his fortune in land in the city of Edinburgh. After several personal legacies, his will directed that the remainder of his property should go to "the Provost, Bailies, Ministers (of the Established Church), and the Town Council of Edinburgh, for founding and erecting an Hospital in that city; and for purchasing land to belong in perpetuity to the Institution, to be employed for the maintenance, relief, bringing up, and educating, as far as the means will allow, of so many poor fatherless boys, freemen's sons of the town of Edinburgh." [1] Heriot had evidently been impressed by Christ's Hospital and had made up his mind to found a similar institution in his native city. In a paper written a year before his decease, he set down his wish "And forsamekle as I intend be Goddis grace, in the zeale off pietie, to found and erect ane publick, pious, and charitable worke within the said burgh of Edinburgh, to the glorie of God, ffor the publick weill and ornament of the said burgh of Edinburgh, ffor the honour and dew regaird quhilk I have and bears to my native soyle, and mother citie of Edinburgh forsaid; and in imitatione of the publict, pious, and religious work foundat within the citie of London called Chrystis Hospital thair, to be callit in all tyme coming Hospital and Seminarie of Orphans." Building commenced in 1628, but the hospital was on such a grand scale that it was not until 1659 that it was ready for the accommodation of thirty boys.[2] By 1695 that number had increased to 130, who, when they were old enough, were sent to the High School.

This practice ceased in 1809 when schoolmasters were appointed for the hospital. In 1835 an Act of Parliament abolished the hospital system and schools for poor children were built in various

---

[1] Dr. F. W. Bedford. *History of George Heriot's Hospital*, p. 33, Bell and Bradfute, 1872.

[2] The architect is reported to have been Inigo Jones, and Archbishop Laud took great interest in the progress of the building. When it was partially completed, in 1650, it was used by Cromwell for accommodating the sick and wounded after the battle of Dunbar.

parts of the city. The Hospital Trust had erected sixteen schools accommodating 4,000 children by 1872.[1] As a consequence of the Colebrooke Commission of 1872, the Endowed Institutions (Scotland) Act was passed in 1878. This Act gave authority to governing bodies to obtain Provisional Orders for the better application of the funds of educational endowments. In 1882 the Educational Endowments (Scotland) Act constituted the Balfour Commission with compulsory powers to settle the endowments. In 1885 the governors of the Heriot Hospital obtained power to discontinue the elementary schools associated with the foundation and to establish George Heriot's Hospital School in the hospital building. This was extended and the governors established, with the Watt Institution and School of Art, the Heriot-Watt College to provide higher and technical education on the lines of the Technical College in Glasgow.

This sketch of the Heriot foundation has been given in some detail as an example of one of the largest Scottish endowed institutions. The burgh schools were very meagrely endowed. The Argyll Commission revealed that in 1868 nineteen burgh schools out of twenty-nine possessed no endowment, and the remainder had together £1,400. The town councils contributed from the Common Good annual payments towards the maintenance of the schools, which in the same year amounted to £5,600. The Edinburgh High School had one of the largest endowments, £513. At this time the endowments of Eton were £20,569 from landed property, the gift of thirty-seven livings worth £10,000 a year, and a probable additional income from lands of £10,000 a year. The Commissioners also drew attention to the fact that the foundations of Eton and Winchester alone were producing a greater revenue than all the burgh schools and universities of Scotland taken together. The lack of endowments meant that the Scottish schools were almost entirely dependent on the grants of the town councils and on fees.

The problems of Scottish education were investigated by the Argyll Commission which reported in 1867. The Commissioners inquired into all types of schools in Scotland and thus the inquiry corresponded "to the Newcastle, Clarendon, and Taunton Commissions rolled into one," as Graham Balfour puts it.[2] The Taunton Commission was sitting in England at the same time and Mr. Fearon

---

[1] In 1854 Dr. F. W. Bedford, headmaster of Leeds Boys' Modern School, was appointed headmaster of Heriot's Hospital and Inspector of the Heriot Foundation Schools.

[2] Graham Balfour. *Educational System of Great Britain and Ireland*, p. 136, Clarendon Press, 1898.

was sent to Scotland to investigate conditions in the burgh schools and compare them with English grammar-schools.

The conclusions of the Argyll Commission as regards elementary education were somewhat similar to those of the Newcastle Commission in England and were characterised by the same note of optimism. In the *Second Report* (elementary schools) the Commissioners drew attention to the deficiencies they had discovered. In the rural districts only 1,133 schools were parish schools, out of 4,451. The remainder were proprietary and private-adventure schools, many of which were hopelessly inefficient. (Pp. clxxiv to clxxvi.)

The Minutes of the Committee of Council containing the reports of H.M.I.s show that these schools were very similar to the type existing in England, *e.g.* "It is difficult to give any adequate notion of the character and condition of most of the adventure School-houses. These Schools are generally taught in apartments of a dwelling-house. The dimensions are contracted; there are no proper means of ventilation; the floor is generally earthen and damp; the walls are frequently unplastered and dirty; the forms and desks are of the poorest description, and frequently incapable of accommodating all the pupils. Little attention is given to neatness and cleanliness of the apartment; the furniture is seldom tastefully and conveniently arranged." (*Minutes*, 1842-3, p. 689.) "These Schools are generally held in small ill-ventilated apartments, unfurnished with the necessary apparatus. The course of instruction includes nothing but reading, writing, and arithmetic; and these are most imperfectly taught. Neither the general character, nor the training and attainments of the teachers, fit them for the discharge of such important duties. . . . The fees were generally paid weekly. This arrangement has been rendered necessary by the improvident habits, by the ignorance or the indifference, by the dissoluteness or the poverty of the parents." (*Minutes*, 1844, Vol. II, p. 326.)

The Commissioners found that most of the schools were in charge of women. The men teachers had often been "parochial teachers at some time, dismissed or superannuated, or they laboured under some physical infirmity, lame of leg, or of an arm, or, as in one case, lame of both legs, or paralysed, or hopelessly crippled, and in the few instances where they were physically competent to teach, they generally had other pursuits to follow." (P. xxxvii.) Their general conclusion was that "for the sake of all concerned, teachers and taught alike, the sooner private adventure schools for the lowest classes ceased to exist the better." (P. li.)   These extracts should be compared with similar ones from the Newcastle Commission given in Chapter vii.

The Commission considered that the parochial school system of Scotland was now no longer adequate; there was lack of organisation and supervision by a competent authority and the only remedy was for the Education Department to take control of the parish schools, and then to fill the gaps by rate-aided schools.   It was thought that this could be accomplished by a 2d. rate in rural districts and a 2½d. rate in Glasgow and the large towns.

In the *Third Report,* which dealt with the burgh and middle-class schools, the Commissioners thought that on the whole secondary education was in a satisfactory condition, but that it required and was capable of amendment. (P. xviii.) They found that thirty-three burgh schools existed, twenty-three academies, and thirty-one parochial schools which carried out the functions of burgh schools.   These were satisfactorily distributed so that only three burghs, Kinghorn, Oban, and Portobello, were without secondary schools.   In addition there were a number of private schools, some being day-schools such as the Edinburgh Institution, some boarding-schools such as Loretto, and others day and boarding schools such as the Aberdeen Gymnasium.   Altogether 15,946 scholars were on the roll of these schools and nearly ninety per cent were in attendance, and the schools provided instruction for more than two-thirds of the Scottish middle-class population.   This represented a proportion of one in 205 receiving secondary education, as compared with one in 249 in Prussia, one in 570 in France, and one in 1,300 in England. (P. viii.) The slender endowments of Scottish secondary schools has already been mentioned, so that the sum of £42,000 per annum was paid in fees by the parents. (P. xvi.)

The prevalence of mixed schools was noted and the Commissioners gave their opinion that "the influence of Mixed schools of boys and girls is not beneficial from a social point of view ; but, intellectually speaking, there is a good deal to recommend in such schools.   There seems to be no reason why girls should not have the same educational advantages as boys, as they appear to make quite as much of what opportunities they have, and in some branches they are distinctly superior to the boys.   If they are taught on the same system, and by the same masters, they should have distinct schoolrooms, and be kept separate from the boys, and under their own lady-superintendent." (P. xiii.) The mid-19th-century point of view is very apparent in this passage.[1]

Pupils came very early to school and left very early. About fifty-six per cent were under twelve and sixteen per cent under eight. In the private schools, pupils came later and remained later. Scholars were extremely hard worked and the Commissioners reckoned that they put in twice the number of hours per week as the pupils at Eton and Winchester. The average worked out at nine hours a day for a five-day week. The Commissioners were of opinion that a good deal of confusion existed as regards the curriculum. In some schools the subjects of instruction were elementary, in others definitely beyond that standard, and, in still others, a mixture of both. The curriculum varied considerably in different parts of Scotland. "Parents look upon education as a means to an immediate end. The great object is to get a lad placed in some situation in which he will gain pecuniary benefit, and keep himself at as early an age as possible. If he can do this by means of classics, as at Aberdeen, they will teach him classics; if by writing, they will teach him writing. If, along with his writing, he can pick up a little Latin and a little French, so much the better, but it is not essential. This is the view of education which is adopted by parents of the middle class in Scotland; and those subjects of instruction which conduce to this end are most appreciated by them." (P. 116.)

The introduction of the Revised Code was not recommended since "the teachers will be compelled to bring their inferior scholars up to the standards required by the Code, and so will have little time to devote to the higher branches. . . . It is of vital importance that every encouragement should be given to that class of young men who, since the foundation of the Parish schools, have risen to eminence through their medium. The number of distinguished men who have risen up in Scotland through these schools and our universities has long been the glory of this country and the wonder and envy of other countries, and it would be a matter of infinite regret if this national feature were to be obliterated." (P. 146.)

They therefore recommended the foundation of district or supplementary schools, and a scholarship system to these schools and to the universities to complete the system and so enable scholars of ability to proceed from the elementary schools to a university career. In addition it was recommended that Treasury

[1] Compare this statement with that of Mr. Fearon which is quoted on p. 535.

grants should be given to parish schools where the schoolmaster carried out the function of a burgh schoolmaster in giving higher education to his pupils. The link between the parochial schools, the burgh schools, and the university, was so essential a feature of Scottish education that it should be maintained, supplemented, and strengthened.

Other recommendations were that the Committee of Council should devise a scheme for the superannuation of schoolmasters, make grants for building, extensions, and repairs, subject to a report from H.M.I., that the tenure of the schoolmaster *ad vitam aut culpam* should be placed on a more explicit basis, and that, apart from these recommendations, no further grants should be made nor any other alterations in the management or superintendence of burgh schools. Finally, the statutes and rules of hospital foundations should be examined, and with the approval of Parliament, alterations with a view to the extension of education should be made.

The Commissioners spoke highly of the private schools which catered for the middle classes and which should not be confused with the "wretched seminaries" for the elementary education which had been roundly condemned in the *Second Report*. One of the reasons given for their efficiency was that most of the teachers had been trained in normal colleges. Also, they were not afraid of publicity, but threw open their doors to teachers and parents. These schools filled an important place in the national scheme by supplementing the education given in the burgh schools. The standard of the private schools in Edinburgh was exceptionally high and it was noted that they had separate departments for girls which carried education to a higher point than the boys' departments. This was because the boys were transferred at about the age of eleven to the high school and academy, but the girls remained until about fourteen or fifteen years of age. The Edinburgh Institution was described in detail in the Special Reports of the Commissioners. (Pp. 313-18.) The school had accommodation for 949 scholars and its fees were moderate. The staff was highly qualified and the object of the instruction was the preparation of the pupils for university entrance, the professions, and business appointments. The general report on the school was that a very good liberal education was supplied at a moderate cost and that there was a sensible earnestness about the teachers and scholars that could not fail to have good results. Similar schools existed in other large towns, *e.g.* the Gymnasium, Old Aberdeen, and Fordyce Academy, Banff. The prospectus of a typical private academy in Edinburgh in 1856 is printed on the opposite page.[1]

Mr. Fearon's report is interesting since he had been appointed as Assistant Commissioner under the Taunton Commission investigating conditions in the English endowed schools and from his experience he was well qualified to draw a comparison between them and the Scottish secondary schools of the period. He thought that the English endowed schools made poor showing in comparison with the Scottish burgh schools. At the conclusion of his report he asked, "Why are these nine Scotch burgh schools so well attended? And why is such good work done in most of them? Because they are constantly stimulated from without. Public feeling, public demand for the things which they produce, make them work; and public interest in the result of their work helps to make that result successful. . . . The mere fact, for example, that 390 children are attending as day scholars at the burgh school of Ayr, a town with less than the population of Reading or Canterbury, is in itself, irrespectively of the quality of the education afforded in that burgh school, a most healthy symptom. Where in England could we produce such an instance of interest and confidence in a public school among the middle classes of our rural

---

[1] The following extracts throw some light upon conditions in Scottish schools during this period:—

(1) Extract from a letter of Mr. T. Christie describing the John Watson's Institution to a friend in England, 30th October, 1855.

"Before leaving Scotland I was appointed to the post which I at present hold in John Watson's Institution. It is only an assistancy, salary £50 besides Bed, board and washing, but such Board as would cost me I should think £50 a year. . . . A few words now as to our School. It numbers 58 boys and nearly 50 girls, both being taught together. We are not at a loss for room, having no fewer than six schoolrooms, besides a chapel capable of holding 6 or 8 hundred, where I have very often to read and pray. There are three resident male teachers, besides visiting Masters for vocal, and instrumental music and dancing. I am sorry to say that the scholars are in a very low educational condition. The new set of teachers, I think, are bringing about a change for the better."

(2) Extract from letter of Dr. Bedford in reply to a teacher seeking a post in Scotland.

George Heriot's Hospital,
Edinburgh.
March 20th, 1855.

". . . Parochial teachers in Scotland are very heavily worked, I hear, but Mr. Christie knows more about them than I do. Many clever young men are glad to get some 50£ or 60£ a year. In a letter which I wrote . . . yesterday I stated that *good* educational appointments are rare in Scotland. I think Mr. Christie will support me in that opinion. . . .

F. W. BEDFORD."

ENGLISH, GEOGRAPHY, HISTORY, &c.

Mr CHRISTIE will open advanced Classes for ENGLISH, &c., at 12 QUEEN STREET, *on Monday, 3d March.*

The Young Gentlemen will meet from 9 till 11 o'clock, and the Young Ladies from 1 till 3 o'clock. Fee, 15s. per Quarter.

Extract from Testimonial in Mr CHRISTIE's favour from Dr BED-FORD, House Governor of Heriot's Hospital :—

"*For four years* Mr CHRISTIE *was one of my most valued Colleagues, when I was Head Master of the Schools with which he is now connected.*

"*As a Gentleman, a Christian, a Scholar, and a Teacher, he stood very high in my estimation.*

"*I have seldom observed Classes so well conducted, and maintaining so superior a tone, as those under* Mr CHRISTIE's *tuition.*"

WRITING, ARITHMETIC, BOOK-KEEPING, & ALGEBRA.

Mr WATSON will resume his MORNING CLASSES at 12 QUEEN STREET, from 7 till 8, *on Monday, 3d March.* Other Classes from 11 till 1, and from 3 till 5 o'clock.

THE LADIES AND GENTLEMEN ARE TAUGHT IN SEPARATE ROOMS.

The next General Quarter Day being *on Saturday 1st March,* Mr WATSON and Mr CHRISTIE will be in attendance at the Class Rooms from 11 till 3 o'clock, to answer enquiries, enrol Pupils, and receive Fees.

Specimens of Penmanship by Mr WATSON's Pupils will be exhibited.

Classes for LATIN, FRENCH, GERMAN, DRAWING, PIANOFORTE, NEEDLEWORK, &c., at different hours, to suit Pupils attending other Classes.

QUEEN STREET ACADEMY,
    February 20, 1856.

population?" [1]   His advice concerning English secondary schools
was, "Let the grammar schools, like the Scotch burgh schools,
assimilate themselves to public requirements; popularise their
education, and condescend to consider things as they are, as a first
practical step towards making things as they should be." [2]

Earlier in his report, Mr. Fearon contrasted the work of
the Scottish burgh school with that of the English grammar-
school in a passage which is well worth quoting in full.
"I wish that I could picture to the Commissioners the interior
of such an English grammar school as I have often seen it
both in town and country at about 3 o'clock p.m. The long room
empty or vacant in the middle, with the massive old fashioned desks
ranged round the walls. The three seats for the teachers, carefully
graduated in size ; the largest and most imposing for the master
at the top of the room; the second at the bottom for the usher;
and at one side a smaller desk, inferior in comfort and dignity,
for the occasional French master. The 30 boys divided nominally
into six forms, of which the sixth contains two or three boys,
boarders, who are reading 'Greek Play,' and one of whom is said to
be preparing to try for an open scholarship at the university. The
fifth form perhaps, 'vacant just at present,' and the bulk of the
scholars in the lower forms classified according to their different
degrees. The master well clothed and fed, lounging in his chair of
state, 'hearing the sixth form,' who sit or lean round him, in every
variety of posture that can indicate indifference and weariness.
The usher, an ignorant untrained drudge ... wearing the listless and
depressed look of one who has known or has been vainly hoping
for better days. The whole scene one of sleepy monotonous
existence; resembling rather a gathering of priests and worshippers
of Morpheus than the Muses.

"And the contrast between such a scene, and that presented
by the class-room of a Scotch burgh school; crowded with 60
or 100 boys *and girls,* all nearly of an age, seated in rows at desks
or benches, but all placed in the order of merit, with their keen
thoughtful faces turned towards the master, watching his every
look and every gesture, in the hopes of winning a place in the class,
and having good news to bring home to their parents at tea time.
The *dux* seated at the head of the class, wearing perhaps a medal;
the object of envy and yet pride to all his fellows; fully conscious
both of the glory and the insecurity of his position; and taught,

[1] *Schools Inquiry Commission,* Vol. VI, p. 60.   [2] *Ibid.,* p. 61.

by experience of many falls, the danger of relaxing his efforts for one moment. In front of this eager animated throng, stands the master, gaunt, muscular, and time-worn, poorly clad, and plain in manner and speech, but with the dignity of a ruler in his gestures and the fire of an enthusiast in his eye, never sitting down, but standing always in some commanding position before the class; full of movement, vigour, and energy; so thoroughly versed in his author or his subject that he seldom requires to look at the text-book, which is open in his left hand, while in his right he holds the chalk or the pointer, ever ready to illustrate from map or blackboard, or perhaps flourishes the ancient 'taws' with which in former days he used to reduce disorderly newcomers to discipline and order. The whole scene is one of vigorous action and masterly force, forming the greatest possible contrast with the monotonous, unmethodical, ill-seconded working of the English teacher." [1]

Mr. Fearon did not agree with the Argyll Commission's opinion on mixed schools. He was convinced that "the presence of the girls both civilises and stimulates the boys, and that the opportunity of working with the boys strengthens the judgment and braces the mental faculties of the girls." [2]

The reports were submitted to Parliament and after two unsuccessful attempts, in 1869 and 1871, to secure an Education Act, Lord Advocate Young succeeded in obtaining the passage of the momentous Act of 1872. The authors of the Act had before them the lessons of the English Elementary Education Act of 1870, and they were determined to produce an enactment of a more thorough and comprehensive nature. Hence the Act of 1872 was concerned with Scottish education as a whole and not merely elementary education. The Act was so great a milestone in Scottish educational progress and marked so fully the distinction between the old and the new, that its consideration is postponed to the chapter dealing with the modern period in Scottish education.

During the 17th century, the universities suffered greatly from the disturbed state of the country due to the continual strife between the Presbyterians and the Episcopalians. It speaks much for the keen interest in higher education of the nation as a whole, that they were able to continue their existence and identity. The outstanding figure in connection with the universities of this period is Bishop Forbes, who in the early part of the 17th century did

[1] *Schools Inquiry Commission*, Vol. VI, pp. 51-2.   [2] *Ibid.*, p. 57.

much to encourage the development of Aberdeen. He established the Chair of theology in 1620, to which his son was appointed, and he gathered round him the famous group of scholars and divines known as the Six Aberdeen Doctors.

To understand the Scottish universities at this time, we must realise that they were to a much greater extent the universities of the people than were those of England. As Graham Balfour said, the university system of Scotland differed at almost every point from the universities of England. However, they were similar to the English universities in one respect: they reached their lowest position during the latter part of the 17th and the first half of the 18th century. The invigorating spirit of the Renaissance and Reformation had exhausted itself and there was a general retrograde movement towards mediaevalism. The faculty of arts dominated the universities, and other faculties such as law, medicine, and theology, had to be content with a subordinate position. The practice of regenting became universal and continued through the first half of the 18th century.

Each regent taught his students, during a course of three or four years, Greek, ethics, pneumatics,[1] logic, mathematics, and physics. The regenting system first came to an end at Edinburgh in 1708. At Glasgow it was abolished in 1727, at St. Andrews in 1747, but although Marischal College abandoned it in 1757, it was retained at King's College until the end of the century.

The burgh schools were justly proud of their Latinity, but at the universities the standards in Greek and Latin were very low and there was no professor of Latin until the beginning of the 18th century. The first professor of Latin (Humanity) was inducted at Glasgow in 1704 at a salary of £20 per annum. The special Chair of Latin at Edinburgh dates from 1708. The opposition to the teaching of Latin in the universities came from the burgh schools, whose masters thought it would lessen the number of their pupils, and therefore their fees.

The teaching in those days cannot have been much more advanced than that given at the grammar-schools. This is evident from the early age at which many students entered. Thomas Reid was twelve when he entered Marischal College and Dr. Chalmers became a student of St. Andrews at an even earlier age. As late as 1830, the royal commission reported students as young as

[1] This study was combined with philosophy and dealt with the nature of angels. of the human soul, and the being and attributes of God.

eleven at Aberdeen and the average age of entrants at Edinburgh was fourteen and a half. There was no entrance examination, and the majority of the students entered the universities without any intention of proceeding to a degree. They selected their own subject for study, and, provided the professor was willing to take them, they attended the course until it suited them to leave. Those who remained to graduate often did so at an age as early as sixteen. Many came to the university ignorant of Latin or Greek and elementary classes in these languages had to be started. All university lectures were dictated in Latin until 1729. In this year Professor Hutcheson of Glasgow broke away from tradition and began to deliver his lectures in English. His example was followed very slowly, and as late as 1776 a student who studied Church History at St. Andrews for three years, left on record that during the whole of that time he never heard one word of English from his professor. During the 17th century the university authorities encouraged students to live in chambers in the colleges, but this custom began to disappear later, partly owing to the increased number of students, which became too great to be accommodated in college, but more particularly because the majority of the students could not afford the moderate charges of the common table. "The great majority of the lads were extremely poor, and lived in mean garrets in the wynds; some were so badly off that old Kirk-Session records mention little doles of a few pence given to lads to help them on their way as they travelled to college. When they went to their classes in October they often took with them a supply of oat and barley meal, which with occasional supplies from home, lasted by careful stinting till the Session was over in May." [1]

If the majority of the students were poor, the salaries paid to the professors were also extremely small. The principal of Marischal College, Aberdeen, received a salary of £60 per annum. The principal of Edinburgh in 1703 received £90, but the principal of Glasgow was given £60 a year and board at the common table. The four regents also shared the table and received a salary of £25 each. The professor of mathematics at King's College, Aberdeen, in the early part of the century, had an income of £10 and board at the common table. His salary was paid out of a tax levied on the ale sold in the town, so that in his case the teaching of mathematics to university students depended on the amount of

[1] H. G. Graham. *The Social Life of Scotland in the Eighteenth Century*, A. and C. Black, 1909.

beer consumed by the populace. Later in the century the salaries of the teaching staffs were roughly doubled. In addition to his official salary, a professor received fees from his students, so that the total income of a professor teaching a large number of students might approximate to £150 a year. Professor Reid, in 1764, as professor of moral philosophy at Glasgow, received a salary of £50. He wrote: "I have touched £70 in fees, and may possibly make out the hundred this session." The cost of living was low, otherwise it would have been impossible for any professor to live on his salary. Small wonder, then, that a university Chair was sought mainly as a stepping-stone to a more lucrative appointment in the Church or as a private tutor to the son of a nobleman.[1]

The condition of the universities slowly improved during the 18th century, which was one of the most brilliant periods in the history of the intellectual life of Scotland. One has to recall such names as Francis Hutcheson, David Hume, Thomas Reid, Adam Smith, James Beattie, Principal Robertson, and many others of European reputation, to realise that in spite of the adverse conditions there was a strong intellectual life in the Scottish universities. A change parallel to that in the burgh schools was taking place. The dominance of the arts faculty was challenged and theology, law, science, and medicine came into their own. The progress of the last-named study was remarkable.

In the early days of the universities, both at Edinburgh and at Glasgow, the medical profession was associated with the barbers, e.g. the Incorporation of Surgeons and Barbers in Edinburgh and the Faculty of Physicians and Surgeons in Glasgow, which included barbers. The barbers not only cut hair but cut veins and arteries in the process of bleeding a person. Hence it was necessary for them to have some understanding of the body. The physicians and surgeons despised their more humble brethren and during the 17th

---

[1] J. Grant, in *History of the Burgh and Parish Schools in Scotland*, gives in an appendix many examples of the salaries and fees paid in the schools. Thus at Edinburgh in 1562, the master received £80 yearly and fees—"so large a salary is given because of the great profit of his school in London, and being very learned in Greek and Latin." But in 1835 the rector's salary was £33 6s. 8d. and each of the four classical masters received £20. The teachers of writing, arithmetic, and mathematics had no salary and depended entirely on fees. Kirkcudbright, which may be taken as an example of a school in a smaller burgh, paid its master £30 in 1787. His assistant received £10. In 1788 the writing and mathematical master received £20 and the following fees from each pupil taking the subject: English, 2s. 6d.; Latin, 2s. 6d.; writing and arithmetic, 1s. 6d.; first six books of Euclid, practical geometry and plane trigonometry, 15s.; navigation, 15s.; geometry, 10s. 6d.; bookkeeping, 15s. These fees applied to burgesses' children only. Others paid higher fees.

century the doctors and the barbers tended to fall apart, and finally in 1727 the two crafts separated. The red and blue stripes on the barber's pole are a reminder of the close association between surgeons and barbers; the red stripes representing arterial blood and the blue that from the veins.

From this date the medical schools of Glasgow and Edinburgh developed rapidly and, thanks to a succession of eminent teachers, they obtained a well-earned reputation. In 1824 a dispute arose in the University of Edinburgh over the introduction of midwifery as a subject for graduation in the medical faculty. The Senate objected to its introduction, but the town council, who were the legal masters of the college, insisted. They proposed a visitation of the college and this caused the Senate to petition for a royal commission, which was appointed in 1826 and took for its field all the Scottish universities. The recommendations of the commission did not receive immediate attention and it was not until 1858 that the University Act was passed.

The Act reconstructed the government of the universities. Previously, the governing body of a university had been the Senate, which consisted of the professors, who were both the teachers and the governors of their institution. The Act created two new bodies, the University Court and the General Council. Thus in Edinburgh, the former consisted of the Rector, the Principal (in Edinburgh, the Lord Provost; in Glasgow, the Dean of Faculties), and four Assessors. The Court appointed the professors, except those nominated by the Crown, and was responsible for the revenues, the regulation of fees, and the internal arrangements of the university. The Council was a larger body consisting of the Chancellor, the members of the Court, the professors, and graduates. Its meeting took place twice yearly and it discussed measures which had been approved by the Senate or the Court. The Senate still retained considerable power, especially in matters concerned with instruction.

The effects of the Act were soon apparent. The basis of the government of the universities had been broadened and the inclusion of the graduates on the Council had considerable influence in bringing university studies into line with the demands of the outside world. The net result was a large increase in both students and graduates. The salaries of the professors were increased and opportunities were given for bringing in lecturers to assist the professors.

Edinburgh, as the original cause of the royal commission, received special treatment. The patronage, which had been in the hands of the town council, was now transferred to seven curators, four nominated by the town council and three by the University Court. The Rector was to be elected by the students and the Chancellor by the graduates and the General Council. To carry out the provisions of the Act, an executive commission was appointed with Lord Justice Clerk Inglis as chairman.

The commission abolished the degree of B.A. and substituted the M.A. as the first degree, to be taken in three stages. Seven subjects were obligatory for the ordinary course in arts: Latin, Greek, mathematics, natural philosophy, logic, moral philosophy, and rhetoric. Honours might be taken in one of four departments: classics, philosophy, mathematics, or science (geology, zoology, and chemistry). In the first three there were two classes of honours, but only one in science. English literature was included under philosophy. Graduates were qualified to become members of the General Council. The elementary classes in Latin and Greek, instituted as a concession in the 18th century to students who were without classical scholarship, were continued as a provisional measure. It was not considered advisable to break the link with the parochial schools in virtue of which bright pupils might pass direct to the university. In pursuance of this policy, the commission did not insist upon the establishment of an entrance examination at the time, but, when secondary education had been reorganised, a Preliminary Examination for university entrance was enforced in 1892.

In conclusion, one very important development should be mentioned. The Andrew Bell Trustees, from 1830 onwards, had been granting money for the building of schools, but after the Education Act of 1872 they found themselves with a surplus of £18,000. With this money they endowed Chairs in The History, Theory, and Practice of Education, at Edinburgh and St. Andrews in 1876. These were the first Chairs in education to be established in Great Britain. The first professor of education at Edinburgh was S. S. Laurie, who in his long life contributed much to the university and to the cause of education in general.

CHAPTER XV

EDUCATION IN SCOTLAND — 1872-1949

The Education Act of 1872 represented such a radical change in the Scottish educational outlook that it will be of value to consider certain broad aspects of this development before examining the details of the Act. The outstanding feature of the Act was the substitution of State for Church control in education. Although this might seem so much at variance with Scottish tradition as it had existed for centuries, it was in fact only a particular instance of the general political changes which were affecting the whole of Europe. This may be summed up by saying that European countries had recognised the importance of education in the secular life of man, and this conclusion was connected with the growing feeling of dissatisfaction with the interference of the clergy in secular affairs. These changes had taken place in Prussia and France early in the 19th century, and the State had assumed responsibility for education in these countries. In Britain the new influences were somewhat later in development. The religious revival of the late 18th century, *e.g.* Methodism and the Evangelical movement, and the general acceptance by all classes of the doctrine of *laissez-faire,* were mainly responsible for the delay. These factors were not so influential in Scotland as in England, with the result that the assumption of control by the State was delayed in the latter country. The Elementary Education Act of 1870 was a measure designed to "fill the gaps" and not to supersede, but rather to supplement, the efforts of the religious denominations. In Scotland, as we shall see, it was otherwise.

The logical mind of the Scot saw quite clearly that if education was to concern the whole of the people, then it must be an affair of the State rather than the Church. This conclusion was strengthened by the fact that after the Disruption of 1843 there was no longer one national Church. In other ways the Church had shown that it was not able to provide an efficient system of elementary and secondary education for the whole of the nation. The Church system had taken the parish for a unit, but in the larger towns the rapid growth in population of the city parishes was breaking down the parochial system. Although the Act of 1872 endeavoured to save as much of the parochial system as possible, this proved one of its weaknesses and eventually the country adopted the county organisation. The schools, when under the control of the Church, had concentrated on giving a liberal education, but the development of industry on a large scale demanded attention to scientific and technical training which the small and often isolated parochial school was unable to supply.

The transition from Church to State control was accomplished with comparative ease because there was little in the school system which had been specifically Presbyterian apart from the assent to the Confession of Faith, and this had already been abolished by the Act of 1861. The religious instruction in the schools, as we shall see, was not changed under the School Boards, and the parochial unit of administration was continued.

The Education (Scotland) Act of 1872 was a much more comprehensive measure than the English Elementary Education Act of 1870. The latter was concerned only with elementary education, but the Scottish Act dealt with both elementary and secondary education. Its object was "to amend and extend the provisions of the Law of Scotland on the subject of Education," and in the preamble its aim was further defined as that the means "of procuring efficient education for their children may be furnished and made available to the whole people of Scotland." The preamble also declared that the religious basis of education was to be retained. "And whereas it has been the custom in the public schools of Scotland to give instruction in religion to children whose parents did not object to the instruction so given, but with liberty to parents, without forfeiting any of the other advantages of the schools to elect that their children should not receive such instruction, and it is expedient that the managers of public schools shall be at liberty to continue the said custom."

The Act created a central authority for education and representative local authorities for administrative purposes. The former was to be the Scotch Education Department which was to consist of "the Lords of any Committee of the Privy Council appointed by Her Majesty on education in Scotland," but to assist in putting the Act into operation, an interim Board of Education of five members sat in Edinburgh. When it came to an end in 1878, its duties devolved on the Scotch Education Department. The president of the Committee of the Privy Council was the Lord President of the

Council. The Committee was given compulsory powers over the local authorities and was responsible for the administration and distribution of the parliamentary grants for education in accordance with an annual Code submitted for the approval of Parliament. The Education Department had authority to conduct an annual inspection of schools and could legislate through Minutes, which, when approved by Parliament, had the same force as an Act. The chief executive officer was the Permanent Secretary, who was directly responsible to the head of the Department.

Local administration was conducted by 984 popularly elected School Boards which corresponded on the whole with the existing parish or burgh areas. The minimum membership of a School Board was five, and the maximum fifteen. All existing schools established by previous Acts of Parliament were transferred to the School Boards and the authority of the Church over these schools was abolished. Thus all schools, parish or burgh, whether academies, high schools, or grammar-schools, were to be handed over to the School Boards. These schools had been the property of the heritors, presbyteries, town councils, and other bodies, but none of these sought or received compensation for the transfer of their buildings. If they did not wish to transfer their schools (as was the case with the Roman Catholics and Episcopalians), they had to maintain them at their own expense. Schools administered by the School Boards were termed "public schools"; the remainder, "voluntary schools."

The first duty of the newly elected School Boards was to survey their districts and estimate the number of school places required to meet the deficiencies. They had the power of levying a local rate and of borrowing money for enlarging existing schools or building new ones. The School Boards also fixed the amount of the school fees, appointed or dismissed teachers, and paid them their salaries. There was as yet no statutory salary scale. In accordance with a conscience clause, the Boards decided upon the kind of religious education to be given and were responsible for receiving and distributing the parliamentary grants paid to them by the Education Department. Since the grants were paid to the School Boards according to the Minutes of the Department, the authority of the Department was assured. All children under thirteen were compelled to attend school, and parents who were unable to pay school fees could apply to have them paid by the Parochial Board. Parents who did not fulfil their duty by seeing that their children received elementary education in reading, writing, and arithmetic, were liable to penalties.

The public schools consisted of two types, State-aided elementary schools and Higher Class Public Schools. The latter included most of the former burgh schools which, unlike the English grammar-schools, now came under the authority of the School Boards. These schools were defined by the Act as those which gave instruction in Latin, Greek, modern languages, mathematics and natural science, and the higher branches of knowledge generally. They received no grant from the Education Department but had to depend upon fees, revenues from endowments, and sums paid from the Common Good. Fees were the chief means of support, and since the Scottish secondary fees had always been moderate, they sufficed to pay only the teachers' salaries. Consequently, for some years the Higher Class Public Schools had a difficult struggle for existence, until in 1892 they were able to share in the benefits of the Education and Local Taxation Act, by which the sum of £60,000 was transferred to the Department to aid secondary education.[1]

It will be seen that although the Act attempted to define a higher-class public school, it made no effort either to define secondary instruction or to limit it to any one type of school. As we saw in the earlier chapter on Scottish education, many parish schools had been providing what was in fact a secondary education for their brighter pupils, and had sent some of them direct to the universities. It was the intention of the Act to encourage this. Clause 67 provided that the Scotch Education Department was to take due care in the construction of its Minutes, not to lower "the standard of education which now exists in the public schools." Thus secondary education could be given both in the Higher Class Public Schools and in the State-aided elementary schools.

In addition, a third type of school, the Higher Class School, was recognised. These schools comprised certain endowed, private, or subscription, schools such as the Academies of Edinburgh and Glasgow, St. Andrews Madras College, the Dollar Institution, Fettes College, Merchiston, and Loretto. Some of these schools eventually came under the management of the School Boards, but the

---

[1] The Elementary Education Act of 1891 for England and Wales provided for a fee-grant of 10s. per year for each child in average attendance. If the managers accepted the fee-grant, no fees were to be charged for children between the ages of three and fifteen. Scotland was entitled to an "equivalent grant" which was applied to assist secondary education in the way described in the text. Certain secondary schools, as in England, were receiving grants from the Science and Art Department, South Kensington.

endowed schools increased in number, and owing to the gifts of wealthy benefactors and to Acts permitting the "diversion" of hospital endowments, they achieved a financially secure position. One weakness of the Act lay in the lack of provision of a common point of contact between the three types of school in which secondary education could be given.

A further defect was the omission of guidance with regard to the aim of secondary education. One might have thought that some reference would have been made to the relations between the secondary schools and the universities, but the only reference to the latter was in Clause 62 which was concerned with the qualifications of teachers. The consequence was that secondary education was left in a state of utter chaos. As in England, there seemed to be no clear ideas about the aim and scope of the secondary school.

Many of the School Boards were responsible for such small districts that they were not adequate to carry out the ever-increasing duties which subsequent Minutes of the Department thrust upon them.[1] Nevertheless, for the first few years there was much enthusiasm shown by the new local authorities and the building and enlargement of schools proceeded rapidly. A modified version of the system of Payment by Results was still in operation and continued for some years, with the effect of narrowing the work and outlook of the elementary schools.

In 1885 the Secretary for Scotland Act reorganised the Scotch Education Department. The Secretary for Scotland became vice-president of the Scottish Education Department. This followed the English precedent of 1856, when the Lord President of the Privy Council became president of the English Education Department. This in effect made the Secretary for Scotland the head of the educational system of Scotland. The secretary of the Education Department was responsible to the Secretary for Scotland, and this ensured that the Department was under the control of Parliament. The first secretary of the Department was Mr. (later Sir) Henry Craik. He

[1] "That there were so many small School Boards may come as a surprise to educationists of to-day. A few cases, chosen at random, are worth recording:

School Board	Total Population of Parish	School Board	Total Population of Parish
Stirling (Landward) ..	85	Cranshaws (Berwick) ..	142
Morham (Haddington)	204	Glendevan (Perth) ..	105
Dolphinton (Lanark) ..	231	Moonzie (Fife) ..	154
Lynne (Peebles) ..	174	Lunan (Forfar) ..	248"

Quoted from the *Centenary Handbook of the Educational Institute of Scotland*, Edinburgh, 1946.

was an extremely able administrator and his previous experience as a senior examiner of the old Department had shown him the needs of Scottish education.   One of his first actions was to rid the schools of any traces of Payment by Results.   His new Code in 1886 contained many changes.   It abolished the examination in the three R's in all classes below Standard III, restricted Specific Subjects[1] to classes above Standard V, and enriched the curriculum by making English, history, geography, elementary science, and drawing, class subjects in all elementary schools.   In 1890 individual examinations were abolished in the senior classes of State-aided schools and at the same time the number of Specific Subjects was reduced. Craik next turned his attention to freeing elementary schools from fees.   By 1893 elementary education was free throughout Scotland for children from three to fifteen years of age.   It was due to Craik that Scotland obtained her share of the money which came through the Education and Local Taxation Act.   The four universities were given £30,000, and, as was mentioned above, £60,000 was assigned for the encouragement of secondary education.   A Secondary Education Committee was established in each county and the five largest towns for the distribution of the grant.   In this way he anticipated the Act of 1918.

Although the Church of Scotland and the Free Church had handed over all their schools to the Department, Roman Catholic and Episcopalian schools remained outside the national system. The Education Department eventually acquired a substantial measure of control over the denominational schools.   This was accomplished through the powers given to the Department to inspect all schools in order to determine how far existing schools were adequate for the educational needs of particular districts.   In addition, schools which satisfied the requirements of the Department were able to receive grants.   This meant that the denominational schools had to bring their buildings and standards of instruction up to the level of the Board schools in order to satisfy the inspectors.

Perhaps Sir Henry Craik's greatest achievement was the institution of the Leaving Certificate Examination.   The Act of 1872 had provided for the examination of the Higher Class Public Schools

[1] The Specific Subjects were introduced by the Code of 1873, which was an attempt to carry out the provisions of Clause 67 of the Act by furnishing instruction in the "University Subjects"—Latin, Greek, and mathematics.   Other subjects were added to these, making a total of thirteen.   Instruction in any of these subjects, under conditions laid down by the Code, could earn a specific grant; hence the name.

by the universities. A further Act of 1878 made it permissible for the Department to examine such schools on the application of a School Board. Higher Class Schools could also apply to be examined by the Department, but they had to bear the expenses of the examination. The Educational Endowments Act of 1882 made it obligatory for the Department to inspect all endowed schools. In 1886 the first general inspection of all secondary schools took place. All these steps led to the introduction in 1888 of the Leaving Certificate Examination. At first the examination was only available for Higher Class Public Schools and Higher Class Schools, but it was not compulsory for them. In practice there were a number of causes which made the examination universally accepted. The Leaving Certificate was accepted as an entrance qualification by many bodies, and it considerably simplified work in the schools by substituting one examination for the variety which had previously existed. In the latter respect it can be compared with the English School Certificate.

The introduction of the Leaving Certificate did much to lift secondary education out of chaos and provide it with an aim and direction. It tended to bring the curricula of the different types of secondary school into line with one another and to set up a link between the schools and universities, since the latter accepted the Leaving Certificate, under certain conditions, in lieu of their own entrance examinations. The Scottish Leaving Certificate was normally taken a year later than the English School Certificate, and thus university candidates often proceeded direct to the universities, entering a year younger than students in England who remained at school to take the Higher School Certificate. It should be noted that in Scotland the equivalent of the School Certificate Examination had been in existence for more than a quarter of a century before a similar idea was adopted in England. Also, while in England the universities examined for the School Certificate, in Scotland the examination was conducted by the Education Department. Some of the Scottish "public schools," such as Fettes, presented their pupils for the School and Higher School Certificates of the English universities.

Originally the Department wished to confine the Leaving Certificate Examination to Higher Class Schools. At the time, however, the greater numbers of university students came from the State-aided schools. By way of experiment, candidates from these schools were admitted to the examination in 1892. The success of the experiment was so decided that there was no further question in the matter. In 1902 candidates were required to pass in certain groups of subjects. An Intermediate Certificate was also introduced, but it was abolished by *Circular 44* in 1922. In 1937 the only obligatory subjects that remained were English, arithmetic, and either history or geography. After 1939 the certificate was known as the Senior Leaving Certificate and testified to the satisfactory completion of a five-year course of secondary education. When the examination was instituted there were three grades: Honours, intended for those preparing for the Indian Civil Service ; Higher, which was an entrance qualification for the arts course at the universities ; and Lower, which was accepted for entrance to the medical faculty. The recent modifications of the Leaving Certificate will be discussed later in this chapter.

In 1892 a leaving-certificate called the Merit Certificate was instituted for elementary schools. The certificate was awarded to scholars over thirteen years of age who satisfied the inspector that they had attained a standard of efficiency in the three R's, in two class subjects, and one specific subject.

Craik also introduced reforms into scientific and technical education, and in 1899 established a system of higher-grade schools. Eventually, pupils were able to continue their education in these schools until seventeen or eighteen years of age and could present themselves for the School Leaving Certificate. As in England, the higher-grade school became, in reality, another type of secondary school.

The school-leaving age was raised to fourteen in 1901, and special courses of instruction were arranged for pupils between twelve and fourteen, thus recognising a break at twelve between primary and post-primary education. The post-primary courses were known as Supplementary Courses, and the Merit Certificate, for which the age-qualification was reduced to twelve, marked the division between primary and post-primary education. In 1903 a qualifying examination was substituted for the Merit Certificate, and its purpose was to select those pupils who would benefit from a course of post-primary education. This was in effect an unfortunate change, since, like the free-place examination in England, the examination tended to turn the upper classes of the junior school into cramming institutions. "On paper the new plans looked promising, but their development was far from satisfactory. A certain element of gradation was introduced into the whole school system. The common foundation was the primary school, terminating for the average pupil about the age of twelve. The successful completion of that stage was tested by means of a qualifying examination implying a knowledge of fundamentals sufficient to justify promotion to a higher stage. A pupil, on passing that examination, was free to go on to secondary education in a higher grade or higher class school, or to enter upon the supplementary course of a primary school. . . . Educationally the supplementary courses did not prove a success except in the larger towns where the work was centralised. . . . The courses were not secondary, and compared with secondary courses they were generally inferior in premises and equipment. . . . In the eyes of the industrial and commercial world they were not considered as equivalent to secondary schools." [1]

Although the Act of 1872 had handed over the schools to the control of the State, the training of teachers remained under the care of the Churches. Until 1901 students in training for the teaching profession were examined and certificated by the Department. Craik abolished the external examination. Training-colleges submitted their own syllabuses for the approval of the Department, from this year, and when approved, the colleges were empowered to conduct their own examination, the inspectors acting as external assessors. Training-college authorities recommended candidates, on the results of this examination, to the Department for certification or failure. The system worked very well and led to a rise in the standards of instruction in the colleges. It was an anticipation of the Joint Board arrangement adopted in England in 1930. The establishment of the supplementary courses led to a demand for increased numbers of well-qualified teachers. To meet the need, a Minute of the Department, January 1905, reorganised the training of teachers and placed the responsibility for it upon four Provincial Committees connected with the universities. The following year new regulations governing the training and certification of teachers were issued and the grants to secondary schools were overhauled.

The Scottish Education Department in its early days had to encounter difficulties similar to those we find in England between 1870 and 1902. The chief problem was that of securing regular attendance. The Act of 1872 had given compulsory powers to the School Boards, but these were rarely exercised. Thus, one inspector reported, "Even in the very centres of population hundreds of

[1] *Centenary Handbook of the Educational Institute of Scotland*, pp. 155-6, Edinburgh, 1946.

children are allowed to absent themselves altogether from school, or to attend so irregularly as to be a constant source of annoyance to the teachers and to render it impossible to give them any effective instruction . . . they know by experience that the threats mean nothing, that the School Board has no intention of proceeding to extremities with them, and things go on as before. In many, indeed in most, School Boards in the rural districts, the members are the employers of juvenile labour. The law says they must see that the children attend school, their own interest says that they must get their trees planted, their turnips thinned, their potatoes gathered, their cattle herded, as cheaply as possible." (*Report of the Committee of Council on Education in Scotland,* 1880-1, pp. 145-6.) In spite of obstacles the majority of the School Boards did their utmost to supply sufficient accommodation in the schools, and the counties which were noted as being the most progressive were Bute, Peebles, Dumfries, Fife, and Edinburgh. The Roman Catholics were foremost in the provision of voluntary schools. Dr. Kerr reported : "I am not aware that a single school has been built in Glasgow for some years by any other religious denomination. The example set by the managers of these schools, in the interest they take in all that concerns their welfare, is worthy of general imitation." (*Report of the Committee of Council on Education in Scotland,* 1880-1, p. 124.)

Sir John Struthers, who succeeded Sir Henry Craik as Secretary of the Education Department in 1904, accentuated the separation between primary and post-primary education, although he realised that this policy was opposed to Scottish tradition which had always considered the parish schools as one of the sources supplying secondary education. The parish schools, especially in rural districts, had neither the buildings nor the staff nor the equipment to undertake successfully the task of secondary instruction. Greater efficiency could be obtained if secondary education were restricted to certain well-equipped schools in each county and the remaining schools concentrated on elementary education. The reorganisation was strenuously opposed by Professor Laurie, who viewed with apprehension what he regarded as an encroachment of a Government department upon the freedom of the schools.

The time was now ripe for new legislation, and the Education (Scotland) Act of 1908 marked an important step towards the unification of Scottish schools. "It gave broader and fuller interpretation to the scope of education. It was the first Scottish Act to recognise that there is an essential unity in educational agencies, and that one of the most important problems of education is the improvement of the physical condition of the people. It enlarged the functions of education till they included practically everything connected with the well-being of the child physically and morally as well as intellectually."[1] The Act retained the School Boards and gave them wide powers of a permissive character. Thus provision was made for the medical examination and supervision of pupils in school. The report of the Physical Deterioration Committee of 1904 had stirred up public opinion, and certain School Boards (Edinburgh, Dunfermline, Kirkcaldy, and Govan) had already experimented with schemes of medical inspection. This was not confined to the State-aided schools but applied to all scholars attending schools in the districts of those School Boards.

The Act empowered School Boards to make special provisions for the education of physically or mentally defective children and prescribed penalties for parents who neglected their children. If, by reason of poverty, a child was unable, because of lack of food or clothing, to take advantage of the education given, the School Board had the power to provide food or clothing for the child. School Boards could also issue orders compelling the attendance of children between the ages of five and fourteen, and were empowered to frame by-laws establishing compulsory continuation classes for pupils up to the age of seventeen. The curriculum of these classes was to include instruction with reference to the crafts and industries of the district (including agriculture and the domestic arts), the study of English language and literature (also the Gaelic language and literature in Gaelic-speaking districts), and instruction in the laws of health with opportunity for suitable physical training.

The Act brought into being a superannuation scheme on a contributory basis which applied to both elementary and secondary teachers. The different sources of income available for higher education were consolidated into one central fund known as the Education (Scotland) Fund. Provision was made for applying the fund to primary, secondary, and university education through the County and Burgh Committees on Secondary Education. This anticipated the next advance in 1918 when the county, instead of the parish, became the unit of educational administration and presented a parallel with England when the distribution of "Whiskey

[1] Alexander Morgan. *Rise and Progress of Scottish Education*, p. 184, Oliver and Boyd, 1927.

Money" through the county councils paved the way for the establishment of the L.E.A.s by the 1902 Act. Thus, for the first time, secondary education was put on a satisfactory financial basis. The teachers' security of tenure was defined and the procedure to be followed in the case of a teacher's dismissal was detailed. The Act also gave power to the School Boards to provide conveyance or pay the travelling expenses of teachers and pupils in sparsely populated districts who were attending a central school, and to award bursaries to enable deserving scholars to proceed to secondary schools and institutions for higher education.

The supplementary courses were retarded by the growth of higher-grade schools, and between 1905 and 1907 the policy of the Department was to bring about a fusion of the curriculum of the higher-grade schools with that of the intermediate departments of secondary schools and to permit the former to offer an intermediate course in preparation for the intermediate certificate. Two distinct types of post-primary education thus came into existence: intermediate, providing a three-year course of instruction in languages, mathematics, and science (cf. the English selective and non-selective central schools), and secondary, which offered a five-year course of instruction leading to the Leaving Certificate. The intermediate certificate was valued so highly that there was a definite tendency for some pupils to remain in the higher-grade schools for more than the three years. Nevertheless, a large proportion of pupils failed to complete the three-year course. The influence of the higher-grade schools was exerted in two directions—their curriculum was of a more practical type than that of the secondary schools and thus helped to widen the conception of secondary education; and, as happened in England, some of them developed into secondary schools presenting their pupils for the School Leaving Certificate and in this way modified the secondary curriculum.

As in England, an Education Act followed the First World War. The Education (Scotland) Act of 1918 was a very important progressive measure. It tackled the problem of the unit of educational administration. For some years it had been generally agreed that the parish, the traditional unit, was too small under modern conditions. If an effective system of secondary and technical education was to be maintained, a larger unit than the parish was necessary. The parochial system resulted in a good many anomalies in taxation; there was considerable interference by localities with services which were more than local; and it led to widely differing standards in buildings and instruction. In spite of these defects, the parochial system had many defenders. The local people did not desire a change, because for many years they had played a conspicuous part on the School Boards, and they were supported by the clergy who feared a diminution of their influence. Strangely enough the Scottish Labour Party were opposed to the change because they believed that the county councils would be reactionary and that it would be difficult for members of the working class to attend meetings. Yet the success of the Act of 1902 in England had proved that the county and the large county borough were the obvious units.

The original intention was to make the county councils the local authorities for education, but this was strongly opposed. The Government saw many obvious advantages that would accrue. The small amount of additional administration could easily be managed by the county councils, which already possessed the appropriate organisation. Better co-ordination between the different social services could be achieved, for the same authority which was responsible for education was also in charge of poor-relief, the sick, the delinquents, and child welfare. On the other hand, it was urged that the best policy was to create a number of *ad hoc* authorities for education. They would be concerned with a single function and so would be more likely to be more efficient in carrying out their task ; they would attract people who had special interests in education, and it was thought that religious education would be better organised. Scottish tradition was all in favour of *ad hoc* authorities and the supporters of this policy won the day. Like the English Act of 1902, the Scottish Act created a partnership between the central and the local authorities. The central authority became the Scottish, in place of the Scotch, Education Department created by the Act of 1872. The 947 School Boards (some had been amalgamated since 1872) gave place to education authorities (five burghs and thirty-three counties). The five burghs were Edinburgh, Glasgow, Aberdeen, Dundee, and Leith. The result was that 5,651 School Board members were replaced by 987 members of the new authorities which were elected every three years by a system of proportional representation. Later, Leith was amalgamated with Edinburgh. Each local authority was given the duty of preparing and submitting to the Department schemes for the constitution of school management committees for managing schools or groups of schools to be placed under their control. Parents were to be

represented on each school management committee, and teachers
could also be nominated for appointment on the committees. The
powers and duties of the committees were limited in regard to
finance and control of expenditure, the acquisition of land, the
appointment, transfer, remuneration, and dismissal of teachers and
certain other matters.

The Act enunciated the principle that no child who was qualified
for entry to an intermediate or secondary school should be debarred
by reason of poverty, and authorities had power to assist by paying
travelling expenses, or fees, or the cost of residence in a hostel, or
to grant bursaries and pay maintenance allowances in cases of hard-
ship. The education authority might also provide books not only
for children and young persons attending schools and continuation
classes but also for adults in the district and for this purpose it
could make suitable arrangements with the public libraries. Every
authority had to submit to the Department its scheme for providing
primary, intermediate, and secondary education in its area and for
the maintenance and support of a limited number of fee-paying
schools. Perhaps one of the most important sections of the Act is
that which directed the authority to institute a scale of salaries for
its teachers in conformity with the conditions to be laid down by
the Department in consultation with representatives of the education
authorities and the teaching profession. Dr. John Strong, then
rector of the Royal High School, Edinburgh, and afterwards
professor of education in the University of Leeds, played a leading
part in the institution of the salary scales.

The education authorities were permitted to aid in supplying
nursery schools for children between the ages of two and five. They
could also contribute, if they thought it necessary, towards the maintenance of schools not under their own management, or to universities. Each education authority was to contribute to the maintenance
of training-colleges such sums as the Department might determine.
The amount of such contributions would depend upon the number
of teachers employed by an authority. The school-leaving age was
to be raised to fifteen on a date to be announced by the Education
Department and no exemptions from attendance were to be granted
to children under the age of thirteen.

Like the corresponding English Act, pupils leaving school at
fifteen were to attend continuation classes till sixteen and eventually
up to eighteen years of age. Schemes for the education of these
continuation-class pupils were to be submitted to the Department

and were to provide for instruction in English language and literature and such other parts of a general education as might be deemed
desirable ; special instruction conducive to the efficiency of young
persons in the employment in which they were engaged or proposed
to be engaged ; and instruction in physical exercises adapted to
their age and physique.   It was hoped that advantage would be
taken of holiday camps, Boys' Brigades, and kindred organisations.
As in England, the instruction was to amount to at least 320 hours
a year, arranged to suit the particular conditions of the district.
Restrictions on the employment of children under thirteen were to
be in force.   (The age in England was twelve.)

Voluntary or denominational schools might, with the consent of
their trustees, be transferred to the local education authority, which
was bound to accept the transfer on terms such as might be agreed
upon.   This amended the Act of 1872 under which School Boards
were not bound to accept the transfer.   Transferred schools became
public schools and teachers appointed to them would have to satisfy
the Department as regards their qualifications and be approved as
to their religious belief and character by the representatives of the
Church or denomination in whose interests the school was conducted.
No school could be transferred later than two years from the passing
of the Act, and after that date no grant could be paid to a voluntary
school which had not been transferred.   Clause 20 of the Act
authorised the establishment, by His Majesty in Council, of an
Advisory Council to assist the Department on educational matters.
The Department should take into consideration any advice or representation submitted by the Advisory Council.   Not less than two-
thirds of the members of the Council should be persons qualified to
represent the views of various bodies interested in education, e.g.
representatives of education authorities, universities, the Educational
Institute of Scotland as representing the teachers and other bodies
connected with education.   The remainder would consist of persons
of wide experience and expert knowledge of the industrial, social,
commercial, and economic aspects of the national life.   The
Council could initiate representations to the Department on matters
of educational policy or administration.   Its functions were therefore wider than those of the Consultative Committee of the English
Board of Education and similar to those of the two Central Advisory
Councils established by the Act of 1944.

Every education authority was obliged, within three months of
its first election, to establish a Local Advisory Council consisting

of persons qualified to represent the views of local bodies interested in education. The Local Advisory Council had the duty of advising the education authority on educational matters relating to its area, and the latter was obliged to consider any advice or representation proferred.

The Scottish Act of 1918 suffered the same fate as the English Act. Owing to the operation of the "Geddes Axe," that part of the Act dealing with the raising of the school-leaving age, and with the institution of compulsory continuation classes, was not carried into effect.

The first Circular issued by the new Scottish Education Department advised each local authority to appoint a full-time Director of Education as technical adviser to the authority and chief executive officer responsible for carrying out the schemes of reorganisation. The duties of the Directors were neither simple nor popular since the Act was resented by many who believed in the tradition of the parish school providing both elementary and secondary education. In 1921 Struthers announced the Department's policy of reorganisation in *Circular 44* which contained many drastic reforms. The issue of the Circular had been preceded by a simplification of the grant system by which a uniform annual grant per pupil was to be paid irrespective of the type of school, primary, intermediate, or secondary. Since the grants no longer depended upon examinations, the qualifying and the intermediate examinations were abolished. This was a much-needed reform, because the examinations had completed their work in raising the standards of all types of school and were now beginning to dominate both the curriculum and the teaching of the schools. Thus only two types of school were now recognised: primary and secondary.

The former was for pupils leaving at the age of fourteen and was organised in the following divisions: Infants (for children under seven), Juniors (ages seven to nine), Seniors (ages nine to twelve), and an Advanced division for pupils between the ages of twelve and fourteen or fifteen. Pupils who had completed satisfactorily a two-year course in the Advanced division could gain the award of the Day School Certificate (Lower). The certificate was issued by the local education authority. For those who completed satisfactorily a three-year Advanced course, the Education Department issued a Day School Certificate (Higher). For this certificate, pupils normally offered four subjects. English, with history and geography, was compulsory. The second subject was determined by the character of the course followed by the pupil: literary (a foreign language), commercial, technical, domestic, or rural. The third was arithmetic, with algebra in commercial courses. The fourth subject could be science, arts and crafts, or any subject not already selected.

The secondary-school course extended for five years, with the Senior Leaving Certificate as its goal. The reorganisation met with much adverse criticism both in the press and from the Educational Institute of Scotland which had for many years urged a national system of education embracing all stages from the primary school to the university and ensuring a full secondary education for all pupils.

In 1920 there was a further development in the arrangements for the training of teachers. The administration of the training scheme was handed over to a National Committee for the Training of Teachers and the four Provincial Committees, who were now relieved from financial responsibility, were given the management of the four training-centres at Edinburgh, Glasgow, Aberdeen, and St. Andrews. By agreement, the Episcopal and Roman Catholic training-colleges were transferred to the National Committee which now controls all the training-institutions in Scotland. Since 1924, except for teachers of handicraft, physical training, art, music, and domestic science, all Scottish men teachers must be graduates.

Since the war, a few non-graduate men teachers, trained under the Emergency Training Regulations, have been admitted to the schools, but this is purely a temporary measure. Women need not be graduates, though a great many of them are. The Educational Institute of Scotland believes that women should be on the same footing as men in this respect, and has been alarmed at the increase of non-graduates among women teachers. Thus, in 1930, women entering the profession were in the proportion of 870 graduates to 301 non-graduates. In 1948 this ratio had become 340 graduates to 630 non-graduates. In 1946 the Advisory Council on Education in Scotland in their report on the *Training of Teachers* showed that they were not in agreement with the views of the Educational Institute, and were reluctant to require all women teachers in primary schools to be university graduates. Scotland is experiencing the same difficulty as England in obtaining honours graduates for the teaching of mathematics and science. The present salary scales are such that a good honours-degree man can obtain a more remunerative post in industry.

As soon as the period of financial stringency had passed, local authorities began to experiment with different types of post-primary organisation. Some preferred to house the advanced divisions and the secondary courses in separate schools. In some districts separate central schools were established for advanced division pupils, whilst in many country areas advanced division "tops" to the primary school were common. Some authorities preferred to include the advanced division in the secondary school and this experiment led to the "omnibus" type of school which is similar in some ways to the English multilateral school.[1]

In 1936 Parliament passed the Education (Scotland) Act which was similar to the English Act of the same year. This Act extended the school-leaving age to fifteen, with certain exemptions, and applied the term "secondary" to all forms of post-primary education. As in England, the outbreak of the Second World War rendered the Act inoperative.

The Local Government (Scotland) Act of 1929 transferred the function of the *ad hoc* education authorities, established in 1918, to the county councils of the counties and the town councils of the four burghs of Edinburgh, Glasgow, Dundee, and Aberdeen. Each of these became the local education authority for its area and was required to appoint an education committee as in England.

After the Second World War, Parliament passed the Education (Scotland) Act of 1945, followed by a consolidating Act in 1946, which brought together all the enactments concerning education in Scotland. The Act of 1945 applied to Scotland the policy that the Government had decided upon with regard to England, but there are certain differences between the Scottish Act and the English Act of 1944. Thus Scottish education did not have to deal with the problems caused in England by the dual system. Other important differences should be noted. The county colleges of the English Act are called junior colleges. Clause 11 provides that primary, secondary, and compulsory further education, in public schools and junior colleges shall be free, but local authorities may charge fees in some or all of the classes in a limited number of primary and secondary schools; but the power to charge fees can only be exercised where it is without prejudice to the adequate provision of free primary and secondary education in schools in which no fees are charged.

[1] For the details concerning experiments in post-primary education between 1918 and 1936, the reader should consult Newman A. Wade, *Post-Primary Education in the Primary Schools of Scotland*, University of London Press, 1939.

Where education is free, there must also be provided, free of charge, books, stationery, mathematical instruments, and other necessary articles. Clause 48 made the appointment of Directors of Education obligatory and Part III of the Act laid down the conditions under which they are to hold office. Clause 78 empowered an education authority, with the approval of the Secretary of State, to make such provision for conducting or assisting the conduct of research as may appear to the authority to be desirable for the purpose of improving the education provided in its area. The Act of 1872 had imposed restrictions on the time during which religious instruction could be given. These are now abolished, but, unlike the English Act of 1944, no specific form of religious instruction is prescribed. All education authorities must submit to the Education Department schemes showing the methods they propose to adopt for promoting pupils from primary to secondary schools.

The Scottish Act grants the central authority more direct and extensive control than has been the case in England. For example, every education authority is required to furnish a promotion scheme for the approval of the Secretary of State, which must show the method of promotion adopted and the means by which a decision is reached regarding the courses from which a pupil shows a reasonable chance of profiting. The English arrangement has been to leave such matters to the discretion of the L.E.A. Again, the Secretary of State is directly responsible for the training of teachers, and has the power by means of regulations to "constitute, alter the constitution of, incorporate and dissolve committees or other bodies for the training of teachers." His control extends as far as prescribing the duties of the committees and the course of training they provide. He also awards certificates of competency to teach, prescribes by regulations the forms of these certificates, the conditions of award, and the conditions under which they may be withdrawn (Section 49). This is a distinct contrast to the English system whereby the Ministry no longer takes an active part in certification, but has delegated the power of examining candidates and recommending them to the Ministry for recognition as qualified teachers to the University Institutes of Education. The Scottish Act provides for a register of educational endowments, but the official appointed as registrar is to be an officer of the Secretary of State.

Another feature worthy of notice is the precision in the definitions of primary and secondary education. It has been noted already that the English Acts have been deficient in this respect.

Thus Section I of the Act of 1945 defines primary education as a "progressive elementary education in such subjects as may be prescribed in the code, regard being had to age, ability, and aptitude of the pupils concerned, and such education shall be given in primary schools or departments. Primary education includes training by appropriate methods in schools and classes—for pupils between the ages of two years and such later age as may be permitted by the code. . . . Secondary education means progressive courses of instruction of such length and in such subjects as may be approved in terms of the code as appropriate to the age, ability, and aptitude of the pupils who have been promoted from primary schools and departments and to the period for which they are expected to remain at school. Such courses shall be given in secondary schools or departments."

The Act also revises the conditions of superannuation for teachers. Each teacher is required to pay five per cent of his salary towards superannuation, and the education authority, governing body, or managers, are required to contribute an equal amount. The minimum national scales of salaries for teachers are abolished and the Act requires all education authorities to pay salaries in accordance with scales to be prescribed by regulations made by the Secretary of State. A National Joint Council had been set up before the outbreak of the Second World War to investigate the problem of teachers' salaries, but the beginning of hostilities postponed a decision. During the war, teachers were given a war-bonus to enable them to meet the rising cost of living. The Advisory Council to the Education Department recommended in 1943 the substitution of standard national scales for the minimum national scales. The National Joint Council was reconstituted and now consisted of twenty-four representatives, half of them representing the authorities and half representing the Educational Institute of Scotland. In addition, six assessors were appointed. Lord Teviot was appointed as an impartial chairman. The Council met in December 1944, and after a lengthy series of negotiations the present Teviot scales were adopted.

The Advisory Council on Education has recently issued three important reports: *Primary Education*, 1946, *Technical Education*, 1946, and *Secondary Education*, 1947.

The report on *Primary Education* emphasises twelve as the normal age for transfer from primary to secondary education. It pays much attention to the problems of school sites and school buildings. Many visitors to Scottish schools comment upon the barrack-like appearance of most of them, especially of those built before the First World War. Even some of the more recent buildings compare unfavourably as regards playground facilities and amenities with English schools of the same type and date. The report recognises that under present conditions, especially in the large towns, the existing barrack-type schools will have to be used for some years, but it recommends that they should be made as attractive as possible internally and the numbers on roll drastically reduced. As outside recreational activities are restricted in such schools, the interiors should be reconstructed to provide the maximum of amenities such as school halls, dining-halls, and gymnasia.

Special emphasis was laid on the colour scheme of the interior. "As children are notoriously fond of bright colours, it seems reasonable that the colour schemes of classrooms should be so designed as to give them pleasure . . . we hope that no school interior will in future be painted in a dull muddy colour which is alleged to be 'restful,' or is guaranteed 'not to show the dirt.' " (P. 8.) It is important that during the whole period of primary education there should be continuous co-operation between home and school and to this end, the report suggests that to encourage a good relationship between the two, visits of parents to the schools should be welcomed and other devices should be tried. It is recommended that the enrolment of a primary school should never exceed 650 and that 400 to 500 could be regarded as a reasonable maximum.

The curriculum and methods of the primary school should be thought out afresh and should follow the child's natural line of development and his delight in all kinds of activity. The "bookish" tradition of Scottish education came in for criticism and the following paragraph is significant of the modern outlook. "It is still assumed in some quarters that those subjects confidently referred to as the ' Three R's ' are the central core of education, and indeed all that is necessary for the great mass of children. The consideration we have given to this matter, and the evidence we have heard, lead us, however, not merely to question but to deny the validity of this assumption under present day conditions." (P. 21.) Instead of a curriculum revolving round the three R's, the report reviews the subjects of the primary school under the broad headings of physical education, hand-work, and speech. It deprecates a preoccupation with school "subjects" in the traditional sense. "A teacher who has realised how futile it is to attempt to teach young children according to a logical scheme will be equally aware that the idea of a school 'subject' is a logical device or abstraction. The giving of separate names to different skills and branches of knowledge and the making of clear dividing lines between them is attractive to the logical mind and is within limits a useful procedure; but it tends to obscure the unity of all knowledge and the infinite interrelation of things in the pattern of life." (P. 29.)

Chapter xi of the report contains many valuable suggestions on teaching method, but the following chapter is unlike anything to be found in the English reports. It is concerned with the place and value of Scottish traditions in the school. Although Scotland has much in common with England, there has been in modern times a growing national feeling which is not "a movement of antagonism to England but a growing determination that Scotland should not be submerged, ignored or treated as a 'province' or a 'region'." (P. 72.) The following are among the suggestions made in this chapter: the allotment of a definite weekly period in the higher classes of the primary school for the study of Scottish traditions and language; the production of anthologies of Scots verse and prose, which should include modern works of good quality; the teaching of the best Scottish folk-tunes; the tradition of using the fiddle as a means of instruction in Scottish songs and dances should be revived; the industries of the district should be reflected in the crafts of the school; all Scottish children should learn something of Gaelic life, legends, and traditions.

Circular 122, which accepts in principle the main suggestions of the report, welcomes the attention to Scottish traditions, but doubts the value of allocating a set weekly period for their study and conveys a warning to over-zealous teachers that in Lowland schools where Gaelic is not spoken, the instruction in Gaelic life and traditions should not go beyond what can be readily related to the natural interest of children at the primary stage.

The report suggests the abolition of compulsory homework and its replacement by different forms of voluntary work, but the Circular indicates that the Education Department is not at present desirous of going as far as this and recommends that homework should be so regulated as to avoid over-pressure. It should involve not only the reading of books, but also research projects making use of purposeful activity and observation out of doors.

The report also stresses the value of organised research into educational problems and commends the policy of the Scottish

Council for Research in Education of providing the great body of Scottish teachers with brief and clearly stated summaries of the main conclusions of recent research work. "Scotland is indeed fortunate in possessing a Council for Research in Education broad enough in constitution and purpose to be a fit instrument for performing the functions we have in view. If up to now their activities ... have been in a sense sporadic, they may with justification plead that they have been to work only under serious limitations of finance and personnel." (P. 113.) Hence, the report recommended that the Secretary of State and the education authorities should take full advantage of the powers given in the Act of 1945 to put the Research Council on a sound financial basis.[1] *Circular 122* accepts this recommendation in principle and points out that the financial assistance asked for has now been provided through the Grant Regulations. The report on *Primary Education* is the most valuable official study yet made on the primary school and contains much of interest for English as well as Scottish teachers.

The report on *Secondary Education* emphasises three general principles. (1) Not only must every child receive a secondary education suited to his age, ability, and aptitude, but his education, whether academic or practical, must have equal importance in the eyes of the community and be provided for with equal care and generosity. (2) The good school must in its variety of types and range of ability reproduce something of the richness of a natural environment. (3) While the school should be large enough to allow of a fully varied curriculum, it should not be of such a size that the headmaster's personal influence is lost and he becomes a mere administrator. In the light of this principle, 600 is suggested as the maximum enrolment number for a secondary school.

The idea of the multilateral school is rejected. "We cannot recommend the setting up of huge multilateral schools on the American model, as favoured by the L.C.C., with 2,000 or more pupils in each. The unity we seek is organic not merely administrative, and we do not believe it can be realised with such vast numbers merely by setting a collection of sub-schools of different kinds on a common campus and calling them one school." (P. 31.)

The English tripartite system of grammar, technical, and modern schools, is severely criticised. It has an obvious attraction of administrative tidiness, but there are decisive reasons against its

[1] The University of London Press publishes works approved by the Scottish Council for Research in Education.

adoption in Scotland. It is so unrelated to the Scottish system that its adoption would mean not a development but a revolution. "The whole scheme rests on an assumption which teacher and psychologist alike must challenge—that children of twelve sort themselves out neatly into three categories to which these three types of school correspond. . . . Status does not come with the attaching of a name or by a wave of the administrative wand, and the discussion to date has left the position of the modern school neither defined nor secure. Indeed, it seems clear to many that the modern school will in practice mean little more than what is left, once the grammar and technical types have been housed elsewhere, and that the scheme will end not in tripartite equality but in a dualism of academic and technical plus a permanently depressed element. . . . If education is much more than instruction, is in fact life and preparation for life, can it be wisdom thus to segregate the types from an early age? On the contrary, we hold that school becomes colourful, rich, and rewarding just as in proportion as the boy who reads Homer, the boy who makes wireless sets and the boy without marked aptitude for either are within its living unity a constant stimulus and supplement one to another." (P. 31.)

On the other hand, the existing Scottish organisation into senior and junior secondary schools is regarded as unsatisfactory because it emphasises the academic tradition in Scottish education and so relegates the junior secondary school to an inferior position.

Hence the report recommends "That the name 'junior secondary school' be no longer used, as it has in fact conveyed a suggestion of inferiority." (P. 35.)

The solution recommended is that of the "omnibus" secondary school.[1] This type of school, however, differs from the multi-lateral school in both size and organisation. Speaking of pupils from twelve to sixteen, the report says: "Within this part of the school [what the Norwood Report called the "Main School," as distinct from the sixth form] we are satisfied that the omnibus principle can operate without waste of staffing, provided the total school roll is about 800. This is a third more than we recommend as applicable to secondary schools . . . where we were specially concerned to ensure the personal influence of the headmaster on his

[1] The organisation of an existing "omnibus" school, the Kirkcaldy High School, is described by Dr. F. M. Earle in his book *Reconstruction in the Secondary School*, University of London Press, 1944.

pupils, but we feel that the concession is worth while, if it secures the advantage of the omnibus school." (P. 39.)

The discussion on examinations and certificates is most interesting, especially if read in conjunction with the English report of the Secondary School Examination Council, 1947. Speaking about external examinations, the Scottish report says: "We do not say that examinations are ruining secondary education in Scotland; but they are gravely distorting it and narrowing its vision." (P. 43.)

The report makes the following recommendations:

(1) That there be no external examination for boys and girls leaving at fifteen.

(2) That each pupil leaving school, either at fifteen or without securing the School Certificate referred to in (3), be supplied with a record giving particulars of his work in the secondary school.

(3) (a) That a School Certificate be instituted, to be taken at the end of the fourth year of secondary school. (This involves two examinations a year, since junior secondary schools have two commencing dates.)

   (b) That this certificate be awarded on the results of internal examinations conducted by the teachers in each school and a process of standardisation carried out by the Scottish Education Department. (The method of standardising the results sent in by different schools is fully discussed in the report.)

   (c) That this School Certificate be not awarded on a group basis, but show the subjects included in the course and those in which a pass has been obtained.

(4) That a Higher School Certificate, also on a subject basis, be instituted, to mark the completion of various types of sixth-form course.

(5) That the external examination for the Higher School Certificate be conducted by the Scottish Education Department.

(6) That on the institution of the School Certificate and the Higher School Certificate the award of the Senior Leaving Certificate be discontinued. (Pp. 52-3.)

The proposed School Certificate would be freed from any relation to university entrance requirements. "Experience on both sides of the Border has shown that the surest way to distort a School

Certificate from its proper function is to peg it to university matriculation requirements." (P. 58.)

The Scottish Education Department, in *Circular 145* of January 1949, accepted the general principles recommended by the Advisory Council's report, but differed as regards certain details. Thus the group system of the Senior Leaving Certificate was abandoned after 1949, but every candidate is required to follow a course of study approved by the Department. For example, although a pass in arithmetic is no longer demanded, yet this subject must be included in every approved course. At the end of a five-year course the school authorities decide the number of subjects each candidate will present for examination, but the certificate is awarded on a subject basis. The value of the certificate depends upon the number and character of the passes recorded on it. A candidate who wishes to satisfy the preliminary entrance requirements of a particular professional body will offer those subjects only which are necessary for this purpose. On the other hand, as in England the Scottish universities have their own entrance regulations and these will influence the curriculum of the school. Although the leaving-certificate is taken at the end of a five-year course, it is still possible, though it is not encouraged, for a candidate to take, in the fourth year of the school course, as many subjects as the school authorities consider he is capable of attempting. These subjects will be taken on the lower grade. This provision, which comes into force in 1951, is to meet the needs of pupils who wish to leave school at the end of the fourth year. It will be remembered that the original Senior Leaving Certificate testified to the satisfactory completion of a five-year course of secondary education. Hence the recent developments are not subject to the criticisms that have been levelled in England about the age at which the General Certificate of Education should be taken. The new examination will in future be known as the Scottish Leaving Certificate.

Chapters ix to xi of the report are concerned with the Secondary Curriculum, Technical Education in the Secondary School, and Secondary Education in Rural and Highland Scotland respectively. The suggestions regarding the treatment of school studies and the place technical education should occupy in the secondary school, will repay study by English as well as Scottish teachers.

The chapter on the Inspectorate emphasises the role of the H.M.I.s as consultants and collaborators, and, although inspection must always remain one of the functions of the Department's officers, the report recommends that "the Inspectorate be renamed His Majesty's Educational Service, the members of the service to be known as His Majesty's Education Officers." (P. 140.)   "And we may properly draw attention to two important respects in which the position of H.M. Inspectorate in Scotland differs from that in England and justifies a relatively larger staff:

(1) In Scotland no share in the work of inspection is taken by officers of the education authorities.

(2) In the conduct of the Higher School Certificate Examination and in the award of the School Certificate the Department and the Inspectorate will perform important and exacting duties that have no counterpart in the work of the Ministry of Education." (P. 141.)

The Scottish Education Department has been very energetic in carrying out the obligation and using the powers conferred by the Acts of 1945 and 1946.   The raising of the school-leaving age in 1947 and the shortage of teaching staff put a heavy strain on the schools, but the output of the training centres and colleges (including those trained under the Emergency Scheme) has relieved the situation.   Some concern is being felt with regard to the supply of specialist teachers of mathematics and science and specialist women teachers of physical training.   The shortage of teachers would certainly have been remedied by 1948 had the Scottish Education Department adopted the short training-scheme for emergency entrants which had been decided upon in England.   The Department, however, took a long-term view and instituted a full course of training, encouraging those who were fitted to read for university degrees.   The Day Schools (Scotland) Code, 1939, fixed the maximum size of classes at fifty in a primary school, at forty in the first three years, and thirty in classes beyond the third year in secondary schools, but these maxima have been greatly exceeded.

Shortage of accommodation has been the principal worry of the authorities.   Large housing estates are springing up in the suburbs of the largest towns and these have to be provided with new schools. The rise in the birth-rate will entail an increase of twenty to twenty-five per cent in the entrants to infant-schools between 1951 and 1953.   Difficulties in regard to labour and materials aggravate the situation.   As in England, the increased accommodation demanded when the school-leaving age was raised is being met by the provision of HORSA huts.   Progress in this has, however, been retarded by a shortage of boilers and radiators, and huts have had to make do with temporary heating expedients.

In spite of these drawbacks, the progress in general has been satisfactory. A Circular of 1945 asked education authorities to begin active experiment to discover the most effective methods of training pupils in citizenship. In 1948 a series of conferences was held with the object of pooling the experience that had been acquired, and a summary of the discussions is to be published in the near future. Some interesting experiments were carried out in regard to education for leisure and social and recreational activities. Thus the Highlands and Islands Film Guild operated six mobile-cinema vans in Inverness, Argyll, and Skye. A similar service was provided by the Orkney Education Authority. A good attendance was secured and many of the islanders saw a film for the first time in their lives. The Department also co-operated with the Scottish Music Committee in encouraging the formation of choral, listening, and instrumental, groups.

One of the most important achievements has been in connection with the youth service. In 1943 the Department asked the Scottish Youth Advisory Committee to undertake an inquiry into the needs of youth, how far they were met by existing agencies, and into the influences that lead to a sound development of character and to the prevention of anti-social conduct and juvenile delinquency. The result was the publication in 1945 of the report entitled *The Needs of Youth in These Times*. The committee, in its report to the Secretary of State, emphasised, "We believe this to be the first occasion on which a Minister of State has given a committee an opportunity of taking into comprehensive review all the needs and possibilities of that stage of human development which we call 'youth,' of considering the vitally important period of transition from childhood to manhood and womanhood as the integral process which it really is." Those who read the report will agree that the committee made full use of the opportunity and produced a valuable and comprehensive report which dealt with the psychological, social, religious, and cultural, aspects of the problem. The first report was followed by another dealing with the way in which the youth service should try to provide for the needs of youth, and how it should be organised, developed, and controlled to this end.

The reports bore fruit in the appointment by the Secretary of State in 1947 of the Scottish Committee for the Training of Community Centre Workers and Youth Leaders. This committee replaced the Scottish Youth Leadership Training Association and has now, with the approval of the Secretary of State, formed a voluntary body known as the Scottish Leadership Training Association. This body held its first training-course of sixty weeks duration in 1948. The youth service has shown a steady expansion. Its units, comprising pre-Service organisations for boys, uniformed organisations for boys and girls, and Church and club organisations for both sexes, by the end of 1948 numbered 12,246, with 487,761 members. Many of these members belonged to more than one organisation, but the figures quoted show the strength of the movement. Education authorities also provided youth clubs and centres for young persons above the statutory school age.

The type of work that can be carried out is illustrated by the following instance. "An interesting example of what can be accomplished in spite of the present difficulties is furnished by the Youth Panel for Eyemouth in Berwickshire. Since 1945 this body has adapted and equipped an old school to provide the locality with a hall and centre for youth and other activities ; established holiday facilities which were used in 1948 by 608 young people, mainly from the Glasgow area ; erected a covered stand for the local playing fields, accommodating 300 spectators and providing dressing rooms, showers and kitchens, which was opened in October, 1948. Much of the work was done by voluntary labour and with second-hand material." [1]

In the earlier chapter on Scottish Education, reference was made to the slender endowments of the burgh schools and universities in their early days. By way of contrast, the 19th century was prolific in the number of bequests for educational purposes. The endowments of Dr. Andrew Bell have already received mention.

Two very important educational endowments are those known as the Dick and the Milne bequests. The former was due to James Dick who in 1828 left a fortune of approximately £113,000 to be applied for the maintenance and assistance of the country parochial schoolmasters in the counties of Aberdeen, Banff, and Moray. The income derived from the bequest was devoted to the augmentation of the very meagre salaries of the country schoolmasters. The bequest was also intended to encourage the "literary elevation" of the schoolmasters, and in order to benefit from it candidates were required to pass an examination of so severe a character that even university graduates of those days are said to have failed. Since

[1] *Education in Scotland in 1949*, H.M.S.O., 1949.

1890, university graduation has been accepted as evidence of sufficient scholarship to enable a teacher to benefit from the fund. The Education Act of 1872 made certain modifications in the distribution of the grants.

The other important endowment was the Milne bequest. Dr. Milne, president of the Medical Board of Bombay, left a sum of about £50,000, in 1841, to be used in a way similar to the funds of the Dick bequest. In this instance, however, the benefits were restricted to the county of Aberdeen. The arrangements of the original trust deed of Dr. Milne were superseded in 1888 by a scheme for using the income in the establishment of bursaries for pupils attending State-aided schools.

Several references have been made in this chapter to the Educational Institute of Scotland. The Institute was founded in 1847. Before this year, certain local associations of teachers had existed, *e.g.* at Aberdeen, 1838, and Glasgow, 1846, but as the first president of the Institute declared, "Scotland is the first country in the world that has a National Association of all her Teachers, resolved and determined to provide their country with the best system of education that they can devise." The Educational Institute of Scotland has been a professional association in the highest sense of the term. During the last hundred years, it not only strove to secure better conditions for Scottish teachers as regards salaries, tenure, and superannuation, but it accomplished important reforms in the schools themselves, maintained the tradition of "sound learning," raised the status of the teaching profession in the estimation of the Scottish people, and encouraged educational experiment and reseach.[1]

There is little space remaining to do more than present the barest outlines of university development after the Act of 1858. Demands for further reforms in the universities brought about the Royal Commission of 1876. As a result of the Commission's recommendations, the Universities (Scotland) Act, 1889, was passed and it completely remodelled the constitution of the Scottish universities. In addition to enlarging the membership of the University

---

[1] In 1944 the Scottish Secondary Teachers' Association was formed within the Educational Institute of Scotland in order to give special attention to the interests of secondary teachers. It broke away from the parent body in the following year. Its objects are "to advance Secondary Education in Scotland, and to safeguard and promote the professional interests of Scottish Secondary Teachers in all matters, particularly in such as affects remuneration and other conditions of service." About twenty-five per cent of Scottish secondary teachers are members of the Association.

Court and more closely defining its functions and those of the Senate, it brought into being a new body, the Universities Committee of the Privy Council, to which all new ordinances were to be referred. Authority was given to affiliate University College, Dundee, with the University of St. Andrews.   The Students' Representative Council, which had originated as a student movement, received official recognition.   New courses of study were established at the universities, the degree of D.Litt. was instituted, and a pension scheme for professors was put into force.   In 1892 women were allowed to graduate.

A further Universities Act, in 1922, made more modifications in the constitution of the universities and brought all members of the teaching staff under the Federated Superannuation Scheme in which nearly all the universities and university colleges of Great Britain participate.

The financial position of the universities was much improved during the latter years of the 19th century.   Earlier in this chapter the allocation of £30,000 per annum from the Equivalent Grant was mentioned.   Like the English universities, the Scottish universities also receive direct Treasury grants.   Under the Act of 1889, the Treasury grant was £42,000, but this has grown to many times that amount and special non-recurrent grants for improving and extending buildings have been made.

One important legacy to the universities calls for mention.   In 1901 Mr. Andrew Carnegie gave £2,000,000 to the Scottish universities for extending buildings, endowing Chairs, and promoting research.   The bequest brings in an annual income of more than £120,000, and, by the terms of the founder's will, half of this amount is devoted to assisting students in the payment of their class fees. Dr. Morgan estimated that as many as seventy per cent of all the university students of Scotland obtain assistance from the Carnegie trustees.

Since the last war, the Scottish universities, like the English, have entered upon a period of expansion.   The number of students has greatly increased, thereby throwing considerable strain on the available accommodation, and for the session 1946-7 it was estimated that the attendance was about 13,000.

CHAPTER XVI

EDUCATION IN H.M. FORCES

It is not generally known that the State created an organised system of education in the Army more than a generation before the Committee of the Privy Council for Education came into existence. As in the case of most other British institutions, Army education owes its origin to voluntary effort. In 1767 an officer of the Queen's Royal Regiment published a set of model standing orders for his unit which at that time was stationed at Dublin. Amongst them occurs the following: "A Sergeant or Corporal, whose Sobriety, Honesty, and Good Conduct can be depended upon and that is capable of teaching Writing, Reading and Arithmetic, is to be employed in the capacity of a Schoolmaster." His duty was to instruct soldiers and soldiers' children, and a room was to be appointed to be used as a schoolroom. How far this order was carried out there is no means of ascertaining, but it is known that at about the same time the 18th Hussars had a regimental school of instruction.

When the Rifle Brigade was founded and placed under the command of Sir John Moore in 1802, instruction in reading, writing, and arithmetic became a regular part of the training. A knowledge of reading, writing, and the first four rules of arithmetic, was expected of every sergeant, and a school was established to enable soldiers to qualify for promotion. In 1811 the commander-in-chief, Frederick, Duke of York, addressed a letter to Lord Palmerston, Secretary-at-War, proposing the establishment of regimental schools. As a result, two general orders, December 1811 and July 1812, were issued. The first appointed one sergeant-schoolmaster, with the pay and allowances of a paymaster-sergeant, to each battalion. His duty was to instruct young soldiers and the children of soldiers, and an allowance of £10 for books was authorised. The second order required a room in every barracks to be set aside for a school, and authorised an allowance of coal.

At this time, a certain number of married soldiers in each regiment were granted the privilege of taking wives and children on service. The parents had so much to do that the children were left to run wild, and it was felt that something should be done for their welfare. In 1811 the Adjutant-General issued an order requiring each regiment to open a school for children, which was to be placed under the charge of the sergeant-schoolmaster. Wellington, during the Peninsular Campaign, ordered schools to be opened in the field as circumstances permitted. Thus, from its commencement in 1811, organised education in the Army developed along two distinct lines: adult education for the soldier, and elementary instruction for the children. The latter at first tended to overshadow the former. It is interesting to note that the Duke of York's instructions required the adoption of Dr. Bell's monitorial system in the Army.

After Waterloo, progress was slow because of the widespread belief that education would upset the *status quo*, and even such a patron of Army schools as the Duke of York considered that a barrack library was unnecessary and objectionable. He did, however, approve the issue of twenty-eight selected and safe volumes, each one stamped "Approved, C. Cantuar, E. Ebor, J. London." "The list included such comforting works as *Kind Caution to Profane Swearers,* Peer's *Companion for the Aged* and *Discourse on a Death-bed Repentance.*" [1]

Thomas Macaulay, when Secretary-at-War, was responsible for two important decisions. In 1839 every barracks was provided with a reading-room and the Stationery Office sent 300 volumes to each. Macaulay is supposed to have personally selected the books and certainly the catalogue at the Record Office shows that the choice involved both understanding and sympathy. In 1840 Macaulay signed a royal warrant appointing a schoolmistress to every regiment or regimental depot. The schoolmistress was to instruct the daughters of soldiers in the three R's, needlework, and housewifery, and to train them in habits of diligence, honesty, and piety. This was the origin of the Corps of Army Schoolmistresses, which afterwards became the Queen's Royal Army Schoolmistresses.

The further development of Army education was due to the Rev. R. C. Gleig, who was appointed Inspector-General of Army Schools in 1846. The previous year, Gleig, then Chaplain-General, met Baring, the Paymaster-General, as he was boarding a river-steamer at Vauxhall. They suddenly resolved to pay a surprise visit to the

[1] Hawkins and Brimble. *Adult Education, the Record of the British Army,* p. 13, Macmillan, 1947.

Duke of York's School.[1] They found the conditions at the school revolting. The buildings were in a filthy state and the sergeant-instructors were both brutal and ignorant. The instruction was educationally valueless and discipline was maintained by flogging and confinement in iron cages so constructed that the children could not stand upright in them. The two visitors were appalled, and approached Sidney Herbert, Secretary-at-War, with proposals for drastic reforms. Herbert enlisted the help of the Committee of the Privy Council, with the result that a royal warrant of 1846 instituted the Corps of Army Schoolmasters. The reason for the new departure was given in the preamble: "Whereas we have deemed it expedient to introduce into our Army a class of man better calculated to perform the duties of schoolmaster . . ." At the same time, the Duke of York's School was completely reorganised and was restricted to boys only. The sergeant-schoolmasters ranked next to the sergeant-major. They were paid 2s. 6d. a day and beer-money, together with an extra 6d. a day for efficiency and good conduct. At first the schoolmaster wore the uniform of his regiment, but in 1854 the uniform prescribed was a dark blue frock-coat and trousers, gold cord shoulder-knots, sash, sword, and a cap with a crown worked in gold thread. At the same time warrant rank was introduced, and commissioned rank a few years later.

Another of Gleig's reforms was the establishment of a normal school as part of the Royal Military Asylum at Chelsea. Its object was to produce efficient schoolmasters, and it gave a two-year training-course. Students were admitted twice a year on the result of a competitive examination, and no fees were charged. Civilians were also admitted as students, but were required to give a bond of £50 that at the end of their training they would enlist as Army schoolmasters. James Thomson, the poet, was one of the earliest students of the college. The course provided did much to raise the standard of Army schoolmasters, and by 1860 there were 244 trained schoolmasters and 242 trained schoolmistresses.

Army schools for adults and children were not only established in Great Britain but also in India and in every part of the Empire where a permanent military station existed. Attendance was voluntary, although a general order signed by Wellington in 1849 attempted to make it compulsory for every recruit to receive instruction from the schoolmaster for two hours each day. The legality

[1] The Duke of York's School had been established in 1801 for the maintenance and support of the children of Regular soldiers.

of the order was questioned and the law officers of the Crown decided that it was no part of military discipline to attend school. The military authorities were unwilling to press for new legislation on the matter and contented themselves with offering strong inducements to soldiers to attend. A general order of 1857 laid down "That no man is to be considered eligible for promotion to corporal, unless in the field, who has not been dismissed the lowest class of the school, and is, therefore, tolerably advanced in reading, writing, and arithmetic."

In 1850 infant-schools and industrial schools for girls were established. Parents sending their children to school were charged small fees which were given over to the use of the schoolmistress. Fees for children attending school in 1858 were according to the following scale: twopence per month for one child, three-halfpence per month for two from the same family, and a halfpenny a month each child if three or four attended. In this year, 11,062 children were being instructed in Army schools. Adults also paid fees. Sergeants paid 8d. a month, corporals 6d. a month, and drummers and privates 4d. a month. The schoolmaster had to provide books and materials from the fees, but in 1854 fees were no longer paid direct to the master, who was relieved of the duty of providing books and stationery.

Gleig was succeeded in 1857 by Colonel Lefroy (later Sir John Lefroy, Governor of Tasmania). The new Inspector-General was an able and zealous man who visited the schools and reported upon the work being done. From his reports, and those of certain H.M.I.s who were placed at the disposal of the military authorities by the Education Department, we learn a great deal about the varied educational activities going on in the Service. "The annual reports speak of unit libraries, managed by committees on which the rank and file were represented, of lantern lectures, community singing, Christy minstrels, dances, and gymnastic classes. In Aldershot, in 1858, there was a garrison list of twenty-seven Army lecturers. Two brigade majors, with 'magic lanthorn,' lectured respectively on 'Wellington' and 'The Australian Gold Diggings.' An artillery officer explained the new electric telegraph, and a corporal of the Devons was found constructing one from his memory of the lecture. Schoolmaster Grant lectured on 'Curiosities of Air and Water, with Chemical Experiments.' But at the other end of the scale was the wretched schoolmaster in Capetown, to whom no sailing ship delivered stores in 1857 and 1858. During these two years, in a dark hut paved with cobblestones, he taught fifty men with the aid of a dozen (borrowed) slates, and a pocket map of the world." [1]

Lefroy introduced a number of reforms during his tenure of office. Fees were abolished in the lowest grade of school which taught the three R's and by 1870 all fees had disappeared. A Council of Military Education was formed in 1857, originally for superintending the education of officers, but in 1860 it undertook the supervision of Army schools. Queen Victoria objected to the Council because it detracted from the authority of the Commander-in-Chief. She had her own way in 1870, when the Council was abolished. Its most noteworthy activity was the institution, in 1860, of Army Certificates of Education. The certificates were in three classes and the standards to be attained by the holders were as follows: First-class—to read fluently any book of ordinary difficulty and write correctly a passage dictated from the same; an understanding of the method of keeping Mess Book, Ledger, and Regimental Savings Bank accounts; ability to work vulgar and decimal fractions and examples in compound proportion; and a fair knowledge of general geography and English history. Second-class—to read a book of moderate difficulty and write fairly a passage dictated from the same, to understand the method of Mess Book, Ledger, and Regimental Savings Bank accounts, and to work examples in practice, simple proportion and interest. Third-class—to read easy narratives and write fairly a passage dictated from the same, and to work examples in the four compound rules and reduction of money.

In 1871 a fourth-class certificate was introduced, but as its standard was too low to be of any value it was discontinued in 1877.

One may be tempted to ask what these early efforts in Army education achieved. Lefroy's reports supply the answer. Illiteracy was widespread amongst the soldiers of the mid-19th century. In 1859, 20·5 per cent could neither read nor write and 18·8 per cent could read a little and just sign their names. By 1868 these percentages had dropped to 9·46 and 10·59 respectively.

The Newcastle Commission included Service schools in their terms of reference and emphasised very strongly the value of Army education. "In the present day the soldier is not looked upon as a mere machine, but is expected to be intelligent and to exercise

---

[1] *Army Education*, Vol. XVII, No. 4, p. 135. "A Note on the History of Army Education," Colonel A. C. T. White, v.c., m.c., June 1942.

self-reliance; it is impossible that he should do so if he has not mastered the rudiments of education and has been subjected to no mental training. Profligacy and habits of excess are no longer tolerated in the soldier; we must, therefore, endeavour by education to raise him above these things, and set before him better objects to wean him from such pursuits: and it must not be forgotten that in many instances soldiers are discharged the service in their prime, and it is obvious that they carry into civil life the habits which they have acquired in the Army. . . . It is most highly important, therefore, in every way that the soldier should be encouraged to attend school." [1]

The Commissioners thought that however desirable it might be to make school attendance compulsory for boys, it should remain voluntary for adults. "A great deal will always depend upon the commanding officer, and upon the interest he shows in the school. It is in his power to stimulate the men to attend, and to give orders that no trivial matters should interfere with the school hours. . . . We think it desirable that an annual report upon these schools should be issued, a copy of which should be forwarded to the commanding officer of every regiment; and that, where the schools of any particular regiment fall short of the average in efficiency and attendance, the special attention of the commanding officer should be called to the matter." [2]

The Cardwell reforms of 1870, the Elementary Education Act of the same year, and the abolition of the purchase of commissions which resulted in a better type of officer, all had their repercussions on Army education. More attention was given to the soldier's welfare, especially in regard to conditions in barracks, and to messing and recreation. The educational system had to be improved to meet the needs of the better type of recruit who was entering the Army. The regulations of 1881 made promotion to the rank of colour-sergeant depend on the possession of a first-class certificate of education. A new drill-book issued in 1892 emphasised that soldiers should be "taught to think and, subject to accepted principles, to act for themselves." The Council of Military Education was replaced by a Director General of Education in 1870, who in turn was superseded by a Director of Army Schools in 1898. New barracks were built in which separate classrooms

---

[1] *Newcastle Commission on Popular Education*, Vol. I, p. 427, H.M.S.O., 1861.
[2] *Ibid.*, pp. 427-8.

were provided. The seating accommodation in children's schools was overhauled and the desks which had been made for adults were replaced by adjustable ones which could serve for adults and children alike. Regular surprise inspections of Army schools became the custom and it has been stated that this caused a definite rise in the standard of the instruction. Published statistics seemed to show a very happy state of affairs. At the end of the century, more than 4,000 men possessed a first-class certificate and 45,000 men a second-class. Much of this progress was illusory The Corps of Army Schoolmasters was hampered at every turn by red tape and the issue of detailed regulations encouraged formalism and stifled initiative. At one time, an exact minimum number of words and sentences was prescribed for the essay examination for the second-class certificate. The spirit bred of Payment by Results invaded and thrived in an Army atmosphere. Under such soul-destroying conditions it is scarcely surprising that the supply of suitable entrants to the educational service dwindled. A committee in 1901, called to consider the conditions of service for Army school-masters, failed to produce any useful recommendations. Another committee, in 1904, suggested a reorganisation which involved a revision of the syllabus and a reduction in the schoolmaster's hours of work. Improved methods of teaching began to appear and the quality of the instruction started to rise. In 1906 proficiency pay was introduced for soldiers, and one of the conditions of earning it was the possession of a third-class certificate of education.

The War Office requested the Board of Education to conduct a thorough investigation into Army education. The inspectors seconded for this duty reported in 1907, and through their recommendations the method of training Army schoolmasters was assimilated to that employed in civilian training-colleges. In 1909 the Board of Education recognised trained Army schoolmasters as certificated teachers, a step which was a boon to those who left the Army after the First World War. It enabled them to enter civilian schools with recognition on the salary scale for time spent in the Service.

Before 1914 the Y.M.C.A. had taken a keen interest in the welfare of the soldier, and in the summer training-camps for both Regulars and Territorials, the Y.M.C.A. tent had become a regular feature. It provided a "quiet room" for reading and writing, and, in off-duty periods, concerts and religious services were held in it, and lectures of an attractive nature given. When the outbreak of war put an end to the educational activities provided by the Army, the Y.M.C.A. stepped into the breach and augmented these facilities for troops in Britain and overseas. In 1915 a committee, with Dr. Temple (afterwards Archbishop of Canterbury) as chairman and Dr. Basil Yeaxlee as secretary, was formed to develop its work in education. The universities and other educational bodies were also providing lecturers, and it became necessary to integrate these different activities. In April 1918 the Y.M.C.A. Universities Committee was created, on which the universities were represented by their Vice-Chancellors and members of their teaching staffs, and other members were elected by the Directors of Education, the N.U.T., the W.E.A., the Y.M.C.A., and Y.W.C.A. The whole of the expense was borne by the Y.M.C.A., which spent about £250,000 on the enterprise. Much of the work was carried out on the different fighting fronts, but the needs of soldiers in training in Britain, and workers in munition factories, also received attention. As the organisation was not supported by public funds, its work was able to develop along liberal lines and freedom in experiment was encouraged. Its object was the personal development of the soldier's interests and training in good citizenship. Owing to the exigencies of the campaign, it was difficult to organise consecutive lectures so that much of the work consisted in single lectures covering a wide variety of topics. Where possible, such as at base camps, regular classes were conducted. At Etaples, early in 1918, over 1,000 men were studying the French language. Voluntary educational efforts started within the Army itself. Thus, at Brocton Camp on Cannock Chase, in 1917, an organised experiment was carried out with certain battalions of young soldiers. The initiative came from the officers of these units and the teachers were supplied by personnel of the camp who had had either secondary education or previous teaching experience. A similar experiment was tried out in November 1917 by the 23rd Army Corps.

All this work attracted the attention of the authorities, and *A.C.I. 322* of 1917 was issued which made elementary education part of the training of the young soldier, *i.e.* recruits under the age of 18½. The next step was the introduction of a definite scheme of education by the Army Council. Its general principles were announced early in 1918, and although the beginning of the scheme coincided with the great German offensive, preparations still went on. The Army was responsible for carrying out the scheme in the forward areas, but the Y.M.C.A. dealt with the provision of educational facilities on the lines of communication. Lectures were provided through the Y.M.C.A. Universities Committee and Sir Henry Hadow went to France as the Y.M.C.A. Director of Education. He was later succeeded by Sir Graham Balfour. Nearly 200 lecturers and teachers volunteered for the work, and classrooms and libraries were established at base camps. By December 1918, on the lines of communication in France, 810 courses of study, covering seventy-one different subjects and attended by 12,235 students, had been organised. The subjects offered included mathematics and science, languages and literature, history, philosophy, business and commercial subjects, and arts and crafts. Attendance at lectures, as distinct from classes, amounted in the same month to 93,380.

The Universities Committee provided educational facilities for officers and men interned in Holland. Music was in great demand there and courses were arranged by Mr. Percy Scholes, who gathered a group of outstanding musicians to carry out the work. Other fronts, *e.g.* Salonika, Egypt, Mesopotamia, and Italy, received lecturers from the Universities Committee. Courses were also arranged for patients in military hospitals.

Meanwhile, the official Army scheme was launched. Lord Gorell was put in charge and was assisted by a committee on which the Armies in Britain and France, the Board of Education, and the Ministries of Labour and Reconstruction were represented. Financial sanction was obtained, and on 24th September 1918 the Army Council issued a special army order (*295* of 1918) which gave official authorisation to the educational work which had been going on in Britain and France. *Army Order 18* of 20th December 1918 extended the scheme to Italy, Salonika, and Egypt. The organisation and supervision of the scheme was in the hands of a Department of the Staff Duties Directorate at the War Office, which was assisted by an Inter-Departmental Committee and a number of expert advisers appointed by the Board of Education and the Scottish Education Department. The scheme provided for the creation of a teaching staff from Army personnel and authorised the appointment of education officers on a scale proportionate to the requirements of the different units. Two schools of education were opened, one at Oxford and the other at Cambridge (later transferred to Newmarket), to train officers and N.C.O.s for teaching. Intensive courses of a month's duration were held at these schools.

In order to unify educational training in the Army, the Army Schoolmasters' Department was transferred to the Staff Duties Directorate. Lord Gorell recognised the significance of this action when he said, "This transference was, as far as it goes, an acceptance of the principle that military training and educational training could be and should be viewed together."

The scheme had barely been launched when the signing of the armistice called for certain important modifications. The citizen armies were looking forward to returning to civil life and the urgent need now was to provide, for the men awaiting demobilisation, training which would assist them in taking up their old occupations or fit them for undertaking new ones. There was also the Army of Occupation on the Rhine to be considered. The task was a gigantic one and the military authorities tackled their problems with vigour. Every unit of 1,000 men in the Home Forces was allotted four officers and twelve N.C.O.s as instructors. Every available textbook was obtained and over three-quarters of a million books were sent overseas. "Colleges in the older Universities were turned into schools for Army instructors, amongst whom were teachers, lawyers, farmers, mechanics, shopkeepers—any class of men that had something to contribute to national reconstruction. Army workshops and military training establishments became vocational training schools, with curricula ranging from linotype setting and stock breeding to English literature and the Malay language. Education officers in hospitals in close touch with the Ministries of Labour and Pensions, worked to facilitate the resettlement of the disabled." [1]

Perhaps the most spectacular effort was made by the Army of the Rhine. Buildings were requisitioned from the German universities and technical colleges and the Rhine Army Colleges developed in which, during the summer of 1919, about 75,000 students were taking regular courses. The Army of the Rhine was allotted double the number of instructors granted to the other armies, and civilian teachers were also employed. In all units, education for one hour each, taken out of parade time, was compulsory. From the units, selected students passed to the Divisional Schools and from these to Corps Schools or Army Colleges.

Mr. Fisher, president of the Board of Education, warmly encouraged the scheme, which he described as the "greatest military invention since gunpowder." Speaking at the Cambridge School

[1] *Army Education*, Vol. XVII, No. 4, pp. 137-8.

for Army Instructors, he said, "Nothing in the shape of adult education has ever been attempted on the same scale in the whole history
of the world."   The final report on Adult Education, published by
the Ministry of Reconstruction, expressed the hope: "It is idle
to prophesy, but we may hope that these are portents of a new
educational era which we are about to enter, an era which will be
marked by a large extension of adult education among the people
generally." [1]

Education in the R.A.F. proceeded on somewhat different lines.
This was due to the fact that the Air Force differed from the Army
in having a larger number of skilled and semi-skilled men.   The
R.A.F. education scheme was approved in August 1918, but before
putting it into operation a census was made of the educational
requirements of Air Force personnel serving in France.   One of
the difficulties encountered was that the R.A.F. had no regimental
system and its units were of all sizes, scattered about the country
and often in out-of-the-way places.   Hence the Air Force scheme
was less centralised and provision had to be made for individual
treatment.   The Air Ministry was convinced that education would
be a permanent feature of the Service, and consequently it prepared
an emergency scheme that could readily be merged into a permanent
one on the return of normal conditions.   Because of the necessity
of decentralisation, Air Force education officers were given more
freedom and responsibility.   The ratio of instructors was the same
as in the Army and their rate of pay was also equivalent.   This was
unfortunate since the pay and allowances were not sufficient to
attract instructors of the best type.   An additional source of supply
was found amongst educated women in the W.R.A.F.   A general
syllabus was issued but each education officer was called upon to
frame courses suited to the requirements of the personnel in his
locality.

A feature of the Air Force was the large demand for vocational
subjects.   A system of correspondence courses was organised to
meet the needs of men and women stationed in out-of-the-way
places.   By March 1919 about 12,300 officers and men were
receiving instruction.   The R.A.F. also drew upon voluntary
sources such as the universities, the Y.M.C.A., and the W.E.A.

The hopes of the president of the Board of Education and the
Ministry of Reconstruction were only partially realised.   "A tremendous task had been attempted and something had been done.

[1] *Final Report of the Adult Education Committee*, p. 349, H.M.S.O., 1919.

Much of the work was slight and ephemeral; some of it was more solid, while occasionally, a little reached a high standard. And when one remembers the conditions under which the work was attempted, one must admire the courage of the men who took up the challenge and achieved what they did." [1]

As demobilisation proceeded rapidly, many people were asking what was to be the future of education in the Army. This question was answered by Mr. Churchill in August 1919, when, as Secretary of State for War, he declared to the House of Commons: "It has been decided that education is henceforward to be regarded as an integral part of Army training." In pursuance of this policy the Corps of Army Schoolmasters was disbanded in February 1920 and Mr. Churchill announced that, in future, regimental officers would be responsible for elementary educational training and would be assisted by an Education Corps incorporating members of the former Corps of Army Schoolmasters and Schoolmistresses.

The constitution and duties of the new corps were laid before Parliament in May 1920, and the establishment, pay, and conditions of service of the Army Educational Corps were set out in *Army Order 231* of 1920. In addition to transferring personnel from the Corps of Army Schoolmasters, officers and other ranks who had suitable qualifications and experience were invited to apply for transfer. A board of selection, under the chairmanship of Lord Gorell, interviewed candidates, and the establishment was made up to 428 officers and 595 warrant-officers and sergeants. Personnel of the corps were allotted on a fixed scale to units and were to be regarded by commanding officers as expert advisers and assistants. They were not only responsible for carrying out advanced instruction, but were also required to supervise the training of regimental instructors who dealt with the more elementary aspects of the training. Other members of the corps were attached to the H.Q.s of brigades, divisions, and commands, and were appointed to the Army School of Education established at Shorncliffe or were given inspectorial posts at the War Office.

The Geddes Axe came into operation in 1922 and the establishment of the corps was cut by one-half. The official textbook of educational principles, *Educational Training, Part I, General Principles*, was issued in 1920, and was revised and enlarged in

[1] Hawkins and Brimble. *Adult Education, the Record of the British Army*, pp. 63-4, Macmillan, 1947.

1923 and again in 1931.   This was an enlightened document which incorporated the principles of modern educational method.   The Army Certificates of Education were restored, with an additional Special Certificate.   A soldier had to gain a first-class certificate before he could receive warrant rank, and the special certificate before he could be commissioned.   The examination for the special certificate included English, mathematics, a classical or modern language, map-reading, and two other subjects selected from a prescribed list.

Vocational training was introduced to fit the soldier to take up civilian employment after his discharge from the Army.   This included gardening, joinery, light metal-work, and elementary electrical engineering.   Special vocational centres were established. At Catterick, soldiers were trained in farming methods and poultry and pig keeping.   Officers and other ranks of the A.E.C. were allotted to the apprentice tradesmen schools and were responsible for the general education of boys who were training to become skilled Army tradesmen.

Between 1920 and 1939, the A.E.C., although suffering from successive economy cuts, took on new responsibilities in Britain and overseas.   Some idea of the success of the Corps is given by the number (18,000) of men who possessed the first-class certificate in 1936 (a standard roughly equivalent to School Certificate) and the fact that ninety per cent of these had left school at fourteen.

When war broke out in 1939, members of the A.E.C. were required to take up Intelligence duties, and it was not until the winter of 1940 that they were able to return to their educational work.   Meanwhile, education in the Forces was left to voluntary associations connected with adult education.   After Munich, a modified form of conscription had been introduced and demands were made by the Y.M.C.A., the W.E.A., and the universities, for the provision of educational training for the young militiamen. These demands were supported by the Board of Education and in consequence the War Office agreed to prepare a scheme in conjunction with the extra-mural departments of the universities. Before the scheme could be put into operation, however, hostilities broke out and the various committees responsible for it were dissolved.

As in the First World War, groups of men within the Army organised educational schemes and called upon the universities and other bodies for assistance.   The need for the co-ordination of these diverse activities grew, and the demand that something should be done was made in the press and by different educational associations. A conference representing the Board of Education and the civilian bodies met and decided upon the institution of a Central Advisory Council for Education in H.M. Forces. The Council had its first meeting in January 1940, and Sir Walter Moberly, chairman of the University Grants Committee, was appointed its chairman, with Dr. A. D. (later Lord) Lindsay, Master of Balliol College, Oxford, as vice-chairman, and Dr. Basil Yeaxlee as secretary. The C.A.C. asked the vice-chancellors and the principals of the university colleges to form Regional Committees through which the C.A.C. could work. Altogether, twenty-three Regional Committees for Education in H.M. Forces were formed, on which the universities and representatives of bodies concerned with adult education served. A full-time secretary, usually a member of the university staff, was appointed for each Regional Committee, and plans were drawn up for the co-ordination of the educational resources of their areas.

The Regional Committees got busy in a very short space of time, and from August 1940 their work was financed by the Government through the War Office. These measures mobilised the whole of the civilian educational resources of the country to deal with the situation. The C.A.C., however, intimated to the War Office that it was important to utilise the educational resources of the Army as soon as possible. The Haining Committee met in March 1940, and recommended the establishment of a Directorate of Army Education. The personnel of the A.E.C. were returned to their educational duties and the increase of the establishment of the corps was authorised. The War Office ordered every unit to appoint a regimental officer as part-time education officer and his duties were to ascertain the needs of his men and make arrangements to meet them.

Some idea of the ground covered by the Regional Committees can be gained from one of the early reports of the C.A.C. for the period April-September 1941. 18,983 single lectures, 1,530 short courses, and 1,075 classes were arranged by the Regional Committees. The total number of meetings was 33,532. In addition, there were classes organised by the L.E.A.s, and between 700 and 800 provided for the Royal Navy and the R.A.F. At this time, the C.A.C. was employing forty-six full-time, and a very much larger number of part-time, lecturers.

In spite of all that was being accomplished by the C.A.C., the L.E.A.s, and the personnel of the A.E.C., the Adjutant-General, Sir Ronald Adam, calculated that nearly eighty per cent of the Army was untouched by any regular educational influence. It was largely due to his advice that the Army Council introduced in September 1941 the Army Bureau of Current Affairs. Sir Ronald Adam decided that educational activities should be compulsory in the Army, but what forms should they take?

The morale of the average soldier was causing the Government considerable concern. The Germans knew quite clearly what they were fighting for, but the same could not be said of many of our own troops. Large numbers had only a vague understanding of the causes which had produced the war, and even those who were adequately informed when they joined the Army, had lost touch with current affairs. It was felt that if the soldier was thoroughly acquainted with the essentials of the cause for which he was fighting, he would be a better soldier and the understanding would give a new direction to both his training and his campaigning. The ideal was that of the Cromwellian soldier who both knew and loved what he was fighting for.

There was to be at least one A.B.C.A. discussion a week and it was to be given by the regimental officer. In order to brief him, a bulletin was issued every week. *Current Affairs* and *War* would be supplied in alternate weeks. Mr. W. E. Williams, the Director of the Army Bureau of Current Affairs, was the originator of this idea. *Current Affairs* provided a background of recent events in their relation to the war effort and *War* was to be a chronicle of the progress of the war on different fronts showing the achievements of the Navy, Army, and Air Force, and the forces of our allies. Each bulletin also contained suggestions about the methods of handling the topics. It was not supposed that every officer would be a capable instructor. Indeed, the majority were faced by a task which was entirely new to them. The method to be employed was that of a free discussion, and the role of the regimental officer was rather that of a group-leader or a chairman than a teacher. He was given the advice, "Take particular care to assure your men that you don't claim to be an expert. But tell them that it's your business, as an officer, to learn the facts about things, so that you can communicate them to the men you have to train. 'I didn't know anything about the Bren gun until I joined the Army. I've had to study it, so that I could teach it. In the same way, I've had to study the origins of this war, so that I can teach you about it. I'm not an expert, but I've collected and examined the facts, and now, as well as I can, I'll try to answer any questions you put about it. I don't say I'll know all the answers, but I'll do my best, and at least I can help you to find them out from other sources.' " [1]

Needless to say, some officers made a great success of their new job while others were complete failures. Everything depended on the attitude of the commanding officer and the zeal and enthusiasm of the regimental officers themselves. On the whole, A.B.C.A. made many men "news-minded" and taught them how to read their newspapers intelligently and to discuss their views with their comrades.

Experience of A.B.C.A. discussions showed that the education of men and women in the forces was lacking in many fundamentals and something more than an hour per week spent at a lecture or in discussion was needed to make good these deficiencies. Accordingly, for the four winter months November 1942 to February 1943, an additional three hours a week were allotted for education from the training time. One period was for the training of the man as a soldier, another was concerned with his education as a citizen, and the third with his education as an individual. The first period was to be at the disposal of the commanding officer, who might use it for map-reading, history of the Army or the regiment, or, in the case of technical units, for mathematics or technical instruction. The briefing for the course in citizenship was by means of the *British Way and Purpose* pamphlets which had been specially written by civilian experts. Whilst the regimental officers continued with A.B.C.A., *British Way and Purpose* was usually given by civilian lecturers from the Regional Committees, personnel of the A.E.C., or specially briefed regimental instructors. The latter were obtained through short courses on subject-matter and methods of teaching held at the universities. Thus, at Leeds, during this period, the writer organised courses of a fortnight's duration through which more than 400 regimental instructors were briefed. Similar courses were arranged at most of the other universities. The third period catered for the individual interests of men and women, and a wide variety of studies and occupations was available. Correspondence courses were arranged to assist those whose professional training had been broken by enlistment. *British Way and Purpose* was such a success that the original series of pamphlets were issued

[1] *Basic A.B.C.A.*, No. 1, November 1942, p. 2.

in book form. A.B.C.A. and *British Way and Purpose* were also taken up by the Royal Navy and the R.A.F.

In November 1942 the A.B.C.A. directorate began the issue of *A.B.C.A. Map Reviews*. Each of these consisted of a large coloured map of the world with arrows pointing to the regions where events of current interest had occurred. The back of the sheet contained comments on recent events illustrated by maps and photographs. They were issued fortnightly to units and formed a running commentary on current affairs. In large units a quiet room was set aside containing current copies of the pamphlets, photographs, wall-newspapers, and selected works of reference.

Music appealed to considerable numbers of men and women. Northern Command was able to produce two orchestras, the Catterick, and the Northern Command Symphony Orchestra, the latter being conducted by Richard Austin. Musical and dramatic performances were arranged by the Entertainments National Service Association (E.N.S.A.) both in Britain and overseas. In some districts, Forces Music Clubs were started and attracted the more serious students of music. The A.T.S. both used and contributed to the different services made available, and special courses in household repairs, handicrafts, and domestic subjects, were arranged for them.

To sum up, these war-time years witnessed the greatest experiment ever conducted in mass adult-education, but this was not the end of it all. As the war drew to its conclusion, serious attention was being given to the demobilisation period. Matters were complicated since no one knew when the war was likely to end, but as early as December 1943 an education scheme for the release-period was being considered. In addition to the Army School of Education, which had moved from Shorncliffe to Wakefield, and the A.B.C.A. School at Coleg Harlech, a new school for training instructors for the release-period was opened at Cuerdon Hall near Preston. The establishment of the A.E.C. was increased so that the corps could adequately supervise the scheme. Most of the actual instruction was to be given by unit education officers and personnel selected from the unit. With the assistance of the Regional Committees, a large number of intensive courses for instructor-training were organised, so that when the time came to put the scheme into operation there would be a sufficiency of instructors. In February 1944 Mr. P. R. Morris was seconded from his duties as Director of Education for Kent to co-ordinate the

Directorates of Army Education and A.B.C.A., and to organise an educational scheme for the release-period. The first Director of Army Education had been Mr. F. W. Bendall, who was released by the Board of Education for that purpose in 1942. He was succeeded by Mr. J. B. Bickersteth who returned to the University of Toronto at the beginning of the year 1944, and, in December of the same year, Brigadier (later Major-General) Cyril Lloyd was released by Field-Marshall Montgomery to take up the duties of Director of Army Education. Sir Philip Morris, who is now Vice-Chancellor of the University of Bristol, brought to the task a long experience of education and administration which was invaluable. He was mainly responsible for the Army Education Scheme (Release-Period), and when, in February 1946, the scheme was fully launched, he handed over the administration to Major-General Lloyd.

The details of the release scheme were given in the *Organisation Handbook*, 16th March 1945. It was planned on a unit basis, an A.T.S. group being regarded as a unit. A minimum of six hours a week was set aside from training- or working- hours for education, and commanding officers could allocate further periods if necessary. Other handbooks were issued which dealt with curricula, method, equipment and materials, correspondence courses, and libraries. The syllabus in each subject was divided into three grades—elementary, intermediate, and advanced. Arrangements were made for a supply of textbooks (eight hundred selected books were printed), stationery, materials, and apparatus.

Classes which could not be organised within units were provided at brigade level. The apex of the scheme was the Formation College, in which students could carry their studies to a more advanced stage than was possible in their units. One college was established in each home command, one in the British Liberation Army, and one each in the Central Mediterranean Force and the Middle East Force. Arrangements were also made for special lecturers, chosen by the C.A.C., to visit the armies in Europe, North Africa, and the Far East. Formation Colleges at home were housed as far as possible in large country houses. Thus Northern Command Formation College was at Welbeck Abbey, the seat of the Duke of Portland, but troops from the London district and Southern Command made use of a hutted camp at Chisledon, near Swindon.

In order to meet the needs of men and women who wished to

enter a university or one of the professions, courses of study leading to the Forces Preliminary Examination were instituted.[1]

The scheme was drawn up in accordance with the prevailing belief that, after the war with Germany had been won, at least another year would be necessary to ensure the defeat of Japan, and that therefore demobilisation would be a gradual process. VE-Day came on 8th May 1945, but by August 10th Japan was also out of the war. As a result, the Government announced that demobilisation would be speeded up. During May and June, units made their preliminary plans and the scheme was to be complete by July 1st. In spite of difficulties caused by the diminishing number of instructors, many of whom were returning to their civilian occupations, in some units the scheme was a marked success. The Army Schools and Regional Committees worked hard to provide training courses for new unit instructors. The pamphlet *War* was discontinued, and in December 1945 the Army Bureau of Current Affairs was replaced by a civilian bureau which, under the control of the Carnegie trustees, continues to issue bulletins, map-reviews, and all kinds of visual aids, including films and film-strips.

During 1947 the Release Scheme was replaced by one more suited to peace-time conditions. The latter differed from pre-war days because a limited form of conscription was continued. The needs of young men drafted into National Service had to be considered, and at the same time arrangements were necessary for the education of Regular soldiers. Plans were prepared for a scheme of general education in which, as in the release-period, the curriculum was divided into three grades in each of the basic subjects—English, mathematics, history and geography, general science, and citizenship with current affairs. *The Handbook of General Education* was issued, 9th April 1948, in which the syllabuses for Grades A, B, and C were given, together with suggestions on teaching method.

The scheme is partly compulsory and partly voluntary. Citizenship and current affairs are compulsory for National Service men and Regular soldiers. Men who have reached the standard of the

---

[1] This examination was in two parts, and, in order to pass, the candidate had to satisfy the examiners in both parts, which could be taken separately. Part I consisted of three compulsory subjects: English, Mathematics or Latin or a subject chosen from Part II, and General Knowledge (including Current Affairs and Citizenship). In Part II, the candidate had to pass in two of the following subjects: Natural Science or Household Science or Latin (if not already taken in Part I), French or German, History or Geography, Social Science, and additional Mathematics or Geometrical and Mechanical Drawing.

Forces Preliminary Examination can continue their education in the form best suited to their needs. Regular soldiers will continue their education until they have served three years or reached the standard of Forces Preliminary, Part I. If they wish to continue voluntarily after this, permission will generally be given. Similar regulations apply to the A.T.S., now renamed the Women's Royal Auxiliary Corps (W.R.A.C.). Soldiers are also encouraged to make use of civilian educational facilities. Correspondence courses are still available, and each course, including the necessary textbooks, costs 10s. per annum.

Two Army colleges in Britain and two overseas are retained, and Army Education Centres up to the number of eighty may be established for garrisons of over 1,500 men at home and abroad. Regimental instructors are being replaced by personnel of the R.A.E.C., but the unit education officer is retained on a part-time basis and the commanding officer is still responsible for the education of his unit. The distinction of the title Royal Army Educational Corps was conferred, 10th December 1946, as recognition for valuable services during the war. Supplies of books, stationery, and other materials are now issued on normal equipment scales.

Two Army Schools of Education were established, one for N.C.O.s, at Buchanan Castle near Loch Lomond, and the other at Eltham Palace, Kent, for officers. In September 1948 the two schools were amalgamated and moved to Bodmin, Cornwall.[1] The whole of Army education is being brought into line with the further education planned by the Act of 1944, and to bring this about the Ministry of Education has arranged for certain H.M.I.s to co-operate in an advisory capacity with the military inspectors of the Army Directorate.

The Northern Command Formation College, Welbeck Abbey, is closed (p. 589) and was re-opened in September 1953 as a college to prepare boys for regular commissions in the technical branches. At present, the public schools in the south of England have supplied the majority of such officers. Few came from the north of England and Scotland or from the grammar-schools. Welbeck Abbey offers a two-year course (16-18 years) and pupils who are recommended by the headmaster will proceed to Sandhurst without being required to pass the entrance examination.

The college is similar to a normal boarding-school and is staffed by civilians. Candidates for entry must be recommended by their

---

[1] The Army School of Education is now at Beaconsfield.

headmasters and should have obtained the General Certificate of Education in three subjects, including science and mathematics. The interviewing board contains a number of civilian members and attention is given to ascertaining those who possess potential officer qualities. The college accommodates seventy-five pupils, but later the number is to be doubled. Emphasis is placed on the study of science and mathematics and every pupil will have workshop training. Tuition is free, but parents are required to contribute to the maintenance of their sons, according to their income. The maximum contribution has been fixed at £90 a year. Many pupils leave the secondary school at sixteen and it is hoped to attract suitable candidates from them to the technical branches of the army.

Another new scheme opens out an opportunity of obtaining a regular commission through national service training. Selected national service officers will enter the Royal Military College of Science, Shrivenham, to read for B.Sc. External of London University. Thus candidates will be able to graduate whilst holding the rank and receiving the pay of an officer without serious disturbance to their academic studies.

The recent reintroduction of Army Certificates of Education has tended to awaken the interest of a certain number and to provide them with a goal towards which to work. *A.C.I. 349*, 20th April 1949, fixed 1st October 1949 as the commencing-date of the examination for the second and third class certificates, and 1st March 1950 for the first-class. The interest is derived from the fact that promotions are to depend on the possession of the appropriate certificate, the details of which are given in the *A.C.I.* mentioned above. The General Officers-in-Chief of commands and districts are responsible for the setting and marking of the two lower certificates, but the first-class certificates are the responsibility of the Institute of Army Education, Eltham Palace, London. For the lower certificates candidates are examined in English (oral and written), elementary mathematics, and in the general paper which includes history, geography, general science, citizenship, and current affairs. Map-reading is an additional subject for the second-class certificate. The first-class certificate consists of two parts. Part I contains the compulsory subjects: English, mathematics, and current affairs. Part II allows the candidate a choice of the following: history, geography, general science, or citizenship. For special requirements, candidates may offer other subjects such as additional mathematics, physics, chemistry, engineering drawing, map-reading, and either French, German, or Russian. All soldiers seeking promotion are given a year of grace in which to qualify.

One problem, the number of illiterates in the forces, has caused considerable concern. In 1943 it was estimated that these represented about $1\frac{1}{4}$ per cent of the intake. Since National Service men have entered the Army, some authorities place the percentage as high as ten with possibly double that number of semi-illiterates. These figures may be exaggerated, but there is no doubt that large numbers enter the Services at eighteen who seem to have retained little that has been taught them at school. These are not always confined to the dull and backward; many with normal, and sometimes high, I.Q.s are almost illiterate. During the war, special courses in basic education were arranged to teach them reading and writing. Special textbooks (*English Parade*) were issued and the teaching of reading proceeded by a combination of "sentence" and "phonetic" methods. Some of these efforts were successful, but many men relapsed a few months after the course. Refresher courses were of value in helping to prevent this. One may ask how it is that men who have attended school until fourteen should become illiterate in the space of a few years. Investigations have shown that many causes have been at work. Some had missed the greater part of their schooling, *e.g.* children of the bargees, gipsies, etc. Another cause was the large numbers in the classes of the junior schools. Under these conditions there was a tendency to neglect the duller pupils, with the result that they left the junior school without being able to read or write. The senior school gave them little help, partly owing to the absence of suitable reading-books for "C-stream" pupils. There were also pupils who, through illness, had missed a large part of the school course. Other contributory factors were the dislocation of the pupils' studies in blitzed areas, the unsatisfactory schooling of many who had been evacuated, and the tendency of some teachers to pay less attention to basic subjects than formerly. Under the new scheme, centres for preliminary education have official recognition and provide a six-week course under specially trained instructors. When the man rejoins his unit, his preliminary education continues. The War Office realises that, under modern conditions of warfare, an illiterate can never make an efficient soldier.

Space will allow only a brief mention of the educational work in the Royal Navy and the R.A.F. during the last war. As in the

Army, education in the Navy has a long history. There were education officers on the ships of the Royal Navy at least as far back as the end of the 17th century. Their duties were to instruct young officers in the three R's and in navigation, and then to teach other young people of the ship. The Newcastle Commission was very critical of the facilities provided by the Admiralty. The Commissioners reported: "The educational arrangements of the navy present a marked difference to those in force for the army. The organisation is inferior, and the Admiralty does not appear to take an equal interest with the War Office in promoting it. The necessity of education for the navy is acknowledged but little earnestness is displayed in carrying it out."[1] Although a seamen's schoolmaster was to be found in all ships with a complement of over 300 men, the Commissioners who investigated the conditions of education in sea-going ships reported that the schools were very defective. The teaching was not of a character to interest or attract the men, and generally no register of attendances was kept. The inadequacy of the schools was largely due to the lack of interest shown by the captain and the senior officers, and the schoolmasters were of an inferior type and would continue to be so until more adequate pay was given. As the Admiralty was not prepared to spend additional money on education, the Commission recommended the introduction of the pupil-teacher system on board ship.

Dr. Wooley inspected the ships in harbour and reported on their schools as follows: "My impression is not favourable; they display an utter want of classification and intelligent system. . . . The records of attendances, if kept at all, are very imperfect. . . . The grand desideratum for these schools is the establishment of some means for providing them with a sufficiency of trained masters. Until this is done, it is useless to suggest minor improvements."[2]

The dockyard schools were also inspected and the unfavourable report which was issued on them resulted in the recommendation that a normal school should be established at Greenwich, similar to the one at Chelsea for the Army, and that a class of assistant schoolmasters and three grades of Royal Navy schoolmasters be established. The report of the Commission was very effective in introducing improvements into naval schools and before the end of the century many of the recommendations had been put into operation.

[1] *Newcastle Commission on Popular Education*, Vol. I, p. 428, H.M.S.O., 1861.   [2] *Ibid.*, p. 435.

The First World War resulted in a large extension of education, but as compared with the Army, it was to a great extent scientific and technical. During the Second World War, when operational activities permitted, education was carried on in a way similar to that in the Army. Technical education has always been important since it is required for the seaman's work, *e.g.* mathematics for his training in gunnery. Courses of lectures, debates, classes in handicrafts, and vocational classes, were provided in the ports, and one interesting feature was a series of lectures delivered on board ship by well-known university professors who were flown to the Grand Fleet at Scapa Flow.

Besides technical education, an hour a week is given to current affairs and citizenship and basic education is compulsory. The work of the Navy demands a high educational standard in its ratings so that the problem of illiteracy does not exist. Basic education roughly corresponds to the Army general education, and is usually given at those times when the seaman is on training courses, mostly ashore. The education centres established at main bases at home or overseas are to be retained and attention is being given to education for leisure and resettlement. The educational facilities of the Navy apply to the W.R.N.S., and civilian lecturers are used at shore stations.

The Royal Navy has its own education officers, two on board each large ship—battleships, aircraft carriers, and battle cruisers—and one for smaller ships. Where the complement of a ship is too small to justify a full-time education officer, one of the ship's officers acts as part-time education officer. The naval education officer has not only administrative duties but the whole of the teaching work falls on him. Every ship has its library containing both educational and recreational books, and men and women preparing for professional examinations can make use of the Army correspondence courses.

The importance of technical training in the R.A.F. was mentioned in the account of education during the First World War. It has become vital under modern conditions. The ground staff includes skilled tradesmen, craftsmen, and mechanics, and many of the officers are required to reach a very high standard of technical fitness. The technical training of the R.A.F. is shared between the technical officers who deal with the practical aspect of training and the educational officers who are responsible for the more theoretical work in mathematics, physical science, and engineering.

During the Second World War, the R.A.F. developed an education scheme similar to that of the Army, and later, in order to prepare personnel for demobilisation, a compulsory scheme known as E.V.T. (Educational and Vocational Training) was organised. The National Service man presents a special problem for the R.A.F. Many trades require more than a year's apprenticeship, so that the National Service man must be allocated to those which require only a short period of training. For boys who intend to make the R.A.F. their career, a scheme for training aircraft-apprentices exists. The course extends over three years and boys are selected by a competitive examination. A third of the time is given to mathematics, physics, mechanics, theory of flight and of structures, mechanical drawing, and the principles of the internal-combustion engine. The remainder is employed in physical training and games, English, history, and geography and current affairs. The largest aircraft-apprentice training-centre is the School of Technical Training, Halton, Bucks. The school not only provides apprentices with a wide general and technical education, but a scheme exists by which some students at the end of a three-year course are given a full university course in engineering to qualify them for commissions in the technical branch. Others may be selected for training as cadets for the flying branch, and one of the main features at the R.A.F. College, Cranwell, is the training of cadets. The R.A.F. is justly proud of its training scheme and a great deal of thought and experiment went into the making of it. Boys who intend to take up clerical and administrative work, and those with more modest attainments, are provided with other courses of training.

The General Education Scheme of the R.A.F. mainly provides for part-time education for officers and men and women in the Service, and the kind of training offered is similar to that of the Army. Each R.A.F. station has its complement of education officers based upon the numbers on the station. They undertake both teaching and administrative duties, but the latter take so much of their time that assistance is obtained from part-time teachers, who may be civilians or members of the Service. Arrangements are made for R.A.F. personnel to use civilian educational facilities in technical schools and evening institutes and help is also given by lecturers from the extra-mural departments of the universities. Before 1st October 1946 the education service of the R.A.F. consisted of civilian graduates, many of whom had been teachers in secondary schools, who were given the status of officers and allowed to wear uniform. After this date an education branch of the R.A.F. was formed. Members are officers holding either permanent or short-service commissions. A recent development has been the introduction of special courses and examinations for officers seeking promotion.

In all three Services, the policy is to bring the education schemes into line with what is being achieved in civilian life and to integrate their efforts with the further education plans proposed by the Ministry of Education. The C.A.C. came to an end on 31st December 1948, but, as the assistance of civilian teachers was still needed by the Services, the universities, through their extra-mural departments, were invited to undertake the work previously carried out by the regional committees. University lecturers have been appointed to deal with students who are of School Certificate standard or over, whilst the W.E.A. and the L.E.A.s have undertaken to give assistance with the remainder. At each university there is a Services Education Committee of the Extra-Mural Board, on which the Services, the university, the W.E.A., and the L.E.A.s, are represented.

The Central Committee for Adult Education in H.M. Forces replaced the C.A.C. and the co-operation with the civilian bodies was continued in a modified form. The final report of the Committee for 1959-60 drew attention to the need for a consideration of administration necessitated by the reduced size and changing character of the Forces because of the ending of National Service. The Committee has been succeeded by a smaller central committee representing the Services and universities only. At the same time the assistance given by L.E.A.s and other bodies was welcomed.

CHAPTER XVII

RECENT DEVELOPMENTS IN BRITISH EDUCATION

A period of about a dozen years after the Education Act of 1944, as regards the schools in England and Wales, was spent in overcoming the lag caused by war conditions, bringing the Act into operation as far as economic circumstances made it possible, and framing of amending Acts to deal with anomalies and omissions in the parent Act. This has been described in Chapter XI. After this, new developments began and events in the field of education have followed with startling rapidity. At the time of writing we are only in the first stage of future development.

It is convenient to start with the issue of the pamphlet entitled *Secondary Education for All: A New Drive* (Cmnd. 604) which was presented to Parliament in December 1958. The object of the publication was to describe the measures the Government had decided to ensure that all children of secondary school age should receive an education based on their ages, abilities and aptitudes. Although a good deal had been achieved since 1944 the time had arrived when much more which was urgently desirable ought to be put into practice. Hence the pamphlet reviewed the progress already made and surveyed the lines which future development should follow.

The first point noted in the White Paper was that since the school leaving age had been raised to fifteen in 1947, pupils tended to remain at school after the statutory leaving age in all types of secondary school. Thus during the years 1948 to 1958 the number staying at school after fifteen had risen from 187,000 to 290,600 and there were indications that the increase would continue. This was not only true of the grammar schools in which the sixth forms had nearly doubled in size, but in secondary modern schools also a new movement was in progress. The number of modern school pupils remaining at school after fifteen was about 12,000. It had increased to 38,000 in ten years.

The same tendency appeared in the technical colleges and the universities. In the technical colleges the number of full-time students had grown from 47,000 to 76,000 and part-time day students from 220,000 to 470,000. Evening students were now nearly two million as compared with one and a half million in

1948. University students were now about double those attending before the War. At the same time, because of the "bulge" in the birth-rate, the school population had increased by more than 25 per cent. The Ministry of Education and the L.E.A.s had planned to meet the challenge of the increased number of entrants. Four thousand new schools had been built and others enlarged with the result that about two million extra school places had become available. The cost had been great but careful planning had resulted in school places costing less than they had at the beginning of this development. This was surprising in face of economic difficulties which beset the nation but it was the outcome of more economic building and the close co-operation of the school architects.

Such rapid development demanded great increases of teaching staffs. The number of teachers had grown by 85,000 to a total of 260,000. Even this figure was not satisfactory. Classes were still too large, especially in the primary and secondary modern schools, though on the whole they were smaller than was usual in 1948.

Growth cannot be reckoned in terms of numbers alone. Education in all types of school was becoming more effective. The White Paper mentioned such activities as the production of school plays and the growing interest in art and the art crafts. On the whole this had been achieved without deterioration in the more formal work of the schools. Reading standards were improving and mathematics and science were growing in importance. The number of pupils in grammar schools who had been successful in the G.C.E. at Ordinary and Advanced levels had increased. Most significant was the number in secondary modern schools who had been successful at G.C.E. Ordinary level.

The general public was becoming more interested in education. This was evident in the attention given to it in the national and local newspapers and in the radio and television programmes. We were realising that our future as a nation depended very largely on the progress being made in the schools. Parents were concerned that their children should have the best opportunities in life. So much for the stocktaking, a process which should review the past and pass on to the consideration of the progress to be made in the future.

The Government thought that 1958 was the most opportune year to begin future planning. For a few years the number of school children would increase and after this the pressure would lessen for a time. After about 1965 there was evidence that a second "bulge" would appear. This left us five or six years during which freedom from the pressure of numbers would offer an opportunity for improving our schools.

There was, however, a serious problem to be solved, the question of the eleven plus examination. It was common knowledge that many children of almost equal ability were receiving their education in schools which varied greatly in quality and the number of different courses they were able to provide. A considerable number of children were not receiving the opportunities they deserved. There were still many districts in which the secondary schools, especially secondary modern, did not have the resources that are necessary. Hence the anxiety parents display in regard to eleven plus. They are inclined to look upon their children as failures if they have not been selected for grammar school entrance. The principle which ought to be followed is to ensure that "every child shall be able to travel along the educational road as far as his ability and perseverance can carry him, irrespective of the type of school to which he goes."

The White Paper supported selection in the widest meaning of the term. Children differ considerably from one another and these individual differences should be met by grouping them into courses suited to their particular abilities and aptitudes. The idea that a child's school career should be determined once and for all by the results of the selection test at eleven plus is entirely wrong. The Government was not prepared to impose a uniform organisation of secondary education on the country as a whole. It did not rule out experiments in comprehensive and similar types of school. In fact there are two particular kinds of area in which there is a case for such schools; rural districts with a sparse population, and industrial areas with extensive new housing estates in which there are no existing schools with an established tradition as grammar, technical, or modern. It would not approve the action of a local authority which closed an efficient grammar school in order to replace it by a continuous building programme for both primary and secondary schools of 2,000 or more pupils are subject to a very real danger. It is not easy to find a sufficient number of teachers able to infuse a spirit of unity in such large schools. The Government was interested in experiments such as those being carried out in Leicestershire, which avoided the disadvantages of the eleven plus test and at the same time, the closure of well established and efficient grammar or modern schools.

What were the Government's plans for the future? It proposed in co-operation with the L.E.A.s and the Churches to embark upon a continuous building programme for both primary and secondary schools from 1960-1 to 1964-5. This would naturally be expensive and to secure this it announced the introduction of a three years' ing more that £1,000 million per annum on education as compared with the approximate figure of £720 million for 1958. In addition to new schools, older ones would be brought up-to-date and L.E.A.s, school governors and managers would be encouraged to undertake improvements because of the increased limit of cost for minor projects from £10,000 to £20,000.

There were still a number of "all-age" schools containing about 150,000 pupils of eleven plus and over. These would be reorganised as quickly as possible and efforts would be speeded up to reduce the size of classes. New buildings would be provided for many ancient grammar schools at present housed in out-of-date premises. In the towns, many voluntary schools would be replaced by modern buildings and it was hoped that the religious bodies would play their full part in the changes. It might be that the Churches would need some further financial assistance.

The Government realised the vital need for well trained teachers and to secure this it announced the introduction of a three years' course in training colleges from the autumn of 1960. The supply of teachers was still a source of anxiety and therefore a plan to increase the available places in the teacher training colleges by 12,000 by 1962 was being carried out. It was hoped that the number of teachers coming from university departments of education would be increased in a similar proportion. The White Paper did not fix dates for the raising of the school leaving age and the opening of the county colleges. It was considered that the immediate policy should be that of encouraging pupils to remain at school beyond the present leaving age. The provision of a variety of extended courses in the modern schools would help. Steps were also being taken to enlarge the universities and to improve the facilities for technical and other courses in further education.

The White Paper was a summary of Government intentions for education in the near future. At the same time more complete investigations into different parts of the educational field were in progress. In March 1956, the Central Advisory Council for Education (England) was requested by the Minister of Education, Sir

David Eccles, to advise him on the education of boys and girls between the ages of fifteen and eighteen. The Chairman of the Council was Sir Geoffrey Crowther and its Report was issued in two
volumes published in 1959 and 1960 respectively under the title of
"15 to 18." Three other committees were also appointed; the first
under the chairmanship of Lady Albemarle dealing with the Youth
Service, another under Sir Colin Anderson to review the system
of grants to university students, and a third, a sub-committee of the
Secondary Schools Examinations Council to consider examinations
other than for the G.C.E.

There is no doubt that the Crowther Report is the most complete
survey of the education of the older adolescent yet undertaken.
Volume I contains the main report and the second volume consists
of a number of special surveys which form the basis of the conclusions and recommendations of the first volume. It is divided into
a Social, a National Service and a Technical Courses Survey. Since
the two volumes cover more than 750 pages, one can do little more
in a short chapter than draw attention to the most important topics
and recommendations of the Report.

The main Report consists of seven sections, entitled Education
in a Changing World, The Development of the Modern School,
Secondary Education for All, The Way to County Colleges, The
Sixth Form, Technical Challenge and Educational Response, and
Institutes and Teachers. The last chapter is a summary of the
conclusions and recommendations of the Report, and Appendix III
gives an account of technical education and vocational training in
western Europe. It was hoped that many who are not professional
teachers would read the Report and to meet their need a Glossary
defining the terms used in the text was included.

According to custom, the Report begins with an historical sketch
of the far reaching changes in education since the Bryce Report of
1895, and the comparisons included provide food for thought. It
is followed by a consideration of the effect of the "bulge" in the
birth rate. When the first volume was issued there were about
2,318,000 boys and girls in the age group considered. This number
will reach its peak in 1965 by which time about 700,000
adolescents will have been added. A second "bulge" is expected
in the middle 1970s. If the legislation dealing with the extension of
the leaving age to 16 and the establishment of county colleges had
been put into force, about $1\frac{3}{4}$ million boys and girls would now be

receiving full-time or part-time education in day schools. Actually in 1957-8 only two-fifths of this number had been realised. Boys and girls in full-time educational establishments were roughly equal in number but those receiving part-time education reveal a different picture. After a natural decrease at 15 plus, the number of girls had fallen rapidly. The majority of boys obtained part-time release during the day but only 5 to 6 per cent. of the girls obtained this. In addition there was a considerable number of both sexes attending evening classes or taking correspondence courses, but a much larger number had no part in educational activities.

The number of pupils in secondary schools had shown a marked increase. In 1894 only about four or five pupils in each thousand proceeded to grammar schools whereas at the present time the number has reached 200 per thousand. Part-time education developed more slowly and in 1911 only about 45,000 of all ages received such education. On the other hand, there was a considerable growth in the numbers who were attending evening classes, but after the day continuation schools of the 1918 Act were discontinued, the pupils receiving part-time education had only increased by about 6,000 in 1938. The raising of the school leaving age to fourteen in 1918 and to fifteen in 1947 removed those under these ages from industry but little had been achieved for those over fifteen. This is one of the main problems considered in the first half of the Report.

Only about one eighth of the pupils in maintained secondary schools are at the age of fifteen or over. The greater number of them are in secondary modern schools, nearly half of which are co-educational. More than 70 per cent. of grammar schools are single sex schools. New types of school have been developed such as multilateral, bilateral and comprehensive, but at present they only contain a minority of pupils of secondary school age. The Report points out that the tripartite organisation of grammar, technical and modern schools is a misnomer because over 40 per cent of L.E.A.s have no technical schools.

Side by side with the development of education, social and economic changes have progressed at a rapid rate, and have to be taken into account when considering plans for the extension of education in the future. The Report discusses such factors as earlier marriage and child-bearing, the decline in the size of families, the increasing number of women in industry and the professions, the growth of delinquency and the effects of rapid technological changes. Can the nation support large-scale extensions of education? The Council saw no difficulty when the expenditure on housing, capital investments and new machinery, or the money spent on drink and tobacco are considered. Education can be viewed from two standpoints, either as a duty which the State owes to its citizens which is one factor of the "welfare state," or as a capital investment which makes for greater efficiency of the nation as a whole. During the last twenty years the expenditure on education has just about kept up with the general growth of the nation's economy.

The next two parts of the Report are concerned with recent developments in the secondary modern school and the arguments for raising the school leaving age to sixteen. There is still a large number of all-age schools in existence but these are decreasing each year. The striking fact is that both parents and pupils are now demanding an extension of schooling beyond the statutory age of fifteen. This leads to the questions of extended courses and external examinations in non-selective secondary schools. It is probable that by 1965 nearly half of the fifteen age group will be following extended courses and L.E.A.s should bear this in mind. Most pupils can be provided with extended courses in the schools they entered at eleven plus but transfers will have to be arranged for children from all-age schools and from very small secondary modern schools.

Careful consideration should be given to the place of external examinations in non-selective secondary schools. The Council remembered the effects of the old School Certificate on the grammar schools, and it would be a disaster if the curriculum and teaching of the modern schools should be conditioned by external examinations. Nevertheless, many of the more able pupils could benefit from them, but the needs of the majority should not be sacrificed to the minority. For some years a few of the brighter boys and girls had been entered for the G.C.E. in selected subjects and had been successful.

It would seem that up to a third of modern school pupils over fifteen might be able to sit for examinations of a lower level than the G.C.E. The Report was cautious about this but acknowledged that the possession of qualifications was becoming an important factor in the choice of a career but it would be wise to experiment with such examinations for a period of about five years before deciding to create a national system. The relative values of subject and group examinations require special study. The majority of pupils would not benefit from such examinations but would gain great value from a choice of extended courses. Small schools could not offer the suitable variety of courses. Hence the preference for larger schools.

The Report strongly advised the extension of the school leaving age to sixteen as soon as this became practicable. This would benefit the individual and also would be in the national interest. The most favourable time should be chosen for this change and this seemed to be between 1965 and 1969, the period between the two "bulges" in the birth-rate. In preparation for this there should be two instead of three leaving dates in the school year—Easter and July. It is also important to select the date for raising the leaving age well in advance so that additional accommodation and supply of teachers would be adequate to cope with the change. There was also the matter of priority. Which should come first, the opening of county colleges or the raising of the school leaving age? The Council was wholly in favour of the latter alternative.

This naturally led to the consideration of the county colleges. "The majority of the boys and nearly all the girls who leave school as soon as they are entitled to do so are without that help in growing up which is acknowledged to be necessary." (Para. 261.) Thus, in 1958 about 60·6 per cent of boys and girls of the ages fifteen to seventeen were not receiving any full-time or part-time education. In actual numbers this amounted to 1,026,000, but this would be reduced when the leaving age is raised to sixteen. The county colleges would be concerned with the sixteen and seventeen year olds.

Although the Education Act of 1944 provides for attendance at county colleges of all young people under nineteen who are not receiving full-time education, it does not give in detail the content of the curriculum. The Act speaks of the duty of L.E.A.s to provide "adequate facilities for—leisure-time occupations, in such organised cultural training and recreative activities as are suited to their requirements, for any persons over compulsory school age who are able and willing to profit" from them. The intention was that the curriculum should be determined by the individual needs and capacities of the students. The latter would fall into two groups— apprentices and those who are "routine process workers." In practice, however, the county college is thought of as applying to the greater number of young workers who neither need nor could benefit from, a purely technical education. In this part of the Report the concern is with those in the latter group. The apprentices are discussed in Part 6 of the Report but here young people who are granted part-time release for general courses of a non-vocational character. The numbers given this opportunity have increased ten times for boys since the War but have only doubled for girls. Hence, "there has been no sign up to the present of any great extension of part-time day education for girls in any sector of employment outside that of the public authorities." (Para. 225.)

In reality, the picture is not as black as it may seem. Many of these young people receive further education in works schools, evening classes, private commercial colleges and correspondence courses. Those in attendance at evening classes comprise 37 per cent of the boys but 40 per cent of the girls give up in less than six months. How far does the Youth Service provide for the needs of those who leave school at fifteen and neither obtain day release nor receive part-time education from the sources mentioned above?

During their school days the majority of boys and girls belong to some type of youth organisation but one-fifth of the girls never belong to any organisation. Many boys continue to play team games after they have left school. A survey of the situation presents the picture "of a Youth Service which attracts many from the abler and steadier elements in the community but fails to retain the bottom quarter or third of the population." (Para. 262.) The Council declined to make specific suggestions on the Youth Service since this task had been allotted to the Albemarle Report. It was agreed, however, that a strong Youth Service is an essential complement to the county college.

Without entering upon a discussion of the details of the curriculum of the county college, it was thought that four strands should be woven into it: an appreciation of the adult world which young workers are entering; guidance for them in working out their problems of human relations and moral standards; development of their physical and aesthetic skills; and a continuance of their basic education with a vocational bias where appropriate. Further experience will be necessary to show in what proportions these strands can best be blended.

The establishment of compulsory attendance at county colleges must avoid the failure which attended the day-continuation schools of the 1918 Act. It would be a mistake to introduce compulsion in one move but the county colleges should be established in three stages. First there should be an intensive encouragement for extending day release to new classes of workers through voluntary means. The next stage would be an exploratory and preparatory one in which experiments should be conducted in various areas and with different kinds of organisation. This might take up to five years. The final stage would be the introduction of compulsory attendance progressively over all the country. This stage should be as short as possible but would probably take three to four years to complete.

Part 5 of the Report deals with the Sixth Form. Up to now the concern has been the pupils who at the age of eleven were of average or below average ability. This part investigates the problems of the more able pupils. In 1958 about 26 per cent (157,000) of the fifteen year-olds were either in selective schools of the statutory system, *i.e.* direct grant grammar schools, maintained grammar or technical schools, or in independent schools which had been recognised as efficient. An additional 9,000 were in comprehensive, bilateral or multilateral schools. By the age of seventeen, when pupils have reached the Sixth Form, the numbers in the first group had fallen to about 5,200 and those in the second to about 1,300. It is obvious that only the schools in the first group are at present making an appreciable numerical contribution to the work of the Sixth Form. About 60 per cent of these pupils are in maintained grammar schools. The number of pupils in the second group is slowly increasing and there is reason to believe that the Sixth Form in these schools will not differ materially from those in the first group. The number of pupils in the Sixth Forms of technical schools is strikingly small compared with those in the other kinds of school in the first group. The idea of a Sixth Form in technical schools is comparatively new and only about half the schools possess one.

The Council believed that most of the pupils aged fifteen in the schools of the first group ought to continue in full-time education up to the age of eighteen. In fact some leave at fifteen and others after they have sat for the Ordinary level of the G.C.E. Some people have suggested that these pupils should not have been admitted to the grammar schools. The Report did not agree with this view. "Unless many are called, few can be chosen." A considerable number who have turned out to be good grammar school pupils would have been excluded if the intake had been drastically cut. Others would have been happier in a technical or a comprehensive school. Nevertheless, early leaving is responsible for a considerable waste of talent. More would remain in full-time education if they had been transferred to another type of secondary school. As it is at present, the first five years of the course represent a fairly good cross-section of the population. One would like this to be more true of the Sixth Form but there is still a sharp distinction between this and the main school.

The Report recommended a reform of the curriculum in the middle school. In planning the curriculum, the background from which the maintained grammar school pupils come should be carefully considered. The majority of pupils come from homes in which both parents left school at fourteen or even earlier. Often parents do not appreciate the value of some of the subjects taught, *e.g.* foreign languages, and many are unable to assist their children in those studies which go beyond the primary school level. Before the institution of the G.C.E., the grammar schools were divided into two unequal groups by the School Certificate examination taken in the Fifth Form and which was a leaving certificate for the majority and a passport to the Sixth Form for those who remained at school. It was hoped that the introduction of the G.C.E. in 1951 would change this but in the majority of schools this has not come to pass. The general practice is for pupils to offer a wide range of subjects at "O" level and if they are successful they enter the Sixth Form to specialise in a few subjects which interest them or in which they have obtained a respectable Pass. They usually sit for the "O" level at sixteen which represents the end of a five year course in maintained schools or three years in independent schools which accept their entrants at thirteen.

The result is that many schools endeavour to present their ablest pupils at fifteen. This is made possible either by an earlier transfer from the primary or preparatory school or by covering the five-year course in four years in maintained schools and in three years in independent schools. Most pupils are restricted in their choice of Sixth Form studies to the subjects they have been taught at the primary or preparatory stage. This is satisfactory for a few pupils but on the whole prevents them from experiencing the full curriculum before deciding on the special subjects they wish to take. This is more common in boys' than in girls' schools in which more time can be allowed for art and music. These so-called "express routes" to the Sixth Form are used more often by direct grant and independent schools than by maintained schools. The consequence is that the majority of boys have practically decided on their special subjects at the age of thirteen or fourteen. The Report would only agree that boys should sit for the "O" level at fourteen in exceptional cases. The writer remembers coming across a boy who was literally a mathematical genius. He was forced to mark time because the G.C.E. regulations at that time did not allow him to sit for the "O" level at fourteen.

As a general policy the Report deprecated a too early specialisation but had no objection to making it possible for very able pupils to move at a faster pace which would enable them to enter the Sixth Form a year earlier, provided that the middle school curriculum was revised and more attention given to non-specialist subjects in the Sixth Form. At present the Fifth Form time-table is too congested, *e.g.* Latin and two modern foreign languages which is a too heavy bias. Also a six period science course could be devised which would enable a Fifth Form pupil who showed promise to take a normal Sixth Form course.

The Sixth Form is so important a factor in our educational system that Chapter XXI is given up to a discussion of the distinctive marks that should characterise a good Sixth Form. These essential marks are in the first place a close link with the university in spite of the fact that not all Sixth Formers will enter a university. The second is specialisation which involves a study in depth of a comparatively small number of subjects. In the Sixth Form the value of independent work should be emphasised. The size of the Sixth Form allows an intimate relation between pupil and teacher which is described as "intellectual discipleship." Finally, an essential mark of the Sixth Form is the development of social responsibility which is measured by the part each pupil plays in the life of the school.

The next chapter presents statistics which emphasise the number of pupils remaining at school in the Sixth Form. During the last decade the size of the Sixth Forms has shown a remarkable increase. In pre-war years the Sixth Forms of the smaller grammar schools contained only a handful of pupils and those who remained up to the age of eighteen seldom exceeded three or four. Larger schools were able to divide the Sixth Form into a first and a second year (Lower and Upper Sixth) and very large schools had sufficient numbers to organise divisions based on the special subjects studied, *e.g.* classical science, modern subjects etc. At the time the Crowther Report was issued, numbers in the Sixth Forms were well over half as great as compared with ten years earlier. This growth is likely to continue and eventually it may be the exception for a boy or girl to leave the grammar school at sixteen.

The success of a Sixth Form depends in part on the staff pupil ratio but still more on the quality of the teachers. In the 1930s, heads and governing bodies were able to select teachers with first or upper second honours degrees. Since then the number of graduates with good honours degrees has declined, though recently there has been a small increase. The situation was very bad in mathematics and science but even in these subjects there has been some improvement. One reason for the decline has been the more attractive prospects offered to suitable graduates in industry, commerce, and the civil and local government services.

The Report concluded that we must not continue to live on capital as in the last few years but "it is necessary to do more than is being done to attract men and women of the highest intellectual calibre into teaching." (Para. 359.) Girls' schools still experience considerable difficulty in obtaining well qualified graduates to teach mathematics and science in the Sixth Form. In some areas they have been forced to appoint men graduates for these subjects. At present, in small country schools, the "Sixth Form is at present often an unsatisfactory unit both for teaching and economy." (Para. 375b.) It is suggested that the problem can be solved either by merging two single-sex schools into one co-educational school, by conversion to a bilateral school, dividing the main subjects between two schools or combining Sixth Forms.

As regards the curriculum, although the Committee supported the policy of specialisation, it was disturbed by the way in which it was working. The heavy demands of the science syllabuses, the unsatisfactory combination of subjects offered by pupils in the Arts Sixth, the tendency for candidates to offer too many "A" level subjects, and the waste of minority time, *i.e.* the periods allotted to non-specialist studies. The minority time should be divided into common elements taken by art and science students, *e.g.* religious and moral education, art, music and physical education, and also complementary subjects. The latter should be designed to secure "the literacy" of science specialists and the "numeracy" of arts specialists. The plans of ensuring this either by the institution of a General Course, or directing arts specialists to take a science course or science specialists to study one arts subject at "A" level were deprecated. The importance of the Sixth Former's minority time can be brought home to them if prospective employers, universities and colleges show that they regard it seriously when they interview the candidates.

The problem of university entrance is a difficult one and leads to considerable controversy but the Committee were unanimous about certain aspects of it. The Sixth Form includes a number of pupils who do not intend to enter a university but who follow the same kind of curriculum as the potential university entrants. The two strands should not be segregated. Hence the "A" level should be regarded as a school leaving examination which tests the work of the upper school rather than a university entrance examination. There is an important distinction between qualification and selection. There are not sufficient university places to accommodate all who are qualified to enter. Also some candidates prefer certain universities or colleges or certain departments to others. Hence the selection of entrants has become extremely competitive. It is obvious that more places for higher education should be made available as soon as possible.

The result is that most applicants fill up entrance forms for several universities. Frequently they accept a place which is their second or third choice but if at a later time they are accepted by a university they put as their first preference, they cancel their previous applications and in some cases, they fail to cancel their previous acceptance. Most university departments require an interview with the candidates but in some cases they are accepted on their achievement at the "S" or "A" level examination. Selection should be more expeditious and universities should notify their acceptances by a common date. This would cause less confusion. The methods of selection should be common to all universities. Selection ought to be based on examination results, the personal qualities of the applicants and the use they have made of their non-specialist time. The Report also recommended an overhaul of the method of allocating financial grants from the L.E.A.s. Since the publication of the Report, the Anderson Committee recommended a revised scale of parental contributions which enables 40 per cent of entrants in place of the previous 25 per cent to receive a full Government grant.

The Report then considered "Sixth Forms with a Difference." It suggested the establishment of courses which are not directly linked with university requirements. On the whole such courses are more useful to girls than to boys since the former often have in mind careers which start at the age of eighteen but which do not necessarily demand "A" level Passes. Such courses would be suitable for girls wishing to enter a teacher training college, nursing, etc. There is now, however, a tendency for training colleges to require one or more Passes at "A" level. Similar general courses might be suitable for boys who wish to take up such professions as banking, insurance or law. These occupations formerly chose their entrants at sixteen but are now changing the age of recruitment to eighteen.

This part of the Report deals with what it terms Neglected Educational Territory. It is concerned with about a quarter of the fifteen to eighteen age group who leave school at fifteen but continue in some kind of further education. Our policy should be to increase the proportion of young people aged sixteen, seventeen and eighteen who are in full-time education. At present it is only one in eight but it should be one in two. Not all of these will be full-time in school but they would give the greater part of their time to further education. Attendance at a county college would not be sufficient though a well organised sandwich course would be satisfactory. Part-time further education courses should not be exclusively technical because the young person also needs a general education.

Many of the further education students are nineteen or over and fall outside the scope of the Report but nearly 43 per cent (about 750,000) in 1957-8 were in the sixteen to eighteen age group. It should not be assumed that all of these are inferior to pupils of the same age in the grammar schools. Indeed, many of them have entered further education from the Sixth Form. The education they are receiving is not inferior to but of a different kind from that they have experienced in the higher forms of the grammar school. So far the field of further education has not been surveyed as a whole and the Crowther Report represents an attempt to review this "neglected educational territory." The Report then summarises the different types of institutions providing further education, their aims and the kind of students who enter them. In addition to the further education establishments, there are the evening institutes which have made most valuable contributions in the past but in the future will be concerned largely with adults pursuing non-vocational studies. Universities and private institutions are not included in the list. There is some overlapping in the statistics because some students attend part-time day and evening classes.

There is a steady growth in the number of full-time students (70 per cent in the last five years) but the most remarkable development is in the number taking part-time day courses, an increase of ten-fold in the last twenty years. The majority of the latter have been granted day release, mostly those in the engineering and building industries. Many of them are working to obtain National Certificates but it is important to note that such candidates must pass in all subjects of the first year before they enter the second year of the course. The percentage of passes is by no means satisfactory. Only 26 per cent gain the Ordinary and 10 per cent the Higher Certificate. The reason seems to be that there is too much reliance upon evening classes and many candidates have an insufficient knowledge of mathematics.

The need for more technologists, technicians and craftsmen was emphasised in the White Paper on Technical Education (1956). Appendix A to Chapter 29 of the Report quotes the definitions of these terms as given in the White Paper and adds the further category of operative. They are men who after a short course of full-time or a part-time training varying from two to three years, are qualified to carry out specific operations in the use of machinery and plant which do not demand traditional craft skills. Some industries such as the chemical industry have no specific place for craftsmen because the operative works under the supervision of a technologist or technician. Craftsmen usually pass one of the craft examinations of the City and Guilds of London Institute. The examination has two levels, an Intermediate and a Final. Problems of further education for agriculture are discussed in the Appendix to Part VI of the Report in which attention is drawn to the recommendations of Lord De La Warr's Committee on Further Education for Agriculture. (1958.)

Sandwich courses are a most important feature in the education of technicians and operatives and are growing in popularity. The students alternate between periods of full-time study for at least nineteen weeks in the year and periods of full-time employment. The sandwich course differs from block release which is equivalent to a day or more a week but is concentrated into about eight continuous weeks in a technical college and then day release for the remainder of the year. The sandwich course should in the future become the standard for the training of technicians and is the most satisfactory method for boys in sixteen to eighteen age group.

The Report selects twelve characteristics of further education to which attention should be directed. (1) Only a minority of industries have a standard pattern of apprenticeship schemes which involve day release and these are only for boys. (2) There is a wide range of ability in further education courses and there should be consistent provision for the training of technicians, operatives and craftsmen.

(3) Because further education developed as "the handmaiden of employment", day release is dependent on apprenticeship. (4) There is, however, no close connection between the organisation and nature of apprenticeship so that the boy is presented with two objectives. (5) Provision for the smooth transition from full-time school to part-time education is often lacking. (6) Many further education students are sons of foremen and skilled artisans and a considerable number of them come from the Sixth Form. (7) Examinations are organised in stages and a student must pass all subjects of one stage before he proceeds to the next. This results in retardation. (8) Because of the different nature of girls' employment there is little day release for them. (9) Full-time students only comprise 5 per cent of the total number who make use of major establishments in the course of a year. (10) Attendance of students in evening classes is irregular and many of them fail to continue their courses. (11) The growth of sandwich courses is a source for optimism. (12) Most of the staff in further education are part-time and include a majority of men. A large proportion of them have had no training in teaching.

Three principles for the development of further education are recommended by the Report. Firstly there must be more integration between schools and further education. More time should be allowed in courses to reduce the rate of failure and no young person should rely on evening classes only. Finally, the eventual aim should be to convert the varied collection of plans for vocational education into a comprehensive and well organised scheme of practical education.

These principles demand steps to extend and foster contacts between schools and further education institutes in their neighbourhood. School teachers should be well informed about what further education can offer and teachers in technical colleges should be aware of recent developments in secondary education. When new students enter the college, they should be separated from those who are returning for continued courses, so that they can receive adequate advice on the most suitable courses they should take. A full induction course of about a month in the autumn term should be organised for those entering on a three or five year course. Some universities have a short introductory course for their entrants and this has proved to be of considerable value. A tutorial group system would develop continuing personal relations between staff and students and would be of advantage to the latter in their study of mathematics.

Chapter XXXIV discusses the problem of time. Wherever agreement is possible, the length of year laid down for county colleges by the 1944 Act (forty-four weeks or 330 hours), should be adopted for day release students. Also "block release" should be substituted for one day a week release. There should be further provision for "college based" sandwich courses for young people aged sixteen to eighteen, if satisfactory arrangements can be made for their industrial training. Students who fail in one subject at one stage should be allowed to proceed to the next stage and repeat the subject in which they failed at a subsidiary examination. At present, boys and girls of fifteen and sixteen have only two alternatives, the full academic course for which they may not be suited and the arduous and time-wasting part-time course. One of the major tasks of English education is that of introducing a new type of education free from the defects of both the part-time course and the traditional academic one. The new form of full-time practical education could be provided in either the schools or in further education but it should not be restricted to technical subjects. Much information might be acquired by studying what is being done in other countries.

Chapter XXXVI deals with the changing pattern in organisation in full-time education and deals with some problems which are highly controversial. The suggestions made are not dogmatic but seek to find a *via media* between conflicting points of view. The aim should be to secure that by 1980 that about half the young people should continue in full-time education (including sandwich courses) until they are eighteen. At present we shall have to use persuasion until this is brought about by legislation. Broadly speaking, the older the pupils are, the larger the school can be. At present many grammar and modern schools are too small to make the provision of extra courses economic beyond the age of sixteen. It is hoped that more secondary technical schools will be built and planned with a Sixth Form in view. This might involve transfer from grammar and modern schools.

The Report's view of the comprehensive school is similar to that we have expressed on pp. 396-7 in this book. The argument about the large numbers in such schools could be satisfied if pupils between the ages of eleven and eighteen were divided between two schools. Areas in which comprehensive schools could be introduced with profit are those described in the White Paper of 1958. (*Secondary Education for All. A New Drive.*) Experiments could be made with special Junior Colleges, parallel with but not replacing Sixth Forms, and which offer a wide variety of both academic and practical full-time courses.

The education advances recommended by the Report will ultimately depend upon the teachers. It is essential to have teachers in the right numbers when the school leaving age becomes sixteen but it is equally important that they should be of the right kind. The qualities which mark out a good teacher need to be analysed. There are still too many over-large classes. The training colleges and the universities form the chief sources of the supply of teachers. The Committee recommended that the National Advisory Council on the Training and Supply of Teachers should be asked to advise on the additional number of teachers required to raise the school leaving age. The third year of training should result in raising the standard reached by training college students.

A vigorous effort should be made to secure the services of highly qualified graduate teachers. The modern schools could benefit from having more trained graduates on their staffs and the grammar schools could do with more college trained teachers. Married women will be required in larger numbers and the conditions of employment amended. Efforts should be made to release teachers from many routine tasks. As regards graduates, "no campaign, however will succeed unless the material rewards of teaching compare favourably with those other professions open to the graduates."

The Report admits that it has presented "a formidable list of recommendations, some of which are more urgent than others." In paragraph 696 it gives the following frank warning. "We do not believe that there is any hope of carrying out the measures we have outlined—or any other list of proposals adequate to the needs —unless they are worked out and adopted as a coherent, properly phased development plan, extending by timed and calculated steps a long way into the future. Nothing of this sort has ever been possible in English education. There has been no lack of aspiration, or of definitions of objectives; but the attainment of them has been left to the mercies of the parliamentary time-table and of financial exigences. Nothing more than this has been possible because there has not been support in public opinion for anything more."

At first the Government was slow to decide what recommendations should be implemented and fears arose that the Report might be put into cold storage. The Ministry was aware of this feeling and in the Introduction to the Report of the Ministry of Education, *Education in 1960,* Sir David Eccles wrote as follows. "The recommendations of the Crowther Report, covering a wide range of complex and controversial issues, took some time to study and many outside interests had to be consulted before the Government could formulate their views. But, as recorded in the Annual Report, the Government are taking action on many of the Crowther recommendations and as time passes it will be seen that this outstanding Report has influenced the thinking of the Ministry on a wide variety of subjects, including the supply of teachers, external examinations, school leaving dates, the integration of school and further education, and courses for technicians."

The earliest impact of the Crowther Report is seen in the White Paper of January 1961. (*Better Opportunities in Technical Education. Cmnd. 1254.*) This proposed that students should start at a technical college direct from school and that preliminary courses at evening institutes should be discontinued. Technical colleges should experiment with full-time introductory courses of a month and with tutorial methods. There should be an improved selection of students for courses which suit their ability. Ordinary National Certificate courses will last for two years instead of three and entry standards will be raised. New general courses will be introduced to lead to either technician courses or Ordinary National Certificate courses. There will be new courses of four or five years for technicians. The craft courses will be modified and courses for operatives developed. More time should be provided under day release schemes so that no student would have to rely wholly on evening classes. Sandwich and block release courses will be developed. The new general courses will include mathematics, English and a grounding in scientific principles. The White Paper appealed to parents and teachers to remain in school after the statutory leaving age of fifteen, and to industry to increase the amount of day release especially for craftsmen and operatives.

A Bill was introduced in the autumn of 1961 and passed in March 1962 which carried out the recommendation of the Crowther Report for only two leaving dates each year. This aimed at leading to a better fourth year in the secondary school for those pupils who would otherwise leave school at the first opportunity. The provision of extended courses has reduced the number of those who would have left at fifteen. Thus those children who reached the age of fifteen in September 1963 will remain at school until Easter 1964, and those who would have left at Easter 1963 will be required to stay at school until the summer holiday of 1964.

Parents are now beginning to realise the value of allowing their children to remain longer at school. The reports of H.M. Inspectors which were quoted in the Ministry of Education Report (*Education in 1960*) showed that extended courses have been for the benefit of the schools and examples of pupils who have won signal successes in examinations and in institutions for further education make it clear that pupils in the secondary modern schools are not necessarily "dogged from the start by a sense of failure." The Ministry Report concluded that "As more and more of these successes are recorded, and as more extended courses are established which in their turn lead on to further education of various kinds, the attitude of parents towards non-selective schools is significantly changing. The effect of the successes is cumulative, and the support for the schools achieving them gathers momentum. It is becoming clear that instead of children having a once-for-all opportunity at eleven, the teachers in our system of secondary education are discovering ways of providing continuous opportunities for all the pupils during the whole of their school lives." (P. 15.) It should be noted that the term "non-selective secondary schools" includes comprehensive and bilateral as well as secondary modern schools. It is hoped that other recommendations of the Crowther Report will be implemented in whole or part in the near future.

Sir Geoffrey Crowther had continued in office as Chairman of the Central Advisory Council for Education (England) at the request of the Ministry. He relinquished office in November 1960 and was succeeded by Viscount Amory who had retired from the office of Chancellor of the Exchequer. The Council was directed "to consider the education of pupils between the ages of thirteen and sixteen of average or less than average ability who are or will be following full-time courses either at schools or in establishments of further education." Lord Amory did not stay long in this appointment because in June 1961 he was selected as United Kingdom High Commissioner in Canada. He was succeeded by the Vice-Chairman of the Advisory Council, Mr. (now Sir) John Newsom, C.B.E., who is Joint Managing Director, Longmans Green and Co. Ltd., and was formerly Chief Education Officer of the County of Hertford.

The development of the Youth Service up to the close of the second World War has been outlined in pages 414-6. Unfortunately the promise of a bright future for the Youth Service did not materialise. In 1945 the Ministry decided to delay putting into force the recommendations of the McNair Report as regards the training of youth leaders. Because of the post-war economic difficulties the question of priorities had to be considered and it was thought it was more essential to concentrate on the building of new schools and the development of technical education. The Jackson Committee (1949) and the Fletcher Committee (1951) studied the conditions of service for professional youth leaders but their recommendations were not accepted. This resulted in the Youth Service being regarded as a poor relation of the other educational services. The enthusiasm of youth leaders was damped and the general public lost interest in the service.

In November 1958 a Committee was constituted with the Countess of Albemarle in the chair to investigate the present situation of the Youth Service. Its Report, The *Youth Service in England and Wales* was presented to Parliament in February 1960. The Report was quite frank about the condition of the Youth Service. It stated, ". . . the Youth Service is at present in a state of acute depression. All over the country and in every part of the service there are devoted workers. In some areas the inspiration of exceptional individuals or organisations, or the encouragement of local education authorities, have kept spirits unusually high. But, in general, we believe it true to say that those who work in the Service feel themselves neglected and held in small regard, both in educational circles and by public opinion generally. We have been told time and time again that the Youth Service is 'dying on its feet' or 'out on a limb.' Indeed, it has more than once been suggested to us that the appointment of our own Committee was either 'a piece of whitewashing' or an attempt to find grounds for 'killing the Service'." (Para. 2.)

The Albemarle committee was firm in the opinion that "a properly nourished Youth Service is profoundly worth while." It demanded a 'new look' which should take into account the characteristics of the post-war generation of young people. Thus Chapters two and three reviewed the problems of "Young People To-day" and the justifications for, and the aims of, the Youth Service. These chapters are marked by their clear understanding of the social, economic and psychological problems of youth.

The Committee was convinced that it was highly important to form a link between those still at school and those who left at the age of fifteen. Thus it recommended that the Youth Service should include all young people between the ages of fourteen and twenty. It advised the Minister to draw up a ten year development plan for the Youth Service, divided into two periods of five years. It should include the formation of an advisory committee of not more than twelve members under the title of the Youth Service Development Council. At least two members of the Council should be appointed because of their specialist knowledge of the problems of Wales.

The Youth Service of the future will depend largely upon the local education authorities." "The Minister may promote, direct and control the many types of provision which create the Youth Service. He will know from H.M. Inspectors what is being done, what they think of it and how they suggest it might be improved. But neither Minister or Ministry can actually do the work. Executive power is plainly fixed upon local education authorities by the Act. The function of the authorities, as we see it, is and should be to determine a policy for their areas in consultation with the voluntary bodies; to establish the machinery for co-operation and for the co-ordination of development, servicing and training; to encourage and give financial aid to voluntary effort through existing voluntary organisations and in other ways; and to ensure that adequate and varied facilities are provided." (Pp. 45-6.)

The Albemarle Report realised that a successful Youth Service demands a partnership between the Ministry, the L.E.A.s, the voluntary Youth organisations, and last, but not the least, the "receiving end", that is the young people themselves who must have opportunities for participation as partners. In addition to the formation of the Development Council, L.E.A.s should constitute a special sub-committee to be responsible for the Youth Service in their areas. It is extremely important to develop the voluntary principle and raise the standards of voluntary youth leaders. The voluntary organisations should have adequate representation on the committees and young people should have opportunities for "association, training and challenge" of the right kind.

The Youth Service had been handicapped by the inadequate buildings in use. "Hitherto much of the work of the Youth Service has been done—in surroundings whose dinginess suggests relief work in the thirties. In the crippling absence of funds, determined leadership and a valiant spirit of self-help have taken derelict chapels and schools, even derelict air-raid shelters, warehouses and decayed town mansions, and turned them into places where young people can meet and pursue certain activities.—But if the Service is to achieve what is expected of it there must be a change of approach." (Para. 220.) Hence the report called for a "generous and imaginative building programme as essential to rehabilitate the Youth Service and to equip it for the expansion that is called for." The extension of residential courses was strongly recommended.

Buildings, however, are only a part of the requirements. At present the Service suffers from inadequate numbers of youth leaders and, in some cases, lack of the necessary experience and qualifications. In the first instance, the Minister should consider long-term arrangements for the training of full-time leaders. This would involve the increase of their number of 700 to a provisional total of 1,300 full-time leaders by 1966. To achieve this it would be essential to open, not later than September 1961, an emergency training college offering a one-year course to men and women. The Area Training Organisations should be invited to accept responsibility for supervision of the courses and to recommend to the Ministry those who are worthy of recognition as qualified leaders. The L.E.A.s should also recommend to the Ministry those full-time leaders who have completed five years of service with satisfaction, but a date should be fixed beyond which other qualifications than experience would be necessary.

L.E.A.s should take steps to increase the number of part-time leaders and should co-operate with the voluntary organisations to organise schemes of part-time training for leaders, both paid and voluntary. The Youth Service will only attract potential leaders if the conditions and the salaries are adequate. Hence it would be necessary to appoint a committee to negotiate salary scales and suitable superannuation arrangements. After five years, when the Ministry grants cease, the L.E.A.s should exercise fully their powers under the Act of 1944 in making capital grants to voluntary youth groups. Suggestions were also made in regard to other financial matters and the Report concluded with a discussion of the priorities of its recommendations.

The Government was conscious of the urgency of the points discussed in the Report and acted quickly. The first step was the creation of a Youth and Adult Services and General Branch in the Ministry under an Under-Secretary with an adequate staff. In March 1960 the Youth Service Development Council met under the chairmanship of the Minister. The Council published in November, *Youth Service,* a monthly review including discussions and exchange of views by experienced workers in the field. This publication was highly popular and its circulation after the first year was so promising that it warranted publication in a revised form. A Youth Service building programme was launched which approved work for the period 1960-2 up to the value of £3 million and later, a £4 million programme for 1962-3 was announced. After a short start, the response of the L.E.A.s and voluntary associations increased sharply, and by November 1961, building applications reached £3½ million.

The premises vacated by the City of Leicester Training College for teachers were acquired to house a National College for the training of youth leaders. Additional residential accommodation became necessary and by the close of 1960 the college was ready to admit ninety students. This number quickly grew to about 140 and a waiting list was opened for the third course which began in March 1963. The existing courses at the University College, Swansea and Westhill Training College, Birmingham, were continued and the courses provided by the National Association of Boys' Clubs and the Y.M.C.A. were lengthened and enriched in content. In 1961 the Youth Department of the Free Church Federal Council, the Services by the Youth Trust and the Youth Hostels Association became recognised for grant.

The committee appointed by the Secondary Schools Examinations Council in 1958 under the chairmanship of Mr. Beloe, Chief Education Officer, Surrey issued its report in 1960 entitled *Secondary School Examinations other than the G.C.E.* From the time of the Hadow Report on the Adolescent, the provision of a leaving certificate for modern school pupils had been discussed but the idea received little encouragement from the local education authorities. When the school leaving age was raised to fifteen in 1947, the situation began to change. There was an increasing tendency for parents whose children attended non-selective secondary schools, to allow them to remain at school beyond the statutory leaving age. The provision of extended courses in non-selective schools accelerated this tendency.

When the C.G.E. at "O" and "A" levels superseded the School and Higher School Certificate examinations, the new examination was regarded as a test for grammar school pupils, but as the G.C.E. came to be thought of as the gateway to higher education, entries from institutions other than grammar schools were received. The G.C.E. is a subject and not a group examination and it was perceived that many pupils who remained in non-selective secondary education after fifteen could offer subjects which would entitle them to the certificate at the "O" level and in a few cases at the "A" level. The average number of subjects presented was just short of four. By 1959, about one-third of the candidates for "O" level came from institutions other than grammar schools. Some of the candidates had left school and sat for the examination from an institute of further education.

It was, however, generally accepted that the G.C.E. was only suitable for a limited number of the more able pupils in non-selective secondary schools. Hence the growing demand for examinations of a different kind and of a lower standard than the G.C.E. The Ministry in Circular 289 of 1955 deprecated the establishment of national examinations for secondary schools in addition to the G.C.E. Circular 326 of 1957 supported the view expressed in the previous Circular but encouraged experiments by groups of schools in developing their own internal examinations with some degree of external assessment. This did not check the demand for another type of external examination. The Ministry referred the problem to the Crowther Committee whose cautious reply has already been summarised.

Meanwhile the number of examinations offered to non-selective secondary schools was growing. The Beloe Report grouped them in four categories. (1) Local examinations conducted by groups of school or by L.E.A.s. These were, as a rule, designed for pupils in their fourth year. (2) School examinations conducted by bodies with regional or national coverage. These may be either for the fourth or fifth year and sometimes for even younger pupils, and may be either group or subject examinations. Among the London based bodies are the College of Preceptors, the Royal Society of Arts, and the London Chamber of Commerce. All these bodies have acquired considerable experience in conducting examinations for schools. The City and Guilds of London Institute also notified their intention of entering this field.

The regional bodies are the East Midland Educational Union (Nottingham), the Northern Counties Technical Examinations Council (Newcastle-upon-Tyne), the Union of Lancashire and Cheshire Institutes (Manchester), and the Union of Educational Institutes (Birmingham), which covers the West Midlands and the south and south-west of the country. Like the London bodies, the regional ones have had long experience of external examining. The first in the field of external school examinations is the College of Preceptors which started its school examinations in 1850. In 1953 it planned the Certificate Examination on a group basis and allowed pupils in the fourth year and even younger to enter. (3) There are a number of further education examinations originally planned for students attending part-time further education courses. (4) Finally there are specialist examinations designed by bodies which generally have a national coverage. They were instituted for pupils who wished to follow certain vocational and professional courses.

The Beloe Committee did not attempt a detailed survey of the specialist examinations because they only influence the curriculum of schools to a small extent. Local examinations in the past had provided a fruitful field for experiment but this stage of educational development was coming to an end and this type of examination was subject to at least two limitations. The Certificates issued tended to possess a local currency only. "The value of a certificate awarded by a group of schools in, say, a north London borough may be well understood by an employer or a technical college principal in that borough, but it may have little meaning or value to an employer or principal in Manchester or even on the other side of London; and this lack of wider currency detracts from its value as an incentive." (Para. 39.)

In addition, most of the local examinations are designed for pupils aged fifteen. The growing tendency for pupils to remain at school after this age and pursue an extended course demands a type of examination suitable for pupils in their fifth year. The G.C.E. examination is suitable for the more able pupils in non-selective schools but does not meet the needs of those in the ability range just below this. At the other end of the scale there is a large number of pupils who should not be entered for any type of external examination.

It was agreed that school pupils should not sit for further education examinations, and that they should not take an external examination until the end of their fifth year. Experience gained from the operation of the School Certificate examination showed that all examinations should be "subject" and not "group" examinations. The new examinations should bear in mind the needs and interests of the pupils but they should not be a watered-down version of the G.C.E. General responsibility for the examinations should be accepted by about twenty Regional Examining Boards but the teachers would be largely in control of the form and content of the examinations. Representatives of the L.E.A.s in each region, one or more persons from institutes for further education in the region, and one or more from the Area Training Organisations and from employers of the region should be included in the Governing Councils of the Regional Bodies, provided that teachers formed the majority.

The Minister of Education should take the initiative and accept the examination for the Certificate of Secondary Education (C.S.E.). He should fix a date from which he would be prepared to consider applications from intending examining bodies who would accept the criteria agreed upon by the Committee. The L.E.A. should pay the fees of candidates from maintained schools who entered for a recognised examination. The Minister had the legal power to reject the C.S.E. but if he did so he would find it extremely difficult to make his prohibition effective. Examinations other than the G.C.E. would continue to flourish but there would be no means of controlling their development.

The Beloe Report was criticised by a considerable number of teachers, L.E.A.s and examining bodies. The College of Preceptors, for example, wished to retain their examinations for pupils in their fourth year. Sir David Eccles was in a difficult position and did not reply at once. He was disturbed about changing the policy of the Ministry and desired time to consider the arguments for and against. At last, in July 1961, he told the Commons that he would accept the Report in principle, but would set up in his department a research and development group to study the problems in greater detail. He also requested the Secondary Schools Examinations Council to decide upon the means through which the general principles of the examination could be applied.

In reply to this request, the Council was reconstituted in October 1961 in order to include an adequate number of members representing technical colleges and people with knowledge and experience of non-selective secondary schools. The Council under the chairmanship of Sir John Lockwood, Master of Birkbeck College, University of London, published its Fifth Report at the end of August 1962. The Report accepted the conclusions of the Beloe Committee and gave guidance for the Regional Examining Bodies. It is entitled—*Examinations in Secondary Schools—The Certificate of Secondary Education*. The comments of teachers and L.E.A.s had been received and the first examinations are to be held in the summer of 1965. Sir Edward Boyle who succeeded Sir David Eccles as a result of the Cabinet reconstruction in the summer of 1962, approved the Report.

In spite of the developments outlined at the end of Chapter XIII, the Government was growing uneasy about the number of technologists and technicians available in comparison with the output from such countries as the U.S.A. and the U.S.S.R. By 1956 the position seemed to be so critical that urgent action became necessary. The White Paper on Technical Education, issued in that year, drew attention to the fact that only about one half of the students who completed advanced courses in technical colleges became technologists and this state of affairs could not be remedied by part-time release and evening classes. It considered "Advanced sandwich courses would therefore probably become the main avenue of progress towards the highest technological qualifications."

After a debate in the Commons, the Minister in June 1956, proposed provisionally to designate eight colleges of advanced technology. These were the Royal Technical College at Salford, the Bradford Institute of Technology, the Loughborough College of Technology, Birmingham and Cardiff Colleges of Technology, and, in London, the Battersea, Chelsea, and Northampton Polytechnics. He told the House that he hoped later to add two more colleges, one in the south-west at Bristol, the other in the north-east, the Rutherford Technical College, Newcastle.

This decision called for far-reaching changes in the colleges. With one exception, in all the colleges, a fair amount of elementary work was carried on, and this would have to be transferred elsewhere. As regards buildings and equipment, only the colleges at Salford and Birmingham and Battersea could reach the requirements in a reasonably short time. These three colleges were designated 1st October 1956, and Loughborough and the Chelsea Polytechnic, 1st January 1957. In September 1960 the Bristol College of Technology was added to the list. The Brunel College of Technology was considered as being up to the required standards as regards its work and the qualifications of its staff. The existing site, however was not suitable for an advanced college of technology, but discussions with the Middlesex L.E.A. resulted in the offer of an alternative site, and the college was designated in 1962. The Minister decided that no further designations and changes in the status of the existing colleges would be made until after the Committee on Higher Education under the chairmanship of Lord Robbins had reported. At the time of designation, all the nine colleges with the exception of Loughborough, which since 1952 had received a direct grant from the Ministry and possessed an independent governing body, were under the control of the L.E.A.s. The other colleges should fall into line with Loughborough and the transfer took place at the beginning of the 1962-3 financial year.

The Colleges of Advanced Technology are at the present time busy with building enlargements, those at Bradford and Loughborough being well advanced whilst Bristol and Brunel are being rebuilt on new sites. The colleges offer courses leading to the Diploma in Technology which demands the standard of a university honours degree, and they are expected to provide the same kind of environment as a university and to grant opportunities for a liberal education. The new buildings at Loughborough, begun in 1959, give an idea of the College of Advanced Technology of the future. "This college is unique in being fully residential, whereas at other colleges of advanced technology only a proportion of the students will live in. At Loughborough extensions costing some £2 million will provide a wide range of teaching buildings for about 1,400 students, of whom over 800 will be living on the campus. A six-storey science block will be the centre of the new teaching buildings. There will also be aeronautical and automobile engineering laboratories (with sound-insulated test houses) and nuclear energy laboratories. A special feature is the workshop engineering block, designed as a miniature factory in which the students will learn production techniques.

The residential buildings are designed as a 'students' village'— the first of its kind in Britain. The area is laid out in streets and closes, with its own village shops, and will house 800 students in two- and three-storey terrace blocks around five courts with one tall building for post-graduate students. Each hostel group has its own dining and common rooms, and accommodation for residential staff, as well of course as well-appointed study bedrooms for the students (of 140 square feet each). Not far away is the new library —with its initial stock of 50,000 books—and the College Union, containing a fully equipped theatre, a games hall of 50,000 square feet, a cafeteria and buttery and a flexible range of small and large rooms to accommodate all the many club and social activities of the students." (Ministry of Education Report, *Education in 1959,* Chapter VI, paras. 33-4.)

In 1956 four types of technical institution were defined; Colleges of Advanced Technology (C.A.T.s), Regional Colleges, Area Colleges and Local Colleges. This classification was not intended to be a hard and fast one for it was made possible for a college to move from its present status to another type, as in the cases of Bristol and Brunel. Some other existing C.A.T.s have found it difficult to expand on their present sites. Thus Chelsea has been contemplating a move to Knebworth Park and Battersea may move to a site at Guildford. The student population of all the ten colleges is expanding rapidly and the number of full-time and sandwich students is expected to reach 15,000 in the near future. There are twenty-five colleges designated as Regional Colleges. Area Colleges in which work of a less advanced level is predominant number about 160, but Local Colleges are expanding and some of them may become Area Colleges in the future.

Several important changes have taken place in the existing universities. The University College of North Staffordshire which received a charter in 1949 and opened in 1950 was a break with traditional policy. Up to this date, university colleges prepared their students for the external degrees of the University of London. The new university college was given the power to grant the degree of B.A. The growing demand for technological training and preparation for such professions as medicine, architecture and others was causing a number of important problems. Were the new universities of the future to develop in technology and science at the expense of other departments?

The new university college was aware of this danger and experimented with a balanced curriculum for the B.A. degree. The course extended over four years. The first year of the course is compulsory for all students and deals with the heritage of civilisation, present-day problems and the methods and influence of the experimental sciences. In the remaining three years students were required to choose not less than four subjects, two of which must be studied for three years and the remainder for one year. The principal subjects must include at least one from the Humanities and Social Studies and at least one from the sciences. In addition to the usual administrative pattern of other universities, a Court, a Council and a Senate, there was an Academic Council, the majority of whose members are representatives of the universities of Oxford, Manchester and Birmingham. The approval of the Academic Council was required on all matters of academic importance. The object of this sponsorship was to guarantee the academic standard of the work. By January 1962, it was considered that sponsorship was no longer necessary and the college received a Royal Charter as the University of Keele. Princess Margaret was installed as Chancellor. The original college started with 150 men and women students. It has now more than 800. The university is completely residential and new buildings are being provided for the increase in numbers which is expected to expand to 2,300.

The separation of the University of Durham into two divisions based on Durham and Newcastle respectively had not been wholly satisfactory. King's College, Newcastle, had grown considerably and for some time had been hoping to become a separate university. This hope has now been realised, and the new University of Newcastle-upon-Tyne aims at a target number of 6,000 students by 1970.

St. David's College, Lampeter, had for some years struggled to obtain recognition as a university but without success. The U.G.C. explored possible means of assisting Lampeter and in the Report on University Development (1952-7), decided that assistance would depend on the college entering into organic relationship with an existing university institution. Efforts to create association with the University College of Wales at Aberystwith were not acceptable to Lampeter. In December 1960, agreement was reached for a sponsorship scheme which would place Lampeter on the grant list of the U.G.C. The B.D. candidates will continue to be examined by the Oxford and Cambridge Board of Examiners according to the Charter of 1852. The sponsorship scheme was made between the University of S. Wales and Monmouthshire, Cardiff, and enabled Lampeter to receive a capital grant for its temporary building scheme. St. David's is now able to expand to 250 arts students with an increase in the teaching staff who will now be paid at the normal rate for universities.

The number of applicants for university places has continued to rise in the post-war period and reached a point where the expansion of existing universities was not adequate for future demands. Several factors have contributed to this state of affairs. The Crowther Report had drawn attention to the growth in the number of

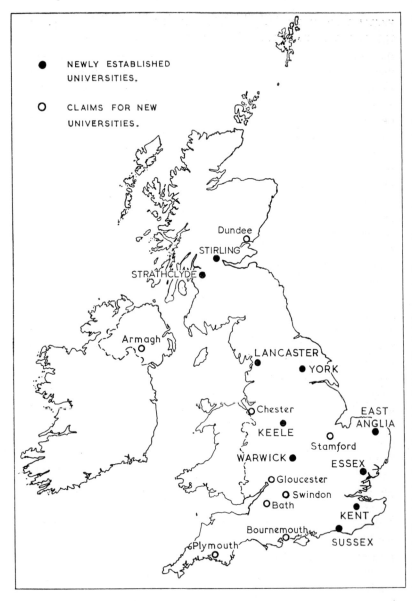

THE NEW UNIVERSITIES, 1964.

pupils remaining at school after sixteen and the steady rise in the size of Sixth Forms. The "bulge" in the birth-rate is now entering the universities and will reach its peak about 1966-8. Another "bulge" is expected in the middle 1970s. Another factor is the rising number of pupils who have pursued a science course in the Sixth Form and wish to continue their studies at university level. Other causes are the growth in the number of over-seas students and an increase in the number of graduates returning to study for post-graduate degrees. The problem of university places is a long term one which can only be solved by looking at least a decade ahead in our planning.

The Government recognised the seriousness of the situation and in 1960 the Chancellor of the Exchequer asked the U.G.C. to consider the establishment of new universities in Sussex, York and East Anglia. The existing universities agreed that they were not prepared to expand beyond 7,000-8,000 for the larger and 4,000-5,000 for the smaller ones.

The first of the new universities was the University of Sussex which is situated in Brighton. It received its charter in 1961 and Viscount Monckton of Brenchley was appointed Chancellor and Mr. J. S. Fulton, Vice-Chancellor. The first students were admitted for the session 1961-2. They numbered fifty-two in that academic year but increased to 432 in 1962-3 and in 1963-4 another 400 were accepted. Further increases are dependent upon the provision of new buildings. The next was the University of York which admitted 200 undergraduates in 1963. It aims to reach 3,000 by 1972. The Chancellor is the Earl of Harewood and the Vice-Chancellor is Lord James of Rusholme who was formerly High Master of Manchester Grammar School. York is being developed on the collegiate system with eight colleges each of which will accommodate about 300 undergraduates. At first the undergraduates of each college are of the same sex but eventually each college will accommodate equal numbers of men and women, a proportion of women greater than the present national average. The university started in temporary buildings but as soon as the permanent buildings are ready, it will offer a substantial amount of residential accommodation. The tutorial system is encouraged because it replaces formal instruction by personal links between the tutor and the students.

The University of East Anglia received its charter in 1963 and a start was made by admitting 100 undergraduates to study English and the biological sciences. At present its administrative head-quarters are at Earlham Hall, Norwich, the birthplace of Elizabeth Fry. When its new buildings are completed it will be able to accommodate about 3,000 students. Special emphasis is placed on the provision of halls of residence. The Chancellor is Viscount Mackintosh of Halifax and the Vice-Chancellor is Mr. Frank Thistlethwaite.

The foundation of these new universities was followed by a change in the policy which had been in operation when the older provincial universities were established from the mid-nineteenth century onwards. The first break in tradition occurred, as we have seen, in the foundation of the University of Keele. When the University of Sussex was established, the U.G.C. decided upon a further step. The new universities would receive their charters at their foundation so a period of apprenticeship or sponsorship would not be required. As each university received its charter, an Academic Committee would be appointed for a limited period. The Committee would include members of existing universities and, possibly, lay representatives.

In May 1961 the U.G.C. was authorised to consider claims for universities in other areas. Many applications were received from different districts. Those which were accepted were:—the University of Essex at Colchester, the University of Kent at Canterbury, the University of Warwick at Coventry and the University of the North at Lancaster. Other applicants included Stamford, Glouces-ter, Bournemouth, Chester, Plymouth and Swindon. Cornwall also asked for a university of the south-west.

The University of Essex envisages a target of at least 6,000 full-time students. Dr. Sloman was appointed Vice-Chancellor in July 1962. Pass degree courses are eliminated and all undergraduates will read for honours. This does not mean that all of them will choose a specialist subject but broader courses will be available. The first school of study will be in the physical sciences because they will give a background for the study of electronics and other branches of engineering which are the chief industry of Essex. The next school of study is that of social studies which include mathe-matics, economics, sociology and government. As time progresses other fields of study will be considered. So far there are no separ-ate faculties of history, classics and modern languages. The tradi-tional halls of residence have been replaced by a pre-fabricated village in which the basic unit is the "apartment." Each is designed to have its own common room and kitchenette and it is planned that every undergraduate will be able to experience at least one year in residence. The first undergraduates entered in October 1964.

The new University of Kent ran into trouble about its title. It had been given the title of the University of Canterbury but the University of Canterbury, New Zealand pointed out that this would cause considerable distress in New Zealand. This point was supported by the U.G.C. The result was that the name finally adopted was "The University of Kent at Canterbury." Dr. Geoffrey Templeman was appointed the first Vice-Chancellor. At first its target was 3,000 students but it is probable that it will be raised to 6,000. The university was to be opened in 1965 but pressure of applicants may result in an emergency opening before this date.

The University of Warwick is on a site close to the City of Coventry and will probably be opened in 1965 when it is hoped to receive the first 200 undergraduates. Mr. J. B. Butterworth, Fellow and Bursar of New College, Oxford, has been appointed Vice-Chancellor. It is expected to have about 3,000 students within ten years. Lord Rootes, chairman of the university's promotion committee, stated that there is need for a graduate School of Business Studies. He hoped that the University of Warwick will help in providing training for high level management. Mr. Butterworth believed that at first the university should choose subjects which were demanded by the undergraduates and which showed signs of rapid development. The university will be largely residential and halls of residence were preferred rather than colleges.

There was considerable discussion about the site for the University of Lancashire and the North-West but eventually Lancaster was chosen. The university is still in the planning stage, and Professor C. F. Carter, formerly Jevons Professor of Political Economy at Manchester, has been appointed Vice-Chancellor. Professor Carter has initiated a new idea. Most of us know that it is possible to possess a competent knowledge of one's subject but little ability in teaching it. There have been criticisms of university lecturers from the students from time to time. The balance between research and teaching raises another problem. Teaching methods in the universities were reviewed in 1962 by a Committee on University Teaching Methods appointed by the U.G.C. under the

chairmanship of Sir Edward Hale. Professor Carter has gone a step
further in the appointment of a Research Fellowship in University
Teaching Methods. Professor Carter believes that a new university
in planning its curriculum should give attention to teaching methods
and the new Fellow should be able to give the members of the
staff up to date information about the experiments and research
which have been undertaken in continental and American universities in regard to teaching methods, and to encourage thought and
experiment on them. He suggested that this appointment might in
the future lead to a department of higher education. Princess
Alexandra will be the first Chancellor of the University.

Scotland had been demanding for some years the establishment
of universities in addition to the four older foundations of St.
Andrews, Glasgow, Aberdeen, and Edinburgh. This desire was only
partially satisfied by the award of university status to the Royal
College of Science and Technology at Glasgow. This College
has a very interesting history. It had developed from the work of
John Anderson (see pp. 471-2). At his death in 1796 he left his
library and collection "to the public for the good of mankind and
the improvement of science, in an Institution to be denominatèd
'Anderson's University.'" In 1913 the Institution became the
Royal Technical College, Glasgow, and in 1963, the University of
Strathclyde.

This, however, did not bring an end to the Scottish campaign.
Glasgow had now two universities but Edinburgh had only one but
it possessed the Heriot-Watt College which was similar to the Royal
Technical College at Glasgow. This has now been promised university status but it will probably have to find a site outside the
capital city for its expansion. It is possible that a site near Falkirk
may be chosen. In July 1964, Stirling was accepted as the third
new university.

In the near future, a fourth university may be recognised at
Dundee. University College, Dundee, founded in 1881, was affiliated to the University of St. Andrews in 1897 but this arrangement proved to be unhappy. The College believed that it suffered
a restriction to its development and made a claim to independent
status. The Secretary of State for Scotland agreed to the request
of the University Court that the problems raised should be considered by an impartial inquiry. This was conducted by Lord
Cooper, President of the Court of Session, and two assessors. The

Report of 1949 recommended the absorption of Dundee into the university. This decision could only be put into force if the colleges which seemed to be centres of discord were dissolved. The University Court accepted some of Lord Cooper's recommendations but it pointed out that if St. Salvator's, the oldest college in Scotland, was closed, this step would meet with strong opposition.

The only solution appeared to be the appointment of a Royal Commission. This was approved in May 1951, with Lord Tedder, Marshal of the Royal Air Force, as chairman. The Commission decided on a scheme of integration to be presented to Parliament for approval. The result was the University of St. Andrews Act, 1953, by which Dundee and the Conjoint Medical School were merged into a new college under the name of Queen's College. This did not satisfy Dundee which aimed at becoming a separate university. If this is realised, Scotland will have eight universities.

It is generally agreed that the new universities should differ from the four ancient universities which by the Universities (Scotland) Act of 1899, have a similar organisation and type of course. It is urged that the new university should be open to new ideas. The Scottish tradition has been to place reliance on the lecture. The result has been that the lecture often became a kind of public oration because of the large number of students attending. Hence the move to experiment with tutorial groups. The majority of Scottish students live at home so that the number resident is comparatively small. It is now acknowledged that a residential university has definite advantages in both academic and social life.

The U.G.C. has agreed to reconsider the claims made by other applicants which had not been accepted and also invited applications from other districts. The closing date was fixed for 31 December, 1963. The reader will realise that this change of policy was the result of the Robbins Report which will be discussed later in this chapter. Two of the applications which had been turned down are specially interesting. The first is that by Chester which is a city historically corresponding in the west to York on the other side of the Pennines. It can offer a site of 220 acres close to the River Dee. The project is sponsored by the local authorities of the city and council and the leading industrialists of the area. The other is Stamford, which, for a short time in the fourteenth century was a university town. (See footnote to p. 59.) Although Stamford in itself is a small town, it has a catchment area of more than a million people and which contains a number of industries. Its claim is strongly supported by Dr. R. W. Stopford, formerly Bishop of Peterborough and now Bishop of London. He is a prominent educationist who has had experience as a schoolmaster, a college principal and has served terms as Secretary and Moderator of the Church of England Training Colleges.

The problems of university entrance had been considered by the Crowther Committee but since then there have been several important developments. The fact that there are more qualified candidates for entrance than there are places available has led to a situation which was becoming chaotic. The universities agreed on a Central Council on Admissions.

Applicants can now send for forms and details of courses from the central office. They complete a single form and are allowed to apply to a maximum of four universities. The central office acts as a Clearing House and sends a copy of each application to each university named by the applicant. For some years the training-colleges had operated a similar scheme with considerable success. The new scheme became operative from 1st September 1962.

Applicants are instructed to decide on their first and second preferences by the 25th of March and their other applications by the 25th of May. The central office notifies the decision of the university selectors to the candidate. Any candidate not chosen will be told of other universities which have vacancies.

Obviously the majority of applicants will have completed their forms and are waiting for the results of the G.C.E. When these are published, outstanding difficulties can be resolved and the provisional acceptance given on successful results in the examination can be confirmed. The scheme does not apply to Oxford and Cambridge where the colleges choose their own undergraduates. Other exceptions are the medical and dental schools of the University of London, Birkbeck College, London, and the University of Belfast. Candidates should make a direct application to these. Candidates who live in Scotland and wish to apply to St. Andrews, Glasgow and Aberdeen only, must also make a direct application.

Although Oxford and Cambridge have not joined the scheme, they have agreed upon changes in the procedure for new admissions, which interfere very slightly with the independence of the colleges but accommodate them to the procedure of the modern universities. The new scheme is fully in operation for the session 1963-4.

The Anderson Committee dealt with the question of university grants and Government grants to other students following comparable courses in further education and to teachers in training. It recommended the abolition of the "means test" by which the amount of grant was based on the income of the parents. The Minister was not prepared to accept the recommendation in its entirety but was agreeable to a modification which raised the number of students in receipt of full grant from 25 per cent to 40 per cent. This resulted in about 10,000 more families who would cease to make contributions. The new rates of grant came into operation in October 1961.

The Committee also recommended the abolition of State Scholarships after 1962. Their place would be taken by the open entry scholarships offered by the universities. The holder of a State Scholarship had the value of the Scholarship deducted from the Government grant. Now the holder of an open scholarship is able to keep up to £100 of the scholarship without deduction from the Government grant. The Committee believed that it would result in a better field of competition for entrance scholarships to the civic universities. The Minister of Education accepted this proposal. The civic universities expressed their fear that this would give a greater "pull" by Oxford and Cambridge. Keele would be worst hit because it had no endowments for entrance scholarships and it was generally felt that the more able students would apply to universities which could offer open scholarships. The colleges of the University of Wales were not disturbed because they had always found a keen competition for their open scholarships. The future will show whether the misgivings of the civic universities are realised.

Ever since the publication of the McNair Report the recruitment and training of teachers has been a major problem for the Ministry of Education. By 1956 it was evident that the yearly increase of six to seven thousand teachers would not be enough to cope with the demand, and even this increase showed signs of falling. Many causes were responsible for this state of affairs. The "bulge" in the birth-rate necessitated an increase in the number of school places which in turn demanded an expansion of the teaching force. The Act of 1944 stated that marriage would not disqualify a woman teacher from continuing in the profession. In spite of this, child-bearing involved a large number of temporary breaks in the service of married women, some of whom never returned to the schools. The McNair recommendation for a third year of training was eventually accepted and the extra year of training came into force from September 1960. This resulted in a time lag of a year in the majority of the output from training-colleges. Although there had been several new salary scales, the increase in number of trained graduate teachers, especially in mathematics and science, was slow. The upward revision of salary scales did not compete with the opportunities offered in industry, commerce, and the civil and local government services.

Two recommendations of the Anderson Committee also affect university entrants. The first was concerned with Government grants to students entering a university, and to others who followed a comparable course in higher education and to teachers in training. The Committee also recommended the abolition of the "means test" by which the amount of grant was dependent on the income of the parents. The Minister was not prepared to accept this but modified the recommendation (p. 627). This resulted in about 10,000 more families who would cease to make contributions. The new rate of grant came into operation in October 1961.

The second was concerned with the abolition of State Scholarships after 1962. The only types of award offered by the Ministry which have been continued are the mature state scholarships and post-graduate state studentships. State Scholarships are replaced by the open entry scholarships offered by the universities. This proposal was accepted by the Minister of Education. Previously the holder of a State Scholarship had the value of the scholarship deducted from the Government grant. Now the holder of an open scholarship can keep up to £100 without any deduction. The Committee believed that it would result in a better field of competition for entrance scholarships to the civic universities. The latter feared that this would intensify the "pull" by Oxford and Cambridge. Keele would be the worst hit because it had no endowments for entrance scholarships and it was generally felt that the more able students would apply to universities which offered open scholarships. The colleges of the University of Wales were not disturbed because they had always found a keen competition for their open scholarships. Time will show how far these misgivings have been realised.

The abolition of State Scholarships resulted in some changes in the G.C.E. examination. These did not affect "O" level candidates nor result in any alteration of the standard "A" level. The old Scholarship level was discarded and the Advanced level results are classified into five main grades of pass awards on the main papers. Grade "A" accounts for about the first 10 per cent of Advanced level entries in a subject. Grade "B" accounts for a further 15 per cent and Grades "C", "D" and "E" account for 45 per cent. These percentages are rough indications. More able candidates can be awarded "Distinction" or "Merit." These are based on the performance in the Special or "S" paper. This paper is designed to test a candidate's intellectual grasp and his power of thinking about his subject. Only candidates who obtain "A", "B", or "C" grading on their basic papers are qualified to have their "S" paper, if offered, taken into account. Supplementary grading can only be awarded to a strictly limited number of candidates. This is approximately about 15 per cent of all "A" level entries in a subject.

The Minister of Education attached great importance in the present competitive situation to ensuring that examination pressures on sixth forms are kept to a minimum. He was glad to find that the universities would continue to use the G.C.E. examination results for selection or qualifying purposes instead of setting their own entrance tests. He agreed that the system of grading is superior to the use of numerical marks. The revision of the "A" level came into operation in the summer of 1963.

The outlook appeared more gloomy when the future was considered. The Crowther Report drew attention to another "bulge" in the early 1970s and if the recommendations concerning the raising of the school leaving age and the opening of county colleges were adopted, there would be a still greater demand for more teachers. In 1959 there was a force of about 326,000 teachers. Various estimates were made about the number of teachers required by 1970 and it was generally agreed that about 94,000 extra would be needed by 1970. At the present rate of increase it was likely that there would be a deficiency of 40,000—50,000 teachers at the end of the decade.

The reaction of the Government was a decision in 1958 to increase the capacity of the training-colleges by 12,000 places. The White Paper of 1958 had suggested that the Churches would be asked to contribute. The Church Assembly co-operated and accepted the responsibility for providing 50 per cent of the cost of capital works necessitated in Church of England training-colleges if the Ministry provided the other half. Up to 1958, the Central Board of Finance co-operating with the Council of the Church Training Colleges had spent over £1 million on capital development.

The Minister recognised that the expansion programme would create difficulties for the voluntary colleges, and amended the Grant Regulations so that a grant of 75 per cent of the cost of approved capital expenditure would be made to enable the voluntary colleges to increase their capacity, in addition. He was prepared to make a grant of 75 per cent towards the cost of new colleges. The extra cost to the Church would be £1 million and this would involve raising a loan.

In addition to the enlargement of the voluntary and L.E.A. training-colleges, new ones have been built at Nottingham, Walsall, Brentwood (Essex), and Cardiff. Christ Church, a new Church of England Training College was opened at Canterbury and another at Lancaster in September 1964. The increase of births in 1938 implied a still greater demand for teachers than had been envisaged and a further 4,000 training-college places would be needed and if later evidence showed it necessary, still more places would be made available. In 1962 the National Advisory Council on the Training and Supply of Teachers published a long-term forecast of the demand for teachers up to 1980.

This evidence led the Ministry in January 1963 to decide that the number of students in the training-colleges would have to be increased to 80,000 by 1970-1. This would make about 23,000 three-year trained teachers a year by 1970, about twice the number of two-year trained teachers supplied to the schools in 1959. We shall see that the Robbins Committee considered that this number was not sufficient. The National Advisory Council concluded that the training of graduates remained on a voluntary basis, 1,000 additional places would be needed by 1968. At present about 6,000 graduates have entered the schools in each year. Of these, more than a half have taken teaching posts either directly after graduation or after a short period in some other employment. The remainder have taken a fourth year of training at a university department of education or in a training-college. As a consequence of the acute shortage of teachers, the Ministry has not felt justified in requiring graduates to train before they can be recognised as qualified teachers.

The Ministry has been worried about the number of women teachers who leave the service after marriage. This has increased because of the earlier date of marriage which was mentioned in the Crowther Report. Since 1961 the Ministry has encouraged these trained women teachers to return to the profession as either full- or part-time teachers. The Kelsall Report of 1963 calculated that one-half of trained graduates and about three-fifths of two-year trained teachers will return to teaching after about nine years absence. Ten years ago about 5,000 teachers entered the schools as part-time teachers and this number had risen to about 25,000 in 1963.

An experiment in day training-colleges was launched at Leeds in September 1959. The City of Leeds L.E.A. secured the premises which formerly belonged to a commercial institute and adapted them for a day training-college. Its purpose was to meet the needs of older students, especially those whose family commitments prevented them from entering a residential college. The college was originally intended for about 150 students but the number of applicants was over 1,000. Some applicants were prepared to travel thirty or forty miles a day in order to attend classes. In 1959, seventy-five students were admitted. "One applicant, a ship's carpenter from Newcastle, would not ask his employer for time off for his interview, but travelled to Leeds for an evening interview and back to Newcastle during the night. He obtained a place and took lodgings in Leeds during the course."[1] In 1963 there were 300 students in the Leeds day training-college.

Other day colleges were opened. One at Manchester started in 1950 and by 1960 had produced four head-mistresses. Other colleges have opened since this time, including four temporary colleges in 1963 and one early in 1964. Many colleges for women students have now admitted men students and some of the residential colleges have opened their doors to day students. The earlier day colleges were intended for older students but the temporary day units attached to existing residential colleges admit well qualified pupils from the schools.

The supply of graduate teachers for mathematics and science began to increase slowly but quickened up when arrangements for deferment of National Service came into force, and the expansion of

[1] Report of the Ministry of Education—*Education in 1959*, p. 63.

the universities resulted in more student places. In June 1962, Sir (now Lord) David Eccles proposed the introduction of auxiliaries in primary schools. The N.U.T. and other professional bodies objected to them on the ground of dilution, that is the use of unqualified people in teaching. The Minister made his intention quite clear. They would not teach but would perform routine duties which would lighten the task of the teachers, especially those in nursery and infant schools.

The Act of 1959 dealt with a situation which did not exist when the Education Act of 1944 was passed. Changes in population distribution such as the new housing estates and towns, had put many children out of reach with existing voluntary schools. At the same time the increase in the birth-rate and the rise in building costs not accompanying any substantial increase in the endowments of the voluntary schools, had thrown a heavy burden upon the Churches if they were to play the part in the developments indicated in the White Paper. The Church of England did not wish to alter the Act of 1944 but pointed out than an increase of the rate of grant for new buildings would be necessary because of the shift of population. The Roman Catholics asked that the increase of grant should apply to all post-war building. The Free Churches were at first critical about the extension of grant to voluntary schools.

Discussions between the Church of England, the L.E.A.s, the political parties and the Free Churches led to a solution based on the analogy with the Education Act of 1936. This had empowered L.E.A.s to pay grants towards voluntary schools for senior pupils which would match voluntary primary schools. The Act of 1944 had honoured agreements which had not been carried out because of the War but omitted selective secondary schools to match voluntary primary schools or any type of secondary school to match aided primary schools built after the War. The Act of 1959 raised the grant from 50 to 75 per cent and authorised the Minister to make grants and to raise loans towards the building and enlargement of aided secondary schools and special agreement schools needed to match existing primary schools. The increased grant only applies to building which had been approved after 15th June 1959. The Bill was welcomed by the Liberal and Labour parties and received the Royal Assent on 29th July 1959.

Because of the sharp rises in the cost of living after the War, the salary scales of the teachers were revised from time to time, but the

increases they received did not keep step with the increased emoluments of those who were employed in industry. Early in 1961,
the teachers' professional associations drew up a new salary scale
which was sent for the consideration of the Burnham Committee.
The case for the teachers was put forward by their representatives
and it was met with sympathy by the L.E.A. panel of the Committee.
The result was the approval of a new salary scale by the whole of
the Committee. The total amount agreed was £47,500,000.

The Burnham Committee sent the agreement to Mr. Selwyn
Lloyd, the Chancellor of the Exchequer. At that time he was concerned with a pay pause policy which limited increases to 3 per
cent and in his Budget he introduced a number of taxation increases
designed to deal with the tendency towards inflation. It was likely
that he would view the Burnham agreement with a critical eye.
Both the panels of the Committee and the teachers were not only
disturbed but were exceedingly angered when he announced that he
rejected the total amount claimed and substituted scales drawn up
by himself and notified that Sir David Eccles would bring in legislation in the autumn to fix the total amount at £42 million. He also
declared his intention to amend Section 89 of the 1944 Act to give
the Chancellor the power possessed by the Secretary of State for
Scotland to modify salary agreements. The Burnham Committee
made a strong protest against the decision but had to admit they
were powerless. Sir William Alexander, the secretary of the authorities' panel declared, "The Burnham Committee as constituted
ceases, as I see it."

Negotiations between the teachers and the Chancellor and Sir
David Eccles made no progress and token strikes in different parts
of the country took place. Some teachers advocated a national strike
but the N.U.T. hoped to avoid this drastic measure. The N.U.T.
decided on a one day token strike and notified that teachers would
refuse to supervise school meals after 1st November. The Chancellor and the Minister of Education compromised by postponing the
proposed legislation and in reply the N.U.T. reluctantly accepted
the award and called off the strike plans. The National Association of Schoolmasters did not agree with the compromise and many
of its members came out in a series of token strikes. The majority
of teachers did not feel that the cuts were sufficiently drastic to cause
widespread distress which would follow strike action but they

strongly objected on principle to the intervention of the Government. Women teachers, whose salaries were now equal to those of the men, were equally indignant.

It was hoped, however, that when the Burnham Committee met to consider the scale which was to operate from 1st April 1963, the negotiations would proceed peaceably, but this hope was quickly dashed. The Committee recommended an increase of £50 throughout the Basic scale which amounted to £21 million. The recommendation was agreed by the authorities' panel and the N.U.T. but was rejected by the National Association of Schoolmasters as being inadequate. The Minister agreed that he was willing to accept the gross amount which he described as a generous increase but he was not ready to sanction any further expenditure on salaries. He could not agree with the recommendation of the Committee about the way the money should be distributed. He believed that a uniform increment on the Basic scale would deter young people who wished to make teaching their life-long career. They would look some years ahead to the amount they would receive after years of experience. Sir Edward Boyle was convinced that the proposed scale did not give satisfactory awards to graduates, holders of graded posts, heads of departments and others who had posts of special responsibility and experience.

The N.U.T. agreed that more experienced and higher qualified teachers should receive higher awards. This would mean an addition to the total sum recommended and the Minister had declared that this was not possible. It was sure that the Minister's plan would deter young applicants for the teaching profession, and therefore, Sir Edward's decision could not be accepted. The Burnham Committee refused to amend their recommendation and a deadlock ensued.

The problem was not an easy one to solve since there is something to be said on each side. It is doubtful whether the Minister has the legal right to reject a recommendation before it has been officially presented to him. The intervention of the Minister is that of a person who is external to the Burnham Committee, and the negotiations which take place are between the representatives of the teachers and their employers who are the local education authorities. The latter contribute nearly half of the cost in salaries. It appears that the whole principle of the procedure of the Burnham Committee as laid down in Section 89 of the Education Act of 1944 needs very careful consideration. Sir Edward Boyle gave notice that he intended to present the case for legislation which would give the Minister a place on the Committee.

In March, 1964, Sir Edward Boyle published his proposals for the reconstitution of the Burnham Committee. In short, he proposed that salary negotiations should take place between the teachers' and the management side. The latter would include representatives of the Ministry with equal voting power with that of the L.E.A.s. If agreement was reached, the Minister would put the negotiations into effect by an order of the Ministry. There would be facilities for independent arbitration. Settlements reached by means of arbitration would normally be put into effect by a Ministry order but in exceptional cases because of weighty reasons of public policy the order would not be made. Sir Edward thought that such exceptional cases would rarely materialise. These proposals were only a framework and some other questions of procedure needed to be settled. The teachers' associations, on the whole, welcomed the proposals and agreed that Section 89 was defective but they would like to know more about certain points such as "weighty reasons of public policy." They wanted to feel that the Minister's views would be expressed in the early stages of negotiation and not as a bolt from the blue at the conclusion.

Another problem connected with this is one which had its beginnings in 1902 and has now become more formidable. This arises as the result of the new valuation and the widespread rise in the rates which has placed a heavy burden on many ratepayers. In this the local contribution towards the cost of education is a chief factor. It has been suggested in many quarters, especially amongst Liberals, that the cost of education should be borne by the central authority. One can sympathise with this view provided that it does not lead to a serious danger. Since 1902, our system of education has been based on the partnership between the central authority, the local authorities, the teaching profession and the parents. The danger is that this proposal, without adequate safeguards, could lead to the breakdown of the partnership and put the Minister in the rôle of a dictator.

The State of our Schools is the title of a survey undertaken by the N.U.T. into the condition of our schools. The Report deals with the Schools of England and Wales and is limited mainly to primary and secondary modern schools. It will be followed by a further report on other schools. The information was gathered by means of questionnaires sent to over 30,000 schools. Answers were received from over 20,000 which was a very satisfactory response. The Report is in some ways comparable to the Taunton Commission of the previous century. Almost every week the Press gives details about the opening of new schools, the enlargement of school buildings, changes in staffing and curricula, and improvements in the equipment of the schools. We can thus find out what improvements have taken place in some areas but so far the general public has had no means of discovering what remains to be done in the country as a whole. Hence the importance of an investigation of this kind.

The survey was compiled by Dr. Mark Abrams and his colleagues on the staff of Research Services Limited. Mr. Tyrrell Burgess, an assistant editor of *New Society,* undertook the study of the replies to the important questions of staffing, improvements in school buildings during the last five years and equipment. It is impossible in a short space to give an adequate summary of the findings and the reader who wishes to seek the details should read the Report. In general, many classes contained a larger number of pupils than the standard laid down by the Ministry; many buildings of the Victorian era, with only minor improvements, were still in use, and there was a great shortage especially of specialist teachers in secondary schools. The overcrowding was worse in the south of England but in the north there was a greater proportion of out-of-date buildings. A large number of primary schools had no adequate space for dining, no staff room, and in some schools, no room for the head teacher. More than a third of primary schools were voluntary schools, aided or controlled. Most of these in rural districts lacked hot water supply and the condition of the toilets was most unsatisfactory. In a few schools the teachers' toilets did not exist and the staff had to share with the pupils. Most toilets were outside the main building and in a severe winter, such as that of 1962-3, they were invariably frozen. Modern equipment was scarce and even some of the larger schools did not possess a library or accommodation for handicrafts or physical education. Often, secondary modern and grammar schools were so overcrowded that groups of pupils had to be accommodated in buildings some distance from the main school. In the district where the writer lives, classes have to travel about three-quarters of a mile for certain lessons and have to cross two extremely dangerous main roads.

The Report did not aim at a condemnation of the policy of the Ministry but was designed to speed up advance in education. Sir Edward Boyle seems to have recognised this but he hoped that the deficiencies in a large number of schools would not turn the minds of the public away from the most serious problems that have to be faced, in particular, the acute shortage of teachers.

Problems in Scottish schools are similar to those in England and Wales but with a different emphasis. Scottish teachers have long been dissatisfied with the salary scales especially in the primary schools. There has been a marked increase in the number of women primary teachers described by some critics using the words of Knox, as "the monstrous regimen of women." On the other hand the secondary scale has been weighted in favour of honours graduates in order to attract those teachers with high academic qualifications. To some extent this reflects the Scottish respect for academic distinction but on the whole it is felt that salary scales are based on the law of supply and demand. There is a strong feeling that Scottish teachers should have the right of free salary negotiation.

The problem is complicated by the acute shortage of teachers after the War. The need for recruiting more teachers has led to what is usually termed dilution. In the earlier days of the century, teachers in both primary and secondary schools were graduates. The exceptions were for teachers of such subjects as art, music, handicrafts, and physical education. The present tendency is to appoint non-graduate teachers of general subjects many of whom are uncertificated. Some of the latter are persons only with slender qualifications.

The discontent reached a head in 1961 when Glasgow teachers came out on a week's strike followed by teachers in other areas. Strike action was a new factor in Scottish education. The Secretary of State for Scotland was not prepared for an immediate change in his policies on salaries and the recruitment and training of teachers. The Educational Institute of Scotland decided in May 1961, to support strike action as a means of forcing the Secretary to a more speedy decision.

The Advisory council on Education in Scotland, appointed in 1957 was discharged in 1961 and its main recommendations were promptly accepted by the Secretary of State at the end of the year. These included the appointment of a Scottish Examination Board and the addition of an advanced grade of the Scottish Certificate of

Education. Since 1888, examinations had been conducted by the Scottish Education Department whose work was on the whole quite efficient. New ideas, however, had developed since that date. The new Board gives the universities a place of influence and it approximates to the Secondary Schools Examination Council in England and Wales.

In the revised system, pupils will sit for the ordinary level in the fourth year of the course and will take the higher grade examinations in their fifth year and can add further subjects at the ordinary level. They will sit for the advanced grade in the sixth year of their course. The fourth and sixth year examinations are comparable to the ordinary and advanced levels fo the G.C.E. The higher grade will then be intermediate to those levels.

As a result of the strikes and threatened coercive measures of 1961, the Wheatley Committee was appointed to consider the conditions of awarding and withdrawing teachers' certificates. A number of practical recommendations were made about the procedure in the appointment of teachers and the conditions of service which should be set out in a written contract. Certain dismissals of teachers had caused a stir and it recommended the Secretary of State to give some guidance in such cases. The teacher should be accompanied, if he wished, by an adviser and the procedure of repeal should be revised. The inquiry into the dismissal should be conducted by an advocate assisted by two persons, one who might be a teacher, and the other a member of an education committee from an area outside that in which the dismissal occurred. This would insure an impartial hearing. Suggestions were also made about consultations between education committees and teachers in regard to school buildings and curricula.

Scottish teachers had little influence on educational policy but now many believe that a body should be created to express the views of qualified teachers to the education authorities. The Wheatley Committee supported this and, after discussion, the Secretary of State accepted the proposal for a General Teaching Council for Scotland. One of its duties would be the issue of a register of qualified teachers. These changes require an Act of Parliament and at the time of writing, a Bill is being considered by the House of Lords.

The Newsom Report (August 1963) was the next stage in what will be a revolution in English education. The terms of reference given to the Advisory Council were as follows:—"To consider the education between the ages of thirteen and sixteen of pupils of average or less than average ability who are or will be following full-time courses either at schools or in establishments of further education. The term education shall be understood to include extra-curricular activities." At the same time, a committee under the Chairmanship of Lord Robbins was appointed by the Prime Minister to report on Higher Education in Great Britain. The Robbins Report was issued in October 1963. Sir John Newsom became Vice-Chairman of the Advisory Council and was followed as Chairman by Lady Plowden. The Plowden Committee was appointed in October 1963 to consider Primary Education and their Report was expected in 1965 but because of the vast field to be covered, it is probable it will not be published until 1966.

The pupils in the age group considered by the Newsom Report are those in non-selective secondary schools, mainly those in modern and comprehensive schools. Some members of this group may be in the lower or middle forms of grammar schools or in institutions of further education, and also include others who left school at the age of fifteen or who have become members of a youth organisation. They are representative of nearly half of the future population of England and Wales. This explains the title of the Report, "Half our Future." The concluding sentences of the Introduction state: "Half our future is in their hands. We must see that it is in good hands."

The Advisory Council carried out a survey of secondary modern and comprehensive schools in 1961. This was necessary for obtaining the facts about the schools, the pupils attending them and the type of education provided in them. It was not possible to survey all the schools of this kind because of time and cost but great care was taken to obtain representative samples. By means of careful sub-sampling the number of pupils was reduced to about 6,000 and great care was taken to secure that the information obtained should be reliable.

At the outset of this task the Council experienced difficulty in regard to the terms average and below average children. It is generally accepted that the terms apply to two large groups of pupils but it is difficult to draw a sharp distinction between them. The term below average ability may give rise to emotional overtones and suggest that such pupils are inferior to the more able ones and therefore are less worth educating. The Council refused to accept this conclusion. The average is not steady but fluctuates over a period of years. The tendency in the last quarter of the century shows a steady rise in the average. "The mysteries of one generation become the commonplaces of life to their grandchildren. In this sense standards do rise."

The Report continues: "This is not often apparent, because we are seldom in a position to compare, directly, the achievements of pupils of one generation with those of another. In a latter part of this report, in which the results are described of a series of tests designed to show the pupils' capacity to read with understanding, there is a clear record of improvement. A test score which even fourteen years ago would have been good enough to put boys or girls well into the above-average category would to-day put them firmly into the below-average group. Over the intervening years the general level of performance has risen. One of the reasons why there is a quite proper anxiety over the general standards of literacy to-day is not that fewer and fewer people can read and write, but that more and more people need to do so with greater competence" (para 8).

The developments recommended in regard to the education of the average and below-average children will be costly. Can we afford this outlay? The answer is that we must afford it. We stand in need of many more skilled workers for existing jobs and a better educated labour force to meet future demands. In spite of the improvements in our educational system, there is still a large amount of wastage. The Council believed that there is a considerable reserve of ability amongst our children which has not been tapped, and one way of dealing with this deficiency is to extend the school leaving age.

In the last decade, the number of pupils remaining in secondary modern schools after the statutory leaving age of fifteen has been increasing and is now more than double what it was in 1958. This tendency will increase and we may find some secondary modern pupils continuing at school until seventeen or even eighteen. We must avoid being too complacent about the situation and think that this can be left to voluntary choice. The school leaving age has been raised in the U.S.A. and France and the Crowther Report recommended a leaving age of sixteen. It suggested that the most suitable time for the change would be in the years 1966-9 when the secondary schools would be less crowded. The delay in bringing into force this advice has made it almost too late to make the change at the most convenient time. Hence the Newsom Report strongly advocated that the school leaving age should become sixteen from 1965 and come into force in the school year 1969-70.

It could be argued that when the new leaving age has become operative, a number of pupils below the age of sixteen will be following full-time courses in further education. The Report emphasised that the schools should be responsible for all boys and girls up to the age of sixteen, but on account of the difficulties caused by the shortage of teachers and the need for additional buildings and equipment, some pupils during the transition period should be allowed after fifteen to enter colleges of further education. This must not become permanent and in this matter co-operation between schools and colleges will be essential.

Chapter 2 of the Report gives a description of the pupils, the schools and the problems that need to be solved. It not only made use of the 1961 survey but included information derived from the National Service Survey in the second volume of the Crowther Report. These sources enabled a rough classification of the pupils' environment. "A third of them live on housing estates, which may be bright and modern, like those of the new towns, or drab and ageing, as are some of those built in the early years between the wars. Just under a fifth live in the old and overcrowded centre of some big city or industrial area, where there are few amenities and often a concentration of social problems; for brevity we later refer to these as 'problem' areas. Another fifth of the pupils is made up of boys and girls from rural and from mining districts; and the remainder come from areas which do not fit into any one of these categories and are generally mixed in character" (para. 31).

Many of the pupils attend schools which possess attractive modern buildings but unfortunately many of these schools are greatly overcrowded. Two-fifths of the schools in the sample carry on in very inadequate buildings. Changes in the teaching staff are frequent. The teachers reported that on the whole the pupils are co-operative and only a minority in the fourth year raise serious problems of class control. The less able pupils are more often absent from school without adequate reasons. Nearly half the boys but only a minority of the girls take up part-time paid employment. The majority of them assist their mothers in the household duties.

There is no evidence that pupils who take up part-time employment suffer from it.

A large number of schools are housed in old buildings while others suffer from a lack of books and inadequate equipment. The picture drawn by the Report supports the evidence presented by the N.U.T. survey, *The State of Our Schools*. The Report states that the Act of 1944 changed the name and status of the previous Senior Elementary Schools to Secondary Modern Schools, but it changed little else for several years. When the school-leaving age was raised in 1947, the problem emerged how to find an effective secondary education for a large part of the population which had become used to leaving school at an earlier age. The teachers were forced to acquire experience in schools which had inadequate buildings and scanty equipment. Even the more recent schools were burdened by the shortage of teaching staff and overcrowded space. Unlike the established grammar schools, the new secondary modern schools had no tradition or reputation to help them. During the last ten years teachers and pupils have been assisted by the schools built as a result of the massive building programmes of the years 1950-5. It is likely that by 1970 about two-thirds of secondary pupils will be attending new schools or older schools which have been enlarged and modernised.

One of the reasons which led to an increasing number of young people remaining at school after the age of fifteen is the development of attractive extended courses, many of which do not involve an external examination. The Report emphasises the extra-curricular activities in the newer schools and pleads for greater publicity concerning them. If the public knew more about these modern developments it would realise that the misbehaviour and delinquency described in the press is often exaggerated. As the Report says, "Education needs a better communications service."

Some pupils say the work of the school bores them while others say they do not see the value of the teaching they receive. Many of these will be equally bored when they leave school and enter industry. The Report stresses that these pupils must be made much more active partners in their own education. They all need to attain self-respect and a reason for wanting to work well. Unless they do this, no one can honestly justify an extra year of schooling for them. They will need all the resources the school can give them. Often linguistic inadequacy or the disadvantage of the pupils' social and physical environment account for their poor attainments at school. It is recommended that the Ministry should organise a programme of research to assist pupils in their linguistic or environmental difficulties. The establishment of an experimental school working in close contact with a teacher training-college in which specially selected members of the staff are appointed for this purpose, is highly desirable.

A very vivid description of the environment of boys and girls who live in the slum areas in London, Lancashire, Yorkshire and the industrial Midlands is given by the Report. In many of these areas there are now considerable numbers of coloured people from India, Pakistan, the West Indies and the new states in former British Africa. In more fortunate districts the disciplinary and social problems which are met with in the schools are usually restricted to a few families but in the slum areas the school has to meet the challenge of the whole neighbourhood. It is good to know that the achievements of these pupils are sometimes equal to or even better than those in schools of better areas.

The Report considers that the staffing of the schools in slum districts is so important that it calls for the establishment of an interdepartmental Working Party to deal with general social problems including education. An increase in the number of teachers will not suffice for the needs of these schools unless the right kind of teachers are appointed. "Whatever happens in the schools depends on the men or women who staff them." Some teachers with a strong sense of vocation volunteer to work in these difficult areas but their numbers are too small. The Crowther Report had recommended that "the bad areas, which pay much more than their fair share of the price for a shortage of teachers, need a direct attack upon their problem." Many of the teachers in slum districts have accepted the posts after their applications to schools in more pleasant surroundings have been rejected. They are looking out for posts in schools which are more agreeable to them and this is the cause of the frequent changes in the very schools which require stability. The Council confessed:—"We can at present see no alternative to some solution involving the recruitment of a special body of teachers who are ready to go where they are needed in return for financial compensation, whether under schemes operated through the Ministry or by groups of local education authorities working on a consortium basis. What is quite certain is that this is a matter of urgent educational concern which must be faced." The chapter concludes:—"But adequate education in slum areas will always be expensive, more expensive than average. It looks to us as if it has often been less expensive than average, and therefore pitifully inadequate. It is time for a change" (para. 74).

Chapter 4 of the Report is concerned with the ultimate objectives of the education of pupils in the age group considered by the Report. It recommends that the basic tool subjects, reading, writing and arithmetic should be reinforced by the whole of the subjects and activities of the curriculum. More demands should be made on the pupils, both as regards the nature and the amount of work required. The value of the educational experience should be judged in terms of its total impact on the pupils' skills, qualities and personal development, not by basic attainments only. The Report is in agreement with the Hadow Report of 1926 when it emphasised the necessity of a practical and realistic approach in framing the curriculum of modern schools. As a result of the Hadow Report, the senior schools of pre-1944 and the secondary modern schools which replaced them, gave a considerable amount of time to practical pursuits. The survey of 1961 showed that many schools were more generously provided with practical work-rooms rather than libraries, which goes to signify that the need for the former was recognised before the need for the latter. At the present the pendulum has swung to a middle point and the need for each is recognised.

The Newsom Report also falls into line with the Hadow Report which complained that there was too great a tendency by some schools to regard the school as an isolated unit and education as something apart from the main stream of life. The Newsom Report does not reiterate the advice of the Hadow but corrects the misinterpretation of it. "Unimaginative exercises can be as dully repetitive in woodwork as they can be in English." During the last two years of school life, a new look should be given to the curriculum, and the general idea should be that of a preparation for adult life.

Pupils in the last two years at school need a unifying theme to give them coherence and purpose. They are ceasing to think of themselves as children and are starting to consider the life they will lead as adults, and they need to feel that the school should help them to do so. Up to this time the curriculum has been prescribed for them but now they should have some choice in their studies.

In many schools this has been offered to the more able pupils but the majority of schools in the survey gave little promise of choice or change of programme for the less able. One difficulty is that whilst many schools would like to agree with this, they are restricted by the teacher accommodation. The best they can do is to place these pupils in school leaving groups. They soon realise that their more able companions are being treated in a different way and this fosters the belief that the school does not cater for them.

Teachers have discovered a reserve of talent among the more able scholars and this suggests that the same may be true of many of the less able. "For these pupils, well-designed courses in schools which, without in any way being narrow trade training, guided their interests and helped them to see the way ahead into future education and future training for a career, could be of great value both to the individuals concerned and to the country's economic resources. We think it vital that increased training provision should be available for such school leavers" (para. 102). Those who are more limited in their capacities should be provided with a programme which makes use of an occupational interest. If this was carried out it could develop a greater stimulating approach to school work and lead to a desire to extend their general education. The proportion of specific content in the curriculum naturally varies in different districts. The schools cannot offer courses which are related to every type of employment they may follow in the future and there is no need for them to do this. The fact that they have some choice will tend to produce a feeling that what they do in school has some value for their future occupation.

This calls for a generous variety of courses, many of which are broadly connected with occupational interests. There is need for a more advanced technical equipment than is possessed by most secondary modern schools, and training in worthwhile ways in which boys and girls can spend their leisure time is very important. These would include different hobbies or imaginative experience through the various arts. Two interesting examples of courses for pupils of very limited abilities are outlined in para. 119. At the same time, attention should be directed to guidance on social manners, in every sense.

Chapter 6, "The School Day, Homework, Extra-Curricular Activities," breaks new ground. It recommends a longer school day for pupils in the last two years at school. At present the majority of boys and girls of fourteen to fifteen spend no longer time at school than they did at the age of seven. "A disturbing number appear to leave school under-equipped in skills, knowledge and personal resources. A characteristic complaint of this group is that they are 'bored'—with school, with life outside school and later with their jobs" (para. 120).

The Newsom Report is in agreement with Crowther which pointed out that the peak period for juvenile delinquency occurs in the last year before pupils leave school. The Crowther Report stated (vol. 1. Para. 63), "There is one aspect of juvenile delinquency with which the schools must be very closely concerned— it is the fact that the last year of compulsory education is also the heaviest year for juvenile delinquency, and that steadily increasing rate in the secondary school years is reversed when a boy goes to work. When the school leaving age was raised from fourteen to fifteen in 1947 there was an immediate change over in the delinquency record of the thirteen-year-olds (who until then had been the most troublesome age-group) and the fourteen-year-olds, who took their place in 1948 and have held it consistently ever since— there is nothing in the state of affairs to make any thoughtful person doubt the value of being at school; indeed, the delinquency may arise, not because boys are at school, but because they are not at school enough.

The Newsom Report goes a step further. In addition to its recommendation about the raising of the school-leaving age, it recommends what may seem revolutionary to some pupils and their parents. The first point is that extra-curricular activities ought to become an integral part of the educational programme. It then suggests that some of the pupils' time could be used for homework. The usual practice in grammar schools is to allocate homework to their pupils and this increases when they begin to study for the G.C.E. Some of the brighter boys and girls in modern and comprehensive schools are given homework which will grow in extent now the C.S.E. is in operation. The Report adds that large numbers of pupils and the majority of "our" pupils, commonly do none. It was reluctant to use the term "homework" and confessed that another name should be found which would be more correct in describing the kind of activities the Council had in mind. In the earlier days of this century the homework demanded of pupils was at first an extension of the work in class and later, intensive study for passing an examination. It often included tasks which more appropriately could be done in school hours. The homework recommended should take more varied forms than that which is generally recognised as homework.

"The task to be undertaken might, for instance, be making a model, or finishing some project in the art or craft room begun in school time. It might be a chance to try some new skill or craft or, for those pupils who wished to learn typing, an opportunity for intensive practice which it may be difficult to provide inside the normal school timetable. It might consist in the group viewing and discussion of a film or television programme. It might be the preparation of material before giving a talk in class, or gathering information for some group project in school: obtaining the information might involve writing letters or direct observation and note making, or visiting an art gallery, the public library or the town hall. It could be working on the school magazine, or balancing the Young Farmers' Club accounts, or mapping the route of a coming school expedition. The possibilities are almost infinitely varied, and the tasks could be purposeful and demanding but adaptable to circumstances or to the pupil's capacities. They could be made the occasion for reading, calculating, recording and discussion, without being confined to the standard written exercises which traditionally make up a great deal of homework" (para. 123).

If it is practicable for some of these activities to take place in the home itself it will bring parents into touch with the work in the school. The picture of the father struggling to assist the children in working out problems in calculation will disappear and instead of being bored, he will be interested in playing a part in activities which interest him as much as the pupil. Some schools have reported that parents have asked for additional homework for their children. Other schools in congested urban areas have stressed the difficulty of obtaining for pupils this privacy and quiet they need to concentrate on what they are doing especially in homes where the radio or television is functioning at full blast. Some local authorities have realised these difficulties and have set aside quiet rooms in the public libraries or in the school itself.

One suggestion is that of a three-session school day. One practical idea is the institution of a morning and a shorter afternoon session followed on certain days by one or two hours in the evening in which pupils could follow up hobbies, or some individual work, or take part in varied group activities. Experiments of this kind should be encouraged. Most teachers have been exceedingly generous in giving their time but if the scheme is developed on a large scale it would not be fair to saddle them with such a heavy burden, especially while the shortage of teachers continues.

A somewhat similar situation occurred when plans were being discussed for the staffing of the Day Continuation Schools of the 1918 Act. The supply of teachers was inadequate and the Board of Education asked retired teachers, clergy, graduates and others with sufficient knowledge to give assistance. The Newsom Report suggests that people with special experience and skills might be invited from time to time to contribute to the courses for older pupils. "If a group of boys and girls want to take up photography or badminton or learn a musical instrument, persons other than qualified teachers may be well capable of instructing and inspiring the group" (para. 143).

In different parts of the country experiments on joint appointments of teacher/youth leaders or teacher/wardens are being tried out. These spend part of their time teaching in school and carry on their work with adolescents in youth organisations in the evening. Another development is an experiment in group living which takes such forms as school journeys or expeditions and camps and residential courses varying from a week-end to a month. Some of the latter emphasise strenuous outdoor activities and some schools have combined this with school work for the Duke of Edinburgh's award. The Report recommends that a short survey by the Ministry and the L.E.A.s should be undertaken with the object of discovering the scale on which residential courses are available. One would also need to know how far the demand for such courses is being met and what would be the cost if they were extended to a larger number of pupils.

Chapter 7, "Spiritual and Moral Development," is again a very important one. Its main concern is with county schools in which the teachers may be committed Christians belonging to different religious denominations, or at the other extreme, non-Christian humanists. Between the two is a middle group whose members are not associated with any particular religious body but who have a respect for the traditional Christian outlook on life and feel that it should be preserved.

On the other hand one must consider the boys and girls who in the thirteen to sixteen age group have entered into what is often termed the middle stage of adolescence. This period has been termed the age of criticism and this is shown by the type of questions they put to their elders. The primary school child, unless he is very precocious, generally accepts the views of his teacher. If he asks a question he does so because he wants to know more about the persons and their actions, but after the age of eieven he begins to open them with the word "what?". He is still asking for further information but at thirteen to sixteen his characteristic question begins with "why?". This does not mean that he is necessarily hostile or critical towards what he has previously been taught but he desires to see how Christianity applies to the problems of the world in which he lives and which he is going to work. He has not sufficient experience to attack what he has been told by parent or teacher but he seeks the reason of it.

Pupils of this age are becoming aware of two facts which puzzle them. The first is why Christians belong to different denominations whose beliefs and practices vary considerably. Secondly they are discovering that so many adults deny in their practice the principles they claim to believe. Some boys and girls come to the conclusion that Christianity has failed but they have not grasped that the apparent failure lies in the individuals and not in Christianity and moral principles. (When the Newsom Report was published the movement towards Christian unity had not developed to the stage it has reached recently.) They have no experience of the bitter controversies of the earlier periods of modern history. Hence they cannot compare the acute attitude of enmity between religious bodies two or three generations past and the greater friendliness between Christians of the present day which are resulting in different forms of co-operation. The recent decrees of the Vatican Council, and the discussions on the subject of unity between the Church of England and the Methodists and Presbyterians give hopes that all differences will ultimately be resolved in one unified Christian Church. It may be that in the future this difficulty of a divided Church will not exist to worry young people. The moral difficulty is probably more essential to overcome at the moment.

The aim of religious and moral teaching in voluntary schools, whether Anglican or Roman Catholic, is to train their pupils to be worshipping members of the Church. The county school does not seek to make converts to any particular religious body. Its duty is to present to its pupils the traditional standards of this country which are based on the Christian way of life. It should never occur that later on in life, a person would be able to say that he knows nothing about the meaning of Christianity.

Secondly there is a problem which springs from the opposing attitudes in society about pre-marital intercourse and the permanence of marriage. The Report gives this sensible advice to the educator. "We can only say that we believe it to be wrong to leave the young to fend for themselves without guidance, and wrong to conceal from them (as if we could) the differences in this issue which separate men and women of real moral sensitivity. For our part we are agreed that boys and girls should be offered firm guidance on sexual morality based on chastity before marriage and fidelity within it. We believe, too, that this is predominantly the standpoint of the schools. It is also important that boys and girls should realise that 'going off the rails' does not involve for Christians losing the fellowship of the church, still less of forfeiting the love of God. There are other, and often graver, sins than those against chastity" (para. 164).

The religious instruction given in the schools should go beyond moral teaching. The Act of 1944 required that religious instruction in county schools should be in accordance with the local authority's Agreed Syllabus of instruction in the Christian religion. This has given rise to some controversy and some schools have sought a way of escape by confining religious instruction to Bible reading with only a minimum of comment. The Report describes this as a sure way of losing the attention of most boys and girls. "A teacher cannot help his pupils unless he can put into words their ill-formulated problems and show them how Christians would set about solving them. He must know his Bible and its teaching, he must have thought about the relation of religion and religious knowledge to other fields of human activity and ways of knowing. . . . His scholarship must be up to date, and he must move on the Christian frontiers of to-day" (para. 169).

An improved supply of suitably qualified teachers is a necessity for religious instruction and adequate time should be allowed for this teaching in schools. For over a century the differences between the Church of England and the Free Churches made religion a very dangerous subject for what are now county schools. This has disappeared and the 1944 Act was based on the conviction that the differences between denominations could be overcome in a way that would not cause obstacles to a real Christian education in county schools. The greater tolerance and understanding was made possible by the use of Agreed Syllabuses. Each syllabus has received the unanimous consent of the local education authorities, the teaching profession, the Church of England and the Free Churches. The faith expressed in the Act has been fully justified.

Many of the Agreed Syllabuses were drawn up during the period between the two world wars and were revised at the time the leaving age was raised to fifteen. Their usual method was to start from the Bible and leave the teacher to build his Christian teaching upon this basis. The consequence was that many pupils in the age range considered by the Report tended to think that the Bible has no significance for modern life. The Student Christian Movement in Schools has reversed this procedure and starting with contemporary problems, led the way back to the Bible. Now when the number of boys and girls remaining in schools until fifteen or later is growing, the Newsom Report quite rightly recommended that local education authorities should think about the revision of the syllabuses on lines suggested in the Report. More attention should be given to the religious and moral instruction for the average and under average pupils. The L.E.A.s have been busy with the revision and some have completed it. Diocesan authorities are considering a revision of their syllabuses and, again, some have completed this work.

The chapter closes with some remarks about the value of corporate worship in schools. This value has been denied by some non-Christian humanists. The Newsom Report points out that the corporate life of the school has a tremendous effect on the moral growth of the pupils. Corporate worship has a similar effect upon their spiritual development. It is in the school assembly that the pupils are able to realise the unity of the schools. The Report says; "Corporate worship is not to be thought of as an instrument of education—though it is that—but as a time in which pupils and teachers seek help in prayer, express awe and gratitude and joy, and pause to recollect the presence of God. We admit we were surprised when one of our number told us that new entrants to industry whom she interviewed soon after their induction period frequently told her that what they missed most now they had left school was school prayers. Reviewing our own experience and the evidence we have received, perhaps we ought not to have been surprised" (para. 174).

Chapter 8 of the Report deals with the school community and the important matter of the relations between boys and girls and their teachers. The views of the Council were largely based on the evidence supplied by the heads of schools in the survey and on a collection of essays by girls who had recently left school at the age of fifteen. The chapter is a long one which gives rise to a number of practical recommendations. These are summarised on page 71 of the Report.

(*a*) Every effort should be made to emphasise the status of the older pupils, through school organisation and in the design of school buildings.

(*b*) We welcome interest in developing group responsibilities, and see a particular value in community service projects.

(*c*) Corporal punishment for the older pupil is likely to delay, rather than promote, the growth of self-discipline. It is humiliating for both the pupils and the staff. We especially deplore such punishment for adolescent girls.

(*d*) There is an urgent need to strengthen all existing links between home and school, and in difficult areas to create new ones, as, for example, in the appointment of members of staff with special liaison or home-visiting responsibilities.

(*e*) Positive and realistic guidance to adolescent boys and girls on sexual behaviour is essential. This should include the biological, moral, social and personal aspects. Advice to parents on the physical and emotional problems of adolescents should be easily available. Schools of whatever type should contrive to provide opportunities for boys and girls to mix socially in a helpful and educative environment.

(*f*) It is of the greatest importance for schools to build up a knowledge of individual pupils and to devise some system of supervising their future welfare.

If the school is to provide a training for life in the greater world outside the school, then it follows that in the last year of its programme there should be a concentration on the preparation of the pupils for entry to the adult world of work and leisure. This is the theme of Chapter 9, "Going out into the World." In the last year especially, the school programme ought to be deliberately outgoing. The pupils should mentally and physically be taken outside the school walls and people from the greater world should be brought into the school. Television constitutes a new resource in the hands of the teacher and its value lies for our pupils in its power to extend their knowledge of the contemporary world and to enlarge their sympathies. Films also serve the same purpose and are more readily available at any time.

The Report recommends that the educational value of television and the film should be more appreciated by the schools and the training-colleges. Both the B.B.C. and Independent Television should pay special attention to the extension of school television and L.E.A.s should base their plans on the recognition that television receivers are part of the necessary equipment of the schools. Training-colleges and university departments of education should include in their programmes the value of films and television as social and educational forces and students should be given instruction in the use of school broadcasts in sound and television. Since the Report was issued, the University of Leeds has been experimenting in the use of closed circuit television and other universities and colleges are doing the same.

One of the things pupils ought to know, and be encouraged to desire to know, is how to continue their education, formally and informally. Older pupils should know about the facilities for further education in the areas of the schools, not only by means of pamphlets on the local courses available, but also by visiting institutes of further education. Invitations to visit the schools should be sent to the principals and staffs of these colleges. There should be a closer liaison with the local youth service and the youth employment service and the personal advisory and welfare services should be extended. Teachers should gain familiarity with industry since all secondary schools need teachers of special responsibilities in career work and should be given time and facilities to do it effectively. In addition training-colleges could consider how their students can obtain this kind of knowledge. The British Employers' Confederation has instituted "Introduction to Industry" schemes for serving teachers and similar experiments should be available for teachers in training.

Chapter 10 discusses examinations and assessments. Some form of leaver's certificate combining assessment with a record of the pupils' school careers would be of value to parents, future employers and colleges of further education. "An assessment of the pupil by the school is essentially what we have in mind. Unfortunately, one of the most sought after forms of assessment, though one that is often misunderstood, is a public examination. We say unfortunately, because we are convinced that for large numbers of the boys and girls with whom we are concerned public external examinations are not likely to offer a suitable means of assessment" (para. 241). It is important to realise that these examinations are not intended for the under average pupils. The Newsom Report agrees with the Beloe that the C.S.E. should not be taken before the fifth year and must not shape the curriculum as the School Certificate examination did. Oral tests of candidates' use of spoken English should be included and the teacher's assessment of the candidate must be taken into account.

If the conclusions of the Report are to be implemented, two factors are necessary without which the changes in the secondary schools will be impossible. The first is the problem of school buildings. Few schools at the present have adequate facilities for the social needs of the older pupils. Much new building is required and the congested areas need special consideration. Chapter 11, "Building for the Future," includes diagrams which are most informative and which have been made available by the Development Group of the Ministry's Architects and Building Branch. In addition to buildings, developments in the methods of education require new equipment or more extensive use of the existing facilities including all the audio-visual aids.

The other essential is an adequate number of teachers of the right type. When the school leaving age is raised, new demands will be made on the teachers and this must be taken into account in their training. Most teachers as well as being able to offer one main subject which they teach throughout the school, should be prepared to teach one or preferably two subjects over a more restricted range. These should include such subjects as housecraft, handicrafts, art, music, drama and physical education. Training-colleges should have this in mind when drawing up their programmes.

The training of all teachers should include sociological and environmental studies with special reference to the problems of pupils in culturally deprived areas. A few joint training courses should be organised for intending secondary school teachers and for those who desire to enter other services such as the youth and youth employment services or who seek posts as social workers. Teaching conditions will be more attractive if non-teaching staff responsible for clerical work, the service and maintenance of workshops, craftrooms and laboratories was available and if expensive audi-visual equipment and so-called teaching machines were supplied in a more generous way.

The Newsom Report seeks to terminate an anomaly which has existed for too many years. This is the appointment of untrained graduates as qualified teachers. The statement of the 8th Report of the National Advisory Council on the Training and Supply of Teachers is quoted. "Here (in the primary and secondary modern schools) teaching methods and techniques with all the specialised knowledge that lies behind them are as essential as mastery of subject matter. The prospect of these schools staffed to an increasing extent by untrained graduates is, in our view, intolerable" (para. 301). The Newsom Report urges that a training requirement for graduates be introduced at the earliest practicable moment. The answer of the Ministry was that this desirable reform cannot be considered until the difficulties of the shortage of teachers are overcome.

Part II of the Newsom Report deals with the "Teaching Situation." For reasons of space this cannot be included in a summary of this kind but the reader is advised to read it and think about its suggestions concerning the curriculum and teaching method. Part III gives details of the 1961 Survey and uses imaginative descriptions of typical pupils who are to be found in secondary modern and comprehensive schools. Appendix II on Sex Education is most helpful and Appendix V is a statistical detail of the Survey.

The Robbins Report is in several aspects different from earlier reports. In the first place the Committee was requested to consider the future pattern of higher education in the whole of Great Britain and it deals with institutions for higher education in Scotland as well as those in England and Wales. Its terms of reference were as follows.

It was "to review the pattern of full-time higher education in Great Britain and in the light of national needs and resources to advise Her Majesty's Government on what principles its long-term development should be based. In particular, to advise, in the light of these principles, whether there should be any changes in that pattern, whether any new types of institution are desireable and whether any modifications should be made in the present arrangements for planning and co-ordinating the development of the various types of institution."

In addition to the main Report there are five Appendices filling six volumes giving the facts and figures on which the main Report is based. The Committee initiated a number of surveys and statistical inquiries which will serve for further observation and analysis. The Appendices cannot be considered in our summary which concerns the main Report solely.

The Report, unlike previous ones, investigates higher education as a whole. In the past there have been Royal Commissions which dealt with particular universities such as Oxford and Cambridge, London, Durham, and St. Andrews. Other committees have reported on different aspects of higher education, *e.g.* technical education and the training of teachers. The Robbins Report was appointed by the Prime Minister and not by the Ministry of Education.

After the historical introduction the Report lays down four objectives which are considered essential to a well balanced system of higher education.

The first is the instruction in skills necessary to play a part in the general division of labour. The Report places this first not because it is of prime importance but because it has been generally neglected. A good general education is important but by itself it is not capable of solving many of the grave problems of the present. The next point is that the aim of producing cultivated men and women must be more important than the creation of mere specialists. Thirdly, views differ considerably about the respective values of teaching and research in institutes of higher education. The search for truth and the advancement of knowledge must always be one of the important functions of higher education. Finally, there is the fundamental function of transmitting a common culture and common standards of citizenship. Higher education must not restrict individuality but like the schools, it should provide in partnership with the family a background of culture and social habit which will ensure a healthy society.

This last function is most important in the present when the idea of equality of opportunity has been accepted. "It is not merely by providing places for students from all classes that this ideal will be achieved but also by providing, in the atmosphere of the institutions in which students live and work, influences that in some measure compensate for any inequalities of home background. These influences are not limited to the student population. Universities and colleges have an important role to play in the general cultural life of the communities in which they are situated" (para. 28).

The functions described will vary in different institutions of higher education as well as in the methods of discharging them. There should be greater emphasis on research and the advancement of knowledge in the postgraduate stage than in the undergraduate but these principles should be present in all the different institutions of higher education. In some institutions the vocational aspects will be more evident than in others. If the system does not provide all of them it must be considered as inadequate.

Chapter 2 then concludes by outlining the main principles which guided the Committee in their enquiries and drawing up their recommendations. The first is the generally acknowledged principle that higher education should be open to all who are qualified to profit by it and who wish to do so. It is essential to make the maximum use of the talent of our people if we are to compete successfully with other highly developed countries in this age of rapid technological and social advance. "But beyond that, education ministers intimately to ultimate ends, in developing man's capacity to understand, to contemplate and to create. And it is characteristic of the aspirations of this age to feel that, where there is capacity to pursue such activities, there that capacity should be fostered. The good society desires equality of opportunity for its citizens to become not merely good producers but also good men and women" (para. 33).

The principle of equal academic awards for equal performance is assumed. The grading of individuals for the purpose of higher education should depend on academic accomplishments rather than upon the status of the institution in which they have studied. There is a need for a variety of institutions with differing functions and with differing emphasis. The Report accepts the inevitability that some institutions will be more eminent than others. The history of education bears this out. "It is in the nature of things that talent should attract talent and that where famous intellectual exploits take place, there should develop some concentration of staff and students especially interested in the subjects concerned" (para. 37). Those who have read the earlier chapters of this book will remember such examples as the pre-eminence of the University of Paris in the thirteenth century and the older universities of Britain in the nineteenth.

The Report gives the warning: "There should be no freezing of institutions into established hierarchies; on the contrary there should be recognition and encouragement of excellence wherever it exists and wherever it appears" (para. 37). Differences in level and function will persist among institutions and are only accept-able if students are able to transfer from one institution to another when their intellectual attainments and educational needs warrant it.

The principle of allowance for free development of institutions must be retained. Existing institutions must be free to experiment without limitations except those which safeguard their essential functions. At the same time there must be freedom to experiment with new types of institution when it is desirable. There must be, however, some co-ordination, commonly accepted principles of policy and an organisation for a reasonable allocation of resources.

Nevertheless, a system must maintain a standard. A sound educational system must include full scope for all kinds of talent at all levels. Historically, our universities have tended to set a standard for other institutions and it is probable that they will con-tinue to do so in the future. It is hoped that their reputation will be sustained and while they broaden the education they provide for first degrees, they will also achieve higher standards for those who are capable of postgraduate work.

Chapter 3 of the Report, "The Growth of Higher Education in Great Britain," is largely historical and shows that in the space of sixty years the number of full-time students in institutions of higher education has increased more than eight times. Chapter 4 sum-marises the different types of institutions of higher education begin-ning with the universities which are classified into seven groups. The reader can gather these if he turns back to Chapter XII in this book, and the new post-war universities are described at the begin-ning of this chapter. In the Robbins Report the new universities are identified by the place in which they are situated.

The next type of institution to be considered are the Training Colleges in England and Wales and the Colleges of Education in

Scotland. There are also specialist colleges for the training of teachers for physical education and domestic subjects. Four colleges for the training of technical teachers have been opened. In Scotland all graduate teachers must be trained. The Scottish Colleges of Education are seven in number including two Roman Catholic colleges. Three of them have less than 450 students. The colleges are supervised by the Scottish Council for the Training of Teachers, and receive direct grant from the Scottish Education Department, and also grants from the education authorities. Their link with the universities consists of university representatives on their governing bodies.

In the 19th century most of further education was provided by evening classes. Towards the end of the century the courses were extended to meet the needs of students who wished to obtain a degree or a professional qualification. It was not until the end of the Second World War that there was a rapid growth in the numbers who followed advanced day courses both full-time and part-time. There are now more than 150,000 students taking advanced courses which lead to a degree or to a qualification of degree standard.

The four categories of colleges of further education have been described earlier in this chapter. In addition to technology and science, there are Art Schools which contain about 8,000 students taking advanced courses full-time. Departments of Regional and Area Colleges provide business studies and there are a few Colleges of Commerce. Besides the Colleges of Advanced Technology and Science (the C.A.T.s), there are certain other colleges which receive direct grant from the Ministry of Education such as the Royal College of Art and the College of Aeronautics at Cranfield.

Full-time advanced further education in Scotland is provided in fifteen Central Institutes, the larger of which correspond to the C.A.T.s. They are handing over to further Education Centres part-time work which is below the level of higher education. The Further Education Centres correspond broadly to the Area and Local Colleges of England and Wales. The Royal College of Science and Technology in Glasgow has now acquired university status as the University of Strathclyde and the Heriot-Watt College, Edinburgh, is promised the same status.

Chapter 5 of the Report compares British higher education with that in Continental countries, the United States and the Soviet Union. The facts about the latter were acquired from the Embassies and the British Council. This initial inquiry indicated the topics in which the Robbins Committee was interested and led to visits to seven countries. Space forbids a full description of the differences found but there are several points which are very important. Thus in Western Europe technology was not generally accepted in the universities whereas in Great Britain technological studies entered the universities during the nineteenth century. In Britain technology is catered for by the university and partly by outside institutions. This weakness of organisation began to be remedied in 1953 when plans were made for a massive expansion of the Imperial College of Science and Technology and other establishments.

The university systems themselves show fewer distinctions in Europe than in Britain, where the prominence of Oxford and Cambridge is very marked. "In the Federal German Republic, in Sweden and in the Netherlands, the older universities no longer have so powerful an attraction for the best students and scholars. The only parallels that are at all close are in France. Here the Sorbonne certainly has a commanding position, but some of this at least is the attraction of Paris itself. The real analogy in French higher education to Oxford and Cambridge is not a university but the small group of Grandes Ecoles, such as the *Ecole Normale Supérieure* and the *Ecole Polytechnique*: these are more exclusive in their spheres than any British institution" (para. 103). Another difference is that the training of primary school teachers which is carried out in "normal schools" is really an extension of secondary education. In Western Europe colleges of education are not usually considered to come under the heading of higher education.

Only a few American states have made efforts towards a co-ordinated development of the institutes of higher education. California is an exception which has made a clean break with American tradition. The State University plans to have 120,000 students on its eight campuses by 1975. Another feature of the plan is the proposed concentration of postgraduate studies in the University. The Soviet Union presents a different pattern. Although there is no caste-system among institutions of different kinds, Moscow and Leningrad have a greater prestige. The universities account for about 10 per cent of the enrolments in higher education. There are many specialised institutions some of which possess a reputation equal to that of the universities. Most of the universities are now devoted to arts and science in their pure forms and give little attention to such studies as law, medicine and economics.

Quantitatively the comparison reveals that France, the Soviet Union and the United States greatly exceed Britain in the number of students following full-time courses in higher education. The Report summarises as follows:—"The output in Britain is equal or superior to that in most of the Western European countries shown. We suspect that a full comparative investigation would reveal that, on its chosen ground, the British university system is among the most efficient and economical in the world. But the output of British higher education is, in very important respects, smaller than that of the Soviet Union or the United States" (para. 126).

So much for the present but when we consider what the future planning is, the difference between this country and the highly developed countries is disquieting. In France *l'explosion scolaire* has been taken into account and the official plans look forward to 1970 when the increase of the university population will be about two and a half times the figures of 1960. The Soviet Union has an equally ambitious programme of expansion. It is clear that immediate action is necessary to improve the situation in Britain. "But at the present time the conclusion is plain: the comparison of numbers likely to qualify is no longer favourable, and the disparity in the numbers entering higher education is even wider than it is to-day. Both in general cultural standards and in competitive power, vigorous action is needed to avert the danger of a serious relative decline in this country's standing" (para. 130).

Chapter 6 deals with the future demand for higher education and the number of places needed to meet it. There are two ways of estimating the number of places required. The first is to estimate the national need for the number who have passed through courses of full-time higher education. The Report decided that this method is impracticable. The reason is that it gives no reliable basis for calculating the national need for a long term policy. The other method is preferred because it is a reasonable estimate of the demand for places in the future and seems to be a more practical approach to the problem. The guiding principle should be that considered in Chapter 2, namely, that all young people qualified by ability and attainment to follow a full-time course in higher education should have an opportunity of doing so.

The Newsom Report had stated that amongst the average and even the under-average pupils there are latent pools of ability so far untouched. The Robbins Committee believed that between the two groups of those who by their natural qualities would attain highest success and those even if they were taught by the best teachers could not reach the required standards, there is a third group whose future depends largely on how they have lived and have been taught before entering upon higher education. The Report states: "But while it would be wrong to deny fundamental differences of nature, it is equally wrong to deny that performance in examinations or tests—or indeed any measurable ability—is affected by nurture in the widest sense of that word. Moreover, the belief that there exists some easy method of ascertaining an intelligence factor unaffected by education or background is outmoded. Years ago, performance in "general intelligence tests" was thought to be relatively independent of earlier experience. It is now known that in fact it is dependent upon previous experience to a degree sufficiently large to be of great relevance. And once one passes beyond tests of this kind and examines for specific knowledge or aptitudes, the influence of education and environment becomes more and more important" (para. 137).

The Committee surveyed a sufficient number of both sexes aged twenty-one in August 1962 and tabulated the results in Table 21. The Robbins Committee agreed with the Crowther Report that there is a close correlation between the occupational level of the father and the achievements of his children at school. Thus, 45 per cent of the children whose fathers were in the higher professional group enter full-time higher education in comparison with the 4 per cent of those whose fathers were in skilled manual occupations. Table 22 shows that children going forward to higher education and whose fathers had continued their own education until eighteen or after, were eight times more numerous than those whose fathers left school before the age of sixteen.

It might be suggested that the great increase of pupils in recent years who leave school with good qualifications is to be found among those whose parents are manual workers. The Tables show that the desire for education which results in improved performance in school is to be found in all classes, and it is reasonable to conclude that this tendency will continue. The statistical tables show that in comparison with the 195,000 places required in 1962-3, the number is likely to rise to 507,000 in 1980-1. This last figure does not include the number of overseas students. The available data makes it more difficult to forecast their number. At present they occupy about 10 per cent of the places in higher education, but it is probable that this proportion will remain for some years ahead; but within this group the number of postgraduate students is likely to increase. The total demand for places in full-time higher education indicates that about 390,000 should be available in 1973-4 and about 560,000 in 1980-1.

Chapter 7 of the Report discusses higher education and the schools. Since the war the pressure to enter universities and training-colleges has increased greatly with the consequence that many applicants who are qualified and acceptable cannot gain a place. The situation in Scotland is not so grave but entrance to a university is becoming more difficult. In other institutions of higher education the pressure is not so great, but even in this sphere there is some shortage of places. "It is not necessary to enlarge at length on the unhappiness and frustration bred in the applicants by this state of affairs. The apprehension among the more gifted boys and girls as they approach eighteen is coming to be as serious as the tension and anxieties caused by the 'eleven plus' examination" (para. 197).

There must be a great expansion of higher education to ease the pressure on the schools. Many schools do all they can to give their more able pupils chances of gaining university entrance but they do not always take full advantage of the flexibility of the G.C.E. Competition to gain a place in "Oxbridge" is more intent than for other universities. The Committee definitely rejected the suggestion that Oxford and Cambridge should become post-graduate institutions. It was thought that the attraction of "Oxbridge" should be lessened by making generous capital grants for the development of other existing universities. There should be a closer relation between the "Oxbridge" colleges and the schools maintained by the L.E.A.s. Institutions for higher education should consider with the Minister of Education and the Scottish Education Department means by which better information can be supplied to pupils and their parents about the courses available.

It is recommended that the faculty and departmental require-ments for entrance should be more uniform in order to widen the choice for applicants and the schools, and the recent moves by the

universities in England and Wales towards making faculty requirements for entry more uniform are welcomed. Selection procedures
are discussed in some detail and it is recommended that all universities should make use of the Central Council on Admissions. In
the selection of entrants greater use should be made of school
records and recommendations and research into methods of selection should be undertaken by a suitable independent organisation.
The schools should collaborate with the teachers in the institutes
of higher education in the improvement of their syllabuses and the
revision of textbooks.

University courses are considered in Chapter 8, the courses for
the education and training of teachers and the relations between
the training-colleges and the universities in Chapter 9, and the
provision of technology both in the universities and other institutions are dealt with in Chapter 10. It is recommended that these
chapters should be read as a single whole because they lead to
Chapter 11 which considers the future pattern of institutions.

One important recommendation is that the universities should
consult together in the establishment of new undergraduate courses
and the provision of more varied facilities for postgraduate study.
There should also be an attempt to secure more uniformity in the
nomenclature of degrees. An article in *The Times Educational
Supplement*, 12 October 1962, pointed out some of the anomalies
in the titles and the contents of the degree courses which are misleading to potential employers and more also to the general public.

The first problem arises from the structure of the first degree
course. In England and Wales it often varies beween universities
and even between faculties. The distinction lies between courses
for honours and those leading to pass or ordinary degrees. In
some cases, undergraduates who have enrolled for an honours
degree course in their first year follow courses in subjects common
to a pass degree and then, after the first or second year, they are
selected to study for a pass or an honours degree. In others, pass
degrees are awarded to those who fail to reach the honours standard in the final examination. In a few universities, students following a pass course and showing distinction in the examination,
may be awarded honours.

The Robbins Committee have received a number of criticisms
about the present pass degree. On the whole they fall into two
classes—those which believe that many of the courses are

overloaded and others which urge that many courses do not satisfy the needs of students who follow them. As the Report states: "The essential aim of a first degree course should be to teach the student how to think. In so far he is under such pressure to acquire detailed knowledge that this aim is not fulfilled, so far the course fails of its purpose" (para. 254). Most of the present courses need thorough revision. Those which specialise on a very narrow front are unsuitable for many students. They would receive greater benefit by following broader courses which would prepare them for their future careers.

Undergraduates roughly fall into two categories: those who have the ability and desire to teach in secondary modern schools or the middle forms of grammar schools, and those who would benefit from specialisation in one or two subjects. The former group would find a wider course more satisfactory, which involved the study of two or three subjects at less depth. Some universities have realised this. Thus in the University of Leeds the courses for the first degrees in arts or science are either for general or special studies. The term "honours" has now its proper meaning. Undergraduates following both types of course can obtain honours if their attainments warrant this. Thus an arts student in either type of course can be awarded first class Honours or second class (first or second division), third class or the simple B.A. A similar scheme applies to science, applied science and law. Some of the courses in special studies include two main subjects, e.g. modern languages.

Undergraduates whose earlier promise does not materialise should be transferred to less exacting courses. The Committee did not recommend the extension of the three-year course to four years. It was thought that the general first degree in Scotland should be retained. Because students can only master the rudiments of their subjects in the first degree course, extension of facilities for postgraduate study is needed. The Committee thought that some Ph.D. theses cover too narrow a field. In some subjects discussion of central problems at a high level is probably more rewarding to the young graduate than an intensive investigation of one problem. This is specially applicable in social science and the humanities. Arrangements for the supervision of postgraduate students should be improved and it is often advisable for many graduates to take their postgraduate course in a university other than that in which they obtained their first degree.

Although the arrangements of the work in colleges for the education and training of teachers differ greatly from those in England and Wales and those in Scotland, the same essential problems apply to both. The colleges feel that they are not fully recognised as institutions of higher education despite that the standards they reach constitute them as such. At one time the colleges concentrated on training non-graduates as teachers but in recent years they have accepted a small number of graduates for professional training. In Scotland most of their students take a combined course of education and training.

Some students prefer to graduate first and follow it with professional training either in a university department or in a training college. Other graduates do not make up their minds to become teachers until the end of the graduate course. The introduction of the three year course in the training-colleges gives the students a better education and nearly half of the students now entering the colleges possess the minimum qualification for university entrance. The establishment of the University Institutes of Education has resulted in closer links with the universities now that the work done in the three-year course approximates to the standard of a pass degree. The Scottish colleges feel they can lay claim to university status in their own right.

It is likely that in the future some colleges will desire to expand their curricula by introducing courses serving as an entrance to a variety of careers in the social services or general courses in the arts and in science subjects. The shortage of teachers will tend to restrict these developments for some years but in the 1970's there will be more opportunities with these kind of courses and some colleges may become constituent parts of a university. Another possibility is that some could combine with the larger technical colleges to form a new university. The recommendations for future developments must vary according to the different positions of the colleges south and north of the Border.

South of the Border many of the colleges are small and eventually a college with less than 750 students should be an exception. The McNair Report had recommended the establishment of University Schools of Education. The present federation of the colleges and the University Departments of Education in the Institutes of Education only goes part of the way. In addition to the three-year course, a four-year course leading to a professional qualification and a degree should be available for suitable students. Some students, after a period in a college, should be able to transfer to a university to graduate in the subjects they wish to teach. Others wishing to teach after their professional training should have opportunities to progress to a degree by part-time study.

After a successful conclusion of the four-year course, students should be awarded the degree of B.Ed. from the university with which the college is linked. The training-colleges should alter their title to Colleges of Education. Each School of Education should be responsible to the university senate for degrees awarded to students in the colleges and the colleges should be financed by earmarked grants from the grants commission made through the Schools of Education. The voluntary colleges with certain modifications should be included in the Schools of Education.

The Scottish Colleges of Education should provide four-year courses for suitable students leading to a degree and a professional qualification. The teaching staff should be represented on the governing bodies of the colleges and the universities should have representative members on the boards of studies in which degree level is established. University graduates intending to enter the teaching profession should normally follow the course for the university Diploma in Education.

The large number of recommendations in regard to institutions for technical education constitute an important factor in the educational revolution. At the higher level, dual policies have been followed, the expansion of technology in the universities and the encouragement of colleges outside the universities. "The most prominent landmark of the first policy was the selection in 1953 of the Imperial College of Science and Technology and other university centres for special development. The most striking feature of the second was the designation in 1956 of the first Colleges of Advanced Technology. All these efforts have notably improved the position. But a great deal more remains to be done. This applies to both science and technology but particularly to the latter" (paras. 376-7).

In this country less attention is directed to technology and more to pure science than in the other countries investigated by the Committee. In Britain pure science attracts greater numbers of students and of higher quality than does technology. Few girls, in contrast to countries such as the U.S.S.R., study applied science. Steps should be taken to attract a larger number of students of high ability into technological courses and this would entail a great expansion of postgraduate work. Although, as regards numbers, technology in Britain lags behind many other countries, our best research is equal in quality to that of any other country.

The Report recommends that as soon as possible we should set our target for five special institutions for scientific and technological education and research. At present, the Imperial College, the Manchester College of Science and Technology and the Royal College of Science and Technology and Science at Glasgow, now the University of Strathclyde, form the nuclei of three. As soon as possible two others should be selected and should receive financial aid on the pattern given to the Imperial College. These two new Special Institutions should be constitutionally independent and provide for about 3,500 to 4,500 students, half of which should be postgraduates.

The Committee considered that since their designation the C.A.T.s have made remarkable progress but they have some difficulties. "We consider that the present powers and status of the colleges are not commensurate with the work they are now doing. They lack many of the attributes of university self-government." They have not full power to grant their own degrees. Many of them have a long history and extensive academic experience. The recently founded universities are able to grant degrees from the start, subject to an Academic Advisory Committee. The C.A.T.s are less attractive to students and their recruitment of suitable staff is impeded.

The Report recommends that these institutions should become technological universities, and if they do not become part of another university, they should have the power to grant their own degrees. The new technological universities should have the forms of government similar to the existing universities. Immediate steps should be taken to grant the charters and until they are ready for full independence, Academic Advisory Committees should be established so that they fall into line with the procedure of the other post-war universities.

Since the Scottish Central Institutions differ in many ways, a varied pattern of development is recommended for them. The larger colleges might either establish links with an appropriate university or have the same status recommended for the C.A.T.s. The smaller ones might adopt a form of academic association with the University of Strathclyde or the proposed arrangements for the English and Welsh Regional Colleges should be extended to them.

In addition to the changes taking place in some universities and colleges, the Report recommends the establishment of two post-graduate schools of management studies. Because they would find it necessary to appoint a proportion of part-time staff they should be situated in large cities where they could secure the best specialists in their work and they should be associated with university institutions. Suitable courses in modern languages should be provided in some of the technological universities and in the Regional Colleges.

The twenty-five Regional Colleges offer a number of full-time and sandwich courses and many of them make use of the external degrees of London. They are not so exclusively concerned with science and technology as the C.A.T.s but possess departments of business studies, architecture and other special studies. It is expected that some of the more developed Regional Colleges will eventually attain university status.

In the large group of more than 160 Area Colleges there are about 9,000 advanced full-time students, less than two-thirds of which are studying science and technology. These are greatly out-numbered by 63,000 advanced part-time students. The colleges mainly cater for those studying for National Diplomas and Certificates. They also include a small number of separate Colleges of Commerce. As the proportion of advanced work increases, some of these colleges may be designated as Regional Colleges. The Area Colleges should continue to be maintained by the L.E.A.s and offer courses connected with local industries. The more successful students should be able to transfer to advanced courses in Regional Colleges and postgraduate studies in a university.

Many colleges outside the London area provide courses for the external degrees of London. These degrees have greatly influenced the development of higher education. Another factor which has produced the high standard of work in the Advanced Colleges of Technology is the National Council for Technological Awards. The Diploma in Technology approximates to the standard of honours degrees and the National Diplomas and Certificates reach the standard of the Pass degree. These awards are usually made for a successful sandwich course of three years.

The situation will change when the technological universities are able to grant their own degrees. The Report recommends that the present Council should be replaced by a Council for National Academic Awards applicable to the whole of Great Britain and its prestige would be enhanced if it could be appointed under Royal Charter.

If these recommendations are accepted, degrees will be more available than ever before in this country, but standards must be fully maintained. Attention is called to the state of the present law which does not restrain the award of degrees by unauthorised bodies or persons. "Unless fraud is to be proved, a 'degree' can be conferred after studies of trivial content, or indeed after no study at all. It is true that such degrees have had limited appeal to residents in this island, but they have sometimes, through ignorance, proved attractive to people abroad, and have caused embarrassment to those concerned with the repute of British education. Action is difficult, not only against those who confer worthless degrees, but also against those who falsely lay claim to genuine qualifications. We recommend legislation to remedy both deficiencies. In future the power to give degrees should be vested only in authorised bodies or persons and abuses should be capable of speedy and effective remedy" (para. 435). The writer has quoted this paragraph in full since he has had a number of experiences of both the types mentioned.

The Report recommends that the Royal College of Art should be treated administratively in the same way as the Colleges of Advanced Technology. In Scotland, the four Central Institutions which provide education in art should develop along one of the alternatives proposed for the other Central Institutions. The College of Aeronautics at Cranfield should be financed through the system for university grants. If it maintains its present size and wishes to grant degrees, it should be linked to a university. Degrees should also be available to students taking courses of degree level at the six National Colleges.

The Agricultural Colleges, five in England and Wales and three in Scotland, provide two-year courses with a minimum entry qualification of the "O" level of the school leaving examinations. In April 1964 they came under the Ministry of Education in place of the Ministry of Agriculture, Fisheries and Food. The Scottish colleges are part of the group of Central Institutions, and each has, or is developing, close links with the university in its area. Those in England and Wales may raise their entry qualification to the "A" level of G.C.E. and develop courses of degree standard.

The future pattern of higher education is discussed in Chapter 11. If the existing institutions are developed along the lines recommended, the establishment of new types would not be necessary. The 560,000 places needed by 1980 should be distributed between different kinds of institutions in order to lessen the pressure on the schools and enable the universities to increase the proportion of their entrants from the 55 per cent of 1962 to 60 per cent in 1980. Immediate action is necessary and 350,000 university places will be needed in 1980. The present number of students is about 130,000 but the development of certain institutions to university status would increase the number to about 300,000.

It must be borne in mind that the new universities require a number of years to become fully established. Although the majority of the places required in the next ten years can be supplied by the expansion of existing universities, the immediate foundation of six new universities is essential, one of which, at least, should be in Scotland. Another would be the new Special Institution for Scientific and Technological Education and Research. This would account for about 30,000 new places by 1980 and the remainder would be provided by the grant of university status to about ten Regional Colleges and Colleges of Education. It is expected that even more places will be demanded after 1980. The Report emphasises that these developments must not lower the standards of degrees or the qualifications of the teaching staff.

The new universities recently founded were largely in cathedral and smaller cities but those of the future should be in the large cities for two reasons: the advantages they can obtain by the environment and those they can confer. There are now two in Glasgow and this policy should be followed in other populous cities. On the whole the Report made few recommendations about the content of courses in particular studies. These are left to the different institutions. Generally the number of science students should be increased and the quality of those following technological courses should be improved but the proportion engaged in studying arts should not be reduced.

Higher education is not confined to the young but many adults experience the need of refresher courses to keep them up to date.

The Crowther Report showed that the age for marriage has fallen and the expectation of life has lengthened. More than half the women engaged in industry are married with the result that a new pattern in careers has developed: a short period of work before marriage and another period starting about fifteen years later and continuing for twenty years or more. This may be more common in the future. Hence the increasing demand of adults for further education which in most cases will be for part-time courses.

There are also many who desire courses in liberal adult education. The Report refers to the work carried out in full-time institutions such as Ruskin College and Coleg Harlech and suitable students should be assisted by capital grants. There is also the work carried out by the Extra-Mural Departments of the universities, the W.E.A., and the classes provided by the L.E.A.s, and there is a further development through the television services.

Chapter 12 is concerned with the problem of staffing. The present student/staff ratios in universities, especially in regard to research and postgraduate training, should be maintained and, if possible, improved. Conditions of service should be such as will attract able recruits and there should be no disparity between the salary and prospects of teaching in similar institutions. Facilities for movement of staff to other institutions of higher education should be improved, and part-time staff should be more frequently appointed so long as the proportion of full-time staff is not reduced. More extensive residential accommodation should be provided for students and the tradition of only one professor to a department is out of date and more appointments of this level are recommended.

With the provision of more student places, the teaching and research staff needs to be increased and the present number of 16,750 must rise to about 45,000 and in other colleges it should be increased from 5,750 to the number of about 14,000. It is not considered that this expansion will produce harm as regards the upper forms of the schools. The newspapers have from time to time published facts about the movement of well-qualified specialists to the Dominions and countries overseas. This can be checked by the provision of more generous salaries, increased secretarial staff and greater facilities for research.

Chapter 13 begins with a discussion of the balance between teaching and research in establishments of higher education. Often discussions on this topic seem to suggest that these two activities are opposed. The Report does not agree with this idea. "There is no borderline between teaching and research; they are complementary and overlapping activities. A teacher who is advancing his general knowledge of his subject is both improving himself as a teacher and laying foundations for his research. The researcher often finds that his personal work provides him with fresh and apt illustration which helps him to set a subject in a new light when he turns to prepare a lecture" (para. 447). The Committee believed that differences in salary and status ought to be abolished and this has happened in some universities.

The Report now passes to consider two main problems, the methods of teaching and student wastage. In 1962 the U.G.C. appointed a Committee on University Teaching Methods under the chairmanship of Sir Edward Hale. This committee also investigated the use students made of their vacations. Methods varied from the large lecture attended by several hundred students to the tutorial in which the tutor discussed the essay written by one student. The latter has been strongly criticised quite recently. Between these two extremes there are forms of teaching varying between lectures to smaller numbers, tutorial groups and seminars of different sizes, and practical work in the laboratory. The lecture system was common in the Scottish universities and in the older civic ones in England. The tutorial system which played a large part in Oxford and Cambridge has now been adopted by the newer universities. Even in the ancient universities tutorial groups of three or five students are becoming more common but in the civic universities where the student/staff ratio is less favourable, a group often varies from seven to ten or twelve.

The Report, however, does not condemn the lecture. "Controversely, we are not in sympathy with the view that the lecture is an archaic survival from the days before printing was invented. We think that a well-planned and well-delivered series of lectures can give a sense of proportion and emphasis lacking in tutorial discussions and seminars where teaching, in following where the argument leads, may often stray into byways. It should bring to students modifications of what they find in their textbooks, suggest wider reading, and, when given by lecturers in touch with recent developments, be a source of stimulus and inspiration. We are particularly thinking here of lectures to large audiences in which a genuinely synoptic view of a subject is given. Lectures of this kind which lay down principles and survey a subject widely are particularly valuable for first-year students. Attendance at lectures gives them a necessary frame to a week's work, makes them feel a part of a community of learning, and leads to a wider intellectual contact with their fellows than membership of small classes alone can give" (para. 568). The conclusion of the Report is that different forms of teaching should be combined.

The practice of assigning a pupil at entry to a tutor or supervisor of his studies is commended. This should not be a mere formality but the tutor should see his students frequently. The regular setting and return of written work is extremely valuable. The method adopted depends to a great extent on the teacher. Some are brilliant lecturers but are not so successful with tutorial groups and others who have marked ability in conducting a discussion are not good lecturers. The latter should be given a smaller share in formal lecturing but more facilities for developing personal relations with the students. Newly appointed junior members of staff should have opportunities of acquainting themselves with both methods of teaching.

Wastage is a term to describe those who enter an institution of higher education and leave without obtaining the qualification for which they enrolled. A certain percentage of wastage is inevitable but it is comforting to know that the average wastage in Great Britain is much smaller than in France or the U.S.A. in which the wastage rate varies between 40 to 50 per cent. Some students leave early because they discover their selection of subjects or courses have proved unsuitable for them. Others are unable to reach the required intellectual standard, and others withdraw through ill health or disturbing personal or financial problems. The average wastage in British universities is about 14 per cent.

The statistics given in Table 50 of the Report show considerable differences between universities and between different faculties in the same university. The Committee could not avoid the conclusion that one of the significant factors accounting for wastage in some faculties and departments is the custom of expecting a fairly fixed proportion of failures. "It should be an essential part of the responsibility of any university department towards its students to investigate this problem carefully, both in regard to the general level of wastage over a period of years and in regard to the individual students who fail in any given year to complete a course successfully" (para. 581).

In the Training Colleges and the Scottish Colleges of Education the average wastage rate is about 7 per cent. One reason for the lower rate may be that the standard is not so high. "Less questionably, it can be argued that the students are committed to a profession and have a sense of purpose in their studies which is lacking in many university students, and that the close contact between staff and students prevailing in all the colleges leads to weaker students receiving more help. We would add that the sense of the urgent need to provide teachers for the nation's schools which rightly permeates the Training Colleges is another motive that impels the teacher in a Training College to make every effort to help weaker students to qualify" (para. 582).

The wastage in the technological colleges and other institutions of higher education is greater. Among the full-time students working for the Diploma in Technology in 1960-1 the wastage rate was 37 per cent and among those reading for a degree of the University of London it reached 62 per cent. A high wastage rate in students working for external degrees is expected. The Committee thought Advanced Technology is leading to higher standards of selection and it is probable that wastage rates will decrease.

The way students spend their vacations is very important. The investigations of the Hale Committee in *The Use of Vacations by Students* (an interim report of the Committee on University Teaching Methods, 1963) showed that during the long vacation, in general, little work is done which is relevant to the students' studies. The Robbins Committee consider that students should be concerned with their studies during ten months of the year. For many of them strictly academic work would not be most appropriate for the whole ten months of the year. Thus the arts student may need access to libraries, the biologists can extend their work in a wider setting, the modern language student could spend some time in the country in which the language he is studying is used and he can extend his knowledge of the institutions and cultural heritage of that country, and those following courses in applied science or in the social sciences can benefit from a period in a related industry or through vacation training schemes.

The chapter concludes with a warning: "In this age and country students are a privileged population; they have exceptional opportunities provided for them by the labour of the community. They are under the obligation to make the best of their three or four years . . . But all those engaged in higher education, both teachers and taught, are privileged persons and we would not wish to end this chapter by suggesting that the privilege is all on one side. The university teacher in particular has a unique freedom in arranging his work and in following his own bent. On paper the hours of work demanded of him are not heavy. He does not have to submit to office hours and has a wide liberty in the interpretation of his professional duties. Such freedom is the condition of the intellectual life. It brings with it a great responsibility. Public opinion will not support the cost of higher education unless teachers are actuated by a high sense of professional obligation and students are actuated by a corresponding sense of the obligation to work" (para. 598).

The next four chapters have met with certain criticisms especially Chapter 17 which deals with the Machinery of Government. Chapter 14 is concerned with the financial and economic recommendations of the Report. In assessing the cost of the proposed expansion, the Committee accepted two assumptions. The first is that incomes in general will only rise with increases in productivity and result in a constant overall price level. In the second place, an average increase of productivity of $3\frac{1}{4}$ per cent per annum can be assumed. The Report cautiously states. "We are not predicting that these assumptions will be fulfilled; we adopt them simply as a suitable basis for calculations." When we consider the growing increases in prices, the unofficial strikes and the gap between imports and exports, many of us tend to be sceptical. The Report considers that the total expenditure on full-time education which in 1932-3 was £206 million will rise to £742 million in 1980-1. The first thought that comes to the reader is, can the country afford such an enormous sum? The view of the Report is that we must. It is honest in the acknowledgement that there does not exist any means of measuring the rate of return on the expenditure. "It is just not true that the rate of return on investment in education is measured adequately by the same yardstick as investment in coal or electricity," but, "on a broad view of history . . . the communities that have paid most attention to the higher studies have in general been the most obviously progressive in respect of income and wealth." The conclusion drawn is that it is possible to spend more on higher education without imposing intolerable strains on the budget or the economy.

The Report makes no recommendations about loans for buildings and equipment but those to students fall into a different category. Loans in place of grants is an alternative which has almost as many supporters as adversaries and therefore are not recommended at present. The decline in tuition fees is regretted and it was agreed that they should be increased to meet at least 20 per cent of current institutional expenditure. In regard to gifts and endowments the Report points out that they do not constitute as large a proportion of the income of institutions of higher education as they did formerly. It believed that gifts and endowments by industry and by private persons should be encouraged.

Chapter 15 deals with the internal government of institutions of higher education. Governing bodies should normally contain a majority of lay members. They bring experience and wisdom to bear upon the governing body and outside bodies who have the right of appointing lay representatives should make sure that they are individuals who can make a useful contribution to the discussion of the affairs of the university. The numbers of academic members should be strong enough to prevent interference with purely academic matters. The importance of Vice-Chancellors is recognised especially during a period of rapid expansion. They have to spend a great deal of time in important administrative affairs and therefore should be relieved of superfluous duties. The repeal of the Universities (Scotland) Act of 1889 is an urgent necessity since it limits independent action by the four older universities.

Oxford and Cambridge present problems and inconveniences arising from their collegiate structure. The Report recognises the distinctive merits of the collegiate system but the difficulty both universities have in arriving at quick decisions about matters of policy under their present constitution and the general obscurity in regard to their administrative and financial arrangements are not compatible with a situation in which they, like other universities, depend on public funds. Both universities recognise these problems and are considering solutions of them but if they cannot solve them in a reasonable time, they should be the subject of independent inquiry.

The federal universities of London and Wales are faced with a different set of problems. The federal system has some advantages. It can more readily adopt a common policy in planning and sharing of joint facilities such as libraries and expensive scientific equipment and can sustain institutions for highly specialised studies. On the other hand, the system has certain drawbacks which increase as the universities grow in size. Power becomes centralised and, "There are real anomalies in a system in which the Vice-Chancellor of a newly-founded university at once has access to the University Grants Committee and the right of membership of the Committee of Vice-Chancellors and Principals, while heads of long established London colleges, each as large as a civic university of moderate size, have no such access or right of membership" (para. 685). The Report gives them the same advice it made regarding Oxford and Cambridge.

The Committee of Vice-Chancellors and Principals meets an important need, namely, it can speak for the universities as a whole. The Report recommends that the Committee should be put on a wider basis. Thus, each university should be represented by its chief administrator and a member of the academic staff elected by the senate.

The scope of academic freedom is discussed in Chapter 16. This is a principle which has been jealously guarded by universities for many centuries and the Report considered that it is essential to a healthy system of higher education. At present the institutions concerned are mainly dependent on State grants instead of fees and endowments. Academic freedom depends upon a balance between the necessary freedom of institutions and the equal necessity to serve the needs of the nation. "For the individual teacher academic freedom means the absence of discriminatory treatment on grounds of race, sex, religion and politics; and the right to teach according to his own conception of fact and truth. It involves, further freedom to publish and, subject to the proper performance of allotted duties, freedom to pursue what personal studies or researches are congenial" (para. 705). As far as freedom of institutions is concerned, it was a stroke of genius which produced the idea of the U.G.C., but it now needs revision since the expansion of institutions of higher education require a Grants Commission of a wider type.

Chapter 17 which deals with the problem of the Machinery of Government is the most controversial of the Report. Although institutions of higher education should be allowed to govern themselves and develop their own policies, their activities must be guided and co-ordinated to serve national needs. This will continue to be the work of the enlarged Grants Commission, but to prevent it from being overburdened, it would be necessary for it to set up ancillary committees. There follows the problem of which minister should be responsible for the Grants Commission. It is obvious that it would be increasingly difficult for the Chancellor of the Exchequer and the Treasury to be at once guardians of the public purse and claimants on it.

Several solutions were rejected by the Robbins Committee which recommended the appointment of a Minister of Arts and Science to be responsible for the Grants Commission, the research Councils and other autonomous state-supported activities. The views of the Secretary of State for Scotland should be taken into account on questions of major concern to the Scottish universities. Responsibility for other institutions of higher education and the schools in England and Wales should remain with the Minister of Education and the L.E.A.s and, in Scotland, with the Secretary of State. The three ministers concerned with higher education should establish a small Consultative Council.

One member of the Robbins Committee, Mr. H. C. Shearman, a former Chairman of the L.C.C., did not agree with the recommendation, and his view is given in the Note of Reservation, pp. 293-6 of the Report. He summed up his conclusion: "I submit therefore that a single Minister of Education . . . with one or two Ministers of State to assist him is the more satisfactory answer. He would take over the present sphere of responsibility of the Minister of Education and that of the Chancellor in respect of the University Grants Committee, and conceivably some of the other functions alluded to in Chapter XVII, but he would be at the head of a new department from which a forward-looking outlook might be expected".

The result was a heated attack on the recommendation of the Robbins Report which was debated in the Lords and the Commons. The Government eventually decided to appoint Mr. Quintin Hogg (formerly Lord Hailsham), Secretary of State for Education and Science. His department was to include two administrative units, one concerned with the schools of England and Wales, the other with science and through the U.G.C. with institutions of university status. The Secretary of State would be supported by two Ministers of State. The Prime Minister, Sir Alex. Douglas-Home, announced that Sir Edward Boyle would become one of these and continue to be a member of the Cabinet.

The General Election of October 1964 led to a Labour Government headed by Mr. Harold Wilson with a precarious majority. The Secretary of State for Education and Science was Mr. Michael Stewart; the two Ministers of State in the Department of Education and Science are Lord Bowden, Principal of the Manchester College of Science and Technology and Mr. R. E. Prentice. Mr. Frank Cousins is Minister of Technology.

To return to the final chapter of the Robbins Report; this under the title of "The Short-Term Emergency", considers the immediate problem. It points out that in the years 1965-6 to 1967-8 we will be confronted with an emergency which demands swift action now. In these years a very large number of boys and girls born just after the war will have reached the age of entry to higher education. If there is no immediate action, the long-term aims of the Report will be more difficult of attainment. Hence it is recommended that the Council for National Academic Awards should be set up at once and the Minister of Arts and Science should be appointed without delay.

We have now to consider the reaction to the Newsom and Robbins Reports. The Government approved the Newsom Report in principle but the delay in putting into force the recommendation for an immediate announcement on the school-leaving age seemed to suggest that the Government was not prepared to accept it. *The Times Educational Supplement* in a leading article of 13th December 1963 declared: "In spite of all the *Aides-mémoires* which have been showered upon them, the Government remain remarkably costive on the question of raising the school age. It will be recalled that it has been before them for a long time. When the Crowther Report came out, a decision was promised before the end of the Parliament. Some weeks after Newsom it has still not been made. The only possible conclusion is that the Government lack enthusiasm for the reform."

It is possible that the Government was over-anxious about the number of teachers who would be needed. Sir Edward Boyle replied that the fears that the Newsom Report would be overlooked were groundless and about six months after the publication of the Report, the Ministry in February 1964 announced that the leaving age of sixteen would apply to pupils entering in September 1965.

The Church of England Board of Education welcomed the Report. "The importance of this report is that it is concerned with attitudes before administration, with persons rather than programmes, with love and not law . . . Convinced Christians and those who do not share our beliefs can, to a very large extent, join together in the task of seeing that these children of average and below average ability are enabled to realise their potentialities, and leave school well equipped to take their place in adult society. . . . Many have already contented themselves with expressing a benevolent and non-committal approval of Newsom, rapidly passing on to speculation about the exciting and costly prospects which Robbins holds out. Robbins has a greater news-value than Newsom and will almost certainly continue to attract greater publicity. But the measure of the integrity with which higher education is expanded and developed will be the determination with which justice for the other half of our future is pursued. And it is the duty of Christians to ensure that Robbins and Newsom become equal partners in one process. This is so because we know that in the mind of God there are no second-class human beings."

Sir John Newsom expressed the view that the cost of raising the leaving age would not exceed £120 million which would be small in comparison with the Robbins estimate of £1,400 million by 1980 and would concern many less people. "If we say we can afford Robbins, by heaven we can afford Newsom."

On page 352 of this book the writer criticised the timing of the Hadow Reports, and the same criticism applies to the sequence of the four recent reports, Crowther, Newsom, Robbins and Plowden. The logical sequence should have been Plowden, Newsom, Crowther and Robbins. The Act of 1944 emphasised that education is a continuous process including the stages of primary, secondary and further education. What occurs in the final stage is dependent to a large extent on what has happened at other levels but Governments have always been slow in discarding the errors of their predecessors.

A few of the recommendations of the Newsom Report have been implemented. The recommendation that the Agreed Syllabuses ought to be revised has led many local education authorities to undertake this task. The Report advised the schools to take the pupils mentally and often physically beyond the school walls and one way of doing this is to make full use of audio and visual means. The Report of the Ministry of Education, *Education in 1963*, p. 7 stated: "Schools are also displaying a greater interest in television, and at Ministry request Leeds University submitted a research plan for assessing the effectiveness of schools programmes. . . . Experiments were also on the increase in the use of closed-circuit television—of advantage both to schools and to training colleges linked to them." Experiments in the use of teaching machines and the techniques of programmed learning were also recommended.

The Government was much quicker in accepting the recommendations of the Robbins Committee. They approved the future status of the Colleges of Advanced Technology and in February 1964, Mr. Quintin Hogg announced a considerable increase of recurrent grants for existing universities for the three years of the quinquennium ending in 1967. This would amount to £20 million. At the same time the increase of building grants to universities would be about £15 million.

One factor which is related to both the Newsom and Robbins Reports is the Industrial Training Act of April 1964. In December 1962 the Government published a White Paper, "Industrial Training: *Government Proposals*" (Cmnd. 1892). It proposed measures for industrial training at all levels of industry and commerce through industrial training boards. These proposals were put to representatives of the L.E.A.s and the teachers. The aims of the White Paper were welcomed and the functions of the education service in the scheme were discussed. As a consequence the proposals were put before Parliament in November 1963.

Conditions vary considerably between industries and the Bill refrained from laying down details about the way the training should be organised. Its object was to present a broad framework on which the arrangements most suitable to the needs of the individual industries could be built. The Minister of Labour would be given powers to establish training boards to cover all activities of industry or commerce. Nationalised industries were included in the scheme which also applied to local authorities in so far as they are concerned with activities in industry or commerce.

Certain modifications were introduced at the Second Reading of the Bill. The Minister of Labour gave an assurance that the Government departments in so far as they were industrial employers would be obliged to equal the standards demanded by the training boards. In general the boards would not be large. It was thought that they should include about five members representing the employers and an equal number from the employees. The Ministry of Labour, the Ministry of Education and the Scottish Education Department would appoint assessors.

The boards would have two main functions. Each would have the duty of seeing that the amount of training in its industry was satisfactory and would issue recommendations concerning the type and length of training for different occupations and the further education connected with it. The Bill asked for power to impose a levy upon employers to secure that adequate funds would be available to meet the training requirements of the industries. Grants would be made from the levies to employers who satisfied the requirements of the board.

An important factor in the development of technical education in the past has been the co-operation between industry and the technical colleges. This training scheme continues the partnership between the education service and the employers and employees and would also provide more industrial training places for both works-based and college-based students. All parties warmly supported the Bill which received the Royal Assent. The Minister of Labour was empowered to set up the training boards and to assist them by grants up to £50 million.

The Act required the boards to make recommendations concerning the further education necessary for the training they recommended. Educationists must be members of each board and of the Central Training Council, six members of which should be appointed after consultation with the Minister of Education and the Secretary of State for Scotland. They should not be mere delegates but should be selected because of their personal capacities and their experience.

The Act will add impetus to the increasing demand for technicians and craftsmen which was mentioned in the Robbins Report, and will also meet the growing expansion of the number of young people who are given day, block, or sandwich release to attend institutions for further education. It should also assist the educational prospects of those mentioned in the Newsom Report, who leave school at the minimum age.

The universities of Oxford and London have started to carry out the recommendation of the Robbins Report; at Oxford the university set up a Commission at Easter 1964 to inquire into the part the university plays now and in the future should play in higher education in Great Britain. Lord Franks, Provost of Worcester College, was the Chairman of the Commission which took evidence contributed by the staff of the university and by some prominent people from outside.

In January 1965 Mr. Michael Stewart was appointed Foreign Secretary in place of Mr. Patrick Gordon Walker, who was defeated first at Smethwick (1964) and then at Leyton (1965). Mr. A. Crosland replaced Mr. Stewart as Secretary of State for Education and Science.

Mr. Crosland agreed with the views of Mr. Stewart concerning comprehensive education. In April he issued a confidential draft circular to the local authorities and others who were connected with education. His object was to discover their views about the organisation of secondary education. The next step was the Circular 10/65 which was sent to L.E.A.s and the governors of Grammar and Direct Grant schools, voluntary aided and special agreement schools. There were certain changes in the text of this circular. Some of these were only verbal but others indicated more clearly Mr. Crosland's objectives. If L.E.A.s had not done so already, they were to submit to him their plans for the organisation of secondary education in their areas on comprehensive lines. The Circular was rather lengthy and only a brief account is given below.

The Government motion in the House of Commons in January 1965 stated that the selection test at eleven plus would be ended together with separatism in secondary education. The eleven plus selection had shown some serious weaknesses. One was that its form varied according to the different local areas. Another was that some authorities had more secondary school places than others. Thus a child who failed to enter a grammar school might have been chosen for one if he had lived in a neighbouring district. Most teachers were alive to this and they felt that the type of test needed a drastic reform or should be replaced by some other system. The Circular pointed out that comprehensive education can be organised in at least six main forms.   Mr. Crosland did not adhere to any one form as being universally applicable.

These forms of comprehensive education were given in the Circular:

(1) The "orthodox" comprehensive school which has an age range from 11 to 18.   Mr. Crosland pointed out that there are strong arguments for adopting it.   He realised that many present school buildings are not large enough to adopt this form, but in areas where such schools are being built, he believed that this is the simplest and best solution.

(2) A two-tier system by which all pupils enter a junior comprehensive when they reach the age of 11 and then at 13 or 14 they transfer to a senior comprehensive school.

(3) A two-tier system under which all pupils leave the primary school and transfer to a junior comprehensive school.   At the age of 13 or 14 some enter a senior comprehensive school while the remainder stay in the same school.   There are two variations of this system.   In the first the comprehensive school has no course which aims at a public examination and the pupils remain at school until 15.   The other is the school which provides courses for the G.C.E. and the C.S.E., and the pupils remain at school to at least 16. They are then encouraged to transfer at the appropriate stage to the sixth form of the senior school.

(4) A two-tier system in which all pupils leave the primary school for the junior comprehensive school and at 13 or 14 can choose a senior school which expects its pupils to remain at school well beyond the compulsory age or to go to a senior school which caters for those who do not.

(5) Comprehensive schools which have an age range of 11 to 16 combined with sixth form colleges for pupils over 16.

(6) A system under which pupils leave the primary school at eight or nine and go into a middle school.   From this middle school they enter a comprehensive school which has an age range from 12 or 13 to 18.

The Circular stated that the type of comprehensive school will depend on the local circumstances and an authority may decide to adopt more than one type of organisation in its area.   Mr. Crosland declared that types 1, 2, 5 and 6 lead to fully comprehensive schools but 3 and 4 are only partly comprehensive since they involve the separation of pupils of differing aims and attitudes into different schools at 13 and 14. Hence these schemes can only be accepted as interim solutions because of the limitations of existing buildings. They are only steps to a fully comprehensive organisation. Many people may be inclined to ask what will happen if after some years of experience of both types of organisation the latter produce results equal or even more effective than a fully comprehensive type. Mr. Crosland's Circular reminds one of the old saying that the man from Whitehall always knows best.

The remainder of the Circular deals with a number of problems such as the difficulties which arise from the existence of a large number of school buildings which are not easily adapted as comprehensive schools. Many such buildings are to be found in rural districts or in large towns which still use buildings erected in the last century. The voluntary schools, whether aided or controlled, and the direct grant schools have their own particular problems. Mr. Crosland admits that they may not find it easy to solve their difficulties. He hoped that the schools, the local authorities and the governors of the denominational schools will get together to discuss ways to deal with their problems. The voluntary denominational schools are much concerned with Mr. Crosland's policy. Most of them are Anglican or Roman Catholic and they find it difficult to find the finances necessary for a wholesale rebuilding. Mr. Crosland realised this but he also realised that he had no power to increase the grants and loans which were authorised by the Education Acts of 1944 and 1959. The only way for this needed a new Education Act but with the small majority of five in the Commons it was not likely that the Bill would be accepted. The General Election of March 31 changed the position and the majority (99) would be more safe. An Education Bill was presented in the autumn of 1966. The amendment for rejection of the Bill was withdrawn and the way was clear for a second reading. This was moved by Mr. Crosland.

The object of the Bill was to enlarge the powers of the Secretary of State to make contributions, grants and loans in respect of aided schools and special agreement schools and to direct local education authorities to pay the expenses of establishing or enlarging controlled schools; and to provide for loans for capital expenditure incurred for purposes of colleges of education by persons other than local education authorities.

Clause 1 provides for increased financial aid to be given by the Secretary of State to aided and special agreement schools. Subsection (1) increases from seventy-five per cent. to eighty per cent. the rate at which contributions are paid under section 102 of the Education Act 1944 towards the cost of alterations and external repairs and the rate at which grants are payable under section 103 of that Act towards the cost of providing buildings for schools transferred to new sites. Sub-sections (2) and (3) enable the Secretary of State to pay grants at the rate of eighty per cent. towards the net cost of building new schools and sub-section (4) enables loans to be made under section 105 of the Education Act 1944 to cover the remainder of the cost. Sub-section (5) provides that the limited powers in existing legislation which are superseded by this new power are to cease to have effect. Sub-section (6) restricts the application of the clause to major projects approved for inclusion in the school building programme for 1967-68 and subsequent years and minor works and repairs approved after the introduction of the Bill.

Clause 2 makes two amendments of section 1 (1) (b) (11) of the Education Act 1946, which as amended by subsequent legislation provides for the cost of enlarging a controlled secondary school to be borne by the local education authority in certain circumstances. The first extends this provision to controlled primary schools. The second removes the restriction which prohibits the payment of the cost where the enlargement is likely to amount to the establishment of a school of a new character.

Clause 3 extends the circumstances in which a local education authority may pay the cost of establishing a new controlled school. Section 2 of the Education (Miscellaneous Provisions) Act 1953 requires that the new school must be needed to accommodate pupils for whom places in some other voluntary school have ceased to be available. Under the clause it will be sufficient if this requirement is satisfied with respect to a substantial proportion of the pupils, provided the new school is a middle school established in accordance with section 1 of the Education Act 1964.

Clause 4 enables the Secretary of State to meet capital expenditure incurred in connection with the premises of colleges of education maintained by bodies other than local education authorities. Clauses 5 and 6 contain financial and supplementary provisions. The increased financial aid under clause 1 will involve recurring payments from the Exchequer, estimated to be about £170,000 in the first full year rising to about £1,500,000 in 1969-70. The exercise of the powers conferred by clauses 2 and 3 will result in additional expending by the local education authorities but this will be offset by corresponding savings on the provision of county schools and no net additional cost will be entailed. It is not possible to estimate the amount of loans under clause 4.

At the second reading of the Education Bill Mr. Crosland said that the money received by the aided and special-agreement schools had proved inadequate to meet the rapidly changing circumstances. The increased grant for the school building work would be criticised from two directions. The Roman Catholic Church thought that the grant should be 85 per cent. On the other hand, Mr. Crosland said that one should consider the increases in the Bill as an achievement at a time of our economic circumstances. To the critics who had supported the amendment, Mr. Crosland replied that public opinion is not ready for reconsideration of the basic principle of the dual system and the reopening of all the bitter arguments of the past.

The strict control over school building would continue and would not be affected by the fact that an increased grant was to be paid nor was there any thought that it would encourage schools at present "controlled" to be changed to "aided". The humanists took a line similar to that of the Nonconformists at the time of the Education Act of 1902; they were afraid that there would be more districts in which the only school was an aided school. Mr. Crosland replied that improved communications would reduce the number of areas in which there was no alternative school. Many of the older Church schools had been closed and the Anglican Church showed no desire to create new single school areas. Some Labour Members opposed the Bill but some Conservative ones supported Mr. Crosland—such as Sir Edward Boyle, now the Shadow Minister of Education; Mr. Redhead, then the Minister of State for Education and Science, agreed with Mr. Crosland and said that the Church of England did not desire to create any new single voluntary school area. The result was that the Bill was given an unopposed reading.

In this criticism of the Circular I wish to make it clear that I am not tied to any political party. I recognise that in some areas a form of comprehensive education is the best solution of their educational problems. When the London County Council shortly after the passage of the 1944 Act decided to adopt the comprehensive idea, it was generally thought that in order to have a vigorous sixth form, the school would be a large one containing 2,000 pupils or more. At that time the objection was made that the headmaster could not be able to know all his pupils and would be a mere administrator. Further experience has shown that a much smaller school could be effective especially if there was an adequate house system in the school. I have come across certain areas in which the grammar school contained little more than one hundred pupils and the sixth form was so small that it had little impress on the younger pupils. In circumstances of this kind, if there was a county secondary school in the neighbourhood, the two schools could be combined either as a bilateral or a comprehensive school. In the new towns, a comprehensive school is probably the best solution and in very large cities there is no reason why the existing grammar schools should remain side by side with a comprehensive school.

From the Circular it seems that the grammar school will be merged in a comprehensive unit. I believe that a grammar school which is fully efficient should not be closed, especially if the majority of the inhabitants of the district wish it to be retained. There is no reason why a grammar school should harbour class distinctions. The grammar school pupils come from the primary schools and any snob ideas about grammar school education are generally due to foolish parents and should not be supported by the school. My criticism of the Circular is that it intends to force the comprehensive system upon pupils and parents who do not wish it. This country believes in democracy and one important point in the philosophy of democracy is that consideration ought to be given to minorities. When the Circular was issued, the Government's majority was so small that the views of the country were shown to be nearly equally divided. The election of March 1966 changed the majority to 99. This does not mean that the reorganisation of secondary school education was one of the chief factors which brought about this change. The majority of the electors were more concerned with the gap between the national earning and the debts which we were owing to other countries, the troubles in industry, the sharp rise in prices and the growth in redundancy among the workers in many industries. They were afraid of a state that was experienced in the 1930s.

Mr. Crosland asked L.E.A.s to submit their plans about the reorganisation of secondary education not later than July 1966. In the spring of that year many local authorities changed in the local elections from Labour to the Opposition. Even before the spring elections, some local authorities had already challenged the Circular. The earliest was the Bournemouth County Borough Council. It stated that "A change to a system of comprehensive schools was unnecessary and undesirable in Bournemouth". The opposition to Mr. Crosland had 39 votes, against the ten who wanted comprehensive schools. A formal reply was sent to Mr. Crosland but no plan was submitted. Westmorland and Worcester, by August 4th, declined to submit a plan. Other L.E.A.s sent plans which did not accept any of the six forms of the Circular. Comprehensive schools were rejected by the council of Poole, Dorset. It has a scheme which covers the next five years. The two grammar schools will be retained and there will be larger G.C.E. streams in the secondary modern schools. Poole has rejected the present method which used the eleven plus test to allocate pupils to the secondary schools. The new plan has been recommended to the County Education Committee, and if the committee agrees it will be used in the next school year.

Birmingham has the fifth largest local education authority in England and Wales. In the May election the Conservatives gained the control of the council. The Chief Education Officer is Sir Lionel Russell. The council substituted "guided parents' choice" of secondary schools for their children instead of the eleven plus selection test. It is likely that in many cases the parents' choice would be based on the advice of the head teacher.

In Ealing a considerable number felt that Mr. Crosland's policy contradicted section 76 of the Act of 1944. "In the exercise and performance of all powers and duties conferred and imposed on them by this Act the Minister and local education authorities shall have regard to the general principle that, so far as is compatible with the provision of efficient instruction and training and the avoidance of unreasonable public expenditure, pupils are to be educated in accordance with the wishes of their parents." Their view was presented to the courts but it was not accepted. Some schools such as Colston's Girls' School at Bristol decided to go independent and considerable financial assistance has been promised. The governors of the Leeds Girls' High School have decided that if necessary the school will revert to the independent status it had from 1945 to 1957.   The Parents' Association of Sheffield's oldest grammar school is fighting to prevent it from being turned into a comprehensive school.   Drax Grammar School, which loses its maintained status with the West Riding County Council, is seeking to become an independent boarding school. The National Association of Governing Bodies of Aided Grammar Schools has declared that under the Act of 1944 an aided grammar school can break off its connexion with a local authority.

The reader who has read chapters XIV and XV will have realised that the Scottish educational system is in many ways different from the English.   Glasgow and Edinburgh have a number of fee-paying schools in their areas.   The Secretary of State for Scotland is pressing the two cities to give up the fee-paying secondary schools and accept an organisation of secondary schools on a comprehensive basis.   The two cities reject this on the ground that the comprehensive system is being urged for political and not educational reasons.

In England the Church has criticised the reorganisation of secondary education in districts which have accepted the three-tier system.   Thus in Dorset the type of comprehensive education suggested is a three-tier system based on that in the West Riding of Yorkshire.   The primary schools would be for pupils from the age of five to nine years.   They would enter the middle school from nine to thirteen years and then go to the upper or high school. Thus it has been proposed that in the area served at present by the Wimborne Grammar School, the high schools would be the present secondary modern schools at Pamphill near Wimborne and at Ferndown.   The feeling of the Salisbury Diocese is against the change from nine to thirteen years.   The result would be that the Church primary schools would become first-tier schools for children from five to nine years and they would enter the middle school at the age of nine or ten years.   The majority believe that the time for entering the middle school should be at eleven.

In the last two years there have been some developments in the Colleges of Advanced Technology.   The Robbins Report had recommended that these colleges should become technological universities with the power of granting their own degrees.   At the time of writing the Colleges of Advanced Technology which have become universities are as follows: the University of Aston in Birmingham, Brunel University (which is at present in a group of buildings on Acton Hill, Middlesex; but a new university is being built about a mile from the centre of Uxbridge), the City University (London), the Loughborough University of Technology and the Bradford University of Technology. In Scotland the Royal Technical College, Glasgow, became the University of Strathclyde in 1964, and was followed by the Heriot-Watt University in Edinburgh in 1966. It is a fallacy to think that these new universities are only concerned with technology. They offer studies in mathematics and pure science, and courses in the social sciences, economics, psychology, education and foreign languages.

As soon as we consider technical education we come up against certain terms and it is important to understand them as far as they can be defined. The most usual ones are those of scientists, technologists, technicians, skilled craftsmen, semi-skilled workers and unskilled workers. The pure scientists are concerned with principles. They are the people who discover new scientific processes and the use of new materials, and they are mostly people who have studied in a university and have been awarded very high degrees. The technologists can understand the discoveries of the scientist and are able to make use of them. They are generally those who have a scientific training and hold university degrees.

The technicians work with the technologists, use their ideas and design the production plant and its products and can supervise the operation of the plants. They will be holders of a degree or a National Certificate. Skilled craftsmen work under the technicians and in many cases have certain certificates. Semi-skilled workers have little knowledge of the principles of the plant but they know how to work it.

These definitions are not hard and fast. Thus a scientist in one industry may be considered a technologist in another. The following example shows the different grades in industry. A scientist has discovered certain principles which he believes will lead to a better engine for a motor car. The technologist uses these principles for the design of the engine. The technician's work is the detailed design of such an engine and the planning of its production. The skilled craftsman is responsible for the means of making the parts for the engine and the semi-skilled craftsman is responsible for working the engine when it is actually assembled in the factory. It is obvious that these different grades will need different types of education.   The higher grades need to study in a technological university.   Others will be trained in a regional or an area college and some will start from a secondary technical school or an evening school.

The Colleges of Advanced Technology have striven to live up to the challenge of the Robbins Report and those which have not yet attained university status are planning for this future.   Most of them have had some experience in research.   Some have to seek other sites for their expansion but others are able to stay where they are and expand into sites which are near.   Among their plans they hope to have available some residential accommodation.   So far, Loughborough is the only one which is fully residential.   The colleges are working on their plans for their degree courses.   Most of their technological courses are based on the sandwich type.   Some have developed Liberal Studies in which there is a mixture of full-time and sandwich courses and Social Studies courses which lead to an M.Sc.

The transition from a C.A.T. to a university brings a number of problems.   For example, some of its teaching staff may be reduced in status by the appointment of new staff to senior positions.   Thus a lecturer who has reached the top of his scale and is looking forward to promotion to a senior lectureship is anxious about his future prospects.   The Robbins Committee realised this.   ". . . there are many persons of first-class ability, particularly in the humanities, who have never engaged in research in the narrow sense or felt any urge to publish, but whose breadth of culture, ripeness of judgment and wide-ranging intellectual curiosity are priceless assets in a department or a college.   There are others who develop powers of organisation and administration that are invaluable for the smooth running of a large department. Like all communities, a university needs a diversity of gifts . . . we think that in the making of appointments and in promotion this diversity of gifts is not sufficiently honoured and that published work counts for too much in comparison with other kinds of excellence."[1]

The C.A.T.s had trained their students for the Diploma in Technology which can be acquired through a sandwich course.   It has

[1] Higher Education Report, paras. 560-1.

been said that the C.A.T.s stood or fell by their performance with
the Dip.-Tech. When the C.A.T.s attain university status with
power to award degrees, the position has changed. The sandwich
course leading to the Dip.-Tech. was the aim of the C.A.T.s, but it
is no longer necessary for the technological universities and they
can drop it. The senior staff at a college realised that the amount
of organisation and administration needed to run a sandwich course
is much greater than that required for running the three-year full-
time course of the university. Hence many of the staff would be
ready to drop the sandwich courses. Further, the sandwich course
demands a longer time than that of a university full-time course.
Some technological universities (such as Brunel) would not agree
with this.

Again, from the educational point of view the sandwich course,
which uses an alternation of periods in college and in industry, may
disrupt the students in their studies and is also detrimental to the
corporate life of the college. The integration of study and practical training is not always effective; and it may be that little would
be lost if the sandwich courses were abandoned by the new technological university.

The Robbins Committee speaking of the C.A.T.s said that they
have made remarkable progress. "We consider that the present
powers and status of the colleges are not commensurate with the
work they are now doing. They lack many of the attributes of
university self-government: they have not full power to award
their own qualifications, and in particular cannot award degrees,
despite the fact that their curricula, staffing and facilities are
adjudged by the National Council for Technological Awards to be
appropriate for work for honours degrees.

"It is anomalous that such colleges should not have the power
to grant their own degrees. Many of them have a long history and
extensive academic experience. While the universities founded in
the last two or three years are allowed to award degrees from the
beginning, subject only to the presence of an Academic Advisory
Committee, these colleges are kept in a position of tutelage so that
they are less attractive to students and their recruitment of staff is
impeded.

"We recommend that in future these colleges should in general
become technological universities, and that this should be recognised in their title if they so wish. We say 'in general' since it is

possible that some of the colleges may reach an agreement to become technological faculties of an adjacent university. But, while this is to be welcomed if there is full consent, some precedents point to the need for caution: on the whole we think that the colleges are more likely to preserve the new look and the new approach to education on which they pride themselves if they develop independently." [1]

The Secretary of State for Education in the debate on Higher Education in the House of Commons on 25th March 1965 said that the shortage of applicants for science or technology has been causing much discussion in the Press. He acknowledged that there is cause for concern. The universities had admitted 1,500 fewer students in science and technology than were places available. This does not mean that the number of entrants for science and technology is falling. The percentage of "A" level passes in science and mathematics fell from 55 per cent. in 1959 to 51 per cent. in 1963. Actually the numbers of such entrants showed that this is a rising total and it is necessary to know more about this. The Council for Scientific Policy invited one of its members, Professor F. S. Dainton, former Professor of Physical Chemistry at the University of Leeds, to report on the situation. He was later appointed Vice-Chancellor at the University of Nottingham. He published evidence which indicated that the situation is more serious than the Secretary of State believed.

The Dainton Report pointed out that the numbers of sixth formers who are preparing for science and technology are not increasing but that numbers of those who studied for "A" level in the arts and a mixed course are growing. The figures for the grammar schools showed that the increase in science between 1963 and 1964 was 8·7 per cent. but those who took the arts course increased by 17·6 and the mixed courses grew by 19·1 per cent. The figures for girls showed only a little difference. Since then the swing to arts has increased. One factor is the growth of redundancy in industry which suggests to young people that appointments in such are not safe jobs for them. It is said that some industrialists think that students trained in the arts serve them just as well for certain posts provided they have some knowledge of mathematics and statistics. Some sixth formers have chosen to study the social

[1] Higher Education Report, paras. 390-2.

sciences rather than chemistry and physics. They find that they become deeply interested in the social sciences and wish to offer these in further education. The result is that the number of these students who choose the social sciences, modern languages and architecture is steadily growing.

One difficulty is that some students feel they have not the confidence to enter upon a university course. Some parents are suspicious of universities and prefer the sandwich course, because part of the time is taken up with actual work in industry. A considerable number of young people did not think of entering a university when they were at school. For some time after the last war they were deeply interested in tanks, aircraft, submarines, the rocket and the atomic bomb. Hence when they entered the grammar school they wished to do a science course rather than an arts course. They became interested in television and motor vehicles. Later they found it was becoming more difficult to obtain the kind of place in industry they had hoped. The number of young folk who wished to study science still increased but at a slower pace. Mr. Porter, H.M. Inspector, tried to account for "swing" towards the arts and the social sciences. He stated that the shortage of science teachers in the secondary schools "is a grievous problem which is especially true in girls' schools". The arts sides in many schools offer a wider variety of courses at sixth form level. The science side can only offer a limited choice of courses.

The C.A.T.s and the new technological universities have included some liberal or general studies in the curriculum. The following is a brief account of the curriculum of the University of Aston in Birmingham (as it now is) which was one of the first to be designated as a College of Advanced Technology, and of Brunel. Both of them attained university status in 1966.

The former began in 1891 when public technical education started in the Birmingham and Midland Institute. At first the classes were of a craft nature and were the nucleus of the new Municipal Technical School (1895). The standard of work and its range developed and the school became the Central Technical College in 1927. In 1951 it became the College of Technology and was designated as a College of Advanced Technology in 1956. In 1962 the government decided that the C.A.T.s should be independent of the Local Authorities and would be financed by direct grant. The College was to provide advanced education in technological, scientific and related subjects and research in connection with these subjects. The students of the College consisted in full-time and sandwich undergraduate studies. It also provided for part-time courses and special short full- and part-time courses at postgraduate level. The sandwich courses led to the Diploma in Technology.

When the Robbins Report recommended that the C.A.T.s should generally become technological universities, the College at Aston began to prepare its plans. It was fortunate to have the guidance of the Principal, Sir Peter Venables, who was appointed the Vice-Chancellor when the College received its Charter. Sir Peter had long experience in the teaching of technology and, more than other principals, he understood quite clearly that technological universities should have a positive philosophy. The new university was not planned on the lines of the traditional universities minus an Arts Faculty. Hence the draft Charter stated, "The objects of the university shall be to advance, disseminate and apply learning and knowledge by teaching and research for the benefit of industry and commerce and of the community generally, and to enable students to obtain the advantages of a university education".

The draft Charter made definite mention of arranging research and services with industrial and research bodies, and of a Research Institute. Representatives of industry and commerce would be members of Convocation, and would also have a significant influence as members of the Council which is the executive body of the university. It was also, on the academic side, intended that distinguished scientists, technologists, economists and others engaged in industry and commerce should be appointed Visiting Professors of the university. They would be full members of it and be eligible to serve on Faculty Boards.

A proper place would be ensured for pure science in the university and courses and studies in the applied sciences and technologies be soundly based on scientific principles. Where it is advantageous, theoretical studies will be closely related to practical training and experience as part of a total educational experience. In this programme sandwich courses have a most important part to play and will be fostered by the university. Professional management studies are very important in the curriculum of a technological university. They should be closely related to the social sciences. The Committee believed that besides the necessary social sciences there is a greater need for the development of practical management studies. Hence the Committee was forced to consider how best the work of the Department of Industrial Administration ought to be expanded to take this much increased work and to fit it in with the general structure of the university. The Committee thought there should be a Faculty of Science, a Faculty of Engineering and a Faculty of Social Sciences. Within the latter there should be strong Departments of Business and Industrial Administration, Economics, Psychology and Sociology.

The Academic Board of the College had already given much time and thought to the future academic policy of the university and the Committee strongly supported the broad lines of development proposed by the Board. The Academic Board stressed the development of general studies and thought that the university should include such services as modern languages, literature and art. The Committee had said, "General studies designed to enable the student the better to understand himself and the world in which he lives, will generally continue to be an integral part of all degree courses". The Academic Board thought that it was important to establish a Department of Education as an integral part providing sandwich courses for the training of teachers. Such a Department would be able to improve the teaching in the university. The establishment of a Medical Faculty was suggested but the Committee felt that it would be better to postpone this proposal until five years' time. It was agreed that the degrees of the university should be B.Sc., M.Sc., Ph.D. and D.Sc.

The name of the university was discussed and it was agreed that the name ought not to be confused with the University of Birmingham. It was agreed that it would be "The University of Aston in Birmingham". The university should be on neighbourly relations with the University of Birmingham and the City Council.

The Brunel College of Technology was considered to be up to the standards required but its existing site was not suitable for an Advanced College of Technology. The Middlesex L.E.A. suggested an alternative site and the College was designated in 1962, the tenth of the C.A.T.s. In July 1966 it received its Charter as a technological university. At the time of writing it occupies a group of buildings on Acton Hill but a new university is being built on a site of 170 acres about ten miles further west at Hillingdon about a mile from the centre of the town of Uxbridge. It will be the first technological university established on a new site in England. Building delays put back plans to move by at least six months.

Meanwhile, the installation of the Chancellor, Lord Halsbury, had to be held at the Hammersmith Town Hall. The delays were partly that the officials did not arrange for the work to start quickly enough and partly because of the redundancy programme of the contractors. It was hoped that the Vice-Chancellor would be able to move in with the administration in September 1966, but his house was not ready and the move was postponed to January 1967. The School of Engineering and the Department of Metallurgy could not enter the new site until April 1967. It is expected that the move to the new site will be completed in 1969, and many students may be in residence.

The undergraduate courses at Brunel differ from other universities. They extend over four years and they are of the sandwich type. The students spend six months in each of the first three years in appropriate industrial training. The courses lead to the degree of Bachelor of Technology which takes the place of B.Sc. in most other universities. The prospectus of the university for 1967-8 stresses the sandwich courses for the first degree. "Over the past decade there has been a great surge of interest in sandwich courses. Brunel has devoted its main effort to these, and may claim to have pioneered in this field ... Brunel University feels it can make its best contribution through courses of this kind. It aims that every student should acquire not only a good knowledge of his field of study, but also a sound understanding of scientific principles and an ability to apply them to new problems and situations. As already suggested, a special aim is to integrate each student's academic study and his practical experience in industry."

The university adopts the Tutor System which has worked so well in the older universities. Each student is allotted a member of the staff who is his tutor not only at the university but also whilst the student is in industry, and keeps in touch with him and his industrial supervisors. This has developed a close liaison between the university and industry in general. Another feature will be a substantial amount of residential accommodation.

For some years Brunel has required the study of subjects from the humanities and the social sciences. It believes in the importance of breadth in education and is aware of the dangers of over-specialisation. This has led to a programme of Subsidiary Studies which enable all undergraduates to have the opportunity of studying at least one subject outside their major disciplines. In the first two years all undergraduates choose from a list of courses which include modern languages, literature, design and the social sciences. The courses are conducted by lectures and tutorials on alternate weeks. Students are required to do such preparation and written work as their tutors see fit, and they are examined at the end of the second year. In the next two years the undergraduates may continue the study of a more detailed aspect of their subsidiary subject or may change to study another subject. "Each student works on an individual assignment which may, for instance, take the form of a project, a design drawing or a piece of creative writing. Performance in these tasks is also assessed."

A number of full- and part-time courses lead to the degree of Master of Technology, and postgraduate students can be accepted for full- or part-time courses of study, and training in research methods leading to the Ph.D. The Departments of the University include Departments of Biology, Chemistry and Industrial Chemistry, Materials, Science and Mathematics in which students have experience in using the computer, metallurgy and physics, pure and applied. There is a School of Engineering which deals with electrical and electronic engineering, mechanical engineering and production technology. The School of Social Sciences includes psychology, sociology and economics. The Department of Education admitted its first students in the year 1967-8. The main emphasis is on training teachers who wish to teach science, mathematics and technological subjects in secondary schools. Successful students are awarded the Bachelor of Technology in Education at the end of a four-year full-time course and will be recognised as qualified teachers.

There is also a Postgraduate Diploma in Education and students who are accepted receive grants from the Department of Education and Science.

The Plowden Report was expected in 1965. The vast field covered made this impossible and it was published late in 1966.

The Report (which was 555 pages in length) took nearly three and a half years to prepare. The last Report on the Primary School was the Hadow in 1931. In addition there was a second volume concerned with Research and Surveys.   The Report gives the warning in chapter 31 that the proposals will be very costly.   The programme is not luxurious or extravagant but it cannot be carried out in the next five years.

It is not possible to give anything like a full account of the Plowden Report since this would need many chapters and not one chapter.   After the introduction, chapter two is concerned with the growth and development of the child and it really brings up to date the findings of the Hadow Report of 1931.   The next two chapters deal with the children and their environment and the participation by the parents.   Since 1931 a great amount of progress has been made.   It is true that the rise in educational standards is the result of improvements in the schools but there has been an important change in the homes of the children.   The Report points out, "Incomes have risen, nutrition has improved, housing is better, the health service and the social services have brought help where it is needed" (para. 78).   The result is that most children are now healthy, vigorous, curious and alert.   It is true that many primary schools were built before 1931 but few children show the effects of lack of food and poor clothing, but even now there are some children who have parents who are well behind in these matters.   The N.U.T. in the survey titled "The State of Our Schools" found many primary and secondary modern schools both in rural districts and in the industrial towns were quite out of date (see pp. 661-2 of this book).

Many schools have Parent-Teacher Associations but the Report did not think that P.T.A.s are the best way of making a close relationship between home and school.   The Report suggests that the child and his parents should be welcomed when he first comes to school.   Other means are meetings between parents and teachers, open days and information for parents, and teachers' visits to the homes of the pupils.   Written reports on the pupils should be made at least once a year and the parents should come to the school to see the work of their children.   The head and the staff should think out ways to gain the participation of the parents such as inviting them to school sports and concerts.   In short, the primary school should be the focal point of a community centre.

The Newsom Report had drawn attention to the slum areas (pp. 667-9 of this book).   The Plowden Report deals with the primary schools in these districts under the name of priority areas in which children are most severely handicapped by home conditions. The programme should make schools in these areas as good as the best in the country. Space will not allow more than the headlines of the remainder of the Plowden Report. Students in a university or a college of education will be able to study the Report in more detail.

Part 5 of the Report is concerned with the structure of primary education, nursery education and the transfer to secondary education. The size of primary schools and education in rural areas are also considered. Part 5 deals with the curriculum and the reader may be interested in religious education in the school, punishment, organisation of primary schools, the education of handicapped children in ordinary schools and the education of gifted children. The curriculum of the primary school is also discussed in detail.

Part 6, the Adults in the Schools, contains such topics as the staffing of schools, use of part-time teachers, the training of primary school teachers and of nursery assistants and teachers' aides. Part 7 deals with independent primary schools. Part 8 examines such topics as the school building and equipment and the status and government of primary education. The last part consists of the recommendations and the conclusions of the Council.

The Plowden Report stated that a series of investigations by the Department of Education from 1948 to 1964 made it clear that the standard of reading in the country has been going up steadily since the war. This was challenged by a report issued by the National Foundation for Educational Research which was given by Dr. Joyce Morris. She studied during a three-year period in ten Kent schools. She was probably right in the cases she studied but her report was concerned with a few schools. On the other hand, the Plowden Report stated that since the war there has been a remarkable improvement in the standards of reading. The Report of the Department of Education and Science agreed with the Plowden Report. The Department said: "Dr. Morris's was a selected survey of a few schools but ours was designed to sample pupils throughout the country".

BIBLIOGRAPHY

SUGGESTIONS FOR FURTHER READING

The following bibliography is not intended to be exhaustive, but gives a selection of books and official publications which the reader will find useful for further study of particular topics.

A. GENERAL HISTORIES OF EDUCATION.

Adamson, J. W., *A Short History of Education*, C.U.P., 1919.

Armytage, W. H. G., *Four Hundred Years of English Education*, C.U.P., 1964.

Barnard, H. C., *A Short History of English Education, 1760-1944*, University of London Press, 1947.

Birchenough, C., *History of Elementary Education in England and Wales from 1800 to the Present Day*, U.T.P., 1938.

Boyd, W., *The History of Western Education*, Black (new edition), 1963.

Cole, P. R., *A History of Educational Thought*, O.U.P., 1931.
 Although this book deals primarily with educational theory, it contains useful sections on the schools and universities of the Middle Ages and the application of educational ideas during the last three centuries.

Craik, Sir Henry, *The State in its Relation to Education*, Macmillan, 1914.

Jarman, T. L., *Landmarks in the History of Education*, Cresset Press, 1951.

Kandel, I. L., *History of Secondary Education*, G. Harrap. (No date given.)
 A general history of secondary education in the U.S.A. and Europe, with special chapters dealing with England.

Kinloch, T. F., *Pioneers of Religious Education*, O.U.P., 1939.

Leese, J., *Personalities and Power in Education*, Arnold, Leeds, 1950.

Lester Smith, W. O., *Education in Great Britain*, Home University Library No. 210, O.U.P., 1949.

Wodehouse, Helen, *A Survey of the History of Education*, Edward Arnold, 1929.

B. Schools of Mediaeval England and the Tudor Period.

Adamson, J. W., *The Illiterate Anglo-Saxon*, C.U.P., 1946.

A collection of essays on mediaeval and modern education. Adamson dispels the belief that England had no elementary schools before the formation of the philanthropic societies of the 18th century.

Brown, J. H., *Elizabethan Schooldays*, Blackwell, 1933.

A very readable description of the Elizabethan grammar-schools, their origin, life, and curriculum; the methods of instruction, punishments, games, and sports, etc. The author has drawn upon Leach and Foster Watson for much of his detail.

Leach, A. F., *The Schools of Medieval England*, Methuen, 1915.

English Schools at the Reformation, Constable, 1894.

These two books are a very valuable contribution to the history of English schools before the Reformation. Mr. Leach was an able historian who, during his period of office as assistant-commissioner of the Charity Commission, had access to most of the important documents dealing with the history of endowed schools.

The reader should also refer to Leach's histories of schools in the different volumes of the *Victoria History of the Counties of England.*

Early Yorkshire Schools. "The Yorkshire Archaeological Society Record Series."

Vol. XXVII, 1899.   York, Beverley, Ripon.

Vol. XXXIII, 1903.   Pontefract, Howden, Northallerton, Acaster, Rotherham, Giggleswick, Sedbergh.

These volumes contain a scholarly introduction and provide a collection of all the documents (mostly in Latin) which relate to the above schools. They form an indispensable source-book for the detailed study of mediaeval schools in northern England.

Marriot, Sir J. A. R., *The Life of John Colet*, Methuen, 1933.

Montmorency, J. E. G. de, *State Intervention in English Education*, C.U.P., 1902.

A much more comprehensive work than its title indicates. The claim to the continuity of elementary education after the Reformation should be noted. The period considered is up to 1833, and there are many useful references to education in other parts of the British Isles and the Empire.

Vincent, W. A. L., *The State and School Education, 1640-1660*, S.P.C.K., 1950.

Watson, Foster, *The English Grammar Schools to 1660*, C.U.P., 1908.

The Old Grammar Schools, C.U.P., 1916.

Specially useful for the Tudor and Stuart periods. They contain much detailed information about the life and curricula of the grammar-schools. The latter has a chapter dealing with the decline of the grammar-schools.

The Beginning of the Teaching of Modern Subjects in England, Pitman, 1909.

The opening chapter is a useful introduction on the development of the grammar-school curriculum in the 16th and 17th centuries. Subsequent chapters describe the introduction of the different studies, such as mathematics, history, and geography, etc.

Wood, N., *The Reformation and English Education,* George Routledge, 1931.

C. ENGLISH SCHOOLS, 1660 TO 1902.

Adamson, J. W., *Pioneers of Modern Education, 1600-1700,* C.U.P., 1921.

In addition to Continental developments, this book deals with the work of Brinsley, the educational legislation of the Long Parliament, Hoole's *New Discovery,* and elementary education during the period.

English Education, 1789-1902, C.U.P., 1930.

A detailed study of great value. Includes elementary, secondary, and university education.

Archer, R. L., *Secondary Education in the Nineteenth Century,* C.U.P., 1921.

Includes an account of the development of the modern universities and pays special attention to Wales.

Arnold, Matthew, *Reports on Elementary Schools,* H.M.S.O., 1910.

The criticism of the Revised Code and its results should be noted.

Baines, E., *The Life of Edward Baines,* Longmans, Brown, Green, Longmans, and Roberts, 1859.

Balfour, G., *The Educational Systems of Great Britain and Ireland,* Clarendon Press, 1903.

Bingham, J. H., *The Sheffield School Board, 1870-1903,* J. W. Northend, 1949.

Binns, H. B., *A Century of Education,* Dent, 1908.

An account of the work of the British and Foreign School Society.

Bowen, W. E., *Edward Bowen,* Longmans, Green, 1902.

Butler, S., *Life and Letters of Dr. Samuel Butler,* 2 vols., J. Murray, 1896.

Carlisle, N., *Endowed Grammar Schools,* 2 vols., 1818.

Clough, B. A., *Memoir of Anne J. Clough,* Edward Arnold, 1903.

Curtis, S. J., and Boultwood, M. E. A., *An Introductory History of English Education since 1800.* 2nd edition, University Tutorial Press, 1962.

Dobbs, A. E., *Education and Social Movements, 1700-1850,* Long-mans, Green, 1919.

Eaglesham, E., *From School Board to Local Authority,* Routledge and Kegan Paul, 1956.

Edgeworth, M., *Practical Education,* 2 vols., London, 1798.

Professional Education, London, 1809.

Findlay, J. J., *Arnold of Rugby,* C.U.P., 1897.

Fitch, Sir J., *Thomas and Matthew Arnold,* "Great Educators Series," W. Heinemann, 1905.

Gautrey, T., *"Lux Mihi Laus," School Board Memories,* Link House Publications.

Gregory, A., *Robert Raikes,* Hodder and Stoughton, 1877.

Gregory, R., *Elementary Education,* National Society, 1905.
An account of the work of the National Society.

Hans, N., *New Trends in Education in the Eighteenth Century,* Routledge, 1951.

Holman, H., *English National Education,* Blackie, 1898.
A very useful account of the development of elementary education before 1897. It contains a sound appraisement of the results of the Revised Code.

Holmes, E., *What Is and What Might Be,* Constable, 1911.

How, F. D., *Six Great Schoolmasters,* Methuen, 1904.
The lives and work of Hawtrey, Moberly, Kennedy, Vaughan, Temple, and Bradley.

Jones, M. G., *The Charity School Movement in the 18th Century,* C.U.P., 1938.
A detailed and scholarly study of the schools of the S.P.C.K. in Great Britain and Ireland.

Kay-Shuttleworth, Sir James, *Public Education,* Longmans, Brown, Green, and Longmans, 1853.

Kekewich, Sir G. W., *The Education Department and After,* Constable, 1920.

Kendall, G., *Robert Raikes,* Nicholson and Watson, 1939.

Kirk, K. E., *The Story of the Woodard Schools,* Hodder and Stoughton, 1937.

Lilley, A. L., *Sir Joshua Fitch,* Edward Arnold, 1906.

Mack, E. C., *Public Schools and British Opinion*, Columbia University Press, 1938 and 1941.

A most important work which should be read by all interested in the relation of the public schools to the national system.
Vol. I, 1780 to 1860.   Vol. II, Since 1860.

McIntosh, P. C., *Physical Education in England since 1800*, G. Bell, 1952.

McLachlan, H., *English Education under the Test Acts*, Manchester University Press, 1931.

Maltby, S. E., *Manchester and the Movement of National Elementary Education, 1800-1870*, Manchester University Press, 1918.

Matthews, H. F., *Methodism and the Education of the People, 1791-1851*, Epworth Press, 1949.

Owen, Robert, *The Life of Robert Owen: Written by Himself*, G. Bell, 1920.

Parker, I., *Dissenting Academies in England*, C.U.P., 1914.

Parkin, G. R., *Life and Letters of Edward Thring*, Macmillan, 1900.

Philpott, H. B., *London at School—The Story of the School Board*, Fisher Unwin, 1904.

Pritchard, F. C., *Methodist Secondary Education*, Epworth Press, 1949.

Raikes, E., *Dorothea Beale of Cheltenham*, Constable, 1908.

Raymont, T., *A History of the Education of Young Children*, Longmans, Green, 1937.

Robson, A. H., *The Education of Children Engaged in Industry in England*, Kegan Paul, 1931.

Rodgers, J., *Old Public Schools of England*, Batsford, 1938.

Rusk, R. R., *A History of Infant Education*, University of London Press, 1933.

Salmon, D., *The Practical Parts of Lancaster's Improvements and Bell's Experiment*, C.U.P., 1932.

Smith, Ashley J. W., *The Birth of Modern Education: the Contribution of the Dissenting Academies, 1660-1800*, Independent Press, 1954.

Smith, F., *The Life and Work of Sir James Kay-Shuttleworth*, J. Murray, 1923.

An interesting and well-written biography.

A History of English Elementary Education, University of London Press, 1931.

Valuable for its relation of educational progress to the political, social, and industrial background.

Spalding, T. A., *The Work of the London School Board*, D. S. King, 1900.

Stanley, A. P., *Life of Dr. Arnold*, J. Murray, 1904.

Stow, D., *The Training System*, Glasgow, 1840.

Strachey, L., *Eminent Victorians* [Life of Dr. Arnold], Penguin Books, 1948.

Tropp, A., *The School Teachers: the Growth of the Teaching Profession in England and Wales from 1800 to the Present Day*, Heinemann, 1957.

Webster, F. A. M., *Our Great Public Schools*, Ward, Lock, 1937.

Wilderspin, S., *The Infant System*, J. S. Hodson, 1852.

Wilkins, H. T., *Great English Schools*, Noel Douglas, 1925.

Wilson, Dover, J., *The Schools of England*, Sidgwick and Jackson, 1928.

Wood, J., *Account of the Edinburgh Sessional School*, Edinburgh, 1828.

Wordsworth, C., *Discourse on Public Education*, F. and J. Rivington, 1844.

D. ENGLISH SCHOOLS SINCE 1902.

Allen, B. M., *Sir Robert Morant*, Macmillan, 1934.

Dr. Allen presents very clearly the part played by Morant in shaping the Education Act of 1902, and the new policy towards education which he developed.

Armfelt, R., *The Structure of English Education*, Cohen and West, 1955.

Badger, A. B., *The Public Schools and the Nation*, Robert Hale, 1944.

Bazeley, E. T., *Homer Lane and the Little Commonwealth*, Geo. Allen and Unwin, 1928.

Curtis, S. J., *Education in Britain, 1900-1950*, Andrew Dakers, 1952.

Dent, H. C., *The Educational System of England and Wales*, University of London Press, 1961.

Dent, H. G., *Education in Transition*, Kegan, Paul, Trench, Trubner, 1944.
A sociological study of the impact of war on English education, 1939-43.

The Education Act, 1944, University of London Press, 1944.

Secondary Education for All, Routledge and Kegan, 1949.
A valuable study of the development of the idea of universal secondary education with pertinent criticisms of the present arrangements.

Growth in English Education, 1946-1952, Routledge and Kegan Paul, 1954.

Earle, F. M., *Reconstruction in the Secondary School*, University of London Press, 1944.
A detailed description of the organisation of a multilateral school.

Edmonds, E. L., *The School Inspector*, Routledge and Kegan Paul, 1962.

Fisher, H. A. L., *An Unfinished Autobiography*, O.U.P., 1941 (reprint).

Graves, J., *Policy and Progress in Secondary Education*, Thomas Nelson and Sons, 1943.
A useful account of secondary education during the past fifty years.

Hall W. Clarke, *Children's Courts*, Geo. Allen and Unwin, 1926.

Hughes, D., *The Public Schools and the Future*, C.U.P. 1942.

Jeffreys, M. V. C., *Revolution in Teacher Training*, Pitman, 1961.

Kitchen, P. I., *From Learning to Earning*, Faber and Faber, 1944.
The story of the Rugby Continuation Schools.

Laidler, J. G., *Voluntary Schools*, Nat. Soc. and S.P.C.K.
Detailed information on the position of voluntary schools under the Education Acts of 1944 and 1946.

Leeson, Spencer, *The Public Schools Question*, Longmans, Green, 1948.
This book develops the views of the Fleming Report.

Lester Smith, W. O., *To Whom Do Schools Belong?*, Blackwell, 1943.

A very able study of the English educational system, introducing the points at issue in current controversy.

Lowndes, G. A. N., *The Silent Social Revolution*, O.U.P., reprinted 1948.

Probably the best study of the development of English elementary, secondary, and technical education from 1895 to the period immediately preceding the Second World War.

The British Educational System, Hutchinson, 1955.

McMillan, Margaret, *The Nursery School*, J. M. Dent, revised edition, 1930.

Mansbridge, A., *Margaret McMillan—Prophet and Pioneer*, J. M. Dent, 1932.

Norwood, C., *The English Tradition of Education*, J. Murray, 1929.

Partridge, E. H., *Freedom in Education*, Faber and Faber, 1943.

A defence of the public schools.

Sanderson of Oundle, Chatto and Windus, 1924.

An account of Sanderson's achievements, compiled by members of his staff.

Segal, C., *Backward Children in the Making*, F. Muller Ltd., 1949.

A sociological study of children in a district of North Kensington.

Selby-Bigge, Sir L. A., *The Board of Education*, Putnam, 1927.

Sillitoe, H., *A History of the Teaching of Domestic Subjects*, Methuen, 1933.

Ward, H., *The Educational System in England and Wales*, C.U.P., 1939.

A concise but interesting description of the different educational institutions immediately preceding the Second World War.

Waugh, A., *Public School Life*, W. Collins, 1922.

Wells, H. G., *The Story of a Great Schoolmaster—Sanderson of Oundle*, Chatto and Windus, 1924.

Wiseman, S., *Examinations in English Education*, Manchester University Press, 1961.

Wolfenden, J. F., *The Public Schools To-day*, University of London Press, 1949.

A spirited defence of boarding-schools, by the late headmaster of Shrewsbury and present Vice-Chancellor of the University of Reading.

Worsley, T. C., *Barbarians and Philistines,* Robert Hale. (No date given.)
A severe criticism of the public-school system.

E. Scottish Education.

Belford, A. J., *Centenary Handbook of the Educational Institute of Scotland,* Edinburgh, 1946.

Boyd, W. (Editor), *Evacuation in Scotland,* University of London Press, 1944.

Cant, R. G., *A Short History of the University of St. Andrews,* Oliver and Boyd, 1946.

Coutts, J., *A History of the University of Glasgow,* James Maclehose, 1909.

Edgar, J., *History of Early Scottish Education,* J. Thin, 1893.

Forbes, F. A., *The Founding of a Northern University,* Sands, 1920.
The story of the foundation of the University of Aberdeen.

Grant, J., *The History of Burgh and Parish Schools,* W. Collins, 1876.
The standard work on Scottish schools before the Act of 1872.

Insh, G. P., *School Life in Old Scotland,* Educational Institute of Scotland, 1925.

Jessop, J. C., *Education in Angus,* University of London Press, 1931.

Kerr, J., *Scottish Education, School and University,* C.U.P., 1910.

Mackenzie, R. J., *Almond of Loretto,* Constable, 1905.

Mason J., *A History of Scottish Experiments in Rural Education,* University of London Press, 1935.

Morgan, A., *Makers of Scottish Education,* Longmans, Green, 1929.
Rise and Progress of Scottish Education, Oliver and Boyd, 1927.
Presents a clear and interesting account of the development of Scottish education including the Act of 1918.

Scottish University Studies, O.U.P., 1933.

Rusk, R. R., *The Training of Teachers in Scotland,* Educational Institute of Scotland, 1928.

Simpson, I. J., *Education in Aberdeenshire Before 1872,* University of London Press, 1947.

Strong, J., *A History of Secondary Education in Scotland,* Clarendon Press, 1909.

Includes the Act of 1908.

Tristan, H. B., *Loretto School,* Fisher Unwin, 1911.

Wade, N. A., *Post-Primary Education in the Primary Schools* of *Scotland, 1872-1936,* University of London Press, 1939.

F.   ADULT, TECHNICAL, AND FORCES EDUCATION.

Abbott, A., *Education for Industry and Commerce in England,* O.U.P., 1933.

A complete survey of the development of technical education up to 1933, by a former Chief Inspector of Technical Schools.   An authoritative work.

Burns, C. Delisle, *A Short History of Birkbeck College,* University of London Press, 1924.

Davies, L. J., *The Working Men's College,* Macmillan, 1904.

Dent, H. G., *Part-Time Education in Great Britain,* Turnstile Press, 1949.

Harrison, J. F. C., *Learning and Living, 1790-1960.   A Study in the History, of the English Adult Education Movement,* Routledge and Kegan Paul, 1961.

Hawkins, T. H., and Brimble, L. J. F., *Adult Education.   The Record of the British Army,* Macmillan, 1947.

Hudson, J. W., *History of Adult Education,* Longmans, Brown, Green, and Longmans, 1851.

A detailed account of the growth of the early adult-schools and the Mechanics' Institutes.

Mansbridge, A., *An Adventure in Working-Class Education,* Longmans, Green, 1920.

An account of the origin and early development of the W.E.A.

Martin, G. Currie, *The Adult School Movement,* National Adult School Union, 1924.

Millis, C. T., *Technical Education, Its Development and Aims,* Edward Arnold, 1925.

Parry, R. St. John (editor), *Cambridge Essays on Adult Education,* C.U.P., 1920.

Peers, R., *Adult Education in Practice,* Macmillan, 1934.

Pole, T., *A History of the Origin and Progress of Adult Schools,* Bristol, 1814.

Raybould, S. G., *W.E.A. The Next Phase*, W.E.A., 1949.

The English Universities and Adult Education, W.E.A., 1951.

Richardson, W. A., *The Technical College*, O.U.P., 1939.

Sadler, Sir M. E., *Continuation Schools in England and Elsewhere*, Manchester University Press, 1907.

Scott, R., *The Story of the Women's Institutes*, Village Press, Idbury, Oxon, 1925.

Smith, Moore G. C., *The Story of the People's College, Sheffield*, Northend, 1912.

Turner, D. M., *History of Science Teaching in England*, Chapman and Hall, 1927.

Venables, Sir P. F. R., and Williams, W. J., *The Smaller Firms and Technical Education*, Parrish, 1961.

Venables, Sir P. F. R., *Technical Education*, Bell, 1955.

This contains chapters by specialist authors.

White, A. C. T., *The Story of Army Education, 1643-1963*, Harrap, 1963.

Wilson, N. Scarlyn, *Education in the Forces—The Civilian Contribution, 1939-46*, Evans, 1948.

Wood, Ethel M., *The Polytechnic and Quintin Hogg*, Nisbet, 1932.

Yeaxlee, Basil A., *Spiritual Values in Adult Education*, 2 vols., O.U.P., 1925.

One of the most important contributions made to the study of adult education.

G. ENGLISH UNIVERSITIES.

Attwater, A., *Pembroke College, Cambridge*, C.U.P. 1939.

Brodrick, G. C., *A History of the University of Oxford*, Longmans, Green, 1886.

Childs, W. M., *Making a University*, Dent, 1933.

Cooper, J. W., *Annals of Cambridge*, 5 vols., C.U.P. (various dates).

Dent, H. G., *Universities in Transition*, Cohen and West, 1961.

Documents Relating to King's College, London, printed for private circulation by Richard Clay, 1933.

Fiddes, E., *Chapters in the History of Owens College, and of Manchester University*, Manchester University Press, 1937.

Flexner, A., *Universities, American, English, German*, O.U.P., 1930.

Gardner, A., *A Short History of Newnham College, Cambridge,* Bowes and Bowes, 1921.

Godley, A. D., *Oxford in the Eighteenth Century,* Methuen, 1909.

Grylls, R. G., *Queen's College,* George Routledge, 1948.

Gunther, R. T., *Early Science in Oxford,* Vol. I, O.U.P., 1921.
Pages 99-107 give an account of Recorde's work as a mathematician.

Hamilton, M. A., *Newnham,* Faber and Faber, 1936

Hearnshaw F. J. C., *The Centenary History of King's College, London,* Harrap, 1929.

Hodgkin, R. H., *Six Centuries of an Oxford College: A History of the Queen's College, 1340-1940,* Blackwell, 1949.

Humberstone, T. L., *University Reform in London,* Allen and Unwin, 1926.

James, L., *A Forgotten Genius: Sewell of St. Columb's and Radley,* Faber, 1945.

Johnson, Brimley R., *The Undergraduate,* Stanley Paul, 1928.
An abridgment of Christopher Wordsworth's *Social Life at the English Universities in the 18th Century.*

Lowe, A., *The University in Transformation,* Sheldon Press, 1940.

Lyte, Maxwell H. C., *A History of the University of Oxford,* Macmillan, 1886.
A detailed account of Oxford before 1530.

Mallet, Sir Charles, *A History of the University of Oxford,* 3 vols., Methuen.

     I.   "The Mediaeval University," 1924.

     II.   "16th and 17th Centuries," 1924.

     III.   "Modern Oxford," 1927.

The most recent authoritative history of the University of Oxford.

Moberly, Sir Walter, *The Crisis in the University,* S.C.M. Press, 1949.
A diagnosis of the dangers which threaten the universities at the present time, with suggestions for meeting them. A valuable study of modern trends in the universities of to-day, based upon the writer's long experience as chairman of the University Grants Committee.

Rait, R. S., *Life in the Mediaeval University,* C.U.P., 1912.

Rashdall, H., *The Universities of Europe in the Middle Ages,* 3 vols., O.U.P., 1936.

The standard work on the mediaeval universities. Dr. Rashdall's theory of the origin of Oxford University is not universally accepted. The original work was published in 1895, but the second edition, 1936 (reprinted 1942), has been re-edited by F. M. Powicke and A. B. Emden, and contains much additional material in the way of notes and corrections. Leach's criticism of Rashdall's theory of the origin of Oxford University has been reprinted in Appendix I, Vol. III.

Roberts, S. C., *British Universities,* Collins, 1947.

Introduction to Cambridge, C.U.P., 1945.

Schachner, N., *The Mediaeval Universities,* Allen and Unwin, 1938.

A useful book for the reader who desires a shorter account than that given by Rashdall.

Smithells, A., *From a Modern University,* O.U.P., 1921.

Stephen, Barbara, *Emily Davies and Girton College,* Constable, 1927.

Thompson J., *The Owens College: Its Foundation and Growth,* Cornish, 1886.

Trevelyan, G. M., *Trinity College,* C.U.P., 1943.

Truscott, B., *Redbrick University,* Faber, 1943.

Tuke, M. G., *A History of Bedford College for Women,* O.U.P., 1939.

Tylecote, M., *The Education of Women at Manchester University, 1883-1933,* Manchester University Press, 1941.

Venn, J., *Early Collegiate Life,* Heffer, 1913.

Caius College, C.U.P., 1923.

Whiting, C. E., *The University of Durham, 1832-1932,* Sheldon Press, 1932.

Wilson, Gordon S., *The University of London and Its Colleges,* U.T.P., 1923.

Winstanley, D. A., *Unreformed Cambridge,* C.U.P., 1935.

Cambridge in the 18th Century, C.U.P., 1922.

Early Victorian Cambridge, C.U.P., 1940.

Later Victorian Cambridge, C.U.P., 1947.

A detailed and authoritative history which performs for Cambridge a service similar to that of Sir Charles Mallet for Oxford.

Histories of particular colleges are published in the *College History Series* published by F. E. Robinson and Hutchinson. Included in the series are : —

Davies, W. C., and Lewis Jones., *The University of Wales,* 1905.

Fowler, J. T., *Durham University,* 1904.

H. A SELECTION OF HISTORIES OF PARTICULAR SCHOOLS.

Histories of all the English public schools and most of the grammar-schools have been published, and the student is advised to read one or more of these with the object of ascertaining how far the particular school fits in with the general line of development. The list which follows is a section from the many histories which have been written and the student will find it useful to choose a school from his own district.

Airy, R., *Westminster,* Bell, 1902.

Anon., *Fifty Years of Fettes,* Constable, 1931.

Ashford, L. J., and Haworth, C. M., *The History of the Royal Grammar School, High Wycombe,* Published by the Governors, 1963.

Austin, R., *The Crypt School, Gloucester,* John Bellows, 1939.

Badley, J. H., *Bedales,* Methuen, 1923.

Barletot, R. G., *History of Crewkerne School,* James Wheatley, 1899.

Bedford, F. W., *History of the George Heriot's Hospital,* Bell and Bradfute, 1872.

Bell, E. A., *A History of Giggleswick School,* R. Jackson, Leeds, 1912.

Bennet, W., *A History of the Burnley Grammar School,* The Grammar School, Burnley, 1940.

Blanch, W. H., *Dulwich College and Edward Alleyn,* E. W. Allen, 1877.

Brett-James, N. G., *The History of Mill Hill School,* Thomas Malcomson, 1923.

Burgess, M. A., *A History of Burlington School,* printed for private circulation, 1924.

Claridge, W., *Origins and History of Bradford Grammar School*, J. Green, 1882.

Clarke, A. K., *A History of Cheltenham Ladies' College*, Faber and Faber, 1953.

Clarke, H. L., *History of Sedbergh School*, Jackson, 1925.

Cobley, F., *Chronicles of the Free Grammar School of Prince Henry at Otley*, W. Walker, 1923.

Cook, A. K., *About Winchester College*, Macmillan, 1917.

Cox, T., *History of the Heath Grammar School, Halifax*, F. King, 1879.

Crump, G., *Bedales Since the War*, Chapman and Hall, 1936.

Cust, L., *A History of Eton College*, Duckworth, 1899.

Davies, J. C., *A History of Borlase School*, Aylesbury, 1932.

Deed, B. L., *A History of Stamford School*, printed for the school, 1954.

Dodd, E. E., *A History of the Bingley Grammar School, Bradford*, 1930.

Douglas, M. A., and Ash, C. R., *The Godolphin School*, Longmans, Green, 1928.

Firth J. d'E., *Winchester College*, Winchester Publications, 1949.
The latest account of Winchester. Very well illustrated.

Fisher, G. W., *Annals of Shrewsbury School*, Methuen, 1899.

Forder, C. R., *A History of the Paston Grammar School* (published by the Governors, 1934).

Forrester, E. G., *A History of Magdalen College School*, Hillier and Sons, 1950.

Garside, B., *History of Hampton School*, C.U.P., 1931.

Garstang, J., *A History of Blackburn Grammar School*, NE. Lancashire Press, 1897.

Gibbon, A. M., *The Ancient Free Grammar School of Skipton in Craven*, University Press of Liverpool, 1947.
An admirable example of the way in which a school's history should be written. The history of Skipton Grammar School is given against the national background of secondary education.

Gilmore, C. G., *History of King Edward VI School, Stafford*, O.U.P., 1953.

Gray, J. M., *A History of the Perse School, Cambridge*, Bowes and Bowes, 1921.

Hill, R. D., *A History of St. Edward's School*, John Sherratt, Altrincham, 1960.

Hinchcliffe, G., *A History of King James' Grammar School in Almondbury*, The Advertiser Press, 1963.
   A graphic account of the foundation and development of an ancient Grammar School. Generously illustrated.

Houseman, J. W., *Hipperholme Grammar School*, Lund Humphries, 1948.

Houson, E. W., and Warner, G. T., *Harrow School*, Edward Arnold, 1898.

Hutton, T. W., *King Edward's School, Birmingham, 1552-1952*, Blackwell, 1952.

Jameson, E. M., *Charterhouse*, Blackie, 1937.

Kay, D. M., *The History of Lymn Grammar School*, John Sherratt, Altrincham, 1960.

Knight, Francis A., *A History of Sidcot School*, J. M. Dent, 1908.

Laborde, E. D., *Harrow School*, Winchester Publications, 1948.

Law, W. S., *Oundle's Story*, Sheldon Press, 1922.

Leach, A. F., *A History of Winchester College*, Duckworth, 1899.
   Leach is writing about his old school and includes many personal reminiscences.
   A History of Bradfield College, O.U.P., 1900.
   History of Warwick School, Constable, 1906.

Lempriere, W., *A History of the Girls' School of Christ's Hospital*, C.U.P., 1924.

Lennox, J. T., *Sevenoaks School and its Founder*, Caxton and Holmesdale Press, 1932.

Lester, D. N. R., *A History of Batley Grammar School*, J. S. Newsome, Batley, 1963.

Lunn, J., *A History of Leigh Grammar School*, Sherrall and Hughes, Manchester, 1930.

Lyte, Maxwell H. C., *A History of Eton College*, Macmillan, 1875.
   Many new editions (1877, 1889, 1899, and 1911). Probably the most complete history of a school yet written.

MacDonald, *A Short History of Repton*, Benn, 1929.

Mumford, A. A., *The Manchester Grammar School,* Longmans, Green, 1919.

Oldham, B. J., *A History of Shrewsbury School, 1552-1952,* Blackwell, 1952.

Peacock, M. H., *History of the Free Grammar School of Queen Elizabeth at Wakefield,* W. H. Milnes, 1892.

Pearce, E. H., *Annals of Christ's Hospital,* Methuen, 1901.

Pine, E., *The Westminster Abbey Singers,* Dennis Dobson, 1953.

Pollard, F. E. (editor), *Bootham School,* Dent, 1926.

Price, A. C., *History of the Leeds Grammar School,* R. Jackson, 1919.

Raine, A., *History of St. Peter's School, York,* Bell, 1926.
A really outstanding school history.

Rivington, S., *The History of Tonbridge School,* Rivingtons, 1935.

Rogers, P. W., *A History of Ripon Grammar School,* printed by Wm. Harrison and Sons, 1954.

Ross, W. C. A., *The Royal High School,* Oliver and Boyd, 1934.

Row, E. F., *A History of Midhurst Grammar School,* Combridge, Hove, 1913.

Sands, P. C., and Haworth, C. M., *A History of Pocklington School,* A. Brown and Sons, 1951.

Sargant, W. L., *The Book of Oakham School* (privately printed), C.U.P., 1928.

Sargeaunt, J., *History of Bedford School,* Fisher Unwin, 1925.
Annals of Westminster School, Methuen, 1898.

Somervell, D. C., *A History of Tonbridge School,* Faber and Faber, 1947.

Sterry, W., *Annals of Eton College,* Methuen, 1898.

Sturge, H. W., and Clark, T., *The Mount School, York,* Dent, 1931.

Talboys, R. St. C., *A Victorian School: the Story of Wellington College,* Basil Blackwell, 1943.

Tanner, L. E., *Westminster School,* Philip Allan, 1923.

Thomas, D. H., *A Short History of St. Martin-in-the-Fields High School for Girls,* 2nd edition, John Murray, 1949.

Thompson, H., *A History of Ackworth School,* Centenary Committee, Ackworth School, 1879.

Thornton, A., *Bridlington School,* Bridlington School, 1930.

Trotter, J. J., *The Royal High School, Edinburgh,* Pitman, 1911.

Wagner, A. F. H. V., *Gillingham Grammar School, Dorset,* Blackmore Press, Gillingham, Dorset, 1958.

Walker, G. W., *A History of the Oundle Schools,* printed for the Grocers' Co. by H. Watson and Viney, 1956.

Ward, B., *History of St. Edmund's College,* Kegan Paul, 1893.

Warner, T. R., *Winchester,* Bell, 1900.

Watney, J., *Some Account of Mercers' School,* Blades, East, and Blades, 1896.

Watson, G. A., *Ayton School, the Centenary History,* Headley Bros., 1941.

Westaway, K. M., *A History of Bedford High School,* Hockcliffe, 1932.

Wheatley, W., *The History of Edward Latymer and his Foundations,* printed for the Latymer Upper School by Wm. Clowes, 1953.

Wildsman, W. B., *A Short History of Sherborne,* Abbey Bookshop, Sherborne, 1930.

Wilson, B., *Sedbergh School Register and History,* R. Jackson, 1909.

Woodruff, C. E., *A History of Canterbury School,* Mitchell, Hughes, and Clark, 1908.

Merchant Taylors' School, Blackwell, 1929.

The Story of St. Bees, Buck and Woolton, 1939.

SELECTIONS FROM OFFICIAL PUBLICATIONS

Again, this list is not intended to be exhaustive, but it attempts to give the names of official publications which may be useful for those studying special topics connected with the history of British education. With the exception of local publications, all the items were issued by H.M.S.O., and in the various sections they have been placed in chronological order.

I. ENGLAND AND WALES

(a) Reports of Royal Commissions etc.

Newcastle Commission (Elementary education), 1861.
Clarendon Commission (Public Schools), 1864.
Schools Inquiry Commission (Endowed schools), 1868.
Royal Commission on Oxford and Cambridge, 1874.
Royal Commission on Technical Instruction, 1884.
Cross Commission (Elementary education), 1888.
Report of the Gresham Committee, 1894.
Bryce Commission (Secondary education), 1895.
Haldane Commission's Report on Technical Education, 1906.
Royal Commission on London University, 1913.
Royal Commission on the University of Durham, 1935.

Hadow Reports—
    The Education of the Adolescent, 1926.
    The Primary School, 1931.
    Infant and Nursery Schools, 1933.
Spens Report, 1938.
Norwood Report (Curricula of secondary schools and examinations), 1943.
McNair Report (Training of teachers and youth leaders), 1944.
Fleming Report (Public schools and the national system), 1944.

OTHER REPORTS—
Final Report of the Adult Education Committee, Ministry of Reconstruction, 1919.
Report on the Differentiation of the Curriculum for Boys and Girls respectively in Secondary Schools, 1925.
The Training of Teachers for Public Elementary Schools, 1925.
Report of the Mental Deficiency Committee, 1929.

The School Certificate Examination, 1931.
Report of the Care of Children Committee (Curtis Report), 1946.
Report on Higher Technological Education (Percy Report), 1943.
Report of the Secondary Schools Examinations Council, 1947.
Reports of the U.G.C. on University Development and the annual
    returns from Universities and University Colleges.

(*b*) *Annual Reports*
Minutes of the Committee of Council on Education, 1839-40 to
    1857-8.
Reports of the Committee of Council on Education, 1858-9 to
    1898-9.
Reports of the Board of Education.
Reports of the Ministry of Education.
Annual Reports of the Chief Medical Officer.

(*c*) *Special Reports*
Committee of Council on Education—Report on Wales, 1847.
Special Reports on Educational Subjects, Vol. I, 1896; Vol. II,
    1897; Vol. III, 1898; Vol. IV, 1900.

(*d*) *Board of Education Pamphlets*
The Course System in Evening Schools, 1910.
The Training of Women Teachers for Secondary Schools, 1912.
The Universities of Great Britain and Ireland, 1918.
Humanism in the Continuation School 1921.
The Development of Adult Education in Rural Areas, 1922.
Adult Education in Yorkshire, 1927.
Examinations for Scholarships and Free Places in Secondary
    Schools, 1928.
The New Prospect in Education, 1928.
Pioneer Work and other developments in Adult Education, 1929.
Education and the Countryside, 1934.
Suggestions in regard to Teaching in Junior Technical Schools, 1937.

(*e*) *Ministry of Education Pamphlets*
The Nation's Schools, 1945.
A Guide to the Educational System of England and Wales, 1945.
Youth's Opportunity, 1945.
Special Education Treatment, 1946.
The New Secondary Education, 1947.
Further Education, 1947.
School and Life, 1947.

Citizens Growing Up—At Home, in School, and After, 1949.

Our Changing Schools (Roger Armfelt), 1950.

Challenge and Response. An Account of the Emergency Scheme for the Training of Teachers, 1950.

The Road to the Sixth Form, 1951.

Secondary Education for All. A New Drive (Cmnd, 604), 1958.

Report of the Central Advisory Council for Education, England, *15 to 18.* (Crowther Report) Vol. I, 1959; Vol. II, 1960.

The Youth Service in England and Wales (Albemarle Report), 1960.

Reports of the Secondary School Examinations Council—

Secondary School Examinations other than the G.C.E. (Beloe Report), 1960.

Examinations in Secondary Schools—The Certificate of Secondary Education, 1962.

Half Our Future (Newsom Report), 1963.

Higher Education (Robbins Report), 1963.

Plowden Report—Children and their Primary Schools.

(f) *Other Publications*

Code of Regulations for Day Schools, 1901.

Regulations for Public Elementary Schools, 1903.

Suggestions to Teachers, 1905. Last Issue, 1937.

Regulations for Secondary Schools, 1907.

Regulations for the Preliminary Education of Elementary School Teachers, 1907.

Examinations in Secondary Schools, 1911.

Circular 1486 of 1939 (Youth committees).

Circular 1503 of 1940 (Grants for youth service).

Circular 1516 of 1940 (The Challenge of Youth).

Circular 1577 of 1941 (Registration of Youth).

Educational Reconstruction (White Paper), 1943.

Abolition of Tuition Fees in Grant-Aided Secondary Schools, 1943.

University Awards—Report of the Working Party on University Awards, 1948.

National Union of Teachers, *The State of Our Schools,* 1963.

II. Scotland

Report of the Argyll Commission, 1869.

Annual Reports of the Committee of Council on Education in Scotland.

Annual Reports of the Scottish Education Department.

Scottish Education Department, Educational Pamphlets—
  The Administration of Public Education in Scotland, 1938.
  School Buildings and Their Equipment, 1939.
  The Teaching Profession in Scotland, 1939.
  The Pupils' Progress, 1939.

Reports of the Advisory Council on Education in Scotland—
  Training for Citizenship, 1945.
  Training of Teachers, 1946.
  Primary Education, 1946.
  Technical Education, 1946.
  Secondary Education, 1947.

Reports of the Scottish Youth Advisory Committees—
  The Needs of Youth in These Times, 1945.
  The Recruitment and Training of Youth Leaders and Organisers, 1946.

Circular 122 of 22nd December 1947. Recommendations of the Report on Primary Education which are accepted by the Scottish Education Department.

Circular 108 of 10th July 1947. Promotion schemes. Deals with the implementation of the scheme for promotion from primary schools to secondary schools.

Circular 145 of 21st January 1949. New conditions for the award of the Scottish Leaving Certificate.

Circular 154 of 30th May 1949. Amendments to the Education Act of 1945.

The Primary School in Scotland, 1950.

III. LOCAL REPORTS

The following have been consulted in compiling this book:—

The Final Report of the School Board for London, 1870-1904, D. S. King, 1904.

Education in Leeds, 1926.

Education in Kent, 1933-8.

Divisional Administration Scheme, 1945, W.R.C.C.

Young Leeds, 1949.

Development Plans of the City of Leeds and the County Councils of the West and North Ridings of Yorkshire.

Reports of Local Education Authorities (Leeds, Bradford, Wakefield, West Riding).

Schools Bulletin (issued monthly by the W.R.C.C.).

Ten Years of Change. Report of the W.R.E.C., 1954.

IV. EDUCATION ACTS

Elementary Education Act, 1870.

Education (Scotland) Act, 1872.

Elementary Education Act, 1873.

Elementary Education Act, 1876.

Elementary Education Act, 1880.

Elementary Education (Blind and Deaf Children) Act, 1893.

Elementary Education (Defective and Epileptic Children) Act, 1899.

Education Act, 1902.

Education (London) Act, 1903.

Education (Local Authority Default) Act, 1904.

Education (Provision of Meals) Act, 1906.

Education (Administrative Provisions) Act, 1907.

Endowed Schools (Masters) Act, 1908.

Education (Scotland) Act, 1908.

Education (Administrative Provisions) Act, 1909.

Education (Choice of Employment) Act, 1910.

Education (Administrative Provisions) Act, 1911.

Elementary School Teachers (Superannuation) Act, 1912.

Mental Deficiency Act, 1913.

Elementary School Teachers' (War Service Superannuation) Act, 1914.

Education Act, 1918. [Consolidating Act, 1921.]

Education (Scotland) Act, 1918.

Mental Deficiency Act, 1927.

Local Government (Scotland) Act, 1929.

Education Act, 1936.   Education (Scotland) Act, 1936.

Education Act, 1944.   Education (Scotland) Act, 1945.

Education Act, 1946.   Education (Scotland) Act 1946.

Education (Miscellaneous Provisions) Act, 1948.

Children's Act, 1948.

Education (Miscellaneous Provisions) Act, 1953.

Education Act, 1959.

Education Act, 1962.

Industrial Training Act, 1964.

DATE CHART

Date	Educational Events		Acts and Official Reports
	England and Wales	Scotland	
397		St. Ninian founds Candida Casa.	
563		St. Columba founds the Abbey of Iona.	
597	Mission of St. Augustine. Foundation of Cathedral School of Canterbury. Cathedral School at Rochester. Cathedral School of London.		
628	Cathedral School of York.		
648	Cathedral School of Winchester.		
664	Synod of Whitby.		
685c.	Cathedral Schools of Worcester, Lichfield, and Hereford.		
705-18	St. John of Beverley, Archbishop of York.		
766	Alcuin master of school of York. Alfred the Great (871-901).		
1005c.	Colloquy of Aelfric.		
1072	Restoration of Cathedral School of York by Thomas I.		
1124		School at Aberdeen.	
1173		Schools at Aberdeen and Perth.	
1185	*Studium generale* at Oxford.		
1191	Order of precedence in school of York settled.		
1231	*Studium generale* at Cambridge.		
1249	William of Durham founded Great University Hall at Oxford.		
1263	Balliol College, Oxford, founded.		
1264	Merton College, Oxford, founded.		
1284	Foundation of Peterhouse, Cambridge.		
1314	Exeter College, Oxford, founded by Walter de Stapleton.		

DATE CHART—*continued.*

DATE	EDUCATIONAL EVENTS		ACTS AND OFFICIAL REPORTS
	ENGLAND AND WALES	SCOTLAND	
1324	Oriel College, Oxford, founded.		
1326	Clare College, Cambridge, founded.		
1340	Queen's College, Oxford, founded by Robert Eglesfield, chaplain to Queen Philippa.		
1348	Gonville and Caius College, Cambridge, founded. Pembroke College, Cambridge, founded.		
1350	Trinity Hall, Cambridge, founded by William Bateman.		
1352	Corpus Christi College, Cambridge, founded.		
1379	New College, Oxford, founded by William of Wykeham.		
1387	Winchester College founded by William of Wykeham.		
1406			Statute of Artificers.
1410	Gloucester Grammar School Case.		
1411		University of St. Andrews founded by Bishop Wardlaw.	
1427	Lincoln College, Oxford, founded by Richard Fleming.		
1438	All Souls College, Oxford, founded by Archbishop Chichele.		
1439	Christ's College, Cambridge (God's House), founded by William Byngham.		
1440	Eton College and King's College, Cambridge, founded by Henry VI.		
1448	Queens' College, Cambridge, founded by Queen Margaret.		
1451		University of Glasgow founded.	
1458	Magdalen College, Oxford, founded by William Waynflete.		
1473	St. Catharine's College, Cambridge, founded by Robert Woodlark.		

DATE CHART—*continued.*

| DATE | EDUCATIONAL EVENTS | | ACTS AND OFFICIAL REPORTS |
	ENGLAND AND WALES	SCOTLAND	
1494		University of Aberdeen founded by Bp. Elphinstone.	
1496	Jesus College, Cambridge, founded.		First Scottish Education Act (James IV).
1509	Brasenose College, Oxford, founded.		
1511	St. John's College, Cambridge, founded by Lady Margaret.		
1512	St. Paul's School refounded by Dean Colet.		
1517	Corpus Christi College, Oxford, founded by Bishop Fox.		
1525	Foundation of Manchester Evening School.		
1542	Magdalene College, Cambridge, founded.		
1545			Chantry Act of Henry VIII.
1546	Foundation of Christ Church, Oxford. Trinity College, Cambridge, founded.		
1547			Chantry Act of Edward VI.
1552	Foundation of King Edward VI School, Birmingham, Christ's Hospital, and Leeds Grammar School.		
1555	St. John's and Trinity Colleges, Oxford, founded.		
1557	Repton School founded by Sir John Porte.		
1560	Westminster School refounded by Queen Elizabeth.	Reformation in Scotland completed. 1st Book of Discipline (John Knox).	
1567	Rugby School founded by Laurance Sheriff.		
1571	Harrow School founded by John Lyon. Jesus College, Oxford, founded by Queen Elizabeth.		
1574		Andrew Melville became principal of Glasgow University.	
1581	Gresham College founded.		

DATE CHART—*continued.*

DATE	EDUCATIONAL EVENTS		ACTS AND OFFICIAL REPORTS
	ENGLAND AND WALES	SCOTLAND	
1583		University of Edinburgh founded.	
1584	Emmanuel College, Cambridge, founded by Sir Walter Mildmay. Uppingham School, founded by Archdeacon Johnson		
1593		Marischal College, Aberdeen, founded.	
1596	Sidney Sussex College, Cambridge, founded. Foundation of University at Ripon proposed.		
1604			Parliamentary representation granted to universities by James I.
1610	Wadham College, Oxford, founded.		
1611	Charterhouse founded by Thomas Sutton.		
1619	Dulwich College founded by Edward Alleyn.		
1624	Pembroke College, Oxford, founded.		
1633			Scottish Act authorising establishment of parish schools.
1639		Hutcheson Hospital founded.	
1646			Scottish Act for founding schools.
1657	Cromwell's College at Durham.		
1659		George Heriot Hospital opened.	
1663	Royal Society incorporated.		
1696			Act for Settling Schools (Scotland).
1698	Founding of S.P.C.K.		
1709		S.P.C.K. (Scotland) founded.	
1714	Worcester College, Oxford, founded.		
1741	Royal Military Academy, Woolwich, founded.		
1761		First Academy opened (Perth).	
1767	First appointment of Army Schoolmaster.		
1779	Nonconformists permitted to teach.		

DATE CHART—*continued.*

Date	Educational Events		Acts and Official Reports
	England and Wales	Scotland	
1780	R. Raikes opens Sunday Schools in Gloucester.		
1794	Stonyhurst College founded.		
1798	Butler becomes head-master of Shrewsbury. Joseph Lancaster in London.		
1799	Royal Military College, Sandhurst, opened.	R. Owen at New Lanark. Birkbeck lectures at Glasgow.	
1800	Royal Institution founded. Oxford Public Exam. Statute. Downing College, Cambridge, founded.		
1801	Duke of York's School founded.		
1802			Health and Morals of Apprentices Act.
1803			Educ. Act (Scotland) fixing salaries.
1805	Leeds Gr. School Case.		
1807			Parochial Schools Bill (Whitbread).
1808	Royal Lancasterian Soc. founded.		
1810	British and Foreign School Society founded.		
1811	National Society founded. Sergeant Schoolmasters appointed.		
1816		R. Owen's infant-school at New Lanark.	
1818			Brougham's Commission of Educational Charities, 1818-37.
1819	Hazelwood School opened by Hill.		Factory Act (Peel). Charity Commission Report (Brougham). Parochial Schools Bill.
1821		Foundation of Dollar Academy.	
1822	Royal Academy of Music founded.		
1823	Beginning of Birkbeck College.		
1824	Infant Sch. Soc. founded.		
1825	Society for Diffusion of Useful Knowledge.		
1826	University College, London, founded.	Glasgow Infant Soc. founded by David Stow.	Royal Commission on Universities (Scotland).

DATE CHART—*continued.*

Date	Educational Events		Acts and Official Reports
	England and Wales	Scotland	
1827	St. David's College, Lampeter.		
1828	King's College, London, founded. Arnold becomes headmaster of Rugby.	Wood's Account of the Edinburgh Sessional School.	
1829		Parochial schools opened to all denominations.	
1832	Durham University founded.		Reform Act.
1833	Oxford Movement begins. Foundation of British Association for the Advancement of Science.		Factory Act (Shaftesbury). Education Bill (Roebuck). First grant for Education.
1834	City of London College founded.		
1836	Home and Colonial Infant School Society founded. University of London established.	Glasgow Normal Seminary opened (Stow).	
1837	Normal School of Design founded.		
1839	Committee of Council for Education.		Grammar School Act.
1840	Kay-Shuttleworth opens Battersea Training College. Appointment of Army Schoolmistresses.		
1841	Cheltenham College founded.		
1842	People's College, Sheffield.		
1843	Queen's College, Birmingham, founded. Governesses' Benevolent Institution founded. Marlborough College founded.	Great Disruption.	Graham's Factory Bill.
1844	Rossall School founded. Y.M.C.A. founded.		
1845	Royal College of Chemistry founded.		
1846	Pupil-teacher system introduced. Corps of Army Schoolmasters founded.		
1847		Educational Institute of Scotland founded.	
1848	Queen's College, London, founded.		

DATE CHART—*continued.*

DATE	EDUCATIONAL EVENTS		ACTS AND OFFICIAL REPORTS
	ENGLAND AND WALES	SCOTLAND	
1849	College of Preceptors incorporated. Bedford College, London, founded.		
1850	North London Collegiate School founded. Hartley Institute (*later* University College), Southampton.		
1851	Great Exhibition. Government School of Mines founded. Owens College, Manchester, founded.		
1853	Department of Science and Art founded. Y.W.C.A. founded Cheltenham Ladies' College founded. Wellington Coll. founded.		
1854	Working Men's College founded. First English Kindergarten opened.		Oxford University Act.
1855			Pakington's Education Bill.
1856	Creation of Education Department.		Cambridge University Act.
1858	Oxford and Cambridge Locals established. Miss Beale appointed to Cheltenham Ladies' College.		University Act (Scotland).
1860	Army Certificates of Education.		
1861			Report of Newcastle Commission. Parochial and Burgh Schoolmasters' Act (Scotland).
1862	Revised Code. Clifton College opened. Haileybury Coll. founded.	Almond at Loretto.	
1864	Cambridge Locals opened to girls.		Report of Clarendon Commission.
1867			Reform Act. Report of Argyll Commission.
1868			Public Schools Act. Report of Taunton Commission.
1869	Girton College founded. Headmasters' Conference founded.		Endowed Schools Act.

DATE CHART—*continued.*

Date	EDUCATIONAL EVENTS		ACTS AND OFFICIAL REPORTS
	ENGLAND AND WALES	SCOTLAND	
1870	National Union of Teachers founded. Keble College, Oxford, incorporated.		Elementary Education Act.
1871	College of Physical Science founded at Newcastle. Newnham College founded.		Abolition of religious tests at the universities. Education (Scotland) Act.
1872	University College, Aberystwyth.		
1873	Beginning of University Extension. Royal Naval College, Greenwich, founded.		
1874	Froebel Society founded. Hertford College, Oxford, founded. Yorkshire College of Science founded.		Report of Royal Commission on Oxford and Cambridge.
1876	Yorkshire College.		Lord Sandon's Act. Oxford and Cambridge Act.
1877	Maria Grey Training College founded.		
1878		Formation of Scotch Education Department.	
1879	Somerville College and Lady Margaret Hall, Oxford, founded.		
1880	Victoria University founded. London University admits women to degrees. Regent Street Polytechnic opened.		Mr. Mundella's Education Act.
1883	University College, Cardiff. Church School Company founded.		
1884	Toynbee Hall opened. Central Technical College opened.		Report of Commision on Technical Education.
1885	University College, Bangor.	Reorganisation of Scotch Education Dept. (Craik, Secretary.)	
1886		Fettes College founded.	
1887	P.N.E.V. founded.		
1888		Leaving Certificate Examination.	Local Government Act. Report of Cross Commission.

DATE CHART—*continued.*

DATE	EDUCATIONAL EVENTS		ACTS AND OFFICIAL REPORTS
	ENGLAND AND WALES	SCOTLAND	
1889			Welsh Intermediate Education Act.
1890	University Day Training Colleges. "Whiskey Money."		
1892		Merit Certificate.	
1893	University of Wales founded. Free Elementary Education achieved.		Elementary Education (Blind and Deaf Children) Act.
1894			Report of Gresham Commission.
1895			Report of Bryce Commission.
1896	Royal College of Art established.		Gorst's Education Bill.
1897	Abolition of Payment by Results.		
1898			University of London Act.
1899	Ruskin College, Oxford, opened.		Board of Education Act.
1900	Cockerton judgment. University of Birmingham created.		
1901	University College, Exeter.		
1902	Hartley University College, Southampton.		Education Act (Balfour–Morant).
1903	W.E.A. founded. Universities of Manchester and Liverpool founded. Common Entrance Examination instituted.		
1904	University of Leeds founded.	Struthers appointed Secretary.	Education (Local Authorities Default) Act.
1905	University of Sheffield founded.		
1906			Education (Provision of Meals) Act. Birrell's Education Bill.
1907	Imperial College of Science founded. Free Place system.		Education (Administrative Provisions) Act.
1908	Boy Scouts founded.		Education (Scotland) Act. McKenna's Education Bill. Children Act.
1909	Queen's University, Belfast. University of Bristol founded.		
1910	Girl Guides founded.		

DATE CHART—*continued.*

Date	Educational Events		Acts and Official Reports
	England and Wales	Scotland	
1911	University Grants Committee.		
1912			Report of Royal Commission on London University.
1914	First World War. Rachel and Margaret McMillan open nursery school at Deptford.		
1915	Women's Institutes started.		
1916	Secondary Schools Examination Council.		
1918	Y.M.C.A. Universities Committee. University College, Leicester.		Education Act (Fisher). Education (Scotland) Act. Teachers' Superannuation Acts.
1919			Burnham Committee.
1920	Women admitted to degrees at Oxford. State scholarships begin. Army Educational Corps founded. University College, Swansea.	National and provincial committees for training of teachers.	
1921	National Council of Labour Colleges formed.		Education (Consolidating) Act.
1922	Geddes Axe.		
1924			Teachers' Superannuation Act.
1925	National Playing Fields Association formed.		
1926	Joint examining boards for training of teachers. University of Reading founded.		Hadow Report (Adolescent).
1928	Cambridge village colleges opened. University College, Hull.		
1929			Local Government (Scotland Act). Report of Mental Deficiency Committee.
1931	Great financial crisis.		Hadow Report (Primary School).
1932	Special Places.		
1933			Children and Young Persons' Act. Hadow Report (Infant and Nursery School).
1936			Education Act (England).

DATE CHART—*continued.*

DATE	EDUCATIONAL EVENTS		ACTS AND OFFICIAL REPORTS
	ENGLAND AND WALES	SCOTLAND	
1936			Education (Scotland) Act.
1937	National Fitness Council.		
1938			Spens Report.
1939	Second World War. Evacuation.		B. of E. Circular 1486, Youth Service. B. of E. Circular 1516, Challenge of Youth.
1940	Institution of Central Advisory Council for Education in H.M. Forces.		
1941	A.T.C. formed. Boys and Girls (16–18) register. Introduction of A.B.C.A.		Green Book.
1942	National Youth Advisory Council.		
1943			B. of E. White Paper. Norwood Report.
1944			Education Act (Butler). Fleming Report. McNair Report.
1945			Education (Scotland) Act. Percy Report.
1946	Army Education Corps receives title of " Royal."		Education Consolidating Act (Scotland). Education Act (England).
1948			Education (Misc. Provisions) Act. Children Act.
1949	Scheme for General Certificate in Education accepted. Universities take responsibility for civilian aid to Forces' education.	Scheme for Scottish Leaving Certificate accepted.	
1950	University College of North Staffordshire (Stoke-on-Trent).		Universities cease to be represented in Parliament.
1952	University of Southampton founded.		
1953		University of St. Andrew's Act.	Education (Misc. Provisions) Act.
1954	University of Hull founded.		
1955	University of Exeter founded		
1957	University of Leicester founded.		
1959			15–18, Report of the Central Advisory Council for Education (England), Vol I.

DATE CHART—*continued*

Date	Educational Events		Acts and Official Reports
	England and Wales	Scotland	
1959			Education Act, 1959.
1960	Official recognition of St. David's College, Lampeter.		15-18 (Crowther Report), Vol. II. Albemarle Report. Beloe Report. Anderson Report.
1961	University of Sussex—Royal Charter. Introduction of third year in Training Colleges.	Institution of Scottish Examination Board. Report of Wheatley Committee.	
1962	University College of N. Staffs. becomes University of Keele. Acceptance of university status for Universities of York, East Anglia, Essex, Warwick, Kent, and Lancaster. Central Council for University Admissions.		Education Act, 1962.
1963	Abolition of State Scholarships (Anderson Report of 1960). King's College, Newcastle, becomes the University of Newcastle-upon-Tyne.	University of Strathclyde (originally The Royal Technical College, Glasgow).	*Half our Future* (Newsom Report), *Higher Education* (Robbins Report), Interim Report of the Hale Committee on University Teaching Methods.
1964	Announcement of date for leaving age of 16. Reconstitution of the Burnham Committee. Ministry of Education becomes the Department of Education and Science.	University of Stirling.	Industrial Training Act.
1966		Heriot-Watt University, Edinburgh. University of Aston in Birmingham. Brunel University. The City University. Loughborough University of Technology.	Plowden Report—Children and their Primary Schools.
1967		Bradford University.	

INDEX

PRINTED IN GREAT BRITAIN BY UNIVERSITY TUTORIAL PRESS LTD, FOXTON
NEAR CAMBRIDGE